BUILDINGS OF THE UNITED STATES

Buildings of Delaware

SOCIETY OF ARCHITECTURAL HISTORIANS
Buildings of the United States

EDITORIAL ADVISORY COMMITTEE

Karen Kingsley
Editor in Chief

Keith Eggener and Michael J. Lewis
Associate Editors

Samuel D. Albert and Gabrielle M. Esperdy
Assistant Editors

George F. Thompson
The Center for American Places
Managing Editor

Osmund Overby
Editor in Chief, 1990–1996

William H. Pierson Jr.
Founding Coeditor in Chief

Damie Stillman
Editor in Chief, 1996–2004

John A. Burns
HABS/HAER/HALS

James J. Malanaphy III
AIA Historic Resources Committee

C. Ford Peatross
Library of Congress

Barry Bergdoll
President, Society of Architectural Historians

Pauline Saliga
Executive Director, Society of Architectural Historians

The Society of Architectural Historians gratefully acknowledges the support of the following, whose generosity helped bring *Buildings of Delaware* to publication:

> Mrs. Lammot du Pont Copeland
> Louisa C. and Robert W. Duemling

Initial and ongoing support for the Buildings of the United States series has come from:

> National Endowment for the Humanities, an independent federal agency
>
> Graham Foundation for Advanced Studies in the Fine Arts
>
> Pew Charitable Trusts
>
> University of Delaware
>
> Ford Foundation
>
> Samuel H. Kress Foundation
>
> National Park Service, Heritage Documentation Programs, HABS/HAER/HALS division
>
> Southeast Chapter, Society of Architectural Historians in honor of Damie Stillman, John W. Shirley Professor Emeritus of Art History at the University of Delaware

BUILDINGS OF
Delaware

W. Barksdale Maynard

*To Tom and Dale Carruthers,
with very best regards —
W. Barksdale Maynard
2008*

University of Virginia Press
CHARLOTTESVILLE AND LONDON

University of Virginia Press
© 2008 by the Society of Architectural Historians
All rights reserved
Printed in the United States of America on acid-free paper

First published 2008

9 8 7 6 5 4 3 2 1

LIBRARY OF CONGRESS CATALOGING-IN-PUBLICATION DATA

Maynard, W. Barksdale (William Barksdale)

Buildings of Delaware / W. Barksdale Maynard.
    p.   cm. — (Buildings of the United States)
Includes bibliographical references and index.
ISBN 978-0-8139-2702-2 (cloth : alk. paper)
1. Architecture—Delaware—Guidebooks. 2. Delaware—Guidebooks.
I. Title.
NA730.D3M39 2008
720.9751—dc22

2007028273

Frontispiece: New Castle Town Hall (NC14). (Historic American Buildings Survey, Prints and Photographs Division, Library of Congress)

CONTENTS

How to Use This Book   ix

Foreword   xi

Acknowledgments   xiii

Introduction   1

Woodland Indians 3 • Swedes, Finns, and Dutch 5 • Colonial (and Colonial Revival) 7 • Nineteenth Century 13 • Architects 16 • Du Pont Estates 19 • Transportation 21 • Suburbs 24 • Historic Preservation 26

Brandywine Hundred   32

Claymont 33 • Arden 37 • Brandywine Hundred South of Arden 41 Vicinity of Brandywine Creek and along Concord Pike 45

Christiana Hundred   55

Northern Christiana Hundred 55 • Centreville 56 • Greenville Vicinity 64 • South of DE 141 70 • Elsmere Vicinity 75 • Newport 76 North along Red Clay Creek 77 • Ashland and Vicinity 79

Wilmington   82

Christina Riverfront and East Side 86 • Market Street Corridor 93 West Center City 111 • Brandywine Village and Park 117 • Northeast Wilmington 126 • West Wilmington 129 • Northwest Wilmington 135

New Castle Hundred   146

North of New Castle 146 • New Castle 149 • South of New Castle 164

Mill Creek and White Clay Creek Hundreds   165

Hockessin 165 • Down Red Clay Creek 166 • Along Limestone Road (DE 7) 168 • Stanton Vicinity 169 • Christiana 170

Newark and White Clay Creek Valley   173

Upper White Clay Creek Valley 175 • Lower White Clay Creek Valley 176
Newark 178 • West of the University of Delaware 188 • South of
Newark Center 190

Pencader and Red Lion Hundreds   192

Glasgow 196 • Along the Chesapeake and Delaware Canal 197
St. Georges and Vicinity 200 • Delaware City 203

Lower New Castle County   207

Port Penn 208 • Odessa 210 • Middletown Vicinity 215
Middletown 216 • Townsend Vicinity 221

Kent County   224

Smyrna 225 • Along DE 9 231 • Camden 234 • Southeast of
Dover 236 • Frederica 240 • Harrington 242 • Milford 243

Dover   246

Eastern Sussex County   258

Milton 260 • South of Ellendale 260 • Georgetown 261 • East of
Georgetown 265 • Lewes 265 • Rehoboth Beach 276 • West of
Rehoboth Beach 279 • South along the Inland Bays and Oceanfront 279

Western Sussex County   284

Bridgeville 286 • West of Bridgeville 287 • Seaford 288 • Woodland
and Bethel 293 • Laurel 294 • Southwest of Millsboro 297

Glossary   299

Bibliography   311

Illustration Credits   321

Index   323

HOW TO USE THIS BOOK

Buildings of Delaware is the first overview of the state's architectural history from every period. All extant structures were eligible for inclusion—houses, schools, churches, dams, highways, bridges, designed landscapes, and more. I have tried to give a balanced presentation of many building types and to do justice to each region of the state. In making difficult choices about which places to include, often the decisive factor was whether sufficiently accurate, detailed, and thought-provoking *architectural* information was available, as opposed to merely historical or genealogical.

Coverage is heavier in *Buildings of Delaware* for New Castle County, northernmost of the three counties. As the twenty-first century began, it had 63 percent of the state's population. Far more students of Delaware architecture have lived there than in southern Delaware, and historical data is much fuller. Relatively more of its buildings are expensive, aesthetically sophisticated, architect-designed structures of masonry, factors which tend to draw maximum attention from historians.

America's superabundant small towns present a thorny problem for any Buildings of the United States author. To include even a handful of structures from every one of Delaware's fifty-seven towns would swell the book. Readers wanting additional information should seek out locally available walking tours and pamphlets, which grow more common every year as historic districts proliferate. Agricultural buildings are hard to treat in this kind of book, too, as they tend to be inaccessible. I have listed a few that the reader can visit. For in-depth discussion, see Gabrielle M. Lanier and Bernard L. Herman's *Everyday Architecture of the Mid-Atlantic* (1997).

I have divided the state into regions convenient for touring, a few of which roughly correspond to the thirty-three political "hundreds" once in use. A "hundred" is an old English land division, smaller than a county. The hundreds of Delaware originally served as judicial or legislative districts, but now they remain only as a basis for property tax assessment; conservative Delaware retained the old English nomenclature. Each region is mapped. Town populations are given for the year 2000; many are growing dramatically as new developments expand. Entries have headings that give the current name of the building (with older designations in parentheses); the date (whenever possible, of design through construction); the architect (if I could discover it); dates of major alterations; and the location. Each building is keyed by its number to a map. Many structures are privately owned. By the time of publication, some of the buildings will have been significantly altered or even demolished.

A word about dates: they are often guesswork for the earliest structures. Many colonial dates are merely traditional, without firm documentation. Not infrequently, home owners insist on one date, architectural experts on another. Published sources may contradict each other. My preference has often been to give conservative ranges rather than repeat precise-sounding but actually flimsy dates.

Not all of the 400-plus buildings included here are aesthetically pleasing. *Buildings of Delaware* gives examples of factories, water pumping stations, airplane hangars, shopping malls, dormitories, housing projects, and subdivisions because they are typical of the modern world we inhabit. To omit a colonial church and include a parking garage may seem a surprising choice—but the former is, after all, extraordinarily rare and used by almost nobody, and the latter extraordinarily common and indispensable to contemporary life.

As the first publication to survey the entire architectural history of the state, *Buildings of Delaware* should be regarded as neither final nor definitive, but as an expression of our current, often limited, understanding and as an invitation to further inquiry.

FOREWORD

The primary objective of the Buildings of the United States (BUS) series is to identify and celebrate the rich cultural, economic, and geographic diversity of the United States of America as it is reflected in the architecture of each state. The series was founded by the Society of Architectural Historians (SAH), a nonprofit organization dedicated to the study, interpretation, and preservation of the built environment throughout the world.

The Buildings of the United States series will eventually comprise more than sixty volumes documenting the built environment of every state of the United States of America, including both high-style and vernacular structures. The idea for such a series was in the minds of the founders of the SAH in the early 1940s, but it was not brought to fruition until Nikolaus Pevsner—the eminent British architectural historian who had conceived and carried out Buildings of England, originally published between 1951 and 1974—challenged the SAH to do for the United States what he had done for his country.

The authors of each BUS volume are trained architectural historians who are thoroughly informed in the local aspects of their subjects. In each volume, special conditions that shaped the state, together with the building types necessary to meet those conditions, are identified and discussed. Barns and other agricultural buildings, factories and industrial structures, warehouses and conservatories, bridges and transportation buildings take their places alongside the familiar building types conventional to the nation as a whole—courthouses, libraries, city halls, religious buildings, commercial structures, and the infinite variety of domestic architecture, from workers' houses to mansions. Although the great national and international architects of American buildings receive proper attention, outstanding local architects, as well as the buildings of skilled but often anonymous carpenter-builders, are also brought prominently into the picture. Each book in the series deals with the very fabric of American architecture, with the context in time and in place of each specific building, and with the entirety of urban, suburban, and rural America. Naturally, the series cannot cover every building of merit; practical considerations dictate difficult choices in the buildings that are represented in this and other volumes. Furthermore, only buildings in existence at the time of publication are included.

The BUS series has received generous and ongoing support from the National Endowment for the Humanities; the Graham Foundation for Advanced Studies in the Fine Arts; the Ford Foundation; the Samuel H. Kress Foundation; and the National Park Service, HABS/HAER/HALS. For this volume, SAH is also enormously indebted to Mrs. Lammot du Pont Copeland and to Louisa C. and Robert W. Duemling, and to the many individual members of the SAH who have made unrestricted contributions to BUS.

The SAH expresses its appreciation to the author, the Center for American Places, the University of Virginia Press, the SAH Board, the current members of the BUS Editorial Advisory Committee (listed on page ii), and that Committee's former members.

Karen Kingsley
EDITOR IN CHIEF
BUILDINGS OF THE UNITED STATES

ACKNOWLEDGMENTS

I am extremely grateful to Mrs. Pamela C. Copeland (1906–2001) and to Louisa C. and Robert W. Duemling. Pamela Copeland and Louisa Duemling are mother and daughter, and *Buildings of Delaware* will be one of the many lasting legacies of their philanthropy.

When I was brought into the project by Damie Stillman in 2002, it was as co-author with Ian Quimby. Unfortunately, Ian passed away before work could begin. Research for *Buildings of Delaware* during the subsequent two years was far more intensive and "from scratch" than I had anticipated, as there proved to be no published book on Wilmington architecture, no countywide survey volumes like those available for Maryland and other states, no Historic American Buildings Survey (HABS) catalogue, and no equivalent (for example) of the *Virginia Landmarks Register*. Therefore, I am especially grateful to experts who shared their personal knowledge. More than two dozen people generously agreed to examine parts of the text, ranging from a page or two to entire sections. Many errors were caught, but others surely remain, and I hope that readers will inform me of them.

For their assistance with the manuscript, I wish to thank Keith L. Eggener, Gabrielle Esperdy, Karen Kingsley, Damie Stillman, and other readers for the Buildings of the United States series. Eliza McClennen provided the excellent maps. At University of Virginia Press, Penelope Kaiserlian and Mark Mones were very helpful. Margaret Dickhart and Laura Armstrong ably assisted in keeping the budget straight and with other logistics. In the Wilmington area, thanks to Doug Andrews, Edward Bachtle, Christopher T. Baer, Reverend Anastasios Bourantas, Jan Gardner Broske, Ann Lee Bugbee, Kim Burdick, Gene Castellano, Susan Mulchahey Chase, Heather Clewell, Constance Cooper, Mrs. Earl Dibble, Governor Pete du Pont, Suzanne L. Gallo, Pam George, Peter S. Gordon, Barbara Hall, Ray and Judith Hester, Thomas E. Higley, Eldon du Pont Homsey, Larry and Susan Hoover, Charles Hummel, David Kee, Joseph and Rosemary Kelly, John and Rosemary Krill, John P. Kurth, Sylvia F. Lahvis, Margaret Lidz, Tom Mallon, Trent Margrif, Debra Campagnari Martin, Alison McKenna, Connee McKinney, Marjorie G. McNinch, David Menser, Maureen Milford, Joseph Mitchell, Thorpe Moeckel, Michael Podmaniczky, Ellen Rendle, Rose Anna Capaldi Richards, Beverly W.

Rowland, John R. Schoonover, Ann Stacy, Kent Steinriede, James Tevebaugh, and Jon Williams. In and around Newark and the University of Delaware: Jennifer Acord, Mr. and Mrs. Edward W. Cooch Jr., Anne G. Copley, Lu Ann De Cunzo, Susan Davi, Richard L. Dayton, Bernard Herman, Carol E. Hoffecker, Ian Janssen, Tracy H. Jentzsch, Mark S. Parker Miller, Rebecca Johnson Melvin, Nedda Moqtaderi, Lenis Northmore, William S. Schenck, Rachael Tezcan, Catherine Walsh, and my students in two graduate courses on Delaware architecture. At the Center for Historic Architecture and Design at the University of Delaware: David Ames, Rebecca Sheppard, Karen Spry, Jeroen van den Hurk, and Emma Young. Elsewhere in New Castle County: Michele Anstine, Jan Crossland, Bruce Dalleo, Laura Lee, David and Alison Matsen, James L. Meek, Joseph and Sally Monigle, Hope Motter, Steven Pulinka, Gerry Scarfe, Mike Schwartz, Tony Shahan, Daniel B. Shutt, and William J. Soukup. In Kent County and Dover: Robin K. Bodo, Dan and Rhonda Bond, Gary Camp, Nancy R. Conlon, Margaret Raubacher Dunham, Bruce C. Ennis, Joseph Gates, the late Edward F. Heite, C. Terry Jackson II, Joan N. Larrivee, Margaret Law, C. Russell McCabe, Denis McGlynn, Dawn E. Melson, Elizabeth G. R. Ross, and Faye L. Stocum. In Sussex County: Susan W. Boving, Ronald F. Bowden, Richard B. Carter, F. Brooke Clendaniel, E. Michael DiPaolo, Ned Fowler, Claudia Leister, Dr. Maynard H. Mires, Kenneth and Frances Novak, Brian Page, David Pedersen, Dr. John Rawlins, Earl B. Tull, and the late William H. Williams. Outside of Delaware: William C. Allen, Gretchen T. Buggeln, John A. Burns, Lael Ensor, Dale H. Frens, Jeff Groff, Evie Joselow, Jeffrey E. Klee, Catherine Adams Masek (who sent many helpful items on western Sussex County), my parents George and Isabel Maynard, Richard Conway Meyer, John D. Milner, Keith Morgan, Timothy Mullins, the late Charles E. Peterson (who reminisced about accompanying Louise du Pont Crowninshield to the opening of Winterthur Museum in the 1950s), Katrina Richter, Sharon Silverman, Mary A. Staikos, my agent Geri Thoma, Franklin K. Toker, David Wilcove, Kristen Wildes, and my sister Mims Maynard Zabriskie. Thanks to others who provided photographs and to several architectural firms. My apologies to anyone I have unintentionally left out in the course of a big project!

As with my previous books I have been helped most of all by the love and support of my wife, Susan Matsen Maynard, who is justly proud of her native state of Delaware.

W. Barksdale Maynard

Buildings of Delaware

Introduction

"Delaware is like a diamond," downstate poet John Lofland wrote in 1847, "diminutive, but having within it inherent specific value."[1] Although ranking just forty-ninth in population, the Diamond State has had a long and colorful history that belies its size. Europeans settled here only a generation after Jamestown. It was one of the original thirteen colonies and the first state to sign the Constitution, a document that gives little states significant power.

Admittedly, its contributions to the architecture of the nation have been modest; as one measure, the National Park Service does not own a single site in Delaware, historical or otherwise, making it the only state thus neglected (although plans got underway in 2003 to change this). Great architecture is often a product of cities, and Delaware is preeminently a place without them: as late as World War II, there was not a single town besides Wilmington with a population of even 5,000. As a result, a great deal of Delaware's historic architecture is rural and vernacular. And because its important buildings almost invariably show the influence of neighboring states, Delaware is mostly a place to study architectural responses rather than bold innovations—responses that are often fascinating in their variety and imaginativeness.

Because of its frontage on Delaware Bay and the Atlantic Ocean, the chief geographical characteristic of the First State is *lowness*: it lies more wholly in the Coastal Plain (95 percent) than any other Eastern Seaboard state except Florida. Delaware's earliest settlers, the Dutch in 1631, must have felt at home as they explored its beautiful saltgrass marshes and sinuous tidal creeks. It was Delaware Bay that was first named for English Lord de la Warr, a name later applied to the entire western shore, today's state of Delaware. The latter forms part of the Delmarva Peninsula, all of which was economically oriented toward the Chesapeake and Delaware bays and away from the wooded central spine, still sparsely populated today. The western boundary of Delaware, almost ninety miles, passes through hardly a town of significant size.

In architecture as in much else, Delaware is delightfully obscure. Few outsiders know much about it, except for having driven through it on I-95 or visited one of its racetracks or beaches. Only one American in 362 is a Delawarean. The state has the fewest counties of any state, just three, compared to 254 in Texas. Even if Delaware were a *city* rather than a state, it would rank only twelfth-largest in the nation, behind San Jose and Detroit. With a population of 853,500 in 2006, it is hemmed in by much larger neighbors with vigorous architectural traditions: Maryland, with a population seven times larger; New Jersey, eleven times larger; and Pennsylvania, fifteen times larger. In the colonial period, in fact, Delaware belonged to Pennsylvania as the Three Lower Counties (it was given to William Penn by the Duke of York to provide his colony with better access to the sea), and northern Delaware's architecture has repeatedly been shaped by Pennsylvania trends and Philadelphia architects. For its part, Maryland claimed chunks of southern Delaware until the 1770s, a legacy of old land disputes between Penn and Lord Baltimore. As Delaware has an average width of only twenty miles, nearly the whole state is

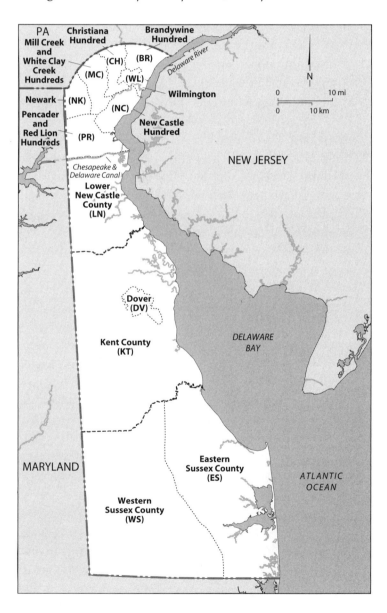

DELAWARE
Divisions of the State

just a short drive from Maryland, making for considerable architectural influence from there, too, especially in the south.

Delaware's relationship to North and South has long been ambiguous. It lies almost entirely south of the Mason-Dixon Line (established 1763–1768)—and at the same time east of it, that famous divider between American regions making a right-angle turn to define Delaware's western border. Delaware was a slave state, yet it did not secede. Quaker abolitionists ferried runaways along the Underground Railroad here, but the state legislature would not ratify the Thirteenth Amendment (outlawing slavery) until 1901! The marked internal division between northward-oriented New Castle County (with only a fifth of Delaware's land area, but today with nearly two-thirds of its population) and the more southern Kent and Sussex counties gives the state much of its sociological interest and architectural variety.

Delaware's prominent, mid-Atlantic location has exposed it to many cultural influences, with a resulting diversity of architectural forms and building types. Take churches, for example: one sees Quaker meeting houses like Pennsylvania's (MC1), Methodist chapels like those on Maryland's Eastern Shore (KT30), and urban Italian-Catholic churches like those of Philadelphia (WL77). There are high-style Gothic Revival Episcopal edifices of stone with soaring towers (CH16), much plainer Presbyterian boxes (NK5), and rustic camp meetings (WS25). The diversity only increases with time, as recent years have brought a Hindu Temple (MC2) built by workers from India and old churches reconfigured for modern social outreach (WL42). One could cite similar variety in other building types. In spite of Delaware's small size—or perhaps because of it—the overlay of architectural cultures and trends here is surprisingly complex and exciting.

WOODLAND INDIANS

Before the Europeans came there were Paleo-Indians in Delaware, highly mobile hunters and gatherers. Starting about 3000 BC in the Woodland Period, they began to settle down for much of each year along rivers and estuaries. Archaeology has lately revealed much about their habitations. Excavation of "pit house features" started in Sussex County, where pits were first recognized (by accumulations of shells and organic matter), then moved north to New Castle County, where numerous pits were found near Delaware Park racetrack. When archaeologists first reported having found pit features, many observers doubted these indicated house sites, for where were the expected postmolds, traces in the earth of upright saplings that supported a wigwam structure? But postmolds were later found ringing a pit feature at the Snapp Site, St. Georges Creek, New Castle County (c. 1000 BC), which had escaped being plowed. The latter discovery clarified the nature of these early houses, as the postmolds formed a ring fully twenty-five feet outside of the pit, answering critics' objections that the pits themselves were too small to comprise a whole house: evidently, the pit was only a small "basement" some dozen feet across and eight feet deep. Probably, the pit houses were occupied during a single winter, then abandoned, smoke escaping through a hole in the structure above. Often the pit had a hearth at its center.[2]

In just a few years, archaeologists went from knowing nothing about Delaware's prehistoric architecture to being able to reconstruct a typical house: a framework of saplings that formed a domical structure over the pit, to which thatch, woven mats, or bark were probably applied. Further excavations have continued to refine the picture, including several undertaken for the Delaware Department of Transportation (DelDOT) just before sites were bulldozed for

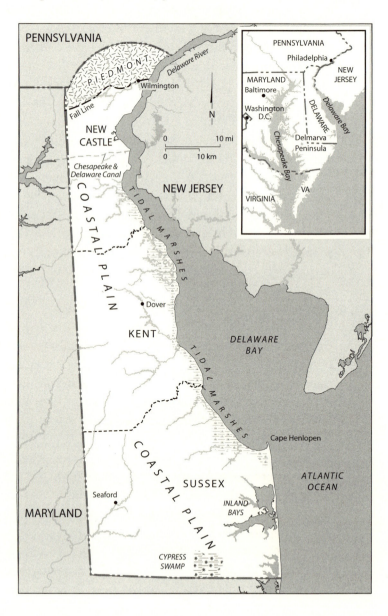

DELAWARE Physiography

road construction (see exhibits at Delaware Archaeological Museum, DV10). Probably, a very few families lived together at each site, so there were no Indian "villages" per se. The total population of Woodland people in Delaware at a given time was astonishingly low, no more than 800 or 1,000.

In the extreme north, a few natural rock shelters existed. Pioneering archaeologist Hilborne T. Cresson excavated one near Claymont (Darley Road at the Baltimore and Ohio Railroad [B&O]) in 1866–1867, identifying four layers of occupation. Another rock shelter at Beaver Valley along the Brandywine was investigated in 1948 (and inspired a diorama at the Hagley Museum, CH15).

At the time of European settlement, the native peoples belonged to the Delaware or Lenni Lenape tribe. Eventually most of them were driven out of the region. In 1990, however, there were still 2,500 persons in Delaware who identified themselves as Native Americans, including members of the downstate Nanticoke tribe, who have their own Indian Mission Church (ES34) and museum.

SWEDES, FINNS, AND DUTCH

With the coming of the Europeans, Delaware formed part of Nya Sverige, or New Sweden, the only Swedish colony in the New World, active from 1638 to 1655. New Sweden was founded when the ships *Kalmar Nyckel* and *Vogel Grip* under Peter Minuit landed at Wilmington (see Fort Christina Park, WL2). Twentieth-century historians searched avidly in Delaware for traces of Swedish architectural influence—and Finnish, as there were many Finns intermingled. But the Swedish colony was never large and was soon swamped by the influx of settlers from England and elsewhere, making Swedish cultural survivals difficult to find. The entire Swedish colony in Pennsylvania, New Jersey, and Delaware numbered only 300 persons when Sweden lost governmental control in 1655; a census taken in 1693 of Swedish families in the southerly half of the old colony, now Delaware, counted just 418 persons; and the 1,200 Swedish speakers in former New Sweden in 1697 numbered only 5 percent of the area's population. Such small numbers mean that there must have been few "Swedish" buildings to start with, and the two famous "Old Swedes" churches in Philadelphia and Wilmington (both begun 1698; WL3) are basically English in style.[3]

Nonetheless, the Swedes and Finns made a crucial contribution to American architecture: the log house. Generations of scholars have concurred that log houses first appeared in the New World in Nya Sverige, debuting within the walls of Fort Christina. From the cultural hearth of the Delaware Valley, log construction diffused widely throughout the colonies, reaching Maryland by the 1660s, North Carolina by 1680, and northern New England after 1760. The crude and inexpensive Finnish cabin, in particular, proved popular in the Delaware Valley and went on to be widely replicated throughout the United

Anglo-American log houses such as Thomas Bird's (WL2.2) followed Finnish practice. Seen here at Prices Corner west of Wilmington, it was removed to Fort Christina as a relic in 1962.

In New Castle, Dutch settlers built crowstep-gable townhouses like ones in Manhattan. On the Tile House, date irons once read "1687." Watercolor by Robert Montgomery Bird, c. 1826.

States, in time spreading from coast to coast as a highly familiar type. It generally featured unhewn, round logs; v-notching; gaps left between the logs and filled with chinking; and a ridgepole-and-purlin roof covered with clapboards. Log houses went hand-in-hand with another Finnish contribution to frontier life, the zig-zag or "worm" fence.[4]

In the 1950s, noted amateur archaeologist C. A. Weslager worked with state archivist Leon deValinger to save several log houses and plank (squared-log) houses from destruction. The Thomas Springer log house of c. 1795 from near Milltown, Mill Creek Hundred, found its way to the Smithsonian Institution in 1962 as a museum exhibit. Log houses of this kind were once extremely numerous in New Castle County. Connecticut diarist Joshua Hempstead visited Ogletown in 1749: "Here are mostly wooden houses Cribb fas[h]ion & old, those that are newly built the logs are hewed & as thick as [a] hog neck."[5] Still today, many early Delaware houses conceal a log portion beneath weatherboarding. Weslager dreamed of finding a purely Swedish or Finnish log house surviving, but probably none exists: all are later Anglo-American adaptations, including Thomas Bird House (WL2.2), "Swedish" Log House (DV3.2), and plank houses in Smyrna (KT10.1) and Lewes (ES16.1).

In addition to the Swedes, the Dutch also settled in Delaware—first at Swanendael (ES13) near Lewes in 1631. Dutch families occupied New Castle, as well (see Fort Casimir Site, NC6), but little or nothing survives of Dutch architecture in either town. (Enthusiasts will need to visit northern New Jersey and New York to see extant examples.) New Castle's Tile House (1687; demolished 1884), known only from illustrations and its surviving iron date numerals, was an exceptionally interesting Dutch townhouse of the kind once common in New York. Its facade with crowstep gable was built of small yellow bricks imported from Holland, which even today are regularly unearthed in yards throughout the town. Still standing in New Castle is the so-called Dutch House (NC7), its modern name cheerfully ignoring the fact that it postdates, by years or even decades, the English takeover of the community. As in the Ryves Holt House (ES18) in Lewes, the H-bent construction suggests typical Dutch practice, but beyond that these houses both seem English. Dutch architectural heritage, like Swedish, proves elusive in Delaware.

COLONIAL (AND COLONIAL REVIVAL)

No architectural era in Delaware has attracted so much attention as the colonial. Early twentieth-century historians, all amateurs, focused enthusiastically on major architectural monuments. More recent historians, including several professionals, have corrected this bias by studying humble structures, pointing out that the vast majority of colonial dwellings were wooden one-story habitations, often well-built and skillfully framed but hardly bigger than shacks. Almost all of these homes have long since disappeared. Experts were once quick to assign extremely early dates to colonial buildings—indeed, seventeenth-century dates wherever possible—but subsequent research has shown that architectural forms often lingered for generations. Buildings from before 1740 are inevitably rare, given that the entire population of New Castle County, for example, was then just 6,000—one-eightieth what it is today. There were few buildings to start with, of which only the tiniest fraction survives (about thirty pre-1740 structures appear in this book). Most likely to persist are churches, of which eighteen are still standing from before 1800. Some remain in active use; Immanuel in New Castle (NC10) is proud of having held services continually for 300 years.

Most architectural motifs and practices came from neighboring colonies. The stone farmhouses of Delaware's Piedmont resemble those of its sprawling neighbors, Delaware and Chester counties, Pennsylvania (see the very early Strand Millas of 1701, CH12). Houses in Wilmington and environs often imitate Philadelphian examples, showing, for example, the pent eave typical of that vicinity as well as the fine proportions and design typical of an urban milieu (John England House, NK6, is a good example). One "Delaware" feature often pointed out is green louvered shutters upstairs, white solid ones below, but this was customary in Philadelphia, too (solid shutters offered security, louvered ones ventilated the bedrooms). Piedmont Delaware, like neighboring Pennsylvania, was a major center of milling, taking advantage of fast, rapidly falling creeks (ten mills above the Fall Line, that point beyond which streams cease to be navigable, are described in this book); downstate, creeks were dammed to provide a head of water—as at the rare survivor of c. 1740, Noxontown Mill (LN20). There were numerous Quakers in Delaware, both upstate and in Kent County, many of them millers, and earlier historians wrote much of the Quaker plan in laying out houses (see Aspendale, KT1). But that plan is no longer considered diagnostic of Quaker architecture. Nor were Quaker buildings "simple," as long held; they basically followed prevailing Anglo-American approaches. In southern Delaware, colonists often employed the Chesapeake custom of earthfast (post-in-ground) construction. Because the posts eventually rotted, these buildings have entirely disappeared. They are known, however, through archaeology—for example, Thompson's Loss and Gain (early eighteenth century), north of Rehoboth Bay, with its hall-parlor plan. As researchers Gabrielle Lanier and Bernard Herman have written, Sussex County builders "developed a regionally distinctive construction tradition of setting durable houses on impermanent foundations. This tradition has persisted to the present," and buildings are frequently moved, as at Lewes.[6]

In all of the eastern United States, wood offered an abundant material for the colonial builder. Even after the white oak of Delaware's Piedmont was depleted, the bounteous supply in the Indian River area, Sussex County, fed the shipbuilding and construction industries for generations. Today, a third of Delaware is timberland, mostly in Sussex County. But wood was sometimes imported from out of state, as was the case in the construction of Wilmington

In colonial times, most Sussex County houses were wooden. Few survive. The paneled Benjamin Potter Mansion, near Milford (c. 1780), was an abandoned wreck when architectural historians studied it in 1985.

Delaware's forests afforded bountiful timber for construction. Nineteenth-century Corner Ketch Barn, north of Newark, was photographed just prior to its 1980s demolition.

INTRODUCTION

Friends Meeting House (1815–1817; WL41), of lumber from North Carolina. Wood was easy and cheap to build with, but, being highly perishable, it produced an ephemeral architecture. Thus, brick buildings survive in disproportionate numbers. Early brick structures are fairly common in New Castle and upper Kent counties but become much scarcer in Sussex, owing both to the paucity of brick clays in sandy southern Delaware and the ready availability of wood there. Perhaps the most interesting brick colonial building in Sussex County is the venerable Maston House (1727; WS8), a Maryland type with lingering seventeenth-century features.

As colonial travelers often noted, stone architecture is confined almost entirely to the 5 percent of Delaware in the Piedmont, a province dominated

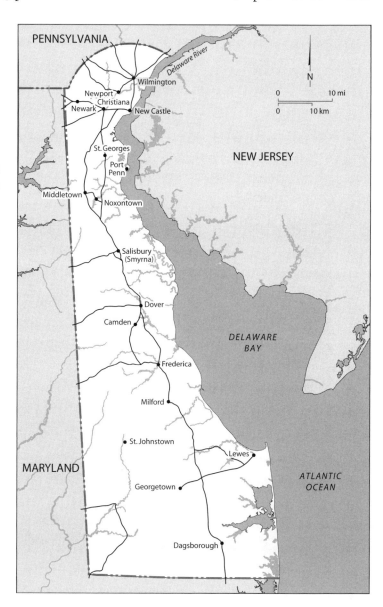

DELAWARE ROADS, 1790s Most colonial Delaware towns were sited at the head of navigation on creeks, which provided power for milling of grain and then shipment via the Delaware Bay to larger markets. These roads and towns—some barely familiar today—are the ones most often shown on contemporary maps.

"Blue rock"—actually Wilmington Complex gneiss—was quarried in the Piedmont throughout the nineteenth century, as here at Brandywine Granite Quarry (BR24).

by ultra-hard, dark-gray gneiss of the so-called "Wilmington Complex." This gneiss underwent metamorphosis unusually deep in the earth (thirteen miles) and was heated to nearly the highest temperature of any Appalachian rock (1,600°F), which accounts for what pioneering geologist James C. Booth called in 1841 its "superior gravity, hardness and toughness" for building.[7] By 1700, Wilmington Complex gneiss was quarried as "blue rock," a name referring to the blue sheen of the quartz that, along with feldspar, distinctively bands the stone. ("Blue granite" is a misnomer, gneiss differing from granite both in being banded and coarser-grained.) Blue rock quarried at Brandywine Granite Quarry (BR24) and elsewhere was used for numerous buildings in Wilmington, including the 1850s stone spire of the Cathedral Church of St. John (WL54). Limestone occurs in a few places, too. More exotic stones have sometimes been imported to Delaware: from Chester County, Pennsylvania, came those Victorian favorites, green serpentine and white Avondale stone (a billion-year-old white quartzite), and Wissahickon schists were brought from areas around Philadelphia (see St. Andrew's School, LN19). Fort Delaware (PR21) is awesomely faced with Quincy, Massachusetts, granite. As a general rule, if you find stone architecture south of the Fall Line, it must be the result of materials brought from a great distance (as at Wilson-Warner House and stable, LN7, or Old Stone Tavern, KT19).[8]

We perceive Delaware's colonial architecture through the lens of the later Colonial Revival, a national movement with special appeal in the First State, which was never more prominent on the national stage than in colonial times.

Small, domestically scaled Colonial Revival has long been popular in the state. When architects Day and Klauder proposed this grandiose design for Memorial Hall, University of Delaware (1919; NK9.9), the trustees told them to give it instead "a more intimate and Delawarean character."

In 1790, one American in sixty-six lived in Delaware, the north–south center of the former colonies; by 1930, just one in 515. The state flag (1913) is, by mandate, "colonial blue," and Delawareans pride themselves in being feisty "Blue Hens," renowned in eighteenth-century cockfighting. Not surprisingly, the Colonial Revival took hold here early and flourished, reaching a peak around 1930, when the University of Delaware campus (NK9) was being steadily expanded, Pierre S. du Pont's campaign of public schools was using colonial exclusively, and a colonial Legislative Hall (DV16) and state government complex would soon be built.[9] *National Geographic* highlighted "Diamond Delaware, Colonial Still" in 1935.[10]

Even the coming of architectural modernism did little to shake the colonial craze. Purely International Style designs were relatively scarce here—and were virtually banned from the University of Delaware so long as wealthy trustee H. Rodney Sharp and other traditionalists dominated the building committees. Modernism was gradually allowed, but only with a certain nod to colonial bricks and white trim (see Smith Hall, NK9.13). In 1962, a Wilmington architect lamented that "contemporary" homes were rare: "Because Delaware was the first state, does that mean we must always live with 'ersatz colonial'?"[11] In the twenty-first century, Colonial Revival remains popular, as clients ranging from individual homeowners to governments and corporations favor the tried-and-true over the experimental. As this book was being written, yet another enormous, red-brick Colonial Revival building was going up in Dover, for Wilmington College (2003–2004, Homsey Architects).

NINETEENTH CENTURY

Socially and politically, nineteenth-century Delaware was conservative. This habit of thought—rooted in an agrarian economy and a palpably Southern mindset—manifested itself in ways both good and bad. "It is not to be wondered that a State which has no free schools should be behind others in civilization," sniffed *Harper's Weekly* in an 1868 cover story denouncing the use of the pillory and whipping post in New Castle (quaint institutions not abolished in the state until 1905 and 1952, respectively).[12] As architectural historian David Ames has written, political and architectural conservatism were tied to Delaware's extremely slow growth: from 64,200 persons in 1800 to 91,500 in 1850.[13] This 7.5 percent increase each decade compared to 34.3 percent nationally. Moreover, Delaware's demographic situation differed from most states: it had no frontier district, no claims to the westward, and little immigration, except to Wilmington. The booming conditions that produced vast expanses of Greek Revival elsewhere in the nation generally failed to occur

In the nineteenth century, baskets of peaches were hauled to market past the Jehu M. Reed House, Kent County (KT29). Ornamental grounds near the home gave way to numerous barns and outbuildings behind, serving specialized functions. In the next century the dirt road would become part of Du Pont Highway.

here, so that signature style of the early nineteenth century is relatively rare, except in a conservative manifestation by which Greek forms and motifs were grafted to old-fashioned Georgian boxes (for example, the house Monterey, built in 1847, on Road 423 near McDonough in southern New Castle County). The paucity of temple-front Greek Revival houses is often commented on, but several have been demolished, including Wilmington-area Draper Mansion (c. 1840) and Ellerslie (1842, home to a carousing F. Scott Fitzgerald in 1927–1929) as well as Lexington (1846, Samuel Sloan) near Delaware City.

If pure Greek Revival was relatively rare, the more flexible Italianate was common. Most examples are quite hybrid, but Ross Mansion, in Seaford, is a perfect pattern-book Italianate villa (WS10). Victorian buildings of many types are abundant in the state, though they are often shorn now of their full complement of decorative details (as at Queen Theater, WL15, or Darley House, BR3). Some locales are especially rich, such as Middletown, and a guidebook was published for Lewes, *Victorian Lewes and Its Architecture* (1986). The houses Rockwood (1851–1857; BR18) and Lesley Manor (1855; NC23) are sophisticated examples of antebellum Gothic Revival, the former being one of Delaware's few nationally important buildings. The subsequent Queen Anne can be found widely, as at Auburn Heights (CH37); Howard Pyle Studios (WL81); turreted and wide-porched Lindale in the town of Magnolia; or in the scenic Victorian Dover Historic District (DV4). Arts and Crafts inspired the unique community of Arden.

As late as the 1920s, it was said that Delaware was the most decidedly agricultural commonwealth in the nation.[14] Some 60 percent of its surface was under cultivation, a greater proportion than in any other state. In 1930, there were nearly 10,000 farms in Delaware occupying 900,815 acres (71.6 percent of the state). These conditions made Delaware, until the last twenty years' frenzy of suburbanization and demolition, a prime laboratory for the study of agricultural buildings and folkways. Rural types consisted of farm houses with their barns (see Cloud's Farm, CH36, and Cherbourg Round Barn, KT21), smokehouses (Corbit-Sharp House, LN6), privies, and other structures, as well as more specialized buildings serving specific needs: corn cribs (Ross Mansion, WS10), sweet-potato houses (Chipman's, WS24), muskrat-skinning sheds (Wilson-Warner House, LN7), and broiler houses for chickens (Mrs. Steele's, DV3.1). Downstate industries supporting agricultural activities included canneries and basket-making factories. The University of Delaware's Center for Historic Architecture and Design (CHAD) has sent fieldworkers to study all of these building types before they are destroyed. Their publications have made nineteenth-century agricultural Delaware perhaps the most intensively studied vernacular landscape in the country. *Buildings of Delaware* gives only a small sampling of vernacular outbuildings, as they are usually difficult to visit. Readers may examine them up close at Allee House (KT16), Delaware Agricultural Museum and Village (DV3), Dickinson Mansion (KT25; reconstructions), and Eleutherian Mills (CH15.6); also, from the road in many

In the pine woods of Sussex County early in the twentieth century, these African American children attended Blocksom's Colored School. After World War I, Pierre S. du Pont would build improved (but still segregated) schools for both blacks and whites in the state.

places, including Achmester (LN11), Cochran Grange (LN17), and Wheel of Fortune (KT17).

African American history and architecture have lately attracted attention (see, for example, the former schools at Hockessin, MC3, and Iron Hill, PR2). Compared to most Southern states, slavery played a lesser role in Delaware, though it was nonetheless a subject of sharp dispute. As early as 1800, freed blacks outnumbered slaves as the state's slave population steadily dropped. By 1860, 20,000 African Americans were free, but 1,800 were still enslaved. Nearly all slaves worked in agriculture. Never numerous, slave quarters subsequently disappeared along with outbuildings of all kinds, and persistent searches have turned up few survivals (but see Causey and Ross mansions, KT38.1 and WS10.2). Delaware lay along the Underground Railroad, and in recent years there has been great interest in locating sites. The Wilmington home of abolitionist Thomas Garrett having long since been demolished, we are left with locales based largely on hearsay or myth. The supposed tunnel that led runaways to safety from the basement of Woodburn (DV6) exemplifies the chimerical nature of many Underground Railroad attributions: no such tunnel ever existed, except in the pages of George A. Townsend's novel, *The Entailed Hat* (1884).[15] More recent African American historic sites

INTRODUCTION   15

are fast disappearing, including the headquarters of a pioneering men's organization, the Monday Club, demolished in 2004 by a Wilmington bank, which had previously razed the United African Methodist Episcopal (U.A.M.E.) Church nearby.[16]

ARCHITECTS

While the state's vernacular builders have lately received considerable attention from historians, its architects remain virtually unstudied. Of the few active here before the Civil War, most were borrowed from Philadelphia and included some of national prominence: Benjamin Henry Latrobe, William Strickland, Samuel Sloan, John Notman, and Thomas U. Walter. Strickland and Robert Mills apprenticed for Latrobe, and all three lived for a time in New Castle. After the war, booming Wilmington at last offered opportunities for a native son, Edward Luff Rice Jr., active from 1870 on and responsible for the frame, Queen Anne style Delaware State Building at the 1876 Centennial Exhibition in Philadelphia.

Ties to Philadelphia long remained close. Frank Furness had several Delaware commissions, including Wilmington Station (WL5) and the ingenious but now demolished B&O Station at Trolley Square, Wilmington, and Stephen

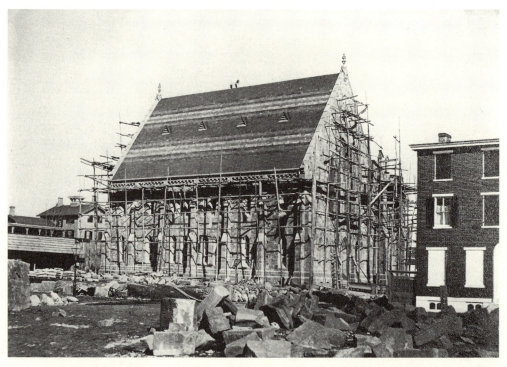

Once the pride of Wilmington, Grace Methodist (WL45) was designed by Baltimore architect Thomas Dixon using green serpentine stone from Pennsylvania, red brownstone from Connecticut, and buff New Brunswick, New Jersey, sandstone. Its Chapel section neared completion in early 1866.

Everything was synthetic in the Nylon Suite at the Hotel du Pont, Wilmington (1948, Joanne Seybold; WL32), a showcase for the revolutionary fiber that epitomized "Better Living Through Chemistry."

Decatur Button concluded his career with Delaware State Hospital, Farnhurst (1882–1884; NC1). A Cope and Stewardson office photograph taken in Philadelphia around 1899 shows several young men who later designed Delaware buildings: James O. Betelle (Delaware public schools), E. Perot Bissell (Winterthur, CH10), Alfred Morton Githens (Wilmington Public Library, WL28), William Woodburn Potter (Wilmington churches), and Herbert C. Wise (University of Delaware). Furness's protégé, E. James Dallett, eventually moved to Wilmington, and the firm of Baker and Dallett was long dominant there. Philadelphian Will Price provided plans for the village of Arden; George I. Lovatt designed Catholic churches in Wilmington; and Wallace and Warner provided nearly two dozen house designs for wealthy Wilmingtonians in the Jazz Age. Some Wilmington architects of the 1920s–1950s who trained with Philadelphia firms or at Philadelphia schools include Weston Holt Blake, William Bonner, Erling Dollar, William Lawler, E. Canby May, Hubert Shelton Stees, and G. Morris Whiteside.

"Most Americans and especially Delawareans have very little conception of what an architect is," Beaux-Arts trained Alfred Victor du Pont lamented in 1933.[17] But this was gradually changing; the year before, Whiteside (Philadelphia born and educated) had organized the Delaware Chapter of the American Institute of Architects (AIA). At that time, the firm of Brown and Whiteside was the state's largest and symbolized the maturing of the architectural profession here (see **Modernism in Delaware** on p. 42). Other firms that contributed early members to Delaware's AIA were Martin and Jeffers (Colonial Revivalists) and Massena and du Pont (specializing in Stripped Classicism and Moderne). Even as several new firms gained hold in Wilmington, the rapidly expanding DuPont Company organized an in-house Engineering Department responsible for the design of chemical plants nationwide, along with Home Office structures in Wilmington. Hubert Stees, for example, spent the 1930s designing for DuPont as it produced more buildings than all the other architectural firms in the city combined. As it happened, the DuPont Building (WL32) housed some of those private firms, too, with Martin and Jeffers

THE DU PONT FAMILY AND ARCHITECTURE

This genealogy is limited to the du Ponts mentioned in *Buildings of Delaware,* down to the sixth generation in America (numbered 1–6). In parentheses appear the names of homes or other edifices associated with them, as builders or residents (plus a key decade of construction or alteration). Buildings that are *starred have entries in the book; demolished ones have a †dagger. Some du Ponts became architects or married one, as indicated.

1 Pierre Samuel d P de Nemours
    2 Victor Marie d P (Lower Louviers 1810s)
        3 Charles I. d P ("C.I.D." house 1820s; Lower Louviers)
            4 Victor d P (Renaud 1880s†)
        3 Adm. Samuel Francis D P (Upper Louviers 1830s†)
    2 Eleuthère Irénée (E.I.) d P (*Eleutherian Mills 1800s, *Hagley Yard 1820s)
        3 Victorine d P (*Brandywine Manufacturers' Sunday School 1810s)
        3 Evelina d P m. James A. Bidermann (*Winterthur 1830s)
        3 Alfred Victor d P (first Nemours 1820s; *First Office 1830s) m. Margaretta Lammot (*Goodstay 1860s)
            4 E. I. d P (Swamp Hall†)
                5 Alfred I. d P (*Nemours 1900s) m. Bessie Gardner (*Chevannes 1920s)
                    6 Alfred Victor d P (*architect*)
            4 Lammot d P (first Nemours) m. Mary Belin (*St. Amour 1890s†)
                5 Louisa d P m. Charles Copeland (Colonial Revival house†)
                    6 Lammot d P Copeland m. Pamela Cunningham (*Mt. Cuba 1930s)
                5 Pierre S. d P (Longwood, PA; *many Del. schools, etc., 1920s)
                5 Henry Belin d P
                5 William K. d P (Still Pond 1890s†)
                    6 S. Hallock d P (Squirrel Run 1920s)
                5 Irénée d P (Square House 1900s, later called St. Giles†; *Granogue 1920s)
                5 Lammot d P (first Iris Brook 1900s†; *St. Amour 1910s†)
                    6 P. S. d P III (Bois-Des-Fosses 1930s, today's *Brantwyn)

on the third floor looking across the courtyard at rival Brown and Whiteside on the second. Both before and after the Great Depression, however—a nadir for architectural commissions—most design work in the state was done by outsiders. In 1946, there were thirty-three Delawareans registered within the state as architects, but sixty-eight registered from outside. Thanks to State Board of Education policy, school commissions went to Delaware architects only, which helped several partnerships thrive.

Like all small businesses, local architectural firms are prone to rapid change and disappearance, and forgotten today are the once-renowned Fletcher and Buck; Martin and Jeffers; Massena and du Pont (later Young and Banwell); Pope and Kruse; and W. Ellis Preston. Nonetheless, at the start of the twenty-first century, there were at least six firms that had operated since the 1960s: Moeckel Carbonell Associates (1909, originally Brown and Whiteside), Homsey Architects (1935), Anderson Brown Higley Associates

   5 Isabella d P (Meown 1930s) m. H. Rodney Sharp (*Gibraltar 1910s, *U. Del. 1910s)
  4 A. Bidermann d P
   5 T. Coleman d P (Du Pont Highway 1910s)
    6 Ellen d P (*Goodstay 1920s) m. Robert Wheelwright (*landscape architect*)
    6 Alice d P m. C. Douglass Buck (*Buena Vista 1930s)
    6 Francis V. d P (U. S. highways 1950s)
   5 A. B. d P
    6 Victorine d P (*architect*) m. Samuel Homsey (*architect*) (*Homsey Architects)
 3 "Boss Henry" d P (*Eleutherian Mills 1850s)
  4 Col. Henry Algernon d P (*Winterthur 1870s)
   5 Louise d P m. Francis B. Crowninshield (*Eleutherian Mills 1920s)
   5 Henry Francis d P (*Winterthur 1920s)
  4 Sophie d P m. Theophilus P. Chandler (*architect*)
  4 William d P (Pelleport 1870s†; Montpelier, VA)
   5 William d P (*Bellevue Hall 1930s)
 3 Alexis Irénée d P (second Hagley house†; *Christ Church C. H. 1850s; *Cath. Church of St. John 1850s)
  4 Eugene d P (Pelleport†)
   5 Eugene d P (*Owl's Nest 1910s)
   5 Amy d P (Pelleport†; Dauneport 1930s)
  4 Alexis I. d P (Rencourt 1880s†)
   5 Philip F. d P
    6 Jane d P m. Harry Lunger (*Oberod 1930s)
   5 Eugene d P (Dogwood†)
  4 Francis G. d P (current Hagley house; today's *A. I. d P Middle School 1890s)
   5 Eleanor d P m. Robeson Lea Perot (*architect*)
   5 A. Felix d P (*St. Andrew's School 1920s) m. Mary Chichester (Elton 1920s†)
   5 Ernest d P (Spanish House 1910s†)
   5 E. Paul d P (*E. Paul d P House 1910s)

(1949, originally Stanhope and Manning, later Dollar and Bonner), R. Calvin Clendaniel Associates (1961), The Architects Studio (1967, firm of Jim Nelson), and Weymouth Architects (1968). All were headquartered in Wilmington except Clendaniel, downstate in Lincoln. These survivors have subsequently been joined by numerous younger firms, listed by AIA Delaware as numbering at least fifteen in Wilmington, two in Dover and Georgetown, and one each in Newport, Christiana, Milford, Lewes, Bethany, and Laurel.

DU PONT ESTATES

Wilmington-area country estates built by wealthy du Ponts and their business associates form Delaware's most famous architectural legacy, sometimes called Chateau Country. Best known is Winterthur, a museum for more than fifty years now. Starting as a gunpowder factory in 1802 at Eleutherian Mills

Hagley House (1814) along the Brandywine was enlarged by Alexis I. du Pont in 1852–1854. Soon after, it was damaged in the powderworks explosion that killed Alexis in Hagley Yard just downhill (CH15.1). Subsequent blasts contributed to the eventual abandonment of the place, which was finally razed in the 1950s.

(CH15.4) on Brandywine Creek, the DuPont Company expanded in the early twentieth century into a gigantic chemical corporation known worldwide. The du Pont chateaux are not a monolithic group, but were built across many decades in a variety of styles. Today's examples are but part of a larger number, the rest having been razed.[18]

Several of the grand houses were made possible by wartime profits from gunpowder in 1914–1918, when just one family member, Alfred I. du Pont, saw his income reach a staggering $3 million a year. He had already built a chateau at Nemours (BR26.1) but now added a Versailles-like garden (BR26.2). All the estates infused Delaware architecture with a flavor of internationalism otherwise lacking, as the family were inveterate travelers—Alfred I. adopted a war orphan off the Paris streets, and H. Rodney Sharp of Gibraltar (WL94) crossed the Atlantic fifty times and would eventually die aboard an ocean liner returning from Italy. Some of the houses were French-inspired, as befitted the origins of eighteenth-century founding father Pierre Samuel du Pont de Nemours, or they emulated one or another of the ancestral homes in France. Several chateau architects were kin to the clannish family by blood or marriage, including Theophilus Parsons Chandler, Robeson Lea Perot, Alfred Victor du Pont, C. Douglass Buck Jr., the Homseys, and Jim Thompson (later a businessman in Asia famous as the "Thai Silk King"). At times, estate architects of regional or national prominence were brought in by the du Ponts or their wealthy neighbors, including Carrère and Hastings (Nemours); DeArmond, Ashmead and Bickley (Oberod, CH1; Gibraltar, WL94); Albert Ely Ives (Winterthur; Chevannes, CH13); Harrie T. Lindeberg (Owl's Nest, CH5); Mellor, Meigs and Howe (Selborne Farms, CH2; Eleutherian Mills); and R. Brognard Okie (Merestone, NK1). Woodwork for sumptuous interiors came from the Mill Department of American Car and Foundry Company, the firm that had taken over the old Jackson and Sharp railroad car plant on the Brandywine in 1901. In 1925, the company switched to making luxury yachts, of which it produced more than 300 before abandoning that business in 1938. In the flush years before the Great Depression, wealthy Wilmingtonians might have purchased both their yacht and dining room from the same firm. Of the chateaux that have been spared demolition, several have been transformed into museums, conference centers, or institutes since 1950, making it possible for the public to gain access to an unprecedented degree. The most recent conversion (2003–2004) was of the Copeland estate, Mt. Cuba (MC4).

TRANSPORTATION

Delaware's entire history could be told from the standpoint of transportation. Water was the first avenue of travel for colonists, and it remains vital today, with countless ships passing along the Delaware River and through the Chesapeake and Delaware Canal. Said to be the only American canal constructed before 1900 that is still in commercial use, the C&D (begun 1824, now hugely enlarged) carries 40 percent of the Port of Baltimore's ship traffic. With its ample frontage on river and ocean, Delaware once had many lighthouses to guide vessels. Eighteen of the original twenty-seven have disappeared, including ones at Bombay Hook (1829, burned 1970s), Port Mahon (1903, burned 1984), and Mispillion (1873–1875, destroyed by lightning in 2002)—all on the Delaware River. However, several survivors are included in the present book (LN1, KT28, ES26, ES43), as are waterfront fortifications that span several centuries.

Water can form a hindrance to travel as well as a help, of course, so the Dutch built dikes—still to be seen at New Castle and Lewes (ES15)—and later came bridges of all kinds. Brandywine Creek saw experimentation with bridge types, including an early chain suspension span, a spillover from innovations at Philadelphia (see North Market Street Bridge, WL51). Northern Delawareans have long taken an interest in covered bridges, a building type derived from Pennsylvania, where they are more numerous than in any other state. The wooden covering serves to keep the structural truss joints dry, so they will not swell or shrink. Delaware once had dozens of nineteenth-century covered bridges, but these were down to twelve by 1930. The rise of automobile and truck traffic resulted in fatal damage to many of the remainder, including three over the Brandywine demolished in 1928–1934. The second-

Ithiel Town's famous lattice truss revolutionized bridge design nationwide in the early nineteenth century, and Delaware had several examples. Wooddale Covered Bridge (c. 1860, CH32; here with its sheathing removed for 1960s repairs) was later pulverized by a flood.

to-last survivor in the state, at Wooddale (CH32), was destroyed by a flood in 2003. It is to be rebuilt by the Delaware Department of Transportation (DelDOT), which takes good care of the state's 1,437 road bridges and recently reconstructed the lost Smith's Bridge (BR37). Recent years have seen continuing bridge innovation. Delaware Memorial suspension bridge over the Delaware River was the sixth-longest in the world when completed in 1951; later it was enlarged as the biggest twin span anywhere. Lately, the state has constructed or planned two cable-stay bridges on the cutting edge of bridge design nationwide (PR13, ES37).

Improved north–south turnpike roads of the early nineteenth century allowed efficient transport of grain from the Piedmont to shipping or milling points in northern Delaware—Pennsylvania farmers driving down the Limestone, Newport and Gap, Kennett, and Concord pikes in huge Conestoga wagons. Centreville exemplifies the towns that sprang up along these routes; Christiana, the point of transfer from wagon to ship; and Brandywine Village, a milling center. All had taverns where farmers could spend the night. Travelers between Philadelphia and Baltimore constantly passed east-to-west through Wilmington, Newport (or New Castle), and Christiana, making these towns familiar to every colonial tourist. George Washington, to take a famous example, is reputed to have slept at taverns along the way (BR1, BR20), held war councils (WL53, MC11), and "kissed the pretty girls" at a New Castle society wedding (NC19). His records confirm that he "lodged at Wil. at O'Flins." tavern (WL12) and spent the night in Christiana as often as five times in a six-month period (MC12).[19] Then, as now, Delaware was frequently a place one passed through on the way to somewhere else.

In spite of modern development and new highways, most of Delaware's roads still follow their ancient routes through the countryside, as a drive with Beers's *Atlas of the State of Delaware* (1868) makes clear. But, as in all states, the coming of the railroad profoundly reshaped the landscape, encouraging the rise of new towns and the growth of formerly remote regions. The New Castle and Frenchtown Railroad, one of the very earliest American lines, cut across Delaware in 1830–1832 (see **New Castle and Frenchtown Railroad** on p. 162). Later came the Baltimore and Ohio Railroad and Pennsylvania Railroad, with various connecting lines: the Wilmington and Western (CH30) served the water-powered industries of the Piedmont, and the north-to-south Delaware Railroad spurred the agricultural development of downstate. Many buildings described in this book owe their existence to the railroad, and not

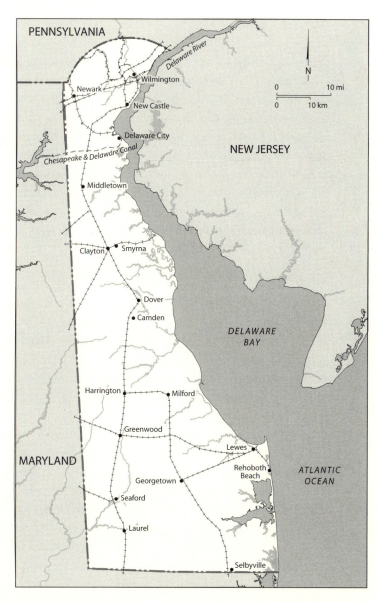

DELAWARE RAILROADS, 1880s
The railroad network shown here dramatically reconfigured commerce and settlement (compare to the map of Delaware roads on p. 10). New towns appeared along the lines, especially in Sussex County.

INTRODUCTION 23

just the railroad stations that are still landmarks in towns from Wilmington (WL5) to Dover (DV9) and beyond. Railroads allowed the importation of eclectic architectural materials, for example, colorful bricks to Harrington (KT34) or concrete blocks imitating stone to Bridgeville. Wealthy manufacturers used the railroad to import raw materials for powdermaking (CH15.1) or building ships (WL8), and on the weekend they took it to country estates (Archmere, BR4; Granogue, CH9), to railroad-company shooting lodges in Sussex County (ES2), or to new vacation communities along the Atlantic beaches. Delaware farmers grew wealthy in the shipment of produce by train and built big houses, sometimes called "Peach Mansions," for the crop that benefited most from rapid transport to urban markets. ("Peach Mansions" is often misleadingly applied to houses that predated both the railroad and the peach boom; see Cochran Grange, LN17.)

The job of shipping agricultural products was taken over in the twentieth century by trucks. Tomato and poultry industries in Kent and Sussex counties were made possible largely by concrete "farm-to-market" highways (see **Du Pont Highway** on pp. 266–67). Later, those highways mostly carried automobiles, as is the case with the new, sprawl-bringing DE 1 (completed 2003). The roads that once benefited the farmer have now put him out of business, as farmland in Delaware declined by 50 percent between 1890 and 1990, owing to urbanization. Roads define and dominate modern Delaware, especially in the congested northern third that is laced by arteries linking it to Maryland, Pennsylvania, and New Jersey, traffic reaching its maximum at a notorious chokepoint near, ironically, the old colonial town that George Washington passed through so often—Christiana.

SUBURBS

Thanks in part to its early road improvements, Delaware is an excellent place to study the development of the modern American suburb. Even as early as 1900–1941, architectural historian Susan Chase has shown, the outskirts of Wilmington saw 143 subdivisions spring up on streetcar lines or automobile routes.[20] Innovative planning was on display at Overlook Colony (BR5), Villa Monterey (BR16), and Union Park Gardens (WL78). The $1.4 million in Works Progress Administration (WPA) funds channeled to the state in 1935–1936 went partly to projects that benefited these new suburbs, including roadwork, stream channelization, and sewer construction. The Depression and World War II curtailed the development of many suburbs, including the exclusive residential park of Henlopen Acres at the beach (ES28). With their varied materials—Brandywine granite, oak, stucco, tile—the pre–World War II suburban dwellings generally form a charming body of work, making subsequent builder-designed tract houses seem anemic by comparison—as, for example, at the development of Fairfax in the 1950s (BR31).

The modern history of Delaware has been defined by its location in the

In May 1940, farm fields in Brandywine Hundred were sprouting houses. The 200 homes of Edgemoor Terrace (priced at $5,000 to $8,000) were under construction, with an old farmhouse and barn remaining nearby. Commuters took the new Governor Printz Boulevard (left) into downtown Wilmington.

Boston-to-Washington megalopolis, said to be the largest urbanized area in world history. Because Delaware remained largely rural until World War II, its subsequent growth (like that of neighboring Maryland) was especially fast and wrenching, causing, by 1969, what a Wilmington architect called "some of the most severe growth problems known in the nation."[21] The changes began when wartime industry brought an influx of workers to Wilmington. Subsequently, growth in the 1950s was astounding. Delaware's population climbed 40 percent, making it the fifth fastest-growing state in America. In just ten years, Delaware added more new residents than its entire population had numbered in 1870. Suburban New Castle County nearly doubled in population; smaller than Wilmington in 1950, it closed the decade at more than twice its size, with new communities sprouting like mushrooms (see Brookside, NK14).

Between 1950 and 1970, Delaware grew twice as fast as the United States as a whole, and explosive growth raised calls for planning. New Castle County had no zoning before 1954. By the time President John Kennedy dedicated the Delaware Turnpike (I-95; PR1) in 1963, only 75,000 acres of open space were left north of the C&D Canal, and these were being swallowed at a rate of 4,000 acres annually. The Delaware AIA warned that, at the current rate of development, northern Delaware would run out of open land by 1982; it called for immediate planning.[22] Architect Samuel Homsey was instrumental in at last getting zoning established. But other architects felt hopeless in the face of the sprawl and bad design, especially as they lost control to the developers, many of whom were from out of state and concerned only with profits. One architect complained in 1962, "We have a hodge podge of architecture in our area put up by builders and owners and sometimes architects who have no conception of good design."[23] In 1967, C. Douglass Buck Jr. was one of many architects who complained bitterly about "the political dominance and red tape which had resulted in bad architecture and unprecedented ugliness throughout our greater community. The evidence screams at us from the edges of our strip zoned arteries"—most infamously, along Kirkwood Highway between Wilmington and booming Newark (see Prices Corner Shopping Center, CH29).[24] Most suburban building was banal, but here and there some examples showed the willingness to experiment that marked the best of the 1950s and 1960s nationwide. Department stores (Wanamaker's, BR22), churches (Aldersgate United Methodist, BR33), and schools (Wilmington High, WL79) were especially interesting. Some reformers have repeatedly tried to improve upon suburbia with innovative, community-building designs—as early as 1966 at Valley Run (BR6) and currently at Town of Parkside (LN12) or Village at Kings Creek (ES33). Today, for all of suburbia's much-publicized flaws, Delawareans continue to crave it.

HISTORIC PRESERVATION

The architect G. Morris Whiteside observed in the 1940s that preservation had been slow to come to Delaware, compared to neighboring states.[25] Nonetheless, a few architectural sentimentalists had been vocal early on. Writers and artists played a critical role as they cast about for picturesque scenes. Wilmington artist Howard Pyle complained of changes at his beloved Old Swedes Church: "Old buildings and fragments of the past are to me very and vitally alive."[26] Between 1877 and 1909, Pyle illustrated no fewer than eighty-seven magazine articles on colonial and Revolutionary subjects, often with architectural backdrops. Local painter Robert Shaw produced numerous prints of old Delaware buildings, writing in 1894–1895 that he was busy with "etchings that I contemplate publishing to preserve some of the old landmarks about our city" and lamenting that "I didn't begin soon enough."[27] Founded in 1896, Friends of Old Drawyers (LN5) was Delaware's first preservation group. Twentieth-century campaigns to save Old First Presbyterian Church (WL58) and Old Town Hall (WL19) in Wilmington (1917), Cape Henlopen Lighthouse (1926), and the Bank of Delaware (WL89; 1931) attracted widespread publicity.

As losses accelerated, the Americana Decade of the 1920s brought a spike in interest. Herbert C. Wise (a designer of the University of Delaware campus) included Delaware examples in *Colonial Architecture for Those About to Build* (1924), and, a year later, he wrote on New Castle's Read House (NC21) for *White Pine*. An issue of that journal in 1926 treated New Castle in detail. Architect George F. Bennett traveled around his native state for twenty-eight months making measured drawings for his *Early Architecture of Delaware* (1932). The Colonial Dames provided Bennett with a supplementary list of historic sites, mostly patriotic in their associations. Bennett's volume was aimed at people seeking elements to incorporate in Colonial Revival homes, and he offered hints on "adapting these early details to modern needs and taste."[28] The automobile allowed easier access to Delaware's historic architecture, which the Historic Markers Commission (first report, January 1931) helpfully began to point out with metal signs. For years, historic churches had hosted annual events such as "Anniversaries" or community festivals, and this idea was now secularized and expanded to whole historic towns with the creation of A Day in Old New Castle (1924) and Old Dover Day (1933).

During the Great Depression, the Delaware office of the Historic American Buildings Survey (HABS) was started under architect Albert Kruse with ten employees in the Old Town Hall, Wilmington (January 1934) and, a year later, under Weston Holt Blake (who presided over the office at 10th and West streets). Blake pointed to some 300 distinctively designed buildings over a century old in the state. By 1941, when funding ran out, 114 buildings had been surveyed in New Castle County alone. Willard S. Stewart provided much HABS photography. The first production of the Federal Writers' Project anywhere—before any of the state guidebooks—was *New Castle on the Delaware* (1936), with abundant information on architecture. It was followed by the indispensable *Delaware: A Guide to the First State,* largely written in 1936 and published two years later, which devoted a chapter to the subject of architecture and described hundreds of significant buildings, many treated in print there for the first time. During those years, New Castle was a major focus of the efforts of Mary Wilson Thompson, who organized the Delaware Society for the Preservation of Antiquities, modeled after the similarly titled group in New England, to "preserve the buildings left to us as a heritage by our forefathers and which are far more beautiful than modern structures," including the Dutch House (NC7).[29] Louise Crowninshield, sister of Henry Francis du Pont of Winterthur and later a founder of the National Trust for Historic Preservation, aided Thompson. The Colonial Dames were also active preservationists. In the matter of rescuing the past, the uppercrust Wilmingtonians' conservative habit of thought proved beneficial—not only in Delaware, but also in their helping to fund the restoration of colonial houses elsewhere, such as Stratford Hall and Kenmore, in Virginia.

Gradually, local historical societies were formed in the face of appalling post–World War II losses of historic fabric. Lewes Historical Society saved and restored the Burton-Ingram House and Early Plank House (ES16.1), the

As Colonial Revival triumphed in twentieth-century Dover, Victorian buildings were purged. The architecturally significant Post Office (1873–1878, William Appleton Potter), seen here being moved in 1934, was demolished four decades later.

former becoming the site of the Second Annual Delaware Preservation Conference in September 1963 (the first had taken place a year before in New Castle). Nearly 200 participants heard architects and historians Albert Kruse, Robert Raley, and Harold D. Eberlein call for restoration of all kinds of historic buildings, even the small and unimportant—presaging today's interest in vernacular structures. Eberlein had just published his landmark *Historic Houses and Buildings of Delaware* (1962), a volume suggested in part by the history-minded Mabel Lloyd Ridgely in Dover (see her home, DV13), who was dismayed at the increasing number of old houses and buildings in the state being torn down. About this time, AIA Delaware had the Junior League undertake a project over two years to identify every pre-1850 building surviving in Brandywine and Christiana Hundreds. Volunteers took 1,615 photographs, now at the Historical Society of Delaware.

The state played an increasing role in preservation under the impetus of longtime archivist Leon deValinger, who sponsored the work of Eberlein and Cortlandt Hubbard. DeValinger arranged the acquisition of several historic houses by the archives commission, starting with the Dickinson Mansion (1952; KT25) and Fisher-Martin House (1962; ES24). Upon turning ninety-five in 2000, deValinger could look back proudly on the whole development of professional historic preservation in Delaware. In 1972, a State Historic Preservation Office had been established under Edward F. Heite. The office eventually found an unlikely ally in the highway department. Long a notorious devourer of old buildings, DelDOT by the 1990s began purchasing them to prevent sprawl (see the Weldin House, BR19). Delaware was late to have state parks, but today there are several that contain important examples of early architecture that otherwise might have been lost. Unfortunately, a number of buildings purchased by the state for preservation, including Buck Tavern (PR10), Lum House (PR11), and Octagonal Schoolhouse (KT18), are currently boarded-up and inexorably decaying.

The University of Delaware has never had a School of Architecture, but several notable programs there allow students to investigate architectural history. The Winterthur Program in Early American Culture (1952), brainchild of Winterthur Museum director Charles F. Montgomery and art historian Frank H. Sommer, derived from Henry Francis du Pont's love of antiques, including old buildings, as manifested at Winterthur Museum. The Hagley Program soon followed (1954), associated with the Hagley Foundation headed by Walter J. Heacock. In the History Department, John A. Munroe, and, later, Carol E. Hoffecker were among the first trained scholars to write about Delaware's architecture. Art historian Alan Gowans ran the Art Department from 1959 to 1966, during which time he published an acclaimed book on architecture, *Images of American Living* (1964). The College of Urban Affairs was founded by a Ford Foundation grant in 1961. In later years came the Art History Department (1966) and the Center for Historic Architecture and Design (1984). These programs have collectively generated considerable scholarship on Delaware's architecture and landscape history.

In spite of increased study, however, much about Delaware's architecture

A home of c. 1810, Middletown's Greenlawn was repeatedly enlarged in the Victorian era, making it an excellent example of the Delaware "evolved house." In the 1990s it was razed for a shopping center as sprawl transformed southern New Castle County.

remains obscure—even as the early examples continue to slip away. "Art builds on sand," reads the inscription on Wilmington's Josephine Fountain (WL59), an appropriate epitaph for the state's architectural heritage. One cause of huge losses is Delaware's high standard of living, which encourages rebuilding. In 1959, Delaware had the highest per capita income in the United States, and, in 2000, its poverty rate remained eighth lowest in the nation. By the latter year, only half of the housing units extant in the state in 1940 still stood, an astounding 40,000 having been destroyed through redevelopment—a preservationist's nightmare. Most Delawareans live surrounded by shiny newness: 40 percent of homes in the state postdate 1980!

Nearly every early building discussed in this book has, at one time or another, been threatened with demolition. Each was saved because one or two people cared enough to speak out. Those who love and respect Delaware's historic architecture owe them gratitude.

NOTES

1. John Lofland, *Poetical and Prose Writings* (Baltimore: John Murphy, 1853), 105.
2. Jay F. Custer, "Stability, Storage, and Culture Change in Prehistoric Delaware" (Dover: Delaware State Historic Preservation Office, 1994).
3. Statistics from Peter Stebbins Craig, *The 1693 Census of the Swedes on the Delaware* (Winter Park, Fla.: SAG Publications, 1993).
4. C. A. Weslager, *The Log Cabin in America* (New Brunswick: Rutgers University Press, 1969); Terry G. Jordan and Matti Kaups, *The American Backwoods Frontier: An Ethnic and Ecological Interpretation* (Baltimore: Johns Hopkins University Press, in association with the Center for American Places, 1989).
5. Springer House in Barbara Clark Smith, *After the Revolution* (New York: Random House, 1985); "Hog Neck" in Joshua Hempstead (1749), *Delaware History* 7:1 (March 1956): 96.
6. Bernard Herman, "Eighteenth-Century Quaker Houses in the Delaware Valley and the Aesthetics of Practice," in Emma J. Lapansky and Anne A. Verplanck, *Quaker Aesthetics: Reflections on a Quaker Ethic in American Design and Consumption* (Philadelphia: University of Pennsylvania Press, 2003), 188–211; Gabrielle M. Lanier and Bernard L. Herman, *Everyday Architecture of the Mid-Atlantic: Looking at Buildings and Landscapes* (Baltimore: Johns Hopkins University Press, in association with the Center for American Places, 1997), 66.
7. James C. Booth, *Memoir of the Geological Survey of the State of Delaware* (Dover: S. Kimmey, 1841).
8. Margaret O. Plank and William S. Schenck, *Delaware Piedmont Geology* (Newark: Delaware Geological Survey, 1998).
9. Ralph Adams Cram, *American Church Building of Today* (New York: Architectural Book Publishing Co., 1929).
10. Leo A. Borah, "Diamond Delaware, Colonial Still," *National Geographic* 68:3 (September 1935): 367–98.
11. Editorial, *Center Line* (AIA Delaware) 4:3 (October 1962): 7.
12. "The Whipping-Post and Pillory in Delaware," *Harper's Weekly* 12:624 (December 12, 1868): 791.

13. David L. Ames, "Architectural Style in Delaware," draft (Newark: Center for Historic Architecture and Engineering, University of Delaware, 1992), 8.
14. 1920s statistics in *Delaware: Its Products, Resources, and Opportunities* (Wilmington: National Publishing Co., c. 1925).
15. George A. Townsend, *The Entailed Hat* (New York: Harper and Brothers, 1884).
16. On slavery, see Patience Essah, *A House Divided: Slavery and Emancipation in Delaware, 1638–1865* (Charlottesville: University of Virginia Press, 1996).
17. Alfred Victor du Pont to A. I. du Pont (June 17, 1933), Accession 1508, Hagley Museum and Library.
18. Destroyed relatively early were Swamp Hall (demolished c. 1910), the original Iris Brook (c. 1925), Rencourt (c. 1950), second Hagley (1950s), Pelleport (1954), and Dogwood (c. 1960). Vanished more recently are Elton (1970), St. Amour (1972), Still Pond (burned c. 1975), Upper Louviers (1978), St. Giles (c. 1980), and Spanish House (early 1990s). Barbara E. Benson, "Vanished Estates of the du Pont Family," *The Hunt* (June–July 2000): 66–78.
19. Jeannette Eckman, *New Castle on the Delaware* (New Castle: New Castle Historical Society, 1950), 88.
20. Susan Mulchahey Chase, *The Process of Suburbanization and the Use of Restrictive Deed Covenants as Private Zoning, Wilmington, Delaware, 1900–1941* (master's thesis, University of Delaware, 1995).
21. "Growth Problems," *Center Line* (AIA Delaware) 10:3 (1969).
22. Ibid.
23. Editorial, *Center Line* 4:3 (October 1962): 7.
24. C. Douglass Buck Jr., *Center Line* 9:1 (Summer 1967).
25. G. Morris Whiteside, "Architecture," in *Delaware: A Guide to the First State* (WPA guidebook; New York: Viking Press, 1938).
26. Charles D. Abbott, *Howard Pyle: A Chronicle* (New York and London: Harper & Brothers, 1925), 153.
27. Thomas Beckman, "The Etchings of Robert Shaw," *Delaware History* 24:2 (Fall–Winter 1990): 75–108.
28. George Fletcher Bennett, *Early Architecture of Delaware* (1932 reprint, Wilmington: Middle Atlantic Press, 1985), 47.
29. Mary Wilson Thompson, "Memoir," pt. 4, *Delaware History* 23:4 (Fall–Winter 1979): 238–66.

Brandywine Hundred

Culturally, Brandywine Hundred in extreme northern New Castle County is oriented almost as much toward Pennsylvania as toward Wilmington. William Penn's Quakers established a seventeenth-century meeting house at Carrcroft, northeast of Wilmington (the current building dates from 1845, with Gothic Revival additions of 1906). The fascinating utopia of Arden was created by Philadelphians (1900), and industrialized Claymont is an extension of the factories in the towns of Chester and Marcus Hook in Pennsylvania. In the early twentieth century, the Delaware River shoreline became increasingly industrial. The DuPont Company's Krebs Pigment and Color Corporation factory (1935) still belches smoke at Edgemoor, near the site of the famous nineteenth-century Edge Moor Iron Works, which closed that same year. Founded in 1869, Edge Moor provided the wrought and cast iron of the Main Building at the Centennial Exhibition in Philadelphia in 1876, rolled iron and steel for the Brooklyn Bridge (1883), and is said to have prefabricated the Transportation Building for the World's Columbian Exposition of 1893 in Chicago.

In the twentieth century, suburbanization swept over the hundred. Architectural historian Susan Chase (1995) has identified ninety-three subdivisions built between 1900 and 1950. In that period, the population increased sixfold; then, in the 1950s alone, it further increased by 142 percent. Post–World War II developments were three times more compactly designed than the land-gulping ones built farther downstate in subsequent decades, but they preserved little open space and usually razed the old farmhouses of stone and frame. Nonetheless, a survey in the 1960s of this and adjacent Christiana Hundred found 486 buildings surviving from before 1850. Most developments were architecturally conservative; the look-alike modernist, corner-windowed houses of the one-street neighborhood of Delwood, east of Blue Ball, is a curious exception (1941). The new suburbs were served in part by International-Style Brandywine High School by Whiteside, Moeckel and Carbonell (1957–1959; 1400 Foulk Rd.).

Heavily traveled Concord Pike (U.S. 202) forms the spine of the westerly district of the hundred. It is practically impossible to imagine the days when this turnpike—a conduit for the shipment of Chester County's grain to mills

Bridge trusses were manufactured at Edge Moor Iron Works, seen in this newly discovered photograph, July 1886.

on Brandywine Creek at North Market Street Bridge in Wilmington (WL51)—traversed fertile farmland. Rapid growth in the 1950s yielded some progressive modernism, much of which is now disappearing, including the glass-fronted library at Talleyville (1957–1959; Whiteside, Moeckel and Carbonell), demolished in 2005. The nearby Charcoal Pit restaurant (1956; 2600 Concord Pike) is a local landmark. A 225-acre park was created in 2002–2007 at the historic site of Blue Ball Tavern (eighteenth century, recently demolished) and around Alfred I. du Pont's Blue Ball Barn (c. 1914). Incredibly, du Pont's nearby Nemours estate (BR26) still contains several acres of virgin forest, a leafy oasis in a district that has seen sweeping changes.

CLAYMONT

For the colonial traveler, arrival in Delaware meant paying a toll at Naamans Creek Bridge, twenty miles from Philadelphia (still indicated by a highway stone). Blue rock was quarried along the creek and transported widely via the Delaware River. Nearby Claymont had charm and convenience and was an attractive locale for a summer home overlooking the water. It was served by the Philadelphia, Wilmington and Baltimore Railroad starting in 1837. Great changes came with the construction of plants for General Chemical (1912), National Aniline Chemical (1914), and Worth Steel (1916), and today Claymont is a good place to study planned worker housing. Much of its early architecture has been lost or spoiled, including the Practical Farmer Inn

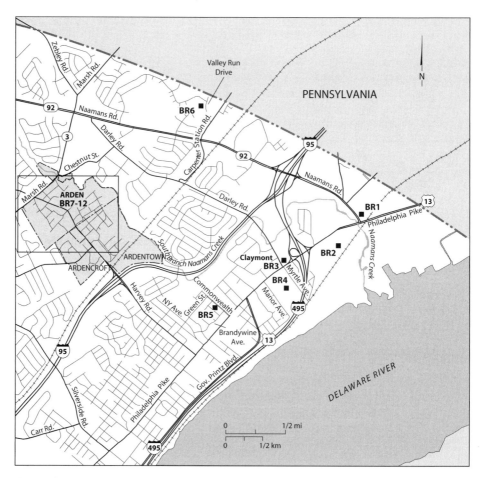

CLAYMONT AND VICINITY

(c. 1750; demolished 1974), famous for having been hit by a British naval shell in the War of 1812. A McDonald's restaurant was built on the front lawn of the demolished eighteenth-century Lackey Mansion and a Burger King in front of the Burr House (1756). The A. A. Grubb House (1783; 1913, Roscoe Cook Tindall) survived as a convent. Road widening has taken many buildings, as have two Interstate highways, I-95 and I-495. With a population of 9,800, unincorporated Claymont is today the seventh-largest community in the state.

BR1 Robinson House (Naamans Tea House)

By 1728 main block. c. 1750 west addition. c. 1790 stone section at east. c. 1914 Doric portico. 1750–1790 "Blockhouse." Philadelphia Pike (U.S. 13) and Naamans Rd.

Thomas Robinson and his descendants owned this inn on King's Highway (now Philadelphia Pike) from 1745 to 1851. Recent investigation showed that its first section is plank-framed, possibly the only example surviving in the Delaware Valley. It has been plausibly argued that Washington stopped here in 1777 when his army camped nearby. A photograph c. 1905 shows the dilapidated house with a portico of slender columns. Students of artist Howard Pyle used it as a studio until its conversion into a popular tea house restaurant in 1914, which operated for fifty years. A five-column Doric portico was added, giving a Greek Revival effect. In 1966, it seemed that the site would be cleared for a motel. State archives director Leon deValinger was mostly interested in the square stone "Blockhouse" at the rear of the site, believed to have been erected in 1654 to protect the sawmill of Swedish settler Johan Rising. Swedes often fortified industrial operations, and slitlike openings suggested embrasures for warfare against Indians. DeValinger thought the Blockhouse might be the oldest surviving building in Delaware, and plans were made to transport it to Fort Christina (WL2). Fortunately, the state archives purchased the entire property in 1967, averting any demolitions. Archaeology later showed, disappointingly, that the Blockhouse was built in the eighteenth century, probably as a kitchen. The Robinson House was restored for the 1976 Bicentennial by architect Robert Raley, and the Claymont Historical Society has made plans to convert it into a museum.

BR3 DARLEY HOUSE, 19th-century drawing prior to alterations

BR2 Clyde Mansion

c. 1800, with additions. On grounds of CitiSteel, east of Philadelphia Pike (U.S. 13) (visible from Robinson House lawn [BR1])

Few historic houses have stranger surroundings—encircled by gigantic factory sheds. Shortly after 1800, Clyde Mansion was home to Swedish painter Adolph-Ulrich Wertmüller, who charged the public admission to see his racy painting, *Danae* (1787). An old photograph shows three sections to the house: the original stone building with heavy, white shutters; a brick wing; and a small board-and-batten extension to that, with jigsaw trim. Claymont Historical Society hopes to save the derelict building, which stands on the grounds of the former Worth steel mill. Nearby is the stone-arched Amtrak Bridge over Naamans Creek (1901). That tributary, now despoiled, was once a fishing place for Indians.

BR3 Darley House

1859 alterations, Felix O. C. Darley. Philadelphia Pike (U.S. 13) and Darley Rd.

Philadelphia-born Felix Darley, America's first important book illustrator, drew pictures for volumes by James Fenimore Cooper, Nathaniel Hawthorne, Washington Irving, Edgar Allan Poe, and others. Upon marrying in 1859, he and Jane Colburn moved to this house along the post road. Darley thereby escaped urban nuisances, yet was within easy train distance of Philadelphia, New York, and Boston. Unsubstantiated local legend says that author Charles Dickens visited him here. As shown in a sketch by Darley, the gambrel-roofed frame house originally had a veranda on the side, an additional window above it, and a door leading to a quaint balcony on the third floor. Gone, too, are the Gothic Revival moldings over the windows. The vacant house was restored in 1991–1992 as a bed-and-breakfast. Next door stands the Church of the Ascension (Episcopal; 1851–1854, Samuel Sloan), built across the road from its current site and moved in 1927, when a stone addition was built. Its facade was reconstructed in 1949. West of the Darley House is Claymont Stone School (1805; enlarged 1905), threatened with demolition in 1987, but subsequently restored (Jim Nelson, architect).

BR4 Archmere

1916–1918, McClure and Harper. Philadelphia Pike (U.S. 13) and Manor Ave.

From 1910 to 1930, this forty-eight-acre estate overlooking the Delaware River was home to financier John Jacob Raskob, protégé of Pierre S. du Pont. The Democratic National Committee met here in 1928, when Raskob managed the campaign of a fellow Catholic, New York governor Al Smith. Later, Raskob oversaw the creation of the Empire State Building (1929–1931), in order to give Smith a new project after his election defeat. Designed by

BR4 ARCHMERE, The Patio

a firm from New York City, Archmere is Delaware's finest example of twentieth-century residential Italianate, both in the main house (The Patio) and nearby Manor Hall, built for Raskob's servants and with room for eleven cars. An underground tunnel connected the two. The Patio was constructed of limestone, with a front porch copied from the famous Pazzi Chapel, Florence, Italy (fifteenth century). The tile-roofed house surrounds a 2,000-square-foot courtyard (or patio, as it was called) with a fountain at the center depicting children—appropriate, as Raskob had thirteen of them. The 4,225-square-foot ceiling of Tiffany stained glass could be opened in summer. The opulent interiors included a paneled library and a music room.

After Raskob moved to Maryland (taking the shrubbery with him), the Norbertine Order purchased the estate in 1932 and established Archmere Academy. A Moderne concrete gymnasium with glass-brick windows (1939; enlarged 1966) survives. Nearby stand St. Norbert Hall (1958–1959, George McDermott) and the modernist Justin E. Diny Science Center, by a Scranton-area firm (1971–1973, Burkavage Design Associates; 2001–2003 renovated and enlarged, Buck Simpers Architect + Associates). McLaughlin-Mullen Student Life Center is the newest addition to campus (2003–2007, Anderson Brown Higley Associates).

BR5 Overlook Colony

1911–1917, John Nolen. Vicinity of Commonwealth Ave. and Philadelphia Pike (U.S. 13)

General Chemical Company developed this planned community for its employees. Nolen, a landscape architect and city planner from Boston, wrote extensively and had been involved in plans for Chattanooga, Tennessee; Glen Ridge, New Jersey; and La Crosse, Wisconsin. The well-designed Arts and Crafts row homes were faced in stucco and had slate roofs. All are privately owned today and have been altered. The restored community center on Commonwealth Avenue received a preservation award in 2000. Additional workers' communities in Claymont include Worthland, for Worth Steel (with a Tudor Revival clubhouse), and Aniline Village. All these bear comparison to postwar Brookview Apartments (1952, south of Darley Road), in a modernist idiom that included steel corner windows. Once a desirable garden apartment complex, Brookview is now slated for demolition.

BR6 Valley Run

1966–1969, with additions, Rahenkamp, Sachs and Associates, site planners, with D'Anastasio and Lisiewski, architects. Valley Run Dr. and vicinity, near Pennsylvania line

As 1960s sprawl filled Brandywine Hundred, some architects called for a new kind of community, a mixed-density development that would combine single-family homes with less expensive townhouses and apartments and leave open space. New Castle County zoning did not allow this approach, so Valley Run Building Corporation and its Philadelphia planners spent three years convincing the government to give them large-scale variances. Weatherboarded apartments form long units that undulate with the topography.

BR6 VALLEY RUN

ARDEN

The "experimental village" along colonial Grubb Road was founded in 1900 with the purchase of 162 acres of farm and forest by two Philadelphians, decorative artist G. Frank Stephens and architect William Price. Stephens was a graduate of the Pennsylvania Academy of the Fine Arts and brother-in-law of artist Thomas Eakins; Price was a successful architect who had studied under Frank Furness and absorbed Emersonian ideas via Furness's father, a close friend of Ralph Waldo Emerson. Funding for Arden was provided by a soap manufacturer of Philadelphia, Joseph Fels. Following the utopian ideals of Henry George, late-nineteenth-century proponent of the Single Tax (he proposed that land only should be taxed), Arden was and remains a community owning its land in common and just taxing land values.

Arden's creation sprang from efforts in the 1890s by members of the Philadelphia Single Tax Society to make tiny Delaware a political hotbed of their ideas. Price had the specific notion of testing the Single Tax theory by establishing a village based on its principles. One model was Elbert Hubbard's Roycroft, East Aurora, New York, founded five years before. Arden, named for the idyllic forest of Shakespeare's play *As You Like It*, was just a summer camp until 1905, when year-round residency tentatively began. Half-acre leaseholds were offered, and all the land was leased by 1909.

There were fifty houses in place by 1908, when 120 people spent the summer, and forty wintered over. The first photographs, dating from 1907, show rustic, shotgun-plan cabins with hipped roofs that extend forward to form a porch supported by two columns. These early so-called "toy houses," a minority among the tents, were faced with plywood and log veneer and topped with tarpaper roofs. Casement-style camp windows allowed ventilation. In 1909, Fels gave $5,000 to encourage better architecture in Arden, and Price turned his attention to the problem. Up to now his energies had been directed to another utopian community of his own creation, Rose Valley, Pennsylvania (begun 1901). Price's layout for Arden, made in December 1910, followed the principles of the Garden City movement in England, as exemplified by Ebenezer Howard's *Garden Cities of Tomorrow* (1902). It retained two "greenbelts," as Howard would have called them, wooded tracts that afforded privacy and access to nature. One lies along scenic Naamans Creek to the east; Sherwood Forest (a nod to Wilmingtonian Howard Pyle's illustrations for *The Merry Adventures of Robin Hood,* 1883) occupies the west and was rescued from development in 2004. In between, the Arden community consisted of two zones, Woodlands and Sherwood, divided by Harvey Road. Each had a central common. Price was commissioned to design four or five cottages in 1909 by Fels, who, influenced by the English Arts and Crafts movement, favored a medieval-style approach. More than sixty houses were built in Arden between 1909 and 1915.

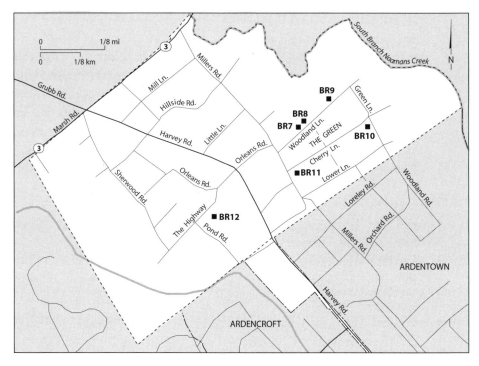

ARDEN

Arden attracted media attention, largely because the famous writer Upton Sinclair briefly lived there (BR9). Mabel Tuke Priestman wrote on "The Summer Camp at Arden" in *American Homes and Gardens* (May 1908), and Gustav Stickley described "Summer Bungalows in Delaware" in *The Craftsman* (November 1909). In the 1920s, the outside world began to impinge upon the colony; there were automobiles and street lamps, though no paved streets and stone curbs until ninety-six WPA workers arrived in 1935.

Arden was added to the National Register of Historic Places in 1973, the only town in the United States placed on the register in its entirety. Today, Arden, population 480, contains many old houses, often as the core of later, weirdly improvisational expansions. An innovative "green" or plant-covered roof was installed on an Arden home in 2003. Residents fear gentrification, and, indeed, the historic Arden Inn was recently replaced by a Nanticoke-brand prefabricated home (see WS2).

In addition to the entries listed here, the following buildings are of interest. The Brambles (1901, George Leach and Harry Vandever; 1910–1912 wings added), at 1901 Millers Road, is one of the earliest Arden homes, famous for having been owned by reformer and labor organizer Eva Reeve Bloor (familiarly known as "Mother Bloor") and her husband. When they wintered over in Arden in 1905, it was the first time anyone had done so. Frank B. Downs added the wings and gave the house running water, a novelty. Friendly Gables (1909, William Price), at 2205 Little Lane, was the first dwelling built with Fels's gift of $5,000 for the architectural improvement of Arden. Here Price copied the Harry Hetzel House he had previously designed in Rose Valley, Pennsylvania. Inside are low ceilings with timber beams, and a stone fireplace stands at the core. The Arden Forge provided hardware for this and other early houses. Owner Fred Steinlein ran the Arden printery in the basement. Built for Lulu Clark, Green Gate (1909, William Price), at 2210 The Sweep, was the second cottage funded by the Fels donation. Across the road at Number 2209 stands another Price house, The Lodge (1910), in a similar Gothic Revival mode.

BR7 Frank Stephens Memorial Theater (Open-Air or Field Theatre)

1905, Frank Stephens. Woodland Ln.

The first area of Arden to be settled was around Village Green, a field in an angle of the woods. A huge boulder suggested a backdrop for an outdoor theater, fronted by a turf stage and originally flanked by two wooden Ionic columns. Patrons sat on grass seats up front or wooden benches; the stage was lit with Japanese lanterns and, later, carbide lights and kerosene footlamps. Plays were a cherished community-building activity, starting with *Merchant of Venice* in 1906 with Stephens as Shylock and William Price as Antonio. In 1909, plays were performed in Esperanto, another of Stephens's passions. During the fall festival of 1912, the Stephens Cottage next door (BR8) was used as a backdrop for *Robin Hood,* illuminated by automobile headlights. In early performances, actors robed at the Craft Shop (BR11), then marched across the Green by candlelight. The boulder provided a balcony for Juliet and a cliff for King Lear. Renamed for Stephens in 1961—his ashes lie buried beside the rock—the theater today hosts concerts and weddings, and Shakespeare is still performed at least once a year.

BR8 The Second Homestead

1909, Frank Stephens. 2311 Woodland Ln.

Arden's founder built for himself a twin-gabled, Old English–style cottage of hollow tile construction. Artists' studios occupied the steeply pitched rooms upstairs, under the red slate roof. The exterior is half-timbered, with leaded windows, and "Tomorrow is a New Day" is carved on a fascia. Behind the house stands the Homestead cabin (1900), the first Stephens residence.

BR9 Mary Bruce Inn (The Jungalow)

1910–1911, Frank Stephens. 1941 alterations. 2321 Woodland Ln.

Famous reformer Upton Sinclair, author of *The Jungle* (1906), lived in Arden from spring 1910 to early 1912, spending the first year in a tent before building a house at the edge of Arden Woods with a $1,250 advance he had received for a book, *Love's Pilgrimage* (1911); the dwelling ended up costing $2,600, however. The main room, of stained wood, boasted a huge fireplace. A high shelf ran all around, holding Sinclair's library. In the 1930s, the place was the Mary Bruce Inn; then, in 1941, it underwent massive alterations. Immediately east is the Scott Nearing Cottage. A Wharton School economist, Nearing paid $13 annual rent for the last available lot on the Green, a low-lying corner. He spent summers here from about 1905 to 1915, building a cabin with, he recalled, a waist-high foundation and huge stone chimney. Sinclair remembered it as being one room and that he himself rented it as a study. Arden helped inspire Nearing's move to Vermont in 1932, in which he founded the modern back-to-the-land "homesteading" movement.

BR8 THE SECOND HOMESTEAD

BR10 REST COTTAGE

BR10 Rest Cottage
1910, William Price. Green and Cherry lns.

Fels's gift of money for cottages made "one stipulation that they should be permanent and artistic in character with stone foundations and cellars, hollow brick and concrete walls, and above all, literally the red-tiled roofs so beautiful in the scenery of Britain and the Netherlands" (see Edwards, 1993). Rest Cottage obeyed these guidelines, and construction photographs show the use of hollow tile on a foundation of native stone. The picturesque dwelling with half-timbered walls, projecting upstairs bedrooms, and wide-eaved shed roofs has recently been expanded by owner-architect Edward Rohrbach. To the south stands Bide-a-wee (c. 1916), home of Don Stephens, furniture maker and son of Arden's founder; beyond that is the Vista, formerly Blue Bird Tea Room (c. 1910), with rustic porch posts of red cedar.

BR11 Red House and Craft Shop
1907 enlargement of original. 1913 Craft Shop, William Price. Cherry Ln. and Millers Rd.

Frank Stephens and Price's philosophies owed much to nineteenth-century English reformer William Morris, who had founded the Arts and Crafts movement with his home at Bexley Heath, Red House (1850s), a name copied here. The little, gable-roofed frame building housed Arden Forge and Stephens's studio. Stephens promoted crafts in order to provide year-round employment for his community. The gambrel-roofed Craft Shop was built next to Red House in a speedy building campaign that used oak and poplar from Arden woods. The concrete basement housed a water pump and bakery; the first floor, a woodworking shop, salesroom, and sewing and costume room; the second floor, facilities for weaving and metalwork, studios, and a classroom. Craft Shop closed in 1936, and later, it served as an apartment house. Across Millers Road is the former Weavers Plant, and at 1806 Millers stands Rest Harrow, now Lone Pine (c. 1913, William Price), part of a row of four low-cost houses—"Little Arden"—aimed at attracting master craftsmen to the nearby shop.

BR12 Gild Hall (Arden Club House)
1909–1910, William Price. 118 The Highway

When the property west of Grubb Road was secured in 1909, it became possible for Arden to expand. The Red House (BR11) having become cramped, the old Derrickson barn was converted into a half-timbered community center. The entire male population of the town, including Upton Sinclair and Scott Nearing, participated in a floor-laying bee in June 1910. The interior was deliberately left rustic. The building has accommodated innumerable town meetings, vespers, theatricals, and pageants. Beneath the structure on the downhill slope was the Moonlight Theater, open on one side to the elements (recently restored). On Sherwood Green nearby stands Buzz Ware Village Center, designed as Arden School by local architect Frances Harrison (1945–1947), who made innovative use of radiant floor heat and sliding interior walls. It was one of the first schools in the state to defy segregation laws (1952).

BR12 GILD HALL (ARDEN CLUB HOUSE)

BRANDYWINE HUNDRED SOUTH OF ARDEN

BR13 St. Francis Renewal Center (Samuel N. Trump House)

1886–1887, Louis Carter Baker Jr. and Elijah James Dallett, for Furness, Evans and Company. St. Patrick's Monastery, Prior Rd., south of Ardencroft

Motorists driving north on I-95 cannot miss the pointy, complex roofline of this house rising above the treetops. Philadelphia architects Baker and Dallett met in the office of Frank Furness and later practiced together (1888–1912). They undertook many Wilmington commissions, as Dallett's wife was a native. Nearly all their houses have been demolished. This one was for the owner of Trump Brothers Machine Company. It recalls, in several ways, Furness's Chalfont House, Kennett Square, Pennsylvania (c. 1884). The tall roof and corbeled chimneys still show a hint of the firm's signature style, despite many exterior alterations. Inside, the central hall contains a fireplace of granite and terra-cotta with a decorative, cast-iron fireback, and a spectacular stair rises three stories. An Irish order of Capuchins established St. Patrick's Monastery at this site, adding an Avondale-stone Friary (c. 1935). Father Thomas Pietrantonio has spent three decades rehabilitating the house, and he installed an upstairs chapel from architectural fragments.

BR14 Silverside Carr Executive Center (Silverside Elementary School)

1947–1948, Robinson, Stanhope and Manning. Silverside Rd., near Carr Rd.

Drastically altered in the 1980s, this was once one of Delaware's most innovative buildings, an elementary school as modern as any in the United States and comparable to Eliel Saarinen's Crow Island School in Winnetka, Illinois (1939). The Wilmington firm built two nearly identical facilities at the same time, this one and Edge Moor Elementary, now demolished (see the illustration on p. 42), both visited by architects from throughout the country. Novelties included sprawling suburban sites (twelve acres each), the series of low wings (more could easily be added) radiating out from the administrative core with its slablike accent tower, extensive use of glass and glass brick, engineered lighting, acoustical ceiling tiles, chimes instead of bells, clocks only in the hallways, and homelike touches, including a fireplace in the front lobby. Construction was of brick and concrete block, without expensive plaster, glazed brick, or tile. Classrooms each had their own bathrooms, were painted in distinctive colors, used varied asphalt-tile patterns on the floors, had colored chalkboards (not black) for use with water-soluble crayons, and opened directly to the outdoors.

BR15 Bellevue Hall

1855–1863. 1931–1933, Bernard T. Converse. 1933 gate lodges, Massena and du Pont. 800 Carr Rd. in Bellevue State Park

So complete was its twentieth-century remodeling, one would never guess that this was once Delaware's most flamboyant Gothic Revival house, with castellated towers and curving verandas of interlacing trusswork. Philadelphia wool merchant Hanson Robinson built the mansion as a summer retreat, naming it Woolton Hall. William du Pont purchased it in 1893 and trained fine carriage and draft horses on the property. Eight years later, he bought Montpelier, home of President Madison in Virginia, to breed trotting horses. His son, William Jr., grew up at Montpelier but returned as an adult to Bellevue, reconstructing

BR15 BELLEVUE HALL

MODERNISM IN DELAWARE

As with states farther south, architectural modernism took only shallow root in Delaware and was usually diluted with historicizing motifs. But as early as the 1930s, a few architects embraced it enthusiastically. Victorine du Pont met her husband and partner Samuel Homsey in an architect's office in Boston. After their practice was wiped out in the Great Depression, they settled in Wilmington and undertook a career that was both historicizing (Mount Cuba, 1935–1937 [MC4], which emulated Colonial Williamsburg) and progressive (their starkly modernist, and now demolished, Henry B. Robertson House in Centreville of 1936 was depicted in *Architectural Forum* in February 1938 and honored by the Museum of Modern Art). For the Delaware Art Museum (WL90), Sam proposed four facade designs ranging from Georgian Revival to Moderne.

About the same time, the arrival of William Moeckel to work for Brown and Whiteside began the transformation of that firm's work from Colonial Revival to International Style. One observes, in microcosm, how the cutting-edge styles of the 1930s, having crossed the Atlantic, now invaded a provincial outpost. The process continued postwar, as even diehard historicists went modern; for example, E. William Martin, renowned for Colonial Revival schools in the 1930s, embraced the International Style by the time of his Newark Elementary School (now much altered as Graham Hall, University of Delaware) in 1948–1949.

Never numerous in Delaware, pure modernist examples are rapidly vanishing. Recently lost to partial demolition (and remodeling of the remainder) is Newark's Chrysler Plant and, in the same city, the Avon Plant (NK7); three automobile dealerships in Wilmington; and the Henry B. Robertson House. Edge Moor Elementary (1947–1948, Robinson, Stanhope and Manning), on the cutting edge of International Style modernism nationwide, with low, radiating wings that allowed every classroom to be bathed in sunlight, was, by 2003, a vandalized wreck awaiting demolition (its twin a few miles away survives in mutilated form, BR14). Edgemoor Theatre (1941, Armand Carroll), Wilmington's best example of Streamline Moderne, was destroyed in 1987. In 1999, a geographer identified Art Deco examples in surprisingly many Wilmington towns but noted their disappearance even as he studied them. Delaware's only building by I. M. Pei, a Wilmington skyscraper (WL37), was "improved" in 2003, prettifying a Brutalist masterpiece of the 1960s—somehow predictable in a state that has shown little sympathy for bold modernist experiments.

EDGE MOOR ELEMENTARY SCHOOL

BR16 VILLA MONTEREY (CORINNE COURT)

it in the 1930s as a Montpelier copy, with the familiar stuccoed walls and big four-column Doric portico of that national shrine. Here he founded a famous racing stable (with gigantic racetrack), and by the time of his death in 1965, he had trained thoroughbreds that won more than 1,200 races. Du Pont's wealth was legendary—he paid $4 million in income tax in 1960. The state bought the 273-acre Bellevue estate in 1976 and opened it to the public as a park.

BR16 Villa Monterey (Corinne Court)

1923, Claude Banta, developer. Philadelphia Pike (U.S. 13), north of Washington St. Extension

As historian Susan Chase has shown (1995), Banta worked as a railroad car builder and carpenter before becoming a land developer with two tracts near Newport: Tuxedo Park and Lyndalia (1920). Typical of the times, he limited his suburbs to whites, calling Lyndalia "The Ideal Restricted American Settlement for American People." More adventurous aesthetically was Villa Monterey, with 350 houses projected as an "enchanting community to make your home." The Mediterranean-influenced style that Banta chose was a radical departure from local precedent. The flat-roofed, cement-block houses were stuccoed and painted "in the brilliant colors of the rainbow." The expensive development was rendered exclusive by the application of fourteen deed covenants, only one fewer than ritzy Westover Hills (CH22). "It takes courage to do anything different in Delaware," a building-trades newsletter said, and Banta only built twelve units, two of which he lost to foreclosure. Arranged around a courtyard and with stuccoed walls and arched openings, they are strikingly different from most suburban development in the state, before or after.

BR17 Laurel (Dudley W. Spencer House)

1956–1961, Frank Lloyd Wright. 619 Shipley Rd., south of I-95

Delaware has few buildings by internationally famous architects. One of Wright's later designs, this small Usonian home was commissioned in 1954. Spencer built it himself over several years, and it was unfinished when Wright died in 1959. He made some changes from Wright's original drawings, for example, strengthening the concrete-pad foundation and moving the house uphill, away from the floodplain of Shellpot Creek, which it faces across a series of terraces on a forested site in Bringhurst Woods. The house turns a solid, though clerestory-lit, fieldstone wall to Shipley Road but opens up with expanses of glass on the curving, woodland side. The form is the "solar hemicycle" Wright sometimes used, the whole copying the Wilbur Pearce House, Bradbury, California (1950). Inside is Wright's trademark central hearth and built-in furniture designed by the architect himself. The stone came from Avondale, Pennsylvania, and Cumberland Ridge, Tennessee (where Wright had built a Usonian house of this type of stone in 1950). The woodwork is Honduras mahogany, and steel supports the cantilevered roof.

BR17 LAUREL (DUDLEY W. SPENCER HOUSE)

The carport was added later. Half a century after it was commissioned, Laurel is one of the very last Wright homes still occupied by the original client.

BR18 Rockwood Museum (Shipley-Bringhurst Mansion)

1851–1857, George Monier Williams. 1913 west wing. 610 Shipley Rd.

Rockwood is nationally important as an intact villa-plus-landscape of the type that Andrew Jackson Downing published in *The Architecture of Country Houses* (1850) and other books. Its taste is directly informed by English precedents. Wilmington-born Joseph Shipley spent his career (1819–1851) as a trader in Liverpool, England, then returned to his native land and built this house on a 300-acre estate, which he called Rockwood for its many boulders. Liverpool architect Williams supplied the designs before Shipley sailed to America, and local contractor Elisha Huxley oversaw construction of the various buildings. Williams had previously designed Shipley's English home, Wyncote (1839–1844). Cast iron and plate glass were imported from Liverpool. Construction was substantial, with meticulously laid, dark gray Brandywine granite exterior walls (they are brick underneath). A light gray cut stone was used lavishly for quoins—even on the chimneys—and other enrichments. The gables have pierced bargeboards and pendant drops, and the roof is punctuated by diamond-shaped red brick chimney clusters. The conservatory, a rare survival, was chiefly of wood with cast-iron detailing; pencil-thin colonettes support an ornamental entablature and parapet enlivened with sprightly finials.

Shipley died in 1867, leaving Rockwood to his sisters, and in 1891, it entered the related Bringhurst family. After 1940, the place deteriorated. In 1963, when Shipley's great-niece was ninety-eight, the edges of the Rockwood property were threatened by proposals to widen Shipley Road and build I-95. Local newspaperman Dudley Cammett Lunt led a campaign to save the Gothic Revival Porter's Lodge (c. 1858, Thomas and James M. Dixon), the childhood home of noted local artist Robert Shaw, whose father was Shipley's

BR18 ROCKWOOD MUSEUM (SHIPLEY-BRINGHURST MANSION)

coachman. When the last Rockwood owner died in 1972, her will left the place to charity. A court order subsequently allowed New Castle County to take charge. A task force in 1999 recommended that the grounds, with their many specimen trees, be restored to their nineteenth-century appearance and the interiors to match a series of photographs taken in the 1890s. As part of this restoration, a visitor center has been skillfully created from a stone carriage house (2003–2004, Moeckel Carbonell Associates).

BR19 Weldin House

c. 1790, with additions. Philadelphia Pike (U.S. 13) and Lore Ave.

Philadelphia Pike has lost many historic buildings, but two stone houses remain on steep Penny Hill, this and the Penny House (BR20). Outcrops of blue rock were quarried nearby from an early date, and the last commercial quarry in New Castle County was in business here making crushed stone as late as 1968 (Philadelphia Pike at Edgemoor Rd). The Weldin House, an L-shaped gable-roofed structure of fieldstone with wood above, housed a popular doughnut shop for two decades starting in 1949. It was the subject of a furor in 2002, when the owner of the dilapidated property announced plans to demolish it for a 7-Eleven store and gas station. Citing traffic concerns, DelDOT announced it would buy the house in order to preserve it.

BR20 Penny House

1749, with additions. North side of Philadelphia Pike (U.S. 13), west of Marsh Rd. intersection

The compact stone colonial home served at various times as residence, blacksmith shop, cabinetmaker's shop, and hostelry. George Washington and the Marquis de Lafayette supposedly stayed here. Nineteenth-century artist Robert Shaw, whose etchings called early attention to Delaware's disappearing colonial architecture, kept a studio inside. A restoration in 1947 added a stone wall (topped with broken glass), partly to protect the building from runaway automobiles, and reversed the orientation of the dwelling. The long, steep descent of Philadelphia Pike here was improved in 1919 as part of the new Lincoln Highway network along the east coast, DuPont dynamite blowing out 5,000 cubic yards of rock to lower the hilltop a dozen feet. The road was then resurfaced in vitrified brick, part of Delaware's pioneering efforts at highway improvement.

BR20 PENNY HOUSE

VICINITY OF BRANDYWINE CREEK AND ALONG CONCORD PIKE

BR21 Augustine Mills

c. 1845 enlargement of earlier facility. Later additions. Park Dr. N. at Brandywine Creek, north of B&O Bridge

Brandywine Creek was a crucible of the Industrial Revolution in the United States, and several early mill buildings survive along its rocky banks. Modern condominiums occupy the remains of this snuff and flour mill purchased in 1845 by Jessup and Moore and converted to papermaking, a trade that originated in the United States on the Brandywine in 1787 (see Rockland Mills, BR36). In 1898, Augustine Mills produced 50,000 pounds of fine book and printing paper a day. Container Corporation of America made sixty tons of paperboard here daily in the 1940s, and the plant remained in operation in the 1970s. A survey during that decade showed seven nineteenth-century mill buildings of brick and stone existing in the complex, some with original iron trusses. The oldest building lay farthest north and alone was spared demolition when the site was redeveloped as high-rise residences, Brandywine Park Condominiums (1983–1984, Homsey Architects).

BR22 Office Building (John Wanamaker Store)

1948–1950, Massena and du Pont; W. Lee Moore, landscape architect. 1962–1963 addition on south, Young and Banwell. c. 1998 adaptive reuse, Planning Design Research Corporation. 1801 Augustine Cut Off

The postwar shift of retail to suburbia was epitomized by the construction of a huge department store in a field outside the Wilmington city limits. Construction proceeded rapidly, with some 300 men employed. Plans were changed in the middle of the process to double the sales space, as a study predicted high local demand. The smooth, streamlined exterior, which culminated in a rounded corner above the downhill entrance, was of Avondale granite and pink-buff Mansota veined marble, with extensive plate glass windows and chrome detailing. A heating system under the sidewalks melted snow. The interior featured escalators, year-round climate control and air conditioning, and both incandescent and fluorescent lighting. The store's Ivy Tea Room overlooked Brandywine Creek. Key to the success of such isolated, "lone wolf"

BR22 OFFICE BUILDING (JOHN WANAMAKER STORE)

stores was a huge parking lot; the one for this building is sufficient for 750 cars, arranged on different levels. The successor firm to Massena and du Pont designed an addition in the early 1960s. Pioneering the suburban-retail model, Wanamaker's was followed closely by Wilmington Merchandise Mart at Edgemoor (1951–1952, Albert D. Lueders). By the end of the twentieth century, newer malls had long since supplanted these early centers; Merchandise Mart was virtually abandoned, with demolition contemplated, and Wanamaker's was converted into corporate offices by a Houston-based firm, with a colorful new Postmodern interior.

BR23 Porter Rapid Sand Filter Plant

1950–1954, Metcalf and Eddy. Porter Reservoir, 0.5 miles north of I-95, east of U.S. 202

Wilmington takes its drinking water from Brandywine Creek. Brandywine Pumping Station (WL50) forced water two miles through a forty-two-inch pipe to a thirty-five-million-gallon reservoir here on McKee's Hill, where the headquarters of 1907 still stands. Far larger is the facility (1950s) of pale brick and Indiana limestone, by a Boston engineering firm. The structure supplanted part of Rock Manor Golf Course (1937, expanded with WPA funds). The filter project was based on Metcalf and Eddy's report in 1948 on Wilmington's ever-increasing water needs. The tall structure with ribbon and corner windows is the Chemical and Filter Building, designed with eight rapid sand filter beds and huge steel washwater tanks on the third floor. Sixteen million gallons could be processed daily. The plant is one of Delaware's best examples of austere, International Style modernism of the post–World War II period—a type fast disappearing today.

BR24 Brandywine Granite Quarry

1880s–c. 1940. East bank of Brandywine Creek near Alapocas Run (not visible from the road)

Blue rock features prominently in Wilmington architecture. Geologist James Booth saw five major blue rock quarries around the city in his 1837–1838 travels, of which Clyde's and Gordon's were probably in this vicinity. In April 1885, the DuPont Company helped develop a large, modern quarry, operated by Locke and Company contractors, who had already extracted the stone for the nearby B&O Bridge (WL62) over the Brandywine. A total of 600,000 tons were removed in 1883–1888. A soaring, 180-foot-high aerial cable system was installed c. 1888 to swing blocks of stone from the quarry on the east bank to waiting Pennsylvania Railroad freight cars on the west (see the illustration on p. 11). Starting in 1889, stockholder William M. Field oversaw the operation, providing stone for breakwater projects at Lewes (see Harbor of Refuge, ES26), Walnut Street Bridge in Philadelphia, and the railroad viaduct through Wilmington (WL10). In 1900, the quarry was 3,000 feet long and 2,000 feet wide, with walls 180 feet high. One hundred fifty men were employed in cutting 350,000 Belgian blocks for paving the streets of Camden, New Jersey. In addition, crushed stone was being sent to Forts Mott and Du Pont on the Delaware River. Today, all the quarries around Wilmington are abandoned, but the name Blue Rocks lives on as the local baseball team. A reconstruction of historic quarrying apparatus can be viewed on the grounds of the Hagley Museum (CH15). Now state-owned

BR23 PORTER RAPID SAND FILTER PLANT

BR25 DUPONT EXPERIMENTAL STATION, photo 1956

parkland, the Brandywine Granite Quarry site was opened to the public in 2004.

BR25 DuPont Experimental Station

1906 established. Along Brandywine Creek south of DE 141 (best seen from Rockford Park)

The DuPont Company undertakes research and development at this facility. A predecessor station was housed in Rokeby mill (near Breck's Mill, CH19), which burned in 1906. Fortunately, larger quarters were already underway at this site, then called Lower Yards. Number 1 Building, housing shops, offices, and laboratories, was built in a Colonial Revival style of glazed-header Flemish bond brickwork, as were several of the early structures at the facility, huddled along the riverbank. By the 1930s, 1,000 scientists worked here in the largest such station in the United States. In Building 228, Wallace Carothers had discovered the chemical forerunners of neoprene and nylon in April 1930 (see Seaford Plant, WS17). Thanks to these and other breakthroughs, company assets grew more than seventy times between 1902 and 1940.

On the hilltop rose the International Style brick buildings of an expansion in 1948–1949, arranged campus-like around a grassy mall. The J. Tyler McConnell highway bridge over the Brandywine (1952) granted access to the enlarged facility. That bridge featured some of the first hammerhead-shaped concrete piers in the United States (currently proposed for replacement, which some have protested on historical grounds). Prominent along DE 141 is the huge, postmodern-style Crawford Greenewalt Laboratory (1981–1984, Kling Partnership). At a 2003 celebration of the Experimental Station's centenary, a time capsule was filled with a hydrogen fuel cell and other futuristic products that, it was hoped, would eventually help revitalize the shrinking DuPont Company.

BR26 Nemours

c. 1909, with many additions. Powder Mill and Rockland rds.

The spectacular, French-style mansion and gardens of Alfred I. du Pont are a much-illustrated symbol of Chateau Country splendor.

BR26 NEMOURS

A. I. du Pont grew fabulously wealthy during the years that the DuPont Company underwent rapid expansion, but he turned his back on both family and company following a messy divorce and scandalous marriage to a cousin. His second wife, Alicia, loved French culture, and Nemours was intended, in part, to gratify her taste. Du Pont assembled 1,600 acres in several parcels, which included a farmhouse of c. 1800 and its stone barn (1842), still extant near the carillon. Hundreds of acres are surrounded by a nine-foot stone wall, the construction of which was overseen by Tom Montgomery, who had helped build "Boss Henry" du Pont's walls (CH11) near Winterthur in the 1870s. Local boys were paid a penny for each glass bottle they collected, which were broken to stud the top of the wall with jagged shards. The story is that A. I. wanted "to keep other du Ponts out," but his third wife, Jessie Ball du Pont, laughed at this notion in an interview in 1937, explaining that the wall with its glass simply suited the Louis XVI, French-chateau theme. She stressed, too, that the grandeur of the estate was intended as a memorial to A. I.'s parents and to his ancestor, Pierre Samuel du Pont—a deeply personal tribute, as A. I. had been orphaned as a boy, and as he was "eldest son of the eldest son" in the du Pont line, with an acute sense of history.

BR26.1 House

1909–1910, Carrère and Hastings

An esteemed Manhattan firm responsible for the New York Public Library and many society mansions designed the seventy-seven-room Nemours house. Presumably, du Pont knew the firm from his frequent vacations in Florida, where they had built Whitehall in Palm Beach (1901) for tycoon Henry M. Flagler. Nemours was one of Carrère's last projects, as he was killed by a taxicab in 1911. Thought to have cost a then-astonishing $2 million, the 102-room home derives from the French chateaux as perfected by eighteenth-century architects A.-J. Gabriel, Alexandre Théodore Brongniart, and Claude-Nicolas Ledoux. It shows similarities to Carrère and Hastings's Vernon Court, Newport, Rhode Island (1901), including a decorative external latticework on one side (the firm's Frick Mansion, New York, of 1913–1914, also had such latticework, removed in the 1930s). The coupled Corinthian columns of the loggia were a favorite device of McKim, Mead and White, with whom Carrère and Hastings had trained. Nemours was built of Nicholson, Pennsylvania, blue stone plus clay tile and concrete, and it has an exterior finish of stucco and Indiana limestone. A third-floor balustraded deck at the foot of the hipped roof affords views of the garden. The contractor was James M. Smyth of Wilmington, with whom du Pont had a famously close and trusting relationship, as indeed he did with Hastings.

Drawings and blueprints survive for a never-executed Gothic Revival chapel connected by a cloister to the house (1920, Carrère and Hastings); a library wing was considered as an alternative. The former Main Gates face DE 141 (1926–1927, Edward Canby May). A late change to the house was the stained glass window of the stairhall (1933–1934, Massena and du Pont). As early as 1936, Jessie declared her intention of keeping the house intact as a memorial to her husband's taste and high standard of culture. Nemours remained astonishingly unchanged, and following her death, it opened to the public as a museum in 1977.

BR26.2 Gardens

1909–1929, Carrère and Hastings

Delaware's largest formal gardens emulate those of Versailles in France. Alfred I. du Pont steadily improved them as the DuPont Company flourished, especially from 1915 on; he was its second-largest shareholder. As seen from the house, the Forecourt Terrace, Tapis Vert, and one-acre Grand Basin (to use A. I.'s names) form a grand vista. Near the Forecourt stand antique garden features imported from overseas, including two marble sphinxes once belonging to French minister Jean-Baptiste

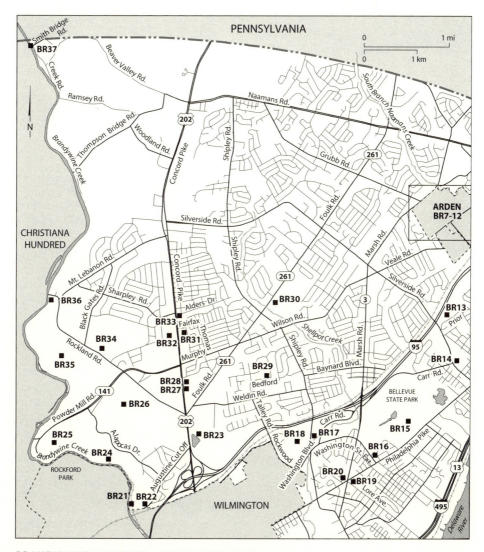

BRANDYWINE HUNDRED—SOUTH AND WEST

Colbert, wrought-iron gates owned by Catherine the Great (c. 1750, Jean Tijou; 2003 restored), and gates from sixteenth-century Wimbledon Manor, England. Blueprints of 1915 show the embellishment of the Grand Basin (Reflecting Pool) and addition of a Maze Garden plus "Pavilion" (called Colonnade when constructed in 1926). At the center of the Maze stands a fountain comprised of a fifteen-ton bowl of red Lavento marble, topped by a sculpture of a heroic male nude, *Achievement* by Henri Crenier (early twentieth century); these were installed in 1929 when Massena and du Pont redesigned the Maze. In 1932–1933, the gardens were opened as a fundraiser for the restoration of colonial-era Stratford Hall, Virginia, one of many preservation projects in that state spearheaded by A. I.'s Virginia-born third wife, Jessie. In 2003, the old, overgrown trees and shrubs of the Tapis Vert and Maze Garden were entirely replaced. New plants of specimen size were imported from throughout the United States and precisely positioned as to height using a laser measure.

BR26.3 The Wren's Nest
1915, E. F. Hodgson Company

Historian Evie Joselow informs me that Alfred I. du Pont ordered this frame, gable-roofed playhouse for his daughters from a catalogue pub-

VICINITY OF BRANDYWINE CREEK AND ALONG CONCORD PIKE

lished in Boston by Hodgson, a manufacturer of sectionally cut, prefabricated homes. In March 1915, crates for one Hodgson Portable Playhouse, Model No. 1541, Plan B, were ordered for a price of $265.00 plus shipment via the Pennsylvania Railroad. Shortly thereafter, crates containing the sectional panels for the floors, walls and ceilings, along with additional structural beams, mouldings and windows, arrived for on-site construction. In the process, the playhouse was enlarged with back rooms, a bathroom, and a kitchen, and a stone chimney also was erected. It is a rare, early example of prefabricated architecture in Delaware.

BR26.4 Sunken Garden

1929–1930, Massena and du Pont; Carlo Sarrabezolles, sculptor. 1931–1932, Temple of Love, Gabriel F. Massena

Alfred I. du Pont's son, Alfred Victor, studied architecture at the Ecole des Beaux-Arts in Paris, where he met Gabriel Massena, a dynamic young Frenchman. Together they formed Massena and du Pont (the former being the design partner) and returned to the United States—before Alfred had quite completed his training—in order to execute a plum commission, a Sunken Garden at Nemours. The idea for such a garden had come about in the late 1920s while A. I. and his son vacationed in Karlsbad. A. I. had paid Thomas Hastings (of Carrère and Hastings) $10,000 for a design just before Hastings's sudden death in 1929—by which time A. I. had already given the project to his son. The Sunken Garden, with its splashing fountains and rich carving, would be the showpiece by which Massena and du Pont hoped to gain fame.

BR26.4 SUNKEN GARDEN, with Colonnade behind

The expensive Roman travertine was novel in the United States, its weathering properties uncertain. Construction was undertaken by Stewart and Donohue of Wilmington. Massena at first called for seashells in the grottolike niches beneath the curving stairs but later changed these to pebbles. Gleaming-white sculptures of frolicking putti by a Paris master of Art Deco, Carlo Sarrabezolles, are unique examples of his work in the United States. Extensive publicity photographs were taken, including aerial views, but these put father and son at cross purposes, as A. I. did not want Nemours to be featured in "society" magazines, especially alongside the gardens of his hated cousin, Pierre, or of John J. Raskob (see Archmere, BR4). Nemours was, however, featured in *Fortune* magazine (November 1934). Last in the huge garden complex came the round-roofed Ionic tholos called the Temple of Love, initially designed by Hastings in 1923 and which A. I. wanted to resemble as nearly as possible that at the Petit Trianon at Versailles, although it was ultimately modified. A bronze copy of Jean-Antoine Houdon's famous *Diana* was installed in 1934.

BR26.5 Carillon

1935, Massena and du Pont

Alfred I. du Pont commissioned a church, tower, and cemetery from his son's firm in 1930, but a commitment to poor relief during the Great Depression put these plans on hold. Eventually the project metamorphosed into a 210-foot, thirty-five-bell carillon as a memorial to A. I.'s parents, to serve as his own mausoleum (he died in 1935), and to celebrate his love of music. Base and quoins are gray Vermont granite, the square shaft pink North Carolina granite facing reinforced concrete. A red light atop the polygonal spire served as a familiar beacon for pilots at Philadelphia airport. Massena later designed Edison Tower, Menlo Park, New Jersey, before his premature death in 1945.

BR26.6 A. I. du Pont Hospital for Children (A. I. du Pont Institute)

1937–1941, Massena and du Pont, with Crisp and Edmunds. 1977–1981 greatly enlarged, Saxelbye, Powell, Roberts and Ponder

Alfred I. du Pont was an orphan and later suffered from partial deafness and blindness. Upon his death, he left a fortune for a children's hospital, one emphasizing research and with no more than $1 million to be spent on the building itself, which stylistically is a stripped-classical offshoot of Nemours mansion. An advisory committee directed the architects to give natural light to every room, include sunrooms, and to be sure that flowers were visible outside. An auditorium was used for plays and motion pictures. A. I.'s widow, Jessie Ball du Pont, advised, and artist-doctor Jack Wilson painted wax-emulsion murals of Dinah Craik's 1875 story "The Little Lame Prince." Architect Alfred Victor du Pont visited similar facilities in California and Colorado and partnered with Crisp and Edmunds, a Baltimore firm specializing in hospitals. By 1974, four years after Jessie's death, the Nemours Foundation was the fourth-largest in the United States and the hospital was soon to be enormously enlarged by a firm in Jacksonville, Florida.

BR27 INDEPENDENCE MALL

ments at Naamans and Foulk roads that pioneered the town-house approach, again following eighteenth-century Philadelphia examples. He planned a series of Independence Malls across the country and had begun one in Dover when he died suddenly at age forty-nine in 1966. The central building and tower were burned by an arsonist in 1980 and have been reconstructed in a less elaborate form.

BR27 Independence Mall

1963–1964, Emilio Capaldi. 1980–1981 central structure rebuilt, Joe Chickadel. U.S. 202, north of Foulk Rd. (DE 261)

This quirky complex—a copy of Independence Hall, Philadelphia, as the centerpiece of a shopping mall—was the creation of Wilmington-born developer Capaldi. A painter by avocation, he sketched historic buildings in Philadelphia and here assembled many of them in a creative combination: the rows of shops that flank the main building individually refer to Philadelphia landmarks, including the Letitia Street House, Carpenters Hall, and Philosophical Hall. In *Center Line*, AIA Delaware blasted the project: "To build such a cheap, commercial imitation of our sacred Hall of Independence would be a disgrace to our community and should outrage each and every citizen." The flanking buildings formed a "mish-mash," and the whole was termed a "discreation." Today one might argue that the Disney-like design blended high and low culture in a way that anticipated postmodernism. Capaldi also designed Olde Colonial Village (completed in 1966), a group of apart-

BR28 Lombardy Hall

1750. c. 1793 south section. Concord Pike (U.S. 202), north of Foulk Rd. (DE 261)

Signer of the Constitution Gunning Bedford Jr. (one of ten contemporary "Gunning Bedfords," to historians' confusion) bought 250 acres as a summer place in 1786, when he was thirty-nine. He first occupied the two-story side-hall stone house in 1792 and enlarged it to five bays, including the so-called downstairs Ballroom on the south. The name Lombardy Hall probably refers to a double row of poplar trees once planted before the door. An exceptional Adamesque chimney-piece was installed in 1820, eight years after Bedford's death here. Over the generations, the estate was whittled down, and a cemetery was created (1889), the dwelling serving as a morgue. Eventually, the crumbling house was occupied by vagrants. Emilio Capaldi purchased it in 1966 with hopes for restoration, but his death put an end to those plans. A new Masonic lodge created to serve the booming suburbs bought Lombardy Hall the next year as the only home of a colonial first Grand Master owned by a Masonic organization. Restored

BR31 FAIRFAX

by 1986, the National Historic Landmark is occasionally open to the public.

BR29 Isaac Budovitch House
1955, Edgar Tafel. 4611 Bedford Blvd., Forest Hills Park

Tafel served as Frank Lloyd Wright's apprentice in 1932–1941 and later practiced on his own in New York City, designing more than ninety houses nationwide, including this one for a client in the construction trades. The stamp of Wright (see Laurel, BR17) is immediately apparent in the horizontal format, long Roman bricks, wide eaves, and second-floor pergola that sweeps out to embrace a chimney. Top-quality materials were employed, including travertine marble for downstairs floors and cork upstairs, copper gutters, and a Ludowici clay tile roof that kicks up at the end, Japanese-style. Occupied by the original owners for half a century, the house today is well-preserved. Its new owners are architecture enthusiasts who have spoken with Tafel about this project and his memories of Wright. The surrounding Forest Hills Park neighborhood boasts an unusual concentration (for Delaware) of modernist houses of the 1950s to 1970s. At 4614 Bedford is another somewhat Wrightian dwelling, low and blending with the forested lot, designed by its owner (1958, Walter Scott Woods). The house at 4615, by Victorine and Samuel Homsey, has twelve rooms on its single, rambling floor. In contrast, the classical-style Dr. Park W. Huntington Jr. house nearby at 1701 Gunning Drive incorporated a room from a seventeenth-century Connecticut saltbox house.

BR30 New Castle County Library Brandywine Hundred Branch
2000–2003, Joseph G. Tattoni and Joseph C. Rizzo for Hillier Architecture, with Jim Nelson for the Architects Studio. Talley-Day Park, east of Foulk Rd. (DE 261)

Rarely is Delaware architecture as cutting-edge as this library, by a prominent firm in Princeton, New Jersey. Its front is a curving wall of gray stone, with a rakish canopy of steel and green glass suspended over the door. From the lobby inside, one sees a long exterior vista of huge stone columns supporting a sculptural, copper-clad roof. This colonnade contrasts with a window-wall behind it. Use of rough-hewn granite (quarried in Media, Pennsylvania) was suggested by the example of historic Rockford Tower (see **Kentmere Parkway and Rockford Park** on p. 140). In contemporary fashion, the building combines a library, community center, and café.

BR31 Fairfax
1950–1955, Alfred J. Vilone, developer. Fairfax Blvd. and Concord Pike (U.S. 202)

The post–World War II pattern was followed again and again—a developer bought a site along a highway and erected signs in a farmer's field advertising a new shopping center, apartments, and homes. "This was a cow pasture out here," Fairfax Shopping Center's current owner recalls. That center, opened in 1950, embodied the customary layout: a strip facility with a parking lot between it and the highway; little stores bracketed by a big anchor store at each end (including a supermarket). Developer Fred Vilone chose Colonial Revival style, complete with a cupola, but the place was twice remodeled after he sold it. Parking ultimately proved inadequate. Behind the shopping center is the residential part of the development; according to historian Carol Hoffecker (1983), "the builder kept his costs low by offering a minimum of variety in his two-story, six-room Colonial houses, which he sold for $15,000 apiece with little or no down payment and an FHA-backed mortgage." Apartments stood as a buffer to the housing tract, all of which is boxy, reductivist red-brick-and-frame. Total housing units numbered 700. In 1951, Vilone's employees erected a granite stone to him by the highway: "One man's vision becomes security and happiness for thousands."

BR32 Office Tower (Rollins International)

1970–1972, Platt Associates, with W. Ellis Preston. 2200 Concord Pike (U.S. 202)

In a rags-to-riches transformation, John W. Rollins, who had grown up poor in Georgia, scraped together $500 in 1954 to start a truck leasing business in Lewes, Delaware. It was the start of an empire that would produce annual revenues of $110 million by 1970. He proposed a city center complex in Wilmington in 1966, but a permit was refused, as many old-line civic leaders looked down on him. Undaunted, he moved his headquarters to suburban Concord Pike, breaking ground for this fifteen-story, white-marble-clad tower. The tallest building in Delaware when built, it proclaimed the presence of Rollins for miles and peered down upon the golf course of the DuPont Country Club (BR34). The soaring white piers culminating in arches beneath the cornice recall the decorative modernism of Minoru Yamasaki's architecture of the 1960s. The Platt firm of Wichita, Kansas, worked with a Wilmington architect, Preston. Pharmaceutical firm AstraZeneca purchased the tower in 2004 and have painted it brown.

BR33 Aldersgate United Methodist Church

1950–1951, Elring G. Dollar for Dollar and Bonner. 1956 enlarged. 1961–1962 sanctuary, Whiteside, Moeckel and Carbonell. 1982 steeple. 1998–2000 addition, William E. Holloway for Bernardon Haber Holloway Architects. 2313 Concord Pike (U.S. 202)

Explosive post–World War II suburbanization in Brandywine Hundred led to the construction of many churches, including the original section of this one in a simplified Colonial Revival mode. The congregation had seventy-six members in 1951 and 1,634 a decade later, when a huge new sanctuary was constructed abutting the highway. Under an A-frame roof are walnut pews and paneling along with cork floors. Designed with soundproofing in mind, the low aisles have walls of brownish-red bricks with strip windows above filled with chunks of colored glass set in thick cement in an abstract pattern. The church can be compared to the contemporaneous St. Albans Episcopal Church at 913 Wilson Road (1958, Victorine and Samuel Homsey) and Hillcrest Bellefonte Methodist Church (1960–1961, W. Ellis Preston) at 400 Hillcrest Avenue, the latter with windows of colored translucent plastics.

BR34 DuPont Country Club

1948–1949, Aymar Embury II. Rockland and Black Gates rds.

A predecessor club for 700 DuPont employees (1924) on the grounds of the Experimental Station was displaced by expansion of that facility in the 1940s. By 1949, there were 4,300 club members, and New York architect Embury's new building was said to be the largest country club in the nation. The 400-foot facade showed the stripped classicism then popular, with a porticoed entry of brick piers modern-looking in its simplification. Inside was a long hall, known as Peacock Alley. The golf course (1946–1947, Alfred H. Tull) was extensively refurbished in 2004.

BR34 DUPONT COUNTRY CLUB

BR35 Brantwyn (Bois-Des-Fosses)

c. 1935, Massena and du Pont. 1939 garden, Frederick W. Holcomb. 600 Rockland Rd.

The 28,000-square-foot, Georgian Revival mansion was home to Pierre S. du Pont III, corporate executive and leader in the development of cellophane and nylon. His son Pete, who grew up here, would later become governor and run for U.S. President. A brick house that suggests the architecture of Tidewater Virginia, with a Palladian window above a Westover-style doorway, the mansion lay at the center of a scenic estate named Bois-Des-Fosses for the family property in France. Following Pierre's death in 1988, the land was subdivided—with more sensitivity than might have been expected—and Bois-Des-Fosses was purchased by the DuPont Company in 1991. Demolition was considered, but instead the place was refurbished as a venue for conferences and weddings and given a new name, Brantwyn. The surroundings are historic; to the east, stone gatehouses mark the entrance to Lower Louviers (1810–1811, much rebuilt), a private estate not visible from the road. Porticoed Lower Louviers was designed for Victor du Pont by his brother and fellow immigrant, E. I., supposedly with the assistance of Thomas Jefferson. Its restoration in the 1930s was the first local design project of architects Victorine and Samuel Homsey. Nearby Upper Louviers (pre-1802, 1830s, and later), immediately east of Brantwyn, was home to Pierre Bauduy and, from 1837–1865, Admiral Samuel F. Du Pont. Despite these associations, Upper Louviers was razed for an extension of the DuPont Country Club golf course in 1978.

BR36 Rockland Mills

19th century and later. Rockland Rd. at Brandywine Creek

Mills were once innumerable on the Brandywine (see Augustine Mills, BR21; Bancroft Mills, WL91; and others). With profits from his Philadelphia bookshop, William Young (printer of the *Columbian Magazine* and chief supplier of paper for the U.S. government) dammed the river here in 1794 and built Delaware Paper Mill. It burned in 1814. By then, he had established Delaware Woolen Factory, making cassimeres, satinette, and fancy cords, and he later added a cotton factory. Operations ceased after a fire in 1846. Young's imposing stone house with fanlight (1801) still stands uphill at 507 Black Gates Road. Later, Jessup and Moore made paper, starting in 1860 and rebuilding after a fire later in the decade. Their long, stone riverside structures with brick arches above the openings were considered quaint as early as 1872, when they appeared in the famous book *Picturesque America*. A map of 1927 shows the plant as making book paper, with bleach and rag houses in the building nearest the road and beater rooms behind them. The facility ceased operation in 1971 and has been converted into condominiums (Peter Jennings and Mary Staikos for Moeckel Carbonell Associates). Rockland Bridge stands nearby, twentieth-century concrete successor to a noted covered span (1823, Lewis Wernwag, washed away 1839). That earlier bridge appeared in two paintings of 1835 by artist John Rubens Smith, along with Young's Mill on the east bank and Kirk's on the west.

BR37 Smith's Bridge

2002 replica of 1839 original, Pocopson Industries. Smith Bridge Rd. over Brandywine Creek

Near Delaware's northernmost point and in sight of the Pennsylvania state line stands a 145-foot covered bridge popular with artists. The first covered span here (1839, copy of a Lewis Wernwag design) suffered damage from truck traffic and was considered ready for demolition in 1954, when state engineer William A. McWilliams successfully pleaded for its restoration as one of the last covered bridges in the state. A steel deck was inserted and the whole Burr arched-truss structure was supported by two stone piers built in the river. The refurbished bridge was burned by an arsonist in 1961, one of several in Delaware to suffer this fate. Its reconstruction forty-one years later came as a result of a campaign by the Centreville Civic Association. The original bridge was of white pine, but the re-creation (awarded a historic preservation award in 2003) employed Bongossi, a fire-resistant African hardwood of rock-hard resinousness. To the east stands the stone Smith's Mill House (c. 1790) and remains of a mill and race, in operation to 1900.

Christiana Hundred

The northern two-thirds of this rolling Piedmont hundred include what is known as Chateau Country, among the most expensive real estate in Delaware. The less scenic southern third, however, consists of dense suburbs and, at the lower edge, the former colonial highway of Newport Pike and the Amtrak line. Red Clay Creek on the west was once lined with mills, including the celebrated snuff mills at Yorklyn, the remains of which were largely demolished in 2003. Several historic bridges cross the creek. The DuPont gunpowder mills at Hagley on the Brandywine still stand (CH15). In the nineteenth century, small farms in upper Christiana Hundred were consolidated into enormous estates of the du Pont family. An early step in popularizing the chateaux was the Garden Club of Wilmington's publication of a map in 1938 highlighting the gardens of its wealthy members. Gradually during the course of the twentieth century, more of the public was invited to visit, and several mansions have become conference centers or museums, including the famous Winterthur Museum (CH10). Christiana Hundred contains the state's best variety of high-style domestic architecture. (As its architectural history is bound up with the history of the du Ponts, a genealogical chart is provided in **The Du Pont Family and Architecture** on pp. 18–19.) With the coming of suburbanization, the Hundred's population grew more rapidly than that of any other district around Wilmington, from 4,700 in 1900 to 18,700 in 1940—and then to 31,700 in 1950. With the south entirely built up, the north continues to grow, with loss of the scenic farmland that gave the area a bucolic character. Accordingly, preservationists are concerned for the future of the region.

NORTHERN CHRISTIANA HUNDRED

CH1 Oberod

1935–1937, DeArmond, Ashmead and Bickley. 400 Burnt Mill Rd., northwest of Centreville

Epitomizing the Christiana Hundred chateau, Oberod stands on a hilltop perch overlooking rolling countryside. Famed horse breeders Harry W. Lunger and his wife, Jane du Pont, built it. As Bickley died in 1938, Oberod is one of the last designs by his Philadelphia firm, which was responsible for several Wilmington mansions, including additions to Gibraltar (WL94). Inspired by farmhouses in Normandy, France, it has a cobblestone courtyard, square tower (a feature of the du Pont estate in France, Bois-Des-Fosses), and unusual masonry: blue stone in wide joints scratched to look rustic; a hint of old whitewash as a patina; wide, stripped-modern limestone trim. Starting in 1979, Oberod served as a church conference center.

CH2 Selborne Farms

1919 and later. Selborne Dr. (private road), north of Centreville

Intending to establish a country club, a syndicate of wealthy Wilmingtonians paid Henry Gause $60,000 for his 600-acre dairy farm in 1917. Plans changed, however, and houses were built instead, most of which are hidden from public view, including the Christopher Ward home, Bramshott, by a top Philadelphia firm (1919–1920, Walter Mellor for Mellor, Meigs and Howe). Ward's house featured steel casement windows imported from England and ironwork by Samuel Yellin. Nearby stood Selborne, home to Colonel Daniel Moore Bates, designed in a provincial French Norman style by Philadelphians (1928–1930, Willing, Sims and Talbutt), also with Yellin ironwork. Visible from Kennett Pike is the stone, Colonial Revival–style Henry Canby House (1919). East of the Selborne entrance road stands Mt. Airy No. 27 School (1863), now a residence.

CENTREVILLE

The village served the Conestoga trade along the Wilmington and Kennett Turnpike (1811–1813), which is still marked by milestones. Its growth stalled when railroads supplanted wagons. In 1918–1920, DuPont Company president Pierre S. du Pont bought the turnpike, widened the roadbed in concrete, and deeded it back to Delaware, all to speed his commute to Longwood, his manor in Pennsylvania. By that time, du Ponts controlled nearly half of the frontage on the road and were building numerous estates. In Centreville itself, boutiques displaced country stores starting in the 1950s. A historic district was established in 1985, and traffic-calming measures were undertaken on Kennett Pike in 2003, in attempts to retain the community's charm in the face of development pressures.

In the middle of town, the brick James Delaplaine House (c. 1820; 5722 Kennett Pike) has a Doric porch and two doors with fanlights; the smaller led to the living quarters, the larger to a general store and possibly a tavern. Southeast of Centreville stands the extravagant chateau Meown (c. 1930), by the architect of Winterthur, Albert Ely Ives; it is distinguished by its tall Norman tower of stone. Irénée du Pont's sister, Isabella (Mrs. Hugh Rodney Sharp), developed Meown as a country retreat, raising horses and Jersey cattle.

CH3 Centreville Lodge No. 37, Independent Order of Odd Fellows (IOOF)

1876. 5725 Kennett Pike (DE 52)

In the 1870s, the town's newly established Odd Fellows Lodge sold stock to build a brick meetinghouse, erected by contractor A. E. Stiner. The three floors, under a gable roof with brackets, still serve their original functions: first floor for retail, second floor a community space, and third floor for IOOF meetings. Dalton's country store was housed here starting in 1877; its successor, Smith's (1931–1966), is remembered for its coal stove, old coffee grinder, dark wooden shelves, and welcoming frame porch. Diagonally across the

CH3 CENTREVILLE LODGE NO. 37, INDEPENDENT ORDER OF ODD FELLOWS (IOOF)

CH4 CENTREVILLE RESERVE

CH5 GREENVILLE COUNTRY CLUB (OWL'S NEST)

street stands another reminder of Centreville's late-nineteenth-century prosperity, the mansard-roofed Chandler-Dixon-Frederick House (1880; 5714 Kennett Pike).

CH4 Centreville Reserve

2000–2003, Jeffrey C. Beitel for Thompson Homes, Inc. Off Owls Nest Rd., 0.3 miles southwest of Centreville

The seventy-acre Dilworth-Phipps Cottage Farm was the last working farm in Centreville; its sale to developers in 1999 was lamented by some as the end of an era. Thompson Homes of West Chester, Pennsylvania, carved out twenty-five spacious lots and erected enormous houses. The first on the right was the showpiece and hosted tours as the *Philadelphia Magazine* Design Home 2002. At 9,384 square feet and $3.15 million, it was "intended to set a new standard for residential elegance in Delaware's Brandywine Valley." The stone exterior was traditional Georgian Revival, but the interior featured twenty-first-century amenities, including a home theater in the basement. Various other homes were modified Tudor Revival in style, and the original Italianate farmhouse (1880) was restored (it looks oddly new). The National Association of Home Builders bestowed awards on Thompson.

CH5 Greenville Country Club (Owl's Nest)

1915–1916, Harrie T. Lindeberg. 1928–1929 garden, Ellen Biddle Shipman. Owls Nest Rd., 0.4 miles southwest of Centreville

Eugene H. du Pont Jr., son of a DuPont Company president, combined parts of three farms into his estate and commissioned an English manor house in medieval style from an inventive New York architect. Built of skintled (lumpy) brick and with irregular massing,

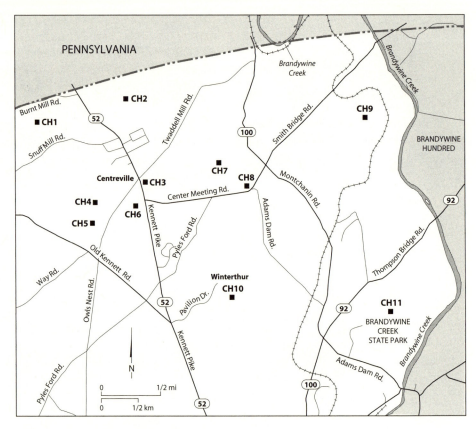

CENTREVILLE AND VICINITY

two-story oriel window, bold chimneys, and a steeply pitched roof of oversized slate shingles, it is one of Delaware's most flamboyant architectural compositions. Lindeberg had published *Domestic Architecture* (New York, 1912) to showcase his estate designs, including several with his trademark "thatched-single roof"—made of modern materials but weirdly undulating, like thatch. Lindeberg had an eye for details: a sheet-copper eagle and scrollwork in the lunette over the front door; real elk antlers affixed high on a gable. The Shipman-designed formal walled garden, for which plans of 1929 survive, was renowned for its lilies. The sensational wedding reception of the owners' daughter, Ethel du Pont, to Franklin Roosevelt Jr. happened at the house in June 1937, with President Franklin D. Roosevelt among 1,300 guests attending. It poured rain, and du Pont family lore insists that the President quipped, "It seems a fine way to soak the rich." Owl's Nest was the first and largest du Pont estate to be sold for development, in 1961, with the main house becoming a country club (expanded in 1987). The boxwood garden is well preserved and includes an oval dancing pavement said to have been installed for the wedding.

CH6 Carpenter House (Riverview)

1847. Kennett Pike (DE 52), west of intersection with Center Meeting Rd.

The J. L. Carpenter family, grown wealthy in the mutton-butchering business, built the bracketed Italianate mansion they called Riverview and raised twelve children there. The ornamental cast-iron veranda is one of Delaware's finest examples of antebellum metalwork. From the cupola, Carpenter could survey his 192 acres, which have subsequently been subdivided.

CH7 Flint House

1978–1980, Robert Venturi for Venturi and Rauch. Center Meeting Rd. north of intersection with Pyles Ford Rd., east of Centreville

This small country house tucked into rolling, unspoiled countryside was built for a grandson of Irénée du Pont. Ostensibly it is a gabled Pennsylvania farmhouse of white clapboards and shingle roof, but Venturi overlaid cutout forms of Doric columns and a huge arch masking a windowed gable. A high-ceilinged music room with organ was given a latticed groin vault with what were described as "Carpenter-Gothic proportions"—another series of cutouts. Big windows in the breakfast area allowed the owners to birdwatch. The Postmodern approach earned a *Progressive Architecture* Honor Award in 1980 and looked ahead to Venturi's burst of public commissions starting in the 1980s (see Trabant Center, NK9.14).

CH8 Center Friends Meeting House

1796. 1870s porch. Center Meeting Rd., east of Centreville

Delaware's first Quaker meetinghouse west of Brandywine Creek was established in this vicinity in 1690. It was called "Center" for lying between New Ark Union (now Carrcroft, northeast of Wilmington) and Old Kennett Meeting, Pennsylvania. The current one-story brick structure has a tall sloping roof and a porch with thin posts and brackets. It is divided inside by a wooden partition in the usual Quaker manner and contains early benches, wainscoting, floors, and stoves (the only source of heat). Rustic-looking sheds outside are divided into stalls for horses, each post supported by a rock. Weathered benches on the little late-nineteenth-century porch overlook rolling countryside. At the rear of the meetinghouse is a graveyard in which markers were forbidden until 1850. The meetinghouse was essentially abandoned from 1907 on, until the growth of the suburbs and renewed interest in Quakerism led to its reopening in the 1950s. Centre Grove School (1854), across the road, operated until 1932.

CH9 Granogue

1921–1923, Albert H. Spahr. South of Smith Bridge Rd. overlooking Brandywine Creek, east of Centreville

Irénée du Pont presided over the family company from 1919 to 1926, years of phenomenal expansion and profitability. He bought four contiguous farms comprising more than 500 acres and began a Colonial Revival house spacious enough for his family of nine children plus six live-in servants. The site was a lofty hilltop with spectacular views across the Brandywine valley. Pittsburgh architect Spahr had been a classmate of Irénée at the Massachusetts Institute of Technology. Construction was of brick faced with Germantown, Pennsylvania, granite; floors were reinforced concrete covered in teak; walls were paneled in oak carved by American Car and Foundry. Metal craftsman Samuel Yellin provided the iron hardware. A garage housed twelve cars. Du Pont collected minerals, and his wife, Irene Sophie, was a horticulturist, so the architect included a museum, solarium, and conservatory. A Maxfield Parrish mural depicting a romantic landscape hangs above a large organ. The basement contained a chemical laboratory and milk-testing facility for the estate's dairy operations. Sophie laid out the gardens with DuPont engineer Albert E. S. Hall. As the twenty-first century began, Granogue remained occupied by Irénée's and Sophie's only son.

CH8 CENTER FRIENDS MEETING HOUSE

CH10 Winterthur

1839 established. Entered by Pavilion Dr., off Kennett Pike (DE 52)

The world's foremost museum of American decorative arts, Winterthur is a monument to the collecting talents of Henry Francis du Pont (1880–1969). In the early nineteenth century, James A. and Evelina du Pont Bidermann named this property, then 445 acres, "Winterthur" after an ancestral village in Switzerland. They built their home at the end of a mile-long driveway. Henry Francis's grandfather, "Boss Henry" du Pont, later bought the estate. The Boss's son, Civil War hero Colonel Henry Algernon du Pont, expanded the house, and Henry Francis continued that process. Some 220,000 visitors tour the collections annually and explore the sprawling grounds.

CH10.1 House and Museum

1839–1842. 1874–1876, 1884, Theophilus Parsons Chandler Jr. 1901–1904, Robeson Lea Perot and Elliston Perot Bissell. 1928–1931, Albert Ely Ives

While living abroad, the Bidermanns hired a French architect, N. Vergnaud, to produce architectural drawings for a house at Winterthur and brought a set of French-style casement windows back from France with them—casements were a novelty in the northeastern United States. As erected under the supervision of Alfred Victor du Pont and builder James Goodman, the squarish, stuccoed-brick dwelling with Greek Doric porticos deviated considerably from the Frenchman's designs. "Boss Henry" du Pont (of Eleutherian Mills, CH15.4) bought the estate in 1867 as part of his immense landholdings and started the process of having Italian work crews build massive stone walls, keeping them busy when not constructing powder yards. He intended the place for his son, Colonel Henry Algernon du Pont. Chandler, a Philadelphia architect married to the Colonel's sister, altered the interior and, in the 1880s, is credited with doing the same to the exterior, giving it a steep roof and tall chimneys.

The next changes came from the firm of Perot and Bissell, who studied at the University of Pennsylvania architectural school founded by Chandler. As young graduates (Perot having married a cousin of the Colonel's), they succeeded Chandler as architects for the extended du Pont family. Working from blueprints of 1901–1903 prepared at their office in the Philadelphia Bourse, they quadrupled the size of the house, encasing the original building within a French Renaissance–style mansion with a red tile roof and terra-cotta cornices. Young Henry Francis du Pont, upon graduation from Harvard in 1903, returned home and became actively involved in the construction of the new edifice, whetting his lifelong interest in design and rebuilding.

Henry Francis became master of Winterthur upon his father's death in 1926 and undertook a $2 million expansion, building a gigantic addition to house his growing furniture collections. His young architect, Bert Ives, had been a draftsman for Addison Mizner in Boca Grande, Florida, where several du Ponts were erecting mansions. Ives moved to Wilmington to build Chevannes (CH13) on Kennett Pike, which evidently attracted the eye of Henry Francis, who ordered the Winterthur designs in 1928. Only thirty when du Pont contacted him, Ives went on to build several country houses outside Wilmington until relocating to Honolulu in 1935. The existing thirty-two-room Winterthur mansion was supplemented by a 145-room fireproof wing designed for good natural light and standing fully eight stories high on the downhill end. Viewed from below, the house was spectacular, tan-colored walls with red shutters soaring up to a stone modillion cornice and tall hipped roofs with clay tiles, dormers, and towering chimneys. There were to be more than 175 period rooms in all, purchased from historic buildings in the thirteen original colonies, following the example of the American Wing (1924) at the Metropolitan Museum of Art, New York. Du Pont worked closely with Ives on matching the design of rooms in the Winterthur wing to the shapes of the historic architectural elements he intended to buy.

The first period rooms, installed 1927–1932 by interior designer Henry D. Sleeper, included, most importantly, elements of demolished Port Royal (1762), northeast of Philadelphia, from which the exterior entrances of the Winterthur wing and its trademark dormers (with a scrolled kick at the bottom) were derived. Installation of further materials was supervised by architect Thomas Tileston Waterman in 1933–1950, with Charles O. Cornelius of the Metropolitan Museum of Art consulting on decoration. The most famous feature of this second campaign was a spiral stair (1936) incorporating parts of one from Montmorenci, a Federal-style house in Warren County, North Carolina, to supplant Colonel Henry's grand marble staircase of 1902–1904. Always interested in family history, Henry Francis preserved original Bidermann-era woodwork in the Winterthur Hall and Bedroom. The Architect's Room showcased historic surveying and drafting instruments. For tax purposes, du Pont incorporated Winterthur as a museum as early as 1930 and opened it occasionally. In 1951, he moved into the nearby Cottage, and Winterthur Museum officially debuted under curator Joseph Downs (formerly of the Metropolitan Museum's American Wing) and director Charles F. Montgomery.

CH10.2 RED LION INN FACADE

CH10.2 Red Lion Inn Facade

c. 1830. 1947–1949 elements installed at Winterthur, Thomas T. Waterman

Fragments of several old Delaware structures were reincorporated into Winterthur. Frank Silver, who owned the brick tavern once known as Red Lion Inn in the Delaware town of that name, offered to sell pieces to Henry Francis du Pont in 1946, prior to demolishing the building. The place was historic: "At Red Lyon we gave the horses a bit of hay," Washington's diary had read in 1791, referring to a predecessor building. For $995, du Pont got 700 feet of "shelving" and cornice, 465 feet of white pine flooring, three doors and their frames, two stairways, and other elements. Parts were used by Waterman to create a mock-facade very different from the original in an interior badminton court in 1948 (where the ancient inn sign is displayed), and other pieces were creatively employed in adjoining rooms.

Other Delaware architecture at Winterthur includes elements of Mordington (KT32), purchased in 1930. Pine paneling from an abandoned log farmhouse near Red Lion was obtained by 1938 for the "Delaware Room." The Wilmington house, Latimeria (best known for the garden structures it provided), also gave interior woodwork, installed 1948. Finally, parts of the Thomas Shipley House in Wilmington (c. 1770, demolished 1957) were added in 1962–1964. In all cases, these were merely pieces of paneling and decorative trim plus, perhaps, doors and windows, which du Pont reassembled, often in a very free way, in his museum rooms. The guiding principle was aesthetics and convenience, not archaeological accuracy; the front door of Mordington became, for example, the entrance to "Massachusetts Hall."

CH10.3 Crowninshield Research Building

1968–1969, James Ford Clapp Jr., for Shepley, Bulfinch, Richardson and Abbott

A series of additions to the museum provided space for staff and projects. The five-story Crowninshield Building, designed with the aid of top consultants and named for du Pont's sister, Louise Crowninshield, housed a library and archives, offices, and state-of-the-art conservation laboratories. Henry Francis du Pont climbed a nearby hill to be sure the building would not block views of the garden and insisted that two full stories be hidden underground. The dedication in May 1969 fol-

DU PONT COUNTRY ESTATES

According to Winterthur Museum historian Margaret Lidz, Delaware's Chateau Country resembles enclaves of the ultra-rich on the Gold Coast of Long Island, New York, and the Main Line grand estates outside Philadelphia, but with differences: a greater physical scale and pervasive Francophilia. Even the railroad stations received French names in honor of the du Ponts' Old World origins: Montchanin, Cossart, and Granogue.

The landscape of northern Christiana Hundred preserves the distinctive impress of the country estate, a phenomenon that reached its peak in 1910–1940. These estates, Lidz notes, showed common characteristics. They were frequently 500 acres or more, embracing diversified agricultural endeavors that were managed scientifically. Huge gardens and conservatories featured rare plants. The company-minded du Ponts ran their estates with corporate efficiency, devising pyramidal charts of organization and paternalistically providing for employees' needs in a way that struck some visitors as feudalistic. The chateaux displayed the genealogical collections of the owners even as they showcased cutting-edge technology from the latest automobiles to innovative mechanical systems—for always the du Ponts were engineers.

Of the many estates, Lidz points to four as especially complex and vast: Nemours (BR26), Winterthur (CH10), Longwood (in Pennsylvania), and Granogue (CH9). The latter is still occupied by the son of its first owner, a remarkable survival of the country estate lifestyle into the twenty-first century.

WINTERTHUR HOUSE AND MUSEUM (CH10.1), MONTMORENCI STAIRCASE

lowed by only a month the death of du Pont. The facility, which many staffers thought ugly, joined the existing South Wing (1957–1959, Victorine and Samuel Homsey), which had provided space for twenty-three professionals plus library, classrooms for the Winterthur Program, a dining room for guests, and a lecture rotunda. Nearby is the latest addition to the museum facilities, the Galleries (1991–1992, Warren J. Cox for Hartman-Cox Architects), built over a creek and repeating motifs from the house, including the clay tile roof and distinctive Winterthur dormers.

CH10.4 The Cottage

1950–1951, Thomas T. Waterman

Waterman studied for eight years under Boston architect Ralph Adams Cram and worked at Colonial Williamsburg during its creation around 1930, playing a crucial role in the design of its major public buildings. His friend, museum director Fiske Kimball, recommended him to Henry Francis du Pont in 1932, and thereafter Waterman was closely involved with the design of Winterthur. With Winterthur slated to become a museum, Henry Francis du Pont converted its bedrooms and bathrooms to display spaces and moved into the Cottage. (Du Pont's life thus came full circle, as he and his father had lived in a predecessor dwelling of 1838 on the Cottage site while Winterthur was enlarged exactly a half-century before.) Waterman's twelfth and final private house commission, this plain stuccoed box with twin Regency-style curved bays facing a creek was completed the year of the architect's premature death at age fifty-one. As historian Margaret Lidz points out, half of the building was servant space, there being eighteen servants and drivers on staff as late as the 1960s.

CH10.5 Pavilion (Garden Tours Pavilion)

1958–1961, Victorine and Samuel Homsey

As big crowds came to tour the museum and gardens, a facility was needed to serve them, well away from the du Ponts' private quarters in the Cottage. The Homseys' son Eldon informs me that this was his father's favorite work, one that "came together very simply" and that was, to the surprise of many, accepted by Henry Francis du Pont in spite of being "such a modern design." Akin to a Japanese teahouse in its extensive glass sidewalls, shingled roof, and wide overhangs, it was originally meant to be open six weeks in spring as a ticket house and restaurant and needed to be contextual in the wooded landscape. Winterthur Museum curator Charles Hummel and other staffers placed stakes so that du Pont could approve the building's location and size. A lecture hall was added in 1964 and, shortly thereafter, the facility was put to year-round use.

CH10.6 Winterthur Farms Dairy Buildings

1918

Before Winterthur was famous for decorative arts, it was known for dairy cattle. Colonel Henry Algernon du Pont kept a herd, which his son Henry Francis greatly enlarged in 1914. Winterthur Farms covered more than 2,000 acres. By 1926, there were ninety houses for workers. Among the Holstein cattle was the second-largest dairy cow in the world (2,225 pounds), which once produced thirty-eight pounds of butter in a single week. Atop Farm Hill, south of the mansion, stood the Main Cow Barn (burned 1930), of hollow tile construction, 329 feet long with big silos at each end. A huge fan could change the air inside every eight minutes. The milk produced (821 tons a year) was screened for purity and sold to the Hotel du Pont and other purchasers in the city of Wilmington. Other buildings (some of which were later demolished or became dilapidated) included the Main Calf Barn, Creamery, and Club House, made possible by huge wartime DuPont Company profits. The farm was served by the fish-scale-shingled Winterthur Railroad Station and Post Office (1890s).

CH10.7 Winterthur Garden

Early 20th century. 1928 and later, additions, Marian Cruger Coffin

Winterthur occupies a virgin tract of hardwoods, and my count of the rings of a white oak on the lawn (sawed down in 1997) showed that it was more than 300 years old. As historian Margaret Lidz describes (1999), Colonel du Pont played an important early role in saving the majestic trees, laying out the road system, and installing the Pinetum (1918). His son, Henry Francis, established March Bank (1902) and consulted Coffin as early as 1910. She was a close friend of the family, had trained at Massachusetts Institute of Technology when Henry Francis was at Harvard, and had afterward traveled with him in Europe. In 1928, following the enlargement of the house, Coffin designed the circular drive at the new front door; the Boxwood Scroll Garden (northeast corner of the house, 1930); the terrace with its existing tulip poplar trees (then sixty feet tall, today closer to 100 feet); and the long stairway to the swimming pool (with James M. Scheiner). In 1955, she was summoned back to turn the tennis courts into a Sundial Garden.

Coffin's designs were executed with plants chosen by Henry Francis du Pont himself. Several garden structures came from the country house Latimeria (1815, E. I. du Pont with William Warner), which once stood on Newport Pike near the foot of Broom Street, Wilmington. From Latimeria, du Pont acquired for the Winterthur garden (1929–1930) an octagonal summerhouse, beehives, a mushroom-top circular bench, latticed Chinese pagoda, and double gates (most have been heavily rebuilt). Near the end of his life, du Pont created a Quarry Garden (1962). Uphill from the museum, a wall from Mansion Farm, south of New Castle, with "1750" set in glazed bricks in the gable, is incorporated into a modern structure (1964) formed from an old water tower.

CH10.8 Enchanted Woods

2000–2001, Buck Simpers Architect + Associates; W. Gary Smith, landscape architect

A prize-winning, $2.4 million landscape garden playground with a fairy theme, Enchanted Woods was meant to boost Winterthur's attractiveness to families. Several elements are architectural, including a rustic Fairie Cottage. Other features make knowing historical references: Tulip Tree House, hewn from a giant tree trunk on the estate, copied an eighteenth-century illustration of a hollow-tree teahouse.

CH11 Winterthur Estate Stone Walls

Late 19th century. Brandywine Creek State Park

For many years following the arrival of the utopian-minded Pierre Samuel du Pont to America, the du Pont family held land in a kind of communistic arrangement. But "Boss Henry" du Pont broke with tradition, seizing for himself huge tracts out of the common holdings, to the dismay of some of his kin. As if forever to mark the landscape as his own, he (and later his son, Colonel Henry A. du Pont) had Italian masons build extensive stone fences around their far-flung estate, using rock from Brandywine Granite Quarry (BR24), which the family partly controlled. The walls at today's Brandywine Creek State Park are good examples—solidly built and with capstones so level on the top that one can easily walk on them. The park property was bought by landscape architect Robert Wheelwright in 1951 and auctioned after his death, at which time developers proposed a housing tract for the 433 acres. Concerned citizens pushed the reluctant State Park Commission to buy the property instead, and today it is cherished open space.

GREENVILLE VICINITY

CH12 Strand Millas

1701. 1760s. South side of Rockland Rd., northeast of Montchanin

The plain stone house is a rare survivor of the dwellings of the first generation of William Penn's Quakers. A datestone gives the very early date of the western part of the building. The dormers are modern. The Gregg family, builders of the house, patented several large tracts here in 1685–1686 and continued to own the property for more than 200 years, pioneering in milling and scientific farming. The name refers to an industrial town near Belfast, Ireland. Near the house (0.3 miles to the west) is the attractive late-nineteenth-

CH12 STRAND MILLAS

century Inn at Montchanin Village, a modern use for a former Italian tenant enclave; it features the distinctive Winterthur workers-housing aesthetic of concrete walls and columns (even a concrete Privy Row) and corbeled brick cornices.

CH13 Chevannes

1926–1930, Albert Ely Ives. 4812 Kennett Pike (DE 52)

Bessie Gardner du Pont's divorce from husband Alfred I. du Pont in 1906 nearly tore the family apart. Alfred's foe, Pierre S. du Pont, sided with Bessie and later gave her this house as thanks for writing a history of the DuPont Company. Ives, architect of Winterthur (CH10.1), based it closely on photographs of Bois-des-Fosses, the Pierre Samuel du Pont house in France (demolished 1970s); the name Chevannes came from a village near that historic home. Brass hardware, parquet floors, and mantels were all imported from France. A walled rose garden copied that at Bois-des-Fosses, from which estate chestnut seeds were brought to establish an allee. H. Rodney Sharp oversaw construction. Historian Margaret Lidz notes how similar the house is to Meown (see Centreville), a nearby farmstead that was built for Sharp's wife, and argues that Sharp was the chief "tastemaker" for the otherwise staid du Pont family during this era.

CH14 E. Paul du Pont House (New Office)

1890–1891. 1914. 204 Buck Rd., east of Greenville

The growth of the DuPont Company after the Civil War was symbolized by a big new headquarters building in High Victorian Gothic, across Buck Road from the family burying ground. When the office staff eventually moved to downtown Wilmington (see DuPont Building, WL32), that headquarters became the William K. du Pont house in 1902 and, after his death five years later, was radically altered into a Colonial Revival–style mansion by E. Paul du Pont. Here Paul built the prototype Du Pont automobile, a 1919 Model A, and oversaw the growth of Du Pont Motors until the Depression ruined his business in 1932. Only 547 Du Pont cars were produced, including the test car for the Model G (1928) now on display nearby in the barn at Eleutherian Mills (see CH15.6). President Franklin D. Roosevelt was received in the parlor at du Pont's home during a visit to Delaware.

CH15 Hagley Museum

1802 and later. Along Brandywine Creek, north of DE 141, east of Greenville

Along a scenic stretch of Brandywine Creek, French emigrant Eleuthère Irénée du Pont founded his namesake gunpowder company in 1802. From this seed would grow the gigantic DuPont chemical corporation of our times. E. I. named the first powder yard after himself, Eleutherian Mills, a name preserved to-

CH15 HAGLEY MUSEUM, staff designing model for Black Powder Exhibit to go in Millwright Shop, c. 1961

GREENVILLE VICINITY

day in his house (CH15.4) that stands overlooking the industrial ruins (also known as Upper Yard). Better preserved is the later Hagley Yard downstream (CH15.1), near which stands a small fraction of the worker housing built by the du Ponts. The various yards remained in continuous operation from 1802 until 1921. Some 42 percent of the gunpowder used by the North in the Civil War was produced here. Today, the architectural remains (thirty buildings of the original 100) are open to the public as a 230-acre outdoor museum under the administration of the Eleutherian Mills-Hagley Foundation, established at the time of the company's 150th anniversary in 1952. Historical materials are housed in the Library (1959–1961, Voorhees, Walker, Smith, Smith and Haines). Hagley is a National Historic Landmark.

CH15.1 Hagley Yard
1820s, with many additions

Long a scene of bustling enterprise and the occasional disastrous explosion, Hagley Yard has been silent since 1921. Following closure, the grounds were divided up as du Pont family holdings and attractively landscaped, and all but two of the thirty iron rolling-mill wheels (seven tons each) were scrapped in 1942 for the war effort. The subsequent creation of an interpretive museum at Hagley involved some of the first industrial archaeology in the United States, building on the example of Saugus Iron Works, Massachusetts. An essay and photo-pictorial by photographer Walker Evans appeared in *Fortune* (May 1957).

Today's visitor enters Hagley Yard through the Centennial Gates, beside the New Machine Shop (1902–1903, Black Powder Operating Department). Henry Clay Mill (CH15.2) lies beyond. Two huge bald-cypress trees near Eagle Mill are all that recall the original, eighteenth-century "Hagley" house of Rumford Dawes (demolished early 1930s), who named it after the estate where he was born in England. (A later "Hagley" uphill is illustrated on p. 20.) The centrally located Millwright Shop (1858, enlarged 1871) appears in a number of nineteenth-century photographs. The modernist Black Powder Exhibit inside (1961–1962) features working models of many building types in the yard, including several no longer extant.

At the upper end of Hagley Yard stands Birkenhead Mills (1822–1824), oldest of all. In typical powder mill design, the stone walls are massively thick and buttressed against explosions, but open on the side facing the creek and with a flimsy shed roof designed to disintegrate in a blast—aiming the fiery concussion away from the yards. At the Birkenhead, E. I. du Pont first used cast-iron wheels to mix powder ingredients in a rolling mill, a means

CH15.1 HAGLEY YARD, Birkenhead Mills, photo c. 1890

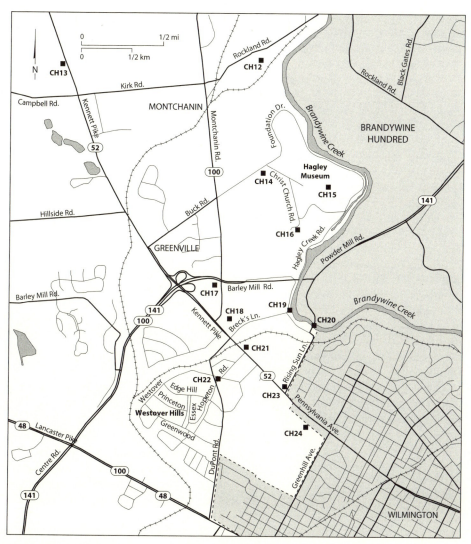

GREENVILLE VICINITY

more efficient than the old stamping process. Massachusetts archaeologist and Saugus veteran Roland Wells Robbins undertook archaeology here in 1955, and the big breast wheel was re-created in 1964. The water level at the dam nearby is thirty-three feet higher than at the one downstream, this fall-of-water once powering the entire yard with its thirty-three mills.

CH15.2 Henry Clay Mill (Metal Keg Shop)

1813–1815. 1954–1957 restored

Opened during the War of 1812 as Duplanty, McCall and Company spinning mill (and contemporaneous with nearby Breck's Mill, CH19), the three-story, water-powered stone factory briefly made fine cotton cloth and yarn but almost immediately switched to coarse goods in an attempt to compete with cheap British imports. The business failed in 1819. Later owners included Victor and E. I. du Pont as shareholders. A cotton-picking machine and dye vats occupied the basement; a carding machine stood on the first floor; and spinning mules and looms were located on the first and third floors. At one end, a small cupola atop a tower housed a bell. Surviving time sheets show that workers (32 percent female) toiled from dawn to eight in the evening, six days a week. By the 1840s, the mill was named for Senator Henry Clay, advocate for American industry. It was converted to the manufacture of metal kegs for powder in 1884.

As leading figures in the DuPont Company began planning the Hagley Museum in 1950, the mill was chosen as the interpretive centerpiece, to be gutted to the walls and have a steel and concrete interior inserted. Walter J. Heacock, director of exhibition buildings at Colonial Williamsburg, came in 1954, and elaborate displays were conceived (1955–1957, Walter Dorwin Teague Associates). A renowned industrial designer who had promoted Streamline Moderne style in the 1930s, Teague was famous for his trade-show exhibits for major corporations, including DuPont's at the World's Fair of 1939 in New York City (in a building by A. M. Erickson). His first-floor exhibits in Henry Clay Mill opened in May 1957 and featured an innovative "talking map" of the Brandywine Valley, possibly the first multilingual museum display in the United States. Miniature working models—marvelously complex and accurate—showed how mill technology worked. Today these exhibit spaces are rare surviving examples of modernist interior design in Delaware, worth preserving in themselves.

CH15.3 Brandywine Manufacturers' Sunday School

1817, with additions. 1850–1851 vestry room

Here E. I. du Pont offered nondenominational general education to the children of factory workers. The institution followed an English reform movement that set up schools in industrial districts. His widowed daughter Victorine threw herself zealously into the enterprise, heading it for decades (1816–1861). A survey in 1826 by Jonas P. Fairlamb offers the earliest (though not very accurate) visual representation of the building, which had been built by local mason William Cleaden. Carpenter James Goodman reconstructed the roof and added a fanlit doorway (subsequently altered) and a "piazza" in 1845. Nineteenth-century drawings thought to be by Alfred Victor du Pont show the Ionic capitals employed here, which may have been recycled from some earlier du Pont mansion. In later years, the building served as the Hagley Yard office of the DuPont Company (1902–1921), after which it was a private home until 1974. A restoration five years later reapplied stucco to the walls and returned the interior to its schoolhouse days, based on an old sketch by Sophie du Pont.

CH15.4 Eleutherian Mills

1802–1803. Before 1809 extended east. 1853–1854 enlarged. 1923–1924 restored, Mellor, Meigs and Howe

Five generations of du Ponts lived in this house. E. I. du Pont built the stuccoed, Federal-style stone edifice with pedimented, fanlit doorway on a bluff above the Upper Yard, so he could keep an eye on the operations. Pierre Samuel du Pont de Nemours illustrated the floorplan in a letter to his wife in France in 1815. Drawings survive that show family activities in the house and on a two-story Ionic piazza at rear. The Marquis de Lafayette stayed here during his American tour. "Boss Henry" du Pont enlarged the house; his son, Henry Algernon du Pont, grew up here and sketched the dwelling and grounds (1852). An explosion in the yards severely damaged the place in 1890, after which it was refurbished as a workers' clubhouse. Henry Algernon's daughter Louise (Mrs. Francis B. Crowninshield) took over the property following the closing of the powder works in 1921 and undertook a restoration with a leading Philadelphia firm. The interior was substantially rebuilt and a lovely spiral stair was brought in. A founder of the National Trust for Historic Preservation, Crowninshield helped restore the Virginia house, Kenmore, in the 1930s, and Independence Hall and Society Hill, Philadelphia, in the 1950s (plus the Dutch House, NC7). Her Eleutherian Mills interiors can be compared to those of her brother, Henry Francis du Pont of Winterthur (CH10). Upon her death in 1958, the Eleutherian Mills–Hagley Foundation undertook further restoration, which First Lady Jacqueline Kennedy came to see in 1961 as she worked with Henry Francis getting ideas for redecorating the White House. Eleutherian Mills opened to the public three years later. Models on display show the development of the house, which underwent refurbishment in 2004–2005.

CH15.5 Eleutherian Mills Gardens
1803. 1972 recreated, William H. Frederick Jr. 1924–1938 Italian classical garden, Francis B. and Louise du Pont Crowninshield

Having declared his profession as "botaniste" on his traveling papers, E. I. du Pont lost no time in having seeds and plants sent from France, including fruit trees and grape vines. His garden (uphill from the house) later vanished, but garden archaeology, one of the first such endeavors in the United States, was begun in 1968. A sketch (c. 1870) by architect Theophilus P. Chandler allowed reconstruction of the pump of 1817. Visitors can study recreated eighteenth-century French garden treatments, including espalier. Near the garden stand several fine trees, including the second-largest Osage orange in the United States and a buckeye thought to have been hybridized by E. I. himself. The Crowninshields established a garden of their own downhill from the house, of entirely different character, an Italian ruin garden on the steep slope. They razed the upper stories of an abandoned saltpeter refinery there and built whimsical brick ruins, designed by Francis, with plantings by Louise. Huge saltpeter kettles of iron served as urns. This ruin garden has been partly razed.

CH15.6 First Office
1837. 1849 enlarged to the east. 1969 restored

For decades the little stone building with brick window arches housed the office of the president of the powder company. Built for Alfred Victor du Pont, it originally measured just 28 × 28 feet. The entire headquarters staff of the company as late as the 1880s consisted of "Boss Henry" du Pont plus bookkeeper, paymaster, bill clerk, telegrapher, and office boy. The building was never electrified, but it was linked to Wilmington by telegraph (1855) and telephone (1883). "Boss Henry" manned the telegraph here in 1860 as election returns for Lincoln came in. Abandoned as a headquarters in 1891 (for the New Office, CH14), by the 1920s it had come to be seen as a cherished relic of the company's past. The current museum display shows it in Alfred Victor's time, with a room in the era of "Boss Henry," too. Horses and mules that hauled powder wagons and rail cars were kept in the barn just uphill (1802–1803, rebuilt 1844, restored 1970), in which a single, enormous structural beam runs wall to wall.

CH16 Christ Church Christiana Hundred
1854–1856, Richard A. Gilpin. 1876 interior alterations, Theophilus Parsons Chandler Jr. 1914–1915 chancel added and interior redesigned, F. Burrall Hoffman Jr., with Henry Francis du Pont. 1951–1952 Education Building and Children's Chapel of the Christ Child, William Heyl Thompson, carvings by Thorsten Sigstedt. 1950s landscaping, Marian Cruger Coffin. Christ Church Rd., off Buck Rd., east of DE 100, Greenville

The first generation of du Ponts in America were Deists, but Victorine became a devout Anglican. From her Brandywine Manufacturers' Sunday School (CH15.3) grew this Episcopal congregation, in which pious Alexis I. du Pont (see St. John, WL54) and Captain Samuel Francis Du Pont were active. After considering architect Richard Upjohn, the captain commissioned English-born Gilpin, a Philadelphia architect and railroad engineer known for rebuilding the Pennsylvania Academy of

CH15.5 ELEUTHERIAN MILLS GARDENS, Italian ruin garden, with ELEUTHERIAN MILLS house (CH15.4) at top (painting 1933)

the Fine Arts after a fire in 1845, to design a stone, buttressed, Gothic Revival church in an oak grove. The soaring, needlelike spire was hoisted in November 1855—knocking off a chimney in the process—and the following April, it was modified with tiny windows for the view, as suggested by Lammot du Pont. Alexis was high-church in his leanings, and debates arose about the chancel arrangement and having a cross on the steeple. Ironically, his was the first funeral here, as he died in a powder-yard blast in 1857. Later explosions, in 1890 and 1920, smashed the lattice-light lancet windows (replaced the second time by Henry Wynd Young of New York City).

The present interior dates to 1914–1915, the alterations overseen by Henry Francis du Pont of Winterthur (CH10), a lifelong member. The parishioners credited "his excellent taste and judgment" and approved the removal of nineteenth-century pews and other trappings: "Gone the hideousness of golden oak!" The truss ceiling has hammerbeams enriched with angel heads in English medieval style. Red sandstone replaced the original plaster for the chancel columns and, in 1929, for the chancel's Gothic arches. President Franklin D. Roosevelt attended the wedding of his son to Ethel du Pont (of Owl's Nest, CH5) here in 1937, one of countless society weddings the church has witnessed. Children's Chapel, by a Philadelphia architect, has decorative painting on the truss ceiling and child-scaled pews by Philadelphian George Ciukurescu. The base of Christ Church tower has been partially enclosed by additions (1957, 2007) that skillfully blend with the original walls.

SOUTH OF DE 141

CH17 St. Joseph on the Brandywine

1841. 1848 enlarged at rear. 1941, Gleeson and Mulrooney. 1950 rear addition. Montchanin Rd. and DE 141

The DuPont Company built this church for its Irish Catholic workers, an early example of benevolent corporate paternalism. Alexis I. du Pont chaired the building committee. Under the supervision of builder James Goodman, DuPont masons working on company time erected the massive stone walls, fashioning them with a durability worthy of the powder yards. Later came the tower (1878) and spire (1887). Alfred I. du Pont, always attentive to the powder workers, electrified the church in 1895 and had the building painted the same color as his nearby house, Swamp Hall—yellow—which it remains today. He also replaced the roof and ceiling. St. Joseph's served as a community bulwark in times of explosion or epidemic. Catholic parochial education in Delaware, so dominant today, got underway with a convent constructed here in 1850. By the turn of the twentieth century, this was the largest Catholic church in the state. In 1941, the front wall was brought forward to mostly enclose the tower; much of the interior dates to this time. The nineteenth-century marble altars and metal communion rails were ripped out in 1974–1975. Twenty years later, the building was refurbished (1994–1995, Homsey Architects).

CH18 Irisbrook

1928, E. William Martin. East of intersection of Montchanin Rd. and Kennett Pike (DE 52)

Home to financier John J. Raskob's brother, William (see Archmere, BR4), the Colonial Revival house is centered on a conservatory and contains a rare Aeolian organ, its 2,400 pipes extending from thirty feet below ground level to the attic three floors above. The announcement party for the engagement of actress Grace Kelly to Prince Rainier of Monaco was held here, as the Kellys and Raskobs were friends, and the bricks for Irisbrook are said to have come from the Kellys' company in Philadelphia. The building now houses the Raskob Foundation for Catholic Activities. Across Kennett Pike to the south is a Colonial Revival hospital (1954–1955) donated by Eugene du Pont of Owl's Nest (CH5); it stands on the site of Pelleport, the William du Pont house, built by architect Theophilus P. Chandler Jr., in Queen Anne Style in the 1870s and demolished in 1954. William du Pont

CH19 BRECK'S MILL, with Walker's Mill at left, photo c. 1910

abandoned it for the historic house Montpelier, Virginia. A granite stables survives at Pelleport.

CH19 Breck's Mill

1813, with later changes. Foot of Breck's Ln. at Brandywine Creek

Beloved of artists, the brick-and-stone mill occupies one of Delaware's most picturesque settings. When the embargo on British goods initiated during the War of 1812 stimulated the U.S. textile industry (see Henry Clay Mill, CH15.2), Wilmington lawyer Louis McLane and his brother-in-law George Milligan erected the cotton-spinning mill on the Brandywine's west bank. Two pencil sketches by the visiting Benjamin Henry Latrobe, dated October 1813, show "Milligan and McLane's New Mills" without its present tower and with a clerestory roof. William Breck took charge in 1832 but sold out to Charles I. du Pont seven years later, who converted the mill to woolen cloth manufacturing and rebuilt the interior and roof after an 1848 fire (his house with "C.I.D. 1823" datestone still stands upstream). Operations ceased in 1854, and by the 1890s, the mill served as Hagley Community House for DuPont.

Mirroring Breck's across the dam is white, bell-towered Walker's Mill (1813–1815, Joseph E. Sims), used for various purposes, including making cotton yarn and muslin and Rowan cassimere. Alexis I. du Pont bought it in 1843 and converted it to weaving. Walker's closed as late as 1938. The so-called "Walker's Bank" beside it provided workers' housing and is now one of the few survivors of the scores of such dwellings that climbed the hills here. Along the west shore between Hagley Yard (CH15.1) and Rising Sun Bridge (CH20), of twenty-seven buildings of various kinds shown on a 1902 survey, only five remain. One of the missing is Rokeby Mill (rebuilt 1840) on Pancake Run, approximately where the driveway to Breck's Mill is today. It served as the first DuPont experimental station from 1903 until it burned in 1906. In their heyday, around 1820, Rokeby and Milligan and McLane's Mills together housed 2,300 spindles, ten hand looms, and twenty power looms, and employed seventy-nine workers. Porticoed Rokeby house (1836), home to William Breck, stands on a knoll above Breck's Lane.

CH20 Rising Sun Bridge

1927–1928, Charles E. Grubb, with Harrington, Howard and Ash. Foot of Rising Sun Ln. over Brandywine Creek, New Bridge

The 123-foot long, riveted Pratt through-truss is the only bridge of this type still carrying highway traffic in Delaware. It rests on abutments from a predecessor of 1883. Climbing down the steep bank, one sees that the roadway is still supported by an early stone arch (c. 1830) that once crossed a millrace. At that time, Rising Sun Bridge was a graceful covered span. Just east is the original entrance to the DuPont Experimental Station (BR25), formerly Lower Powder Yard. Along the west

CH20 RISING SUN BRIDGE

SOUTH OF DE 141

bank runs a sewer line, blasted into solid rock by the WPA in one of its most difficult Delaware projects (1935–1936).

CH21 Alexis I. du Pont Middle School (Public School, United School Districts 23 and 75)

1892–1893, Theophilus P. Chandler Jr. c. 1918, Brown and Whiteside. 1938–1939, enlarged. Later additions. Kennett Pike (DE 52), southeast of Breck's Ln.

Intended to be the finest public school building in the state outside of Wilmington, the Avondale-stone structure with curving half-timbered ornamentation was erected in nine months in a field donated by the DuPont Company. Chief benefactor Francis G. du Pont (for whose father the school was named) stressed at the dedication that it was not a du Pont family school but a truly public facility. The project was the first major one for James M. Smyth, later one of Wilmington's busiest contractors, thanks in part to the patronage of Francis. An arched, stone entrance porch with a polygonal roof stood between two big, turretlike classroom bays, and chimneys rose above the stone ends. Lattice windows were replaced at an early date. The much-enlarged facility became a high school in 1952, then a middle school (a new concept at the time) in 1966.

CH21 ALEXIS I. DU PONT MIDDLE SCHOOL (PUBLIC SCHOOL, UNITED SCHOOL DISTRICTS 23 AND 75), photo c. 1907

CH22 Westover Hills

1926–1935, Allen J. Saville Inc. and John W. McComb, for Delaware Land Development Company. Westover and adjacent rds.

By 1929, there were an estimated sixty-eight millionaires in Delaware, and many of them lived in this exclusive tract. Three years earlier, William du Pont had transferred 600 acres to the Delaware Land Development Company, which he controlled. The layout was provided by Saville, a Richmond, Virginia, firm. Restrictions included fifty-foot setbacks for houses and ninety for garages, following the model of the early-twentieth-century Guilford development in Baltimore. Roads wound gracefully with the topography. Spanish-type domestic architecture, popular in the United States at the time, was discouraged in favor of English styles. When the Great Depression struck, some nicknamed the expensive neighborhood "Leftover Bills." Ironically, sewer service for the heavily Republican enclave was provided by President Franklin D. Roosevelt's WPA program, the pipe being laid down Thundergust Run and along Brandywine Creek (1935–1936).

Mansions here combined historicizing detail, first-rate design, and every modern amenity. The Royal C. Hull House (1100 Westover Rd., by Albert Ely Ives) is Tudor Revival with a crowstep gable and carved American walnut paneling inside. It is brick, with a tile roof, steel window sash, and attached three-car garage. At 801 Edgehill Road, the stone Colonial Revival James L. Luke Jr. House (1939) still has its original, nautical-themed lounge in the basement, with portholes for light fixtures, a bar of glass bricks that glows from within, a ship's stair with canvas sides, and a seascape mural.

Many noted architects were involved here, including the Philadelphia firm of Wallace and Warner (1109 Hopeton Rd.) and locals Brown and Whiteside. Philadelphia architect William Woodburn Potter designed the first house to be completed in the development at 1006 Westover Road. The Tudor Revival home of Foxcroft stone has a tall slate roof and herringbone brick nogging by the door. Massena and du Pont designed a "Low English Georgian" house of stone for Pierre S. du Pont III at 1102 Hopeton Road (1934–1935). R. Brognard Okie contributed one of his trademark Colo-

CH22 WESTOVER HILLS, photo 1930

nial Revival–style farmsteads across the street at number 1101, a lot bought by Thomas Edison in 1926 for his son, William L. Edison. The younger Edison lived in this house with his wife and butler until his death in 1937. He carried out experiments with a novel one-tube radio receiving set in a laboratory in the basement. Architect Alfred Victor du Pont (see Nemours, BR26) rented 907 Edgehill Road in the 1930s, where writer H. L. Mencken often visited him and his wife, Marcella.

Huge houses have continued to be built in the exclusive district. The chopping up of the George P. Edmonds estate in the 1990s produced several new lots, on one of which rose the Tudor Revival, stone-and-stucco house at 906 Westover Road (1999, Montchanin Design Group).

CH23 St. Amour Site

1890–1892, Albert W. Dilks. 1918 garden, Marian Cruger Coffin. North corner of Kennett Pike (DE 52) and Rising Sun Ln.

Here stood a famous chateau, now demolished. Mary Belin du Pont, widow of Lammot (who died in a chemical plant explosion in 1884), had a Queen Anne–style stone mansion with turrets and tower built by a Philadelphia architect. Her son, Pierre S. du Pont, twenty-two years old when the house was finished, helped supervise construction and lived here as he began his career with the family company after graduating from Massachusetts Institute of Technology. Brother Irénée (see Granogue, CH9) helped design the original garden. Another brother, Lammot, purchased the home following his mother's death in 1913 and expanded it to forty rooms. All three men eventually headed the DuPont Company. The du Pont family celebrated its American centennial at St. Amour in 1900. The mansion was acquired by adjacent Tower Hill School (WL93) and demolished in 1972 as too expensive to heat or keep up. All that remains are some garages—presumably those erected by Smyth Construction Company after World War I—and an abandoned, walled garden.

SOUTH OF DE 141

CH24 Goodstay

c. 1740, with additions. 1924, 1933 additions, Edmund B. Gilchrist. 2600 Pennsylvania Ave., west of Greenhill Ave.

"Green Hill," as it was known from at least 1732 until the du Pont family purchased it in the nineteenth century, was a desirable farmstead, right on Kennett Pike and within sight of downtown Wilmington. The original stone house was enlarged c. 1780 (to fourteen rooms) and again c. 1855; the barn bears a datestone (1807) with the initials of then-owner John Hirons. A sale in 1846 noted the excellence of the outbuildings: barn, granary, two carriage houses, plus hen, smoke, wash, and spring houses, all of which were built out of stone; a corn crib and summer house were frame. Ornamental trees occupied the grounds, perhaps including the huge ginkgo extant today. Howard Pyle's father bought Green Hill in 1853, and the artist spent his early childhood here. At what he called "the quaintest, dearest old place you can imagine," young Howard pored over picture books while lying on a rug in the library by the fire, rolled down the "terraced bank" in front of the house, and watched Conestoga wagons rumble by on the turnpike.

The Pyles soon sold the house and moved to town. Widow Margaretta E. du Pont bought the place in 1868 and changed the name to Goodstay, a nod to Bon Sejour, the New Jersey home where the du Pont family first settled in America. T. Coleman du Pont purchased it in 1911 and gave it to his daughter, Ellen, in 1923. Ensuing alterations gave the Colonial Revival ensemble a complex plan. Standing with one's back to downtown and facing the original stone house, a joint shows the break between the oldest section (right) and second-oldest (left). The frame parts of the house to extreme left and right date to 1924, with a major facade on the left looking toward the garden and away from automobile traffic on the turnpike; its doorway emulates New England colonial examples. On the far side of the house, facing a parking lot, is the addition of 1933.

CH24.1 Garden

1924 and 1937 garden redeveloped, Wheelwright and Stevenson

Robert Wheelwright, noted landscape architect who designed the Goodstay gardens, later married Ellen du Pont and lived here. Young Howard Pyle had played on a big rock by the wall of what he recalled as "such a garden as you would hardly find outside of a story book"; Wheelwright retained the ancient, four-square plan and old shrubs in fashioning a new knot garden like those of the Tudor period. A Garden Club of Wilmington pamphlet said in 1938, "Mrs. Wheelwright's garden belonged to her grandmother and she has kept all the charm of its age." The year before, her husband had added a cutting garden plus Magnolia Walk (redone 1997), terminating in a pool with an Aristide Maillol bronze sculpture, *Venus*. Wheelwright later designed the 102-acre Valley Garden on Campbell Road, Wilmington, making use of plants rescued from the flooding of adjacent Hoopes Reservoir (CH33). Ellen Wheelwright gave Valley Garden to the public in 1943, and, in 2003, the state expanded it. She was preservation-minded—saving the Howard Pyle Studios (WL81) in 1950—and upon her death, she willed Goodstay to the University of Delaware, which opened it as an educational facility in 1969.

CH24 GOODSTAY

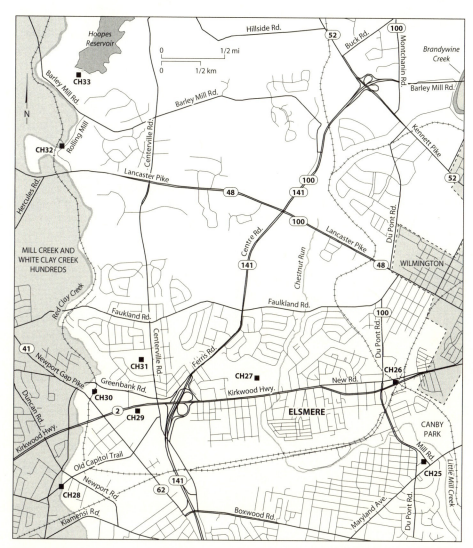

ELSMERE VICINITY

ELSMERE VICINITY

CH25 John Richardson House (Brick Mill House)

c. 1723. 3 Mill Rd., on Little Mill Creek, off Maryland Ave. at southwest corner of Canby Park

Swedish engineer Peter Lindeström showed "Little Falls Kill" on a map of 1654, but soon the name was Anglicized to "Mill Creek"—appropriately, as milling took place here continuously from 1669 to 1923. Quaker John Richardson, miller and trader, possibly built the two-story brick house in 1723 when he bought the mill. Of glazed-header Flemish bond, the irregular and ancient-looking little dwelling stands on a high stone basement and has a watertable at the level of the windowsills. Richardson's son built the large stone house just uphill (1765 datestone); lawyer and historian Henry C. Conrad owned it as "Glynrich" starting in 1887 and subdivided its farm in 1905—one of the first streetcar suburbs on the fringes of Wilmington.

CH26 Elsmere Viaduct

1945–1949, W. W. Mack, chief engineer. Kirkwood Hwy. (DE 2) over train tracks, east of DuPont Rd.

Highway construction stalled in Delaware during World War II but rebounded afterward. This was the state's first postwar project. The viaduct eliminated a grade crossing of seven railroad tracks and, connecting with the dual highway through Elsmere, seemed essential to the growth of the suburbs. Both state and federal funds were employed in this project, which pointed to the great freeway-building campaigns of the 1950s–1960s. The upper parts have been rebuilt, but some of the reinforced-concrete piers still show decorative profiles that are almost classical—a historicizing approach that soon would be considered unthinkable on an engineering structure.

CH27 Veterans Administration Medical and Regional Office Center

1946–1950, Massena and du Pont. 1601 Kirkwood Hwy. (DE 2), Elsmere

This eight-story, post–World War II federal project rose amid the fields of Hollingsworth

CH27 VETERANS ADMINISTRATION MEDICAL AND REGIONAL OFFICE CENTER

farm. A big, muscular Art Deco building in brick and limestone, the hospital had 320 beds, rooms wired for radio reception, and an auditorium where movies could be shown. The specifications (1947) contained seventy-eight sections and hundreds of pages of type. Elsmere grew phenomenally with suburbanization and was, for a time around 1960, the third largest incorporated town in the state.

NEWPORT

Founded in 1735, the town was described by *The Traveller's Directory* in 1804 as occupying "a pleasant situation, and [it] has a considerable trade with Philadelphia in flour," owing to its location on the Christina River. Later it became a stop on the Philadelphia, Wilmington and Baltimore Railroad. Only a handful of colonial buildings can still be found in this community of just over one thousand people, including a long brick house with gables on Market Street and a vinyl-sided brick gambrel-roofed house on John Street. The two other colonial houses mentioned in the WPA *Delaware Guide* (1938) are gone. St. James Episcopal (1948–1949, William Heyl Thompson, with William E. Grancell) at 2 Augustine Street is Colonial Revival, with stained glass by Frank Schoonover. The Newport vicinity was industrialized by the coming of Krebs Chemical and Pigment Company on the riverfront and, after World War II, the modernist brick General Motors Plant on Boxwood Road (1945–1946).

Newport. Krebs factory and Christina River in foreground, photo 1931.

NORTH ALONG RED CLAY CREEK

CH28 Marshallton Bridge

1930–1931. Old Capitol Trail over Red Clay Creek

The low span consists of a pair of 113-foot-long through-plate girders, studded with rivets. The girders arrived by railroad from Bethlehem Steel and were hoisted into place by crane. Tall, daggerlike, cast-in-place light standards of pebbly concrete rising from stepped bases look 1930s-modernistic. Much of the Delaware Hard Fibre plant of 1906 survives as a modern factory upstream, remnant of the many industries that once thrived on Red Clay Creek.

CH29 Prices Corner Shopping Center

1962–1963. Kirkwood Hwy. (DE 2), west of DE 141

Instead of enlarging their store built in 1950 in northeast Wilmington, Sears, Roebuck and Co. decided to build a huge new facility on thirty acres in the booming suburbs. A marketing study showed that Prices Corner was the best location in the entire county, with over forty thousand households within a ten-minute drive. A 20 percent growth in population was expected by 1970, Wilmington and Newark growing together along Kirkwood Highway (modernized 1957–1958). Working with Philadelphia developers Jardel Co. and Richard I. Rubin, Sears erected their largest outlet between Philadelphia and Washington, with a special suburban emphasis: the biggest garden and "outdoor living" center on the East Coast. A series of low, freestanding buildings were arranged in an arc and fronted by a continuous pedestrian portico. The various stores stood in a sea of parking lots big enough for 2,400 cars. By 1969, this kind of development was being decried by Wilmington architects, who in the AIA journal *Center Line* called for careful planning "to avoid future Kirkwood Highways."

CH30 Wilmington and Western Railroad

1872, with additions. Along Red Clay Creek; station at Greenbank Rd., northwest of Prices Corner

This ten-mile short line offers a rare, working glimpse at what nineteenth-century railroading was like. Enthusiastic volunteers keep it running for tourists. Wilmington and Western trains originally hauled kaolin clay, vulcanized fiber, snuff, iron, and coal along Red Clay Creek valley, serving the many mills as well as ferrying passengers to the picnic grounds at Mt. Cuba or to Brandywine Springs (MC5). The train is now boarded at Greenbank (see MC6), where the station was replaced in 1968 with a little steep-roofed one from farther up the line at Yorklyn (1873). The railroad repeatedly crosses the twisting creek, and during Hurricane Floyd in 1999, two bridges were destroyed by flooding and four others were severely damaged. Reconstruction of the lost bridges at Greenbank and Brandywine Springs involved the replacing of wooden trestles with steel, with the number of supports, or "bents," reduced in order to improve the flow of debris in floodtime. In 2003, a worse flood (in which the creek rose five-and-one-half feet in an hour) spared the new bridges but destroyed most of the surviving old ones, a stunning setback for the railroad, which again began a process of rebuilding.

CH31 Marbrook Elementary School

1965–1966, Dollar, Bonner, Blake and Manning. 2101 Centerville Rd., north of Kirkwood Hwy. (DE 2)

Six schools approved in the district in 1965 incorporated innovative educational concepts: clusters, pods, centrums, and carrels. Marbrook was the first completed. In a break from the rectilinear school designs of the 1950s, the facility consisted of three hexagonal, red brick and concrete wings (or pods), two containing classrooms and one an open-air gymnasium. Wedge-shaped classrooms were clustered around a centrum, or communal teaching space, with study carrels lining its walls. Several schools in the state following this now-discredited educational model have lately been demolished.

CH31 MARBROOK ELEMENTARY SCHOOL

CH32 Wooddale Covered Bridge

c. 1860. Scheduled for rebuilding. Foxhill Ln. over Red Clay Creek, north of Lancaster Pike (DE 48)

The fifty-four-foot, Ithiel Town wooden lattice truss bridge was reinforced with steel I-beams in 1969 (see photograph on p. 22). It occupies a steep, wooded valley where Red Clay Creek makes a hairpin turn and is twice crossed by the Wilmington and Western Railroad (blasted through an adjacent ridge in 1871–1872, a cut so narrow that fast trains risked scraping against the sides). A station was built near the bridge and Wooddale became popular with picnickers. North of the bridge are traces of Delaware Iron Works (active 1814–c. 1890), a sheet-iron rolling mill operated by Philadelphia entrepreneur Alan Wood. A village was centered at Wooddale in the 1890s but disappeared after the last factory, a paper mill, burned in 1918. Of the Red Clay Creek's thirteen bridges shown on an 1868 map, only Wooddale and its near-twin at Ashland (CH35) survived to 2003, when the former was destroyed by the record flood. It is scheduled for rebuilding.

CH33 Hoopes Reservoir Dam (Old Mill Stream Dam)

1929–1932, E. G. Manahan for Fuller and McClintock, engineers, with W. Compton Wills. Visible from Barley Mill Rd., northwest of Rolling Mill Rd.

Drought-prone Wilmington needed a storage reservoir, so scenic Mill Stream Valley was dammed, destroying a colonial mill (1732 datestone) that T. Coleman du Pont had restored and enlarged (c. 1908). Local soils

CH33 HOOPES RESERVOIR DAM (OLD MILL STREAM DAM), photo 1933

proved inadequate for an earthen dam, so 105,000 cubic yards of concrete were used instead. Poured in 1930 by contractors from Long Island, the structure was 135 feet high, 90 feet thick at the base, and 900 feet long. A hopper-bottom railroad car delivered cement from Hercules Cement Company. The material was pumped 2,000 feet from the railroad siding to a concrete mixer, from which conveyor belts carried it up the hillside to the dam. The structure is V-shaped to take best advantage of underlying rock layers. The reservoir was not needed until 1941, but water consumption has increased enormously since then, making it critical today.

ASHLAND AND VICINITY

West of this pleasant rural crossroads along Red Clay Creek stands Ashland Nature Center (established 1976), where modern buildings (Cooperson Associates) blend with an old farmstead. Along the brow of a hill curves the Center's award-winning Lodge, a crescent-shaped wooden building elevated on concrete posts (1989–1990, Homsey Architects). East of the covered bridge stands "Ashland Mills," the William Gregg House (corner of Creek Rd. and Ashland Clinton School Rd.), which shows fine glazed-header Flemish bond. Pent eaves above both first and second stories recall Chester County, Pennsylvania, practice. A carved-brick plaque bearing the date 1737 must have been inspired by a similar one of 1726 at the much-altered Cox House, near Yorklyn, because such plaques are rare. Southeast of Ashland is the house Mt. Cuba (MC4).

CH34 Pratt Truss Bridge

Late 19th century; moved here 1907. Over Red Clay Creek, near Creek Rd., northeast of Ashland

Wilmington and Western Railroad (CH30) was owned by the Baltimore and Ohio starting in 1883. This iron bridge was hauled in from the B&O's Wheeling, West Virginia, division, where heavier locomotives had made it obsolete, and today it is an extremely rare example of a Pratt through truss still carrying railroad traffic. Wrought-iron members are connected by pins and eye bars.

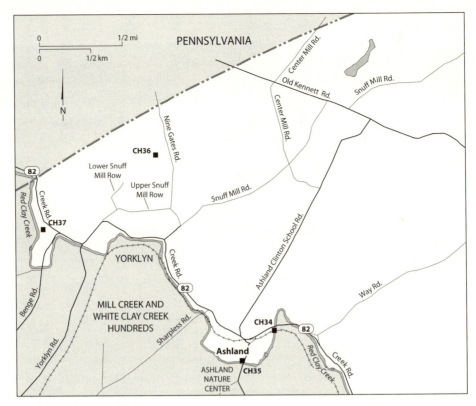

ASHLAND AND VICINITY

CH35 Ashland Covered Bridge

c. 1860. Barley Mill Rd. over Red Clay Creek

The fifty-four-foot, one-lane covered bridge is "plank-pin," its beams secured with big hardwood pegs or "trunnels." It uses the densely latticed timber-truss construction popularized nationally in the nineteenth century by architect Ithiel Town. Covered bridges were once numerous in the United States but have dwindled to only 800 or so, with just one original left in Delaware, now that Wooddale Bridge (CH32) has washed away. There were twelve as recently as 1930. Steel I-beams were inserted under the deck in 1982.

CH36 Cloud's Farm

1802–1848. West side of Nine Gates Rd., 0.4 miles north of Snuff Mill Rd., Yorklyn

The valley of upper Red Clay Creek is unusually rich in stone farmhouses, which often stand on steep slopes in this hilly terrain. Cloud's is considered an exemplary farmstead unit for its two houses (1806 and 1848) and large stone barn (1802). The roof-ridge of the older house is directly aligned with that of the barn in an arrangement architectural historian Henry Glassie calls typical of folk building in the southeastern Pennsylvania cultural region. The barn is noteworthy for four deep arches that lead to each inner bay. Hay mows, now missing, stood on three sides of the structure.

CH37 Auburn Heights

1896–1897. 3000 Creek Rd., 0.5 miles northwest of Yorklyn

One of numerous industries on Red Clay Creek was the manufacture of vulcanized fiber, which was a cotton cellulose treated to form a hard substance used for products from insulators to suitcases. Northern Delaware was the world center for production of this fiber. On a hilltop above the creek, the owner of National

CH37 AUBURN HEIGHTS

Vulcanized Fiber Company built one of Delaware's more exuberant Queen Anne mansions, of shingles and rockfaced stone. One pointed turret stands above a broad porte-cochere; another caps a corner tower that rises rocketlike from a wide porch at its base. In the 1970s, the builder's grandson, Tom Marshall, operated a museum on the property devoted to Stanley Steamers. Marshall has announced that he will leave the beautifully preserved mansion to the state, and it will become a state park.

Wilmington

With a population of approximately 73,000 in 2006, Wilmington is Delaware's largest city, twice as big as its nearest rivals. (Only four states have smaller leading cities, however.) Founded along the Christina River, Wilmington's history is long and colorful, going back to Swedish immigrants in the seventeenth century, followed by the English. On land west of the site of the small Swedish settlement, Thomas Willing laid out "Willingtown" in 1731, following the grid of his native Philadelphia. A brick house that once stood at the foot of Market Street and bore the date tablet 1732 was reputedly the first dwelling. Seven years later, a royal charter changed the local designation to "Wilmington," apparently to honor the earl of that name. The market town grew rapidly. Similar to Philadelphia, Wilmington was predominantly built of brick, but blue rock was readily available, too.

Milling of grain brought wealth to Revolutionary-era Wilmington. Later, it was fortunate to lie directly along the line of one of America's first railroads, the Philadelphia, Wilmington and Baltimore (1837), which triggered an industrial boom: shipyards, tanneries, carriage and railroad-car factories, and textile and flour mills. Among many nationally known firms were Jackson and Sharp (railroad cars) and Harlan and Hollingsworth (ships; WL8). Two bird's-eye views captured Wilmington's industrial heyday (1864–1865 by Edward Sachse, and 1874). If Delaware as a whole grew slowly in the nineteenth century, Wilmington experienced rapid growth, especially in the final decades. By 1900, it housed more than 40 percent of the state's population—on less than 1 percent of its land area. Civic boosters bragged of its sixty churches and an array of public buildings. Many of the proudest monuments built in this period are gone today, including the spire of Central Presbyterian Church on King Street (1856), the post office, the county courthouse, the high school, the tallest downtown buildings (Eden Hall and Equitable Building), two hospitals, and Washington Street Bridge. Somewhat more survives of the large number of nineteenth-century houses, which included handsome villas in the fast-growing western districts.

A milestone occurred in 1905 when DuPont's headquarters staff left the banks of the Brandywine and broke ground for a downtown office tower

(WL32). As the company grew phenomenally, so did the city, which became the wealthiest per capita in the United States following World War I. By 1926, Wilmington's population had reached 124,000, and up to 1,363 building permits were issued annually between 1921 and 1930. Dozens of housing developments went up, often with restrictive covenants, as architectural historian Susan Chase has explored. This was the golden age for architect-designed houses, with many firms founded, but it also saw the rise of big contracting companies headed by John A. Bader, Allen L. Lauritsen, James M. Smyth, and others. Oberly Brick Company provided large quantities of brick (1889–1958), including two million burned for Pierre S. du Pont High School (WL65), built on Oberly land near the northeastern edge of town in 1932–1935. Woodlawn Trustees, Inc., a philanthropic trust, built more than 400 homes between 1903 and the 1940s for working men to rent. Wilmington benefited from an influx of Italian craftsmen, such as Frank Giovannozzi, who had run a cut-stone establishment at Teramo before immigrating in about 1914. He installed, among

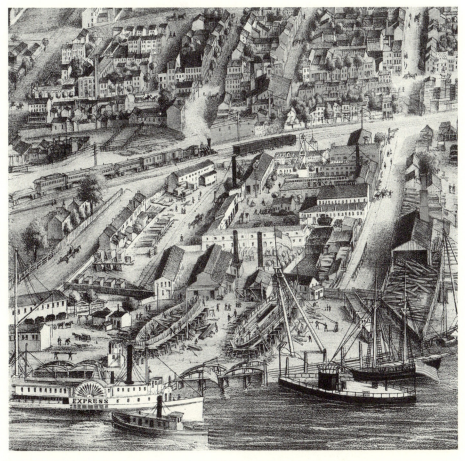

In the Sachse bird's-eye view, made during the Civil War, ships are under construction in the Wilmington riverfront yards, including a newly completed U.S. Navy monitor.

Wilmington, 1938. From Christina River (upper left) to the Brandywine (lower right), the city showed extraordinary density of settlement, with one neighborhood grading imperceptibly into another. Economic power was concentrated in the colossal DuPont Building (WL32) at center. Within thirty years, urban renewal, parking lots, and an interstate highway would clear huge swaths.

other projects, the 13,000 cubic feet of decorative limestone at Emalea Pusey Warner School (1928–1929; 801 W. 18th St.).

During the 1950s, Wilmington's stature swiftly collapsed as industries vanished and the population of its suburbs nearly doubled, and it ignominiously fell out of the list of American cities of 100,000 for the first time in fifty years. The DuPont Company remained, however, and, as a result, the Wilmington urban area in 1955 was the sixth wealthiest in the United States in terms of average family income ($6,900). By 1960, DuPont was the seventh largest industrial concern in the nation. Money was available for a vast rebuilding of downtown, centered on a key question broached as early as a Wilmington Chamber of Commerce publication in 1926: "'Where shall we park the car?'—that is the burning question before the shoppers." As an answer, in the 1960s, twenty-two blocks of the east side were leveled for urban renewal and parking lots. That same decade saw the blasting of I-95 through the densely populated western edge of downtown. These decisions have subsequently been condemned for exacerbating, not curing, the ills that afflicted the city and contributing to race riots in 1968, which were followed by a nine-month military occupation by the National Guard.

"Is Wilmington Dying?" asked the local reporter Bill Frank in 1964. Starting in the mid-1970s, however, the city showed slow but hopeful signs of recovery. Sobered after its orgy of blockbusting, it rediscovered its architectural history, establishing eleven historic "overlay zoning" districts between 1975 and 2003. DuPont shrank, but the Financial Center Development Act of 1981 brought in many banks. MBNA America, a gigantic credit card bank, built

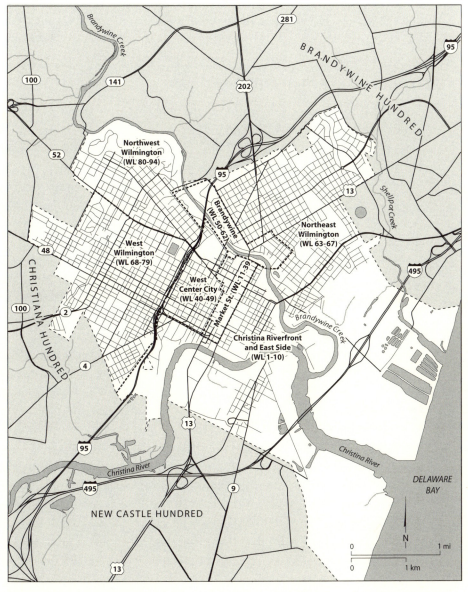

WILMINGTON NEIGHBORHOODS

or refurbished eight large office buildings after 1994 and occupied 1.75 million feet of office space. By 2005, the downtown was enjoying a boom, and new office construction grew at a rate equaled by few American cities. Even as new corporate buildings are erected, millions have been spent converting old, empty offices into residences downtown. Between 1995 and 2003, about $1 billion in public and private money was spent to rehabilitate rundown real estate. Nevertheless, the city's population continues its slow decline and is currently lower than it was in the 1890s. Those who remain are largely poor (21 percent live in poverty) and African American. One in ten housing units stands empty, and more than 2,000 homes need major repairs. As with all American cities, Wilmington has changed profoundly over the years, building and rebuilding, growing and decaying in a pattern of ceaseless change.

CHRISTINA RIVERFRONT AND EAST SIDE

The riverfront district was settled extremely early. Here the Swedes gained a foothold in the New World in 1638, just three decades after Jamestown; here Willingtown was founded; here the shipbuilding industry thrived. The bustling nineteenth-century riverfront was depicted minutely in the Edward Sachse bird's-eye view (1864–1865). As late as the mid-twentieth century, Front Street was dense with old buildings, but most have subsequently been destroyed, including the Thomas Mendenhall House (1790), documented by the Center for Historic Architecture and Design (CHAD) at the University of Delaware in 1980 before demolition. Recent decades have brought expensive efforts to revitalize the riverfront. A governor's task force that included fourteen architectural firms released a *Vision for the Rivers* report in 1994, and the Riverfront Development Corporation was established by the legislature a year later to begin the process of implementing improvements, including a riverwalk. No such revitalization seems in store for the rundown East Side, however, between Old Swedes Church (WL3) and King Street, one of the poorest sections of the city. This area housed factory laborers and has been studied by CHAD for the evidence it provides of working-class life. The City Planning Department surveyed architectural resources throughout Wilmington in 1978–1985 and established three historic districts on the East Side, embracing those rowhouse blocks not scoured clean by urban renewal. The East Side includes some historic churches, including Asbury Methodist at 3rd and Walnut (1789, 1885) and St. Mary's at 6th and Pine (c. 1860) by a New York architect, Patrick Keely.

Christina Riverfront, still industrial in 1931, with Harlan and Hollingsworth shipyard (WL8) at center and the railroad swinging through (see WL10). The Delaware River lies in the far distance.

WL1 Kalmar Nyckel Shipyard

1987 established. Christina River at 7th St., east of Fort Christina Park

Looking ahead to the 350th anniversary of Swedish settlement in Delaware, the Kalmar Nyckel Foundation purchased land beside Fort Christina Park (WL2)—appropriately, a former shipyard—and set out to reconstruct the vessel that brought the first twenty-four Swedes in 1638. Master shipbuilder Allen Rawl and naval architect Thomas Gillmer researched the historical appearance of the three-masted, Dutch-built pinnace *Kalmar Nyckel* ("Key of Kalmar") and ordered 50,000 feet of purpleheart wood from South America for the frame. The keel was laid in 1990, and the $4.3 million craft was launched seven years later, a living laboratory of seventeenth-century sailing. It has nine miles of rigging. The shipyard is used for public instruction in carpentry and other trades.

WL2 Fort Christina Park

1937–1938, Wheelwright and Stevenson, landscape architects. Christina River at 7th St., east of Swedes Landing Rd.

European settlement of the Delaware Valley began with the landing of Swedish ships *Kalmar Nyckel* and *Fogel Grip* here at the Rocks in 1638 and the construction of a fort designed by engineer Peter Lindeström. As the Tercentenary approached, commemorations were planned, and it was noted that two million Americans were of Swedish descent. The Swedish Crown Prince Gustav Adolf solicited donations from all citizens of his country for the erection of a monument, and 170,000 persons contributed. The park was a joint effort; Swedish sculptor Carl Milles provided the sculpture (plus an exact replica for Goteborg, Sweden) and a Philadelphia landscape design firm prepared the site, a former dump in the midst of an industrial district along an oily river. Ameri-

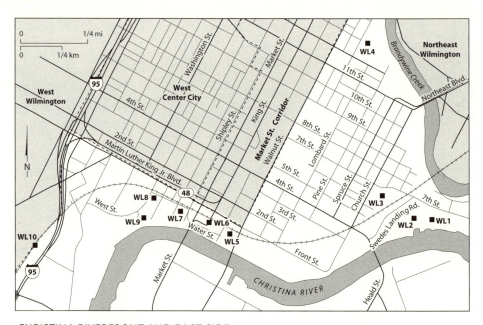

CHRISTINA RIVERFRONT AND EAST SIDE

can Car and Foundry stood directly across the street, and not a trace remained of the fort the Swedes had built or of the marshes that surrounded it protectively upstream and down. A high wall was erected (of 300,000 handmade Virginia bricks and 6,000 cubic feet of granite), paths were laid, sweetgum trees planted, and stone bollards erected at the edge of a plaza beside what remained of the Rocks. During the dedication in June 1938, an entourage of Swedish dignitaries disembarked from a ship in a lashing rainstorm, accompanied by President Franklin D. Roosevelt. The park, born in such a spirit of enthusiasm, subsequently saw little use despite its status as a National Historic Landmark.

WL2.1 Fort Christina Monument
1937–1938, Carl Milles, sculptor

Milles (active at Cranbrook Academy of Art, Michigan) created an Art Deco monument of black Swedish granite from two quarries. A stylized ship and wave stands atop a curve-faced column on which scenes from New Sweden are depicted. Per A. Palm, the carver who worked from Milles's model, supervised the installation of the thirty pieces of granite, with lead beneath each section. The ship carving alone weighs 7.5 tons. A time capsule was embedded in the base.

WL2.2 Thomas Bird House (John Stalcop Log House)
Possibly early 19th century

Fort Christina has been called the birthplace of the American log cabin, as Swedish and Finnish settlers built dwellings inside the fort, presumably of logs. None survives, but the Delaware State Archives brought one to the park to commemorate the important cultural achievement. The 18 × 20–foot "Swedish" log house had deliberately been spared destruction by the Fenimore family near Prices Corner, west of Wilmington. Log construction expert C. A. Weslager examined it just before the move, finding the oak logs mostly left in the round, although crudely hewn on front and back surfaces; both V and saddle notchings were used, not dovetailing (see photograph on p. 6). These are standard log house methods from all periods; and archaeology at the site suggested the building was no older than the 1820s. Its relocation to Fort Christina in 1962 saved it from demolition for a Shell gasoline station, but today it is boarded up.

WL3 Old Swedes Church (Holy Trinity)
1698–1699. 1740s north porches. 1762 south porch. 1774 gallery. 1802 tower, Thomas Cole. 1842 restored. 1898–1899 restored, William H. Mersereau, with Ferguson and Brown.

1964 restored after fire in roof. Church and 7th sts.

A National Historic Landmark and said to be the oldest church in North America still standing as originally built and holding regular worship services, Old Swedes celebrated its 300th anniversary in 1999. With its massive gray stone walls, red brick belltower with white-painted cupola atop, and verdant churchyard, it has attracted artists since at least the 1840s, including Howard Pyle, Robert Shaw, and the young Andrew Wyeth. Aesthetically and historically, this is one of Delaware's premier buildings.

Fort Christina settlers buried their dead on a slight rise here just inland from the river (although the oldest legible gravestones date from almost a century later, c. 1720). Three Lutheran missionaries arrived from Sweden in 1697, including the energetic Reverend Eric Björk, who pressed for a new church to serve inhabitants north of the Christina. These were descendents of the pioneers of six decades earlier, a Swedish enclave in a region that had by this time become heavily English. This larger cultural context explains why there is little or nothing "Swedish" about the church. A mason named Yard brought his crew down from Philadelphia, as did carpenters John Smart and John Britt. Of the other men involved, whose names are recorded in detailed church records, only a handful were Swedish. Although Björk offered design suggestions, the building they created was ultimately English-Colonial: a rectangular plan with compass-headed windows and jerkinhead roof (like the Anglican and Presbyterian churches in New Castle, built shortly after; NC10 and NC12). The cornerstone (supposedly at the northeast angle) was laid in May 1698, and the stone walls were up by the fall of that year. Lime was brought from Maryland by boat, and mortar joints are studded with pebbles ("galleted"). The building was consecrated on Trinity Sunday, June 1699 (hence the name Holy Trinity).

The oak-framed A-trusses of the roof exerted tremendous thrust on the tops of the stone walls, which were laid in soft riverine soils and soon began to bow outward, as can be seen today from the upstairs gallery. In response, two heavy porches were built against the north wall and a subsequent one against the south, the latter during the tenure of Reverend Israel Acrelius. In 1774, the spacious, sloping gallery containing twenty-five additional box pews was added, which is well preserved today. Access was via a stair in the south porch (the current one is a replacement). The congregation, by then Episcopalian, moved to a new building in downtown Wilmington in 1830, and Old Swedes was left empty. Some of the penknife graffiti on the south porch doors, recently uncovered, date from the dozen years of abandonment, though much is eighteenth-century, too. In a pious spirit of preservation—and augmenting a bequest by Henrietta Allmond—parish women raised money to save the old church and return it to regular use by 1842. The downstairs box pews were done away with and the windows given red sandstone sills.

WL3 OLD SWEDES CHURCH (HOLY TRINITY), photo c. 1870

Aside from electrification in 1886–1887, the next structural changes came with the church's bicentennial. Mersereau, a New York architect, and the Brooklyn firm of Ferguson and Brown returned the gallery stairs to the south porch and added the iron gates there, rebuilt the belfry, recreated the box pews based on those in the gallery, and returned the pulpit to the north wall where it had stood until moved to the east end in 1793. The changes pained the artist Pyle, who loved the ancient building and always pointed it out to companions from the train. He complained to Mersereau of "the garish yellow shingles and the crass new woodwork" (Abbott, 1925). In 1928, the raised wooden floor of the east end was replaced in brick. There have been few subsequent alterations, except for the reconstruction of the roof following a lightning-strike fire in 1964, steel trusses reinforcing the charred originals. The altar was replaced with a free-standing one in 1984.

A walk around the outside shows that no two elevations are alike, thanks to the several additions. Only the east wall with its clipped gable is largely unchanged from the seventeenth century. The smith Mattias de Foss wrought dozens of letters for inscriptions on every outside wall, but only here on the east are a few still in their original places, forming a fragment of "LUX-L.I. TENEBR. ORIENS-EX ALTO" ("Light from on high shines in the darkness"). Other walls show letters and numbers rearranged in the nineteenth century to spell, for example, the date of the church's construction. Dutch houses often had dates in iron numerals (famously, "1687" on New Castle's Tile House), but the lengthy inscription on Old Swedes is unique in any known Dutch or Swedish Colonial building. Even more surprising is that it survives.

Inside, the north porches are now enclosed as sacristy and vesting room. The original exterior wall of the 1698 nave can be studied here, protected and hence unweathered. Inside the nave itself, the austere, plastered interior suggests great age, although the once-clear lights have been filled with glass of delicate beauty (1885–1897). A rare survival is the brick floor of the center aisle. The gigantic hinges of the doors are notable. The walnut pulpit with canopy is said to be the oldest in the United States. Early portraits of Björk and other pastors hang along the gallery.

WL3.1 Hendrickson House

c. 1690. c. 1800 addition. 1958–1960 moved and rebuilt, William Moeckel with Robert L. Raley

Now relocated to the grounds of Old Swedes Church, the gambrel-roofed stone farmhouse was built by a Swedish settler late in the seventeenth century at Eddystone, Ridley Township, Pennsylvania (at the mouth of Crum Creek, a few miles up the Delaware River). The Federal Direct Tax of 1798 noted its original dimensions, 30 × 20 feet, and already called it "old." In the twentieth century, it stood abandoned, surrounded by quarries and brickyards. Baldwin Locomotive Works safeguarded the house for thirty years, but when Vertol Aircraft took over, they prepared to demolish it. Eventually, they were convinced to donate the building, which was disassembled and moved in fall 1958. Only the stones of the walls and the chimneypiece of the first-period hall (south end) are original. Other details are re-creations or miscellaneous salvage. Beams were finished with an adz for authenticity. Hendrickson House serves as a visitor center and genealogical library for Old Swedes Church.

WL4 Howard High School

1927–1928, James O. Betelle. 13th St.and Clifford Brown Walk

Generations of African American students passed beneath the Ionic portico of this brick school, the first secondary school for blacks in Delaware, its construction funded by P. S. du

WL5 WILMINGTON STATION (PENNSYLVANIA RAILROAD PASSENGER STATION)

Pont. The institution was originally founded in 1867 by the Association for the Moral Improvement and Education of Colored People and named for Civil War General O. O. Howard of the Freedmen's Bureau. It was declared a National Historic Landmark in 2005 for its role in the *Brown v. Board of Education* (1954) desegregation case (see also former Hockessin School, MC3).

WL5 Wilmington Station (Pennsylvania Railroad Passenger Station)

1905–1908, Furness, Evans and Company. c. 1980 restored and altered, Moeckel/Carbonell + Partners. Front St. between French and Walnut sts.

The Italian Renaissance–style station concluded the career of legendary Philadelphia architect Frank Furness. With an expensive project to elevate the Pennsylvania Railroad tracks on a viaduct through Wilmington (WL10) came the need for a new station on the site of the old one (of the 1870s). Furness faced a challenge—the trains would run right across the top of the first floor, and an ancient riverbed underlay the foundations (for this reason, two hidden rows of brick arches rest on piles). The station is faced with Kittanning (Pennsylvania) brick and robust red terra-cotta—Furness trademarks. A square clocktower rises above one corner. High-quality materials were employed: copper and tile for the roofs, white oak interior paneling, tile floors, and marble in the bathrooms. By 1925, 185 passenger trains stopped at the bustling station daily. Today, it is the eleventh busiest in the United States and forms part of the largest surviving complex of Furness railroad buildings anywhere. Renovations in the 1980s saw the introduction of tile mosaics by nationally known artist Joyce Kozloff, part of a series of public art projects she was then undertaking at train stations. Behind the station stands Furness's Pennsylvania Building (1905–1906), which served as the office for the Pennsylvania Railroad in Wilmington. It was redeveloped by a Philadelphia firm for ING Direct bank (2003, IEI Group), with the unfortunate removal of an ornate staircase spared in a previous (1980s) gutting of the building.

WL6 Riverfront Parking Deck

2002–2004, John Hynes and Richard Stratford for Tevebaugh Associates. Water and Market sts.

Another piece in the Riverfront Development Corporation's reconstruction of the once-blighted district, the 425-car parking deck's red brick color and detailing harmonizes with Furness's Wilmington Station, which it serves. The design process began with pencil sketches and led eventually to pencil-on-vellum renderings, computer-generated details, and digitally created prints showing the complex as it would look when finished. Its lowrise, stepped form avoids blocking the view of the river from the train tracks, which 1.5 million travelers ride annually. Ironwork railings and grillwork add a decorative touch, and landscaping and espaliered fruit trees soften the whole. To the west is another Frank Furness–designed building, Water Street Station for the B&O (c. 1886–1888), rescued by the City of Wilmington. Small but lively and with complex rooflines, it had decayed almost to the point of collapse before being restored by ING, working with a Media, Pennsylvania, firm on its exterior (116 Technologies) and Tevebaugh on the interior.

WL7 ING Direct (Kent Building)

c. 1885. 2000 renovation, Tevebaugh Associates, with Cecil Baker and Associates. Orange and Water sts.

A Dutch banking firm, ING, helped transform Wilmington's riverfront starting in 2000 by renovating three old structures. This rather plain brick warehouse had long loomed above the waterfront. Photographs from the 1920s show it as Bird Transfer Company, a hauling and storage facility. Tevebaugh's initial plan was for thirty-two apartment units, but this proved unfeasible. ING then bought and renovated the building, calling it "The Pakhaus," Dutch for warehouse. The nearby J. Morton Poole Buildings, of about the same date, once housed a firm that manufactured metal rollers for papermaking. A part of the Poole complex was renovated by a Wilmington firm (1984, Moeckel Carbonell Associates) as architectural offices in the earliest phase of riverfront improvements.

WL8 Office Building (Harlan and Hollingsworth Company Office Building)

1910–1912, E. James Dallett. West and Water sts.

Founded in the 1840s, over the next forty years the Harlan and Hollingsworth company constructed 232 vessels, including *Saugus* (1863) and two other Civil War monitors. A William Boell lithograph shows the sixty-building facility in 1878. In 1887, the works covered forty-three acres, and by 1900, the Harlan firm was one of the top four shipbuilders in the nation, famous for, among other things, the palatial steel steam yacht *Alva* for William K. Vanderbilt. Business boomed during World War I, with twenty-four ships produced, and the company hired legendary Joseph "Shoeless Joe" Jackson to play on its wartime Steel League baseball team. Shipbuilding ceased in 1926, but the construction of railroad cars continued for a time. The three-story headquarters, a Colonial Revival late work by Frank Furness-trained architect Dallett, was spared the wrecking ball and restored in 1987. Much of the building's interest lies in its retaining its original, many-paned metal windows and copper bays.

WL9 Juniper Financial Corporation (Gates Engineering Building)

Late 19th century; 1998–1999 rehabilitation, Design Collaborative, Inc. West St. at Christina River

A boiler shop for Harlan and Hollingsworth (WL8) was transformed in the 1990s into 38,000 square feet of office space. Little remains of the original building except the brick walls with elliptical-arch windows, a fire having ripped through just as the project began. A unique barrel roof design with dormers offered four additional floor levels. Not long after, a headquarters for the American Automobile Association (AAA) was built just south, in a historicizing, red-brick-warehouse style (2004–2005, Tevebaugh Associates). Big shipbuilding gantry cranes still stand along the riverbank nearby.

WL10 Amtrak Viaduct Arches (Pennsylvania Railroad)

1901–1908, William H. Brown. Visible at Beech St., west of I-95

The rapidly expanding Pennsylvania Railroad built viaducts in several cities to eliminate dangerous grade crossings. Wilmington's viaduct snakes for almost four miles starting northeast at Wilmington Shops (WL63), where construction began. It featured walls of building stone on concrete foundations and a fill of earth, but deep mud southwest of downtown required a switch to arch construction. Pads of concrete, eight feet deep, were poured to receive the arches, which were supposed to be stone entirely, only the supply was limited. Bricks were laid instead, in rings up to fifty-five inches deep, forming a series of arches eight feet high and forty-one feet in span. Working for the Engineering Department of the Pennsylvania Railroad, Brown promoted heavy masonry-arch construction throughout the company's works.

WL9 JUNIPER FINANCIAL CORPORATION (GATES ENGINEERING BUILDING)

WL10 AMTRAK VIADUCT ARCHES (PENNSYLVANIA RAILROAD)

MARKET STREET CORRIDOR

Nearly a century passed between the landing of the Swedes at the Rocks (see Fort Christina Park, WL2) and the founding of Wilmington (1731). The latter settlement was located on the Christina, too, but farther west along today's Market Street. Emulating that of Philadelphia, Wilmington's grid plan began along the waterfront, then marched up the hillside. From the start, there were two rival markets, at 2nd and 4th streets (the latter in the middle of the street). These were repeatedly enlarged and rebuilt, as, for example, the reconstruction in 1846 of the one at 4th (George Read Biddle), which included a public room where Abraham Lincoln addressed a Whig rally in June 1848. Fourth

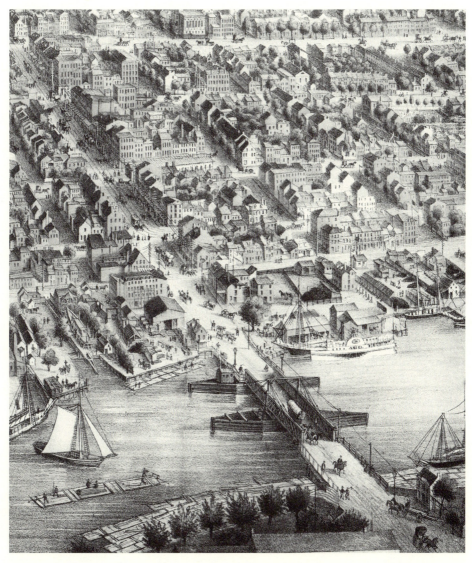

Market Street descends to the Christina River in the Sachse bird's-eye view, 1864–1865.

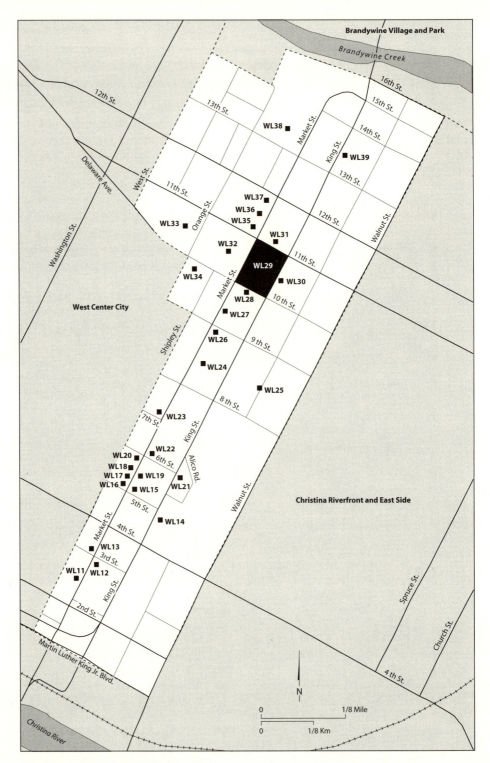

MARKET STREET CORRIDOR

Market Street and its early telegraph line were recorded in a rare daguerreotype, c. 1850. Some of these buildings survive today as Ships Tavern Mews (WL11).

Street Market was removed in 1875 as the one at 2nd Street was rebuilt (1876, Jacob Jefferis). Market Street in the early twentieth century was a thriving retail district with fashionable storefronts designed by Wilmington's leading architects. But by the 1920s, lower Market was failing, and a Wilmington Civic Association was formed to deal with the problem. They demolished the rat-infested market at 2nd, but Market Street continued to decline. The historic Bringhurst Drugstore at numbers 317–319 (1793) closed in 1939 and was eventually moved to Mystic, Connecticut, as a museum display. Turning the street into a pedestrian mall was proposed by the Wilmington Planning Commission in a report in 1955 and carried out in 1974, but this hurt businesses, and in 2002–2006, it was redesigned and reopened to traffic. At that time, redevelopment of buildings at both ends of the thoroughfare was aimed at luring renters and creating a safe residential and commercial district. Much of Market Street below 10th Street is included in a historic overlay zoning district, the first in the city (1975).

WL11 Ships Tavern Mews

18th century–early 20th century. 1998–2003 restored, Curtis Harkin of Homsey Architects, with Struever Brothers Eccles and Rouse and Wilmington Renaissance Corporation. West side of Market St., between 2nd and 3rd sts.

This important commercial grouping has survived intact and conveys the flavor of the mid-nineteenth-century Wilmington business district. Some buildings already appeared in a daguerreotype (c. 1850) made not long after a telegraph line was strung down the street. In 1998, a plan was devised to spend $107 million transforming six blighted blocks into a vibrant Ships Tavern District, the most ambitious preservation effort in Delaware history (honored with a National Trust for Historic Preservation award in 2005). Starting with this block, twenty-two old buildings were gutted and converted into eighty-six apartments, no two alike. Developers and city officials hoped to lure "upscale-funky" renters. The project was plagued by construction delays and lack of parking, and in 2006, Struever Brothers announced it would undertake no further development here, a setback to the entire Ships Tavern District effort.

WL12 Sign of the Ship Tavern

c. 1740. 3rd and Market sts.

This brick building is the last of the thirty or so Wilmington taverns of the eighteenth century, which had colorful names (Bull Frog, Foul Anchor, Golden Swan, Weeping Willow). A certain John Marshall ran the Sign of the Ship in Revolutionary days, and American officers had headquarters there. After the war, it was O'Flynn's, and Washington's diaries show that he occupied the "best room" on the second floor whenever (as in 1787) he "lodged at Wil. at O'Flins." Thomas Jefferson, John Adams, Aaron Burr, and others stayed here, too, and the proprietor feted the Marquis de Lafayette at Old Town Hall (WL19) in 1824. After 1835, it housed a clothing outlet, then a shoe store, but, as late as 1930, the owner preserved the front room where Washington supposedly slept. Little survives externally of its colonial appearance, except for its massing, a hint of a watertable, and the coves on the front facade and gable end.

WL13 Delaware State Bar Association (Farmers Bank)

1913–1914, Edward Canby May. 301 N. Market St.

Founded in Wilmington in 1813, the bank built a neoclassical building on this site in 1836. It was remodeled in 1889 and finally replaced by the current one, for which the Wilmington architect made extensive use of white marble in a Roman Revival composition. Behind a massive portico of coupled Doric columns and pediment, walls of Flemish bond add a note of Colonial Revival. As neighborhood revitalization got underway around 2000, the structure was refurbished to house the Delaware State Bar Association.

WL14 New Castle County Courthouse

2002, Buck Simpers Architect + Associates. 4th and King sts.

King Street was once famed for retail, with 240 stores and businesses in 1900. From 1863, this corner was the site of the Farmer's Market. Twentieth-century urban renewal swept it all away, creating barren parking lots. Relocating the county courthouse here formed part of a larger effort in the 1990s to shift downtown activities toward the riverfront. At 572,000 square feet, the fourteen-story tower in a chilly modernist idiom was the largest nontransportation building project ever undertaken in Delaware. Architect Simpers had earlier been a National Guardsman patrolling this area after race riots in 1968.

WL11 SHIPS TAVERN MEWS

WL14 NEW CASTLE COUNTY COURTHOUSE

WL15 Queen Theater (Clayton House Hotel)

1871–1873, Thomas Dixon and Charles L. Carson. 1915–1916, with later changes. 5th and Market sts.

The Indian Queen Hotel that once stood here was Wilmington's finest from the coming of statehood until 1871. The present structure, originally with a fashionable mansard roof, was built by the Baltimore architects (partners in 1871–1880) who also designed the Grand Opera House (WL24). Carpentry, brickwork, plastering, painting, and stonework were done by local firms; the ironwork by a Baltimore company; the slate roof by Philadelphians. It opened as the 105-bedroom Clayton House and promised to lure visitors away from the best hotels of Philadelphia. Newspapers described its sumptuous fittings, and toasts at the opening banquet hailed Wilmington's newfound stature and predicted a population of 100,000 in the city by 1900. The coming of the Hotel du Pont (WL32) and the shift of lower Market Street toward grocery trades eventually killed the Clayton House, however, and military bandages were rolled in the grand dining room in 1914–1915. Thereafter, the interior was gutted, and the building reopened in 1916 as the 2,000-seat Queen movie theater. The cream-colored terra-cotta facade dates to this campaign. Inside, lobby walls were of rare Alaska marble. The theater was remodeled in 1942 (with further alterations to the facade) and closed in 1957, the start of a half-century of near-abandonment. Redevelopment plans were announced in 2004 with talk of "partial demolition."

WL16 Levy's Loan Office (Central National Bank)

1889–1890. 501 N. Market St.

The Queen Anne red brick and sandstone facade has lost much of its decorative detail, including fine window grilles, but retains four carved lions' heads. The bank at first occupied only the front ground floor, with a real estate firm, Gibbons and Moore, on the Shipley Street side. The upper floor housed the nascent DuPont Engineering Department (1904), by which dynamite plants and other facilities were designed. Harris Jewelers eventually took over the building and remodeled the ground floor (1956, Morton Bleich).

WL17 Historical Society of Delaware (Artisan's Savings Bank)

c. 1930, Brown and Whiteside. 1972 restored, Whiteside, Moeckel and Carbonell. 505 N. Market St.

Delaware's historical society was founded relatively late, in 1864—twenty years after Maryland's and forty after Pennsylvania's. It occupied the Old First Presbyterian Church (WL58) from 1878 to 1916, then Old Town Hall (WL19) before moving into this Art Deco bank building in the early 1970s. Across the street, the Society owns the former F. W. Woolworth Store (1940, closed 1971), the third-largest in the United States when built, with a steel lunch counter a city-block deep. Woolworth's has been converted into the Delaware History Museum (1994–1995, Homsey Architects). The same firm spanned Market Street with a decorative steel arch that calls to mind the series of four arches erected on the thoroughfare for the Marquis de Lafayette in 1824.

WL18 Willingtown Square

18th century. 1976, houses moved here

Six historic brick townhouses form Willingtown Square, a refuge for buildings spared the wrecking ball during the era of urban renewal. In 1964, the director of the Wilmington Housing Authority telephoned the director of the Historical Society of Delaware to alert him to the imminent destruction of dozens of houses on the East Side. The Society moved quickly to identify those especially worth saving, recognizing that "very few, if any, homes of working class peoples in urban America had been preserved" before. About this same time, the Dingee Houses were scheduled for demolition for the Government Center project—only an outcry arose from preservationists, including one who wrote the Housing Authority in 1965, "One wonders that you would have the temerity to pull down such buildings." Working under the auspices of the Delaware Society for the Preservation of Antiquities, Albert Kruse proposed that all the preserved houses be assembled near the threatened Old Custom House (WL21) as a "village." A later scheme (1971, George M. Whiteside) would have located them at Old Swedes Church (WL3) as the Delaware Ethnic Studies and Cultural Center. Fundraising for that location proved difficult, and, finally, the mayor of Wilmington pushed for a home adjacent to the Historical Society. They were finally moved here in 1976.

The pent-eaved Jacobs House, with 1748 in glazed bricks (formerly called the Zachariah Ferris House and dated c. 1715), from 414 W. 2nd Street, was long thought to be the oldest house in Wilmington. The Cook-Simms House (1778), originally at the northeast corner of 4th and King streets, was built by a Quaker and served as Simms Pharmacy for decades. The conjoined Obadiah and Jacob Dingee Houses (1771 and 1773, respectively), from 105–107 E. 7th Street, were built by owners who were themselves house carpenters, joiners, and cabinet makers. The double Thomas Coxe Houses (c. 1801) remained in the family of the first owner, a stone mason, until 1957. All these buildings emulate Philadelphia townhouses of the day, with neat Flemish-bond brickwork (sometimes with glazed headers), projecting brick stringcourses, classical moldings under the eaves, and arched passages once leading to rear yards. As restored, they were intended to house the ethnic center, an entity that fizzled, and today are used as Society offices and storage. Like the Market Street pedestrian mall of which it formed a component, Willingtown Square represents an earnest attempt in the 1970s at addressing urban blight.

WL19 Old Town Hall

1798–1800, Peter Brynberg and John Way. 1926–1927 restored, Edgar V. Seeler. 1964–1966 restored, Whiteside, Moeckel and Carbonell, with Lee Nelson and Henry Judd. 512 N. Market St.

Along with Philadelphia (1787–1789), Lancaster, Pennsylvania (1795–1798), and New Orleans (1795–1799), this is one of the oldest surviving town halls in the United States. By the 1790s, fast-growing Wilmington had a population of 3,000 and needed a new governmental facility. French immigrant Pierre Bauduy was long credited with the design, without much evidence. Documents point instead to major roles played by council members Brynberg and Way. A near-copy of Philadelphia's Congress Hall, the edifice cost $4,400 and hobbled the town's budget for years. Atop the brick, five-bay, Federal-style edifice with stone stringcourse, panels, and central pediment, a rooftop walkway looked to the river; a tall cupola made the building the most prominent in town for half a century. Quaker miller Joseph Tatnall donated the English-made clock and bells. Inside the building, the spacious main room occupied 2,000 square feet with four central Doric columns with their own entablatures supporting a ceiling seventeen feet high. This room saw elec-

WL19 OLD TOWN HALL interior

tions, town meetings, and trials, as well as a popular ventriloquist (1817), a steam locomotive that visitors could ride (1831), and Henry Clay briefly lying in state (1852). The three upstairs chambers included the Long Room at rear, a meeting place for the town council and rented out to every kind of organization. The Marquis de Lafayette was hosted here in 1824. Outside the Town Hall, a garden of lombardy poplars and elms added a touch of civic gentility. Wrongdoers feared the place, as the cells under the building's rear bow were infamously unheated (until 1845).

The Town Hall was Victorianized and given a taller cupola in 1875. Abandoned in 1916, the building's future was uncertain, and within a year it bore signs, "Subscribe Here to Save the Old Town Hall," "The Center of the Patriotic and Civic Life of Wilmington for Nearly One Hundred and Twenty-Five Years." With the help of Pierre S. du Pont, the Historical Society of Delaware bought it in 1917, and a decade later it was restored to its original appearance (based on an old photograph) to serve as the Society's headquarters. Philadelphia architect Seeler was an appropriate choice; a former employee of Frank Miles Day, he had worked with Charles A. Ziegler on the restoration of Congress Hall in 1911, which Day had advocated. A document room was later added (1938, Massena and du Pont), and there have been several renovations.

WL20 Kuumba Academy Charter School (Security Trust and Safe Deposit Company)

1885, Furness, Evans and Company. 1908 enlarged to the north. 1927 extended at rear and interior reconstructed, Brown and Whiteside. 6th and Market sts.

The trust company was created along with Central National Bank (WL16), which moved into a separate building at 5th and Market streets in 1890. The facade of Security Trust was derived from the Penn National Bank in Philadelphia (1882–1884, later demolished), also designed by the Furness company. In *Frank Furness: The Complete Works*, the authors give Security Trust to Furness directly, but it is plausible that draftsman E. James Dallett played an important role in both it and Penn National, his father being head of the latter bank. Security Trust featured innovations, including fireproof steel vaults and safe-deposit boxes. It was originally just three bays along Market Street, but was expanded to six in 1908 (making it even more like Penn National), with changes to the fenestration. In 1927, Brown and Whiteside remodeled the interior and, in 1930, it became the National Bank of Delaware. Alterations were made to the facade in 1961. The building is now used for a charter school.

WL21 Old Custom House (Old Federal Building)

1852–1855, Ammi B. Young. King and 6th Sts.

Appointed Supervising Architect of the Office of Construction of the Treasury Department in 1852, Young became the first American architect with a nationwide sway. This building, the finished drawings for which are dated February 1853, was among the first he executed after his appointment. Construction was fireproof: walls were three feet thick, wooden floors were supported by structural brick arches on wrought-iron beams, and iron was used for columns, stairs, and roof trusses. The style was austere Italianate under a hipped roof. A post office occupied the main floor, and the courtroom upstairs saw important Civil War trials. The front balcony is gone. Delaware WPA occupied the building in 1937 when the post office moved to a new home on Rodney Square. After 1960, as King Street underwent massive urban renewal, the vacant Old Custom House was the subject of debate, AIA Delaware declining to recommend its preservation, fearful of antagonizing city officials who wanted to demolish it. Mayor Harry G. Haskell Jr. told a Wilmington reporter it was not "worth a damn . . . absolutely nothing. Its preservation will threaten the economic future of the city." His successor, Tom Maloney, disagreed, and eventually the Custom House became the first example in Delaware of a private building on the National Register being renovated for public use (1975–1976, Richard L. Dayton for Homsey Architects). Following another remodeling (1981, Kenneth M. Freemark Jr.), it housed fast-growing Wilmington College. In 2004, the college announced it no longer needed the building, the fate of which became again uncertain.

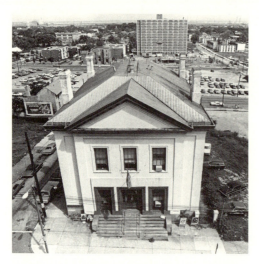

WL21 OLD CUSTOM HOUSE (OLD FEDERAL BUILDING), photo c. 1970 with urban renewal behind

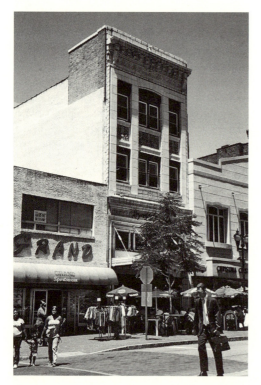

WL23 CAVANAUGH'S RESTAURANT (REYNOLDS CANDY STORE)

WL22 Delaware College of Art and Design (Delmarva Power and Light Company)

1931–1932, Reah de B. Robinson for Brown and Whiteside. 6th and Market sts.

Construction of Delaware's largest Art Deco building was considered a hopeful sign in the depths of the Great Depression. The exterior, of Mansota stone and light brick, was dramatically illuminated at night. The interior boasted many amenities, including gas heat (allowing for a coal-free basement), central air, and automatic elevators with fancy doors. The huge ground-level showroom had big windows, fittings of black marble and chromium metal, and a terrazzo floor. The building housed the most sophisticated retail display yet seen in Wilmington, with stylish new appliances from refrigerators and washing machines to radios, percolators, and waffle irons. In opening ceremonies, Mayor Sparks turned on all the lights by training a flashlight across an "electric eye." In the 1990s, the abandoned building was converted into an art school in an effort at neighborhood revitalization. Across 6th Street stands the former Mullins Store (1940–1941, G. Morris Whiteside).

WL23 Cavanaugh's Restaurant (Reynolds Candy Store)

1924, Clarence R. Hope. 703 N. Market St.

This facility was said to be among the finest candy stores in the country, with one of the longest soda fountains anywhere, measuring seventy-five feet along the south wall. Two hundred persons could be served lunch in one sitting. A counter on the north wall displayed 500 varieties of Reynolds candies. The mezzanine was used for dances. American Car and Foundry provided interior woodwork. Outside was an ornate terra-cotta facade fronted by a bronze marquee by the local firm, William Shinn and Company, with bulbs to bathe the front in a flood of light. Display windows were framed in walnut. Ice cream was manufactured in the basement and candies upstairs in facilities that included mechanically cooled chocolate coating rooms. Sold in 1955, the building today houses a restaurant.

WL24 Grand Opera House

1870–1871, Thomas Dixon and Charles L. Carson. 1974–1976 restoration, Grieves, Armstrong-Child, and Baird. 818 N. Market St.

In 1869, local Masons offered stock to fund a combination Masonic Hall and Opera House. Dixon and Carson of Baltimore, the former having designed Wilmington's finest new building, Grace United Methodist Church (WL45), were selected from five finalists. A photographer recorded the cornerstone ceremony. The Opera House went up rapidly in 1871; foundations were dug in the spring, with the gala opening taking place before Christmas. Royer Brothers of Philadelphia erected the elaborate, Italianate cast-iron facade. The auditorium, which seated 1,400 and held the third largest stage in the United States, was reached through a narrow hall with stores occupying spaces on either side—rented over the years to sewing machine companies and music shops, among others. The Masons met privately on the third floor, their ownership of the building announced by symbols on the facade: "G" for God and Geometry; an all-seeing eye, also for God; "AF & AM" for Ancient Free and Accepted Masons. The interior was redone in 1909 and the facade given an electric sign reading GRAND. Motion pictures had been shown here as early as 1896, but only now did the place become primarily a movie theater.

Business suffered after 1913 from competition with the Playhouse at the Hotel du Pont, and, although the Grand continued to operate until 1967, it grew increasingly rundown. So, too, did downtown Wilmington, and it was with great hope that some proposed a restoration of the building as the keystone of a larger plan to revitalize the city. A nonprofit group was established with the goal of creating Delaware's first performing arts center, and a team of architects was assembled. Stephen Baird had restored the facade of a nineteenth-century department store in Salt Lake City; James R. Grieves of Baltimore had been involved with the adaptive reuse of an old mill to make the Brandywine River Museum, Chadds Ford, Pennsylvania (1971). First to be restored was the cast-iron facade—Delaware's finest example—in 1974, under the supervision of Baird.

WL24 GRAND OPERA HOUSE

This involved the re-creation of the entire fourth story, lost in a fire in 1934, and the arch of the central door. Replacement pieces, based on old photographs, were cast in Salt Lake City. The interior was gutted, except for the original balcony with its cast-iron columns. Windows were returned to the interior walls, but they are blind, to keep noise out. Decorative details in the interior are mostly modern interpretations, although a few are based on surviving fragments. A statue of Thomas Maloney, a Wilmington mayor involved in the renewal of the Grand, has been installed nearby (2004), a late work by octogenarian sculptor Charles C. Parks.

WL25 Government Center

1970–1972, with additions. Bounded by 8th, 9th, King, and Walnut sts.

A goal of urban renewal planners and the Greater Wilmington Development Council was to disperse civic activities away from congested Rodney Square (WL29). The present Government Center, consisting of several buildings planned in concert, owes its origins to a plan by architect W. Ellis Preston, published in October 1961, that showed a similar complex to the one eventually built, except that the entire block between King and Market and 7th and 8th streets was to have been razed for a public information building (to be a copy of Delaware's expected pavilion at the New York World's Fair of 1964). Not long after, the local AIA sponsored "Concepts for the Decades Ahead," a collaborative project in which

Samuel Homsey and the firm of Whiteside and Carbonell were active. The report (November 1963) called for wholesale redevelopment of downtown into a series of four "centers," including this Government Center. Two years later, the planning firm of Wallace, McHarg, Roberts and Todd put forward "a total design concept" closely following the earlier "Concepts" proposal. It emphasized the needs of pedestrians and, at the same time, "addresse[d] itself boldly to the major complaint of most Wilmingtonians—PARKING." The first buildings of the complex, on King Street, were finished by 1972 and soon followed by others, including the Wilmington City-County Building (1975–1977, Whiteside, Moeckel and Carbonell, with Vincent G. Kling and Partners). Why is the center so bland and beige? This was a deliberate effort to humanize the architecture and escape "the travesty of glass block buildings." The empty plaza was supposed to be enlivened with a shopping complex, but this never happened. Some works of public sculpture were scattered about, including one by Richard Stankiewicz (1980) and three by local son Charles C. Parks. Recent changes include the reconstruction of Carvel Plaza by Breckstone Group and the interior renovation of twelve-story Carvel State Office Building by Buck Simpers Architect + Associates.

WL26 Wilmington Savings Fund Society

1920–1921, Hoggson Brothers. 1959 interior reconstructed, Hoggson Brothers. 1963 addition to south, George W. Clark. 838 N. Market St.

A slew of banks statewide attested to Delaware's economic vitality in the 1920s. This one (WSFS) was designed by a New York City firm to replace the Gothic Revival original (1886–1887, Addison Hutton). The thirteen limestone columns on the side, copies of those on the Tower of the Winds in Athens (c. 50 BC), are engaged; to vary the theme, the four across the front are free-standing. For the bank's centennial, N. C. Wyeth—trained in Wilmington at the Pyle studio (WL81)—painted an enormous, 60 × 20–foot mural, *Apotheosis of the Family* (1930–1932). By 1949, it was said that every third Wilmingtonian was a depositor at the bank. Across the street stands an Art Deco drugstore, formerly Woolworth's (1939–1940). In 2007 it was announced that WSFS would leave the building and remove the *Apotheosis* mural, which several museums nationwide clamored to obtain.

WL27 Residences at Rodney Square (Delaware Trust Building)

1919–1921, Ethan A. Dennison and Frederic C. Hirons. 1929–1930 wings, Bernard T. Converse and Philip T. Harris. 2002–2003 converted to apartments, Buccini/Pollin Group. 902 N. Market St.

After Alfred I. du Pont of Nemours (BR26) quarreled with cousin Pierre and withdrew from the family company, he built his own office tower to rival the nearby DuPont Building (WL32). He took out a construction permit for $1.2 million, the largest to date in the city. New York City architects Dennison and Hirons designed the fourteen-story, classicizing structure; they had studied at the Ecole des Beaux-Arts in Paris and became partners in 1910. The wings, when added by a Philadelphia firm, cost another $1.2 million and featured a great novelty, an underground parking garage. In order to retain the Hercules chemical company, a major tenant, a twenty-two-story International Style tower clad in pink porcelainized enamel was inserted within the light court (1958–1960, W. Ellis Preston), at which time the cornices were removed from the original building. At 679,000 square feet, the resulting office building was one of the state's largest. Its fate seemed uncertain after a fire in 1997 forced its closure. Subsequently, developers converted it into 280 upscale apartments, removing the tower of the 1950s in the process. Their conversion formed part of several ongoing efforts to establish a residential district downtown—a complete reversal of the ill-fated urban renewal principles of the 1950s that deliberately sought to minimize such residences in order to reduce congestion.

WL28 Wilmington Public Library (Wilmington Institute Library)

1921–1923, Edward L. Tilton and Alfred Morton Githens. 1969–1971 interior altered, Joseph E. Carbonell Jr. for Whiteside, Moeckel and Carbonell, with James Ford Clapp Jr. of Shepley,

WL28 WILMINGTON PUBLIC LIBRARY (WILMINGTON INSTITUTE LIBRARY), side view

Bulfinch, Richardson and Abbott. 10th and Market sts.

The library as an institution was already 134 years old when the cornerstone of its new building was laid in 1922. Its previous home, the Wilmington Institute at 8th and Market streets (1860), had been deemed ugly and potentially combustible. In his first major expression of philanthropy, Pierre S. du Pont bought land on Rodney Square (WL29) in 1915 from First Presbyterian Church. A cemetery had to be moved to make way for the new building. The New York City architects, known for their Carnegie libraries, drew up designs in 1916 in which the Rodney Square facade had a dozen engaged columns and a projecting portico. This was later simplified by the omission of the portico and reduction of engaged columns to eight, resulting in the unusual final design in which the center of the composition is flat and relatively unadorned. Sculpted owls of wisdom perch on second-story window sills. The continuous frieze of colored terra-cotta derives from the Temple of Antoninus and Faustina in Rome (141 AD), with the addition of modern symbolism, including swastikas. Githens spoke of this emblem as "originating far beyond the beginning of history and common to most of the primitive races of the world, its meaning not always the same, but always beneficent."

Inside, the central reading room was a two-story, skylit atrium. Black Greek Doric columns with painted capitals supported a plaster copy of the Parthenon frieze in Athens. Yellow Ionic columns graced the second floor. Nearly all the books were stored in the basement, the architects having created what they called an interior "of openness and of light, strong, flooding, brilliant light." Githens was proud of the open plan for libraries as developed here. The building won an AIA prize in 1925 and pointed the way to the firm's much larger Enoch Pratt Library, Baltimore (1929–1933). In a ruthless remodeling first outlined in 1965, an extra floor was inserted between the first and second all around the reading room; the upper part of the atrium was destroyed, the ceiling lowered, and the Parthenon frieze cut into pieces and remounted between the Doric columns. In its elimination of old-fashioned bombast and formality, this campaign was considered highly progressive, making the interior, according to the architects, "decidedly more inviting, more refreshing and more human"—questionable to our eyes today.

WL29 Rodney Square

1917–1921, Zantzinger, Borie and Medary. East side of Market St., between 10th and 11th sts.

Occupying the hilltop at the center of downtown, the park called Rodney Square was in-

WL29 RODNEY SQUARE, photo 1941; DUPONT BUILDING (WL32) at left, POST OFFICE (WL31) at center, PUBLIC BUILDING (WL30) at right

tended to take the adjoining Public Building, the DuPont Building, and a planned library and "unify them into a single scheme of civic adornment." A million-gallon water reservoir (1827–1877) originally occupied this site, which was replaced by the New Castle County Courthouse (1880, Theophilus P. Chandler; demolished 1919–1920). The subsequent courthouse would have stood here, too, except that John J. Raskob of the DuPont Company wisely suggested placing it farther east in order to create a square. With funds from Irénée du Pont, a Center Square competition was held in 1916–1917 by the Park Commission, conducted by University of Pennsylvania professor Warren P. Laird, who was assisted by a board of experts, including architects William M. Kendall, Charles A. Platt, and John Russell Pope. This kind of professional, nonpolitical jury was typical of the reformist City Beautiful movement of the early twentieth century. Of the five plans submitted (including one by Carrère and Hastings), that of the Zantzinger firm of Philadelphia had, according to the judges, "the requisite simplicity and dignity." The winners worked with the Onondaga Litholite Company of Syracuse, New York, suppliers of the cut cast stone. Bronze lanterns on pylons were illuminated by electric lights. From the time of its completion, the square has been a favorite gathering place, and 30,000 people assembled here to cheer pro-business Republican presidential candidate Wendell Wilkie in October 1940. Rodney Square had its pavements redesigned in the 1970s and again in 1996–1997 (Rodney Robinson).

WL29.1 Caesar Rodney Equestrian Monument

1917–1922, James Edward Kelly, sculptor

Cast by Gorham Manufacturing Company and standing on a litholite base, the bronze sculpture commemorates a patriot's ride from Dover to Philadelphia to give the deciding vote in favor of the Declaration of Independence in 1776 (it should read "July 2"). Kelly was known for sculptures of Civil War heroes. It took so long for him to complete the bronze tablets at its base (until 1925, when he was seventy), that the art committee grew "tired, disgusted

& through with him." The well-known statue has appeared on a U.S. coin, the Delaware state quarter of 1999.

WL30 Public Building of the City of Wilmington and County of New Castle (former)

1914–1916, Palmer, Hornbostel and Jones, with John Dockery Thompson Jr. 1000 N. King St.

Until its conversion into office space in the early-twenty-first century, the Beaux-Arts, granite City and County Building had "City Hall" carved over its southerly door, and "Court House" over its northerly, emblematic of the original dual nature of the structure. Its design—a long Corinthian colonnade linking two triumphal-arch motifs—was a collaboration between a New York firm and Thompson, a Wilmington architect. They won a competition, judged by a jury assembled by Professor Warren P. Laird of the University of Pennsylvania (consisting of architects Paul Cret, William M. Kendall, and H. Van Buren Magonigle). The competition disallowed towers and domes, reminders of unfashionable Victorian civic styles. New York City artist Charles Keck carved the reliefs over the exterior doors. Fast-growing MBNA, the second largest credit card bank in the world at the time and Delaware's largest nongovernment employer, purchased the building in 2002. The conversion by Homsey Architects included dismantling the front steps, which had been integral to the 1914 design, and removal of the historic, walnut-lined courtrooms.

WL31 Wilmington Trust Center (United States Post Office, Court House, and Custom House)

1933–1936, Associated Federal Architects: E. William Martin (design), Brown and Whiteside (specifications), and Robinson, Stanhope and Manning (working drawings), with Walker and Gilette. 1982–1983 tower, Robbi Cox for Curtis Cox Kennerly. 1100 N. Market St.

Completing the Rodney Square complex and echoing the colonnade of the City-County Building (WL30), this classical-style former federal building was constructed using work relief funds initially authorized by President Hoover. The historic Winchester mansion on the site was condemned to make way for

WL30 PUBLIC BUILDING OF THE CITY OF WILMINGTON AND COUNTY OF NEW CASTLE (FORMER), early view

it. Owing to the Great Depression, work was shared among many local architects. Martin's chief designer, Albert Kruse, contributed much of the exterior detail. The building was fully equipped with eighty electric clocks and sixty telephones. Small murals were installed in 1938, *Chemistry and Industry* and *Chemistry and Agriculture* (Herman H. Zimmerman), and *Landing of the Swedes* (Albert Pels, later well known as an artist in New York City). In the 1980s, a Philadelphia firm's transformation of the public edifice into a highrise bank office tower, involving radical revisions to the interior and the facade, was controversial.

WL32 DuPont Building

1905–1906, Manufacturers Contracting Company. 1910–1911 southeast extension. 1911–1912 east extension, including Hotel du Pont. 1913 Playhouse Theater. 1915–1916 extension, F. W. Russum. 1917–1918 north extension. 1930–1931 west extension, Hubert Sheldon Stees. 1007 N. Market St.

Pierre S. du Pont oversaw the reorganization of the family company in 1904, called by historians Alfred Chandler and Stephen Salsbury (1971) a "revolution in administrative control . . . capped by the construction of an office building to house the many new executives, managers, and their staffs." The pragmatic Pierre wanted to call it the Wilmington Trust Building, to advertise the company's new banking venture, but cousin Alfred I., always sentimental about family history, insisted on "du Pont de Nemours." The massive DuPont "home office," a gray and restrained Beaux-Arts box, appears virtually seamless, but was erected in six sections over a period of more than a generation, starting at the south corner and moving generally counterclockwise. Construction of the first, twelve-story section was recorded in a series of more than thirty photographs, beginning with demolition of the nineteenth-century buildings on the site. Indiana limestone faced the first four floors. The sections to the north were built during World War I, when the company expanded rapidly and profits skyrocketed, from net earnings of $5.3 million in 1913 to $82.1 million in 1916.

By the time the last section on the west was planned, architectural modernism had arrived, and this part of the building is stylistically distinct from the older ones. The steel skeleton was fabricated using a new technology, welding instead of riveting, sparing office workers the noise of rivet guns. So unfamiliar was welding, a sign was posted, "DANGER TO EYES. Do not look at electric welding." The ninth floor of this last section contained the new Board of Director's Room (1931, Raymond M. Hood) with a huge oval table, portraits of former company presidents, and walls paneled in a stylized Adamesque manner. Above the building's cornice, two attic stories were added in Moderne style (1937, Hubert Sheldon Stees), by which time the edifice housed 3,300 employees. After World War II came various mutilations: the ornate copper cornice on big scrolls gave way to a minimalist aluminum one in 1950, and, in 1955–1957, stone balconies on the hotel facade were stripped off as a safety precaution. The interiors, too, have seen many changes, including a remodeling of the Market Street Lobby and Corridor (c. 1948, George E. Pope and Albert Kruse).

Completely enveloped within the DuPont Building is the long-running DuPont Theatre (Playhouse Theater) of 1913. Designed by New York City architect Charles A. Rich, the Playhouse was built in just 150 working days. Its exterior brick walls were unadorned, as it was to be hidden as the larger edifice grew around it. Its fireproof construction was of reinforced concrete, including the roof slab and the massive, eighty-five-foot girders (at the time, the third largest ever fabricated). It was built by William Eckhart of New York City, with J. A. Bader and Company, Wilmington contractors. The Playhouse was funded by leading citizens Robert Carpenter, Pierre S. du Pont, and John J. Raskob, and it opened in a gala event. It was a 1,200-seat facility, the stage larger than all but three in Manhattan. Motion pictures were shown within a month of its opening—and they were talkies, thanks to the innovative magnaphone device invented by Wilmingtonian George R. Webb.

Also incorporated within the DuPont Building is Hotel du Pont (1911–1912, 1917–1918, Frederick Godley, J. André Fouilhoux, and Joel Barber, with Raymond M. Hood; 1937 enlarged; 1955–1958 and later, alterations, Edward C. May Jr.). The placing of a hotel within a corporate headquarters complex is said to be unique to this institution. Pierre S. du Pont made the hotel his special project and maintained an apartment here for Delaware voting purposes (he actually lived at Longwood, Pennsylvania). The hotel interiors were kept secret during construction in order to surprise the public. Materials were sumptuous and varied: Italian marble, Caen stone, mosaic, terrazzo, scagliola columns, oak paneling. Framed Howard Pyle paintings decorated the walls. The hotel was said to have cost more, per room, than any other in the world. When it was doubled in size within a decade, the entrance door was

WL32 DUPONT BUILDING, fifth section under construction 1918

moved five bays west and the spectacular original lobby became a soda shop (cut up in 1955). Little survives of the interiors created in 1912, except a section of mosaic floor.

The lobby of 1918 is presumably by Hood, as is certainly the adjoining Ballroom Suite. Huge walnut doors set in a rose marble frame open into a spectacular, travertine-walled stairhall. This leads up to the Colonial-style du Barry Room and down to the dazzling Gold Ballroom, opened in October 1918. In a French eighteenth-century style, it measures 88 × 49 feet, with a twenty-nine-foot-high ceiling; 250 couples could dance comfortably. Sgraffito decoration by New York designer Duncan Smith was carried out by thirty Italian artisans working for a year, scratching through three layers of colored plaster. The theme is Muses and dancing girls. "The beautiful women of history" were portrayed in twenty medallions in the spandrels, by Violet Terwilliger. Four cartouches over the doors in the corners, depicting amorous themes, were by Hood himself, executed by a builder of architectural models, M. R. Giusti, who also created decorative plaster ceilings and other elements throughout the hotel's public rooms. Scene of countless weddings and high school proms as well as the annual DuPont stockholders' meeting, the room was renovated in 1966 by William Moeckel.

The Ballroom Suite is a key surviving example of the early work of Hood, an architect later renowned for his role in the establishment of Art Deco skyscrapers of the 1920s, culminating in Rockefeller Center. Hood apparently credited the DuPont project with giving him his start. He made a sketch, published in *Architecture* (March 1931), showing a scheme for rebuilding the center section of the Rodney Square facade as a ziggurat-form skyscraper.

The hotel boasted several sumptuous dining rooms. The Green Room featured oak paneling rising two-and-one-half stories high, and six Spanish-made chandeliers each weighing 2,500 pounds. On the eleventh floor was a private dining room, the Georgian Room (1936–1937, G. Morris Whiteside II). The Brandywine Room opened in 1941. It has subsequently been redesigned, but originally it was the work of Godley and interior decorator Barber, both of New York City. Big mahogany doors came from a mansion on Fifth Avenue, Manhattan. Paneling was American walnut, and the pillars were covered in DuPont's Fabrikoid, an imitation leather. Over the years, the hotel has been a showplace for many DuPont materials, as in the Nylon Suite (1948, Joanne Seybold; see photograph on p. 17).

WL33 Nemours Building

1935–1937 and 1939–1941, Hubert Sheldon Stees for DuPont Engineering Department, with F. A. Godley. 1999–2001 remodeled, Buccini/Pollin Group. 1007 Orange St.

This fourteen-story annex to the DuPont Building (WL32) matched the Moderne style of the section of 1930–1931. It was linked to the DuPont Building by a streamlined aluminum sky walk (since removed). Stees, who had spent three years in the office of Will Price in Philadelphia, designed or helped draft 110 structures, mostly industrial, for what he called the DuPont "plan factory" over fourteen years, starting in 1928. He was proudest of this building, he told an interviewer in 1982; like the other Home Office structures, it was not meant as any kind of publicity statement, hence its plainness, but instead was focused entirely on employee comfort. At that time it was said to be the largest office building ever air-conditioned, and building managers from Rockefeller Center, the Empire State Building, and elsewhere came to Wilmington to study its systems. Godley, a New York City architect, was responsible for the exterior design, with setbacks to meet new city zoning regulations. At the Tatnall Street entrance hung the painting *Better Things for Better Living Through Chemistry* by John W. McCoy Jr., brought here after exhibition in the DuPont pavilion at the World's Fair of 1939 in New York City (now at the Hagley Museum). The Soda Shop contained murals on linoleum by a New York artist (1942, Mortelido). The Nemours Building coincided with DuPont's golden age, nylon having been announced to the public at the fair as "strong as steel, as fine as a spider's web." An eighteen-story tower was intended to fill the unfinished notch on the building's southwest corner (1945–1947) but was later scaled down. Following the sale of the 450,000-square-foot edifice in 1999, it underwent conversion to mixed-use, with gutting of the asbestos-filled interior, replacement of all windows, and construction of a new lobby, theater, and eighty-five upscale apartments.

WL34 Community Service Building (Montchanin Building)

1958 remodeling of an earlier building. 1995–1997 renovated, Buck Simpers Architect + Associates. 100 W. 10th St.

The boxy, twelve-story office building was remodeled into one of the most austere examples of curtain-walled International Style in the state. It housed Wilmington Trust and, later, 600 DuPont employees. The latter firm sold it in 1995 to a nonprofit organization, which renovated it as general headquarters for many local nonprofit groups. Today it is occupied by seventy-four such organizations, making it the largest building in the nation entirely devoted to nonprofits.

WL35 First and Central Presbyterian Church

1929–1930, Brown and Whiteside. 1101 N. Market St.

According to the historian Barbara McEwing, commercial and civic development on Market Street led the First and Central congregations, merged in 1920, to seek a new home across Rodney Square (WL29). Given the venerable history of the congregations, the Colonial Revival style seemed an obvious choice, and moreover the committee held that "no design more aptly bespeaks a building of the Presbyterian faith than does our own Georgian or Colonial." The exterior face brick supplied by a York, Pennsylvania, firm "resembles the hand-made clay brick used in Colonial days." It was laid in Hytest mortar and sand, which "produced the desired effect of resembling a building built fifty years or more ago." The tile roof was "made to resemble an aged split shingle roof." Marble trim came from West Rutland, Vermont. The gabled portico echoed that of the historic Greek Revival Draper Mansion (c. 1840), demolished to make way for the church. A 115-foot spire was topped with a fish emblem. The church was set back from the city streets behind a wall of brick piers, iron fence, and boxwood hedge. Inside, the nave has old-fashioned box pews and arches supported by Roman Doric columns. For all the traditionalist touches, the building was highly modern: it was made with fireproof construction, it was fully wired for staunchly fundamentalist broadcasts on radio station WDEL, and it had a motion-picture booth in the Social Hall. The church was one of the last collaborations of Walter Stewart Brown (design partner) and G. Morris Whiteside II, as Brown died in 1931. Much of the design work was by draftsman Reah de B. Robinson.

WL36 Wilmington Club

1864, Edmund G. Lind. 1103 N. Market St.

John Merrick, a carriagemaker grown rich in the Civil War, hired Baltimore architect Lind to design an ostentatious brownstone mansion, now a lone survivor of the big townhomes that once dominated the vicinity of today's Rodney Square (WL29). Its heavy Italianate forms, including massive scroll-supported window heads and an oversize bracketed cornice, recall Lind's famous Peabody Institute, Baltimore, the first section of which had re-

WL36 WILMINGTON CLUB

cently been erected (1858–1862). Since 1900, the Merrick mansion has housed one of the country's oldest social clubs, founded in 1855. Generations of civic elites traditionally came for lunch or afternoon bridge games.

WL37 1105 North Market Street (Wilmington Tower)

1963–1971, I. M. Pei and Araldo Cossutta. 2004 alterations, Thomas E. Hall and Associates. 1105 N. Market St.

AIA Delaware's "Concepts for the Decades Ahead" plan of 1963 for the redesign of downtown called for a tall slab on this site. The 210,500 square foot, twenty-two-story tower that was finally completed nearly a decade later is often referred to locally as "the I. M. Pei Building," so famous has its architect become worldwide. At 286 feet in height, it was a landmark, although newer tall buildings have subsequently lessened its impact. Its sculptural massing in reinforced concrete combined with elegant, greenish windows in long, apparently seamless bands typified Pei's approach during the 1960s, when he followed the Brutalist aesthetic of Le Corbusier and Marcel Breuer (he had studied with the latter at Harvard). When the tower was announced (as the American Life Insurance Building, or Alico), the Wilmington newspaperman Bill Frank wrote a story headlined, "We Love You, Mr. Pei," and predicted that "we will be as proud of [it] as we are of Old Swedes Church." This was not to be.

When planning began in 1963, Pei was completing the cast-in-place concrete Society Hill Towers, Philadelphia (1957–1964). Wilmington Tower is closer, however, to Pei's Municipal Center in Dallas (1966–1977) or to his colleague Cossutta's Christian Science Administration Building in Boston (1968–1973). The great expanses of raw concrete were, until a coating was applied in 2004, a warm sand color with the imprint of the formwork still crisply visible. The large size of the window panes was typical of the Pei firm's experimentalism, which would culminate in the disastrous cracking of the huge windows on the John Hancock Tower, Boston (by partner Henry Cobb, 1966–1976). Until the radical redesign in 2004, the Wilmington lobbies were

WL37 1105 NORTH MARKET STREET (WILMINGTON TOWER), on right

granite-walled and solemn. This is Pei's only building in Delaware, but Cobb's World Trade Center, Baltimore (1966–1977) employs many of its motifs, including the sunken channels beneath the windows. The forceful massing of heavy volumes of masonry at Wilmington Tower looks ahead to Pei's East Building for the National Gallery of Art, Washington, D.C., in planning as this skyscraper was being finished. Pei liked Wilmington Tower enough to propose two virtually identical buildings for Columbia University in 1970 (not executed).

The superstructure mostly went up in 1968–1969. Wilmington history buff Doug Andrews informs me, "Construction was loud. I believe this was the first 'pre-stressed on site' concrete mid-to high-rise building. This was achieved by having the concrete poured into metal forms that were then vibrated to compact the material. All of the structural elements were designed into the forms including the unique pocket grid ceiling. Even the horizontal indentation along each floor of the building's facade is a structural component. . . . a two-story segment of the building was constructed at the then-Wilmington Airport for testing of each process and feature before they did it on site." The new techniques maximized column-free space inside. Wooden falsework was moved up floor-by-floor, as can be seen in the repeating patterns in the concrete on the exterior.

Unfortunately, the innovative building was plagued by problems. The expanses of single-glazed windows caused climate-control difficulties inside, especially as the tower was narrow front-to-back. Tinted films eventually peeled and discolored. Exterior concrete spalled. In 2003, new owners announced plans (formulated for them by Thomas E. Hall and Associates of Wayne, Pennsylvania) to replace all the windows, paint the concrete with white elastomeric coating, add decorative brackets to the exterior, reconstruct the lobby, and eventually build a larger tower next door. "Oh, it was awful. All concrete, all concrete, all concrete everywhere," complained an agent for the building, referring to Pei's Brutalist style. Wilmington architects and others rallied to oppose these prettifying alterations, with partial success.

WL38 Hercules Inc. Headquarters

1980–1983, Arthur May and Robert Evans for Kohn Pederson Fox. 1313 N. Market St.

The New York City firm of Kohn Pederson Fox became famous for an office tower in Chicago, 333 Wacker Drive, begun just a year before this Wilmington commission for a chemical company. Both projects raised expanses of blue-green glass against the sky. Postmodern contextualism called for bulky highrises to relate sympathetically to their historical surroundings, and here the glass tower rises from a lower section of stone, a false-front (complete with faux cornices) mimicking a series of older, discreet buildings. The firm followed an identical approach in a hotel on Logan Circle, Philadelphia (1979–1983). Rockville, Minnesota, granite was cut at a fabrication plant into two-inch-thick panels. The designers attempted to give the illusion of depth to the detailing, but it is nonetheless cold and mechanical compared to genuine nineteenth-century stonework. A hugely overscaled clock perched on a roofline offers a note of Postmodern whimsy. Inside the 680,000-square-foot, fourteen-story building is a towering atrium with a gridded framework in colors inspired by the Dutch artist Piet Mondrian. Soaring piers and globe lighting fixtures were derived from Frank Lloyd Wright's Larkin Building, Buffalo. Postmodernism was then new, and Hercules proved controversial. In an interview, the local architect Harley Funk, still committed to modernism, called it "an unfortunate building . . . arbitrary in a stylistic way, to have a glass box rising out of imitative eclectic stone fragments at the bottom" (Athan 1982). Across Market Street stands the Beneficial Building, with a curved corner, one of the first International Style structures in Wilmington (c. 1952, Walter Carlson).

WL39 Starr House

1804, Michael Van Kirk. 1310 King St.

Stonecutter Van Kirk built this Federal-style brick townhouse for himself and fabricated the marble exterior trim (the lintels banded with stone and brick are distinctive) and interior chimneypieces. He sold it to Jacob Starr, waterman, in 1806. It survived the explosion of three DuPont powder wagons on a nearby street in 1854, which cracked its yellow pine doors. The house remained in the Starr family until 1945, at which time it was recognized as one of the best preserved historic houses in Wilmington. Albert Kruse restored it for the new owner in 1946–1947, adding modern facilities, a shingle roof, and shutters. It became an attorney's office in 1954 and remains so today.

WL38 HERCULES INC. HEADQUARTERS

WEST CENTER CITY

Quaker millers spurred the growth of Wilmington in its first decade, the 1730s, and settled on the slopes of a hill west of the town center, where they built a meetinghouse in 1739. A handful of colonial buildings survive on Quaker Hill, including 310 West Street (c. 1750). The brick house at the corner of 4th and West streets is said to date back to 1737. Far more numerous are mid-to-late-nineteenth-century houses, including 401 Washington Street (1881, Edwin Thorne), supposedly built by a local architect to demonstrate his skills. Abolitionist Thomas Garrett's son Ellwood, a daguerreotypist, built the townhouse at 609–611 Washington Street (c. 1848). The *History of Wilmington* (1894) noted that the residential district centered on West Street had enjoyed its heyday from 1864 to 1874, when it witnessed "the first attempt to break away from the rectangular, steep-roofed houses of the colonial period," the new homes being "pushed back from the street, and their fronts . . . adorned with the then fashionable cast iron piazzas or porches." Six major churches were erected between 1865 and 1871, an achievement "unsurpassed by any community in the United States." By the mid-twentieth century the area had slipped economically, however, and the old mansions on West Street were being subdivided for apartments or demolished. The riots of 1968 (centered around Jefferson and 6th streets) led to wholesale abandonment of much of the area through the 1970s. Some urban homesteading has subsequently occurred, and historic districts, including Shipley Run, Trinity Vicinity, and Quaker Hill have been established, with ongoing restoration. The last, embracing the old Quaker Meeting House and extending from Tatnall to Jefferson and 2nd to 8th streets, is especially rich in historic rowhouses.

WL40 Education and Technology Building, Delaware Technical and Community College

1999–2000, Thomas E. Higley for Anderson Brown Higley Associates. 2nd and Orange sts.

This urban school began with a large building by a Houston firm (1973–1974, Caudill Rowlett Scott). The addition of 1999 won an AIA Delaware award. Brown bricks at the foundation relate to the original building, but everything else is Postmodern, including the use of curved walls, strong color, and varied materials: tan and orange bricks, gray aluminum panels, and green window glass. The campus entrance pavilion, with its patterned brickwork and bright-green metal (the school color), is eye-catching. The college was built on the site of the Thomas Garrett House, from which the abolitionist is said to have ferried 2,700 slaves north via the Underground Railroad.

WL40 EDUCATION AND TECHNOLOGY BUILDING, DELAWARE TECHNICAL AND COMMUNITY COLLEGE

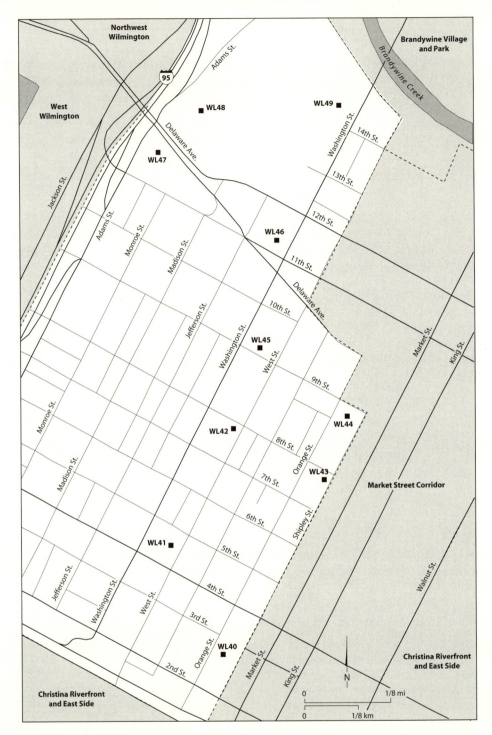

WEST CENTER CITY

WL41 Wilmington Friends Meeting House

1815–1817, William Poole, Jacob Alrichs, and Benjamin Ferris. 1951 annex on west, Weston Holt Blake. 401 N. West St.

This two-story, gable-roofed brick building is the third structure on the site. A three-man committee was "appointed to prepare a ground-plan and Elevation," with Ferris keeping a diary of the process. The plan was adjusted to make the building relatively longer (48 × 76 feet) so as to "enable us to divide the house to greater advantage" between men and women. A separate elevation showed the Dividing Partition and "the manner of raising [it from the floor and simultaneously] lowering it [from the ceiling] as now practiced at Friends meeting house in Green Street Philadelphia." Some 10,000 feet of yellow pine boards were ordered from Wilmington, North Carolina. Recorded Ministers sat in so-called facing benches looking out at the membership; children sat in the Youths Gallery.

WL41 WILMINGTON FRIENDS MEETING HOUSE, photo c. 1870

WL42 West Presbyterian Church

1870–1871, Samuel Sloan. 1994–1997 rebuilt, George Yu Architects. 500 W. 8th St.

This steep-roofed, Gothic Revival structure by a prominent Philadelphia architect used red pressed brick and Ohio stone for Ruskinian Gothic color contrast, including banded arches. In an audience room larger than that at nearby Grace Methodist (WL45), nearly a thousand people could be accommodated in seats made by Jackson and Sharp Car Works of Wilmington. Heavily in debt, the church nearly faced a sheriff's sale during the Financial Panic of 1873. In the 1940s, West was one of the largest congregations in the city, but after many of its white congregants fled to the suburbs, it shrank to just 148 members by 1993, the year it was gutted by fire. As rebuilt by a Philadelphia architect who had studied under Louis I. Kahn, the church differs greatly from the original building, incorporating only a few architectural fragments from the old structure—even retaining the fire-damaged walls was deemed too expensive—and devoting the great majority of its interior space not to worship but community outreach.

WL43 Episcopal Church of Saints Andrew and Matthew (St. Andrew's)

1840. 1854 enlarged, Thomas Dixon. 1890 interior alterations, E. James Dallett for Baker and Dallett. 1917 Parish House, E. James Dallett. 1954 addition. 8th and Shipley sts.

This urban church memorializes Bishop Alfred Lee, who led the revival of Episcopalianism in Delaware and who was rector at St. Andrew's starting in 1841, the year after the original edifice of 1829 burned. The blocky tower and heavy facade detailing later added by Dixon are typical of the overscaled design forms popular in the 1850s. Walls are stuccoed and scored to resemble ashlar. The wide interior was entirely redone by Dallett, who attended the church; he added three huge Romanesque arches of Caen stone in front of the chancel, with intricately carved capitals, the whole effect recalling the work of Boston architect H. H. Richardson. The original stencil work on the chancel walls has been replaced by garish gold paint. The 1890s taste is exemplified by the pews with their almost Art Nouveau carving; the pale, abstract stained-glass windows with chunky bull's-eyes; and the mosaic floor at the entrance. In 1907, a triptych was added over the altar, and ten years later Dallett inserted a baptistry niche in a side wall and built the Parish House. Recently, the font (1890) was moved to a new location and surrounded by a marble pavement (2002, Lee Sparks). St. Andrew's was the largest church in the diocese around 1950, but its congregation was decimated by white flight. Subsequently, it merged with an African American congregation, St. Matthew's, that had split off from it in the nineteenth century.

WL44 Mid-Town Parking Center
1957, Whiteside, Moeckel and Carbonell. 9th St., between Orange and Shipley sts.

Described in a 1957 Wilmington newspaper as "an answer to the harassed motorist's prayer," this 522-car Wilmington Parking Authority garage addressed the postwar commuter crisis by clearing an entire block. The facility was so novel, the public had to be educated about using its spiraling ramps and obeying an elaborate system of signs and warning lights. Treadles electronically counted the number of cars entering (it was only the sixth garage in the world to do this). Each level had a color (white, yellow, blue, green), as "color technicians insist that feminine users will remember the color of the floor they are on." The garage itself was of unpainted concrete and gray bricks, but the 9th Street facade housing retail establishments (originally Eagle Restaurant and Epicure Shop) was supported by piers clad in polished granite, with "Mid-Town Parking Center" in aluminum cursive letters above. An important desegregation case argued before the U.S. Supreme Court in 1961, *Burton v. Wilmington Parking Authority and the Eagle Coffee Shoppe*, was brought by an African American man who was denied a cup of coffee here in August 1958.

WL44 MID-TOWN PARKING CENTER

WL45 Grace United Methodist Church
1865–1867, Thomas Dixon. 9th and West sts.

Here is Delaware's best surviving example of High Victorian Gothic, a richly ornamental mode imported from England. The style was short-lived and many examples have been demolished, making this one especially valuable. An enthusiastic Sunday School association emerged at St. Paul's Methodist at 7th and Market streets in the early 1860s, organizing mission work in poor neighborhoods. The wealthy leaders of the group, including the heads of Jackson and Sharp Car Works and Harlan and Hollingsworth (WL8), wished to expand the campaign but met with resistance at St. Paul's. They formed a new congregation in 1864 and set out to build Delaware's finest church. Architect Dixon, a Wilmingtonian who moved to Baltimore, had added a tower to nearby St. Andrew's (WL43). Ground was broken in April 1865 on the Chapel—the section of Grace Church to the west—where the first service was held in March 1866, in the Upper Room (600 seats). The raising of the spire that year was considered an exceptional feat, recorded in photographs. The main body of the church, or sanctuary (800 seats), opened in January 1868. It bears a plaque outside, "A Centenary Offering 1866," referring to the 100th anniversary of Methodism. The Chapel was then put to Sunday school uses.

Polychromy, the use of intrinsically colorful building materials, is fundamental to High Victorian Gothic. Dixon used serpentine, a green stone from Brinton's Quarry near West Chester, Pennsylvania, a few years in advance of its great, though fleeting, regional popularity. Reddish Connecticut brownstone forms the lowest courses, and the trim is buff New Brunswick, New Jersey, sandstone. The serpentine and brownstone have deteriorated badly, owing in part to twentieth-century sandblasting. Grace Church bears comparison with Dixon and Charles L. Carson's serpentine Mount Vernon Place Methodist Episcopal Church, Baltimore (1872), similar in plan though with a different arrangement of towers. Both churches would have been at home in Great Britain in the 1860s, showing close affinities to the work of architect George Gilbert Scott and his contemporaries, which in

WL45 GRACE UNITED METHODIST CHURCH, photo c. 1870

turn was inspired by architect A. W. N. Pugin. The detailing of Grace Church's stone walls and its intricate, historically accurate Gothic Revival window shapes are fascinating to study, with so much variety and deliberate contrast.

Some original stained glass windows survive, splendid examples of tracery and fiery with ruby-reds and purples. The big window over the gallery in the sanctuary was recently restored; equally valuable, though rarely visited, are the somewhat similar windows in the now-empty Upper Room and the round windows in the disused tower. The lancets along the side walls of the sanctuary were replaced in 1913–1914 with muted, opalescent-glass copies of famous religious paintings (William Reith Studios, Philadelphia). An apsidal stained glass window is extraordinary, lit from behind, originally with sixty lightbulbs, now by fluorescent tubes. Given by Melville Gambrill and his wife, it stands nearly thirty feet high, weighs more than two tons, and contains 18,000 pieces of glass, with its subject being "Come Unto Me" (1924, H. B. Hankinson and Charles Mente). The church received an addition in 1942, and the original polychrome slate roofs were replaced with unaesthetic gray metal in 1949. In 1995, the sanctuary floor plan was altered to allow better visibility for arts performances, the urban congregation now emphasizing such activities to boost community involvement. A major addition (2001, Anderson Brown Higley Associates) unfortunately included removal of a set of triple lancet windows in the Upper Room, so distinctive of English Gothic; worse, it involved destruction of the serpentine stone parsonage adjacent to the church, Bassett Hall (c. 1890, Baker and Dallett).

WL46 Central Young Men's Christian Association (YMCA)

1928–1929, G. Morris Whiteside for Brown and Whiteside. 501 W. 11th St.

The YMCA Central Branch marked the heyday of Brown and Whiteside, when talented Reah Robinson and Albert Kruse worked as designers. The building's style, described by the architects as "northern Italian," featured lower stories of Indiana limestone with "a light tapestry brick" above, as popularized by the Shelton Hotel, New York City (1924, Arthur Loomis Harmon). The entrance hall had rich marble panels, figured glass lighting fixtures, silver and gold gilt trimmings, and subdued colored tiling. A Spanish Colonial Revival–style cafeteria had exposed beams and ironwork balconies facing a courtyard. "Youth Division" still appears in gilt lettering on the south door, which is surrounded by elaborate relief sculptures in limestone. Inside that entrance was the half-timbered Boys' Department, one room made to resemble the poop deck of an old ship of the line, its walls of ship siding and beams, with ship lanterns

WL46 CENTRAL YOUNG MEN'S CHRISTIAN ASSOCIATION (YMCA), early view

WEST CENTER CITY 115

for illumination. New York City men's clubs of the 1920s often displayed such theatricality. A Gothic Revival chapel was upstairs. Buck Simpers Architect + Associates undertook renovation of the building (2003–2004).

WL47 Trinity Episcopal Church

1889–1890, Theophilus Parsons Chandler Jr. 1909–1911 Parish House and Rectory, Frank Miles Day (Day and Klauder). 1924–1925 broach spire, Day and Klauder. 1952–1953 Chapel, Victorine and Samuel Homsey. Delaware Ave. and Adams St.

Trinity claims descent from the Old Swedes (WL3) congregation of 1638. An in-law and favorite architect for the du Pont family, the Philadelphian Chandler designed the Gothic Revival church of rockfaced Avondale, Pennsylvania, quartzite stone. The expenditure was insufficient for a spire, which came decades later. The interior has a dramatic, oak hammerbeam ceiling with angels. Originally, walls were painted terra-cotta color and lit by gas jets. A later era brought the involvement of Philadelphia architect Day, who had produced two homes for Wilmingtonian Henry B. Thompson, the congregant who commissioned him for Trinity in 1909. A trustee of Princeton University, Thompson had also arranged for Day to design the Freshman Dormitories there (1908–1913). In his presentation drawing, the new buildings for Trinity are similar in fenestration and other details to Princeton, though less so as actually built. As Day scholar Patricia Keebler notes (1980), "the interior furnishings use the same Perpendicular Gothic motifs as the Princeton dining halls, planned in 1913." In 1911–1913, Day designed Caen stone additions to the church interior: altar, reredos, sedilia, Bishop's throne with paneled wings, and communion rail—plus sanctuary wainscoting and oak choir stalls. As at the Cathedral Church of St. John (WL54), Edward Maene did the sumptuous Gothic Revival carving, although Philadelphia stone masons B. Ridgway and Son advertised themselves in 1913 with a photograph of the intricate throne.

Trinity retains much of its early interior, including the font (1872, from the predecessor church downtown) and brass lectern (1892). Stained glass by Tiffany Studios (1890s) abounds. Two lancets in the left aisle, at the transept, are by Charles J. Boston (1928); the big, pale window at the back of the nave is by American Decorative Glass Company (1911); lancets in the chapel of the 1950s are by Wilbur Herbert Burnham of Boston. Near the main nave door to outside is a brilliantly colorful window imported as part of the Senator Willard Saulsbury bequest of English glass to four Delaware churches (1929, James H. Hogan), which includes a scene of the Swedish landing; it incorporates expensive ruby glass made with gold. Beside that door are two new windows by a Philadelphia artist depicting contemporary urban themes (2002, Joseph Beyer). The residential neighborhood adjacent to the church, known as Trinity Vicinity, was named a historic overlay zoning district in 2003 and is undergoing homesteading and gentrification, a process that began with DuPont lawyer (and eventual city mayor) Dan Frawley's purchase of a house for $1 in 1973.

WL48 Wilmington and Brandywine Cemetery

1843. 1913 chapel, E. James Dallett. Delaware Ave. and Adams St.

The rural cemetery movement left few examples in Delaware. Behind this cemetery's entrance gates is a rare Cedar of Lebanon tree, brought here by botanist James Canby c. 1850. To the right is the late-nineteenth-century caretaker's office. A straight avenue leads past the Gothic Revival chapel of fieldstone, the last work of Dallett, whose casket would lie there four years later. A cast-iron dog guarding the Néo-Grec Cleaden monument (c. 1873) recalls memoirist Henry Seidel Canby's recollections of the many such dogs beside doorsteps in the Wilmington of his youth. On the right side of the cemetery is the white marble, Egyptian-style obelisk dedicated to Alexander Porter, who drowned in a shipwreck off Africa in 1827 (brought from the Old First Presbyterian burying ground; see WL58); the Néo-Grec Robinson monument with small, polished red columns (c. 1878); and the Adams mausoleum, also Néo-Grec, with a fine gate (1887). On the left side are the matching,

Gothic Revival Harlan and Gause mausolea (c. 1880). An additional graveyard was located just east of the cemetery but was razed for a parking lot in the 1950s and forgotten. Hospital expansion on the site in the 1990s led to its surprising rediscovery and a controversial archaeological excavation in which hundreds of bodies—many of them Irish paupers—were removed for reinterment elsewhere.

WL49 Wilmington Hospital (Delaware Hospital)

1940–1942, Massena and du Pont. c. 1964–1966 and later, additions. Washington and 14th sts.

In the 1940s, the busy downtown hospital was mostly razed and rebuilt at far greater scale in Art Deco style. The reinforced concrete frame was covered with brick facing shaded progressively lighter from base to coping, a coloristic touch popular at the time in New York City, but unknown in Delaware. Interior innovations included an unprecedented use of sound-deadening material, lights instead of loudspeakers or bells to send calls, and operating rooms with year-round air conditioning and blue tile walls to ease eyestrain. Less progressive was the racial segregation of the facility by wards, a system abolished gradually in the mid-1950s. The entrance lobby, now remodeled, retains some Art Deco touches. Green marble pilasters and muted, green-and-blue terrazzo floors form a cool contrast to the warmth of the exterior walls, which suggest a Navajo rug in their patterned brickwork of yellows and reds, along with limestone trim, white paint, and green marble panels. A side entrance for nurses has a polychrome terracotta relief over the door. The suggestions of handicraft that add interest and variety to this bulky building would soon be abandoned with the coming of post–World War II modernism.

BRANDYWINE VILLAGE AND PARK

Brandywine Village Historic District, north of Brandywine Creek, preserves the flavor of early-nineteenth-century Wilmington, when the city was famed for its many mills. A dynasty of millers established itself downstream from North Market Street Bridge (WL51): Oliver Canby, Thomas Lea, James Price, and Joseph Tatnall. Artist Charles Willson Peale sketched their lofty mill buildings in 1789. Disappointingly, almost nothing survives of these nationally renowned structures, although brick arches on the north bank, incorporated into a residential highrise (1979–1983, first section, Richard D. Chalfant), mark the foundations of Lea Mills (1880s, burned 1933).

Brandywine Village existed as a separate town until 1869, when it became part of Wilmington's Ninth Ward. As an expanding city lost most of the colonial buildings along its outskirts, those in slow-growth Brandywine Village survived. In 1928, architect Edward Canby May lauded "their beautiful doorways, cornices and dormer windows," noting that such antiquities were "fast disappearing and giving way to the 'store front,' 'apartment house,' and 'gasoline stations.'" By 1960, Ninth Ward was suffering white flight and its old buildings faced demolition. Robert L. Raley and Albert Kruse, of AIA Delaware, championed the formation of Old Brandywine Village Inc. to buy the historic Lea House (WL52) in 1962–1963, the first of a series of preservation purchases. "It would be a crime to tear these buildings down," said Kruse.

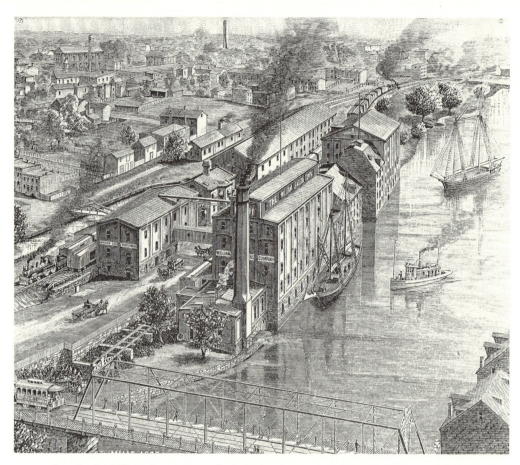

Brandywine Village. Downstream from Market Street Bridge (WL51) stood Lea Mills, seen here in the 1880s. As in the 18th century, ships pulled right up beside the mills to receive loads of flour.

These successes promised a bright future for the neighborhood, but this was never quite fulfilled. In the latest attempt, a Baltimore urban design firm prepared a revitalization plan (2001, Allison Platt and Associates), and a large Federal Job Corps Center got underway (2002–2004, Tevebaugh Associates). AIA Delaware remains active in the vicinity, occupying Brandywine Academy (WL55) and, in 2003, having renovated the Art Deco Wilmington Trust Building (Brandywine Trust and Savings Bank) at 2120 Market Street (1929–1930, L. Waring Wilson).

WL50 Brandywine Pumping Station and Waterworks

1905–1906, Theodore A. Leisen. 1907–1909 additions. 1932–1934 Office Building, G. Morris Whiteside. Southeast of Market Street Bridge

Grain mills operated on this riverbank as early as 1671. In 1827, the city installed a water-powered pump below the bridge to feed a reservoir at today's Rodney Square (WL29), supplying citizens with a reliable drinking supply. A steam pump was added in 1861 and several buildings were constructed, including City Mill Pumping Station in 1872, now demolished. A huge increase in city population led to the construction of the current station, in the Roman Revival style popular for civic structures after the World's Columbian Exposition in Chicago of 1893, and with a grand Palladian motif defining the central block's facade. Its walls are brick with Brandywine granite trim; the steel-reinforced interior is spanned by concrete floors. It was designed to house two Holly steam engines, manufactured in Buffalo, New York, that each weighed 500 tons and could pump twelve million gallons per day. They operated until 1968, when replaced by electric motors. One was removed in 1976; the other, preserved, is now among just sixteen in the United States. Tunnels in the basement, used for sand filtration of the water, remain from the building's predecessors. The waterworks still takes its supply from the millrace (rebuilt). The pumping station and subsequent buildings are said to stand on the venerable foundations of the colonial mills themselves, but, if so, this is not apparent from outside. The Public Works Administration–funded office next door (slated for demolition) has a colorful Art Deco relief inside, above a revolving front door. Brandywine Pumping Station received a new roof and windows in a major restoration (2002–2003, MGZA).

WL50 BRANDYWINE PUMPING STATION AND WATERWORKS

WL51 North Market Street Bridge

1928, Harrington, Howard and Ash, with Charles E. Grubb. Market St. over Brandywine Creek

A respected bridge-building firm of Kansas City, Missouri, designed this, the sixth bridge to span the river at the historic crossing on what was the main north–south road in colonial America. The first bridge here went up in 1764. Its replacement was a pioneering chain-link suspension span (1810, washed away 1822), itself followed by two covered bridges (1822, Lewis Wernwag, washed away 1839; its successor, demolished 1887) and then a wrought-iron Pratt through truss (demolished 1928). The current bridge was built to handle increased automobile traffic, which toward the end of its predecessor's life made up 85 percent of traffic across the river here. The Harrington firm had competed unsuccessfully for the Washington Memorial Bridge (WL57) a few years before. The structure is of steel girders, though those at the sides are encased in concrete, and the whole is made, decoratively, to resemble a masonry arch. The single, clear span measures 150 feet. The bridge was rehabilitated in 2002.

WL52 Thomas Lea House

1770. 1963 restoration, Robert L. Raley and Albert Kruse. 1801 Market St.

In 1770, a decade after the first overshot mills were begun on the south bank of the Brandywine, James Marshall excavated a millrace on the north. With the granite thus made available he built this five-bay, two-story Georgian house, which Thomas Lea, prominent miller and banker, bought in 1785. It survives as the oldest dwelling in the vicinity, emblematic of the prosperity that water-powered industrialization brought. Old Brandywine Village, Inc., was organized to buy the threatened structure in 1963. The group undertook a restoration in which nineteenth-century accretions—fully half of the building—were demolished and interiors were returned to a colonial appearance. Original partition walls were identified by ghost-marks on the floors. The old exterior doorframe was discovered beneath one from 1830. In a then-pioneering preservation strategy, adaptive reuse, the house was turned over to the Junior League of Wilmington in 1965 as

WL52 THOMAS LEA HOUSE, under renovation 1960s

a headquarters. The house has variously been known as the Lea-Derickson House and the Harvey-Derickson-Bringhurst House.

WL53 Market Street Houses

c. 1770, with additions. 1800 and 1900 blocks Market St.

This handsome row of early stone houses extends up the street from the Lea House (WL52) and, like it, was saved by Old Brandywine Village, Inc. The Tatnall Houses, at 1803 (c. 1770 with alterations of the 1840s) and 1805 (c. 1850) Market Street, were rescued from being demolished for a high-rise apartment building. The former was famed as Revolutionary War general Anthony Wayne's headquarters, where Washington held council. Restoration in the 1970s removed nineteenth-century porches and mansard roofs. Edward Tatnall, nineteenth-century botanist and owner of Wawaset Nursery, kept a telescope on the balustraded rooftop of his house at 1805 Market. The titanic explosion of some DuPont powder wagons on 14th Street in May 1854 smashed windows here. The Tatnall-Febiger House is at 1807 (1735 rear section; c. 1807 front); the William Lea House at 1901 (c. 1800, restored 1963–1966). Old Brandywine Village razed an incompatible nineteenth-century townhouse at 1903 and restored the houses at 1905 (c. 1805) and 1907 (c. 1785) in the 1970s, removing a commercial storefront from the latter.

WL54 Cathedral Church of St. John

1857–1858, John Notman. 1885 Sunday School. 1919–1921 chancel lengthened, Lady Chapel and wing, and Rectory, Zantzinger, Borie and Medary. 1951–1954 additions, Victorine and Samuel Homsey. 1960s interior remodeled. Concord Ave. and Market St.

With walls of Brandywine granite and a soaring, sixty-five-foot buttressed tower and spire, St. John's stands as a symbol of stability in a deteriorated neighborhood. It is the final documented church by Notman, noted Philadelphia architect. Alexis I. du Pont, congregant at Trinity (WL47, but then at 5th and King sts.) and recent convert to high-church Anglicanism, led the way in establishing this offshoot in the flourishing residential district north of the river. It stood at the corner of two important roads and replaced the notorious Green Tree Inn, the bar of which supposedly lay where the altar is now. Notman employed features advocated by the Ecclesiological movement: orientation to the east, cruciform plan, deep chancel, and exposed wooden beams. The style is Early English Gothic with Decorated touches and recalls his St. Mark's, Philadelphia (1847–1852).

"We are today building better churches than any other people in the world, with the exception of England," said Gothic Revival architect Ralph Adams Cram in 1929, pointing to such Philadelphia firms as Zantzinger, Borie and Medary, creators of St. Paul's, Chestnut Hill, Philadelphia (1928–1931), and the exquisite Valley Forge Memorial Chapel in

WL54 CATHEDRAL CHURCH OF ST. JOHN, photo c. 1893

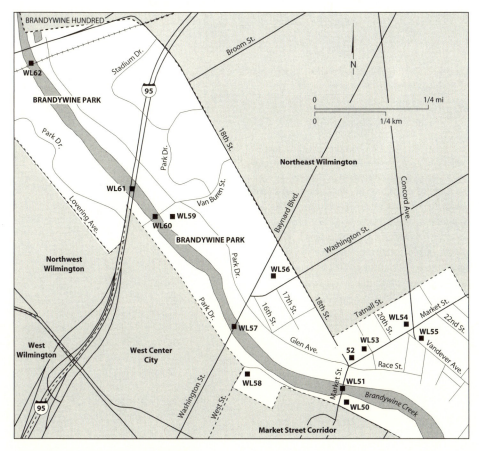

BRANDYWINE VILLAGE AND PARK

Pennsylvania (1917), as well as Rodney Square (WL29). They skillfully added to St. John's in 1919–1921. In the chancel, the arches of the sedilia (seats) have carved ornament even on their not-visible inner sides—meant for the glorification of God, not gratification of man. Additions at that date, in English Perpendicular style, included the Lady Chapel, Delaware's finest example of Cram-derived Gothic Revival. Wood carving was provided by American Car and Foundry Company. The splendid organ screen was carved in oak by Belgian-born sculptor Edward Maene of Philadelphia, who created the Valley Forge work, too. The Zantzinger firm's work here bears further comparison to their Foulke and Henry Dormitories, Princeton, and Philadelphia Divinity School (all 1923). The church has served as the diocesan cathedral since 1935, the year one of several new stained glass windows by Philadelphian Henry Lee Willet was dedicated.

WL55 Brandywine Academy

1798. c. 1820 cupola, Benjamin Ferris. 5 Vandever Ave.

Money for this blue-rock schoolhouse was donated by residents of Brandywine Hundred. The first neighborhood institution in Brandywine Village, it served many purposes, and all religious denominations except Catholic were allowed to meet here—even Millerites, who anticipated the end of the world in 1843. Ferris's design drawing for the "steeple house or Bellfry" survives (at Winterthur) and evidently copies that of Old Swedes Church (WL3), which he sketched at about the same time. The Academy served as a school until 1870 and a branch library from 1915 to 1943. When HABS was established in Delaware in January 1934, this was one of the first four buildings surveyed. The city gave the building to Old Brandywine Village, Inc., in 1963, which restored it and, for a time, re-created a

BRANDYWINE VILLAGE AND PARK

schoolroom inside. In 2001, it was refurbished as headquarters for AIA Delaware.

WL56 Todd Memorial (Soldiers and Sailors of Delaware Monument)

1925, H. Augustus Lukeman, sculptor. In Brandywine Park at Baynard Blvd. and Washington St.

Rags-to-riches shipbuilder William H. Todd gave this $100,000 war memorial, which consists of a granite obelisk and a triumphant bronze *Victory* figure derived from Augustus Saint-Gaudens's statue of *William Tecumseh Sherman,* New York City (1903). Nine thousand people gathered for the unveiling. That same year, Lukeman went to Georgia to carry out his most famous work, the giant relief sculptures of Stone Mountain (1925–1928). Todd Memorial, its avenue of cherry trees, and nearby Washington Memorial Bridge together form a City Beautiful ensemble. To the west are memorials to the Vietnam War (1983) and African American soldiers (1998) by local sculptor Charles C. Parks.

WL57 Washington Memorial Bridge

1919–1922, Benjamin H. Davis and Vance W. Torbert. Washington St. over Brandywine Creek

Before I-95 was built, this bridge was the main civic gateway to Wilmington when coming from the north. The state legislature approved a memorial bridge in 1919 to replace a metal span (1893, Edge Moor Bridge Company) too weak for modern traffic. Alfred I. du Pont chaired the bridge commission and initially corresponded with Carrère and Hastings (architects of his house, Nemours, BR26) about possible designs. Six firms were invited to submit proposals for a bridge strong enough to hold two trains consisting of sixty-ton electric railway cars, plus two lines of twenty-ton trucks. The winning New York City team of Davis (engineer) and Torbert (architect, a former associate of Carrère and Hastings) proposed a 720-foot structure of five reinforced-concrete arches, the longest of 250-foot span—Delaware's only open-spandrel concrete highway bridge.

The span was dedicated on Memorial Day 1922 in honor of the 10,000 Delawareans who served in World War I, with additional reference to Washington's role in the historic Battle of the Brandywine, fought upstream in Pennsylvania. A parade of 1,200 girls strewed flowers on the water. General James H. Wilson gave a speech in which he reminisced about building bridges for Grant at Vicksburg and called the new structure "a permanent utility and convenience to our city." The seventy-two-foot-wide causeway lined with balustrades made a grand statement, especially with its tall concrete cenotaphs adorned with eagles, of Onondaga litholite, and bronze plaques and lanterns. These details were supplied by Torbert. *Scientific American* in 1924 considered it "the longest, low-rise, skew arch span"

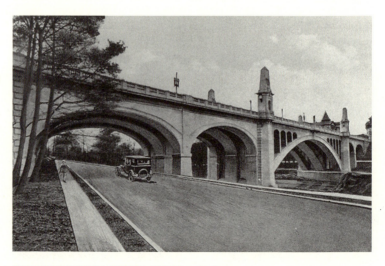

WL57 WASHINGTON MEMORIAL BRIDGE, early view

BRANDYWINE PARK

Brandywine Creek had long afforded Wilmingtonians with recreation: walks, picnics, bathing, skating. A proposal for the city to buy land on its banks was rejected in a town meeting in 1865. Three years later, the threat of houses going up between Wilmington and Brandywine Cemetery (WL48) and Rattlesnake Run upstream led to an outcry. A committee was established in 1868–1869 and recommended a Brandywine Park, the fast-flowing rocky river being a scenic amenity few other American cities could boast. Still, nothing was done.

In Brandywine Park, Wilmington, Del.

E. S. R. BUTLER & SON, WILM., DEL.

In 1881, textile magnate William P. Bancroft complained that Wilmington was growing fast, with scarcely any provision for parks or open spaces of any kind—except cemeteries. Two years later, he pushed the state legislature to set up the Wilmington Board of Park Commissioners, to which his cousin, banker and botanist William M. Canby, was appointed. Canby wrote to Frederick Law Olmsted, famous Boston landscape designer, who accepted an invitation to visit Wilmington. Olmsted reported (in December 1883) that the city should move quickly to purchase both banks of the river, which it did, buying 115 acres in 1886–1887. Olmsted did not design the park, however. Instead, credit should go to the Wilmington Board of Park Commissioners, along with Samuel Canby and Theodore A. Leisen.

By 1908, the park embraced 178 acres, and the scenic Brandywine raceways were depicted on innumerable postcards. Recent years have seen an effort to rid the park of invasive plant species, and Brandywine Zoo has been refurbished (Homsey Architects). The State Division of Parks took over Brandywine Park in the 1990s, with positive results, and scholar Susan Mulchahey Chase has recently written a history.

in the United States and perhaps the world. Davis went on to design memorial bridges in other cities, including Wilkes-Barre, Pennsylvania (1926–1929). Washington Street Bridge underwent major repairs by DelDOT in 2000.

WL58 Old First Presbyterian Church

1740. 1917–1918 relocated and restored, Edward Canby May. West St. and Park Dr.

The one-story, gambrel-roofed brick church was moved to Brandywine Park from downtown early in the twentieth century as a historic shrine, having been built just nine years after the founding of Willingtown. Originally, it stood at the intersection of Market Street and the thoroughfare called the "great road leading to the rocks" where the Swedes had landed. (In today's terms, the church occupied the site of the rear corner of Wilmington Public Library [WL28], for the construction of which it had to be relocated.) Facing two major roads, it had two entrances. Its construction date is marked on the north wall in glazed bricks. Zigzag patterning in the brickwork recalls southern New Jersey practice. It became a school in the 1840s after a larger church was erected nearby. Bancroft Mills executive Henry B. Thompson (see WL91) had Frank Miles Day prepare plans for its restoration in 1910 for the Historical Society of Delaware; these were never executed.

When the venerable building was threatened with demolition not long after, the Society of the Colonial Dames and the Society of Colonial Wars helped pay for its move to Brandywine Park in October 1917. The old mortar was so hard, many bricks could not be salvaged, so only three-quarters of the walls are made of original material. The leaded fanlights of the windows, long hidden, were a surprising discovery during the building's disassembly. The entrance doors are May's design based on historical precedent, as is much of the interior. Its successor congregation is First and Central Presbyterian Church (WL35), in which a Stanley Arthurs painting (1930) shows the colonial building in its heyday. Between the church and the riverbank runs Brandywine race (1900), which still supplies the city with water. North of the church is a sculpture, the President McKinley Memorial (1908, moved here 1971).

WL59 Josephine Fountain (Josephine Tatnall Smith Memorial Fountain)

1931–1932, Edward Canby May; John Brockhouse, sculptor. Brandywine Park, east of Van Buren St. Bridge

Grieving husband J. Ernest Smith, author of Delaware's historic General Incorporation Law that first made the state a business haven, donated the fountain along with 115 Japanese cherry trees (planted 1929). Wilmington architect May copied the design from a fountain at Villa Petraia, Florence, Italy (sixteenth century, Niccolo Tribolo), and a Philadelphia sculptor executed the work. Water sprayed down from near the crowning figure's feet, enveloping the tall, sculptural base in a veil of mist. The soft marble has suffered from weathering and vandalism. In the rose garden (1933) nearby stands Ferris Bringhurst Fountain (1872), said to be of red Aberdeen (Scotland) granite, which was moved here from the corner of Delaware and Pennsylvania Avenues.

WL60 Van Buren Street Bridge and Aqueduct

1906, Concrete-Steel Engineering Company, with Theodore A. Leisen. 1997 rebuilt. Van Buren St. over Brandywine Creek

The 353-foot bridge of eight arches, an early example of reinforced-concrete construction,

WL58 OLD FIRST PRESBYTERIAN CHURCH, in original location on Market Street

WL61 I-95 BRIDGE

WL62 CSX RAILROAD BRIDGE (BALTIMORE AND OHIO RAILROAD BRIDGE), under construction c. 1910

contained a pipe that carried water from Porter Reservoir on Concord Pike to the Wilmington filter station. The first of many concrete highway bridges in Delaware, it used a variety of early reinforcement methods: latticed and Melan-type rolled I-beams as well as Thacher bars, the last named for the noted Edwin Thacher of the New York City firm, Concrete-Steel Engineering Company, which designed some 300 reinforced-concrete bridges between 1895 and 1904. This bridge was meant to spur development on Wilmington's northeast side. Constant internal leaking led to a recent reconstruction of the bridge, generally along the lines of its original appearance. Downstream, a pattern of ripples marks the site of Barley Mill Dam, which served a millsite on the west bank—scene of the first milling on the Brandywine (before 1687) and rebuilt in the mid-eighteenth century. A millstone survives as a lone relic of those early days.

WL61 I-95 Bridge

1963–1967, Howard, Needles, Tammen and Bergendoff, engineers. Over Brandywine Creek

This massive bridge over the gorgelike valley of the Brandywine epitomizes the challenges inherent in constructing I-95 through northern Delaware, the last gap in the planners' dream of driving from Washington to Boston without stopping. It was a dramatic and controversial process. The first section of I-95, then known as the Delaware Turnpike, was dedicated at the Maryland-Delaware line in 1963 (see PR1). Extension of the road through Wilmington to Pennsylvania was completed in 1968. As historian Carol Hoffecker has described (1983), President Dwight Eisenhower's Commissioner of the Bureau of Public Roads, Francis V. du Pont, pushed for a highway directly through the city rather than around its eastern edge, although this involved wiping out a series of city blocks between Adams and Jackson streets—destroying 652 homes and dislocating 926 families. Among the public buildings lost were the brick and terra-cotta Willard Hall School (1884–1886, Edward Luff Rice Jr.; demolished 1962). The 1,870-foot bridge over the Brandywine, designed by the firm that built the Delaware Memorial Bridge (NC3), won an award from the American Institute for Steel Construction. The bridge's most dramatic aspect is the leglike, sculptural concrete piers that support the steel superstructure of twelve plate girders, each eight feet deep. The concrete deck has been replaced twice (1978–1982, again in 2003).

WL62 CSX Railroad Bridge (Baltimore and Ohio Railroad Bridge)

1909–1910, A. W. Thompson, chief engineer. Over Brandywine Creek, south of Augustine Cut Off

Nationwide growth in railroading in the 1890s triggered, paradoxically, a revival of an ancient architectural type: the heavy masonry bridge, of which this is an awesome example (650 feet long, 115 feet high). Built by contractors C. A. Sims and Company of Baltimore, it supplanted the old Augustine Bridge just upstream and cut running time between

Washington and New York by five minutes, its massiveness allowing trains to cross it safely at high speeds. There are seven arches in all, three of them of 100-foot span. Considerable concrete was used for foundations and for the core of the structure, which is faced with stone, half of which is buff sandstone from Berea, Ohio. Construction took only fourteen months, and just one workman was killed, by a falling bolt. The bridge remains in constant use by CSX Corporation trains today.

This scenic locale features three bridges close together. Augustine Bridge (1883–1885) stands to the north, originally a pin-connected Pratt-type deck truss nearly 1,000 feet long and 110 feet high that was converted to automobile use in 1920. Its rusted steel superstructure was entirely replaced in 1980, atop the original piers of blue rock from Brandywine Granite Quarry (BR24). Downstream is the diminutive Wire or Swinging Bridge (1910, restored 1975), a suspension span that gave workers access to Augustine Mills (BR21). Popular with Sunday strollers, it originally stood 100 feet further upstream until displaced by the B&O Bridge. Its form calls to mind a much earlier suspension span on the river, the short-lived but historic chain bridge at Market Street (1810). On the east bank stands the modernist W. Compton Mills Pumping Station (1959).

NORTHEAST WILMINGTON

Samuel H. Baynard opened up the Ninth Ward with his North Side Improvement Company in the 1890s. Baynard Boulevard Historic District commemorates those streetcar suburb days, when the newly wealthy were attracted to the area. It is an excellent place to study the variety of house types and styles popular c. 1900, many of them outstanding in their inventiveness, fine proportions, and craftsmanlike use of materials. Prominent along the parkway is the former No. 30, or Shortlidge School (1913, Edward Luff Rice Jr.), one of at least seven Wilmington schools designed by this pioneering local architect; it is of rough gray stone with red sandstone trim, culminating in a big turret. Also on the parkway is Beth Shalom synagogue, by New York City architect Raphael Courland (1949–1953). Several postwar schools were built in northeast Wilmington, including Salesianum at 1801 N. Broom Street (1952–1957, Gleeson and Mulrooney).

WL63 Amtrak Wilmington Shops (Pennsylvania Railroad)

1902–1904. East of Todds Ln.

The Pennsylvania Railroad enjoyed 78 percent growth in net earnings between 1897 and 1902 and invested heavily in new facilities. At Todd's Cut near Wilmington it gathered major repair facilities on a single site. A Mammoth-type steam shovel helped bury a wetland under ten feet of fill, on which twenty-seven buildings were erected in a plan carefully devised for efficiency. Tracks generally entered one side of the structure, exited the other. A forty-four-stall roundhouse of 363-foot diameter was the most notable feature (mostly demolished by 1976). Main Locomotive Shop, 500 feet long, had an erecting shop running down the middle, with a machine shop in one aisle, a boiler shop in the other. All were served by giant overhead cranes and lit by skylights. The zigzag roof outlines of the adjacent Car Paint Shop (to the west) and Car Erecting Shop (east) are still landmarks as seen from the windows of commuter trains zipping by. These were the only buildings on the site with wooden-truss roofs, not steel. Each was 300 feet long and skylit. Wilmington Shops was the scene of a bitter strike in 1922–1923. Amtrak took over in 1976 and considered moving its maintenance facili-

WL63 AMTRAK WILMINGTON SHOPS (PENNSYLVANIA RAILROAD)

ties to Boston, but Delaware Senator Joseph Biden successfully protested. At that time, 734 workers were employed, only half the number as in the 1920s.

WL64 Village of Eastlake (Eastlake Public Housing Project)

1943, G. Morris Whiteside. 2000–2005 rebuilt, Wilmington Housing Authority with developer Leon N. Weiner and Associates. Vicinity of 26th and Locust sts.

Wilmington Housing Authority was founded in 1938 to clear slums and build new homes for the poor. This neighborhood, first of its kind in Delaware, was hastily created to provide wartime housing, for whites only. It followed the standards of the Federal Public Housing Authority. Always interested in enlightened city planning for Wilmington, architect Whiteside saw these housing developments as pieces of a larger civic improvement puzzle and promising in their break from the old pattern of rowhouses crammed together. Rather suburban in its approach, Eastlake consisted of semi-detached units surrounded by grass. Along with nearby Riverside and Eastlake Extension, it later offered shelter for the city's poorest residents, mostly African American. By the 1990s, Eastlake was blighted with drugs and violence. Federal funds allowed a $30 million "Hope VI" reconstruction designed to create a mixed-income community and promote home ownership. The design of the new buildings, with sash windows, gables, and porches, somewhat recalled the old Wilmington rowhouses Whiteside had decried. The Weiner firm of Wilmington is well-known for its work in providing housing for low-income residents, having erected 10,000 apartments and homes throughout the Mid-Atlantic. The Eastlake redevelopment scheme was plagued with problems: the discovery of asbestos and lead delayed construction, and renovation did nothing to solve the crime problem in the surrounding areas or to bring in grocery stores and services. Some displaced residents complained that the new rules for admission, including holding a job and having no rent delinquencies for a year, were too harsh.

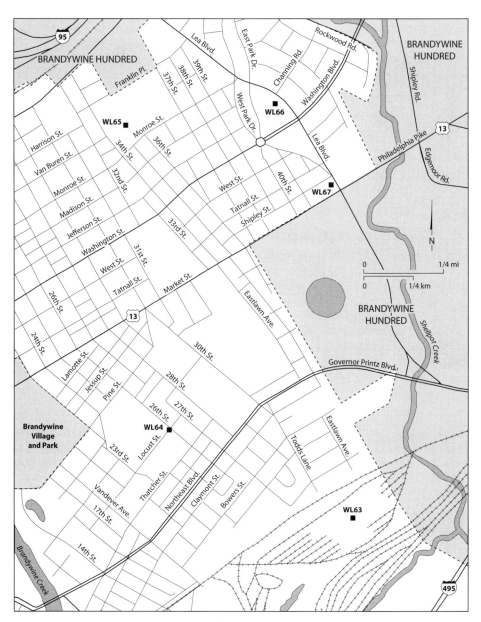

NORTHEAST WILMINGTON

WL65 P. S. du Pont Elementary School
(Pierre S. du Pont High School)

1932–1935, E. William Martin. 34th and Monroe sts.

The number of high school graduates in Wilmington jumped 265 percent during the 1920s. Continuing his extraordinary philanthropy towards Delaware education, Pierre S. du Pont funded the construction of this new institution. A committee spent more than a year studying modern educational needs. The Colonial Revival building needed to be massive (150,000 square feet, with forty-one classrooms) to serve a student body of 2,250. Du Pont chose Martin for his proven record on three Chester County, Pennsylvania, schools. Construction by a Trenton, New Jersey, contractor took 500 days, starting with the laying of the cornerstone in a Masonic ceremony in October 1934. The steel skeleton was clad with "Old Swedes" dark red face brick from Oberly

Brick Yards, which also supplied 45,000 specially cut and shaped brick. Artificial cut stone trim was employed, in addition to Indiana limestone, with classical detailing provided by Martin's designer, Albert Kruse. Angled wings maximized sunlight. An expensive limestone Ionic portico on a rusticated, arched base defines the entrance, and a multitiered octagonal cupola with balustrades and urns makes a grand show against the sky. Inside, floors were covered with linoleum; gypsum-block partitions divided classrooms; ceilings were fire-resistant metal lath and plaster; a furnace was fueled with 400 tons of soft coal. Innovations included a telephone system with outlets in every classroom, fire alarm boxes, built-in vacuum cleaning, and automatic coal stokers. Outside there was parking for 400 cars, and 100 workers laid out the streets and grounds in the first WPA project in Delaware (fall 1935). Du Pont told the architect he was "lost in admiration of the beautiful simplicity of treatment, finding the perfect balance between aesthetics and function." With the coming of court-ordered busing in 1978, the school ceased to be a high school, and it currently houses an elementary facility.

WL66 Beth Emeth Synagogue

1953–1954, Bloch and Hesse. 300 W. Lea Blvd.

Founded in 1905, Temple Beth Emeth was Wilmington's first Jewish reform congregation. It occupied a site at 904 Washington Street from 1908 to 1954, when it joined the general migration to the suburbs. As with most International Style buildings, traditional ornament is dispensed with, and, instead, simple geometric masses interact in complex ways. The New York City architects used long, thin

WL66 BETH EMETH SYNAGOGUE

pieces of tan-colored sandstone called Adirondack ashlar—never before seen in Delaware—plus blue stone from Binghamton, New York. Roofs are of reinforced concrete. The interior is paneled in oak, and the stained glass is by D'Ascenzo Studios, Philadelphia. Alterations by a Maryland firm, Levin/Brown and Associates, began in 2006.

WL67 Wilmington Drama League

1939, Victorine and Samuel Homsey. 10 W. Lea Blvd.

Delaware's oldest community theater, the League at first met in Lea Mills on the Brandywine before moving into this severely stripped-modernist, 300-seat brick facility. Along with five other Homsey buildings, it was listed in John McAndrew's *Guide to Modern Architecture: Northeast States* (1940) on architectural modernism. Early contributors pressed their hands into cement on the sidewalk, as in Hollywood. The lobby has been enlarged and a thrust stage added to the auditorium.

WEST WILMINGTON

Ethnically diverse, this extensive residential section contains two historic districts, 8th Street/Tilton Park and Cool Spring. Farther west is the hilltop neighborhood of Little Italy, recently marked by special signage and streetscape improvements (Design Collaborative). Concerned with the shortage of affordable rental housing for workers, William P. Bancroft's civic-minded real estate concern, Woodlawn Trustees, developed brick rowhouses west of Union Street between 4th and 7th streets ("The Flats"). Twenty rows were built in the first phase, 1902–1912, and offered unusual amenities: up-to-date utilities, maintenance service, front and back yards, and a park. Woodlawn Trustees still operates these units today. Far more upscale are fine homes along Bancroft Parkway. Wawaset Park (1919), near Pennsylvania and Greenhill avenues, was built for DuPont employees on the site of the fairgrounds that witnessed the pioneering flight of the homebuilt Wilmington Aero Club aircraft, *Delaplane*, in 1910. Wawaset's winding streets with Arts-and-Crafts and other stylish houses bears comparison to contemporaneous Union Park Gardens (WL78). West Wilmington has a number of interesting churches, including modernist, A-frame Zion Lutheran at Lancaster Avenue and Bancroft Parkway, by Philadelphia architect Harold Wagoner (1960–1961).

WL68 Delaware Children's Theater (New Century Club)

1892, Minerva Parker Nichols. 1014 Delaware Ave.

Nichols was a pioneering woman architect who, during a brief career in Philadelphia, designed that city's New Century Club (1891, demolished 1970s) for a women's group. Delaware's New Century Club played an active role in reforms of the day: creation of the Women's College in Newark (NK9.12), cafeterias and penny savings banks in schools, Christmas Seals (first in the nation, 1907), child labor laws, juvenile court, garbage wrapped for collection. Nichols's homelike, Colonial Revival three-story clubhouse of brick and pargetting has brick quoins, twin Palladian windows beside the front door, and a central dormer with a curved gable. The place served as a hospital during the flu epidemic of 1918. Plans survive at the Historical Society of Delaware for the building and later additions (1910, 1930, Brown and Whiteside).

WL69 Ursuline Academy Performing Arts Center (First Church of Christ Scientist)

1912, Solon S. Beman. Van Buren St. and Pennsylvania Ave.

The work of Chicago architect Beman attracted the attention of the founder of the Church of Christ Scientist, Mary Baker Eddy, at the World's Columbian Exposition of 1893. She hired him to build a Christian Science church in his native city, based upon the Fine Arts Building at the exposition. This, in turn, became the model for his subsequent churches across the nation. The Wilmington building, of limestone, used a favorite Beman device, a six-column pedimented Ionic portico—Delaware's finest example of this form. The classical interior is also noteworthy. The building has recently become part of Ursuline Academy, most of the campus of which is Gothic Revival by a Philadelphia architect (1927–1954, Paul Monaghan).

WL70 Cool Spring Reservoir Pumping Station

1878. 10th and Van Buren sts.

"Coolspring" was the country house of Caesar A. Rodney Jr. at 11th and Broom streets. A pile of stones marked the site as late as the 1940s. A reservoir was built nearby in 1877 and a fashionable neighborhood sprang up. Cool Spring Park, originally with fountains and

WL68 DELAWARE CHILDREN'S THEATER (NEW CENTURY CLUB)

rare trees, long hosted the Wilmington Flower Market (1920s–1950s). The pumping station, a compact brick building of Queen Anne style with elaborate corbeling, a clipped gable at the back, and a big, octagonal cupola at the front, contained an engine and two boilers. After it was decommissioned, it housed the Society of Natural History of Delaware from 1910 to 1949, which was founded by botanist William M. Canby. Postwar growth in Wilmington required the pumping station to return to service, and its windows were replaced with glass blocks. Later, it was renovated by a Baltimore firm (1978, Whitman, Requardt and Associates, engineers) and again in 2003 by the Wilmington firm MGZA.

WL70 COOL SPRING RESERVOIR PUMPING STATION

WL71 St. Paul's Catholic Church

1869. c. 1910. 1010 W. 4th St.

The church's green tile roof and tall belltower are familiar landmarks seen from I-95, which wiped out part of the neighborhood it served. The congregation today is mostly Puerto Rican and Mexican. A cornerstone gives the date of the first church, 1869, a brick edifice hidden by the twentieth-century granite skin. Buff terra-cotta trim contrasts with gray stone walls and green copper cornices. The church is entered through a Corinthian porch of terra-cotta into a narrow cross-hall with an attractive tiled floor. In the nave, slender columns support a graceful arcade. Decorative details are painted on the walls and arched ceiling, and stained glass abounds. The rectory (1930) next door continues the Italianate theme. The church makes an interesting comparison to twin-spired St. Hedwig's Roman Catholic (1904–1905) nearby at 408 S. Harrison Street, by a Milwaukee architect, E. Brilmaier, who was known to the pastor from his seminary days. That church, noted for its scagliola work and decorative painting, dominated a Polish neighborhood called Hedgeville.

WL72 Holy Trinity Greek Orthodox Church

1949–1952, Ernest K. Eugene. 808 N. Broom St.

This church served a scattered Greek community that drove here from four states every Sunday. A Chicago engineer who specialized in Byzantine designs was hired for the Greek Cross plan building. Above a slate roof rose a lead-covered dome and two spires (forty and seventy-five feet each). Terrazzo floors originally had a double-eagle design, and a ceiling mosaic featured God Pantocrator. Thirty windows were added in 1954 (Llorens Stained Glass Studios, Atlanta), and Newark, Delaware, artist Leo Laskaris was hired to paint 2,000 square feet of murals on canvas (1957–1958). The water-damaged murals were later replaced in a new campaign of iconographic decoration by a Crete-born painter now living in New York City (2003, George Filippakis). The resulting dome shimmers in gold leaf and vibrant color. At the same time, a raised sacramental platform or *solea* was added to the sanctuary, of yellowish Brazilian granite. Some 800 families, still from four states, currently attend the church.

WL69 URSULINE ACADEMY PERFORMING ARTS CENTER (FIRST CHURCH OF CHRIST SCIENTIST)

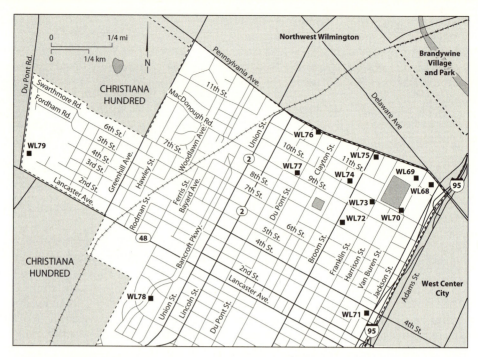

WEST WILMINGTON

WL73 Frank Pyle House

1891, Frank Miles Day. 10th and Franklin sts.

Philadelphia architect Day opened his own practice in 1887 and, three years later, designed a house for Bancroft Mills (WL91) executive Henry B. Thompson (1305 Rodney Street, demolished). The Pyle House, for a patent-leather manufacturer, probably followed as a result of the Thompson commission. According to architectural historian Patricia Keebler (1980), it is "one of the few Day houses that exists virtually unaltered. . . . Deep porches, turret and undercut breezeway combine aspects of both the Shingle Style and the Queen Anne"—a steep-roofed, red brick ensemble of great robustness with a massive round corner tower. Day would eventually design the campus for the University of Delaware (NK9), in an entirely different idiom, Colonial Revival.

WL74 Mauchline

c. 1914–1917, Wilson Eyre and John Gilbert McIlvaine. 1401 10th St.

The half-timbered, Tudor Revival home with two prominent gables was illustrated in *Architectural Forum* (August 1919), and drawings survive at the University of Pennsylvania. Owner Frank G. Tallman came to Wilmington in 1905 as a DuPont executive and assembled a nationally famous collection of Lincoln memorabilia, now at the University of Delaware. The rough-faced brick used on the dwelling was a recent innovation of English-born mason Edward L. Johnson, who came to Wilmington in 1868 and trained as a journeyman bricklayer under builder Thomas B. Hizar.

WL73 FRANK PYLE HOUSE

WL75 Church of the Holy City (Swedenborgian)

1857–1858, attributed to Edmund G. Lind. 1917 moved and altered, William Woodburn Potter. 1118 N. Broom St.

Twenty "receivers" of Swedenborg's religious ideas, mostly relatives of local enthusiast Daniel Lammot, established this New Church temple at Delaware Avenue and 11th streets, from which location it was later moved by Lammot's great-grandson Pierre S. du Pont when he widened the avenue. The original, Early English Gothic Revival building is attributed to the Baltimore architect Lind, who had trained in London and immigrated in 1855. Potter, a Philadelphia architect who had worked with Cope and Stewardson in 1897–1903, rebuilt it in a different form—the lancet windows were lowered, the doorway moved, and the conical, shingled steeple replaced by a broach spire entirely of stone, matching the church walls of blue Brandywine granite. The reredos and altar are of imported Caen stone, carved with grapevines and oak leaves. An oak-and-leaded-glass screen at the north end recalls one that Potter installed at Westminster Presbyterian (WL84). He also added a parish house, with an inglenook and a cloister. (Several interesting buildings across Pennsylvania Avenue are discussed in the Northwest Wilmington section.)

WL76 Automobile Row

Early 20th century to present. Pennsylvania Ave., between Clayton and Union sts.

Car dealerships sprang up along the commuter thoroughfare from wealthy residential districts to downtown, with the name "Automobile Row" being applied as early as 1912, just five years after the first car was licensed in the state. By 1927, Delawareans owned 44,000 cars. Bill Moeckel designed Porter Showroom (c. 1938, now altered) in the new International Style. "There wasn't a modern building in Wilmington at the time that I arrived here in 1936," he later recalled.

Another modernist dealership was Union Park Pontiac (1949, W. Ellis Preston), with a glass-and-porcelainized-steel front and soaring pylon. The last to survive intact was the red-and-yellow brick Art Deco Delaware Motor Sales (1938–1939, Massena and du Pont). This Cadillac dealership was owned by Eugene E. du Pont, who relocated it from near Rodney Square (WL29). Its design was meant to offer the greatest possible area of show-window glass. The second floor, reached by a circular stair, displayed used cars. In 2003–2004, Delaware Cadillac was rehabilitated by Buck Simpers Architect + Associates, who covered the historic building with an encrustation of Indiana limestone, a nationwide requirement of General Motors for all Cadillac dealerships. A spokesman told the Wilmington *News-Journal*, "The integrity of the building won't be affected. . . . It's still an example of Art Deco." Preservationists vehemently disagreed.

WL76 AUTOMOBILE ROW, Union Park Pontiac, before alteration

WL77 St. Anthony of Padua Church

1925–1948, Gleeson, Mulrooney and Burke. 1952–1953 school, Gleeson and Mulrooney. 1960–1961 rectory, Leon Fagnani. 901 N. Du Pont St.

For generations, the church's tall campanile has soared above Little Italy, cherished symbol in a state in which almost one person in ten claims Italian ancestry. Architect Thomas F. Mulrooney, a native Wilmingtonian with his

WEST WILMINGTON 133

WL77 ST. ANTHONY OF PADUA CHURCH, with school behind, photo c. 1953

office in Philadelphia, traveled to Italy with the congregation's Father Francis Tucker to study churches. The Italian Romanesque–style edifice the firm designed was usable by 1926, but full completion took decades; the 125-foot campanile (with radio-electric chimes) was erected only in fall 1937 and the ceiling given its barrel vault in 1948. Outer walls are gray Wissahickon schist from Pennsylvania. Based on the church of St. Zeno Maggiore, Verona (1123–1135 AD), the entrance porch is of orange terra-cotta on limestone columns. Polychrome sculpture hints at the spectacle that awaits one inside: a huge, echoing nave; a wide ceiling enriched with colorful coffers; ten bronze coronas hung from long chains; arcades supported by columns of scagliola (over structural steel) with richly modeled capitals depicting rams' heads and peacocks. The mosaic over the sanctuary arch consists of several million tesserae, fabricated at the mosaic studio of the Vatican and shipped in sections in 1949, the year the Siena marble altar was added. A Philadelphia artist, Paula Himmelsbach Balano, designed the stained glass. The aisles are dense with candle-lit shrines, statuary, and more scagliola, examples of nearly forgotten arts. One enters the memorable church through bronze doors (1966) by local architect Leon N. Fagnani and Italian sculptor Egidio Giaroli.

WL78 Union Park Gardens

1918–1919, Ballinger and Perrot, with John Nolen. Vicinity of Bancroft Pkwy., south of Lancaster Ave. to Barry St.

Union Park fairgrounds was a popular venue for sports and amusements, and Buffalo Bill starred there in 1916. Responding to a housing shortage for wartime shipbuilders, U.S. Shipping Board officials met with Wilmingtonians in 1918 to plan a community of 506 rental homes on the fifty-acre site. The architects, with town planner Nolen (who had designed Overlook Colony, BR5), laid out curving streets and designed homes using just five different floor plans. Monotony was avoided by gables, setbacks, and intelligent use of materials: varied brick bonds, tile roofs, stucco walls. The results, embodying the principles of the English Garden Suburb of the early twentieth century, have ever since been hailed for successful design. Union Park Gardens properties were auctioned off in 1922, and most homes have since been altered, with some dilution of their original character. Neighborhood associations have been vital here and helped prevent the proposed construction of I-95 down Bancroft Parkway.

WL79 Cab Calloway School of the Arts (Wilmington High School)

1958–1960, Whiteside, Moeckel and Carbonell. 100 N. Du Pont Rd.

WL79 CAB CALLOWAY SCHOOL OF THE ARTS (WILMINGTON HIGH SCHOOL)

The previous Wilmington High School, on Delaware Avenue (1899–1901), was ultimately deemed dark and dreary and a fire hazard; it was razed in 1964. Its datestone and gate are preserved on the grounds of the present facility, the largest high school in the state when built. A pamphlet explained, "The elements of the building express light, order, beauty, color, line and quiet—attributes which foster study and growth." In fact, its stern International Style aluminum-framed windows and brick walls were relieved only by a few colored glazed-tiles, including green ones that form a block at the entrance (penetrating the building internally as well as projecting externally). Over the front doors stands a shallow roof supported by slender, cruciform steel *pilotis*. Built for 1,350 pupils, the school was overcrowded as soon as it opened, and an extra floor was added. Rioting in its hallways in 1968 led to a plunge in enrollment. When court-ordered desegregation of Delaware schools ended in 1994, numbers dropped still further, culminating in temporary closure five years later. It has reopened as a magnet school for the arts. Next door stands corner-windowed Westcourt Apartments (Foster Park Apartments; 1940–1941, Morton Keast, with Massena and du Pont, associates).

NORTHWEST WILMINGTON

Joshua T. Heald opened northwest Wilmington to development with his horse-drawn railcar line along Delaware Avenue in 1864. Today, the area is divided into two sections by the tracks of the former Baltimore and Ohio Railroad. The eastern section comprises dense, relatively affordable residential neighborhoods closer to downtown, including Trolley Square, former site of the railcar depot; the western section includes the expensive Highlands. The Delaware Avenue historic overlay zoning district in the eastern section, established in 1979, is a showcase for late-nineteenth-century architectural styles. Other such districts embrace Kentmere Parkway and the outstanding collection of early-twentieth-century houses near Rockford Park in the vicinity of Willard Street. A lost landmark is the B&O Station of Frank Furness (designed 1886), one of the most innovative buildings ever erected in Wilmington and the scene of whistle stop speeches by Presidents Franklin D. Roosevelt and Harry Truman in the 1940s. Disgracefully, it was demolished for a grocery store parking lot in the fall of 1960. A Furness design survives at 1315 Delaware Avenue, a c. 1887 addition to a house of the 1870s.

WL80 Fountain Plaza

1968–1969, Edward Bachtle. Delaware and Pennsylvania aves.

The triangular park occupies the site of Kennett Apartments, which civic leader Henry Belin du Pont deemed ugly. He bought them in 1965 to demolish them and create this park, among the first works by Bachtle after establishing a landscape design practice in Wilmington in 1965—the first person, he thought, ever to do so (Wilmingtonian Robert Wheelwright, for whom Bachtle briefly worked, was based in Philadelphia). The park has ivy-covered earth mounds, curving benches, and stone paving in biomorphic patterns. Bachtle, who attended Harvard University for his graduate studies and cited landscape architect Roberto Burle Marx as a chief influence, chose plant types resistant to gasoline vapors. A focus is the sculpture of a boy and two dogs, *American Youth* (1967, Charles C. Parks), a welcome addition to Wilmington's park statuary, which, in 1964, numbered just ten pieces, compared to Philadelphia's 150.

One block north is another triangular park, Columbus Square (1956–1957, Leon N. Fagnani), featuring a 1,600-pound bronze statue of the Genoese explorer modeled in Rome by Egidio Giaroli, a sculptor later favored by Pope Paul VI. The Italian Societies of Wilmington conceived of Columbus Square.

WL81 Howard Pyle Studios

1883. 1900 School Studios. 1305 Franklin St.

The quaint complex tucked into a narrow lot amid hollies and hemlocks is a rare, unaltered survival of nineteenth-century artists' studios still used for their original purpose. The famous illustrator Pyle returned to his native Wilmington from New York in 1879 and built the first studio (at rear) in this growing district. The cottagelike Queen Anne–style building stood eighty feet back from the street, where the lot widened. Inside were brick fireplaces; heavy, curved ceiling beams; skylights; and rustic-looking walls of unpainted shingles (white today). The Old-English flavor befitted the Anglophilia of Pyle, illustrator of the *King Arthur and His Knights* series of books (1903–1910). A shingled section of the house to the west has a doorway and marble steps that appear to be recycled from a townhouse of c. 1800, typical of Pyle's acquisition of historical fragments.

Pyle taught summer sessions at Chadds Ford, Pennsylvania, and, in 1900, built three

WL80 FOUNTAIN PLAZA, photo 1969

WL81 HOWARD PYLE STUDIOS, school studios, photo c. 1910

WL82 QUEEN ANNE HOUSES

attached studios along the southwest edge of the lot for "the boys" of the Howard Pyle School of Art. That institution trained N. C. Wyeth (who arrived in fall 1902), Frank Schoonover (see WL86), and other painters of the Brandywine group. Like Pyle's studio itself, the school buildings epitomize the Queen Anne style, with complex massing, jutting half-timbered gables, and tall chimneys. Big windows and skylights admitted the coveted north light. In Pyle's day, the complex was open and sunny, its brickwork cloaked in ivy. Repointing has obscured the original mortar joints, thin and dark. Millstones and a datestone (1799) dot the pavement outside. Pyle died in Italy in 1911, and pupil Stanley Arthurs owned the studio from 1920 to 1950. The Studio Group of local painters has preserved the property since 1964.

WL82 Queen Anne Houses

c. 1880. Pennsylvania Ave., west of Franklin St.

These are among the last survivors of dozens of Queen Anne–style houses that once lined this busy route. Unrestored and venerable-looking, these three-story homes are characteristic of that picturesque and medievalizing style, with red brick laid in thin, red mortar joints, slate pantiles on upper walls, pargetting, and steeply pitched roofs. One has eyebrow windows in rakishly pointed, slate-shingled twin gables. The area eastward has still more Queen Anne–style houses surviving from its heyday as an enclave for streetcar commuters in the late nineteenth century.

WL83 1401 Condominiums

1959–1960, Milton Schwartz. Pennsylvania Ave. and Broom St.

In the heyday of the DuPont Company in the 1950s, greater Wilmington became the sixth wealthiest city in the United States, which attracted Philadelphia developers to build a series of luxury apartment towers just west of downtown. This sixteen-story tower for developer Mayer I. Blum and Sons contained 182 units, all air-conditioned. Construction was delayed by the blue rock boulders encountered when sinking the seventy-six caisson pilings. Openwork concrete-block screens at the side of the projecting balconies add a rare decorative touch. The fifteen-story Dorset (1959–1960) stands nearby at 1301 Harrison Street. Designed by Wilmington architect Morton E. Bleich for Philadelphia developer Ephraim J. Frankl, the Dorset featured Vermont granite trim at the foundations and projecting concrete slabs as sunshades at each floor.

WL84 Westminster Presbyterian Church

1910–1911, William Woodburn Potter. 1923 Parish House, Edward Canby May. 1992–1993 Community Hall, George Yu Architects. Rodney St. and Pennsylvania Ave.

This Gothic Revival group has a complex building history. Attached to the present church is the earlier Rodney Street Chapel (1882–1883 chancel, Chauncey G. Graham; 1888 nave and transepts, Edward Luff Rice Jr.; 1904 addition, Rice). The chapel was refaced in stone when the larger church was built and,

WL83 1401 CONDOMINIUMS

WL85 SOLDIERS AND SAILORS MONUMENT, photo c. 1900

WL86 FRANK E. SCHOONOVER STUDIOS

subsequently, was altered by May (1917–1923; Weston Holt Blake, draftsman), then again by G. Morris Whiteside (1950), and yet again in the 1990s. Only the ceiling remains from the 1880s. The church proper, by Philadelphia architect Potter, has extensive stained glass. The Community Hall and long covered walk with stone buttresses were added in 1992–1993. In the once-highly fashionable neighborhood nearby stand Immanuel Episcopal at 2400 W. 17th Street (1915, Frederick E. Mann, with Brown and Whiteside, and stained glass by Frank Schoonover, 1929–1930) and St. Stephen's Lutheran (1926–1927, Clarence R. Hope) at 1304 N. Rodney Street.

WL85 Soldiers and Sailors Monument

1871, Alfred B. Mullett, incorporating a 1799–1801 column by Benjamin Henry Latrobe; Harry Lowe, sculptor. Delaware Ave. and Broom St.

This column was the first public monument ever erected in Wilmington and incorporates a fragment of one of America's most historic lost structures. In 1868, Latrobe's Bank of Pennsylvania, Philadelphia, was demolished to make way for the U.S. Appraisers' Stores Building. Delaware Civil War veteran Albert S. Nones suggested to U.S. Congressman Charles O'Neill of Philadelphia that its columns be made into war memorials to be designed by the architect Mullett. Congress passed a bill of authorization. Through Nones's leadership, the Soldiers and Sailors Monument Association, Delaware, successfully applied for one of the columns, which formed the basis for the state's only Civil War soldiers memorial. (Other Latrobe-column memorials survive at Adrian, Michigan, and Dayton, Ohio.) Lowe fashioned the globe and eagle (which grapples with the serpent of rebellion), cast at Pusey and Jones Company in Wilmington from donated cannon bronze. The monument was dedicated in May 1871 by General Oliver O. Howard of the Freedman's Bureau. Debts went unpaid, and the sheriff seized the monument for a time. Willam du Pont enclosed the plot with granite copings in 1893 as Monument Place. The landscaping is modern (1978, Edward Bachtle). The surrounding neighborhood has interesting houses of the 1870s–1880s era, although the childhood home of memoirist Henry Seidel Canby (*The Age of Confidence*, 1934) at 1212 Delaware Avenue was torn down for a 1920s-era apartment house.

WL86 Frank E. Schoonover Studios

1905–1906, Edward Luff Rice Jr. 1616 N. Rodney St.

Art collector Samuel Bancroft built four attached studios for illustrators studying with Howard Pyle. The architecture is simpli-

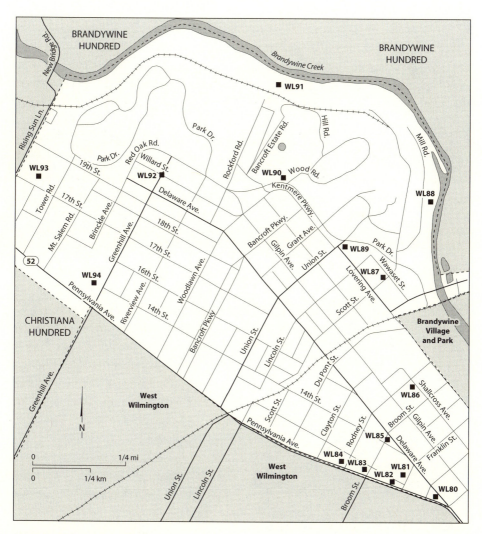

NORTHWEST WILMINGTON

KENTMERE PARKWAY AND ROCKFORD PARK

Breaking with the city grid, the sinuous Kentmere Parkway was meant to connect the two new parks, Brandywine and Rockford. William P. Bancroft, who donated the latter, designed a 150-foot-wide parkway in 1889 and sent the blueprint to John C. Olmsted in Boston, who corrected it with a more graceful curve. The aging master Frederick Law Olmsted visited Wilmington in December 1892 to meet with William Canby of the Park Commissioners to discuss the delays in implementation of the scheme—owing, he thought, to mutual misunderstanding. In driving over the parkway, Olmsted saw that his plans had been deviated from, the Wilmington parties having proceeded without him in 1891. Impatient with continuing slow response from the Olmsteds, the park board severed ties in 1893.

Kentmere Parkway is lined with expensive homes of the early twentieth century. At the northern end is a statue, cast in England, of Wilmingtonian Thomas F. Bayard (1907, Michael Stillman; Effie Stillman Ritchie, sculptor). Farther on stand the lightning-scarred nineteenth-century oaks of Rockford Grove.

On the west side of Rockford Road is Rockford Park. Bancroft, who prevailed upon the state legislature to form the Wilmington Board of Park Commissioners in 1883, provided land for the park in 1889 and 1895, totaling some 200 acres. In the latter year, DuPont donated the steep, scenic hillside overlooking today's Experimental Station (BR25), where now sits the William M. Canby Memorial—a bench of Barre, Vermont, granite designed by a leading Boston architect (1905, Guy Lowell). Canby, president of the park board, was a botanist who once visited Alaska with John Muir, who attended the park's dedication. Historian Priscilla M. Thompson wrote in 1978, "Scholars do not consider the Wilmington parks to be one of [Frederick Law] Olmsted's significant projects, and yet his influence and genius is inescapable. He suggested acquisition of Brandywine Park; he made a plan for Kentmere Parkway; and his firm unofficially advised and planned Rockford Park on William Bancroft's blueprint." A statue of Civil War Admiral Samuel F. Du Pont (1884, Launt Thompson) was moved to the park from Du Pont Circle, Washington, in 1920, when displaced by a fountain.

Rapid urban growth demanded a water tank on Mount Salem Hill, encased in a decorative, 115-foot tower with round-arched observation deck atop. Construction of Rockford Tower made use, in part, of boulders from old farm walls on the park grounds. Some of the stones are truly cyclopean. Edge Moor Bridge Works provided the 500,000 gallon steel tank (replaced 1983–1984). The interior of the Norman-style tower was lined with white-glazed brick, and the roof was supported by a spidery metal truss system (restored 2002, MGZA). When Rockford Tower opened, ten million gallons flowed through the tank annually—compared to four million gallons daily at present, so greatly has water demand increased.

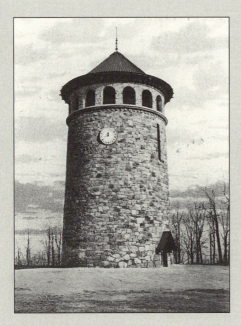

ROCKFORD TOWER

WL87 HOMSEY ARCHITECTS

fied Tudor Revival, with half-timbering, by the leading Wilmington architect of the day. Each studio has a big brick chimney against an end wall. Among the first four tenants were Schoonover and Wyeth, paying $17.50 a month. Wyeth stayed just two years (1906–1908) before moving to Chadds Ford, but Schoonover—illustrator of more than 150 books—remained for decades and bought all four studios in 1970, two years before his death. Architect Richard Chalfant then bought the place, planning to redevelop it, but neighbors convinced him to undertake a restoration instead. He sold the refurbished studios to artists, and today, Schoonover's grandson runs a gallery here. The entire facility was restored again in the late twentieth century by Design Collaborative.

WL87 Homsey Architects

1960–1962, Samuel and Victorine Homsey. 2003 N. Scott St.

Architecturally, this is the most interesting architects' office in the state, for almost half a century home to a prominent firm. The Homseys, who lived in a top floor apartment, had a sensitive feeling for architectural materials, using stone from a pre-existing retaining wall and wood to add a human touch to the International Style, structure-revealing design of concrete, steel, and glass. The artfully designed Cartesian composition of the front facade repays careful study: each floor is different (columns on the first level suggest weight-bearing; above comes progressively more glass) and horizontals and verticals are thoughtfully juxtaposed. The translucent, honeycomb front door, of "Panelux" plastic materials in a mahogany frame, is one the Homseys saw advertised in a trade journal and ordered from its Florida manufacturer, Monostructure Inc.

WL88 Three Mill Road

1988–1989, Eldon Homsey for Homsey Architects. 3 Mill Rd., on Brandywine Creek

This 60,000-square-foot office building by the son of the architects Victorine and Samuel Homsey employs exposed I-beams and mirrored glass to express structure directly. The steel beams supporting the floors are painted green. Vertical posts, more slender and rising the full height of the building, are painted brown, as are the diagonals that brace the cantilevered floors. Most slender of all are the mullions, painted black. The whole frame forms an open cage, a dramatic complement to the scenic riverbank site.

WL89 Office Building (Bank of Delaware)

1815–1816. 1931–1932 moved here, Charles O. Cornelius of Holden, McLaughlin and Associates. 1958 wing, Albert Kruse. Lovering Ave. and Union St.

Constructed for the first bank in the state (established 1795), this is one of Delaware's finest public buildings of the Federal era. For generations it was a familiar presence in downtown Wilmington, at the busy northeast corner of 6th and Market streets. It contained both banking house (front entrance) and cashier's residence (side). White marble was employed extensively, including for the thin, monolithic

WL88 THREE MILL ROAD

WL89 OFFICE BUILDING (BANK OF DELAWARE), photo 1931 at original location on Market Street

Ionic columns and tympanum at the main entrance, stringcourse, and cornice. The words "Bank of Delaware" carved on the stringcourse may be original; some dates added later, perhaps in 1907, refer to the chartering (1795) and re-chartering (1865) of the bank. An earlier generation of historians attributed the building to Pierre Bauduy, without evidence. The interior was remodeled in 1907 and windows were inserted into formerly blind openings beside the front door.

The Bank of Delaware was liquidated shortly after 1929, and Delmarva Power and Light (WL22) planned to demolish it to erect a corporate headquarters. In response to this threat, Mary Wilson (Mrs. Henry B.) Thompson founded the Old Delaware Bank Association and interested the recently formed Delaware Academy of Medicine in utilizing the relocated building as a medical library and meeting place. Thompson was jeered as a balmy sentimentalist but pressed ahead. Charles O. Cornelius, former curator of the American Wing at the Metropolitan Museum of Art, New York, and designer of a home for the Thompsons, was hired to adapt the building. He took pious care to rebuild the structure accurately on its new suburban site at the foot of Kentmere Parkway. Citing an inability to expand, the Academy of Medicine sold the historic building in 2002 to a law firm, which undertook a renovation (2003–2004, Bernardon Haber Holloway).

WL90 Delaware Art Museum (Delaware Art Center)

1937–1938, Victorine and Samuel Homsey and G. Morris Whiteside, II. 2003–2005 enlarged, Ann Beha Architects. 2301 Kentmere Pkwy.

The Samuel Bancroft collection of Pre-Raphaelite paintings was offered to the Wilmington Society of the Fine Arts if a suitable museum could be established. Four drawings in 1937 by Samuel Homsey proposed various facades for the building: Georgian Revival without a portico; stripped classicism akin to Eliel Saarinen's design for the Cranbrook Academy of Art; Moderne; and the arcaded Georgian Revival that was finally chosen. The final design resembled one of several proposed for the Portland Art Museum, Oregon (1930–1932, Pietro Belluschi) before a modernist scheme was picked—the opposite of how the Delaware project turned out. Subsequent additions were designed by Homsey Architects (1955–1956, 1987). In time, the decision was made to spend bond monies rebuilding the facility, gutting and refurbishing the Georgian Revival building in the process, which would form the centerpiece between two rambling wings. A competition was held, which Boston architect Beha won against top national firms (Frank Gehry, Michael Graves, the Gwathmey Siegel firm, and Robert Venturi). Beha had experience in similar projects in the Taft Museum, Cincinnati (2003), and the Portland Museum of Art, Maine (2002), and intended to use

Brandywine Valley materials in the design, which she likened to a country house gently integrated with its surrounding landscape. Traditional materials were to be employed, though sometimes in unusual ways, such as in using copper as a wall cladding (pre-patinated to prevent color change over time). A sculpture garden was designed around an old reservoir by Harvard landscape professor, Michael Van Valkenburgh, who had worked with Beha on a project at Walker Art Center, Minneapolis (2005).

WL91 Bancroft Mills

Mid- to late-19th century and later. Foot of Rockford Rd. at Brandywine Creek

English-born Quaker Joseph Bancroft was trained in cotton weaving in Lancashire. He bought a grist mill here in 1831, at a time when grain milling was on the decline. He switched it over to cloth making, specializing in glazing fabric for awnings, tents, and especially window shades. In 1859–1860, Bancroft added bleaching and dyeing equipment. By the 1880s, the firm was the largest textile finisher in the nation, with its brick and stone mills sprawling along the riverbank. Bancroft built worker housing in Rockford Village on Rockford and Ivy roads. His son donated land uphill from the mills for Rockford Park in 1889 and 1895 (see **Kentmere Parkway and Rockford Park** on p. 140). As late as the 1940s, this was called the largest cotton dyeing and finishing plant in the world, with a soaring, 250-foot yellow-brick smokestack (by Heinecke, a New York firm, 1911). Bancroft Mills was bought out in 1961 and later closed. Only part of the extensive original complex survives, and, in 2007, a developer proposed demolishing most of the toxics-laced remainder and building condominiums.

WL92 Willard Street Vicinity Houses

c. 1901–1905 first nine houses built. Willard St., between Rockford and Red Oak rds.

When William P. Bancroft helped establish Rockford Park (see **Kentmere Parkway and Rockford Park** on p. 140), he had his Woodlawn Company purchase adjacent land for deed-restricted development. To some, the site seemed inconveniently remote, but, in fact, an electric trolley ran nearby; the park was adja-

WL91 BANCROFT MILLS, photo 1931, with Rockford and Ivy roads in foreground, and BRANDYWINE GRANITE QUARRY (BR24) at top

WL92 WILLARD STREET VICINITY HOUSES, Stirling H. Thomas House

cent; and one could enjoy "a high elevation, excellent water, sewers, gas, electric light and telephone service." As an affluent and daring group of young "progressive folk" shook off "the spell of Wilmington's [architectural] conservatism," they commissioned homes from Philadelphia architects in Colonial Revival, Tudor Revival, and Arts and Crafts styles, as described in a Boston magazine, *Indoors and Out* (October 1905). The first house was the outstanding, half-timbered Stirling H. Thomas House at 2501 Willard (c. 1901; addition c. 1916, DeArmond, Ashmead and Bickley). Local building codes mandated its brick first floor; the omission of a veranda and dormers, features still popular at the time, was considered innovative. The next resident of the neighborhood was Bancroft and Sons engineer (and newlywed) Daniel Moore Bates, who built at 1903 Greenhill Avenue a Colonial Revival farmhouse of brick covered with "vigorous roughcast" (c. 1902, Frank Miles Day and Brother). Young lawyer Christopher Ward visited him and liked the area; he bought a big lot at 8 Red Oak Road and erected a low, brick Colonial Revival, which included a large library and rooms for two servants (1904–1905, Charles Barton Keen). Keen simultaneously designed the Thomas F. Bayard House at 9 Red Oak Road (featured in *Brickbuilder*, February 1908), deriving it from the Maryland house, Mount Clare (1757–1760); its projecting front porch has been removed. An old farmhouse was remodeled as the Colonial Revival "Little White House" at 2425 Delaware Avenue. Bancroft, Ward said, "foresaw a lot of cheap little houses only" at his Rockford Park development and was surprised at the expensive ones that went up. For a time, the settlement remained isolated; Ward recalled (1973), "We lived as a sort of separate community, much at each other's houses in the winter, sitting out on porches in the warmer weather." Envious locals called the upscale place "Snobtown."

WL93 Tower Hill School

1919–1920, Brown and Whiteside. 1948–1949 gym, G. Morris Whiteside II. 1962–1963 preschool, Dollar, Bonner, Blake and Manning. 1970–1973 Library-Science Building, Peter C. Anderson and John Bue for Dollar, Bonner and Funk. 1994–1996 Arts Center, Moeckel Carbonell Associates. 17th St. and Rising Sun Ln.

Founded to educate the children of Wilmington's elites, Tower Hill School occupies a neighborhood once thick with du Pont family mansions (see St. Amour, CH23). Irénée du Pont and his cousins established the school, construction of which cost more than twice the $300,000 estimate. It was the most important early commission of Brown and Whiteside. A rendering of the Colonial Revival facade survives by Reah de B. Robinson, chief draftsman for the firm, and construction by DuPont Engineering Company was recorded in a series of photographs. In his 1970s design for the Library-Science Building, architect Anderson recalls being influenced by "the brick structures, concrete frames, and waffle slabs" popularized by The Architects Collaborative in Cambridge, Massachusetts. The main building was renovated by a Wilmington firm, Kelly and Johnson Architects, in 1999–2002.

WL94 Gibraltar

1844. 1915 enlarged, DeArmond, Ashmead and Bickley. 1927 enlarged, Albert Ely Ives. Pennsylvania and Greenhill aves.

Wilmington cotton merchant and agriculturist John R. Brinckle owned an extensive farm here and landscaped the grounds elaborately. His boxy, three-story dwelling with low hipped roof is austerely plain, of squared stone blocks. The name "Gibraltar" is derived from the Mediterranean promontory of Gibraltar in reference to the house's perch on a rocky ledge. H. Rodney Sharp purchased the house in September 1909, although it was

WL94 GIBRALTAR, solarium prior to collapse of its roof in 2004

"quite desolate"; he had fallen in love with the "marvelous staircase." Wilmington's quarries provided convenient stone for expansion, and Sharp tripled the size of the house. He died in 1968, and by the mid-1990s it seemed that rundown Gibraltar would be demolished. Preservation Delaware took over, hoping to find an adaptive reuse for the building. In the meantime, deterioration sadly continued.

WL94.1 Garden

1916–1923, Marian Cruger Coffin

H. Rodney Sharp worked for industrialist Pierre S. du Pont and was married to his sister, so the development of the six-acre Gibraltar gardens can be compared to Pierre's contemporaneous Longwood Gardens a few miles north. (Pierre often visited the Sharp's garden at lunchtime and, in 1915, proposed to his wife amid the roses.) Coffin created a series of "rooms" (1916) and designed a curving marble stair that sweeps down from the house. Photographs of the 200-foot bald cypress allee (designed 1919) appeared in garden magazines. The twenty-four cypresses, planted in spring 1921, were cut into formal specimens to answer the same purpose as a hedge, though today they are towering. A one-foot-high ivy-covered wall, smoketrees, and statuary lined the path, which terminated at a three-arched Italian-style tea house with imported *rosso verona* columns. Garden restoration was undertaken in 1998–1999 by Rodney Robinson.

New Castle Hundred

The low-lying region south of Wilmington, bounded by the Delaware and Christina rivers, was long agricultural but is now laced with divided highways and densely built-up. There were a number of country seats in this fertile area, but they have nearly all been destroyed. Eden Park, where colorful French immigrant Pierre Bauduy raised Merino sheep in the early nineteenth century, was leveled in 1892–1895. Swanwyck, one of several buildings that have been attributed to Bauduy, was hailed by architectural historians in the 1930s as a rare, Regency-style villa; it was already rundown, and what remained was spoiled by remodeling in 2003. Dunleith (1847, John Notman) was torn down about 1962. Long Hook, on the Christina River near I-495, part of which may have been seventeenth century, was demolished after a fire in the 1980s. Boothhurst (1842 addition by John Notman), home in the early twentieth century to architect Laussat Richter Rogers, burned in the 1990s and has been replaced with a housing development. Philadelphia architect Thomas U. Walter listed the Holcomb mansion, Devondale Hall, among his top professional accomplishments, but all traces of it have vanished beneath New Castle County Airport. This record of disappointments is redeemed, however, by Delaware's architectural showpiece, the town of New Castle, where many outstanding old buildings survive. And of quirky interest along Christiana Road west of Hare's Corner is an Egyptian Revival style house (early 1960s, Jack Hawkins Sr.) still occupied by its builder, who admires that ancient civilization.

NORTH OF NEW CASTLE

NC1 Delaware Health and Social Services Herman M. Holloway Sr. Campus (Delaware State Hospital)

1894–1895 Main Building, Elijah James Dallett for Baker and Dallett. Many additions. U.S. 13 and I-295

This facility on more than 100 campus-like acres contains only a fraction of the buildings it had at the time of World War II. The remnant will probably continue to shrink, as several structures now stand empty. The Wilmington Almshouse, founded in 1785, moved here in the 1880s as Delaware Almshouse, developing the Blandy Farm at Hare's Corner. Its red brick Italianate headquarters was the last commission of a noted Philadelphia architect (1882–1884, Stephen De-

NC1 DELAWARE HEALTH AND SOCIAL SERVICES HERMAN M. HOLLOWAY SR. CAMPUS (DELAWARE STATE HOSPITAL)

catur Button). The later Delaware Hospital for the Insane next door was a near-twin; it survives today as Main Building, whereas the Almshouse was razed in 1967. Main Building housed women downstairs, men upstairs, with a machine shop and kitchen in the basement; the attached Annex at rear was for "colored" patients. Nearby, Brown and Whiteside designed two H-shaped facilities in Art Deco style (1930–1932), Continued Treatment Building and Re-Educational Building; the former is today's Debnam Building and the latter sits abandoned. Du Pont Highway in front of the campus was made into a divided road, the Delaware Dual Road (see **Du Pont Highway** on pp. 266–67) as a work relief project in 1933.

NC1.1 Chapel
1938–1939, G. Morris Whiteside II

This frame chapel in Colonial Revival style was partly funded by the WPA and built by seventy-two workers. It featured a modernist novelty, the first "color organ" installed in a church. Designed in the 1930s by Mary Hal-

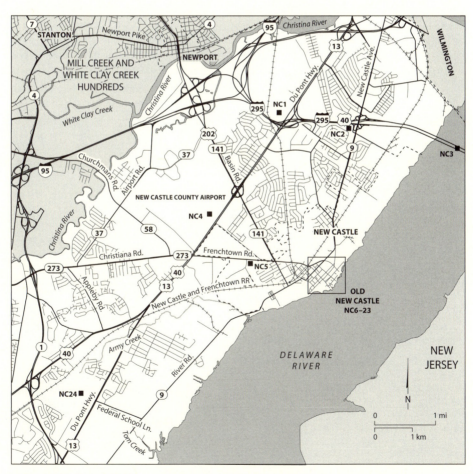

NEW CASTLE HUNDRED

NC2 MIKE'S FAMOUS ROADSIDE REST

lock Greenewalt, known as a "pioneer in color music," it was meant to enthrall mental patients with the sight of colors flowing through long glass tubes rising from behind an altar made of structural glass as well as through lamps in niches in the walls. This experiment seems to have been shortlived, as the interior was redesigned and given a conventional wooden altar, reredos arch, iron railing, and cork floor (1955–1956, Victorine and Samuel Homsey).

NC2 Mike's Famous Roadside Rest

1997–1998, Joseph Chickadel for Design Collaborative Inc. DE 9 and I-295

The award-winning, 40,000-square-foot retail complex strategically positioned along a busy highway at the approaches to the Delaware Memorial Bridge (NC3) combines a Harley-Davidson motorcycle dealership, restaurant, and museum, built around an existing Howard Johnson motel registration booth. Market studies were carried out to determine what visitors would potentially like to see. Various themes were combined: old warehouses, Art Deco design, oversized signage, and Route 66 nostalgia. Extensive use was made of reclaimed materials: 100-year-old yellow pine flooring, bricks from abandoned buildings, a wooden steam shovel. Seats and doors were made from machine-part molds. The result is some of the most theatrical architecture in Delaware.

NC3 Delaware Memorial Bridge

1947–1951 south span, Howard, Needles, Tammen and Bergendoff, engineers, with O. H. Ammann for Ammann and Whitney, and A. G. Lorimer for Lorimer and Rose, architect. 1964–1968 north span, Howard, Needles, Tammen and Bergendoff, with E. Lionel Pavlo. I-295 over Delaware River

Building on their enthusiasm for good roads, some Delawareans had advocated a bridge to New Jersey as early as 1917, and more seriously in 1927–1928 (a tunnel was suggested, too). The legislature approved a bond issue for a World War II memorial bridge in April 1945, and New Jersey soon agreed to participate in the project. The 2,150-foot main span of the bridge was sixth longest in the world (all the rivals being in the United States). Its design resembled Oakland (number four) and Bronx-Whitestone (number five) bridges, both about 2,300 feet in span. The steel towers, of cellular construction with riveted plates and weighing 4,000 tons each, rose 440 feet above the river and, being free from diagonal bracing, displayed breathtaking verticality. The east tower, from its base on marine clays to the top, was 559 feet, taller than the Washington Monument; 12,600 miles of twenty-inch cable were used, each composed of 8,284 wires. Including approaches, the bridge measures 3.5 miles.

NC3 DELAWARE MEMORIAL BRIDGE, under construction 1967

By 1961, bridge traffic was 53 percent heavier than predicted a decade earlier, and plans were launched for a second span, the whole forming the longest twin span in the world. Vice President Hubert Humphrey helped dedicate the new bridge in 1968. The two spans look nearly identical, but the second rests mostly on steel piles, not the concrete bases of the first, and it is heavier, for increased rigidity (the greatest pull on any one cable being twenty-two million pounds, versus eighteen million for the first bridge). Today the Delaware Memorial Bridge is one of the state's best-known structures.

NC5 AIR SERVICE HANGAR

NC4 New Castle County Airport (Greater Wilmington Airport)

1941, established. Basin Rd. and U.S. 13

Laid out in farm fields at sleepy Hare's Corner, Delaware's first public airport was just begun when Japan attacked Pearl Harbor on December 7, 1941 (see also Dover Air Force Base, DV18). The U.S. Army leased it for a dollar a year starting in 1942 and hastily built seventy-nine buildings in ninety days, 300 in a year. New Castle Army Air Base housed 5,000 men. From here, bombers and fighters came and went from Europe, and C-54 Skymasters ferried supplies to India. Little, if anything, survives of the wartime facilities. A control tower and terminal were built postwar (1954–1956, W. Ellis Preston). The terminal has lost some of its original touches, but retains colored terrazzo floors and plate-glass windows. A stair with aluminum handrails leads past a big aerial photograph taken in the 1950s of a sparsely developed New Castle County to an observation deck overlooking the runways. Nationwide, few terminals of this vintage survive intact.

NC5 Air Service Hangar

1936. DE 273 and Centerpoint Blvd.

The abandoned hangar is all that remains of Bellanca Airfield, famous in aviation history. Henry Belin du Pont, avid promoter of flight, purchased a 360-acre farm and lured legendary, Italian-born aircraft designer Giuseppe Bellanca from Staten Island in 1928. In a factory here, Bellanca would build more than 1,000 airplanes, including *Miss Veedol*, first to cross the Pacific nonstop (1931). The Air Service, Inc., hangar—the original of 1928 was replaced by this one after a fire—was not officially part of the Bellanca factory but was used by public pilots. Bellanca remained in business until 1954. In later years, Centerpoint Boulevard was built down the main runway and the site developed for business. The lone surviving hangar (closed 1960) was threatened with demolition in 2003, but a grassroots group mobilized to save it.

NEW CASTLE

This time capsule of a riverfront town (pop. 4,862) was founded by the Dutch in 1651 as Fort Casimir, later New Amstel; its current name dates from the British takeover in 1664. The fort has long since vanished, but Dutch dikes are obvious at Wilmington Road (Broad Dyke) and 2nd Street (Dyke Street, terminating in Foot Dyke north of town). This was the first community in Delaware deliberately laid out, with Front Street, or the Strand, paralleling the busy waterfront and a Green two blocks inland. One stepped-gable Dutch house, the so-called Tile House (1687), survived at 54 the Strand as late as

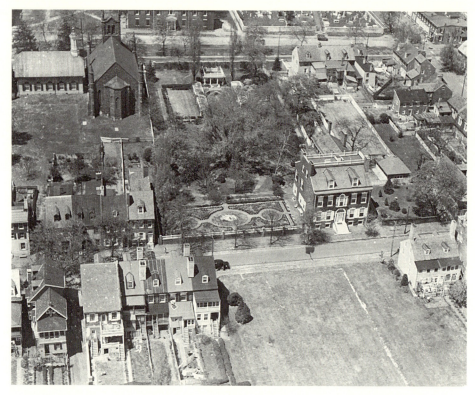

Aerial View of New Castle. In the foreground, houses along the Strand (NC20) have gardens running down to the banks of the Delaware River. Beside the large George Read House (NC21) lie its formal gardens. Inland on Second Street stands, at upper left, the Presbyterian Church (NC12), with its Gothic Revival successor next door. Photo c. 1945.

1884 (see p. 6). A handful of extant buildings have been attributed to the late seventeenth century, including the Dutch House (NC7), William Penn Guest House (206 Delaware St.), and Rosemont House kitchen wing (110 Delaware St.), but all of these may possibly be early eighteenth century.

William Penn landed in America at New Castle in 1682, and the Court House he established here (first edifice, c. 1689; see NC16) formed the eighteenth-century seat of government for Pennsylvania's "Three Lower Counties," today's Delaware. Tradition holds that the Court House cupola was appointed the center of the twelve-mile circle drawn as Delaware's northern border (1750), a circular boundary unique in America. (The circle was difficult to draw and came out somewhat irregular.) At the heart of town lies the Green, overseen by the Trustees of New Castle Common, an institution unique to this place and dating back centuries. By 1704, the Common consisted of 1,068 acres outside of town held in trust for the community; today these lands have been sold or developed, and the trustees manage the endowment. The trustees planted trees on the Green in 1807. The seventy-five elms added in 1851 grew to huge size and were an unforgettable feature of New Castle until killed by disease.

English-born Philadelphia architect Benjamin Henry Latrobe—who lived for a time on the Strand—was commissioned to survey the streets, a project carried out in 1805 and resulting in an ink-and-watercolor depiction of many of the buildings in town, drawn by his twenty-three-year-old assistant, Robert Mills, later a famous architect in his own right. This *Survey of New Castle* offers a level of architectural documentation rivaled by few American places of the period. Two versions survive, one at the Delaware Public Archives (DV15) and the other at the New Castle Historical Society (NC19). They record the appearance of the community before a disastrous fire burned the southern half of the Strand in 1824. Its houses were promptly rebuilt in Federal style.

In time, New Castle's outlying districts became industrialized. New Castle Manufacturing Company (active 1833–1857) was the only Delaware firm to make locomotives, of which one survives, *Memnon* (1848, B&O Railroad Museum, Baltimore). Late-nineteenth-century commerce mostly bypassed the center of New Castle, although a general prosperity was suggested by the Opera House (1879, Theophilus P. Chandler Jr.), which has lost its attractive tower and which is where Wild West Show star Annie Oakley and opera singer Enrico Caruso once performed. A restoration of the building's sheet-metal cornice in 2003 involved microscopic paint analysis to ensure accuracy of color for repainting. The old part of town mostly slumbered until its rediscovery by tourists in the early twentieth century. By the 1920s, a process of gentrification had begun that continues to this day.

New Castle has fascinated generations of architectural historians. Philadelphia antiquarian John Fanning Watson twice paid historical visits in the 1820s to the Tile House. Souvenir bricks from that building circulated widely in the last decades of the nineteenth century. Early-twentieth-century photographers recorded the town's architecture extensively, and a 1926 issue of *White Pine* was devoted to it: "There are few communities to-day which have retained their early American flavor as completely." "A Day in Old New Castle" debuted in May 1924 as a means to raise money to repair Immanuel Church (NC10), with 800 visitors each paying fifty cents to tour historic homes and buildings. From this beginning—sometimes said to be the first "open house day" anywhere—grew the largest such event on the East Coast. The *Baltimore Sun* newspaper said in 1932, "For architects, especially, it is a field day. They come from Boston and New York, Philadelphia and Baltimore to take notes on design and detail; everywhere they may be seen sketching." *National Geographic* in 1935 called New Castle "one of the most charming old towns in the United States . . . entirely unspoiled and 'unrestored.'" By that time, a local historical society was thriving. The following year saw publication of the WPA guidebook *New Castle on the Delaware*.

Prominent Wilmingtonian Colonel Daniel Moore Bates campaigned in the

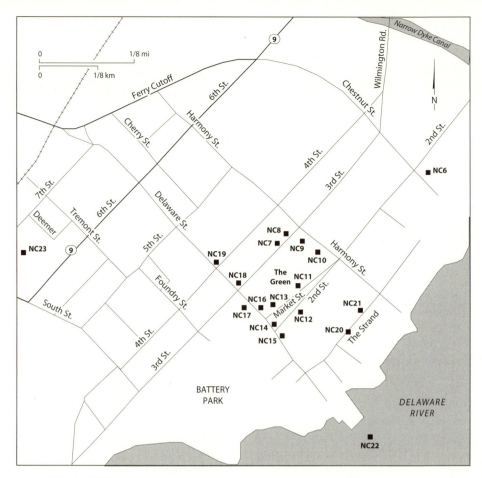

OLD NEW CASTLE

1940s for turning the town into a second Colonial Williamsburg, but little came of this, thankfully, as many nineteenth-century buildings would have been demolished under the plan generated by Boston architects Perry, Shaw and Hepburn. The town's quaint courthouse square appeared on the cover of *Saturday Evening Post* in March 1962. The First Delaware Preservation Conference, organized by architects Al Kruse and Robert Raley for the AIA, was held in New Castle the following September. In 1967, New Castle was named a National Historic Landmark. The town celebrated its 350th anniversary in 2001.

NC6 Fort Casimir Site

Fort extant 1651–c. 1679. 2nd and Chestnut sts.

Following establishment of the fort by Peter Stuyvesant, Dutch traders built homes along the riverfront just south—the genesis of New Castle. 2nd Street, oldest in town, approached the fort across a narrow isthmus, and the stronghold had marshes on three sides. Probably it resembled Dutch forts at Manhattan and elsewhere, square with earthen bastions at the corners. A contemporary account gives its riverfront length as 210 feet. It was garrisoned by nine soldiers with thirteen cannons (but no powder) when captured by the Swedes. The fort was demolished in the 1670s, and the site may have become a tannery. Fortunately, the "Fort Lot" was little-developed over the centuries. Starting in 1925, it served as a busy ferry terminal to New Jersey (ruined piers survive offshore). All traces of the fort were assumed to have washed away, as a stone marker of 1905 says, but limited archaeology in 1986 showed that it probably still exists beneath six feet of fill under a grassy lot. A ditch was found that may have formed part of the defenses. Various seventeenth-century artifacts came to light: yellow Dutch brick, majolica pottery from the Netherlands, and gray Rhenish stoneware.

NC7 DUTCH HOUSE

NC7 Dutch House

1690–1710 period, with later changes. 1938 restored, George E. Pope, Albert Kruse, and James H. W. Thompson. c. 1939 garden, Robert Wheelwright. 32 E. 3rd St.

The tiny brick-and-frame house with a steep roof was long thought to date to around 1660, the product of Dutch builders. Historians pointed to, among other things, the very wide overhang of the front eave (with a matched-board soffit below), this being a feature of several Dutch dwellings in America, including the Holmes-Hendrickson House, Monmouth County, New Jersey (mid-eighteenth century). By the early twentieth century, the house's quaintness was irresistible to artists, such as the young painter shown with her easel "in front of a famous Dutch colonial house" in *National Geographic* (1935). Looking to the town's Tercentenary, Mary Wilson Thompson's Delaware Society for the Preservation of Antiquities bought the place in 1937. The group toyed with calling it the "Old Swedish House." Kruse restored it, rebuilding the south wall and replacing the floorboards downstairs (using them, it seems, to build the garden fence). He roofed the house with "old moss" asbestos shingles and painted the interior light "Quaker gray," except the kitchen windows which were colored "Dutch blue." Louise du Pont Crowninshield furnished the rooms. On opening day, Mrs. Thompson greeted guests in the kitchen, showing the fireplace Kruse had uncovered.

The Dutch House has for decades been operated as a museum by New Castle Historical Society. Their repainting in 2001 of the exterior trim in red, based on paint analysis, caused a stir. Two years later, architectural historian Jeff Klee removed some wall plaster and floorboards in an attempt to resolve the date of the house. He discovered that the building was fashioned with a series of heavy timber frames or "H bents"—sometimes, but not always, a sign of Dutch construction. As with the Ryves Holt House, Lewes (ES18), the house originally had exposed ceiling joists with chamfered edges and lamb's-tongue stops, and wall posts. Between the posts is brick nogging. According to Klee's analysis, the building was originally all-frame, consisting of a single room with a big cooking fireplace on the north wall; later in the eighteenth century the interior was partitioned and the house encased in a brick exterior wall, as one sees today. In the early nineteenth century, the end chimney was replaced with a center one, the roof was raised, and the interior refinished. It seems likely that the present front eave represents a rebuilding of that element higher on the front of the house following the raising of the street level here (one now steps *down* from the sidewalk into the entry). Why the eave is so wide is unclear, unless it provided storage space. Nothing is indisputably Dutch about the place, and none of the owners' names was ever anything but English. "Not Really So Dutch After All," read a Wilmington *News-Journal* newspaper headline reporting the new findings.

NC8 Old Library

1890–1892, Furness, Evans and Company. 40 E. 3rd St.

New Castle's Library Company, founded in 1812, was housed in the Academy (NC9) for decades before this facility was commissioned. Furness was then completing the University of Pennsylvania Library, which made him a good choice. Local contractor H. McCaulley, who was busy at the Delaware State Hospital (NC1), erected a high fence that kept the public wondering what the library would look like. The authors of *Frank Furness: The Complete Works* (1996) attribute the design to a member of his firm, William M. Camac, but note the difficulty of assigning credit precisely during these years when the office was busy and expanding. Whether by Furness or an assistant, the octagonal structure with tall roof and cupola is an extremely clever synthesis of Queen Anne style and glazed-header-brick Colonial Revival, the oversized fanlight and wind vane making witty reference to Federal-era features elsewhere in the historic town. As in Furness's design for the University of Pennsylvania Library (1888–1890), illumination comes from skylights and is admitted to the basement through glass panels on the floor. When the building eventually became a museum, paint analysis (1982) by Matthew Mosca, who also worked on the George Read House (NC21), allowed the restoration of the original color scheme.

NC9 Old Academy

1799, with additions. 3rd and Harmony sts.

A resolution in 1798 by the Trustees of the Common called for "the funds arising from the lands" they oversaw to be used "for the erection and support of a college." This nicely proportioned, seven-bay, two-story brick school (never actually a college) was built on a corner of the Green. Stylistic similarities between it and the George Read House (NC21) have led to its being attributed to Read's contractor, Peter Crouding, without evidence. Inside the pedimented entrance bay (with Palladian window) stands a glorious, unrestored "antler stair" that divides as it descends. A cupola was added to the building in 1811. The Academy remained a school until 1930, following which, a restoration filled in a big arch that had been cut at the front door. The building remains in use as a Sunday school.

NC10 Immanuel Episcopal Church on the Green

1703–1706 nave. By 1727 south porch. 1820–1830 transepts and tower, William Strickland. c. 1850 chancel, John Notman. 1859–1860 transepts lengthened and east apse, Stephen Decatur Button. 1980–1982 reconstructed, John Milner Associates. 2nd and Harmony sts.

The oldest Anglican church in the United States with continuous Sunday services, Immanuel is the most venerable survivor of the Delaware Valley churches established by the London-based Society for Propagation of the Gospel. The brick building of the early eighteenth century—today's nave—was unchanged when architects Benjamin Henry Latrobe and Robert Mills depicted it on their survey of 1805: a simple rectangular box with compass-headed windows and clipped gables. It was then in disrepair following the post-Revolutionary de-

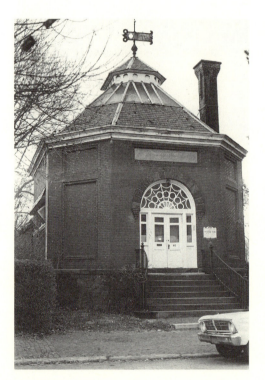

NC8 OLD LIBRARY

cline of Anglicanism. The walls were stuccoed by 1817, and Strickland was hired to greatly enlarge the building along the lines of an English parish church with a tall spire on a square tower over the crossing of the nave and transepts. The Trustees of the Common maintained the four-dial town clock in the tower, the original mechanism of which ran faithfully until 1945. The rise of the high-church Ecclesiological movement in the mid-nineteenth century saw further changes to the church. Notman created a chancel by recessing the center of the west wall seven feet into the tower; he then inserted a stained glass window above the altar. Button lengthened the transepts. Laussat R. Rogers redesigned the interior in a Colonial Revival manner in 1918, a direction continued by the firms of Pope and Kruse (1951), the Homseys (1958), and Fletcher and Buck (1966), so that the building became decidedly a hybrid, with a mid-nineteenth-century plan but twentieth-century pseudo-colonial fittings.

In February 1980, a fire in a marsh wafted sparks that ignited the cedar shake roof, and the building was gutted. History-minded parishioners narrowly prevented firemen from demolishing the leaning north nave wall. Restoration architect Milner and his associates studied the ruins and discovered much information about the building's history, including the fact that the various additions were "almost improvisatory" in their physical connections to each other (*Restoration and Rehabilitation*, 1984). The first step was to correct these serious structural flaws. Six bodies were found buried beneath the floor, as was a cannonball, which seemed to confirm the tradition that Immanuel had been built atop a seventeenth-century fort or blockhouse. The restoration sought historical accuracy, but with fireproofing and modern amenities. Clay tiles were used instead of wooden shingles on the roof; the new roof was ten times heavier than the original and had to be borne on steel trusses. Inside, Milner proposed a return to 1822, this being the date the transepts were first completed and well before the muddling modifications. It was not a purist approach, Milner admitted, given that the present, longer transepts had come decades later; moreover, the chancel was to be retained for liturgical purposes even though it had not existed in 1822.

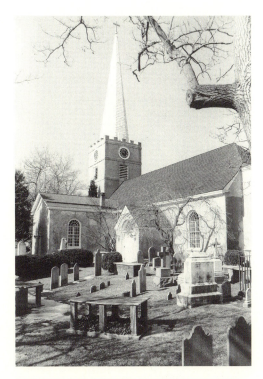

NC10 IMMANUEL EPISCOPAL CHURCH ON THE GREEN

Almost nothing was known of the interior's early appearance. The result is, therefore, not an exact replica of any one historical moment in the life of the church but rather a "reconstruction in accordance with an interpretation of the aesthetic standards of an 1820–1822 interior," as Milner explained.

Immanuel stands in a singularly appealing churchyard, where weathered monuments in a variety of styles press close upon each other and thirty-one Revolutionary patriots are buried. Granite gateposts were added in 1843 (east) and 1855 (south).

NC11 Arsenal

1809–1811. 1854–1855 enlarged, John G. Lankey. 1935–1936 remodeled, Laussat R. Rogers for WPA. Market St., east side of the Green

The U.S. government allocated money for arsenals in 1804, and a year later Benjamin Henry Latrobe and Robert Mills marked the future site of this one on their town survey. The original one-story building, perhaps with arched wagon entrances into the gable ends, housed cannon, grape shot, powder, and supplies.

NC11 ARSENAL

Later, it served as a barracks, cholera hospital, post office, custom house, and railroad office. The Trustees of the Common took over in 1852 and established the New Castle Institute, adding a second story (as seen in the brickwork) and Italianate cupola and changing the fenestration and doorways. It remained a school until 1930. A remodeling moved the spirited cannon-and-eagle bas relief from north gable to south and replaced the cupola with a more Colonial-style one, eliminating, according to a WPA newsletter, the "excrescences of the rococo period of American architecture." For years, the building has housed a restaurant. A renovation (1999–2001, Bernardon Haber Holloway) replaced the cedar shake roof with terne metal (steel sheets covered with a protective alloy finish).

NC12 New Castle Presbyterian Church

1707. 1712 extended. 1949–1950 restored, Albert Kruse. 25 E. 2nd St.

Dutch Calvinists worshipped in early New Castle. By 1699, their church had decayed and the congregation had become Presbyterian, headed by a Scotsman. In 1706, it joined with six other congregations officially to found the Presbyterian Church in the New World. A year later, this brick building was erected, with a gambrel and jerkinhead roof, and compass-headed windows. Unusually, the cove cornice rose into the gables. The Presbyterians resented the fact that the rival Anglicans had built directly on the Green (Immanuel Church, NC10), on a site they considered their own as successors to the Dutch. The 2nd Street location was as close to the Green as possible, and an Anglican complained that "our troublesome neighbours have builded themselves a chapel in the very shadow of Immanuel." The Presbyterians became still more troublesome in the 1720s, with the arrival of an "inundation" of Scots-Irish "fiery zealots," "the bitterest railers against the [Anglican] Church that ever trod upon American Ground" (Bankert, 1989). Charismatic Reverend Gilbert Tennent, later a founder of Princeton, served them here in 1726. A balcony was added in 1801 by Jacob Belville. Pews were installed in 1818 and the interior rearranged; the big end window was sealed up and a pulpit placed before it, following what a trustees report called "the most approved plan of modern-built churches by making single pews all fronting toward the pulpit." The exterior colonial brickwork was hidden by stucco in 1833, scored on the front facade to resemble stone.

The building became a Sunday School with the construction of a brownstone Gothic church immediately north in 1854. Over time, the latter structure proved poorly built and expensive to maintain, and in 1946 the congregation voted to destroy it and restore the colonial church as a place of worship. Demolition took place four years later, amid controversy. In a restoration in which Perry, Shaw and Hepburn of Colonial Williamsburg advised, Kruse removed exterior stucco on the eighteenth-century building, which revealed the remains of a string course and keystones that had been chiseled off. He remodeled the interior based on the extant one at Christ Church, Laurel (ws23), reconstructing the high pulpit on the long wall opposite the door, which he unsealed, along with the big window on the end-wall. The hook for the pulpit canopy survived. Floorboards were taken up to reveal the original brick floors. Oak roof trusses were reinforced with steel and all windows were replaced. The "mysterious blue-green" paint scheme inside was based on a single section of surviving cornice, under ten coats. Where the brownstone church had stood, Kruse built an education building (1957–1958)—Colonial Revival, of course.

NC13 SHERIFF'S HOUSE AND JAIL SITE

NC13 Sheriff's House and Jail Site

1857–1858, Samuel Sloan. Market St., between Court House and Arsenal

The brownstone Italianate Sheriff's House runs counter to the local colonial, red-brick aesthetic. It is a remnant of a much larger correctional complex by a prolific Philadelphia architect, who modeled it on a facility he had completed in Norristown, Pennsylvania. (Later, in 1871–1872, he would design the Kent County prison and sheriff's house in Dover.) The New Castle Sheriff's House was erected by a renowned masonry firm of the Quaker City, Carman and Dobbins. Behind and extending north was the thirty-eight-cell jail (the whole forming an L), and towering stone walls on three sides enclosed a prison yard. Inside the wall (just back from the sidewalk and about half-way to the Arsenal) stood the infamous whipping post and pillory, long decried in the national press as "a Relic of Barbarism which the state refuses to abandon." This "disgrace" made a lurid cover story for *Harper's Weekly* (1868), and the writer Theodore Dreiser denounced it after a visit in 1901 (Hakutani, 2003). Sturdy construction of Trenton, New Jersey, brownstone aimed to "impress one with an idea that escape would be almost impossible." The jail was closed in 1901 and demolished a decade later, except for a few surviving cells, two doors to which are visible high on the rear wall of the Sheriff's House. The pattern of the jail's foundations is visible in the grass during droughts, and archaeology suggests that whole cells may remain buried underground. The Sheriff's House served as the New Castle Club in the mid-twentieth century. In 1963, the state senate voted money to pay for its demolition, one critic in the Wilmington newspaper calling it "the world's worst monstrosity," but a campaign by a local editor helped save it. The town police occupied it from 1971 to 1997 but then moved out, citing its disrepair.

NC14 Town Hall

1823. 2nd and Delaware sts.

England has many "head houses" like this one—town halls at the front of a series of market stalls—and one can still be seen in Philadelphia at New Market (c. 1805). The New Castle market stalls were entered through the big arch and once extended down the grassy median on Second Street; although demolished c. 1880, traces of their roofline are faintly visible today against the rear of Town Hall. The three-story brick hall—in basic form, about a forty-foot cube—housed the town council on the second floor. The cupola, with ball-and-sail weathervane, is one of Delaware's best (see the frontispiece on p. iv). The edifice now houses the zoning office, a newspaper, and the office of the Trustees of the Common. A renovation (Buck Simpers Architect + Associates) brought the building up to code so that town meetings could again take place inside. Behind stands a statue of William Penn (1984, Charles C. Parks).

NC15 Cloud's Row

1803–1804. Delaware and 2nd sts.

Delaware's oldest rowhouse block suggests the ambitious, urbanistic pretensions of early-

NC15 CLOUD'S ROW

nineteenth-century New Castle. It was built on speculation by merchant Harlan Cloud of Pennsylvania, who was recalling Philadelphia. Five tenements and a store are lined up in a row, multistory but originally just one room deep, with shared chimneys and winder stairs in a corner. These units changed hands many times before 1850. Cloud's name is recalled today partly because his then-new brick row with stone string course and lintels appeared on the Latrobe-Mills *Survey of New Castle* of 1805.

NC16 Court House

c. 1730–1731. 1765 wings, Richard McWilliam. 1771 roof altered. 1802 east wing extended. 1840–1845 new west wing. 1867 bay at rear. 1935–1936 restoration, Laussat R. Rogers. 1956–1963 restoration, Albert Kruse for Pope, Kruse and McCune, with Perry, Shaw and Hepburn. 211 Delaware St.

One of the oldest public buildings in the United States and now a state museum, this National Historic Landmark is Delaware's most significant English-colonial edifice. It served as meeting place of the Delaware General Assembly (1704–1776) and as state capitol (1776–1777) in addition to housing all state and federal courts for generations. Restoration architect Kruse made sketches that showed four stages in its development, starting with an earlier courthouse (c. 1689), established by William Penn and burned in a failed jailbreak in 1729. Its stone foundations, excavated by C. A. Weslager, are visible though an opening in the floor. The central block of the present building replaced it, originally with a hipped gambrel roof and plaster cove cornice. A dog-legged stringcourse steps up, not once, but twice, upon turning the corner, as on the Town Hall, Philadelphia (1707–1710, demolished 1837). Two small wings were added, the east one (sometimes wrongly said to be seventeenth century) having been altered by the time Benjamin Henry Latrobe sketched the building from across the street in 1805. At various times the roof was rebuilt, the cupola replaced, and the building stuccoed and given a heavy, Gothic Revival porch around the door. The west wing of the 1840s was fireproof, with stone sleepers from the New Castle and Frenchtown Railroad (see **New Castle and Frenchtown Railroad** on p. 162) used in its foundations. In time, there was talk of replacing the aging structure, but nothing was done, and in 1881, the county government moved to Wilmington.

For years subsequently, the building was managed by the Trustees, who leased it to various parties. During the period that New Castle lay on a main U.S. north–south automobile route, Horace L. Deakyne operated a popular Colonial Revival tea room (1926–1942). The first restoration removed the porch and salmon-colored stucco and introduced the balcony; a second, more sweeping, stabilized the structure, lowered the windows to their original level, and returned the building to a colonial appearance inside and out. (Deep cracks were discovered, which might eventually have caused the building to collapse.) Fortunately, local objections forestalled the planned demolition of the west wing and rebuilding of the roof. In 1957, Kruse acquired 18,000 old bricks for restoration purposes by demolishing the abandoned Maple Lane Farm north of town.

The mellow, weathered walls of the Court House show how bricklaying changed over time, from English and glazed-header Flemish bonds of the 1730s to common bond of the 1840s. The terrace in front of the building, approached by deeply worn steps and surrounded by an iron railing (1830), postdates the leveling of the streets as stipulated by the Latrobe-Mills survey. This has long been a popular place to congregate, and deep grooves at the east corner are attributed to shad fishermen loitering and sharpening their knives.

NC16 COURT HOUSE

Prominent in the spacious courtroom is a pair of tall Doric pillars supporting the ceiling. All else in the room is restoration. This space has witnessed many historic events, including Catherine Bevan being sentenced in 1731 to be burned alive for the murder of her husband; also, the trial in 1848 of abolitionist Thomas Garrett, presided over by the Chief Justice of the U.S. Supreme Court, Roger B. Taney. The second floor originally housed the colonial assembly and, later, jury rooms. Thousands of tourists and schoolchildren visit these historic chambers annually. The exterior has been refurbished (2003, Frens and Frens and Bernardon Haber Holloway) and the white trim repainted in colors found by paint analysis: creamy yellow on the older parts, gray on the wing of the 1840s.

NC17 James Booth House

1713–1719 section at right. 1795–1797 extended. 1860s frame section. 216 Delaware St.

Deed records for the lot go back to 1670. The original brick section was built by merchant and innkeeper Sylvester Garland for his daughter, Soetje; decades later it was extended eastward, with no attempt to emulate the fine early-eighteenth-century brickwork of the original. The front door with bull's-eye windows dates from the first period of construction; its surround, from the second. The early stairway inside has heavy, turned spindles. Federal-era chimneypieces are richly ornamented. The house changed hands many times before prominent Delawarean James Booth Sr. bought it in 1785. Nine years later he sold it to John Bird, member of the committee that hired Benjamin Henry Latrobe to survey the town. His son, Robert Montgomery Bird, born in the enlarged house, became a famous novelist and playwright. Judge James Booth Jr. later lived here, and when juries deliberated late into the night, he would pull on slippers and gown and dash across the street to hear the verdict.

NC18 Kensey Johns House

1788–1789. 1795 rear wing. 3rd and Delaware sts.

One of Delaware's best-known Federal dwellings, this side-passage, double-pile brick

NC18 KENSEY JOHNS HOUSE

townhouse stands in a prominent location in town. Johns, later Chief Justice of Delaware, corresponded with his carpenters and himself sketched at least eight possible house plans (now at the Historical Society of Delaware), "a rare and meticulously kept body of written material" that has been analyzed by architectural historian Bernard Herman (Garrison, 1988). Almost half the cost of the house went to carpenters—Joseph Baldwin was lead carpenter as well as contractor and builder, working closely with Johns himself. Another 34 percent went to bricklayers, 4 percent to common laborers, and 8 percent to painters and plasterers. A wing at right housed Johns's office; an added rear wing accommodated cooking and casual dining, replacing a cellar kitchen. The front door with its flanking Doric pilasters and small pediment derives from Abraham Swan's *The British Architect* (1757), as do details of the richly paneled interior. Some door hardware was donated to Mount Vernon in 1910. On the back of the lot rose a house for Johns's son (1823). In 1925, architect Kenneth Clark did measured drawings for *White Pine*, spreading the fame of this attractive Federal home.

The passage of 200 years has hardly touched 3rd Street just north, and all its dwellings are interesting. Rodney House (1831), Number 16, has housed many lawyers and judges. Number 18 is the John Wiley House (c. 1801). It appears on the Latrobe-Mills survey, along with the Alexander House (c. 1804). Remarkably, some residents of this prestigious street are descendants of early settlers.

NC19 Amstel House

c. 1738. c. 1904 restored, Laussat R. Rogers. 4th and Delaware sts.

This outstanding brick colonial dwelling should properly be called the Dr. John Finney House, for its builder. Its current name, a reference to New Amstel town of the Dutch, was applied by an early-twentieth-century owner, Professor Henry H. Hay, probably following an idea of his restoration architect, Rogers. It has been claimed (doubtfully) that the back service wing is older than the single-pile main block. The front-gable shape of the house is unusual, but other examples exist (with cove cornices, too), such as the stone house Mt. Pleasant, Chester County, Pennsylvania (also 1730s), plus a few later ones on the Eastern Shore. The outstanding Doric front doorway must be an addition, perhaps 1760s, as its fanlight resembles one of that date at Mount Pleasant, Philadelphia. Several prominent New Castle citizens have owned the house, with surnames including Van Dyke, Johns, Bird, and Burnham. A stone slab on the floor of the hall (or "music room") refers to George Washington attending a wedding here in 1784, a witness reporting that he "stood upon the hearthstone and kissed the pretty girls—as was his wont." Paneling is extensive, though some was removed in the nineteenth century. In June 1929, just as Colonial Williamsburg got underway in Virginia, New Castle Historical Society bought the Amstel House for a museum, reportedly saving it from imminent destruction. The exceptionally quaint kitchen came to house the largest collection of colonial artifacts in the state, photographed by David Reyam for the WPA Index of American Design. Wealthy Wilmingtonians led the way in restoring Amstel House. The coves and the upper parts of the chimneys were rebuilt (1943–1944), but thankfully, the house has never been over-restored—thereby preserving the feeling of extraordinary age both outside and in.

NC19.1 Garden

1932–1937, Charles F. Gillette. 1938 toolhouse, Victorine du Pont Homsey

The Colonial Revival garden was designed by a Richmond landscape architect under the auspices of Mrs. E. Paul du Pont. Thirty drawings (1932, 1937) specified every detail, down to the hardware of the door in the garden wall. This garden wall of old brick (some graffitoed) was funded by the Colonial Dames, who hired a Williamsburg bricklayer; for some reason the sandstone coping was considered a distinctively Delawarean feature. Brandywine Garden Club installed the plantings. The sundial, supposedly incorporating a London Bridge baluster, came from Ashley Park, Walton-on-Thames, England, a gift of Mrs. A. Felix du Pont, whose walled garden at Elton near Wilmington was contemporaneous (begun 1929, William Wains; now demolished). The toolhouse was built of timbers from the old Pocopson Bridge, Pennsylvania, with windows and door from the razed Perkins House on Penny Hill, Wilmington (see BR19). Stepping stones came from historic sites in each of the thirteen colonies. Restoration was undertaken in 2000–2001, with much of the overgrown boxwood replaced with a Korean dwarf variety.

NC20 The Strand

18th century and later. Near riverfront

Now a prized address, this ancient street once lay directly on the river, but gradually land was reclaimed on the water side. On April 26, 1824, a fire whipped by a gale destroyed more than twenty houses at the south and east parts of the Strand. The area was quickly rebuilt in a homogeneous Federal-style aesthetic. In the twentieth century, the Lairds, then owners of the Read House (NC21), worked to preserve the streetscape. A proposal in 1950 to remove the 135-year-old cobblestones caused public

NC19 AMSTEL HOUSE, photo 1934

outcry. The whole ensemble of buildings is charming; individually, there are several noteworthy structures, nearly all of brick. At the south end stands the eighteenth-century Van Leuvenigh House, with glazed-header brickwork. Jefferson Hotel, Number 5, went up on the lots where the fire had begun and was enlarged in the 1890s. The Old Farmers Bank (c. 1850, J. McArthur) has cast-iron quoins and unusual all-header brickwork on a curving wall behind. The Gunning Bedford House (c. 1730), Number 6, was stripped of its longtime coat of stucco in 2003; the double watertable shows how the street level was lowered subsequent to the Latrobe-Mills survey (on which this house appears). A restoration in the 1990s returned the pent eave and removed stucco from the eighteenth-century house next door, too. Architect Benjamin Henry Latrobe's residence in New Castle was in one of the Aull Houses, Number 55. At the corner of Harmony Street rises the tall, handsome Immanuel Parish House (Charles Thomas House) of c. 1801, built as a hotel and identical to contemporaneous structures in Philadelphia. A presentation watercolor survives for its Colonial Revival wing (1913, Laussat R. Rogers).

NC21 George Read House

1797–1803. 42 the Strand

Delaware's best-known historic house is a masterpiece of the Federal style. The lawyer George Read grew up in the home of his father (a signer of the Declaration of Independence), which was located where the garden now stands; it burned in the fire of 1824. Young Read spent considerable time in Philadelphia and intended to imitate the townhouses of that city. Construction of this house is extensively documented in his papers, in which four plans survive. He built a wharf to receive foundation stone from Chester, Pennsylvania, as well as bricks transported from Philadelphia by shallop boats at a dollar per thousand. Carpenter Peter Crouding of Philadelphia was hired, and he visited sawmills to price lumber, choosing a supplier near Dagsboro, Sussex County. Drawings made by Crouding in December 1797 show decorative window heads for the facade, "one with stone kee [key] and brick arch the other all Stone";

NC21 GEORGE READ HOUSE, photo pre-1950

Read requested instead the same pattern as on his brother-in-law's house at 260 Arch Street, Philadelphia. These window heads were executed in marble in that city, stored for a year during which Read indecisively halted work, then finally delivered in June 1799. A shipment of 250,000 bricks came from Philadelphia in 1801, and Wilmington bricklayer Thomas Spikeman was engaged, the bricks to be laid "in the best manners according to the mode fashion and Stile of working & finishing the front Walls of the best Buildings in the City of Philadelphia." Stylistic similarities to that city were profound—for example, in the Palladian window centered above the fanlit front door, an arrangement found at Philadelphia's William Bingham Mansion (c. 1786, burned 1823).

After the exterior was finished, decoration of the interior commenced. Benjamin Henry Latrobe offered to furnish patterns for the cornices, though apparently he never did so, and later he privately faulted Read's "enormous house, in bad taste . . . close by the water, of which to enjoy a scanty view he sacrifices a range of the most valuable lots in town, by not building upon them, and he has then planted a range of Lombardy poplars which exclude the prospect as effectually as a brick wall." Crouding found mahogany for the doors, for which Read was eager. Composition ornament for chimneypieces was supplied by Philadelphian Robert Wellford in 1803. Subjects include "the triumph of *Mars* returning from Battle" and "*Diana* giving command to her hounds."

By constantly wetting the roof, the house was saved from the Strand fire of 1824, and subsequently it passed through the generations virtually unchanged. When an owner died

NEW CASTLE AND FRENCHTOWN RAILROAD

New Castle was the eastern terminus for one of America's earliest railroads, among the half dozen or so lines begun in 1828–1832 at the dawn of railroading (starting with the famous Baltimore and Ohio). As with earlier cross-peninsula turnpikes, the railroad was meant to speed travel between steamship lines on the two bays. New York engineer John Randel Jr. surveyed the sixteen-and-one-half mile route in spring 1830, as he had done for the Chesapeake and Delaware Canal six years earlier.

About 1,100 men were at work within a year. They affixed Georgia pine rails to tens of thousands of stone blocks, as was typical of the earliest railroads. The blocks were quarried at Port Deposit, Maryland, and Robinson and Carr's quarry in Pennsylvania and were brought here by boat. (Delays in delivery of the blocks led to part of the railroad being built with innovative white oak sleepers instead.) The wooden rails were capped with steel strips imported from Britain. The first horse-drawn passenger train ran across the completed line in one hour and twenty minutes on February 28, 1832; that fall, the locomotives *Delaware* and *Pennsylvania*, built by famed designer Robert Stevenson of Newcastle, England, came into use, traveling at a speed of fifteen miles an hour—alarming to some travelers.

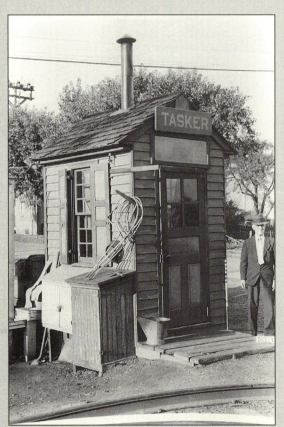

NEW CASTLE AND FRENCHTOWN RAILROAD TICKET OFFICE, PRIOR TO MOVE AND RESTORATION

In 1837, a second track was added, but that same year saw rival railroads connect Baltimore, Wilmington, and Philadelphia, leading to the obsolescence of the western portions of the line in 1856, one of the first railroad abandonments in the country. The distinctive stone blocks with paired drill holes were recycled for pavers or foundation material throughout New Castle. The eastern portion of the route (with modernized tracks, of course) is still used by Conrail today.

The railroad's ticket office (c. 1832; 1953 restored, Albert Kruse) in Battery Park is the second-oldest station extant in the United States, after the B&O station at Ellicott Mills, Maryland (1831). It resembles one built by the B&O in Baltimore in early 1830 (demolished). In later years, it was used as a farm shed until repaired in 1908 as a crossing watchman's box for the Pennsylvania Railroad. In 1946, its use was discontinued, and a Philadelphia museum nearly removed it. Instead, it was stored until re-erected here in New Castle.

in 1919, a Wilmington newspaper warned, "It would be a grave crime to let the old house fall into inappreciative ownership. To think of its being gutted of its treasures makes one shudder." Indeed, large sums were offered for the woodwork and the old boxwood shrubbery. Fortunately, investment banker Philip Laird and his wife, Lydia, bought the place and undertook a sensitive renovation (1920, Brown and Whiteside) and added the brick garden wall. New steps and railings followed the design of architect E. William Martin. The house was ivy-covered in 1925 when architect Kenneth Clark made measured drawings for *White Pine*. During this decade it attracted widespread attention in magazines as an ideal type of American residence. Wallpaper installed in the dining room (1927, Chapman Decorative Company, Philadelphia) showed scenes of New Castle history and architecture, including the Court House, George Read I House, and William Penn's landing in 1682.

Today, the Read House is a museum operated by the Historical Society of Delaware, its owner since 1975, when Lydia Laird died. Restorers mistakenly removed shutters from the exterior on the basis of there being none on the Latrobe-Mills survey (which omits shutters as a matter of course). In an ambitious campaign inside (1981–1986, Martin Rosenblum), spaces were refurnished according to the inventory of 1836, "the Goods & Chattels of George Read deceased," which organizes items by room (front and back parlors, entry, store room, kitchen, cellar, rooms upstairs, garret, nursery, library, yard, wash house, stable) and lists everything from mahogany chairs to oyster knives.

NC21.1 Garden

1847, attributed to Robert Buist

The extensive garden, consisting of a "parterre," "park," and kitchen garden at successively further distance from the street, was installed by then-owner William Couper. He may have hired Philadelphia nurseryman Buist, author of *The American Flower Garden Directory* (1832)—the evidence is a single bill for arborvitae. (Persistent attributions to Andrew Jackson Downing are baseless.) Over the years, this became quite a famous place, depicted, for example, in *House and Garden* in November 1901. A yulan magnolia from Buist's day fell in a storm in 1992, but one of his pear trees still stands, among many other specimen trees. Archaeology has uncovered garden features, as well as evidence of the first George Read house. The garden is undergoing restoration (begun 1991); a trellis and two gazebos were reinstated in 1996, based on nineteenth-century photographs.

NC22 Ice Piers

1803–1882. In Delaware River (visible from foot of Delaware St.)

Ice floes could crush wooden-hulled ships, so piers were built to form a barrier sheltering New Castle harbor. These were the first constructed anywhere on the Delaware River. An initial set of three was funded by state lottery and installed in 1795 and 1801. An act of Congress in 1802 appropriated $30,000 for many more Delaware River piers, provided the sites were ceded to the federal government. The Latrobe-Mills survey of 1805 shows four "U.S. Piers," results of the first nonmilitary federal funding applied to the Delaware. Further piers were added later, until the ascendancy of iron-hulled ships rendered them unnecessary. Today there are seven in all. The two oldest, square in plan, lie at the foot of Harmony Street and along the silted-up shoreline at Alexander's Alley. The five hexagonal-plan piers, left to right as seen from shore, respectively date to 1874, 1879, 1882, 1875, and 1854 (the last now linked to shore by a walkway). The piers are rubble-cored with ashlar granite blocks outside, resting on wooden cribwork (visible at low tide). Some granite mooring posts and iron straps survive. The Ice Piers were a precursor to a much larger project at Lewes (ES25).

NC23 Fox Lodge at Lesley Manor (Allen Lesley House)

1855, Thomas and James M. Dixon. 123 W. 7th St.

One of Delaware's best examples of Gothic Revival (along with Rockwood, BR18), this thirty-five-room stuccoed-brick house with ten fireplaces was built by Philadelphia-born surgeon Allen V. Lesley, whose father had served on the board of the C&D Canal company. The

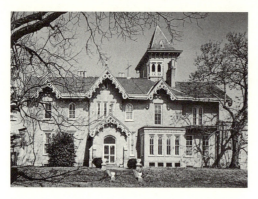

NC23 FOX LODGE AT LESLEY MANOR (ALLEN LESLEY HOUSE)

noted architects Dixon of Baltimore designed the house, which bears a resemblance to their Sheppard and Enoch Pratt Hospital there (begun 1858). Augustin Van Kirk of Salem, New Jersey, built it. The roofline is studded with tall gables with massive, pierced vergeboards, and a square tower with a tall pointed roof soars overhead. Window sills and hood moldings are cast-iron. Inside are an oak stair, speaking tubes, and original gas lighting fixtures.

SOUTH OF NEW CASTLE

NC24 Buena Vista

1845–1847. 1930–1932 library wing, R. Brognard Okie. West side of U.S. 13, opposite Federal School Lane, 4 miles southwest of New Castle

Prominent Whig John M. Clayton, secretary of state under President Zachary Taylor, named his house for a victory of Taylor's in the Mexican War. The dwelling shows Greek Revival detailing grafted to a conservative five-bay, center-passage, brick form. The low-pitched roof has parapets at the ends, capped with stone; a Greek Doric piazza extends across the front. No architect has been identified. Kentucky senator Henry Clay visited Clayton here. Later, Clayton's great-nephew, Depression-era Delaware governor C. Douglass Buck, was born (1890) and died (1965) at the estate. Clayton promoted construction of the Delaware Railroad; for his part, Buck was chief architect of Delaware's highway system. Buck donated the building to the state in 1965, and it serves as a conference center. A handicapped-accessible entrance has been added (1999–2003, Bernardon Haber Holloway).

NC24 BUENA VISTA

Mill Creek and White Clay Creek Hundreds

Mill power was long a key to the prosperity of hilly Mill Creek Hundred, its technologies having been transformed nationwide by the innovations of Oliver Evans of Newport, Delaware, author of *Young Millwright and Miller's Guide* (1795). Mill Creek Hundred is traversed by colonial Limestone Road (the Simon Hadley Barn of 1717 survives from this era) and the later Newport and Gap Turnpike toll road (1808), which formerly were arteries for grain transport. Farmers and their animals were refreshed at taverns, including Tweed's (1796), a two-story, V-notched log building that was moved and restored in 2005 (Limestone and Valley rds.). Agriculture sputtered by the 1950s, a decade during which the population of Mill Creek Hundred grew 205 percent, tract housing spilling over the hills. Serving a new suburban population, many churches and schools were built in a modernist idiom (to cite but two Newark-area examples, St. Paul's Lutheran Church at 701 S. College Avenue, and St. Philip Lutheran at 4501 Kirkwood Highway, both by T. Norman Mansell, 1957–1958). Delaware's Financial Center Development Act of 1981 made the state a tax haven for banks, and, subsequently, the Pike Creek and Hockessin areas of Mill Creek Hundred lost 10,600 acres of open space to the bulldozer in 1982–1987 alone. What historic architecture survives is often difficult to find in a massively altered landscape of rerouted roads and wall-to-wall development.

Most of White Clay Creek Hundred is treated in the Newark chapter, but its eastern portions are discussed here.

HOCKESSIN

MC1 Hockessin Friends Meeting House

1738. 1745 frame addition. 1501 Old Wilmington Rd.

Among early members of this hilltop meeting was miller William Cox of Ocassa Farm, hence the name "Hockessin," today a community of 12,900, seventh-largest in the state. The meetinghouse walls—long white-plastered but now bare stone and recently repointed—are of billion-year-old Baltimore gneiss, which occurs in Delaware only in this vicinity. The pent hood is early but not original, which is also true for the furnishings, hardware, and exterior trim. General Charles Cornwallis's troops spent a night here in September 1777. The long carriage shed has been converted into a Sunday school. Three miles southwest stands another Quaker outpost, Mill Creek Friends Meeting House (1841), at Doe Run Road near the Pennsylvania line. That meeting was moribund in 1930–1949 but restored in 1954.

MC2 Hindu Temple of Delaware

2000–2001, Jag Deshpande. 760 Yorklyn Rd.

This white temple, or *mandir*, adorned with Indian capitals and cornices is topped by a pyramidal *shikhara* peak above the shrine room, symbolizing the link between heaven and earth. The peak and other decorative touches were crafted by seven workers brought from India. Inside the temple are sixteen imported statues of divinities, principally Mahalaxmi, goddess of prosperity, dressed in colorful clothing and seated in a niche. With increased immigration, the Hindu community in the region has grown, enriching Delaware's architectural diversity.

MC3 Hockessin Community Center (Hockessin School 107-C)

1920. 4266 Mill Creek Rd.

Like other African American schools in the state, the little brick Hockessin Colored School was funded by P. S. du Pont. In 1950, Sarah Bulah wanted her seven-year-old daughter, Shirley, a pupil here, to ride the bus to

MC3 HOCKESSIN COMMUNITY CENTER (HOCKESSIN SCHOOL 107-C)

school, a privilege granted only to whites. Bulah turned to attorney Louis L. Redding, who filed suit demanding that Shirley be admitted to the nearby white school, Hockessin Elementary. This and a case from Claymont were decided in the plaintiffs' favor in 1952. Appealed to the United States Supreme Court, they became part of the famous *Brown v. Board of Education* case (1954)—its only component lawsuits in which a state court struck down segregation. After *Brown* ended segregation nationwide, School 107-C closed in 1959. It appears virtually unchanged today, but an addition is planned for its new use as a community center.

DOWN RED CLAY CREEK

MC4 Mt. Cuba

1935–1937, Victorine and Samuel Homsey; Thomas Warren Sears, landscape architect. 1949–1950 formal gardens, Marian Cruger Coffin. 2003 adaptive reuse, Homsey Architects. 3120 Barley Mill Rd., southeast of Ashland

Colonial Williamsburg defined the style of this home, built by Lammot du Pont Copeland and his wife, Pamela Cunningham Copeland. The hilly district, said to have been named for a locale in Ireland, was a popular picnic area even before the Wilmington and Western Railroad (CH30) established a station nearby in 1872. Pamela liked the 400-foot hill, among Delaware's highest, for its resemblance to places in her native New England, and they built their Georgian Revival mansion in a cornfield near the summit. It was one of the first commissions of the Homsey firm, relatives of Lammot. On a frame of steel and concrete, the Homseys erected walls of Williamsburg Genuine Handmade Colonial Brick, manufactured by C. H. Locher of Glasgow, Virginia—just like the bricks used in restoring the Williamsburg Gaol in 1935. Paneling of outstanding quality was brought in from colonial homes in the Carolinas, Massachusetts, New Hampshire, and Virginia, with a stair (c. 1800) from Charleston. American Car and Foundry repaired and painted the paneling in its Wilmington plant. The living room contains bold paneling from the Old Brick House, Pasquotank County, North Carolina: Ionic pilasters and a huge scroll above the fireplace, that Winterthur Museum director Charles F. Montgomery traced to Batty Langley's *Builder's Jewel* (1751). (Ties were always close between the Copelands and Winterthur, CH10.) The conservatory has a trompe l'oeil latticework mural (1953, Robert Bushell). Lammot, an arts enthusiast who once had Salvador Dali paint his portrait, was the son of the woman who founded the Delaware Art Museum (WL90), the facade of which would imitate this conservatory. Lammot liked to shoot in the pistol range in the Mt. Cuba basement. The mansion became widely known: it was featured in *Antiques* (October 1952) and in a book, *The One Hundred Most Beautiful Rooms in America* (1958). Following Pamela's death here at age ninety-four in 2001, Sotheby's auctioned the furniture for $12.5 million, a symbolic end to the great twentieth-century era of du Pont family collecting.

Philadelphia landscape architect Thomas Sears, designer of many estates, met with the Homseys as early as December 1935 to discuss the integration of house and grounds. His major contributions were the forecourt with its Williamsburg-like walls, sweet gum allee, lilac allee, and also the south terrace and cutting garden. The formal gardens of the south terrace are among the last by Marian Coffin, who had designed Lammot's grandparents' garden at St. Amour in 1918 (CH23). She reworked Sears's south terrace and added a Round Garden. Pamela Copeland developed a naturalistic garden in the 1960s that became famous. Following Mrs. Copeland's wishes, Mt. Cuba has been restored as a center for the study of Piedmont flora. Its hand-wrought en-

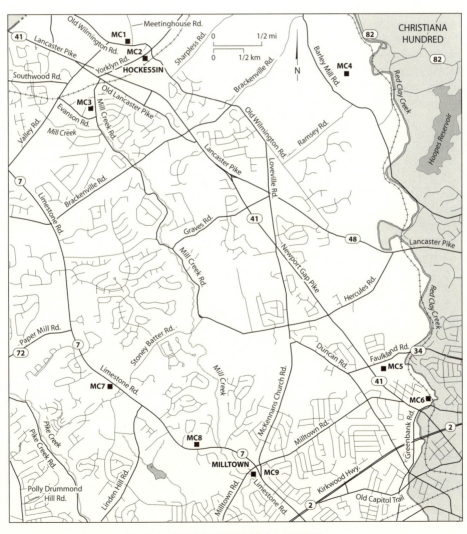

MILL CREEK AND WHITE CLAY CREEK HUNDREDS—NORTH

trance gates replicating trees and plants are by Greg Leavitt of Berks County, Pennsylvania.

MC5 Brandywine Springs Park
1826 and later. Faulkland Rd. and DE 41

Only foundations suggest the dozens of structures that made up a nationally famous mineral spring resort (1826–1852) and, later, amusement park (1886–1923). From the foot of the ridge sprang foul smelling but healthful chalybeate (iron rich) springs. Above the historic brow of the hill stood the Council Oak, labeled by resort promoters as a meeting place of George Washington and the Marquis de Lafayette; it died in 1993. Ground-penetrating radar has revealed the site of a group of Greek Revival houses designed by Thomas U. Walter for Philadelphian Matthew Newkirk (1835–1836), where a basketball court is now. Just east was the great Saratoga-like colonnaded hotel (1826, burned 1853). That hotel may have been the work of Benjamin Ferris, whose survey and sketches survive. Along Red Clay Creek runs the Wilmington and Western Railroad (CH30), the groundbreaking ceremony for which was held at this site in July 1871. Brandywine Springs became Delaware's first state park in 1951 but later came under county control (1970). Bridges have been rebuilt and signs installed to display historic photographs. Near the railroad, archaeology undertaken in 1993–1994 located the electrified entrance archway. Dozens of light sockets were unearthed, some still in working condition.

MC6 Greenbank Mill
1983–1996 rebuilding of c. 1760 and 1810 structures, Charles du Pont and others. Greenbank Rd. at Red Clay Creek, 0.1 miles northeast of Newport Gap Pike (DE 41)

A Swedish mill operated here in the late seventeenth century. The Philips family of Quakers later ran a wooden merchant gristmill to grind

MC6 GREENBANK MILL

flour (1790–1888), modernizing the facility with Oliver Evans equipment in 1793. Their nearby stone farmhouse bears a datestone, "IRP 1794" (for John R. Philips). In 1810, they erected a stone addition to the mill complex as the Madison Factory to process Merino wool. A mansion was built on Newport Gap Pike in 1852 and named Greenbank, the Madison Factory by then making hubs, spokes, and felloes (wheel rims) for the Wilmington carriage industry. The gristmill was still operating in the mid-1960s when Historic Red Clay Valley bought it. In 1969, some youths burned the place, but it has been rebuilt and serves as a living history museum. (A small part of the original survives at the Hagley Museum [CH15.2], to which it was transported in the 1950s.) The deteriorated and fire-weakened Madison wing was removed, but subsequently reconstructed, though with stone walls merely as a veneer over frame. Since 1992, many improvements have been carried out, including excavating the extensive raceway and rebuilding the eighteen-foot waterwheel. Archaeology is ongoing beneath the Madison Factory, where a dye house has been identified, a rare find. Future plans call for replicating the kitchen building in which two slaves were housed c. 1820, reconstructing a vertical sawmill, and renovating the bank barn of c. 1850.

ALONG LIMESTONE ROAD (DE 7)

MC7 Mermaid Tavern
c. 1746, with additions. 4900 Limestone Rd.

Limestone Road, a colonial route now much-widened, crosses five miles of undulating Piedmont terrain from the Pennsylvania line to Milltown. It linked the fertile farms of southeastern Pennsylvania to shipping points at Newport and Stanton, Delaware, from which grain traveled by boat to Philadelphia's burgeoning markets. Its long, steady downgrade made it popular with teamsters even after the Newport and Gap Turnpike opened in 1808. At the geographical center of Mill Creek Hundred and originally on a crossroads, the Mermaid is said to have opened in 1746 and remains in the original family. It retains an old liquor cabinet, money drawers, postal cabinet, and ballot box. A James K. Polk campaign flag was discovered in the attic. The stone part of the house is oldest, having replaced a log dwelling. The building operated as a tavern until 1869, witnessing the Civil War "Battle of the Mermaid," a scuffle in which Democrats tried to prevent the Fourth Delaware Regiment from voting.

MC8 McKennan-Klair House

Early 18th century. 1818 enlarged. 3401 Limestone Rd., near Milltown

The use of fieldstone here is typical of the rocky Piedmont, as is the way the house was elongated over time in varying materials (the brick-and-stucco half is older). A datestone gives 1818 for the stone end, which has Federal detailing inside. Scots-Irish immigrant William McKennan, for half a century the pastor of Red Clay Creek Presbyterian Church, bought the place in 1756. After his death in 1809, the next owner, Frederick Klair, moved down from Montgomery County, Pennsylvania, and improved the property. His stone bank barn (1823) across the road was demolished in the 1970s; a spring house near the dwelling survives. One researcher argues that its cellar kitchen (entered through the gable end of the house) copies Swiss or German bank houses of Chester County.

MC9 Harlan Mill

1815. Milltown and Limestone rds., Milltown

Mill villages were keys to the prosperity of northern New Castle County. Farmers raised barley, corn, oats, and wheat, ground at water-powered establishments. Woolen mills allowed them to raise sheep, too. Modern commuters are hardly aware of Milltown today; the old five-points arrangement (radiating starlike in five directions) of colonial roads was cut off by highway rerouting in 1964. Milling got underway at this site on Mill Creek by 1747. Caleb Harlan was involved from 1771 to 1815, when his will conveyed "mill, millstones and every other appurtanances" to his sons and the present structure was built, as shown in a datestone. Abram Chandler purchased it in 1852 and, by 1871, had erected the extant brick house nearby with its elegant cast-iron veranda. The mill's rectangular plan and huge corner chimney (once warming an enclosed office inside), as well as its having the race flow through the building to turn the waterwheel and grinding machinery at one end, are derived from Chester County, Pennsylvania, practice (as disseminated widely by Oliver Evans's book of 1795 on mill technology). Harlan Mill ceased operation in the 1890s and was gutted by fire in the 1940s. Today it is a private home. To the west (on the current site of Dickinson High) stood the Thomas Springer log dwelling (c. 1795), installed at the Smithsonian Institution as "the Delaware Plank House" (1958–1963, Robert L. Raley, with curator John Pearce). Barbara Clark Smith's book *After the Revolution* (1985) discusses its former neighborhood.

STANTON VICINITY

MC10 St. James Episcopal Church Millcreek Hundred

1820–1823. c. 1895 belfry. Old Capitol Trail and St. James Church Rd., 0.8 miles northwest of Stanton

Another Anglican congregation founded by the Society for the Propagation of the Gospel, St. James served English and Swedes who had settled at Stanton, forming a serious rival to Immanuel Church at New Castle (NC10).

The present stone building with doors on three facades replaced a wooden one of 1717 that burned in 1820. The cozy interior, refurbished in 2003, has a barrel-vaulted ceiling, a gallery on three sides (its posts replaced), and box pews. The curved apse originally held a Palladian window, for which a Gothic stained-glass window was later substituted. The stone tower is original, with modifications: the arched window is now a Palladian one that curves outward—evidently the apse window,

MC10 ST. JAMES EPISCOPAL CHURCH MILLCREEK HUNDRED

MC11 HALE-BYRNES HOUSE, photo 1930s

moved here—and a belfry has been added above (the mansard roof that it supports has been reshingled without its graceful kick). The old stuccoed walls are rough and mellow. The churchyard is believed to have tombs dating as early as 1726; the carving on one black slate of 1743 is whimsically crude. The stone wall dates to 1817. A century later, the churchyard was noted for its firs and lindens and was a popular picnicking spot. In the early twentieth century, blackbirds were so thick in the trees that a rector used roman candles to scare them off, briefly setting the church on fire.

MC11 Hale-Byrnes House

c. 1750. c. 1772 extended north. Stanton-Christiana Rd., on White Clay Creek

Samuel Hale was a potter who used White Clay Creek to transport his wares. In 1772, he sold the riverside house to Daniel Byrnes, a miller, who enlarged it. Flemish bond brickwork on the front facade (unfortunately sandblasted) contrasts with mingled English and common bonds on sides and rear. General George Washington convened a council of war with the Marquis de Lafayette and others here in September 1777. By 1961, the house was boarded up and about to be demolished for a highway realignment, but Mrs. Harry C. Boden of the revived Delaware Society for the Preservation of Antiquities successfully campaigned for its preservation. Her group restored the house (with G. Morris Whiteside II and Albert Kruse; landscape by Edward Bachtle), giving it to the state in 1971. The gnarled sycamore outside may be as old as the house. Nearby stands abandoned Stanton Bridge (1940–1942), unique in Delaware as a C-shaped concrete "rainbow arch," with a span of 119 feet.

CHRISTIANA

Old-timers still call this tiny village "Christine." The crossroads settlement remains largely intact, although highways and developments have ringed it. It is hard to conceive of this inland village as a port, but it does lie at the head of navigation on the Christina River. Although the river is only a few yards wide here, the town served as a major grain depot. In addition, the main north–south colonial highway ran directly through town, as did an important east–west county road. Ten or so structures existed by 1739. Joshua Hempstead of Connecticut, coming from Ogletown in 1749, was surprised to pass from a region of log houses to "a Clump of very fine brick houses a Dozen or more & Several Taverns," it being "a place . . . of much Business." *The Traveller's Directory* of 1804 said, "It was built by the Swedes in the year 1640, on the side of

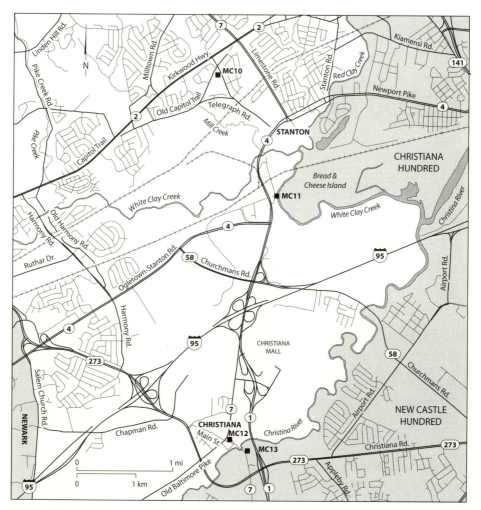

MILL CREEK AND WHITE CLAY CREEK HUNDREDS—SOUTH

a hill, commanding a beautiful prospect of the surrounding country" (Moore and Jones, 1804). With fifty dwellings and a Presbyterian Church, "it is the principal carrying place between the waters of the Chesapeak and Delaware" and traded extensively with Philadelphia in flour. When a concrete bridge was built over the river (1936–1937), a Revolutionary cannonball was discovered.

Evidence of the community's substantial eighteenth-century wealth is that no fewer than nine brick structures stand in the historic district. The fine, eighteenth-century Hillis Mansion House (29 S. Old Baltimore Pike) belonged to a cordwainer who also owned wharves and stores. The Brinckle-Maxwell House (c. 1786), 29 E. Main Street, was originally side-hall. It is the only brick Federal-style building surviving in the village and has a parapet wall. Solomon Maxwell, its owner after 1787, ran the shallop boat trade with Philadelphia. The stone foundation is typical of several buildings in town. The Gothic Revival Presbyterian Church (1857, replacing one of 1738) emulates one in Newark.

MC12 Shannon Hotel

By 1766 east section. c. 1817 enlarged to west. Old Baltimore Pike and Main St.

MC12 SHANNON HOTEL, photo prior to facade reconstruction

"There are good Houses of Entertainment at Christiana Bridge," said the *Pennsylvania Chronicle* in 1767, a year after this brick tavern first appeared in the historical record (in a will). George Washington visited the town often in his travels—five times between July and December 1795 alone—staying, presumably, here or diagonally across the street at the still-extant but sandblasted Christiana Inn (pre-1770, enlarged 1842). William Shannon took over in 1800 and was succeeded, after his death, by Isaac Price, who filed a tavern petition in 1817 for the "old established" inn. In 1855, the place became half dwelling, half general store, but it was a hotel again by the 1880s. HABS researchers found its condition "poor" in 1975, and it remains so today. Severe cracks eventually developed in the historic, first-period three-bay facade, which had to be entirely rebuilt in March 2000. Its excellent, unrestored pent eave, so typical of northern Delaware and Pennsylvania, was removed during that project and has not been replaced.

MC13 John Lewden House

1770. 1815 enlarged. 107 E. Main St.

Further evidence of the early wealth and importance of Christiana, this brick Georgian dwelling stands on what the Lewden family called the "Fishing Place," right on the Christina River. The construction date of 1770 is said to appear in a foundation stone. Lewden's firm was prominent in the West Indian grain trade and helped plantation owners flee to Wilmington after the slave revolt of 1802 on Santo Domingo. Lewden was first cousin to William Corbit of Odessa, and the house is similar in plan and finish to some buildings in that town. The fine Doric surround to the door, with shutters, is quite similar to one at Odessa's Wilson-Warner House (1769; LN7). Both Lewden and Corbit were tanners and the leading citizens of their respective shipping communities. The traditional attribution of the Lewden House is to one Robert May of Head of Elk, Maryland, who might have been the same Robert May whose carpenters carried out the Corbit-Sharp House (1772–1774; LN6) and perhaps the Wilson-Warner House. Alternatively, the Lewden House, like the Wilson-Warner, simply obeys an established Delaware type: brick, center-passage, single-pile. The house fell into disrepair under a succession of tenant occupants—chickens were cooped in the living room—but was restored in the mid-twentieth century.

Newark and White Clay Creek Valley

Situated at the northwest corner of the state, Newark has grown to be Delaware's third-largest town (population 28,500), nearly as large as Dover and dominated by a sizeable university. Historically, the community was exclusively strung along Main Street. Its growth was extremely slow, reaching only 4,500 by 1940, but then it exploded to more than 15,000 by 1965 with the expansion of the University of Delaware and construction of two DuPont facilities and a Chrysler plant. As early as 1951, there were complaints about the town's traffic problem, an issue that has grown more troublesome. Newark's explosive growth doomed much historic architecture. A typical local newspaper headline of the post–World War II period read, "Razing of Pre-Revolutionary War House at Newark Starts; Will Allow Wider Road" (1957). The covered bridge (1861) at Paper Mill Road over White Clay Creek was removed in 1947, and an important Greek Revival house, Linden Hall (1845), was demolished at the Chrysler plant. The Frank Furness–designed B&O train station was replaced by a characterless brick box. The town planning department belatedly catalogued historic buildings in 1983, but within fifteen years several of the most prominent were swept away, including Deer Park Farm (1840) and Granite Mansion (1844). The brick Thomas Montgomery House (c. 1740), with paneled interiors, was in good condition in 1991 just before demolition. Curtis Paper Company operated on White Clay Creek at the edge of town from 1789 until 1997, the longest-running paper mill in the nation, but was demolished in 2007.

The entries begin in the upper White Clay Creek Valley, north of Newark. DuPont bought much of the valley starting in 1956 to dam it and create a huge reservoir. Environmentalists eventually defeated these plans, and, in 1984, the company donated the land to the state as White Clay Creek State Park (now 3,384 acres). Because it was sequestered by DuPont and spared almost thirty years of sprawl, the park is the best-preserved rural landscape in northern Delaware, where one can still walk unpaved country roads and see the ruins of old barns and stone farmhouses.

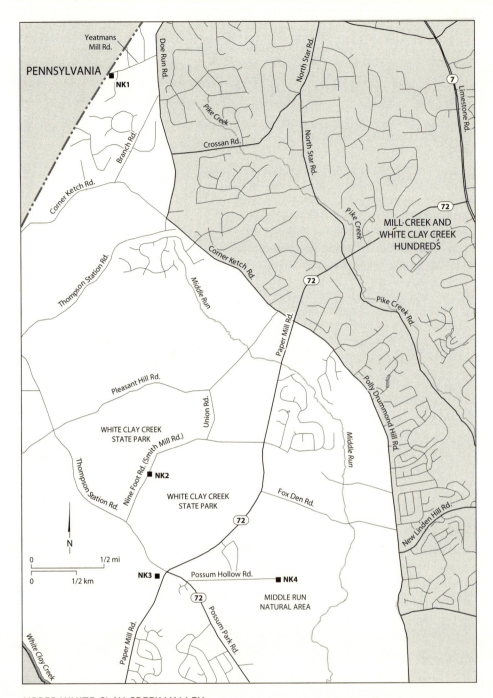

UPPER WHITE CLAY CREEK VALLEY

UPPER WHITE CLAY CREEK VALLEY

NK1 Merestone

c. 1738 log house. 18th century frame addition. c. 1804 stone section. 1940–1942 restored and east wing added, R. Brognard Okie. 1610–20 Yeatmans Mill Rd., near Pennsylvania state line

This many-sectioned farmhouse, typical of Chester County, Pennsylvania, was enhanced by a Philadelphia architect for twentieth-century owner John Reese. The name means "boundary stone," referring to a nearby marker on the circular border between Pennsylvania and Delaware. In the eighteenth century the Evans family owned the house and operated a mill nearby. Okie had designed the S. Hallock du Pont House, Squirrel Run, at 5 Old Barley Mill Road, near Hagley (1927), as well as a home for Henry Belin du Pont near Mt. Cuba (1935; MC4). He was known for his pleasing Colonial Revival style based on Pennsylvania farmhouses—white trim, shutters, stone chimneys, porches—which here harmonizes perfectly with the original colonial fabric. He died in 1945, not long after this commission.

NK2 Nine Foot Road (Smith Mill Road)

1928. White Clay Creek State Park; intersects Thompson Station Rd. northwest of Paper Mill Rd.

The nine-foot-wide road of concrete, recently restored, is the last survivor of several funded by the state highway department during 1928–1933. Atop a dirt track of the 1870s, the George Lynch Company of Wilmington poured a continuous ribbon of cement, seven inches thick. Rubber-tired vehicles could use the concrete; metal-wheeled ones, the wide shoulder. At the north, it terminates into a never-paved, vehicle-free road, now the Tri-Valley Trail, which offers a stroll along an antebellum route through unspoiled countryside. A quarter-mile east, the trail crosses another early-nineteenth-century road, now largely overgrown. Not so long ago, all Delaware roads resembled these.

NK3 Office Building (Louviers Building)

1951–1952 Wings 1 to 3, Voorhees, Walker, Foley and Smith, with Hubert Sheldon Stees, consultant. 1973–1974 Wing Five. Thompson Station and Paper Mill rds., 2 miles north of Newark

As corporations joined the post–World War II exodus to suburbia, DuPont decided in 1950 to decentralize the Home Office and, at the same time, consolidate the Engineering Department from eight office locations in Wilmington (see DuPont Building, WL32). It examined a dozen rural sites before choosing this remote location at Milford Crossroads. On 850 acres, DuPont planned a facility with enough room for expansion and with parking to accommodate twenty years' growth. A famous New York firm was called in as designer, one known for its industrial facilities going back to Bell Telephone Labs, New Jersey (1937–1949). The Louviers Building was fully modern, with hung metal acoustical ceiling pans, air conditioning, recessed fluorescent lighting, moveable partitions, and escalators. The steel frame allowed large, open workrooms (when work habits later became more solitary, these were subdivided). The sleekly modern lobby had bookmatched marble panels on the walls. A pioneering UNIVAC 1 computer was installed in 1954. In the 1960s, the corporation planned to dam White Clay Creek to create a reservoir, a plan thankfully abandoned. MBNA, the credit card company, bought Louviers in the mid-1990s and painted the brick walls their trademark dollar-bill green. At that time, the rural surroundings were rapidly being subdivided.

NK1 MERESTONE

NK4 Frink Center for Wildlife, Tri-State Bird Rescue Center

1989–1992, Mary Staikos for Staikos Associates Architects. End of Possum Hollow Rd. at Middle Run Natural Area, 2.5 miles northeast of Newark

Only rarely did pell-mell farm abandonment in New Castle County lead to adaptive reuse of agricultural buildings instead of destruction. This converted farmstead lies at the end of a little-used country road that now terminates at a bucolic county park. An old barn was converted into a bird hospital. Outside, wooden stairs lead up and around an old concrete silo to an elevated deck with a view down onto a warren of tin-roofed wooden aviaries, some on stilts. The naturalistic landscaping preserves the old-farm feeling.

LOWER WHITE CLAY CREEK VALLEY

NK5 White Clay Creek Presbyterian Church

1855. Kirkwood Hwy. and Polly Drummond Hill Rd.

Scots-Irish immigrants built a log structure on nearby Polly Drummond Hill in 1721. George Whitefield preached to 8,000 there in November 1739, which contributed to a subsequent rift among Presbyterians, with "New Side" Presbyterians, who liked him, departing to establish this church. ("New Side" or "New Light" referred to fervent revivalists inspired by the Great Awakening, as opposed to the more orthodox "Old Side." Their local leader was Reverend Charles Tennent, son of the founder of the famous Log College, Pennsylvania.) This church was established in 1752, replaced in 1785, and again, in 1855, with the present structure. The current building is brick, of Greek Revival style with the sanctuary upstairs, Sunday school below, in an arrangement that was popular in the mid nineteenth century. Sanctuary walls and ceiling are covered with decorative sheet metal in Gothic and other historical patterns, and cast-iron columns support the floor. A dedicatory inscription of 1752 is displayed, along with a folk-art mural showing all four historic churches. Gravestones in the sizeable cemetery are said to go back to 1734; among the many made from marble stands a single green stone, apparently serpentine (1757). The lumpy cemetery wall of whitewashed rocks dates to 1785. The temple-form purity of the hilltop church was marred in 1996 when a stumpy tower was built beside it to house an elevator.

NK6 John England House and Mill

1747, with additions. 81 Red Mill Rd. at White Clay Creek, south of Kirkwood Hwy.

John England immigrated from Staffordshire to operate Principio Furnace, Maryland, and three years later, in 1726, bought 400 acres on White Clay Creek. The brick house erected by his brother and heir, Joseph, bears a datestone of 1747. Historian Harold D. Eberlein says the brick wing at right was already standing, though it looks later; it shows traces of a Dutch oven, which connected to the huge fireplace inside. The section of 1747 has glazed-header brickwork with a scattering of putlog holes (holes where bricks were omitted so scaffolding could be inserted for construction or repair); pent eaves; and a wavy diaper pattern in one gable, somewhat recalling that of Wilmington's Presbyterian Church (WL58) of the same decade. The mill stands on massive stone foundations, one stone supposedly inscribed "I E 1789," and has changed little since visited by HABS in 1937, at which

NK6 JOHN ENGLAND HOUSE AND MILL, photo 1937

time it was still grinding feed. It retains elements of its sideshot water turbine, which replaced the original undershot wheel (metal turbines were more efficient than the larger old wooden wheels).

NK7 Avon Products Northeast Regional Headquarters

1961, Whiteside, Moeckel and Carbonell. 1998–2001 remodeled, Marjorie Rothberg Architecture. 2100 Ogletown Rd., 1.2 miles east of Newark

NK7 AVON PRODUCTS NORTHEAST REGIONAL HEADQUARTERS

One of the world's largest sellers of cosmetics, fragrances, and toiletries, Avon had a facility in Newark starting in 1954. This building's original curtain wall, dramatically low and long at 500 feet, employed vibrant color: yellow-enameled metal panels and green glazed brick. The panels floated in front of the wall, as did the aluminum mullions and honeycomb-pattern bronzed grills as sunscreens. Rothberg's exterior modernization, undertaken for aesthetic purposes, involved replacement of the entire curtain wall with a more massive structure. Gone was the minimalist lightness of the original conception; gone, too, was color, eradicated in favor of aluminum panels in a smoky gray. The results are attractive—but at the cost of a modernist classic of the 1960s.

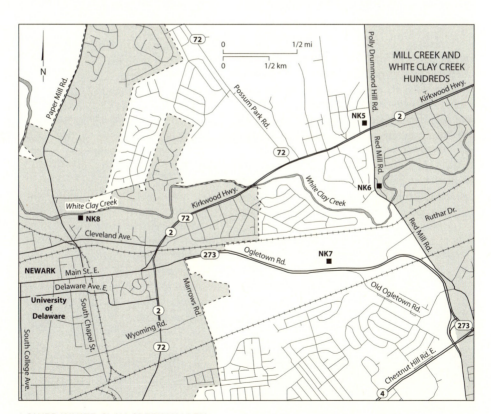

LOWER WHITE CLAY CREEK VALLEY

NEWARK

The town's Main Street has several buildings of note. The former Rhodes Pharmacy (1916–1917, Richard A. Whittingham) translated Gothic architecture into concrete, complete with gargoyles. Wilmington Trust Bank (1926, originally Farmers' Trust Company; 82 Main St.) is neo-Roman with big Corinthian columns. Green Mansion (c. 1882; 96 Main St.) is named for its colorful facade of serpentine. Klondike Kate's Restaurant (1880; 158 Main St.) served originally as a store and grange hall. Its mansard roof of patterned tiles was repaired after a fire in the 1990s. St. John the Baptist Roman Catholic Church (1883; 200 Main St.) occupies the site of an earlier Presbyterian church. The present brick edifice had a rose window by a Philadelphia artist inserted (1946, Paula Himmelsbach Balano), and its belfry was modified after lightning struck it in 1953.

NK8 The Mill at White Clay (Joseph Dean and Son)

1830s–1840s, with additions. Late 1990s adaptive reuse, Design Collaborative, Breckstone Group, and Landmark Engineering, Inc., for Commonwealth Development Group. Creek View Rd., off Paper Mill Rd. at White Clay Creek

On twenty riverfront acres north of the University of Delaware lies a brownfield redevelopment. An early grist mill (c. 1702, of which part of the race survives) burned in 1831 and was rebuilt. English-born Joseph Dean took over in 1845, converting the operation to spinning wool. He later expanded into the manufacture of Kentucky jeans, blankets, and Civil War military clothing. The company's Indigo Sky Blue Army Kerseys were famous, their "clear color and finish" attributed to crystalline White Clay Creek water. The mills burned in 1886. In the twentieth century, they were converted into a paper and vulcanized fiber mill. Following abandonment in the late 1980s, the polluted site was redeveloped as forty-eight apartments along with shops and offices, utilizing the old structures, including the tall, stuccoed-stone Main Building, which, in 1886, had been used for carding, spinning, and finishing, with fulling in the basement. Nearby stands a nineteenth-century neighborhood of former tenement houses for the mill workers.

NK9 University of Delaware

1833 to present

The tiny school, established in 1833 as Newark College and renamed Delaware College in 1843, was reborn in 1914 through the efforts of Pierre S. du Pont, then crusading for the improvement of education statewide. The same year, a women's college was established adjacent to the men's campus and was linked to it administratively. In 1921, the University of Delaware was created from the two colleges. The university was racially integrated in 1950.

Du Pont's gifts to Newark College were ostensibly anonymous, channeled through his secretary and brother-in-law, Hugh Rodney Sharp (see Gibraltar, WL94). Du Pont and Sharp drove down to Newark together on the initial visit, and, Sharp said, "Pierre agreed

NK8 THE MILL AT WHITE CLAY (JOSEPH DEAN AND SON)

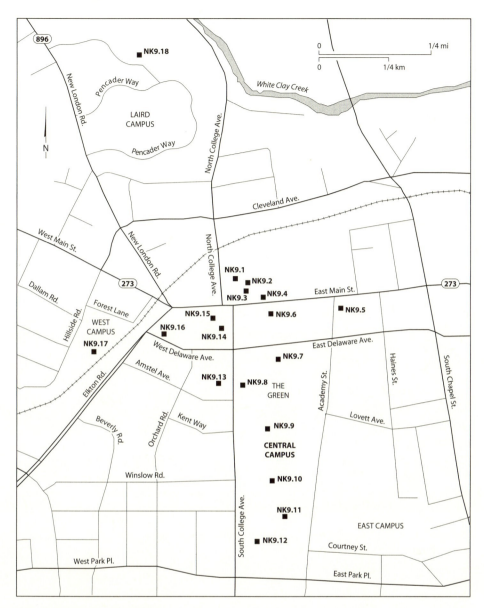

UNIVERSITY OF DELAWARE

that the place was as shabby as it could be." Also involved were Lammot du Pont, Henry F. du Pont (of Winterthur, CH10), and Bancroft Mills (WL91) magnate Henry B. Thompson, a Princeton University trustee who played a critical role—he brought in the celebrated architects of that campus, the Philadelphia firm of Day and Klauder. Their Gothic Revival Freshman Dormitories at Princeton (begun 1909) were already famous. The original Delaware campus had huddled around Old College (NK9.1); now Day and Klauder created an expansive Green running south of Main Street. The Green somehow came to be called "The Mall" for generations, but at the turn of the twenty-first century, the original nomenclature was revived. The trustees played an active role in the campus plan's conception, and it is said that Thompson had the idea for it "flash upon his mind" during a train ride from New York City. With Memorial Hall (NK9.9) at its head, the Green is often said to copy

Thomas Jefferson's design for the University of Virginia, but, more accurately, it is one of several campuses built in the United States around 1900–1915 that blended Jefferson's design with Beaux-Arts planning principles in new, creative ways. At Delaware, Day and Klauder neatly combined the grand axiality of the University of Virginia with the relative narrowness and intimacy of the old yards at Harvard and Yale.

Thompson first approached Day about designing the campus in December 1914, and he immediately agreed, with "very lively pleasure." Day visited the next month and urged the purchase of the land that forms the Green. His involvement was critical but relatively brief, just three years, for he suffered a fatal stroke at the age of fifty-seven in June 1918, leaving Klauder and staff to carry on (both here and at several other campuses nationwide). Architectural historian Patricia Keebler has written of the university (1980), "The designs were really advanced and executed after Day's death, with the exception of the restoration and renovation of Old College. Correspondence shows Herbert C. Wise had the major responsibility for their construction. Only the basic development plan can be given wholly to Day." Wise, a friend of Klauder's since they had worked together for Cope and Stewardson, specialized in Colonial Revival. He wrote *Colonial Architecture for Those About to Build* (1924) and, with Klauder, *College Architecture in America* (1929).

Growth was slow at the university: in 1938, the state of Delaware had the lowest rate of college attendance in the nation. But the school exploded in size in the suburbanizing decades following World War II, going from 2,400 undergraduates in 1957 to 6,500 in 1967. Sharp and others saw that additions to the Green continued to follow the original Colonial Revival aesthetic. Elsewhere on campus, there was greater architectural experimentation— most of it rather tame, however. From time to time, noted architectural firms were called in. The New York City firm of McKim, Mead and White designed Squire, Sypherd, and Thompson Halls in 1957–1958. Amy du Pont Music Building (1973, Vincent G. Kling and Associates) was by the firm that had just completed the Annenberg Center, University of Pennsylvania. More recent years have brought the Lammot du Pont Laboratory (1992–1993, Ay-

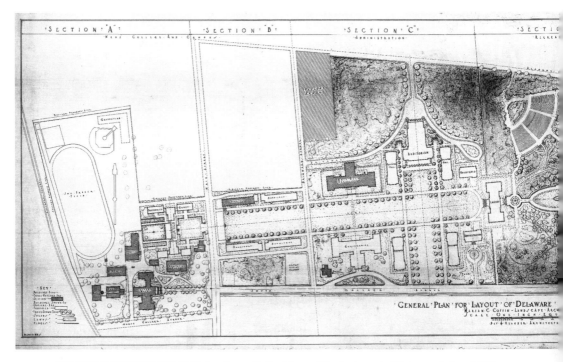

NK9 UNIVERSITY OF DELAWARE, Marian Cruger Coffin, "General Plan for Layout of Delaware College," 1919, showing the Day and Klauder design for campus

ers/Saint/Gross and Moeckel Carbonell Associates) and Bob Carpenter Center (1992, Hellmuth, Obata and Kassabaum, with Tevebaugh Associates). Roselle Center for the Arts was built in 2004–2006 (Ayers/Saint/Gross).

NK9.1 Old College

1832–1834, Winslow Lewis. 1885 expanded at rear. 1902 enlarged, Richard A. Whittingham. 1916–1917 renovated, Day and Klauder

Three pediments of Greek Doric style, the middle one approached by tall steps, form the keynote of the most memorable building on campus. Once the charter of 1833 had established Newark College (or Delaware College, as it was renamed in 1843), a new building was needed, for which a tract owned by Alexander McBeath was purchased at what was then the west end of Main Street. Winslow Lewis, a Bostonian, was contractor and presumably also designer of the edifice; a former sea captain, he was a renowned builder of lighthouses and possibly had in mind William Strickland's Naval Asylum, Philadelphia (1827–1833), and Minard Lafever's Sailor's Snug Harbor, Long Island (1831–1833). In 1826, however, the

NK9.1 OLD COLLEGE

trustees had paid Bostonian Charles Bulfinch, then architect of the United States Capitol, for a college plan. Because it is lost, there is no way of knowing if Lewis followed it; but Bulfinch's first design for University Hall, Harvard, does resemble Lewis's building. Newark College was Greek Revival, with a four-columned temple-form center flanked by long wings unadorned except for applied wooden pilasters (removed 1902, their outlines faintly visible today). Plans called for it to be greatly extended as funds allowed, from 180 to 260 feet, with Ionic pavilions at each end. This was never done. It contained a kitchen, dining hall, classrooms, plus student rooms; the largest space was the auditorium, or Oratory. A cupola was added in 1853. The Whittingham renovation created Doric pavilions by enlarging the ends of the wings to front and rear.

When du Pont and Sharp organized the rebirth of Delaware College, they were insistent that the old building be preserved. To Day's suggestion that it could be replaced more cheaply than restored, du Pont replied, "Mr. Day, we shall have many occasions to put up new buildings, but this is the only old one we have." The architects were allowed to undertake an overhaul, however, gutting the structure and stripping off its columns and steps. (Boston and Delaware newspapers of mid-1833 were found inside a column.) The handsome exterior of today largely dates from this restoration. New steps were of a granular concrete or "caverite." The lobby's Colonial Revival stairs are particularly attractive, with gracious balustrades terminating in huge twists. If this interior in a style of the 1700s seems anachronistic inside a building of the

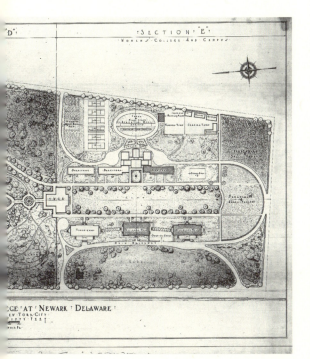

1830s, it can be explained by Day's leading role in the restoration of Congress Hall, Philadelphia, in 1911. There he had reconstructed a grand double set of colonial stairs.

Old College, as it has been known since 1918, today houses academic programs related to the study of art and architecture. Its interior has been renovated (1977–1978, Whiteside, Moeckel and Carbonell). "Linden Avenue," leading to the building, consisted of sixteen trees possibly planted in 1833; the last few survivors were removed in 2005.

NK9.2 Recitation Hall Annex (Agricultural Experiment Station)

1888, Lewis R. Springer. 1996 renovated, Moeckel Carbonell Associates

The college expanded in the 1880s with federal funds, as the Hatch Act made money available for the establishment of an agricultural experiment station. This 43 × 27–foot brick building in Queen Anne style has wrongly been attributed to Frank Furness, confusing it with next-door Recitation Hall (NK9.3); it does closely resemble some Furness designs, however. The architect, Springer, remains obscure, except for having bid unsuccessfully on a Delaware State Hospital job (NC1) in 1895. Chemical laboratories occupied much of the first floor, with the director's office slightly projecting at right of the front door. Upstairs were botanical, bacteriological, and entomological laboratories, plus a darkroom. Nearby stand two unassuming brick buildings, Mechanical and Electrical Hall (1898, Frank R. Carswell; enlarged 1904 and 1911; restored 2003), once home to the engineering department, and Taylor Hall, built as a gymnasium (1905–1906, Robeson Lea Perot).

NK9.3 Recitation Hall

1891–1892, Furness, Evans and Company. 1963 altered, Howell L. Shay

Delaware College began to awaken from a long stupor around 1890, and enrollment soared to ninety-seven. A combination auditorium, laboratory, and classroom building was needed, and the General Assembly appropriated funds for the construction of Recitation. Its style was an agglomeration of Colonial Revival and Queen Anne. The Day and Klauder campus plan of 1916 called for its removal.

Marian Cruger Coffin's landscaping report of three years later termed it "of a later and less fortunate period of architecture" than Old College (NK9.1), but allowed it to remain. At times, it housed the university's administrative offices on the first floor, lecture halls on the first and second, and library on the third. Alterations made in 1963 removed the four chimneys and added a new portico with gangly Colonial Revival columns. More recently, the interior was renovated (1996, Moeckel Carbonell Associates).

NK9.4 Elliott Hall

1760–1780 period. Mid-19th century, with additions

Long a private home, this university building is one of Newark's few colonial survivors. To historian Harold D. Eberlein, the pediment formed by running a pent eave across the bottom of the gable suggested Chester County, Pennsylvania, practice. The lighter brick of the nineteenth-century eastern extension is said to have come from the George Evans brickyard on Elkton Road. The enlarged building housed the town's post office and drugstore before the place was bought for the university in 1915. To the west stands fanlighted, side-passage Alumni Hall, formerly Purnell or Evans House (1809), a private residence until purchased by the college in 1903 and put to use as the library (1909–1916) and then, later, as a World War I county draft board. Day and Klauder's campus plans called for the demolition of these historic buildings, but by 1936, the decision had been made to keep them. Elliott Hall has been renovated and enlarged (1993–1994, Homsey Architects).

NK9.5 Academy Building

1841 west section. 1842 east section (dormitory). 1872 middle section

Delaware Governor John Penn chartered the Academy of Newark in 1769, granting permanent status to a school founded by Dr. Francis Alison at his home in New London, Pennsylvania, in 1743. Academy Square was Newark's town marketplace (the markethouse was removed c. 1840), and proceeds from weekly markets and the annual fair were directed to constructing, in the late 1760s, a two-story stone schoolhouse on the site of the current building. In the struggle between Presbyterian factions, the Academy of Newark was promoted as a traditionalist "Old Side" rival to enthusiastic "New Side" Princeton University (see White Clay Creek Presbyterian, NK5). The splenetic Alison served as president of the Academy's board for the first decade. Eventually, the trustees applied for a state charter, granted in 1833; at that point, the institution split into a preparatory school and Newark College, today's university. Old College hall (NK9.1) was built across town for the latter. A few years later, the Academy Building was erected, an economical, cupola-topped brick edifice with a dormitory beside it, facing a lawn with trees. Edgar Allan Poe charmed an audience here at Christmastime 1843, lecturing on "American Poetry." As Delaware College grew over the years, the Academy was overshadowed, and it closed in 1898. Today the building contains university offices.

NK9.6 Harter Hall

1915–1917, Day and Klauder

The architectural development of the Green—a name alluding to historic Greens in Dover (see **The Green** on p. 254) and New Castle—began with two buildings, this 100-student dormitory (begun November 1916) and nearby Wolf Hall (started six months earlier). It is legendary that trustee H. Rodney Sharp urged Klauder to look at Delaware architecture and toured the state with him, and Day and Klauder did publish a prospectus for the campus that illustrated the Parke-Ridgely House (DV13); New Castle's Immanuel Church (NC10) and Court House (NC16); and Old Drawyers (LN5). In truth, there is little about Day and Klauder's architecture at the university that can be ascribed to Delaware examples, beyond, perhaps, a predilection for intimacy of scale. Instead, they employed generic colonial elements long familiar to them in their practice. With its rowlike form and gambrel roof, Harter derives from well-known college dormitories of the colonial period, such as Yale University's Connecticut Hall (1752). As built, Harter differed from the presentation drawing of 1916, the entryway system used at Princeton being modified in favor of hallways and expensive Ionic porticos being dispensed with.

NK9.7 Wolf Hall

1915–1917, Day and Klauder. 1962–1964 extended at rear, Whiteside, Moeckel and Carbonell

The first structure to be erected in the Day and Klauder plan, this 45,000-square-foot agriculture building originally housed science laboratories, classrooms, and an auditorium. Its hipped-roof, five-part massing—a seventeenth-century English country house type with central pediment and pilasters—recalls the Law School at the University of Pennsylvania (1899–1900) by Cope and Stewardson, for whom Klauder had worked. Wolf Hall also resembled laboratories at Johns Hopkins University, Baltimore, for which school Day served as advisory architect. Perhaps the University of Delaware's most architecturally distinguished building, it stands near the middle of the long Green, lined until recently by the great elms of 1917. Wolf has been restored (2002–2003, Ayers/Saint/Gross). Across the Green diagonally is a domed auditorium, Mitchell Hall (1927–1930, Charles Z. Klauder).

NK9.8 Gore Hall

1995–1998, Allan Greenberg

This 65,000-square-foot classroom building and its gracious companion across the way, Du Pont Hall (1998–2003), are creations of Washington, D.C., architect Greenberg, a leading contemporary proponent of classical revival in the U.S. Gore Hall and Du Pont completed, at long last, Day and Klauder's plan for the Green; they make an interesting comparison to much older Wolf Hall (NK9.7), from which

NK9.6 HARTER HALL

NEWARK 183

NK9.7 WOLF HALL, early photo

they borrow motifs and a distinctive "monk bond" brickwork (Flemish bond, except the stretchers are doubled, with a red mortar joint between). Expensive and massive, Gore indulges in a lavish use of materials, to a degree almost unheard of nowadays, including interior woodwork of mahogany, painted white, and extensive plasterwork in lieu of drywall. The octagonal atrium has a colorful terrazzo floor. Behind the building, an existing pedestrian overpass was given a Classical Revival dressing, its brick supports swelling in size far beyond structural necessity, to an enjoyable sculpturalism almost Baroque. On the main facade, Greenberg introduced a triumphal note to the Green with his overscale Doric columns of concrete, manufactured in Louisiana, that are thirty-one feet tall and weigh 24,000 pounds each. His showpiece buildings seek to prove that Classical Revival style can remain vital in the twenty-first century.

NK9.9 Memorial Hall

1919–1924, Charles Z. Klauder. 1939–1940 extended at south and wings lengthened. 1998–1999 restoration, Anderson Brown Higley

The university needed a library, for which President Walter Hullihen and Newark citizen Everett C. Johnson pushed, envisioning a dual use as the statewide memorial to those killed in World War I. Porticos on each main facade were expressive of the building's double role in serving both the men's and women's campuses. Renderings of 1919 (see the illustration on p. 12) show that the porticos were to have had six columns, not four as finally built, and there was to have been a cupola atop; these first Klauder plans were rejected by trustee H. Rodney Sharp, who desired a building "of a more intimate and Delawarean character." Budgetary constraints, too, favored simplification. The central block as redesigned in 1923, with its tall profile, was apparently derived from the Indiana War Memorial, Indianapolis, by Frank B. Walker and Harry E. Weeks, who won a nationwide competition that year. The Indianapolis design was based, in turn, on the ancient Mausoleum of Halicarnassus (351 BC) in Turkey.

In Memorial Hall's central room is the "Book of Memory" with 270 names of war dead created by Everett C. Johnson's Press of Kells (NK13); the book's pages are turned daily. (Day and Klauder had installed a similar memorial room at Princeton University's Nassau Hall in 1919–1920.) Following a flood in the basement, Public Works Administration funds helped pay for an enlargement of the library, which included raising the flat roofs of the wings. In 1937, a year before his death, Klauder had called for connecting Memorial Hall to the buildings he had designed on either side (erected 1937–1940), and brick-arched curving screens were completed in 1940. They hearken back to the Johns Hopkins University, Baltimore, campus plan and ultimately to Independence Hall in Philadelphia. When the library vacated the building for larger premises in 1963, the collection was ten times larger than it had been in 1925. Two years later, the English department took over. A restoration in the 1990s altered much of the interior and re-created lost decorative medallions on the outside walls.

NK9.10 Magnolia Circle

c. 1935 installation based on 1919 proposal, Marian Cruger Coffin. 2005, Rodney Robinson

Starting in 1918, Coffin served as landscape architect for the Day and Klauder campus redevelopment, and her eight-foot-long plan for the grounds survives (1919). This pioneering woman professional was brought from New York City by H. Rodney Sharp and other du Ponts on the board, for whom she had provided estate garden designs (at Winterthur, CH10; St. Amour, CH23; and Gibraltar, WL94). Historian Nancy Fleming writes (1995) that the campus is her "most significant professional achievement.... Much of Coffin's plan survives: the circulation system of paths and drives, the lamp-posts, the wall enclosing the women's campus, the oval, and the Magnolia Circle, which disguises the misalignment of axes between the men's and women's colleges. The rows of honey locust on the women's campus and the allee of paulownia on the oval are also intact." Actually, the oval planned in 1919 was not laid out until 1935, and then as a rectangle. Its paulownia trees—recently replanted—are a rarity on college campuses but were a du Pont family favorite. Magnolia Circle was also established in 1935, an enlarged version of the small circle originally proposed; it was redesigned in 2005 and given a brick central fountain. To the east survives a section of Coffin's arboretum.

NK9.11 Sussex, New Castle, and Kent Halls (Women's Dormitories)

1918–1956, following a design of 1916 by Day and Klauder

Klauder adopted the butterfly plan for women's dormitories (used, for example, at Stanford University in 1917) as a means of breaking a single monolithic structure into a more domestic and picturesque arrangement of small wings, as was considered suitable for housing young ladies at the time. These Delaware dormitories follow closely a Klauder rendering of 1916, but, in fact, the complex was built over many decades. First, Sussex Hall (1918), then Kent Dining Hall and New Castle Hall (1926). Probably, Herbert C. Wise played the leading role in all three, which had gable roofs of slate supported by modillion cornices. Kent Hall, lofty and approached by a double stair, was not added until 1955–1956. The irregular plan of the dormitories allowed for doorstep gardens designed by Marian Cruger Coffin. To the south and built in a compatible style is Hartshorn Hall, originally the women's gymnasium (1929–1931, Louis Jallade).

NK9.12 Warner Hall

1913–1914, Laussat R. Rogers

The first sign of improving twentieth-century conditions at Delaware College was the state legislature's funding of two Colonial Revival buildings for the new women's college, this and adjacent Robinson Hall, both by Rogers. Until 1913, Delaware was the only state in the nation with no provision for the higher education of white women; black women could attend Delaware State College. Newark resident Everett C. Johnson (of Press of Kells, NK13) led a crusade to remedy this "burning injustice," culminating in the purchase of the twenty-acre Wollaston farm. A crowd of 3,000 gathered for the dedication of Robinson and Warner halls, the latter originally called Residence Hall, to which a driveway made a close approach so the women could hurry inside after dark. An inventive touch is the Beaux-Arts wooden portico of coupled Doric columns with an unusual segmental pediment (a windowed dorm room occupies this lofty perch). Equally surprising is the tall fanlight over the pedimented front door. Robinson was originally called Science Hall; Warner was named for Emalea Pusey Warner, champion of women's education. The colorful Rogers, of New Castle, was an artist who studied architecture at Harvard and entered practice in Washington, D.C., with classmate Charles Totten before setting up his Delaware practice in 1903.

NK9.13 Smith Hall

1967–1970, John M. Adams for Whiteside, Moeckel and Carbonell

Even unattractive buildings have stories to tell. This facility occupied the site of an old house called "The Knoll" and contained classrooms and offices for arts and sciences, serving a booming campus (its population had increased from 5,500 students in 1963 to 13,000 four years later). Colleges nationwide rushed to build similar multipurpose facilities, many with this kind of brick-and-concrete aesthetic that projected a modern look yet employed a traditional red-brick-and-white-trim color scheme. Here the two materials were deliberately used in similar proportion of light and dark to that of the main campus. Design associate Adams was a former student of architect Louis Kahn. The challenge in the design was to move crowds through the building, so it was made accessible from all four sides and free from constricting corridors. Three auditoria could be entered from outside. Classrooms and offices faced a large central atrium. The basement housed what was then a great novelty, a computer center, and the public could watch the machines behind a glass partition. Fear of water damage to the computers led to a change in plans, and skylights were never installed above the atrium, leaving it gloomy, which a recent redecoration did little to alleviate.

NK9.14 Trabant University Center

1992–1996, Venturi, Scott Brown and Associates (VSBA)

When a previous student center (1957) proved inadequate for a greatly enlarged enrollment, a new one was planned closer to the westward-shifted geographical heart of campus. Five architectural firms competed, and the famous Philadelphia group VSBA (see Flint House, CH7) won with this design that incorporates a kind of indoor street, as at their Seattle Art Museum (1991). Its angled direction follows a preexisting student shortcut. The food court and shops are mall-like and huddle beneath a long, colorful row of oversized and glowing plastic letters that spell PIZZA DELI SNACKS FRIES, etc. Blue and gold neon lights (the University colors) buzz overhead, giving the

NK9.14 TRABANT UNIVERSITY CENTER

illusion of a vault. "We really like the fact that it is just a little vulgarly commercial in there," said the architects (Kershaw, 2001). Outside, the long descending arcade is marked by a deliberately complex arrangement of pilasters with wide-mullioned windows between, the whole creatively extrapolating from the brick Georgian Revival aesthetic of the rest of the campus. At either end, three mega-columns are in essence signposts that shout "Entrance," amusing in their unwarranted bombast and in that they support only the slenderest of roof slabs.

Opinions about the design were divided. Admirers cited the building's intelligent accommodation to the many complex functions of a modern student center, even as it nodded to colonial traditions and incorporated the old Gothic Revival church, Daugherty Hall. (Similar virtues were evident at other university student centers of the 1990s by these architects at Pennsylvania, Princeton, and Harvard.) They also enjoyed its witty play with a wide range of allusions, from American Main Streets (the arcade) to the Greek Parthenon frieze (the row of letters) to the architects' own design for Guild House (1960–1963) in Philadelphia (the fat columns). Detractors complained, however, of the jarring termination of the arcade at its roofline and where it meets the barren rear elevations and at the undignified, carnival atmosphere of the neon interior—which was, the architects admit, deliberately designed to please students, not their elders.

NK9.15 Daugherty Hall (Old First Presbyterian Church)

c. 1867–1871, Thomas Dixon and Frank E. Davis

Baltimore architect Dixon designed Grace Methodist Church (1865–1867, WL45) and Mount Vernon Place Methodist Church, Baltimore (1872). Newark's former Presbyterian church is far simpler than either of those elaborate Gothic Revival urban churches and uses wooden tracery instead of stone, but its stained glass is artful. Dixon and Davis briefly ran a firm together in 1867–1868. Eventually, the Newark Presbyterians moved to a more suburban location, and the university took over this stone-walled building in 1967 as a student center and dining facility. The 100-foot spire was unfortunately removed. A rear wing (1920s) was demolished in 1994 when the building was incorporated into Trabant University Center (NK9.14).

NK9.16 Bayard Sharp Hall (St. Thomas Church)

1843–1844. 1866–1867 tower and chancel

A recent addition to the university's holdings, this was one of the first churches founded as the Episcopal denomination returned to vigor in Delaware under Bishop Alfred Lee. The nave is flanked by buttresses and has a crenellated tower in front. Brick walls were later covered with stucco scored to resemble ashlar. Other Gothic Revival churches of this form exist on the Delmarva peninsula, including St. John's Chapel, Talbot County, Maryland (1835). The architect of St. Thomas is unknown; it might have been the famous Richard Upjohn, with whom a vestryman corresponded in summer 1843, or perhaps the commission ultimately went to the competing architect (not named in the correspondence). About 60,000 "good, well burnt, merchantable bricks" came from the George Evans brickyard on Elkton Road. Philadelphia bricklayer Joseph Hicks agreed to lay them "with all possible dispatch" and to erect buttresses and "front and back battlements." After World War II, the growing congregation moved to a new facility (1954–1959, Victorine and Samuel Homsey) on S. College Avenue and sold the old church to the town, which used it as a library from 1956 to 1974. Subsequently, there were plans to demolish the dilapidated building, but the university eventually purchased it and undertook a thorough renovation for a performing-arts center (1998–1999, Homsey Architects). Epoxy was injected to strengthen water-damaged walls and all the stucco was replaced.

NK9.17 Rodney Complex (West Complex)

1964–1966, Geddes Brecher Qualls Cunningham, Architects (GBQC)

This often-slighted dormitory and dining hall group is architecturally important, being derived from the innovative work of the great Louis Kahn in Philadelphia. Kahn's Richard Medical Research Building (1957–1965) and Erdman Dormitory, Bryn Mawr (erected 1963–1965) had awed a younger "Philadelphia School" of architects, including the architects of this building, who imitated Kahn in their Pender Labs, University of Pennsylvania (1958–1960). The choice of GBQC for the 796-student Delaware dorms came about after it was determined that Howell Lewis Shay and Associates, long favored by the university, was too busy to execute the project. The design called for six houses and three house lounges, the latter with walled garden-terraces. The lounges were communal meeting places with an apartment for a resident supervisor. The arrangement of the buildings was dense, to

NK9.17 RODNEY COMPLEX (WEST COMPLEX)

suit the site, and construction was massive, to deaden train noise. Recalling Kahn's Richard Labs, the blocky, apparently free-standing stair towers were, to use Kahn's terminology, "servant" spaces to the "served" houses. The chimney that floated free of the lounge walls was a Kahn device, as were the steel windows in a variety of shapes, including tall and narrow. Lantern-windows on the dining hall roof followed those at Erdman. The design won an award from the Pennsylvania Society of Architects in October 1964.

The conservative and frugal university was not quite ready for GBQC's kind of modernism. The estimated cost of $5.6 million shocked the trustees, who called it "unacceptably high" (they were accustomed to the cheap-and-quick dormitories of the 1950s). As costs mounted toward an eventual $6.7 million, the architects were repeatedly urged to compromise. Smooth bricks and "flamingo tinted mortar" were deemed unacceptable, as the trustees did not wish to deviate from "red Sayre Fisher brick with natural mortar of Delaware sand and finished with ivy joints," as used for half a century on the Green; eventually the smooth bricks were allowed. Exposed brick walls in corridors and lounges were questioned on the grounds of cost, at which architect Robert L. Geddes argued passionately for "the human scale of brick, its warm color" as part of an interior ensemble of muted lighting and wooden doors and benches. Rodney was designed for a new way of living, co-education, but within strict parameters, and the university overseers expended great energy in finding ways to refine the design in order to keep men and women apart. Mingling was allowed in the lounges, however. When lounge hours were lengthened to midnight (and to two on weekends), it was considered a victory for student rights.

NK9.18 Christiana Towers Apartments

1970–1972, Charles Luckman Associates

Bigger enrollments in the 1960s produced a need for two seventeen-story high-rise towers with commons. Some 1,300 students were to be housed in 452 units. The Luckman firm, of Los Angeles, planned steel-frame structures for the Delaware commission until they realized that the English precast-concrete industrialized housing systems just becoming available in the United States offered a better solution: same price, bigger rooms, soundproofing. The towers were built entirely of concrete slabs manufactured by a Baltimore firm and hoisted into place by crane. Windows were aluminum-and-glass infill within precast spandrels. The towers were pioneering in another way: concerns about wind stresses were resolved using a computer program.

WEST OF THE UNIVERSITY OF DELAWARE

NK10 Deer Park Tavern (Deer Park Hotel)

1851, with additions. 108 W. Main St.

This three-story brick building, dispenser of drink to innumerable students, replaced the log St. Patrick's Inn (1747), a headquarters for Charles Mason and Jeremiah Dixon during their famous survey in the 1760s, which stood just east. Edgar Allen Poe reputedly lodged there. The B&O Railroad was laid behind the hotel in 1886, over local opposition. The place has endured its share of drunken sprees, including one in 1974 that saw a mob of 4,000 students and others battle 200 police for hours. The Deer Park had its porch

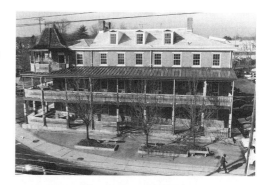

NK10 DEER PARK TAVERN (DEER PARK HOTEL)

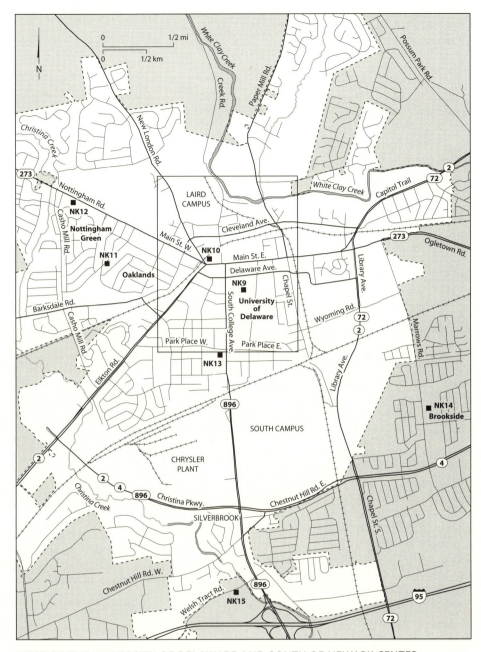

WEST OF THE UNIVERSITY OF DELAWARE AND SOUTH OF NEWARK CENTER

and balcony (later accretions) torn off in 1951, then replaced in a restoration (2001, Design Collaborative).

NK11 Oaklands and Nottingham Green

1956 established. South of W. Main St., from Hillside to Casho Mill rds.

The city charter of 1951 expanded Newark nearly a mile in all directions, the same year the Chrysler tank plant was built for the Korean War. Newark resident Hugh F. Gallagher left his father's Pontiac business for a career as a developer, starting Newark's first planned subdivision that year, Silverbrook (south of the plant). Once it was finished, Gallagher bought the ninety-one-acre Oaklands estate, laying out streets and demolishing a stately but rundown mansion of that name (1843). The tract houses he built here in 1963 were relatively upscale and in various styles and plans, including Colonial Revival, ranch, and split-level. The model home was a split-level at 114 Cheltenham Road (1956). More affordable and modernist were the houses of nearby Nottingham Green (Radcliffe Drive and west), developed out of the Ryan Farm by the nationally known firm of Leon N. Weiner and Associates, also starting in 1956. These subdivisions are typical of their period, with various models offering such amenities as brick and aluminum siding, dishwashers, garbage disposers, carports, and basements designed to accommodate game areas and hobby-workshops.

NK12 Gastho Etzel House

1939, Roscoe Cook Tindall. 417 Nottingham Rd.

In striking contrast to the builders' houses of the 1950s in Oaklands and Nottingham Green (NK11) is this two-story architect-designed house nearby—meticulously conceived, handcrafted, and making historical reference to the Old English cottage. A slate roof rises over stone walls, and the original steel casements have happily been retained. Tindall, who practiced in Wilmington and helped found AIA Delaware, prepared twelve pages of blueprints that showed such details as downspout heads, a china cabinet, kitchen bench and cabinetry with linoleum baseboards, and a paneled Game Room in the basement. An elaborate garden with stone walls was installed c. 1955.

SOUTH OF NEWARK CENTER

NK13 318 South College (Press of Kells)

1915–1916, Everett C. Johnson. 1925–1926 expanded to west. 1965–1966 altered, Whiteside, Moeckel and Carbonell. S. College Ave. and Park Pl.

This much-altered building was the printing plant of Johnson, founder of the *Newark Post* in 1910 and famous as a civic-minded publisher and progressive Republican secretary of state in the reform era of Delaware politics. When his first plant on Main Street was acquired for demolition by the expanding university, Johnson moved here, a then-rural district well south of the town center, to avoid taxes. He had visited Elbert Hubbard's Roycroft community in upstate New York in July 1911 and was inspired to replicate its Arts and Crafts flavor, fashioning a cardboard model to guide the workmen. A square stone tower with crenellations, copying one at the Roycroft Inn, rose above the Tudor Revival wings with walls of pebbledash. Stone came from farmers' fields on Iron Hill and was laid by two Italian craftsmen who sang opera as they worked, to Johnson's delight. A linotype operator chose the name, based on the famous medieval manuscript, the Book of Kells (800 AD). This was fitting, as Johnson, in the tradition of John Ruskin, William Morris, and Hubbard, emphasized neo-medievalism, handicraft ("Head, Heart, and Hand" was his motto), use of local materials, and capacious hearths (such as one in "The Whim," a lounge named after a line in Emerson's essay *Self-Reliance*). Just west is Johnson's irregular, self-designed Tudor Revival home (1921), with Cape Henlopen lighthouse carved on the cedar mantel; Johnson campaigned to save that threatened colonial landmark and proposed moving it to the university campus. In financial turmoil even before Johnson's sudden death in 1926, Press of Kells was sold in 1935 and was eventually turned into apartments. The YMCA purchased the building in 1961 and made regrettable changes.

NK14 Brookside

1952 established. Marrows Rd., north of Chestnut Hill Rd. (DE 4)

Raymond A. Burkland, a developer of Trenton, New Jersey, helped create the famous postwar suburb of Levittown. He brought that kind of tract housing to Delaware with a densely planned residential development on 285 acres. Sample homes of varying degrees of cost were erected along busy Kirkwood Highway, where commuters would see them (still extant east of Polly Drummond Hill Road). Burkland's development coincided with the opening in 1952 of DuPont's Louviers facility (NK3), and Brookside was occupied by young, white-collar families, including many engineers. Deed restrictions governed even the size of backyard clothes-lines and mandated a civic association to which residents paid dues. In the 1960s, Brookside abruptly changed: the proportion of college-educated adults dropped from 90 percent to less than 10 percent as engineers moved out. Only a quarter of the residents of the 1950s stayed to 1973, and some houses turned shabby. Brookside has attracted architectural historians interested in the ways that home owners alter the houses they inhabit, as the standard Brookside models have been tinkered with, especially their carports (see *Material Culture,* Spring 1997). A neighborhood landmark is the Kingswood United Methodist Church (1954–1955, George D. Savage; 300 Marrows Rd.), of brick and limestone with a spire of translucent green plastic, through which a beam of light was trained. The architect, of Narberth, Pennsylvania, designed several Colonial Revival churches in northern Delaware. With a population of about 15,000, unincorporated Brookside is today the state's sixth-largest conurbation.

NK15 Welsh Tract Baptist Church

1746. Welsh Tract Rd., 0.1 miles west of DE 896

The third Baptist congregation in the United States was established here at the foot of Iron Hill in 1703 by sixteen immigrants from Wales on the 30,000-acre "Welsh Tract" granted them by William Penn. The current building of glazed-header Flemish bond brickwork replaced a log original. Jerkinhead gables recall those at several of Delaware's early-eighteenth-century churches (for example, NC10). The two front entrances emulate Quaker practice. Steps, foundation corners, datestone

NK15 WELSH TRACT BAPTIST CHURCH

(with relief numerals and Catherine wheel), table tomb bases, and several tombstones are of red sandstone, perhaps imported from New Jersey. A greenish rock is evident for tombstones dating back to the 1720s, and there is much marble, suggesting an extensive trade in stones. As recorded by a University of Delaware professor in the 1920s, the oldest stone (1707) was in Latin; others were Welsh, dating as late as 1759. In 1936 the old markers were crumbling, and today, the table tombs in particular are disintegrating. American soldiers made a last stand in the churchyard after the Battle of Cooch's Bridge in 1777, and a cannonball struck the building (or, alternatively, went in one window and out another). Once renowned for its huge "Three Sisters" white oaks, the now-treeless yard is surrounded by a heavy wall (1827 and later; recently refurbished). In the 1990s, the church's brickwork suffered an awful repointing with hard, white cement. Across the road are an ancient sexton's house of stone and a shed with tree-trunk posts. As in the early twentieth century, the church houses a tiny Primitive Baptist congregation that meets one or more Sundays a month.

Pencader and Red Lion Hundreds

This section of Delaware roughly corresponds to the boundaries of two historic New Castle County hundreds, embracing fertile agricultural land on the upper margin of the Coastal Plain. Along its southern edge runs the Chesapeake and Delaware Canal; at its northern rises a geological anomaly, Iron Hill, a mass of the dark, igneous rock called gabbro protruding above the soft silts and clays of the surrounding fields. For thousands of years, Iron Hill attracted Native Americans who quarried jasper on its slopes and established stone-tool workshops. European settlers mined the hill for iron ore from the early eighteenth century until about 1890. Historically, its greatest fame came during the British campaign for Philadelphia in 1777: General George Washington, Nathanael Greene, and the Marquis de Lafayette reconnoitered the advancing army of General William Howe from the summit, and the Battle of Cooch's Bridge raged at its base. Elsewhere in the region, prosperous farms and towns developed at an early date and grew gradually. In the twentieth century, the convulsive growth of the 1950s brought the construction of an enormous oil refinery in Red Lion Hundred. For its part, Pencader Hundred became the fastest-growing section of New Castle County, its population increasing by 259 percent that decade. The area has subsequently been overrun almost entirely by sprawl, eventually obliterating even the last surviving farms along the southernmost fringe. Many old farmhouses and outbuildings have been destroyed, including any surviving traces of the log house inhabited by the architect Benjamin Henry Latrobe on the summit of Iron Hill, where he lived in summer 1805 during construction of the Feeder Canal (part of the first, abortive attempt to build a ship canal across the peninsula). Latrobe's probable house site was developed for houses in 2000.

PR1 I-95 Newark Toll Plaza (John F. Kennedy Memorial Highway, Delaware Turnpike)

1962–1963. I-95 at Maryland line, southwest of Newark

No man-made achievement has affected northern Delaware so much as this interstate, a key link in East Coast megalopolis (see also its bridge at Wilmington, WL61). Ten thousand people gathered at the state line west of the toll plaza on November 14, 1963, for the dedication of the Maryland and Delaware turnpikes, limited access superhighways that symbolized America's preference for automobile transportation and allowed motorists to drive from Newark to Baltimore without

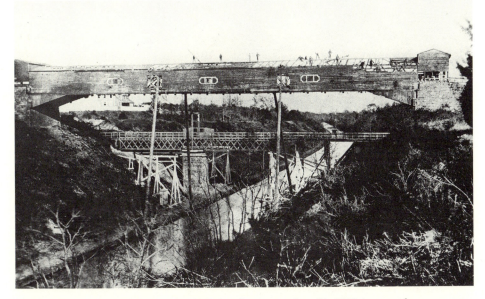

Summit Covered Bridge. When the C&D Canal was completed in 1829, its most famous feature was Summit Bridge at the Deep Cut—a covered wooden truss 247 feet long and a dizzying 90 feet above the water. As seen here, it was removed in 1865–1866 and replaced with a lower drawbridge.

stopping (the equivalent stretch of old U.S. 40 had nearly 100 dangerous at-grade intersections). At four o'clock in the afternoon, President John F. Kennedy alighted from an Army helicopter and gave a speech referring prophetically to the future, when the Boston-to-Washington corridor would be "one gigantic urban complex." Governor Elbert N. Carvel said to him, "We in Delaware look forward to your presence at the dedication of the second Delaware Memorial Bridge, which we expect will take place some time during your second term, probably in 1967." Kennedy snipped a ribbon to unveil a replica of a Mason-Dixon crown stone, a copy of several originals that still mark the eighteenth-century boundary between the two colonies. Six days later, he flew to Dallas.

PR2 Iron Hill Museum (Iron Hill School No. 112C)

1923, James O. Betelle for Guilbert and Betelle. 1355 Old Baltimore Pike, 0.9 miles west of DE 896

Delaware's ensemble of one-room schoolhouses shrank from 178 in 1930 to just fourteen in 1962, including this one for African Americans on the lower slopes of Iron Hill. In 1920–1935, Pierre S. du Pont gave over $6 million for new Delaware schools. By 1938, he had expended $2.6 million on eighty-seven facilities specifically for African Americans. The Guilbert and Betelle firm of Newark, New Jersey (carried on by Wilmington-raised Betelle after Guilbert died in 1916), received its professional direction from the du Pont commissions, eventually designing hundreds of schools in five states, with an office staff of up to seventy-five. A museum has occupied the building since 1964, and its director informs me that "the smaller black schools were commissioned after a population study (financed by du Pont, and conducted by Columbia University) determined that scattered populations of African Americans would make larger consolidated schools less feasible." Betelle brought skill and sensitivity to even the most economical schoolhouses, the example here showing good proportions and design within the context of a simple frame structure clad in shingles and with a pedimented portico. As a group, the former du Pont schools have attracted great interest in recent years, but most are dilapidated.

PR3 COOCH HOUSE, photo 1930s

PR3 Cooch House

1760. c. 1822 enlarged. Old Baltimore Pike, 0.4 miles east of DE 896, at Christina Creek

In 1746, miller Thomas Cooch bought the property with its early iron furnace, only the third in British America. The nearby road bridge (1922) stands on the site of the colonial one that saw the only Revolutionary War battle fought in Delaware, the Battle of Cooch's Bridge. Lord Cornwallis was headquartered in the Cooch House following the September 1777 skirmish. Cooch, a leading patriot who was then eighty years old, had fled to Pennsylvania before the armies arrived. A monument (1901, 1932) and four Civil War cannons (1863) commemorate the fight—according to legend, the first conflict in which the Stars and Stripes flew. The brick house was originally two stories high, but was later raised one story and stuccoed. A porch of four fluted Doric columns overlooks the creek. The slender columns of the small, gabled side porch are said to have come from the old colonial front porch and were, according to tradition, originally ship masts. Owner Edward W. Cooch, later lieutenant governor, had Wilmington architect Edward Canby May install Colonial Revival stairs inside (1919–1920), although in a different location from the original ones. Several outbuildings survive, including some of board-and-batten construction. Edward Cooch's son still occupies this oasis of green just south of I-95 and has placed the land in a conservation easement.

PR4 Cooch-Dayett Mill

c. 1822; c. 1894 enlarged, with later changes. Dayett Mill Rd., 0.2 miles southwest of intersection of Old Baltimore Pike and DE 72

Industry flourished early along this stretch of Christina Creek. The boxy brick mill stands almost in sight of the Cooch House (PR3). Up-

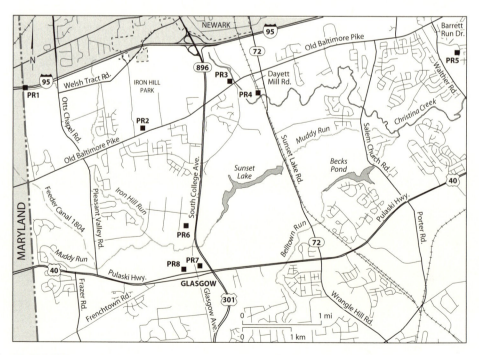

GLASGOW

stream from that house once stood Lord Keith's iron smelting furnace and drop hammer mill (c. 1720), the dam for which was raised in 1792 and restored after damage by Hurricane Floyd in 1999 by Landmark Engineering, Inc. Ruins of several other eighteenth-century mills still exist, and a barn just east of Cooch's Bridge with a datestone of 1792 in the foundation incorporates one wall from William Cooch Jr.'s grist mill. The 2,700-foot mill race of 1792 can still be traced, as well as the 1,300-foot-long extension of 1822, elevated above the surrounding fields. It fed Dayatt Mill, built by Cooch but expanded following its purchase by John Dayett in 1894. Dayett (locally pronounced "diet") added boilers and engines to supplement waterpower and could grind seventy-five barrels of flour per day here. The facility was restored after fires in 1916 and 1933. In 1981, it was one of only two mills in the state still in operation (the other was Hearns Mill, Seaford) and used a water turbine of 1918. Subsequently abandoned, Dayatt is undergoing long-term restoration.

PR5 Thurgood Marshall Elementary School

1991–1993, Buck Simpers Architect + Associates. 101 Barrett Run Dr., off Walther Rd., northwest of Bear

As explosive development overtook New Castle County south of I-95 in the 1990s, the Simpers firm designed a series of Postmodern elementary schools for the fast-growing district: the 64,000-square-foot Marshall School and two others: William B. Keene School (c. 2000, 200 LaGrange Ave., Glasgow) and May B. Leasure School (c. 2000, 1015 Church

PR6 ASTROPOWER (FORMER)

Rd., Bear). All followed a standardized "learning pod" design, with classroom wings arranged around common spaces. Interiors are filled with light, and, to ease young children as they enter the building, the school entrances make reference to familiar childhood objects, in the pop-cultural manner of Philadelphia architect Robert Venturi (see his Flint House, CH7, and Trabant Center, NK9.14). At Keene School, those objects are huge building blocks; at Leasure, Lego blocks; and at Marshall, gigantic crayons supporting the metal canopy as columns. The colors of the crayons are continued inside as distinctive pod colors for various grades. With rapid growth, unincorporated and formless Bear has become the fifth-largest community in the state.

PR6 AstroPower (former)

2000–2001, Bernardon Haber Holloway. 300 Executive Dr., west of U.S. 301, north of Glasgow

A solar electric power company built this showpiece headquarters in the sprawl belt south of Newark. The 160,000-square-foot facility combined headquarters and manufacturing space. A "green" structure, its dramatically curving blue facade contains solar cells in the spandrel glass of the curtain wall. A solar-electric system on the roof can produce more than 300,000 kilowatt-hours of power annually. Inside, a colorful lobby floor is made of recycled glass. The company only occupied the facility for eighteen months before going bankrupt. Plans were subsequently made to convert the empty building into a school.

PR5 THURGOOD MARSHALL ELEMENTARY SCHOOL

GLASGOW

Originally named Aikentown, this unincorporated historic village is bisected by the maelstrom of a modern highway, but still retains a short stretch of north–south colonial road (DE 896 north of U.S. 40), along which 4,000 British troops marched to the Battle of Cooch's Bridge. A brick Presbyterian parsonage stands on the east side of this road (early nineteenth century); farther north and on the west, beside the creek historically known as Five Mile Run, is a nineteenth-century schoolhouse. The run was considered as a possible route for Benjamin Henry Latrobe's Chesapeake and Delaware Canal of 1804. Although the canal was never constructed, its feeder was, and can still be seen as a ditch north of U.S. 40 and west of Pleasant Valley Road (west of Glasgow). The original Aiken's Tavern (Glasgow Hotel) was destroyed in 1943 when a truck crashed into its living room and burst into flames.

PR7 Pencader Presbyterian Church

1852. DE (BUS) 896 and U.S. 40

William Penn's grant in 1701 of 30,000 acres to Welsh settlers gave rise to two churches, this one and Welsh Tract Baptist (NK15). Pencader is Welsh for "chief seat." The early-eighteenth-century frame chapel that stood nearby was replaced by a brick building in 1782–1783, later demolished for the current one, also brick, in a plain Greek Revival style with very tall second-floor windows. The pedimented front-gable form of the church, engaged brick pilasters, and a sharp steeple on a square base resemble several other churches of the period in Delaware (e.g., PR14, NK5). In 1899, the "audience room" (sanctuary) was replastered, pews and woodwork grained, and the building roofed with tin. During that decade, a tomb of 1712 could still be seen in the churchyard; further examination in the 1930s revealed some gravestones in Welsh. The sycamores probably date to the 1780s. Directly opposite stands the handsome brick Cann Store of the nineteenth century.

PR8 La Grange

1815, with additions. North of U.S. 40, 0.2 miles west of DE (BUS) 896

Dr. Samuel Henry Black bought 225 acres in the old Welsh Tract (see PR7) in 1799 and built this Federal-style brick dwelling, notable for its attractive front facade of big sash windows, nine in all with a total of nearly 200 panes. A medical doctor trained at the University of Pennsylvania, Black named the place for the Marquis de Lafayette's estate in France. Black practiced scientific farming, wrote on medicine and agriculture, and made a public demonstration of the smallpox vaccine on his own son. A drawing of the house in 1817 shows it before the addition of the pleasing Greek Revival portico around the door. The Steven B. Barczewski family bought the deteriorated place in 1942 and undertook restoration, doing the work themselves, as labor was unavailable in wartime. They whitewashed the gray-painted house, added shutters, rebuilt the

PR7 PENCADER PRESBYTERIAN CHURCH

PR8 LA GRANGE, early 19th-century drawing

kitchen, and installed bathrooms. As suburban development later choked the DE 40 corridor, La Grange survived intact. When efforts failed to have the property incorporated into a new Glasgow Regional Park (2003–2005, Wallace, Roberts and Todd, landscape architects), it became apparent that the historic and beautiful house would be sold to developers.

ALONG THE CHESAPEAKE AND DELAWARE CANAL

PR9 Summit Bridge

1958–1959. DE 896 over Chesapeake and Delaware (C&D) Canal

The steel-truss high bridge stands just west of the site of earlier Summit bridges over the Deep Cut of the canal. A four-lane highway bridge here was considered essential for the state's growth. Shrewd Delaware lawmakers forced the federal government to pay by citing the canal company's charter of 1801, which required that company (bought out by the United States in 1919) to provide "good and sufficient bridges across the canal." To the east stands the Pennsylvania Railroad bridge (1965–1966), at the time the third-longest railroad lift bridge in the world and cited for excellence by the American Institute for Steel Construction. An intriguing iron pivot bridge (1852) just north of the railroad bridge was unfortunately removed in 1967.

PR10 Buck Tavern

1821. 1963 moved. Red Lion Rd., Lums Pond State Park

Now an immediate neighbor to the relocated Lum House (PR11), this austere, three-bay brick Federal building with arched dormers and a narrow, fanlit front door formerly

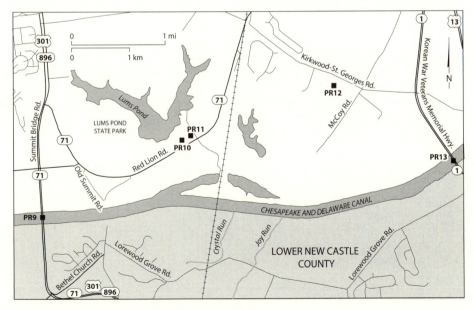

ALONG THE CHESAPEAKE & DELAWARE CANAL

CHESAPEAKE AND DELAWARE CANAL

So potently does the canal divide Delaware into northern and southern cultural zones, it is sometimes hard to recall that it is a man-made feature. Eighteenth-century Philadelphians clamored for such a transpeninsular waterway, as it would open them to western markets via the Susquehanna River, and one was abortively begun by Benjamin Henry Latrobe in 1804. In summer 1822, Latrobe's former pupil William Strickland surveyed two possible routes, Latrobe's and one farther south. After furious debate, the canal company chose the latter, to the surprise of many, and it was dug across Eastern Shore Maryland and Delaware in 1824–1829 (Benjamin Wright and John Randel Jr., engineers).

A force of 2,600 men at a time, Irish with some African Americans, did the work, cutting the fourteen-mile channel and building locks. The difficulties were enormous, as was the cost—about twice the original estimate of $1.2 million, and at $165,000 per mile (compared to $19,000 for the Erie Canal). The canal cut 286 miles off a trip from Baltimore to ports on the Delaware River. The canal company never recovered from the enormous expenses of digging the waterway and remained in debt until the Federal Government bought it in 1919 and undertook enlargement.

Several bridges are interesting, as is the rare surviving Delaware Tide Lock at Delaware City (PR20). As widened in the 1960s, today's sea-level canal is 450 feet wide and thirty-five feet deep. Complex electronic devices are used to monitor ship traffic, under the auspices of the U.S. Army Corps of Engineers at Chesapeake City, Maryland. A Canal Museum there occupies a historic pumphouse.

BOATS ON THE C&D CANAL ORIGINALLY PASSED THROUGH A SERIES OF NARROW LOCKS, AS HERE AT ST. GEORGES; ALL BUT THE DELAWARE TIDE LOCK (PR20) WERE ELIMINATED IN A MASSIVE ENLARGEMENT OF THE CANAL AFTER 1919.

stood south of the C&D Canal at Summit. Over the years, confusion arose as to which building had actually been Buck Tavern and whether this one—considered the most likely candidate—was old enough to have hosted George Washington, who occasionally "Din'd at the Buck." In 1963, the U.S. Army Corps of Engineers, altering the route of the canal, intended to demolish the building. Instead, the Corps donated it to the state under the condition that it be moved within weeks. As the structure was dismantled brick-by-brick under the supervision of architect George F. Bennett, it was discovered that a carpenter had written in red crayon inside an attic dormer, "John Bayly June 19, 1821," which rules out any visits by Washington. Like the Lum House next door, it is now boarded up. In 2004, the state announced a plan to have "resident curators" pay to restore Buck Tavern and the Lum House, then live in them rent-free for life.

PR12 AU CLAIR SCHOOL (MCCOY HOUSE)

PR11 Lum House (Lums Mill House, Samuel Davies House)

c. 1730, with additions. Red Lion Rd., Lums Pond State Park

This early, three-bay, pent-eave brick house was probably built by Samuel Clement, who bought the property in 1724 and established a mill in 1736. Traditionally, it was the birthplace of Andrew Jackson's grandmother and also a home of Samuel Davies, a founder of Princeton University (the latter claim is doubtful). Two John Lums owned it successively, and their millpond provided water for the summit pool of the C&D Canal. The common-bond east wing was added later and heightened post-1809; a strange rear wall of boulders is apparently later still. The dwelling is much altered inside. The vicinity was the scene of extensive dumping when the canal was widened, a process involving steam shovels and train cars (1921–1923). The road in front of the house was once forty feet lower than today. By 1962, the Lum House was rapidly disintegrating and at risk of destruction by the Army Corps of Engineers. Attention was drawn to it by a resources survey commissioned by the National Park Service, Philadelphia, under John S. Cotter. Repairs were made, but today the front wall of the boarded-up building shows an alarming bulge.

PR12 Au Clair School (McCoy House)

1892–1897. 4185 Kirkwood-St. Georges Rd., 0.1 miles west of DE 1 Bridge

Dr. John C. McCoy became wealthy by developing a patent-medicine catarrh remedy. He was also a horse breeder and operated a public harness-racing track here starting in 1892, with a 3,000-seat grandstand. His twenty-eight-room mansion is unusual in Delaware for its Germanic flavor, and family legend attributed the design to McCoy's student days in Germany. Extremely steep roofs employed ninety tons of brown glazed tiles from Belgium, and walls two feet thick were faced with yellow brick. The home was familiarly known as the Gingerbread House for its picturesque qualities. Inside, pine paneling and decorative woodwork is copious, and there are massive brick chimneypieces. A mosaic of a Greek goddess was derived from a coin in McCoy's collection. In the late 1960s, the house became a pioneering school for autistic children.

PR13 Senator William V. Roth Jr. Bridge (DE 1 Bridge, St. Georges Bridge)

1992–1995, Figg Engineering Group. DE 1 over the Chesapeake and Delaware Canal, 0.4 miles southwest of St. Georges

ALONG THE CHESAPEAKE AND DELAWARE CANAL   199

A fifty-one-mile divided highway built over more than a decade (1987–2003), DE 1 was a project of extraordinary intricacy and expense. Intended as a "relief route" for the benefit of beachgoers, it had the side effect of triggering boundless sprawl. Houses along the corridor multiplied by 42 percent in the 1990s alone. The striking, 4,650-foot bridge over the canal—already considered a landmark in the state—was the work of a Florida-based firm known for its Sunshine Skyway Bridge, St. Petersburg (1987), which, as here, used cable-stay technology: cables radiate out from tall concrete pylons. With a span of 750 feet, the Delaware bridge is a little more than half the size of its Florida predecessor. It is the longest concrete span in the northeast United States.

ST. GEORGES AND VICINITY

Before envelopment by sprawl, this was northern New Castle County's least-changed settlement, partly as a result of its having been bypassed by the highway bridge of 1940. Some streets are still paved with their first concrete surface. A mill dam stood on a creek here in the early eighteenth century, and a village sprang up around it. When the creek was enlarged into the Chesapeake and Delaware Canal, rapid growth followed. Twentieth-century widenings of the canal wiped out the lower part of the town, but the upper sections remain largely intact. A relic of the earliest period is the brick Robinson House (1750s) at 213 Main Street. The Sutton House (1792, date irons on rear wing), corner of Broad and Delaware streets, was enlarged c. 1820 and was embellished with Queen Anne motifs in the late nineteenth century; it remained in one family for generations. Several buildings on its block are on the National Register, including the mansarded brick International Order of Odd Fellows (IOOF) Lodge (1875), reminder of a flourishing decade that saw the town's population reach 500. The frame Gam's Store (c. 1855) at Delaware and Main streets has long housed a business. On the north edge of town stands the Classical Revival Commodore Macdonough School (1923–1924, Guilbert and Betelle), praised by Leo Borah in *National Geographic* (1935) as "a fine example of the schools that resulted from Pierre du Pont's program."

PR14 Presbyterian Church

1844–1845. Main St. at Church St.

The front-gable brick design and the specific steeple form (needle-shaped atop a square base) are similar to several other churches in the county, including Pencader Presbyterian Church (PR7). The St. Georges church has big Greek Revival front doors and an Ithiel Town lattice truss roof, said to be the only one surviving in the state. The church reached its nadir in the 1980s, when the congregation disbanded and the structure was condemned by the county building inspector. Fortunately, the St. Georges Historical Society was formed to save the building, which is now restored as a community center, and the steeple is again illuminated at night. Across the street is a cottage with fish-scale slate shingle roof (c. 1860).

PR15 Old St. Georges Bridge

1939–1941, Parsons, Klapp, Brinckerhoff and Douglas, engineers, with Aymar Embury II, architect. U.S. 13 over the Chesapeake and Delaware Canal

In January 1939, the steamship *Waukegan* crashed into the original St. Georges Bridge, which collapsed. This high-level replacement bridge spans 540 feet and stands 135 feet over the canal. A New York City engineering firm provided a tied-arch design (where the arch's horizontal forces are borne by the bridge deck rather then the bridge foundations), a type more common in Europe than in the United States. Architect Embury had consulted on the Triborough and Bronx-Whitestone bridges, New York. Plans survive (at Hagley Museum) that show construction details down to the last rivet. The bridge utilized 7,500 tons of steel, fabricated by Phoenix Iron and Steel. Its opening in January 1942 was timely, as the war brought a boom in canal and highway traffic. Once the new DE 1 bridge opened (PR13), demolition of this earlier span was considered but rejected. Flaking lead-paint chips have raised health concerns among local residents.

PR16 Fairview

1822. 1885 enlarged, Furness and Evans. Cox Neck Rd., 1.5 miles southwest of Delaware City

"AH 1822" in glazed bricks on an end gable commemorates the first owner, Anthony Higgins. His grandson, John Clark Higgins, founded Wilmington's Vulcanized Fiber Company and served as President William McKinley's consul in Scotland. Here, at Fairview, the gentleman farmer bred Guernsey cattle. Frank Furness enlarged the house for him, adding a third floor in his inimitable manner without regard for the clash of styles. The effect is bizarre, the Queen Anne additions with fish-scale shingled siding, wide eaves, and swelling chimneytops sitting like a fancy hat on top of the sober old Federal walls. Higgins may have preserved these walls, though outmoded, in homage to his grandfather.

PR17 Delaware City Refinery (Tidewater Delaware Refinery)

1955–1957. Wrangle Hill Rd. and River Rd., 1.8 miles west of Delaware City

Tidewater Oil Company marketed its products nationwide as Flying A Gasolines and Veedol Motor Oils. It examined thirty sites on the Eastern Seaboard before choosing this one, 5,000 acres of farmland centered on the historic Philip Reybold peach mansion, Lexington (1846, Samuel Sloan). The company torched the mansion (July 1955) and erected the largest refinery ever built at one time, a facility that could process 130,000 barrels of crude oil per day. Nine thousand men were at work erecting the plant in 1956. At its heart was the twenty-five-story-high Fluid Catalytic Cracker for converting gas oils into gasoline, said to be the largest in the world at the time. A huge marine terminal was dredged, and nine million barrels of river water were pumped through the refinery per day for cooling, more than the volume used by Philadelphia. Indeed, the gigantic facility resembles a city in itself when its towering smokestacks

PR15 OLD ST. GEORGES BRIDGE, photo 1950s, with town in foreground

PR16 FAIRVIEW, showing Frank Furness enlargement of house

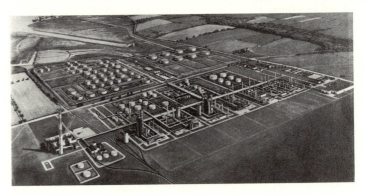

PR17 DELAWARE CITY REFINERY (TIDEWATER DELAWARE REFINERY)

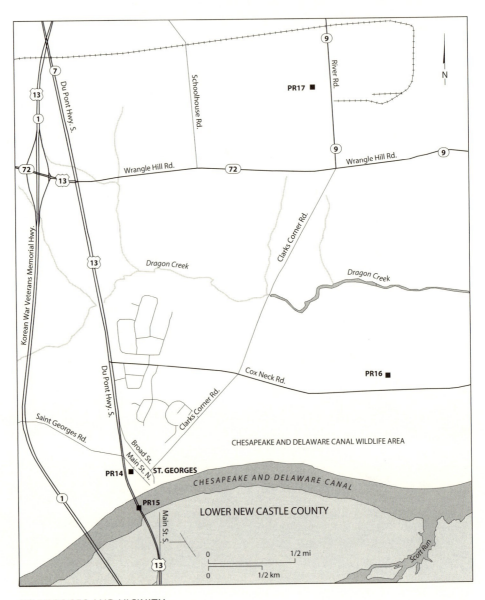

ST. GEORGES AND VICINITY

and thousands of lights are seen from across the fields at night. Delaware City welcomed the plant eagerly, but some residents later grumbled about the limited financial benefits to the town and the acrid smells. From his farm at Buena Vista (NC24), former Governor C. Douglass Buck complained in 1958 that the plant had turned "peaceful" farmland into "a smelly unattractive section." Fearing more refineries, the state legislature eventually passed the historic Coastal Zone Act banning heavy industry (1971). Tidewater Refinery has subsequently changed hands many times and remains controversial for its groundwater pollution and toxic releases.

DELAWARE CITY

Unique in the state as an antebellum boom town, Delaware City (pop. 1,453) was born of the Chesapeake and Delaware (C&D) Canal. The Newbold family, proprietors of Newbold's Landing, drew a town plan and invented the optimistic title of "city." The main street was named for Erie Canal promoter and New York governor De Witt Clinton. Speculators drove up land values between 1826 and the opening of the C&D Canal in 1829, but the bubble burst. Subsequent growth was slow, the population peaking at 1,355 in 1860. The town was stranded when an enlargement to the canal, in 1927, was sited two miles south. *National Geographic* (1935) called Delaware City "the seasonal center of shad and sturgeon fishing and reed and railbird hunting," but river pollution soon ended the lucrative fishing industry. By the 1980s, the town was struggling. Over the past forty years, a series of proposals has been put forward for touristic rehabilitation, and they are finally showing signs of success.

Christ Church (1849–1851; 222 Clinton Street) is one of several congregations established in Delaware after Episcopalianism returned to life under Bishop Alfred Lee. Parish tradition points to a Philadelphia oddity, The Floating Church of the Redeemer (1849), as inspiration. The rectory and parish hall were added in 1870 and 1894–1895, respectively. The building has lost its steeple. Also in town is the Ebenezer United Methodist Church of 1875, restored after a fire in 1946 (306 Clinton St.). At 300 Clinton Street is a bungalow said to have been designed by Gustav Stickley and illustrated in his magazine, *The Craftsman* (1912). Near Reedy Point Bridge (1965–1968), south of town, stand the scattered buildings of Fort DuPont (1899–1915), which originally provided artillery support for Fort Delaware (PR21) in the Civil War.

PR18 Polk-Henry House
1839. 2nd and Washington sts.

In this big, three-story wooden house with corner pilasters one sees a Greek Revival approach relatively rare in Delaware, where few places truly boomed during that architectural era. The house's first inhabitant, Robert Polk, was also owner of Polktown, a community for free African Americans just outside of town. He soon sold the house to coal merchant James Henry. The abandoned place was nearly razed in 1999 for a fire station, but the town sold it five years later to a developer who planned to create a bed-and-breakfast and redevelop the rest of the spacious, grassy lot. The bank next door dates from 1849. A walk along Washington Street shows that scattered brick townhouses were built on the wide nineteenth-century thoroughfare in expectation of an urban density that never occurred. One house has a porch supported by bundled, lotiform (lotus-shaped) colonnettes, rare in the state.

PR19 Central Hotel (Sterling Hotel)

c. 1830. Clinton St. facing Battery Park

Promoters of the boom town built several hotels that catered to business travelers as well as excursionists. This wedge-shaped, Federal-style brick edifice is one; another was the Delaware City Hotel on the same street, at Number 30 (1829). The celebration in 1927 for the opening of the widened canal was held at Central Hotel, but subsequently the hostelry declined along with the town, and today it stands empty and dilapidated, though still a reminder of flush times. Recent improvements nearby include a massive seawall and promenade alongside the canal. Old storefronts along Clinton Street, which are gradually being restored, show the "lay-on-your-belly" third story windows typical of antebellum Delaware (small windows that sit close to floor level).

PR20 Delaware Tide Lock, Chesapeake and Delaware Canal

1824–1825, Benjamin Wright and John Randel Jr. 1851–1854 rebuilt and enlarged. Battery Park at the riverfront

The only surviving lock of the original canal and an engineering landmark of national significance, the Delaware Tide Lock was spared destruction only because the enlarged waterway of the 1920s was shifted two miles south. Engineers Wright and Randel, brought down from the Erie Canal in 1823, designed the lock to be 100 feet long and twenty-two feet wide, with a lift of seven feet. What exists today is the replacement of the 1850s, much longer and somewhat wider; it has been partly filled in, along with the Basin westwards. (A lock pumphouse of 1850s date, similar to the kind that would have stood here, can still be seen at Chesapeake City, Maryland, where a museum is devoted to the canal.) The lock is of stone on wooden underpinnings, with a wooden floor. Underwater mechanisms were repaired by means of an iron, Philadelphia-made diving bell (1839), which stands nearby. A restoration in 1999 recreated the gravel towpath. Battery

PR20 DELAWARE TIDE LOCK, CHESAPEAKE AND DELAWARE CANAL

Park itself dates back to a U.S. Navy fortification of 1814 protecting Newbold's Landing.

PR21 Fort Delaware

1853–1859. 1890s altered. Pea Patch Island (reached by ferry from Delaware City)

As early as 1794, the architect Pierre-Charles L'Enfant recommended a fort on this muddy island to protect Philadelphia from attack. The War of 1812 confirmed that forts needed to lie at a considerable distance from the cities they defended, and an ambitious series of national fortifications was planned. A fort in the traditional "star" shape was built here (1816–1827), but its foundations shifted in soggy ground, and it was demolished after a fire in 1831. A second fort was begun but was damaged by a flood, and all work stopped during a lawsuit over ownership of the island. Clearing, foundation work, and pile driving for the present edifice took place in 1848–1852, and stone walls began to rise, with outer facings of Quincy, Massachusetts, granite. Work dragged on until 1868, by which time the island had served as a fetid detention camp for thousands of Confederate prisoners, with more than forty buildings surrounding the fort. All evidence of this sprawling wartime facility was later buried under dredge spoils. Fort Delaware was modified during the Spanish-American War by the insertion of a Three Gun Lift, a hulking concrete-with-sand-core battery to house disappearing guns. One of the two original Officers' Quarters and half of the barracks were demolished. The fort was abandoned after World War II, having never

PR21 FORT DELAWARE, view from atop terreplain looking across parade to three-arched sallyport, with officers' quarters at right

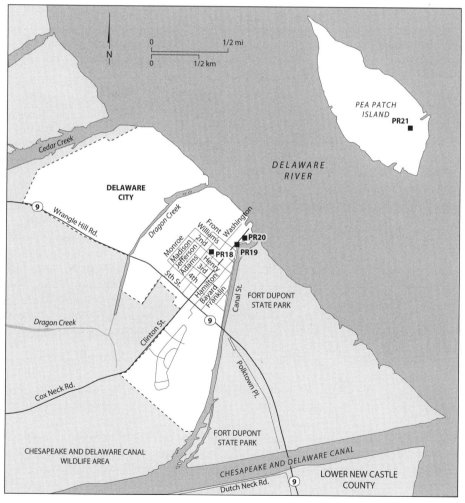

DELAWARE CITY

fired a shot against an enemy. Vandals worked the place over even after the state park was established in 1951. Professional restoration and interpretation of the imposing ruins began in 1995, and 40,000 tourists now visit annually. Prison barracks have been re-created; staff offices, mess halls, supply room, and officers' quarters have been restored; and fiberglass replica cannons added. There has been talk of over-restoration by eliminating the historic, concrete additions of the 1890s.

The six-acre fort consists of five polygonal bastions at the corners, with three-story ramparts between. The outer granite wall, or scarp, rises steeply above a water-filled ditch. One enters over a drawbridge and through a pedimented sallyport with massive doors. Inside is a grassy parade ground. Guns were mounted inside the walls as well as on the terreplain on top, which offers sweeping views of the river. The gun emplacements have iron rails in the floor (along which the carriages swiveled) and embrasures cut into the massive stone walls. Heavy, yet graceful, brick arches (in utilitarian English bond) form complex geometries, as do circular stairs of granite. The whole comprises a fascinating labyrinth of dark, dripping, echoing corridors with slimy walls. Fort Delaware is one of the state's most significant buildings, its rugged construction insuring exceptional preservation in spite of the vandalism. A must-see for any Civil War buff, it is far better preserved than the more famous, war-shattered Fort Sumter at Charleston.

Lower New Castle County

The Dutch settled in the seventeenth century along the Appoquinimink River at present-day Odessa, starting the local pattern by which towns sprang up along river wharves from which produce could be shipped to larger markets. Agriculture was intensive in this fertile region of the Upper Coastal Plain, and soil exhaustion set in by the early nineteenth century. As historian Bernard Herman has described, scientific farming sought innovative solutions to the crisis and brought new prosperity, which in turn triggered a great antebellum renewal of homes and outbuildings. One of the northernmost outposts of slavery in the United States was here, although most slaves in the state had been freed by 1840. By that time, the Chesapeake and Delaware (C&D) Canal had divided this section of the county from the part farther north, "Below the Canal" becoming shorthand for the more Southern culture detectable here. The coming of the north–south Delaware Railroad in 1855 allowed perishable fruits to be sped quickly to markets in ice-cooled cars, triggering a boom in peach production. Fortunes made in the 1860s and 1870s were followed by a sudden failure around 1890, owing in part to a dread agricultural disease, "peach yellows." A second wave of growth in this region, infinitely bigger than the first, came in the form of late-twentieth-century suburbanization. Current lot sizes are three times larger than those in the developments of the 1950s in northern New Castle County, and open space is disappearing with incredible rapidity, along with old farmhouses. No part of Delaware has been more thoroughly studied by architectural historians, thanks to the Center for Historic Architecture and Design at the University of Delaware. Many of the structures they surveyed in the 1980s and 1990s are already gone, as are many of those discussed in Herman's *Architecture and Rural Life in Central Delaware, 1700–1900* (1987).

LN1 Liston Range Rear Lighthouse

1876–1877. 1906 moved here. East of U.S. 13 on Port Penn Rd.

The U.S. Coast Guard still operates this archaic-looking lighthouse, part of a historic network serving Delaware River ship traffic. River range lighthouses are rare today nationwide. The 120-foot tower was fabricated of wrought iron by Kellogg Bridge Company of Buffalo, New York, and originally stood a few miles east, where it was coated with a protective layer of coal tar and held a fixed white light. Dwellings, a barn, and an oil house were

LN1 LISTON RANGE REAR LIGHTHOUSE

LN2 JOHN ASHTON HOUSE

built to serve it on its current site, to which it was moved. It was electrified and automated in the 1930s and recorded by the Historic American Engineering Record in 1976. The lighthouse is unusual for being of wrought iron rather than cast iron. Raised on a stone base and with a narrow central column and a skirtlike array of stays radiating from the top, Liston bears a close resemblance to the later Reedy Island Range Rear Light, Taylors Bridge (1909–1910).

LN2 John Ashton House

c. 1700–1730 period, main block, with additions. Thorntown Rd., west of DE 9, north of Port Penn

Historians disagree regarding the date of this simple two-story house, which stands atop a rise in open country south of the C&D Canal. Quaker Robert Ashton, a cousin of William Penn, was granted 900 acres here in 1686, and some think the hall-parlor-plan residence was built about the time of his death in 1706, at which point his lands were divided between his two sons. Others believe that his grandson, John Ashton Jr., built the house when he inherited the property in 1728. Either way, it is one of the oldest brick dwellings in Delaware. Early features include the steep roof pitch, doglegged (or stepped) stringcourse on the gable end, shaped chimneys, small windows, and pent eave. In the vicinity, too, stands the early brick Dilworth House (c. 1700), off DE 9, west of Port Penn, originally just one room in plan.

PORT PENN

In 1763, Dr. David Stewart ambitiously planned a grain-shipping town around his existing brick house in this marshy district along the Delaware River. He dreamed of someday rivaling Philadelphia, but success eluded him and Port Penn remains tiny today. In their book *Everyday Architecture of the Mid-Atlantic*, architectural historians Gabrielle Lanier and Bernard Herman discuss the town and its architecture in detail. Seeking to preserve this unique enclave, the State of Delaware bought several properties in the 1990s. A Port Penn Interpretive Center has been established in a schoolhouse of 1886. The Stewart House (1740s) on Stewart Street is an outstanding, virtually unrestored cen-

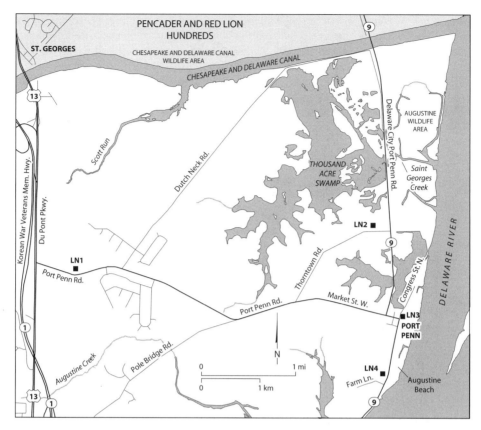

PORT PENN

ter-passage brick house that lies somewhat askew from the streetgrid. Various features point to its early date: glazed-header Flemish bond brickwork, with extensive English bond; stringcourse; a pent eave and cove cornice (both now missing). Windows were replaced with large panes of glass in the nineteenth century.

LN3 Cleaver House (Linden Hall)

c. 1834. Congress and Market sts.

The Cleaver family dominated Port Penn throughout the nineteenth century. Joseph built this Federal-style brick house, which included an office and store at right, divided from the residence by a firewall. The whole resembles two urban townhouses. Cleaver maintained the adjacent wharf, practiced law, founded an insurance company, served on the board of a bank, and was local postmaster. The contents of the house are known by a room-by-room probate inventory undertaken after his death in 1858. In 1977 a new owner altered the interior for rental units and redesigned the roof of the wing, which caused the front wall of that section to collapse. In 1994 the State of Delaware bought it.

LN4 Augustine Inn (Augustine Beach Hotel)

1814. 0.7 miles south of Port Penn on DE 9

This two-and-a-half-story brick hotel facing the Delaware River, its tall original windows remarkably intact, was built by Messrs. Grier and Aiken to serve ship travelers. Later in the nineteenth century, St. Augustine Piers became a popular pleasure ground, with beach, bath houses, and amusement park, the excursion boat *Thomas Clyde* bringing Philadelphians here as late as the 1920s. During the Great Depression, the place was the scene of the Farmer's Day Picnic in late summer. World War II brought a slump, but the resort revived somewhat in the 1950s. In 1963, the state Board of Health closed the beach due to bacterial pollution and the hotel was sold by sheriff's sale. Today, it houses a bar popular with motorcyclists.

ODESSA

This historic little community was long called "Cantwell's Bridge" for a toll bridge built in 1731 over the Appoquinimink River, a name that the town's twentieth-century benefactor, H. Rodney Sharp, always preferred. "Odessa" was applied in 1855 as appropriate to the town's prosperity in the grain trade, like the port city of the same name in the Crimea. As John Sweeney showed in his classic study of the Corbit-Sharp House (LN6), *Grandeur on the Appoquinimink* (1959), taste in the colonial village followed that in Philadelphia, as the leading families, the Corbits and the Wilsons, engaged in trade with that city and cultivated social ties there. Cantwell's Bridge had 211 residents in twenty-five houses in 1800. Growth was rapid after 1820 and, contrary to myth, did not slow after the railroad came through rival Middletown in 1855, although the latter town grew much faster and larger. There are fine examples of Italianate houses of the 1850s, the new mode being grafted onto a lingering Federal-style brick template during the peach-growing boom. By 1900, however, trade and prosperity had passed Odessa by, and a long slumber began. Sharp taught school here after graduating from the University of Delaware and later, having grown rich in the service of Pierre S. du Pont, returned to purchase and restore fifteen colonial properties. Later, Winterthur (CH10) took them over for many years as museum sites (an affiliation that ended in 2003). Du Pont Highway (U.S. 13) cuts through Odessa, causing traffic woes. The town itself had just 195 homes in 2003, but was soon to be ringed by mushrooming developments. Historical zoning is stringent, and painful debate erupted about loosening these rules to bring in business to the sleepy Main Street. A Winterthur guidebook, *Discover the Historic Houses of Odessa* (1999), lists thirty-six old buildings in Odessa, including some that are partly of log covered with weatherboards. Among these is the venerable-looking Starr-Lore House (mid-eighteenth century) at 310 Main Street.

LN5 Old Drawyers Church

c. 1773. U.S. 13 at Drawyer Creek, north of Odessa

Historian Harold D. Eberlein ranked Old Drawyers with the very finest Georgian churches in America. It was one of the first two Presbyterian congregations in Delaware (see also NC12). The present brick church on a scenic bluff above the tidal creek replaced a dilapidated one of logs. A building committee was appointed in 1769, but "the house was not erected until 1773," according to an account of 1842. Are we to understand that the church was begun in 1773, or finished then? It seems certain that it was underway at the same time as the Corbit-Sharp House (1772–1774; LN6), as Corbit bought "plank at meeting hous" to

LN5 OLD DRAWYERS CHURCH, rear view, in a rare photo of July 1899

use in his project (Sweeney, 1989). No written evidence links Robert May, the Corbit-Sharp House carpenter, with the design of Old Drawyers, but a link is plausible, as the two buildings (plus the Wilson-Warner House, LN7) share an extremely high level of finish and use a similar-looking foundation stone brought from a distance. Old Drawyers must have been substantially complete by 1776, although many more years were required to finish it completely. Its bricks were burned on a nearby farm; the remains of the kiln were evident as late as the 1840s.

As is typical for rural Presbyterian churches, Old Drawyers is plain in form, without belfry or steeple. Its beauty lies in its refinements: the monumental Doric doorway, pedimented and with engaged columns; segmental-arched windows on the first floor (with curving hinges); big gable-pediments at each end, with bull's-eye windows (a rarity in Delaware; restored 1983). The proportions are impeccable, and even the abundant putlog holes (holes where bricks were omitted so that scaffolding could be inserted for construction or repair) form a pleasing pattern. The superb colonial interior is organized around a raised pulpit, approached by double stairs, above which stands a canopied sounding board and golden dove. Behind is a small window flanked by two giant, round-headed windows with eighty-five panes each and fitted with interior, slatted shutters. A gallery surrounds three sides of the room, supported on Tuscan columns. The woodcarving is said to be by John Weaver, partner of local clockmaker Duncan Beard. A new roof was put on in 1811, and the mahogany-trimmed box pews and pulpit were altered in 1833. When a new church was opened in Odessa in 1861, regular services were discontinued, but an annual one has been held since 1896 under The Friends of Old Drawyers, which is part religious service, part history lecture, part picnic. HABS produced fourteen sheets of drawings in 1936. For decades the building was cloaked in ivy, but today its beautifully laid brickwork is again exposed.

LN6 Corbit-Sharp House

1772–1774. c. 1790 kitchen wing. 1938–1940 restored, Harry L. Lindsey; garden, H. Rodney Sharp and Marian Cruger Coffin. 118 Main St.

William Corbit, tanner, apprenticed in Philadelphia before returning to his native Delaware in 1767. His tannery on the Appoquinimink River thrived, as did his farm holdings, and soon he built a five-bay, twenty-two-room mansion, Delaware's finest pre-Revolutionary house. It faced a now-vanished road that led to the tannery and boat landing. The 89,250 bricks may have been burned locally, but stone for the cellar, stringcourse, and lintels was brought in, with "Stone from Chester [Pennsylvania]" listed in Corbit's account of construction costs (Sweeney, 1989). A Philadelphia lumber firm provided pine and cedar boards; hinges, screws, and locks came from Wilmington or Philadelphia. Nails and window glass were shipped, too. The cornice, with big mutules instead of modillions, is exceptionally grand. The Doric front door, or "frontispiece," is like the one at the now-demolished Stamper House, Philadelphia (1764). From a lead-covered roof deck or "terrass" with "Chineas Lattis" railing, Corbit surveyed his business and farm operations. Painting the house inside and out with "Oyl & Whitelead & paints" cost Corbit a large sum.

Exterior and interior woodwork was fashioned by the otherwise-unknown Robert May and Company, an educated and skilled craftsman, and his crew of carpenters. May left an invaluable itemized list of his activities in the bill for Corbit, part of the reason the place is, in Winterthur Museum curator John Sweeney's words, "one of the best-documented houses in America." The center passage, double-pile plan is the embodiment of full Georgian ar-

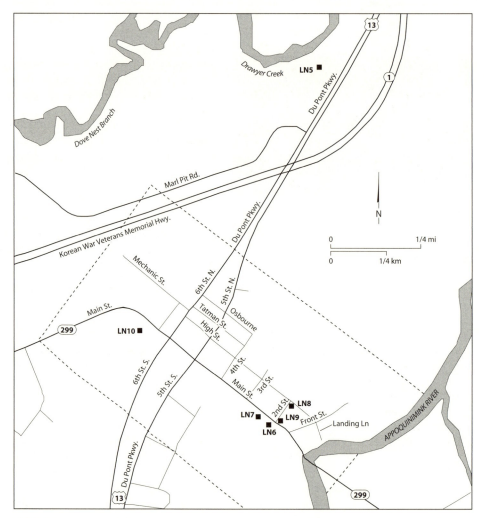

ODESSA

chitecture. The largest space in the house is upstairs, the "long room" or drawing room, which bears an uncanny resemblance to that of the Powel House, Philadelphia (1765), with some of the fretwork moldings (described by May as "Base & s[u]r base a frett in each") literally identical. In both houses, Abraham Swan's *Designs in Architecture* (London, 1757) provided inspiration. May's bill refers to the drawing room's ornamental details: "Pilasters," "Tabernacle frame," "Mantle cornice." Splendid carpentry throughout the house consumed almost half the construction budget.

Corbit, twenty-seven years of age when construction began, may have expected a thriving city to develop around his homestead, but this never happened, and "Castle William" (as locals called it in the nineteenth century) loomed over the modest community for generations. H. Rodney Sharp fell in love with the old house when he lived across the street in the Brick Hotel in 1900. Years later, in 1938, he heard that the building, then empty except for a charwoman inhabiting the upper floor, was slated to be converted to apartments. He bought the place and, with architect Lindsey, reversed nineteenth-century changes and returned original elements to their proper locations in the house, which was exceptionally intact, even to the Chinese railing atop the roof. Sharp donated the mansion to Winterthur Museum (CH10) in 1958, which long operated it as part of the Historic Houses of Odessa, toured by 9,000 visitors annually. Furnishings in the National Historic Landmark follow William Corbit's 1818 inventory.

LN6 CORBIT-SHARP HOUSE, with **LN6.1** SMOKEHOUSE at left

LN6.1 Smokehouse

18th century

Colonial farm structures hardly ever survive, but this is a rare exception. Historically, smokehouses were among the most common outbuildings. Only a handful were brick, as this one is. Meats were hung from hooks attached to poles that ran from wall to wall under the roof. Benches allowed one to sit while salting and packing meat—part of the curing process. Smokehouses are typically windowless, with a single batten door (this one is especially ancient-looking). In masonry examples, a few bricks are omitted for ventilation, as here. The Center for Historic Architecture and Design at the University of Delaware has called increased attention to smokehouses, which are rapidly disappearing, many of the best examples they studied in the 1980s now having been razed. Nearby, H. Rodney Sharp demolished some nineteenth-century outbuildings to create a Colonial Revival garden.

LN7 Wilson-Warner House (David Wilson House)

1769. 1960s restoration, Robert Raley.
202 Main St.

This somewhat more modest, but exquisitely proportioned, brick predecessor to the Corbit-Sharp House (LN6) was built for Corbit's brother-in-law, a local dry-goods merchant who sold imported goods bought from Philadelphia dealers. Iron numerals give the date. No evidence links Robert May, carpenter for the Corbit-Sharp House, with this building, but it seems plausible that he was involved, given the similarly high level of finish and interior paneling (see also John Lewden House, MC13). Four rooms occupy the main block of the Georgian dwelling, with nine more in a tall wing. As Sweeney recognized, the narrow format (five bays wide but just one-pile in depth) was frequent in upper Delaware. Stone for foundations, lintels, and steps was imported from outside the state. The builder's son, David Wilson Jr., went bankrupt, sold the house in 1829, and moved to Richmond, Indiana, as a brush peddler. Documents relating to his legal woes give invaluable information about the contents of the house. Mary Tatnall Warner, daughter of Mary Wilson and Daniel Corbit, bought the place in 1901 to preserve it as a family shrine. In 1924, it became the first historic house in Delaware to be opened to the public, under David Wilson Mansion, Inc., which ultimately donated the property to Winterthur in 1969 after restoration. Refurnishing in 1984 followed the documents of 1829. A nineteenth-century muskrat-skinning shack was moved to a location behind the house as a museum exhibit, recalling the once-lucrative pelt trade. The nearby stable is of stone, brought here from outside of Delaware; its datestone reads, "Built 1812, Rebuilt 1877."

LN8 COLLINS-SHARP HOUSE, before restoration

LN8 Collins-Sharp House

Early 18th century. 1962 moved here and restored, Albert Kruse. 2nd and High sts.

Planned construction of a giant Shell refinery threatened to doom this early house, which then stood in a scenic spot along Road 493 on Thoroughfare Neck near Taylors Bridge, overlooking a marsh and surrounded by centuries-old trees. Sharp paid to move the building to Odessa. The foreman supervising the difficult, sixteen-mile overland trip had a nervous breakdown, but the house arrived safely. The long, one-and-a-half story gambrel-roofed form is a common Eastern Shore type. Its structure is frame with brick nogging, covered by wide, irregular weatherboards. A change in the weatherboarding from matched to overlapping suggests that two houses were joined. Inside, the paneled end-wall is notable. A big fireplace long served as the Winterthur hearth-cooking site.

LN9 Brick Hotel

1822. 2nd and Main sts.

The north side of Main Street was not divided into lots until 1822. Merchant William Polk built this five-bay Federal-style hotel, which was soon bought by J. F. Mansfield of Middletown. A newspaper advertisement for "Cantwell's Bridge Hotel" said that the latter had "taken and furnished that large and commodious New Brick House, lately erected by the Messrs. Polk . . . where he is prepared to accommodate travellers and others, with the best the country affords." The hotel operated into the twentieth century. Sharp lived on the second floor front when he became schoolmaster in Odessa in 1900, and decades later (1960s) he restored it. To the rear stands Janvier Stable (1791 appears in a brick), brought here from across town, with fencing re-created from a 1798 watercolor of its original lot. East of the hotel is the brick, gambrel-roofed Leftovers House (1955), built by Sharp as a guesthouse with leftover historic materials. Across 2nd Street stands the bracketed Italianate town bank by famous Philadelphia architect Samuel Sloan (1855), who had designed the Greco-Egyptian St. Paul's Methodist Church at the west end of High Street (1851). As late as 1945, the bank's cashier slept upstairs above the bank vault with a shotgun he could point through a hole in the floor.

LN10 Appoquinimink Friends Meeting House

c. 1785. Main St., west of U.S. 13

David Wilson Sr. built this toylike gable-fronted brick structure—one of the smallest public places of worship in the nation, just 20 × 20 feet in area—and donated it to the Quaker congregation. Many Corbits and Wilsons are buried in the graveyard. Supposedly, the building served as a stop on the Underground Railroad, with slaves hiding in the loft. The congregation turned Hicksite (after followers of Elias Hicks, who separated from the main body of the Society of Friends) in 1828. By the time the place closed c. 1880, there were only two members remaining. H. Rodney Sharp and Rosanna Evans restored it c. 1938, and public worship resumed in 1946. Next door stands the Gothic Revival Zoar Methodist Church (1881).

LN10 APPOQUINIMINK FRIENDS MEETING HOUSE

MIDDLETOWN VICINITY

LN11 Achmester

1829, alterations through c. 1850. Marl Pit Rd., 0.5 miles east of U.S. 71, north of Middletown

When agricultural reformer General Richard Mansfield lived here, this low-slung, single-story frame house looked Georgian, as recorded in a rare oil painting of the estate. After his death in 1846, his son-in-law added stylish jigsaw work along the eaves and the dormer windows, giving it a Gothic-cottage-like flavor. Mansfield kept account books for eighteen years that record construction of the house by carpenters named McFarlane in the summer of 1829, as well as scientific farming practices, such as liming the clover and grain fields with plaster dust. According to his will, Mansfield owned an extensive library. Huge ornamental trees shade the lawn. At the rear of the dwelling stand a frame granary, smokehouse, and v-notched log granary (c. 1820), the last a rare survival. Achmester stands vacant and weathering.

LN11 ACHMESTER

LN12 Town of Parkside

2003-present, Keith Adams, developer, with land planner Richard Woodin. Marl Pit and Cedar Lane rds., north of Middletown

This new development, one of many around Middletown, differentiates itself by including diverse housing types, ranging from estates to small homes. The developer's promotional literature calls it Delaware's first example of "Traditional Neighborhood Development," or New Urbanism. Consisting of 492 houses on 300 acres, it seeks to turn back the clock to before the time when "the post–World War II era gave birth to Levittown. Parkside will be a place where sidewalks and pedestrian traffic trump highways and automobiles. Where community parks and a community club house foster neighborhood gatherings. Where front porches replace rear decks." Philosophically similar developments are Kentlands in Gaithersburg, Maryland, and Eagleview in Downingtown, Pennsylvania, although the styles of the houses differ there. The "two-story, neo-traditional homes reflecting a mid-Atlantic or Southern heritage" have garages at the rear only, on alleys. Three home-building companies have contributed. Narrow, tree-lined streets with "traffic circles, pocket parks and a variety of traffic-calming devices" are designed to slow automobiles. An eight-acre park is at the center of the town, with a community center. Parkside is the latest innovation among many in the long history of tract-house suburbanization in Delaware.

LN13 The Maples

c. 1860. 1880s altered. Bunker Hill and Choptank rds., west of Middletown

This frame house built for the Derrickson family stands among old trees at the heart of a 200-acre farm in an area fast filling with development. Its appearance is little-changed: pilastered porch; odd center gable, much like an oversized dormer with mansard profile and a wide, pierced bargeboard; and a slate roof with colorful, patterned shingles (recently replaced). These embellishments were added in the 1880s to bring the simple, vernacular house up-to-date stylistically, as was often the case in prosperous nineteenth-century rural Delaware.

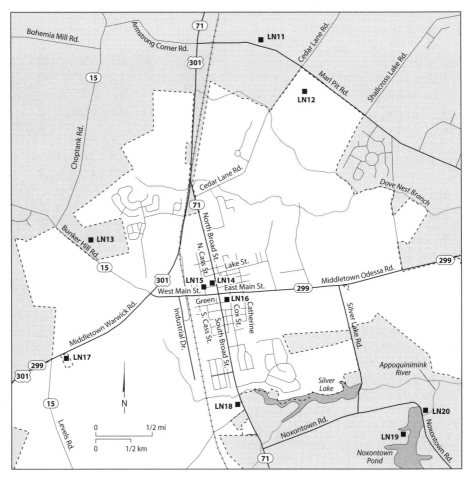

MIDDLETOWN

MIDDLETOWN

Unusual in Delaware for having been founded away from any navigable river, Middletown coalesced at an early crossroads, a tavern stop at the "middle" of the Delmarva Peninsula, halfway between landings on the Appoquinimink River on the east and the Bohemia River, Maryland, on the west. Its present appearance is largely late nineteenth century and later, as the place experienced rapid growth after the railroad came through in 1855. Peach farming on the fertile "Levels" brought prosperity. Cass and Broad streets have sizeable nineteenth-century houses, and the mid-nineteenth-century brick Italianate house at 123 W. Main St. sports an ornate cast-iron porch, a feature somewhat uncommon in the state. Wilmington contractor John A. Bader kept a minute record (now at the Hagley Museum) of the construction of Middletown Theater on Main Street (1922), now the Everett Theater, where a venerable carbon-arc movie projector is still operational. At the town center is a small civic plaza by a New York designer (1980, Ben-Ami Friedman and Associates).

The adjacent Witherspoon Building contains parts of a tavern built in 1761 that survived a fire in 1946. Starting in the 1990s, Middletown's population exploded, and the town's acreage was tripled. Among many new buildings is the Volunteer Hose Company (1999, Richard Conway Meyer and Lawrence D. McEwen). A recently printed walking tour by the Downtown Revitalization Office discusses forty-five historically significant structures in town.

LN14 Academy Building

1826–1827. c. 1875 enlarged. 216 N. Broad St.

A $10,000 lottery was authorized by the General Assembly in 1825 to fund a school building, and, in February 1826, Henry Little was awarded the contract for $5,000. He was to build a two-story edifice "of the best materials and in a plain but substantial manner." A trustee visited Philadelphia in 1827 to study the latest methods of stuccoing masonry. Called by children the "Yellow Prison" for its exterior paint color, the plain, Federal-style edifice with cupola served as a school until 1929, after which it became dilapidated. In the 1940s, a post office was nearly erected on the lawn in front of it, but a historical society mobilized to prevent this, and court battles ensued. Starting in 1960, it was owned by the town and functioned as a town hall. Rapid growth of Middletown led the mayor to announce in 2004 that he would sell the building and build a larger town hall elsewhere. The old Academy now houses a chamber of commerce and the historical society.

LN15 North Cass Street Houses

Late 19th century. N. Cass St., between W. Main and W. Lake sts.

The most fashionable street of Middletown's flourishing Victorian era boasts a series of ostentatious homes. They include the Queen Anne–style house (1890s) at 12 N. Cass Street, with generous porch and fish-scale-shingled upper walls, which was erected by a lumberyard owner. Former Governor Benjamin T. Biggs, farmer and railroad director, built the three-story Italianate house at Number 210 in 1876, with one of the first central heating systems in the state.

LN16 St. Anne's Church

1871–1872, Catanach and Son. 1882 restored. 1948–1949 Barr Memorial Chapel and Parish House, William Heyl Thompson. 15 E. Green St.

Successor to Old St. Anne's (LN18), this Gothic Revival church by a Philadelphia firm burned in May 1882, a decade after it opened. The buttressed, green serpentine walls trimmed with red sandstone survived unharmed. The original wooden spire was octagonal with four flanking pinnacles, but as rebuilt it is four-sided, with pinnacles omitted. The slate roof was replaced in 2002. Tiny-windowed and intimate, the attached Barr Chapel uses serpentine, too—a rare twentieth-century example. A pencil rendering of Thompson's interior scheme survives.

LN17 Cochran Grange

c. 1840. South side of U.S. 301, east of the intersection with Levels Rd.

Southern New Castle County's nineteenth-century agricultural heyday is recalled in this two-story brick house, the consummate "Peach Mansion" (though it predates the height of the peach boom), crowned with a square, windowed observatory overlooking the wide fields of The Levels. Built by John P. Cochran, largest peach producer in the area and governor of Delaware (1875–1879), the house was one of several family dwellings in the vicinity; the frame Hedgelawn (1856) and Summerton (c. 1850) stand to the west. Though built in

LN17 COCHRAN GRANGE

stylish Greek Revival style, Cochran Grange is often said to show the conservatism of Delaware architecture, as Georgian massing and Flemish-bond brickwork were holdovers from a bygone era. The two-story square porch pillars were once green with white panels. Sources differ as to the date of the building, ranging from 1834 to 1842. The farmstead remained in the family for generations, but plans in 2007 called for much of the site to become an auto mall.

LN17.1 Outbuildings

c. 1830–1860 period

The collection of outbuildings, some older than the house, is exceptional. One barnlike wood and brick structure behind the house served as a combination dairy, storehouse, smokehouse, and workshop; the brick room at the end of the structure may have been a slave quarter. The brick bank barn (said to be 1830–1835) retains its complex roof framing, in which diagonal struts brace canted queen posts that support the purlins. A rare, highly specialized type of agricultural building is the wooden threshing barn (of the same date as the bank barn), a long, narrow structure.

LN18 Old St. Anne's Church

1768–1771. DE 71, 1.2 miles south of Middletown

The Anglican parish dates back to 1704, when "poor Brother Jenkins at Appoquinimink" was "baited to death by mosquitoes and bloodthirsty gal-nippers," as a contemporary account described; but the present church was erected during the tenure of Reverend Philip Reading, famous in the Revolutionary War for locking up the facility rather than omit the prayer for the King (1705–1955, *Celebrating the 250th Anniversary*, 1955). Reading replaced the earlier log church with this five-bay brick box, which closely resembles a dissenters' meeting house. Its rectilinear severity is subtly relieved by variations in the brickwork: segmental arches over first-story windows, stringcourses of differing lengths, bricklaying that ranges from English bond to Flemish bond according to the relative hierarchy of the facades (the back wall is all-English). Some have thought the building must be earlier than the traditional date, given the old-fashioned cove cornice, but a letter in 1772 from Reading back to friends in London shows that he was proud of its up-to-date appearance: "This Church is designed and constructed in a manner that would do credit to a populous city." Reading called attention to the east window "finished in the Venetian form"; to the "elegant" pulpit and reading desk on the north wall; the "large, handsome gallery" on the south; and the "spacious, convenient pews." In short, "the inside work of this edifice is much applauded by all who see it, for its elegance in the execution, and for its well-proportioned disposition of its several parts."

During the revival of Anglicanism under Bishop Alfred Lee, the building was restored in the summer of 1847, its high-backed box pews cut down and rearranged facing east, where the pulpit (reduced in size) was moved. The congregation was meeting in town by 1867 (see LN16), and, subsequently, the building has been open only occasionally, in summertime. A project begun in 1952 by Albert Kruse, who had just finished another restoration (NC12), reversed the 1847 alterations. He removed a termite-damaged exterior vestibule; returned the gallery to its original, smaller size; rebuilt the pulpit in its original position and form (with three levels and sounding board); returned the architrave over the Palladian window to a slender profile; and replaced the window framing. His south door copies the surviving west one, with its tall panels. The altar has been said to be the only pre-Revolutionary one surviving in an American church.

LN18 OLD ST. ANNE'S CHURCH

LN19 ST. ANDREW'S SCHOOL

The churchyard, walled in 1913, is memorable for its nineteenth-century tombstones and cast-ironwork and includes the contents of several family graveyards removed here from the countryside. An enormous white oak may be 330 years old.

LN19 St. Andrew's School

1929–1930, Arthur Howell Brockie. Wheelwright and Stevenson, landscape designers. Noxontown Rd., 2 miles southeast of Middletown

Working for DuPont during World War I, A. Felix du Pont was directly responsible for providing France with gunpowder. Pacifists branded him a "Merchant of Death." A devout high churchman, his zeal for the creation of this Episcopal school possibly owed something to postwar guilt. He searched widely for the perfect rural site until the Episcopal Bishop Philip Cook of Delaware suggested scenic Noxontown Pond, in a historic and unspoiled district only a mile from Du Pont Highway. The 360-acre Comegys Farm was purchased in 1928, and Brockie, a Philadelphia architect who had worked for Cope and Stewardson, was hired, with the contractor, Turner Construction Company, to provide stone construction in Collegiate Gothic Revival style: irregular massings, mullioned windows with leaded lights, a crenellated tower, and cloisters. Main Building and the master's house nearest it were finished when the school opened with thirty-two boys in fall 1930; "the house on the point" (a dwelling overlooking the pond) came in 1932; the original boat house and headmaster's house in 1934; gym, 1935–1937. In November 1988, the affluent and idyllic campus provided the setting for a Hollywood movie, *Dead Poets Society* (1989). An elementary school, St. Anne's, was created on land nearby (2002, Doug Proctor for Anderson Brown Higley Associates), its buildings imitating agricultural structures.

LN19.1 Founders Hall (Main Building)

1929–1930, Arthur Howell Brockie. 1936–1937 Middle Wing, Brockie. 1954–1956 New Wing, William Heyl Thompson, with William E. Grancell

Italian stonemasons working for Joseph Mandes Company of Philadelphia (famous for college campuses) built the Gothic Revival walls with rock from quarries around that city. Middle Wing contains a chapel with dec-

LN20 NOXONTOWN MILL

orative carvings by sculptor Karl Sigstedt, as well as an enlarged dining hall for which Irene Sophie (wife of Irénée) du Pont, sister of the founder, gave an N. C. Wyeth mural (1938) that shows the committee studying the St. Andrew's building plans as an inspiring vision of English cathedrals rises up behind them. The wing of the 1950s includes a tower, a cloister garth with Tudor Revival arches, and a War Memorial Room honoring twenty-six alumni who died in World War II.

LN19.2 Kip du Pont Boathouse

1988–1989, Richard Conway Meyer

This rustic-looking facility housing crew shells stands at the head of a new inlet. Outer walls are of a single layer of cedar clapboarding, so the building can breathe. The bow-shaped roof of the lower section is fashioned from exposed wooden trusses. Over a repair bay stands a nave-like social space, the warming room, with a deep porch framed in bold trefoil arches. In a playful Postmodern touch, corner posts betray their nonstructural nature by being whittled to a point. Meyer, its Philadelphia architect, admires the work of architect Robert Venturi. The boathouse was honored by *Time* magazine in its "Best of 1990" list: "An enchanting building, as graceful as the sculls inside. . . . With its timber framing and clover-shaped arches, [it] could make one yearn to be sixteen again." Meyer went on to transform the St. Andrew's campus with a series of new buildings and renovations, including an arts center (2001–2004) adjacent to the boathouse, sensitively adapted to its site and broken into small masses to reduce its apparent scale. The arts center employs standing-seam, lead-coated-copper panels for its complex roofscape.

LN20 Noxontown Mill

c. 1740. Noxontown Rd. at Appoquinimink River, southeast of Middletown

Here is a rare survival, a frame industrial structure from the eighteenth century, analogous to Maryland's famous Wye Mill on the Eastern Shore. Thomas Noxon, born in Kingston, New York, in 1669, owned several mills in Delaware. He settled here on the Appoquinimink in 1735 and built the brick house that still survives (1740 datestone). Noxon lived to see his mill seat expand into a little town, chartered in 1742, a year before he died. An annual fair became popular, and the patriot Colonel John Haslet wrote to Caesar Rodney in 1776 worrying that "the People [would] attend Noxontown fair rather than the Election, and sell their Birthright for a piece of Gingerbread." By the time adjacent St. Andrew's School (LN19) was founded, the mill was seasonally busy pressing apples for cider and grinding corn, and it found a new function in providing wheat for bread in the dining hall. The structural fabric of the now-idle building is well preserved, though its bakehouse, brewhouse, and malthouse are gone, and the machinery has been changed over the years. Architectural historian Bernard Herman has studied the framework (1987): "In this small-scale industrial structure, the principals carry the major elements of the wall framing [as well as] a timber girder that spans the length of the building and which is supported at mid-point by a decorated chamfered edge post and pillow."

TOWNSEND VICINITY

LN21 Brook Ramble

1804–1806. Grears Corner Rd., near intersection with Green Giant Rd., northwest of Townsend

James Crawford, a gentleman farmer, employed the so-called townhouse (or side-passage) plan that was popular in the late eighteenth century for urban and rural dwellings alike. According to a tax roll of 1816, his brick house was one of only twenty-eight of that material in today's Appoquinimink and Blackbird hundreds, putting it in the top 9 percent of local building stock (50 percent of dwellings then were log, 41 percent frame). It remained in the Crawford family for generations and was never altered, still retaining its punch-and-gouge Federal chimneypieces and fine staircase. The current owners rescued the house from abandonment in the 1970s and restored it again after a disastrous attic fire caused by lightning in 2003. The cruciform, Gothic Revival Greenlawn Farm Manager's House (c. 1860), only survivor of a historic farmstead razed for a shopping center on North Broad Street in Middletown (see photograph on p. 29), was moved here to the Brook Ramble grounds in 1992.

LN22 Old Union Methodist Church

1847. Union Church Rd. and U.S. 13, southeast of Townsend

Standing on a knoll beside the busy highway on a site where the congregation had worshipped since 1789, this unadorned, gabled brick box is one of the best-preserved Methodist meetinghouses in Delaware, a rare survivor of a once-common type. Early Methodism stressed austerity. The entrance door faces the former highway location, east of the building. The Gothic Revival pulpit and other interior fittings may date from a renovation in 1877.

LN23 Huguenot House (Elias Naudain House)

c. 1735 section at left. After 1749 enlarged. c. 1825–1850 period kitchen wing. DE 9 at Taylor's Bridge

Marshy Blackbird Creek provides the scenic locale for this primitive-looking brick dwelling. Historians have recently moved its construction two decades later than the long supposed date of 1711. They believe that Huguenot colonist Elias Naudain purchased the

LN23 HUGUENOT HOUSE (ELIAS NAUDAIN HOUSE), photo 1936

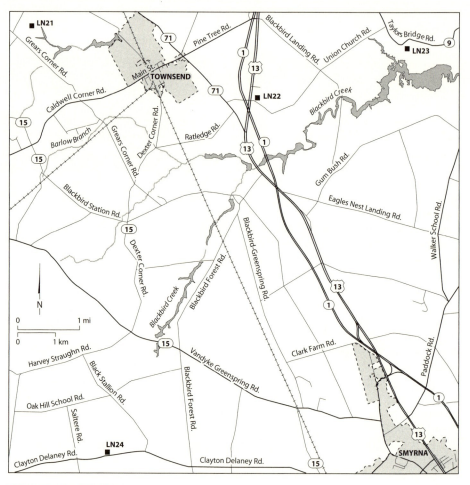

TOWNSEND VICINITY

property in 1735 and probably built the first, eastern section of the main block, 22 × 35 feet, with a pent eave (the joist-holes of which remain) and little porthole windows in the attic of the gable. (Historians once thought that the west part of the main block was first, plus the wing.) Naudain's son Andrew lived here from 1749 to 1769, and presumably it was he who extended the house twenty-five feet, making it center passage. The extensive paneling inside the dwelling dates from this campaign. William Corbit owned the house starting in 1816. Fortunately, the tenant farmers who long occupied the place made few changes. Architect Laussat R. Rogers studied it for HABS in 1936 and noted the stateliness of the first story, with its big, twelve-over-twelve lights widely spaced and the lofty stringcourse. The roof is low-pitched, adding to the walls' apparent immensity. A giant sycamore before the door—its companion appears as a stump in photographs of the 1930s—recalls the account of Peter Kalm, who traveled in the Mid-Atlantic in the 1740s, of the popularity of this species in dooryard settings. A barn (1827) survived in ruinous condition until it was demolished in the early 1990s, a period during which the Huguenot House was, for a time, abandoned. It grew dilapidated and had its front doorlock, cupboard doors, and several huge floorboards stolen. New owners since 1995 are gradually refurbishing the place. Also in the Taylors Bridge vicinity stood the important brick gambrel-roofed Liston House (1739), destroyed by fire a few years ago.

LN24 Marim-Dawkins House
(Ye Olde Log Cabin)

Early 19th century. 2003 rebuilt, Bill Dawkins. Clayton Delaney Rd., 0.6 miles east of Saltere Rd., northwest of Clayton

LN24 MARIM-DAWKINS HOUSE (YE OLDE LOG CABIN), prior to reconstruction

Thomas Marim bought the Blackiston family farm in 1834 and became responsible for 375 acres with two log houses, a kitchen, barn, two outhouses, and two slaves. The extant one-story log house is presumably one of those then standing. It is v-notched and chinked with mortar and stone rubble. A frame addition came around 1860 or later. When Marim died in 1874, his son, Richard, only survivor of eleven children, inherited the farm. Bill Dawkins, its owner since the 1960s, stripped off the early, protective weatherboarding over the logs and removed structural walls inside, and a Center for Historic Architecture and Design investigation in 1998 showed that the house was fast deteriorating. Experts regretted the drastic transformation undertaken by Dawkins in 2003, when he replaced nearly all the walls with new wood—white oak logs cut on his property and squared by Amish workers with a portable sawmill. For him (age seventy-five) and his two helpers (ages seventy-seven and eighty-seven), however, it was a labor of love and far preferable to demolishing the termite-weakened structure.

Kent County

"Where the wheat fields break and billow, In the peaceful land of Kent," goes the state song, "Our Delaware" (c. 1906). In this rural heart of the state, bounded by the Smyrna River on the north and the Mispillion on the south, small towns lie amidst big farm fields and roads intersect at variously named "Corners." Several brick houses survive from the eighteenth century—including Eden Hill (1749; Water St., Dover) and Great Geneva (c. 1760; DE 356, 3 miles south of Dover)—reminders of the wealth that some Kent County gentry attained, including a number of Quakers. The National Register of Historic Places lists 140 sites in the county, including architecturally rich historic districts in such towns as Felton, Frederica, Kenton, Smyrna, Wyoming, and Milford; Dover, the state capital, appears in its own chapter. The register highlights several rural churches, for example, the colorfully named Cow Marsh Old School Baptist Church, near Sandtown, of 1872. The region remained farm-centered until after World War II, when its population suddenly surged by 70 percent in the 1950s. Growth has continued; in the 1990s, Kent County was the fastest-growing metropolitan statistical area in eleven northeastern states. There were about twice as many residents of Kent in 2000 as there had been in 1960, and one in four housing units standing in 2000 had been built since 1990. Not until 2003 did the county have development ordinances that required protection of woodlands, wetlands, and historic sites. The flavor of the past is perhaps most apparent along scenic DE 9, which parallels the bay shore in both New Castle and Kent counties; several of the entries that follow lie in close proximity to this road, as does the nineteenth-century Raymond Neck Historic District, north of Leipsic.

KT1 Aspendale

1771–1773 brick section. DE 300, 1 mile west of Kenton

An inscription on the stringcourse gives the date of completion of the brick section, which was added to an existing frame structure. The brick portion exemplifies what historians once called a "Quaker plan," a single large room with a pair of small rooms to the side, this being a somewhat rare Delaware example. The extensive interior wooden paneling has been compared to that in simpler rooms of the contemporaneous Corbit-Sharp House (LN6) and still shows some original coats of paint. A National Historic Landmark, the home remains in the family of the original owner, Charles Number.

KT1 ASPENDALE

KT2 PROVIDENCE CREEK ACADEMY (ST. JOSEPH'S INDUSTRIAL SCHOOL)

KT2 Providence Creek Academy (St. Joseph's Industrial School)

1895–1896, George I. Lovatt. 355 W. Duck Creek Rd. at Clayton Ave., Clayton

Philadelphian St. Katharine Drexel (canonized in 2000) founded the Sisters of the Blessed Sacrament for Indians and Colored People in 1891, which financed this school for African American boys. It occupied six buildings on 289 acres. The centerpiece is the frame chapel, a rare Delaware example of an Italianate basilica form, long and narrow, with a wide cornice of painted tin and stained glass windows. Unfortunately, the tall campanile tower has been removed. The architect, Lovatt, was a young Philadelphian just starting a long career as a designer of Catholic churches and schools. For eighty-two years, St. Joseph's, run by a Catholic society in Baltimore, educated 7,000 students from as far away as Texas. A Clayton resident recalls that the students, upon leaving the grounds, always marched in a line with a Josephite father at either end and were "as isolated from the community as people with leprosy." The facility closed in 1972 and stood vacant until its conversion into a charter school in 1999. The town of Clayton has a number of old buildings, including the one-story, wide-eaved Pennsylvania Railroad Station (1885).

KT3 The Lindens (Miller's House)

1765 or earlier. Duck Creek Rd. (N. Main St.) at Duck Creek, north of Smyrna

Founded by 1705 where the King's Highway forded a navigable creek, Duck Creek Village was the oldest settlement in northern Kent County. By the Revolution it had three churches. Later, the creek silted up and nearby Smyrna became ascendant. Nothing survives of the churches but their graveyards, and the village vanished except for an 80 × 100–foot gristmill and a miller's house (The Lindens). The mill (1820s and later) was dilapidated when recorded by historians in 1981 and was subsequently razed. The dwelling, a brick gambrel-roofed structure four bays wide, was threatened with demolition by the highway department in 1960, but the state archives department rescued it. A marbleized dado inside is rare, although Brook Ramble (LN21) has one, too.

SMYRNA

Originally called Duck Creek Crossroads, where two colonial highways intersected and grain could be shipped by water, the town became Smyrna in 1806. Its architecture is unusually rich, with good examples of colonial and nineteenth-century buildings side-by-side in picturesque groupings along the grid of streets. The National Register District includes nearly 500 structures, many

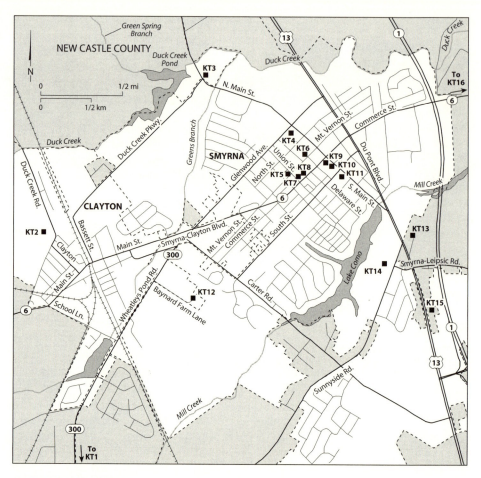

CLAYTON AND SMYRNA

of which appear on a bird's-eye lithograph of 1885. At the center of Smyrna is the Four Corners crossroads, with an eclectic grouping of commercial buildings. N. Main Street is marked by interesting nineteenth-century houses in a variety of styles, including the Alexander G. Cummins House (1874–1875), at 107; its owner was rector of the local Episcopal Church, which explains the unusually literal treatment of the Gothic Revival in his house, with a variety of window shapes and a colorful slate roof. On the south side of town is Odd Fellows Cemetery; its rare wooden gate (1864, recently restored), with lifelike hands reaching down from a round arch and holding three links of chain, was illustrated by John Maass in his groundbreaking book on Victoriana, *The Gingerbread Age* (1957). The Du Pont Highway came through just east of Smyrna in 1923. John Bassett Moore Intermediate School (1920–1936, Ballinger Company; 29 W. Frazier St.), renovated in 2003, contains six Federal Arts Project murals by Edward L. Grant, Walter Pyle, and Stafford Good, including the latter's *Cavalcade of Delaware* (1935–1936). Highway DE 1 has lately eased the commute to Wilmington and Dover, bringing extraordinary development.

KT4 Cummins Stockly House

Late 18th century. 215 N. Main St.

The lowering of the street has made this 18 × 26–foot brick townhouse stand unusually high off the sidewalk. As often in the late eighteenth century, "stone" lintels were cut from one piece of wood, with joints carved in and a keystone nailed at center. Certain details are especially interesting: the nicely shaped wooden bedmold (a classical molding supporting a cornice) is much shorter than the cornice above it, and the big stringcourse is fully five bricks high. The long-neglected building was owned by Duck Creek Historical Society until bought by a private individual c. 1980 to restore it. He spent a year cleaning out pigeon and bat droppings. Today it again stands empty.

KT5 Pope-Mustard Mansion

c. 1768. c. 1850 altered. 204 W. Mt. Vernon St.

Delaware has several colonial homes that were drastically altered in the nineteenth century. In its original form, this side-passage brick townhouse with double stringcourses must have resembled the Cummins Stockly House (KT4), down to the wooden, keystoned lintels that imitate cut stone. Italianate alterations

KT5 POPE-MUSTARD MANSION

involved removing the gable roof and adding a third story topped with a flat roof and wide, bracketed eaves. All the windows were replaced with large-paned ones. A wing at the side leads to a detached brick kitchen. The mansion's unrestored wooden doorway of the Doric order is especially fine, recalling one at the now-demolished Stamper House, Philadelphia (1764). As at the later Corbit-Sharp House (LN6), the outer door has wooden jalousies that form a geometric pattern.

KT6 Asbury United Methodist Church

1871–1872. 24 W. Mt. Vernon St.

At 135 feet, the church's octagonal spire soars above the town. The original building (1844–1845) burned in 1869 and was restored, with the addition of a big, two-towered Italianate front of red pressed brick, which still retained the three-tall-windows arrangement of the first facade. A lithograph made in the 1880s shows fancy finials on the gable, on the gablets of the spire, and elsewhere, enlivening the facade (these details were mostly removed by the 1950s). The interior has been altered, especially the chancel end, but the wide nave is still dominated by a dark walnut gallery on three sides, with heavy moldings, supported on slim cast-iron columns. The frame parsonage (1867) was eventually replaced by a Colonial Revival–style education annex (1962–1965, W. Ellis Preston). Across the street is the Second Empire–style Hudson Mansion (1887, R. Graham and Sons). At 35 Mt. Vernon Street is the McLane-Spearman House (c. 1790, extensively changed in the nineteenth century and given a mansard roof), with a quaint board-and-batten outbuilding and a barn. Mt. Vernon was once Smyrna's most fashionable street.

KT7 St. Peter's Episcopal Church

1827–1829. 1859 enlarged. 1885 alterations. 1901–1902 alterations, Charles M. Burns. 22 N. Union St.

The present church supplanted a brick edifice of 1744 at Duck Creek Village, which was demolished in 1827. The new lot was provided by the Cummins family, memorialized by the altar window. Eben Cloak built the brick

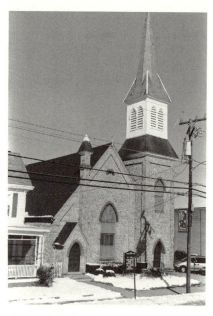

KT8 FIRST PRESBYTERIAN CHURCH

was erected on busy Commerce Street, the form of its facade emulating that of the much larger Asbury Methodist (KT6) nearby. Brick was used as trim. There were never any buttresses (unlike the serpentine St. Anne's, LN16), as neighboring buildings pressed close on both sides. The interior is little changed, with original pews, hammerbeam ceiling, and stained glass that predates the fashion for opalescent glass in the 1890s. Its grisaille stenciling is faded, but it remains a valuable survival. The organ of 1904 no longer works, but the painted pipes are preserved.

KT9 Citizens Bank (Fruit Growers' National Bank and Trust Company)

1925–1926, Tilghman Moyer Company. 5 W. Commerce St.

This bank was founded in 1876 to serve the booming peach business, as fruit-basket sculptural reliefs on the facade acknowledge. The current boxy Georgian Revival building with Corinthian columns was conceived by an Allentown, Pennsylvania, firm specializing in banks. The fireproof steel frame is clad in rough-textured red brick and cast limestone. Inside, floors are pink Tennessee marble with accents of Levanto and Botticino marbles from Italy. The money vault of concrete and steel was twenty-one inches thick. The vault door alone weighed 20,000 pounds. Overlooking the banking room is a directors' meeting space, typical of banks of the period. At the rear, the building nearly touches the similarly designed PNC Bank (National Bank) of 1925, except the tapestry brick used there is yellow, not red.

structure, which was enlarged in 1859 into a cruciform plan. A chapel was added later. The tower, with octagonal wooden spire rising from a square base, was in place by the time of the lithograph (1885) of Smyrna. A new chancel window came in 1885 and a vaulted arched ceiling in 1902; the latter was designed by a Philadelphia church architect and subsequently replaced in oak. North of the building stands Fisler Memorial Chapel (1872), originally a Sunday school and one of the state's best examples of board-and-batten Gothic Revival.

KT8 First Presbyterian Church

1883–1884. 118 W. Commerce St.

The original Duck Creek Presbyterian Church (1733, abandoned 1846) was located at today's Holy Hill Cemetery on Lake Como, where a historical marker was erected in 2003. A primitive painting (discovered in a Michigan attic in 1961) shows that it had a jerkinhead roof, like several early Delaware churches. In the nineteenth century, the congregation moved into town, building a church that was later turned over to Methodists and that burned in 1996. The present simple Gothic Revival edifice of green serpentine (with a hundred-foot broach spire rising from an attached tower)

KT10.1 PLANK HOUSE, with KT10 SMYRNA MUSEUM (THE BARRACKS) at rear

KT11 SMYRNA OPERA HOUSE AND OLD TOWN HALL

KT10 Smyrna Museum (The Barracks)

c. 1795 and later. 11 S. Main St.

The six-bay, two-story, Federal-style brick house south of Four Corners was later given a front porch and bracketed Italianate cornice. The first Delaware state draft lottery took place on this porch in 1863. The traditional name, The Barracks, referred to its supposed use by militia in the War of 1812. Duck Creek Historical Society took over the property in 1981 and operates a museum. Across the street stands the former Colonial Revival brick post office (1915–1916, James A. Wetmore), on the steps of which President Warren G. Harding briefly spoke in June 1923.

KT10.1 Plank House

Possibly 18th century. 11 S. Main St.

This little single-story house originally stood on N. Main Street. In deteriorated condition by the 1950s, it was rescued and brought to The Lindens (KT3) in 1962. In the 1990s, it was moved to the Barracks and restored, which included solicitously lowering the floor so modern visitors would not hit their heads. The neatly sawn and dovetailed planks represent high-quality log construction.

KT11 Smyrna Opera House and Old Town Hall

1869, Richard Mitchell. 1886 wing. 1998–2002 restored and addition, Cooperson Associates. South and S. Main sts.

Constructed quickly, this brick facility fulfilled a longstanding dream of the citizenry. On the first floor, it housed a town commissioners' room and library, jail, and engine house; a meeting hall above; and Masonic Lodge within the mansard roofed top floor. Abolitionist and author Frederick Douglass spoke here in 1880 and presidential candidate William Jennings Bryan in 1900. An addition in 1886 housed the engine room of Citizens Hose Company No. 1, with a stage for the hall above (a hall now called the Opera House). Fire destroyed the upper floor and tower on Christmas Day, 1948. Decades later, architect Jay N. Cooperson restored the building with its tall second floor windows, adding a mansard roof and a central tower with a cupola based on the original. A four-story brick addition features a glass-fronted stair tower.

KT12 Bannister Hall

1865–1866. Baynard Farm Ln., off DE 300, south of Smyrna

John Anthony of Troy, New York, came to Delaware to participate in the booming peach market. He ordered plans, elevation, and specifications (which survive at Duck Creek Historical Society) and then, unusually for the time, had the house prefabricated, shipping the parts to Delaware by train. As assembled here, Bannister Hall (indicated as "New Home" on D. G. Beers's Delaware atlas of 1868) was a big, fourteen-room frame box with a veranda across the front, a wing at the rear, and an observatory atop a hipped roof (both with brackets). Weathered and unrestored, it stands at the end of a long drive, surrounded by an arboretum of rare varieties of trees. The brick dwelling behind the house

KT12 BANNISTER HALL, rear view

(c. 1754) was the original home place on the plantation, most of which has recently been subdivided.

KT13 Belmont Hall

c. 1770–1800 period. U.S. 13, north of Smyrna-Leipsic Rd.

This stately colonial home was erected by Revolutionary governor Thomas Collins. The flat-topped gable pediment that embraces the full five-bay width of the facade is an unusual form in Delaware, though Philadelphia had several examples. On the roof is a deck with balustrade. Dates for the construction of Belmont Hall have ranged widely, some sources giving 1686 for the rear wings and 1753 for the front; today, it is generally held that the entire house was built in one campaign after Collins purchased the property in 1771. The house was featured in Marion Harlan's *More Colonial Homesteads* (1899), showing exterior changes that have since been removed. By Harlan's time, interiors were marked by the new Colonial Revival fashion, with a spinning wheel beside a blue-and-white-tile fireplace and a grandfather clock on the stair landing. Already Belmont Hall had attracted artists: Howard Pyle visited in 1879 to write and illustrate a *Harper's New Monthly Magazine* article. Two workmen spent the summer of 1920 scraping nineteenth-century paint from the colonial bricks with wire brushes and acid. The top floor was destroyed by fire two years later; subsequently, the house was restored and dormers were added. Owner Cummins Speakman drove down from Wilmington to show a *National Geographic* reporter through in 1935 and repeated one of the cherished legends of the place: "On the roof of Belmont Hall one of Washington's sentries was shot. Mortally wounded by a British sharpshooter, he crawled to a bedroom to give the alarm." The house was sold in 1984 to the state, and it is now used as a conference center. In front of the house stretches a spacious lawn with large trees, 100 of which blew down in a tornado in 1988.

KT14 Delaware Hospital for the Chronically Ill (State Welfare Home)

1931–1933, Massena and du Pont. Sunnyside Rd., near U.S. 13

Millionaire Alfred I. du Pont showered largesse upon the state's poor, so he had much sway with Governor C. Douglass Buck in steering the Welfare Home commission to his own architect-son in the depths of the Great Depression. The Administration and Hospital Building, a large-scale exercise in red-brick Colonial Revival in a composition of three main blocks, has a muscular, curving Doric portico of limestone that recalls Massena's contemporaneous Temple of Love at Nemours (see BR26.4). Walls inside were warm-colored, for psychological benefit.

KT15 Thomas England House Restaurant (Woodlawn)

18th century. 1853 temple front. 1165 S. Du Pont Hwy. (U.S. 13)

Few stately, temple-fronted, Greek Revival homes survive in Delaware. The pedimented

KT14 DELAWARE HOSPITAL FOR THE CHRONICALLY ILL (STATE WELFARE HOME), early view

portico was added to this two-story house in 1853 for George W. Cummins, whose family prospered through ownership of boats and wagons for agricultural trade with Philadelphia. Cummins was one of the wealthiest citizens in Kent County, with 2,500 acres under cultivation. The portico with its six fluted Doric columns is of wood imitating stone, with beveled joints incised in the planks of the walls and the whole coated with sand-textured paint. The additions disguise an older house: a log structure later given a frame upper story. The original section, which can be seen behind and to the right of the portico, was subsequently extended in brick. The ensemble is an excellent example of what historian David Ames calls "the Delaware evolved house," in

KT15 THOMAS ENGLAND HOUSE RESTAURANT (WOODLAWN), photo 1960

which major nineteenth-century additions made no effort to resemble the original style. Woodlawn now houses a restaurant.

ALONG DE 9

KT16 Allee House

c. 1765. Dutch Neck Rd., Bombay Hook National Wildlife Refuge

One of the earliest surviving Delaware deeds records a Dutchman's purchase of "Bompies Hook" from the Native American, Mehocksett, in 1679 for gun, powder, clothes, liquor, and a kettle. A Huguenot farmer, Abraham Allee, built the brick house decades later in a center passage, single-pile plan. Local tradition gives 1753 as the date, but a brick (left of the front door) reads "BR 1765," perhaps, some have thought, the initials of the builder. The exterior is distinguished by a cove cornice, the interior by considerable paneling and a spacious wooden stair and cupboards. The rather extensive use of glazed-header bricks on the *rear* elevation is unusual (there are few elsewhere on the house). Allee's inventory (1770) included four slaves and an eight-day clock, his most valuable possessions. The extant outbuildings were in place by 1790. Time seemed to have passed the place by when, in 1937, the surroundings were condemned by the federal government for 11,000-acre Bombay Hook Migratory Waterfowl Refuge, and the Civilian Conservation Corps (CCC), using African American labor, erected an intricate system of dikes. In 1963, the government planned to demolish the abandoned house—in spite of its high quality and undeveloped setting—but state archivist Leon deValinger convinced them to lease the property to the state. George F. Bennett undertook a restoration (1963–1966). By 2007, another was needed, and the house stood empty.

KT17 Wheel of Fortune

c. 1807–1815. West side of DE 9, 0.2 miles south of Leipsic Rd.

Only the wealthiest farmers of Little Creek Hundred could have afforded so fashionable a two-story brick dwelling. Not until recently have historians proposed a date later than mid-eighteenth-century for the very conser-

KT16 ALLEE HOUSE, rear view, photo 1930s

vative house. The plan is five bay, single-pile, center passage, and with the usual rear wing. The front and side porches are later additions. The farmstead—named "Wheel of Fortune," probably as a play on the name of its 1738 owner, John Chance—comprises 235 acres in an as-yet-unspoiled agricultural landscape. The WPA *Delaware Guide* (1938) noted its excellent preservation, being then occupied not by tenant farmers, as usually the case, but by the owner, a U.S. senator. A brick smokehouse, brick milkhouse, granary, corn cribs, and dairy barn together form a surprisingly intact complex. The dairy business was once lucrative in Kent County but subsequently faded away.

KT18 Octagonal Schoolhouse (District No. 12 Public School)

1830–1831. DE 9 east of Cowgill's Corner (visible from Edgewater Farm Ln.)

Delaware was early in establishing a system of free public schools (1829). Prominent citizen Manlove Hayes Sr. helped build this one, of stone with a corbeled brick cornice like those of two nearby houses associated with him (see KT19). Octagonal schools were popular in Chester County, Pennsylvania, and there were several in New Castle County, including the "Eight Square School" near Summit Bridge (1813, burned 1936). The date of construction of the Cowgill's Corner school is often given as 1836, but a public meeting was held at Pleasant Hill Academy as early as October 1831 (this

KT18 OCTAGONAL SCHOOLHOUSE (DISTRICT NO. 12 PUBLIC SCHOOL), photo 1936

being the school's original name), and glass was puttied here and walls whitewashed in 1833. Up to eighty-seven students sat at desks arranged in circles, boys on the outside and girls inside. The dilapidated facility closed in 1929. Restored by the state in 1971, it is currently boarded up.

KT19 Old Stone Tavern

c. 1822. East side of Main St., Little Creek

The settlement of Little Creek grew up at a wharf on the line between neighboring plantations. This building was never a tavern but rather a house, built by Manlove Hayes Sr. and his wife's cousin, John Bell. A prosperous farmer and politician who operated a steamship line to Philadelphia, Hayes built three nearby structures of stone with corbeled brick cornices: this building; an addition to his house, York Seat (1826, recently demolished); and Octagonal Schoolhouse (1830–1831; KT18). The so-called tavern is of gneiss rich in muscovite. The state geologist, William S. Schenck, tells me that Hayes probably brought the stone by boat from Chester County, Pennsylvania, or possibly from Maryland. Ashlar is used on the front, rubble on sides and back. The stone was stuccoed, traces of which remain. A tax assessment of 1828 for Little Creek Hundred demonstrates the uniqueness of these stone buildings: there were ninety-seven local structures of frame, sixty of log, twenty-seven of brick, and only two of stone. Stone Tavern was restored in 1978 by the state.

KT17 WHEEL OF FORTUNE

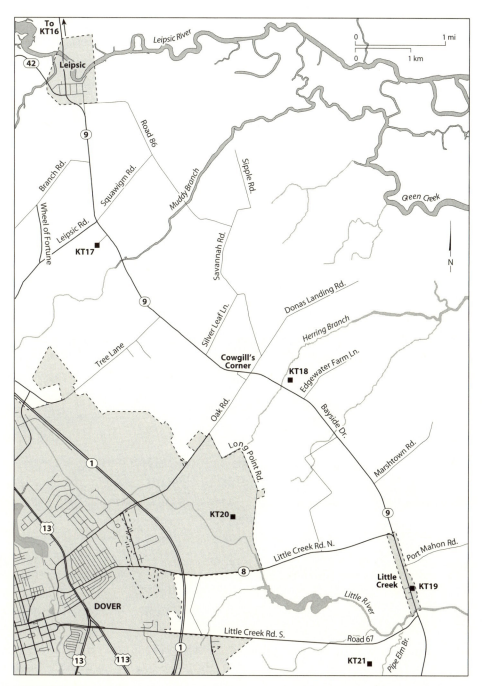

ALONG DE 9

KT20 Sally A. Sipple House

c. 1750. 633 Long Point Rd., west of Little Creek

Surrounded by fields, this white-stuccoed brick house on a high base exemplifies a relatively rare Georgian type in the state: a shallow, single-pile plan with the facade topped by a big, sheltering gable-pediment. Two other examples are among Delaware's esteemed buildings, Amstel House (NC19) and Belmont Hall (KT13); but unlike them, Sipple House (named for an antebellum owner) is unrestored and workaday. Its late-nineteenth-century crib barn is noteworthy, too.

KT21 Cherbourg Round Barn

1912–1918. 2000 roof rebuilt. South of Road 67, southwest of Little Creek

The eighteenth-century house Cherbourg was demolished in 1953, its woodwork used in restoring Dickinson Mansion (KT25). This was a major twentieth-century dairy farm, and the surviving agricultural complex is unusually varied and complete, with some rare types. Its centerpiece is the Round Barn, unique in Delaware, with poured concrete walls seventy-two feet in diameter. Harry McDaniel built it during his ownership of the farm in 1910–1935. The barn's immense frame loft dispensed grain to the cattle below. The round plan maximized floor space and made cleaning convenient. Despite its size, the roof was supported only by rafters and plates, without cross bracing or collars. (As an index of the rarity of the circular barn, all of Maryland's Eastern Shore has but one example.) Four silos are attached, as are a milking parlor and hipped-roof milkhouse with ventilator. A granary, a rock-faced concrete milkhouse, and dairy barn stand nearby. The Round Barn's roof collapsed in a storm in August 1999, but it has been rebuilt in as similar a form as modern building codes allow.

KT21 CHERBOURG ROUND BARN, under construction

CAMDEN

At first called Mifflin's Crossroads, Camden was established in 1783 and grew rapidly, as attested by the many fine brick houses of Georgian derivation just starting to turn Federal in style. There are so many of these dwellings, one can find motifs that repeat, including stucco scored to resemble ashlar, or rows of glazed bricks in the common-bond of gables. Greek Revival is represented by the Hunn House (1830s; 3 S. Main St.), frame with chamfered blocks to resemble ashlar and with small, third-floor attic windows typical of Delaware practice. With many Quakers in the area, the Underground Railroad is said to have been active here. The actual railroad ran west of town in 1856–1858 through what became the community of Wyoming, but no great boom followed, and Camden remained small. Architect G. Morris Whiteside wrote approvingly (1938) of its "numerous buildings well worth study, as they are only slightly altered." Camden Historic District consists of sixty-five structures. The town's population was 2,100 in 2000, but explosive growth was underway.

KT22 Brecknock (Howell's Mill Seat)

Early 18th century, with additions. Brecknock County Park, 80 Old Camden Rd.

This historic farm and millseat on Isaac Branch (a stream) was converted into an eighty-six-acre county park through the generosity of its last occupant, Elizabeth Goggin, descendant of a man who bought it in 1761. English-born mariner Daniel Toaes acquired the 600-acre tract called Brecknock in the 1680s for payment of one white servant and 4,000 pounds of tobacco in casks. Subsequent owners enjoyed prosperity from milling; fragments of Howell Mill, described in an insurance policy of 1851 as two stories of frame on a brick footing, are visible from the park's nature trail. The centerpiece of the park is Brecknock house, one of the oddest colonial dwellings in Delaware, a conglomeration of four sections built at different periods. The first part is especially enigmatic, a somewhat crudely built brick shed that Camden-based architect George F. Bennett thought was seventeenth century, though its common bond would surely rule this out. A larger brick addition (c. 1740) is also shed-roofed, a rare form for the state; it contains fine paneling around its fireplaces, which are, exceptionally, placed in the corner. Heavy stair balusters suggest a date before 1750. The last two additions (mid-eighteenth century and 1880s) are frame. One of these transformed the c. 1740 addition into a gabled house; the other is a one-story lean-to in the right-angled space between the two brick sections.

KT22 BRECKNOCK (HOWELL'S MILL SEAT), rear view

KT23 CAMDEN FRIENDS MEETING HOUSE, photo 1936

KT23 Camden Friends Meeting House

1805. 1957 Annex, Albert Kruse. 122 E. Camden-Wyoming Ave.

Camden town was laid out by a Quaker, Daniel Mifflin, and was long a downstate outpost of that faith. Built on a square plan, the brick meetinghouse sports a gambrel roof, unusual for such buildings in the Delaware Valley. The gambrel is explained by the presence of a schoolroom upstairs, which retains its desks and black-painted plank chalkboards, although no pupils have studied in it since 1882! Thanks to the finished upstairs room, men and women could conveniently hold their monthly business meetings in segregated spaces, which eliminated the need for the usual dividing wall downstairs. Another unusual feature is that the two entry doors to the meetinghouse are not side-by-side, as was Quaker custom, but in opposite walls. The massive original key is still used to unlock them. Camden is one of just three Delaware meetinghouses in continuous operation (for the others, see WL41 and MC1).

KT24 Morning Star Institutional Church of God in Christ (Whatcoat Methodist Episcopal Church)

1856–1857. 255 Camden-Wyoming Ave.

This somewhat dilapidated front-gabled brick edifice has housed four religious denominations in 150 years. Although the church originally served a white congregation, historians of the Underground Railroad point to two tunnels beneath the building as possible hiding places and note that among the bricklayers were free blacks Absalom Gibbs and his son Abraham, the latter known to have worked with Harriet Tubman. Stained-glass windows are said to be English-made. The current, African American congregation took over the vacant structure in 1986 as their second choice to building a new facility in the countryside. Other historic black congregations in town are Star Hill A.M.E. Church (1866; Voshells Mill–Star Hill Rd.) and the Classical Revival, frame Zion A.M.E. Church (1889; Center St.).

SOUTHEAST OF DOVER

KT25 John Dickinson Mansion

1739–1740. 1752–1754 western extensions. 1804–1806 rebuilt. U.S. 113 and Kitts Hummock Rd.

A National Historic Landmark, state museum site, and one of Delaware's most famous buildings, this was the childhood home of "Penman of the Revolution" John Dickinson, who drafted the Articles of Confederation in 1778. His father, Judge Samuel Dickinson, built the brick Georgian dwelling (of Flemish bond with glazed headers) on his 13,000-acre plantation along the St. Jones River. Two wings, each progressively smaller, were later added to the west, housing a dining room plus bedroom above and (in the second extension) a kitchen and slave quarters. John Dickinson lived here as a child before moving to Philadelphia to study law. His famous political document, *Letters from a Farmer in Pennsylvania* (1767), in fact refers to this Delaware farm (Delaware then forming the three lower counties of Pennsylvania). A destructive fire in 1804 spared only the walls. By then a resident of Wilmington, Dickinson rebuilt the place via a series of letters he sent to his workmen, highly informative to historians. The house went from three stories to two. Interior finishings were far simpler than before, as only tenants would occupy it.

By 1950, the kitchen was starting to collapse; two years later, the whole mansion was threatened with demolition. When archivist Leon deValinger visited, the front room had four tons of grain in it. The Colonial Dames and the State of Delaware bought it in 1952 and opened it as a museum four years later. Woodwork used for the restoration is of a finer character than originally. The grounds were restored by Alden Hopkins, with help from Donald H. Parker of Colonial Williamsburg (1954). Further restorations took place after 1980 and included re-creation of the cove cornice and porches with built-in benches and repainting the house both inside and out based on microscopic paint analysis. Modern climate control and other improvements have been introduced (1999–2003, Bernardon Haber Holloway). A feed barn was rebuilt (1985–1986) based on specifications of c. 1800; another barn (1988–1989) has no precedent here but was needed as a modern visitor center.

KT26 Kingston-upon-Hull

Early 18th century, first three bays and two-bay kitchen addition. Mid-19th century, second story. On St. Jones River in Ted Harvey Wildlife Area, entered off Kitts Hummock Rd., 1.8 miles east of U.S. 113

Listed by Preservation Delaware as threatened, this ancient, abandoned brick building stands empty along the riverbank. The tract that it occupies was patented in 1671. The date of construction is unknown, and even the nomenclature is confusing; the dwelling has sometimes been called Town Point, and nearby Dickinson Mansion (KT25) has been called Kingston-upon-Hull. Early-twentieth-century historians mistook it for a relic of the seventeenth century, calling it "Kent County's first courthouse." In fact, it was always a home, owned by the Dickinsons for genera-

KT25 JOHN DICKINSON MANSION, photo 1950s

KT26 KINGSTON-UPON-HULL

tions. They added the frame second story during the years when tenant farmers occupied the place. The much-remarked colonial brickwork of the walls, nearly sixty feet in length on each long side, shows English, Flemish, and common bonds, with treatments changing over time as the building was enlarged. Earliest are the splendid sections with glazed headers and a doglegged watertable.

KT27 Matthew Lowber House

1774. 1980 moved and restored. East side of Main St. N.(U.S. 113A), Magnolia

For seventy-one years this three-bay, hall-and-parlor brick house stood alone at the crossroads where Magnolia (pop. 226) later grew. Its construction date appears in glazed headers in the gable, along with Lowber's initials. Frame wings were eventually added and the house was painted white. In the 1960s, archivist Leon deValinger heard that the "White House" was to be demolished for a gas station. Peeping through the windows, he saw some of the finest colonial paneling in Delaware, a fireplace with classical surround, and an unusual winder stair approached by four free-standing

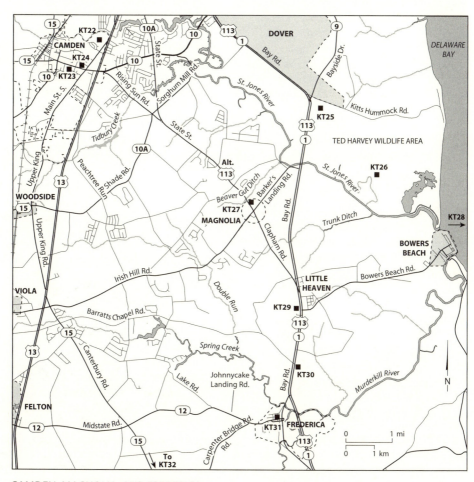

CAMDEN, MAGNOLIA, AND FREDERICA

SOUTHEAST OF DOVER

KT27 MATTHEW LOWBER HOUSE, during move

steps with elaborate banister (somewhat like Aspendale's, KT1). He decided to launch a campaign of preservation—what turned, ultimately, into a comedy of errors. The state bought the house only to give it to a local fire company that then moved it 100 yards and cut down the two colossal sycamore trees in the yard (planted 1786 and 1823).

Elsewhere in Magnolia, on Main Street South is a prominent late-nineteenth-century Queen Anne house, Lindale, with turrets and wide porches.

KT28 Fourteen Foot Bank Lighthouse

1885–1886, D. P. Heap, with Anderson and Barr, engineers. In Delaware Bay, 11 miles east of Bowers Beach (not visible from shore)

The lighthouse guards the south end of dangerous Joe Flogger Shoal along the central shipping channel of Delaware Bay. "On the cutting edge of lighthouse technology in the United States," according to historians Jim Gowdy and Kim Ruth (1999), it was the first to be built by pneumatic caisson, in the dramatic manner of the Brooklyn Bridge's footings. The wooden caisson was floated out from Lewes, then sunk at the site and filled with compressed air, which allowed men to work inside it. Three brave gangs of eight laborers each toiled by the light of paraffin candles, digging through sand until the caisson had sunk twenty-three feet beneath the surface of the submerged shoal. The caisson was then filled with 2,000 cubic yards of concrete. Already, the three lower tiers of the cylindrical, cast-iron lighthouse base stood atop the caisson, and once it was fully sunk the superstructure (by H. A. Ramsay and Son, Baltimore) was erected. It resembled a multigabled Queen Anne house, oddly enough, but was built entirely of cast iron, even the roof. A square, three-story central tower was surmounted by an octagonal cupola containing the light, and a neat little iron privy overhung the waves. The lighthouse remains in use, though it has been unmanned since the last two-person crew moved out in 1973. Former keepers tell of the intense loneliness of the winter months, with ice floes crashing against the metal sides. Lately, it has found a new function as an improvised platform for environmental-monitoring sensors.

KT29 Jehu M. Reed House

1771. 1868. West side of U.S. 113 near Bowers Beach Rd., Little Heaven

Another fascinating Delaware "evolved" house (see KT15 and WS21), this brick colonial dwelling beside the highway turned Italianate after the Civil War and seems a strange fusion of styles and periods. The property belonged to the related Newell-Sipple-Reed families for centuries (1685–1912). The first section (a side-passage house consisting of the three

KT28 FOURTEEN FOOT BANK LIGHTHOUSE

KT29 JEHU M. REED HOUSE, lower stories colonial and upper story Victorian

bays at right) was built for Henry Newell in glazed-header Flemish bond. Jehu M. Reed's father moved in upon marrying in 1827, and three years later he planted a peach orchard—introducing, some have said, this fruit as a crop to the United States (see the illustration on p. 13). The younger Reed took over in 1858, expanding the farm to 250 acres and making it highly profitable via scientific farming. He transformed the house by adding the two bays at left and an upper story, and running a wrought-iron porch across the front. The rooftop observatory was gone by the 1930s. The house is threatened with demolition.

KT30 Barratt's Chapel

1780. U.S. 113, north of Frederica

Wide fields of Kent County—now starting to sprout houses—embrace the famous "Cradle of Methodism," Barratt's Chapel. In this barnlike building, 42 × 48 feet in area, the Methodist Church in America was founded in a series of meetings between Thomas Coke and Francis Asbury in 1784. Brickwork is used to signal the hierarchy of the various facades of the church, there being (as at the more elaborate Old Drawyers, LN5) two major facades and two minor ones. The major facades are both Flemish bond (one of them with glazed headers); the minor are common bond. Glazed-header lozenges, as seen in the gables, are rare in Delaware, but the McComb House elsewhere in Kent County has two nested lozenges in its gable, and there are examples on the Eastern Shore as well. Entering the ancient western door, one originally faced a high pulpit. As Methodism became more consciously plain, however, the congregation resolved in 1800–1801 "that the old pulpit be taken away." The present pulpit and altar are thought to date to 1841. A visitor of four years later found that "the interior has been considerably repaired and altered," and benches had long since given way to rail-backed pews (one of which says "Made by Jas. G. Harrison, Oct. 19th, 1826"). A relic backless bench is preserved in the museum here as the one on which Coke and Asbury sat. The doors flanking the front door (c. 1860) replaced windows, allowing persons seated in the three-sided gallery (including African Americans) separate egress.

In 1880, the Philadelphia Conference of Methodists called Barratt's a "sacred landmark of Methodism." During the next four years, there were various proposals for "improvements," including making single, tall windows in place of each two colonial ones. Thankfully, funds were lacking, and a young pastor, Sewell N. Pilchard, summoned his parish in a newspaper, *Barratt's Chapel Centenary* (1884), "to restore to the church its former quaint styles of furniture and surroundings.... [We] do not think that the all-prevailing spirit of 'change' will serve to keep the past in remembrance." Such conservatism has ensured the excellent state of preservation of Barratt's to this day. The present wood floor was installed in 1933.

KT30 BARRATT'S CHAPEL

A restoration forty years later put on a wood shingle roof, the seventh in the history of the church, and removed the stucco of 1885 from east and south walls, exposing the historic brickwork.

The chapel is surrounded by an unusually large country churchyard, which had 6,500 tombs by 1938. A surviving ledger records payments to brick masons for constructing its wall in 1839.

FREDERICA

This small community on the Murderkill River, originally settled in colonial days, is dense with old houses crowded up against each other and pressing close to the streets. Its nineteenth-century shipbuilding industry and twentieth-century canneries are a distant memory. Hardly anything has been restored in this working-class community, and all seems threatened with gradual decay or piecemeal demolition. Glazed-header brickwork of the eighteenth century peeks through the stucco at 123 Front Street, a facade elongated over time, with tiny, irregular windows upstairs. Residents protested when the road was widened into its front yard. Union Hotel (eighteenth century, now Robbins Hardware Store), at the corner of Front and Market, is perhaps Delaware's only example of a type of brick bond familiar in colonial Maryland, all-header. Red-brick Trinity Methodist Church (1856; 4 Front St.) follows the temple-form of several Delaware churches of that decade. Its brick pilasters are scored down the middle with a channel. The exceedingly sharp-pointed spire supports a fine ball-and-arrow windvane. A corner of the church collapsed in a hurricane in 1954, but has been rebuilt. The Tudor Revival public school (1931–1932; 124 Front St.) is a rarity in Delaware; locals at the time called its style "Swedish." The brick Town Hall and Firehouse (14 E. David St.) was erected as a WPA project, one of the most ambitious in the state (1935–1936). More than 100 properties in Frederica have been added to the National Register.

KT31 Hathorn-Betts House (Hathorn-Lowber or Peter Lowber House)

1730–1750 period. 1979–1981 restored, William Harkins and Geron S. Hite. 5 Market St.

The five-bay, single-pile Georgian house with steep-pitched roof literally stands in the street, as it predates the laying out of the town in 1770. Over time, it had twin trees planted in front of the door and acquired a veranda in the nineteenth century. Local lore held that the little sealed-up windows in the gable end were gun mounts, used to ward off Indian attacks. By 1979, the dwelling had been abandoned for twenty-five years and was overgrown with vines. Vandals had stripped it of everything from linens and Tiffany lamps to beds and brass door fittings. A Ms. Dodd, raised in the

KT31 HATHORN-BETTS HOUSE (HATHORN-LOWBER OR PETER LOWBER HOUSE), pre-restoration

KT33 VOGL HOUSE

house, undertook a restoration with a $25,000 matching federal grant. Removal of stucco revealed that no fewer than three sides of the house were glazed-header Flemish bond, a generous use of this decorative treatment, and that even the English bond below the watertable showed considerable glazing. These first-rate exterior walls are well preserved, but interior trim was mostly replaced in the early nineteenth century.

KT32 Mordington

c. 1770–1800 period. Canterbury Rd. (DE 15) at McColley Pond, southwest of Frederica

An ironmaster and miller built this elegant, side-passage brick house on an upper branch of the Murderkill River, overlooking a millpond. It shows the moment of transition between Georgian and Federal; new are the side hall or townhouse form (popular in adjacent Maryland) and double-pile plan, fashionable keystoned lintels (of wood, painted to resemble stone), and the absence of a watertable. In an unusual touch, the stringcourse runs around the entire structure. In 1930, during the Great Depression, the owner agreed to sell the interior woodwork to H. F. du Pont of Winterthur (CH10). For $3,500, du Pont bought eight doors and their trim, six window trims and reveals, all the carved cornices and chair rails, two mantlepieces, the staircase, porch columns, and even the old beams in the garage. Virtually all that was spared was the chimneypiece of the southwest room. Du Pont's architect, Burt Ives, measured the material prior to removal. "Sixth Floor Hall" and "Wisteria Hall" at Winterthur were adorned with Mordington fragments in 1930–1931, and the front door of the house became the entrance to "Massachusetts Hall." Unlike many of the buildings from which du Pont removed materials, Mordington was in little danger of demolition and still stands today, making it, for some, an egregious example of the collecting practices of the 1930s. The house briefly stood vacant before the Leslie I. March family purchased it in 1941. Its stair and other woodwork have been replicated, and the present front door came from a house in historic Berlin, Maryland.

KT33 Vogl House

1915, Wilhelmine Vogl. North side of Road 277, west of Road 78, southwest of Mastens Corner

Bohemian immigrants John and Wilhelmine Vogl raised chickens on this farm southwest of Felton, supposedly having seen the property advertised in a Prague newspaper. They purchased a concrete-block-making machine from Sears, Roebuck (it still survives) and built their own H-shaped house with hipped roofs, with the help of their eight children, in a folk style recalling the stone architecture of their native Bohemia. The concrete blocks are rusticated for the quoins and smooth for the walls, and the cornice is adorned with a concrete egg-and-dart motif. There is a strange Ionic porch with a balcony above, also of concrete, as are the various outbuildings: silo, milk house, garden house, chicken house, even a dog house. Concrete statues of animals adorn the lawn. Inside the home, Wilhelmine painted pictures on fibreboard walls and ceilings, completing an exuberant tableau unique in Delaware.

HARRINGTON

"Clark's Corner" developed in the eighteenth century and became a railroad link in the 1850s. Renamed Harrington in 1862, the town was a key downstate junction, and, as late as 1960, the railroad remained the top employer. By that time, the automobile was fast supplanting trains, and a stagnating Harrington was best known for the nearby state fairgrounds. On the Du Pont Highway south of town stands the Tharp House (c. 1835), part brick, part frame. Asbury Methodist Church (1890; 200 Weiner Ave.) has a Stick Style belfry. W. T. Chipman Middle School (former Harrington High School) at 101 W. Center Street offers a striking contrast between the original red-brick structure (1929, Guilbert and Betelle) and International Style additions. The latter consist of curtain walls with aluminum mullions, tinted glass, and lime-green enamel panels. The town's boxlike, brick Colonial Revival post office (1936, Louis A. Simon) contains a Depression-era mural by Eve Salisbury titled *Men Howing*.

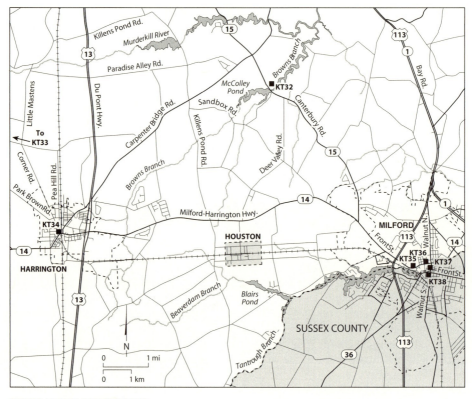

HARRINGTON AND MILFORD

KT34 First National Bank

1887. Mechanic St. and Railroad Ave.

In this colorful Queen Anne–style jewelbox of a building, hard, pressed bricks of red, yellow, and black are set in thin black mortar (crudely repointed in recent years with white cement). Segmental brick arches over the windows and a semicircular one above the porch opening are jauntily zebra-striped. Decorative brick corbeling undergirds a wide tin cornice. The polychromy recalls the Central Law Building at 314 S. State Street, Dover (1888). The bank has lost its roof cresting and big iron gates. A rare note of color in a town of grayish vinyl siding, it stands vacant, as do several commercial buildings nearby.

MILFORD

The sinuous Mispillion River bisects Milford, Delaware's fourth-largest incorporated town, subdivided by Joseph Oliver out of his farm in 1787. By agreement, Reverend Sydenham Thorne—a founder of the Episcopal church in the United States—simultaneously built a dam and wharves at his adjacent millseat. By the mid-nineteenth century the community had begun to spread south of the river (South Milford is in Sussex County, but discussed here for convenience), its growth fuelled by shipbuilding and, in 1859, the coming of the railroad. Great quantities of peaches were canned and shipped. When surveyed in 1979, North Milford Historic District was found to contain ninety-five noteworthy buildings (23 percent of them brick), of which more than half predated 1860. Front Street shows surprisingly many early-nineteenth-century buildings, some with Queen Anne embellishments. Several, including Number 129 with its date spelled out in black bricks (1816?), are in poor repair. Prominent in the South Milford Historic District is the former Schine Theater (Plaza Theater), built in 1922, the same year as the Everett in Middletown. It was the largest in the state when rebuilt with 1,800 seats after a fire in 1946. It closed in the 1970s. In 2003, a child knocked over a candle in an upstairs apartment on S. Walnut Street, starting a fire that unfortunately gutted a quarter of the historic district. Among the nineteenth-century homes in South Milford is the rambling, frame Vaules-Grier House, or Draper House (1872, altered 1907; 200 Lakeview Ave.), built for a railroad station agent.

KT35 Parson Thorne Mansion

1730–1735 rear wing. 1745–1750 main section. 1879 remodeled. 501 N.W. Front St.

A strange fusion of colonial and late-nineteenth-century styles, Milford's most famous building was home to Reverend Sydenham Thorne, co-founder of the town. It was once thought that he built the house c. 1785, but, in fact, it is considerably older, consisting of a center passage Georgian structure added to an existing frame wing (at rear; with brick nogging). Wooden lintels imitate stone, as of-

KT35 PARSON THORNE MANSION

ten seen in Kent County. In the 1870s, Colonel Henry B. Fiddeman, banker and president of railroad and steamship companies, added sharp gables to the main block and wings and heightened the roofline. "Rebuilt the house frame," a carpenter wrote on a board inside. Fortunately, the interior was not touched and retains its colonial paneling. Tenant farmers lived here in the early twentieth century, when the Draper family owned it. Milford Historical Society, founded by Catherine Downing and others, took over in 1962 and has restored it several times, initially under Albert Kruse (1963), who removed the Fiddeman front porch, renewed the windows with colonial-type sash, and found bits of original weatherboarding under imitation brick siding on the rear wing. Fortunately, funds were lacking for removal of the weird late-nineteenth-century accretions of gables and trim at the roofline that made the house, for an unsympathetic Harold Eberlein (1962), "a monument to insanity."

KT36 The Towers

Late 18th century. 1891 remodeling. 101 N.W. Front St.

This house's occupants have included poet John Lofland (the "Milford Bard") in 1808–1838 and, later, Governor William Burton, whose wife occupied it until 1885. Her daughter, wealthy widow Rhoda B. Roudebush, returned from New York to undertake extraordinary Queen Anne–style transformations. The frame house became a riot of roof-shapes, window types, shingle patterns, and decorative details. One end of the dwelling has a storybook turret and a red-brick chimney with black bricks that spell "1783" (the supposed original date of the house) and "1891," along with a checkered pattern cleverly alluding to glazed-header colonial brickwork. Interior woodwork is elaborate, including a sycamore-wood coffered ceiling in the music room. Late-nineteenth-century architecture was rarely mentioned in the WPA *Delaware Guide* (1938); this was an exception, but only because of its association with Lofland. At that time, it was painted red and green. As part of a transformation in the mid-1980s into a bed-and-breakfast, it received a dazzling scheme of pinks and purples, which landed it in the popular book by Elizabeth Pomada, *America's Painted Ladies* (1992). Fender-benders sometimes occur on the street as drivers slow down to stare.

KT37 Mispillion Riverwalk and Greenway

1991–2002, Davis, Bowen and Friedel, engineers. Center of Milford

Studies in the 1970s called for more parks in Milford and for the Mispillion River to be redeveloped for recreation. The thoughtfully designed western extension of the riverwalk features a meandering boardwalk over a streamside meadow, the path elevated as required by regulations for floodplains. Plans call for extending the walk west to Silver Lake.

KT38 Causey Mansion

1763. c. 1855 alterations and wings. Causey Ave. and Walnut St., south Milford (in Sussex County)

A landmark older than the town, this yellow-painted brick house was built for Levin Crapper. Its design was long attributed, obscurely, to an English architect named Mitchell; certainly it was one of the most substantial Georgian houses in Sussex County at that date, Crapper being the wealthiest man around. Next it was home to Colonel Daniel Rogers, governor of Delaware in 1797–1799. Another governor, the Know-Nothing politician Peter F. Causey (elected 1855), bought the house in 1849 and transformed it to Greek Revival, with delicate iron grilles in the low horizontal windows of the added third floor, low pediments over the other windows, and a one-story central porch with paired Ionic columns. He reversed the orientation of the dwelling to

KT36 THE TOWERS, rear view prior to restoration

KT38 CAUSEY MANSION

face the growing town of Milford. New owners restored the mansion in 1986–1988 as a bed-and-breakfast. They show guests how the walls of the hallway are ornamented with Lincrusta, a linoleumlike embossed fabric imitating tooled leather.

KT38.1 Kitchen and Slave Quarter
c. 1806

The probate inventory of Colonel Rogers (d. 1806) listed large numbers of bricks, suggesting that this building was then under construction (he owned about fifteen slaves). Later, Causey raised the roof on the kitchen-quarter, increasing the height of the cramped garret inside. This room is a rare Sussex County survival of a slave habitation. Both the stuccoed kitchen-quarter and nearby smokehouse-with-icehouse eventually became decayed; the latter is now ruinous, but a restoration of the former is contemplated.

Dover

Rich with colonial associations, Dover was established along the St. Jones River by William Penn in 1683, though not actually laid out until 1717, following Penn's original plan for the town. The second largest city in Delaware (32,100 population in the year 2000), it has served as state capital for more than two centuries (replacing New Castle in 1777). In the early nineteenth century, the community was torn by political divisions, abolitionists versus slaveowners. Modern Dover essentially dates from the completion of the Du Pont Highway (U.S. 13) in the mid-1920s, which attracted such industries as International Latex (1937; DV5). World War II brought the famous Dover Air Force Base, which today employs 6,000 people. After World War II, Dover grew rapidly, increasing by 137 percent in the 1960s alone, and growth continues with much new construction. The city shows a marked contrast between the sometimes unsightly sprawl belt on its perimeter and the charming historic neighborhoods and districts closer to the center.

With the rise of the automobile, springtime pilgrimages to old houses and gardens became widely popular, and, in 1933, the first "A Day with the Storied Houses and Gardens of Old Dover" (Old Dover Day) attracted 2,000 tourists. This annual event raised money for the Friends of Old Dover and continues today in a modified form. Construction of Legislative Hall (DV16) and a capitol complex in the 1930s developed the Colonial Revival theme already established in Newark at the University of Delaware campus (NK9), these two planned institutions firmly establishing it as a dominant twentieth-century style in Delaware. And when modernism fully arrived in the 1950s, Colonial Revivalists kept it at bay in Dover. Wesley College's Gothic Revival main building had been erected as Wilmington Conference Academy by a Philadelphia architect (1873–1874, James H. Windrim; 1876–1878 restored after a fire); now it got a Colonial Revival makeover by another Philadelphia firm (1941–1942, Wenner and Fink). Delaware Trust Bank was similarly converted from Italianate to Colonial Revival by a Philadelphian (1949–1950, Philip Thomas Harris).

A corollary to the stress on Colonial Revival was that the center of Dover was purged of much of its mid-to-late-nineteenth-century architecture, including Hotel Richardson (1881–1882, demolished 1954), one of Delaware's

Dover. Historic view down the main business thoroughfare, Loockerman Street, to the Post Office (1873–1878, William Appleton Potter).

best Queen Anne–style buildings. Also razed was the High Victorian Gothic Post Office, later City Hall, designed by the U.S. Supervising Architect of the Treasury (1873–1878, William Appleton Potter). This important building (see photograph on p. 28) was demolished in February 1973, in spite of some protest, and replaced with a Virginia-style Colonial Revival structure (1972–1974, R. Calvin Clendaniel). Dover lost another historic building in 2005 with the demolition of the Timothy Hanson House (c. 1730), a gambrel-roofed frame dwelling.

DV1 Dover Downs and Dover International Speedway

1967–1969. 1980s–1990s enlarged, Becker Morgan Group and others. 2000–2002 hotel, Cope Linder Architects, with interiors by Mitchell Associates with Marcia Davis and Associates. U.S. 13 and Leipsic Rd.

The track was originally conceived for harness racing and thoroughbreds, but entrepreneur John W. Rollins (see BR32) got involved during construction, completing the facility and insisting that it be modified to include automobile racing. Richard Petty won the opening race in 1969. By 1982, the track had lost millions of dollars and seemed a hopeless boondoggle. The explosive growth of NASCAR racing saved the day, however, and Dover Downs underwent sixteen consecutive years of expansion, growing from 22,000 seats in 1985 to 140,000 in 2001, by which time each NASCAR race weekend pumped millions of dollars directly into the Delaware economy, with 92 percent of the fans from out-of-state. An

DV1 DOVER DOWNS AND DOVER INTERNATIONAL SPEEDWAY

adjacent casino attracts 2.5 million customers annually (three times the population of Delaware!); to serve them, a ten-story hotel was added. Removal of all "architectural barriers to access" and the addition of 300 wheelchair-accessible seats came as a result of a 1990s settlement agreement with the U.S. government, one of the first results of the Americans with Disabilities Act.

DV2 Delaware State University

1892, with additions. Old College Rd., west of U.S. 13

"Del State" was founded in 1890 as the State College for Colored Students, providing education in agriculture and the mechanical arts. It now offers a full range of undergraduate programs in seventeen modern buildings on its 400-acre campus. The most venerable building is the five-bay house (c. 1780) called Loockerman Hall. Its pedimented end gables, unusual in Delaware, are handsomely adorned with modillion cornices. The pioneering historian Thomas Scharf wrote (1888), "The slave quarters were a short distance away. Here Mr. Loockerman lived in the easy style of the old-time Southern gentleman"—ironic, given the subsequent history of the house as this historically African American college's main building and, later, women's dormitory. A drive to restore the house began in the late 1960s, but a fire was a major setback, and a shortage of funds meant that the project dragged on for years. Recently, Homsey Architects has done much work on the Del State campus, including the William C. Jason Library (1990–1991), with its curving wall of blue glass, and the state-of-the-art Claude E. Phillips Herbarium, with a skylit reading atrium (1999–2000).

DV3 Delaware Agricultural Museum and Village

1979–1980, Diamond State Engineering. 866 N. Du Pont Hwy. (U.S. 13)

The nonprofit museum includes a "village" of farm and rural buildings brought in from elsewhere, including a log corncrib (c. 1825), blacksmith's shop (c. 1850), schoolhouse (c. 1850), railroad station (c. 1864), and fully stocked general store (c. 1873). St. Thomas Methodist Church (1857, later altered), from Shortly, Sussex County, was moved here in 1994. It features original pews, chairs, pulpit, altar table, and cast-iron stoves, the latter made in 1878. A mill was built from scratch on the village grounds, incorporating milling equipment of 1862. Carney Farm (1893) gives a good idea of old-fashioned rural living. Fully one-quarter of the house was devoted to the parlor, a mark of status, and ample porches offered space for work and relaxation. The outdoor or summer kitchen is a late survival of this type of feature. Given that Delaware loses 10,000 acres of farmland every year, this museum may be as close as tomorrow's schoolchildren get to experiencing farm life.

DV3.1 Mrs. Steele's Broiler House

c. 1925. 1973 renovated. Exhibited indoors at museum

In 1923, Ocean View housewife Cecile Steele received a shipment of 500 chicks from a hatchery, ten times more than she had ordered. Making a virtue of this crisis, she raised them to two pounds each, then sold them. Surprised by the profit she made, the Steeles began raising chickens for sale as broilers—young chickens meant expressly for eating. By the third year, they were growing 10,000 birds. From this beginning sprang the Sussex County broiler industry, which revolutionized the raising of chickens in the United States. Consumption nationwide went from fourteen pounds of chicken annually in 1934 to seventy-five pounds in 1997, with 600 million broilers produced annually on Delmarva alone. The same period saw Delmarva's share of American broiler production decline from 66 percent to 8 percent, but the industry remains a major (and highly polluting) employer here, with 14,000 workers. Mrs. Steele's Broiler House, sixteen feet square, commemorates the early days when 500 broilers were housed in little sheds heated by a coal stove.

DV3.2 "Swedish" Log House (Josh's Cabin)

Probably 1750–1800 period. 1980, exhibited indoors at museum

Driving to Wilmington one day about 1950, state archivist Leon deValinger spotted this old house in a field near the junction of U.S. 13

and U.S. 40 in New Castle County. It turned out to be a one-room log cabin, 14 × 18 feet, with three small windows and a door (a second door has been cut in). It had been abandoned for about thirty years since its elderly African American resident, Josh, had died. White oak logs were hewn on two sides and chinked with clay mixed with rye or oat hulls. V-notching was crude. The interior showed fifty-five layers of plaster, suggestive of great age. Stairs to the loft were carved from a single log. C. A. Weslager undertook an archaeological investigation in 1951–1952, one of the first digs at a log cabin anywhere (his classic book is *The Log Cabin in America*, 1969). Under the floor were bones of various animals, including rats, and 244 buttons from generations of human residents. Clay pipes dated the house to the second half of the eighteenth century. To Weslager and deValinger, the importance of such Delaware log houses was the evidence they provided of the Swedish origins of log architecture in America. Josh's Cabin was far too young to be Swedish, but Weslager believed it reflected Scandinavian influences (see also Bird House, WL2.2).

DV4 North State Street Houses

19th and 20th centuries. N. State St.

Among the notable homes is Number 2, the Mifflin House (1879–1885), built in green serpentine and brick by a peach canner. Dr. Henry Ridgely erected Number 6 (1869) on a busy corner, a towered house of brick with red stone quoins. Richardson Hall (c. 1890 and later), Number 29, was built by Senator Harry A. Richardson, a wealthy canner.

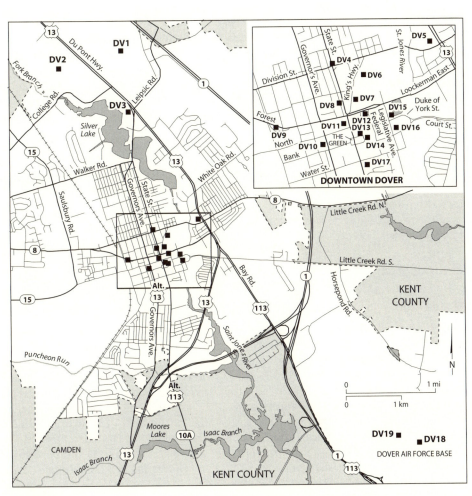

DOVER

Its brick turret was added between 1904 and 1910. The family sold the place to Wesley College in the 1950s. Redevelopment schemes for Richardson Hall (as it was named) were controversial for years. An assisted living facility was built on the grounds in 1999 and Richardson Hall was restored. The house at Number 300 was originally the Allee Mansion, remodeled as the Tudor Manor Hotel (1929–1930). The Delaware corporation law, under which, by 1938, one-fifth of U.S. corporations were chartered in Dover, hugely increased the need for hotels in town. Owing to the Great Depression, this one was never completed to its intended size.

DV6 WOODBURN, rear view

DV5 Playtex Products (International Latex Company)

1937, with additions. U.S. 13 and Division St.

Russian immigrant Abram N. Spanel moved his latex company here from Rochester, New York, building a 100,000-square-foot factory of brick in a cow pasture near the U.S. 13 bypass, the beginning of big industry in Dover. In the Moderne style facility, he manufactured baby pants and ladies' girdles. Foreseeing war in the Pacific, Spanel bought a reserve of Southeast Asian latex just before Pearl Harbor, stashing it on-site in underground vaults (extant until the early 1990s) lined with chemically treated beeswax. During the war, the entire U.S. supply of latex was here, used by Spanel's workmen to make inflatable assault boats, floatable stretchers for the injured, and other materiel.

DV6 Woodburn

c. 1798. c. 1914 portico at rear; terraces.
151 King's Hwy.

This Federal house was built as Charles Hillyard's country seat well outside of town. The date of construction is unknown, but a diary of 1798 refers to "Hillyards New Brick House." Brick side-passage dwellings were popular at the time. Some features are conservative, such as the extensive interior paneling with dog-ears. Nineteenth-century owner Daniel Cowgill, a Quaker, allegedly made the place available as a stop on the Underground Railroad, as dramatized by a scene in George A. Townsend's novel, *The Entailed Hat* (1884). But Cowgill actually lived on another farm and rented the house, and the tunnel that supposedly helped slaves escape from the cellar to the St. Jones River is merely imaginary, though at least one Doverite today recalls playing in it as a child, and published sources continue wishfully to refer to it. The ivy-covered house was illustrated in Marion Harlan's *More Colonial Homesteads* (1899). At the behest of Governor Charles Terry, the state bought Woodburn in 1965 and restored it for use as the official mansion for the state's governor, the first Delaware ever had. Gubernatorial events find a handsome backdrop in the unusually large Federal stairhall (forty-one feet long), which Harlan found as spacious and shadowy as "an ocean cave." The early-twentieth-century portico has grouped Doric columns.

DV7 State Office Building (Richardson and Robbins Cannery Complex)

1881 with additions. 1979–1983 restored, Moeckel Carbonell and Partners.
89 King's Hwy.

Dover was once famed for canneries. This red-brick one produced nationally known brands of canned chicken and plum puddings and was described in the WPA *Delaware Guide* in 1938 as having "white tile walls, painted cement floors, and men and women workers clad in spotless white." After 1959, it manufactured Underwood Red Devil ham spreads. The complex was recorded by HAER prior to its sensitive conversion into a state office building.

DV8 Rose Cottage

c. 1855. 102 S. State St.

Cottages showing the impact of Andrew Jackson Downing's designs published in his influential books, including *The Architecture of Country Houses* (1850), are rare in Delaware. This frame house was built for Presbyterian minister Thomas B. Bradford and shows the signatures of the style: decorative bargeboards, a wooden porch with Tudor Revival arches, and bay and casement windows. (Smyrna, too, has a similar cottage built for a minister, the Cummins House of 1874–1875 at 107 N. Main St.) Nearly razed at one point, Rose Cottage was bought for a dollar by the Friends of Old Dover and given to the state, which uses it as headquarters for the state museums.

DV9 George V. Massey Station (Pennsylvania Station)

1911, William H. Cookman. West end of Loockerman St.

Railroad stations once served as triumphal portals to American towns and cities, as this temple-form building recalls. Its Doric portico of wood is heroically massive, as are its wide eaves with mutules. It is reminiscent of Thomas Jefferson's Pavilions at the University of Virginia. The brick building's facade is composed of a series of pilasters and relieving arches under a hipped roof. Massey, a lawyer for the Pennsylvania Railroad, convinced the company to replace the original Italianate station built by the Delaware Railroad (1853–

DV8 ROSE COTTAGE

1860), the coming of which had invigorated the southern part of the state. Adaptive reuse (1998–2002, Bernardon Haber Holloway) has converted the interior to office space. Nearby rises the new Social Security Administration Office (2003–2004, C. Terry Jackson II), which similarly attempts to revive the western edge of downtown.

DV10 Delaware Archaeological Museum (Old Presbyterian Church)

1790. 1949–1950 restoration, Albert Kruse. 316 S. Governor's Ave.

The Dover plat of 1717 set this lot aside as Meeting House Square, and already a log church (c. 1715) stood here. This brick former church was still new when Delaware's constitution, drafted by John Dickinson, was ratified inside in 1792. The Square was spoiled by a gas works in the late nineteenth century, not removed until the 1950s. In 1923, the congregation started meeting elsewhere and, in 1947, sold the building to the state, which opened the Delaware State Museum here three years later (today it houses the Delaware Archaeological Museum). Kruse replaced the boxy steeple with a Colonial Revival cupola. Inside, the outstanding feature is the circular stair to

DV7 STATE OFFICE BUILDING (RICHARDSON AND ROBBINS CANNERY COMPLEX), pre-restoration

the gallery. In the churchyard stands a monument (1841, incorporating a tablet of 1783) to Revolutionary patriot Colonel John Haslet, killed in the Battle of Princeton and reinterred here from Philadelphia. A brick Sunday School building (1880) contains a museum that includes carpenter's tools and sections of Wilmington's early wooden waterpipes.

DV11 Schwartz Center for the Arts (Dover Opera House)

1904. 1920s facade. 1929–1934 interior. 1999–2001, C. Terry Jackson II. 226 S. State St.

With this Opera House completed, Dover became the first town in Delaware outside Wilmington to have a facility devoted entirely to the arts. Actually, it was built to house touring vaudeville shows, not operas. By the 1920s, motion pictures predominated. The film *Birth of a Nation* played here in 1922, the year before a former MGM film distributor for Philadelphia, George M. Schwartz, bought the place. He built a new facade and marquee, expanded the seating to 900, refashioned the interior in Art Deco style, and renamed the building the Capitol Theater. It flourished for decades, not closing until 1982. The abandoned facility has found new life following a restoration that gutted the interior (the old fittings were auctioned off). The lost marquee was replaced, and seating was reduced to 600.

DV12 Wesley Church Educational Center (U.S. Post Office, Federal Building)

1931–1933, Massena and du Pont, with James A. Wetmore. Federal and E. Loockerman sts.

Architect Alfred Victor du Pont was repeatedly frustrated in trying to get commissions for state projects, because, he thought, Pierre S. du Pont held an old grudge against his father, A. I. du Pont. This federal commission was highly welcome. The limestone portico consists of two big columns copied from the Tower of the Winds in Athens, Greece (50 BC), set in antis beneath a pediment. The walls are of Williamsburg-type bricks with limestone quoins, under a hipped roof with widow's walk and cupola. Inside is a work-relief mural by a Wilmington artist, *Harvest Spring and Summer* (1936, William D. White). The building was too small for its purpose and was supplanted in 1962 by the Colonial Revival post

DV11 SCHWARTZ CENTER FOR THE ARTS (DOVER OPERA HOUSE), pre-renovation

DV12 WESLEY CHURCH EDUCATIONAL CENTER (U.S. POST OFFICE, FEDERAL BUILDING), early view

office nearby, which resembles a motel—the contrast demonstrating a striking postwar decline in the quality of public architecture.

DV13 Parke-Ridgely House

1728 main section. 1764 rear wing. 1767 first floor of west end. Later alterations. 9 the Green

One of Delaware's most famous colonial houses faces the Green (see **The Green** on p. 254) just feet from the Old State House (DV14). Its name refers to Thomas Parke, who built it, and Dr. Charles G. Ridgely, who bought it in 1769 and in whose family it has remained ever since. The original four-bay section was hall-and-parlor, and the construction date, it is said, appears on both a rafter and a brick. Walls are Flemish bond with glazed headers under a handsome modillion cornice; the pent eave is now missing. Inside is extensive paneling (some of it brought from other houses by twentieth-century owners) and, in "The Hall," a fireback from Batsto Foundry, New Jersey, and a much-remarked corner stairway. A room-by-room inventory was taken when Ridgely died in 1785 and included the contents of the "Physick Shop" that he conducted, apparently in the west end. Here in town and at his plantation he owned nineteen slaves. The house has many political associations, including the visit of abolitionist Lucretia Mott in 1841 as an angry crowd gathered outside. Interiors and the rear garden of the Ridgely House are illustrated in Marion Harlan's *More Colonial Homesteads* (1899).

For decades (1894–1962) this was home to preservationist Mabel Lloyd Ridgely, who refurbished the house and made changes, including adding the present front door with its Colonial Revival coved doorhood (in place by 1914). That door recalls the Newport, Rhode Island, work of Norman M. Isham, who would later design Legislative Hall (DV16) at Ridgely's request; but she herself might have designed it, too, as she had studied some architecture in her youth at the Metropolitan Museum of Art under Arthur Lyman Tuckerman. The garden was an Old Dover Days attraction in the 1930s, and a color photograph in *Saturday Evening Post* (1949) showed Mrs. Ridgely serving tea in the parlor. Following her death, another refurbishment was undertaken (1966, Robert Raley).

DV14 Old State House

1787–1792, Alexander Givan and others. 1873–1875 altered, James H. Windrim. 1909–1912 restored, Edward L. Tilton. 1973–1976 restored, John F. McCune III and William Harkins (for Pope, Kruse and McCune). East side of the Green

The present structure, center of Delaware government from 1792 to 1932 and now a state museum, replaced the Kent County Courthouse of 1722, supposedly reusing its bricks. The State House's form may have been derived from the Court House in New Castle (NC16), former seat of colonial power. The building became exclusively the capitol when the county moved out in 1873, at which time it was modernized with the addition of a mansard roof and a tower, which historian Harold D. Eberlein later called "ignorant and hideous." The interior was gutted. In the early twentieth century, preservationist Mabel Lloyd Ridgely

DV13 PARKE-RIDGELY HOUSE, photo c. 1960

DOVER 253

THE GREEN

William Penn called for a market square in Dover, but one was not laid out until c. 1720, on either side of S. State Street. Revolutionary soldiers are said to have mustered here. Since the 1840s, it has been a park. Many of its trees are unusual specimens or were planted to mark an occasion. The tall elms (1849) were a favorite subject for postcards; a survivor is the second-tallest tree in the state at 136 feet, after a tulip poplar at Winterthur (CH10.7).

In recent years, residents defeated a plan to close the area to traffic and remodel buildings back to a "colonial" appearance as "Constitution Place" (1986–1987, Norman Day Associates). Many attractive old houses surround the Green, the whole forming a delightful, storybook ensemble not to be missed. The big, brick Greek Revival house at Number 10 was built c. 1854 for Sally A. Sipple (see also KT20). The State Historic Preservation Office at Number 15 is the former Henry Todd House (1859), a tall brick dwelling with marble steps and watertable; a print shop was added at the side. Number 16 is one of Delaware's best cottages, influenced by the mid-nineteenth-century designs of Andrew Jackson Downing, with vertical boarding and a Gothic Revival porch. The Century Club (Number 40, remodeled 1897) is a good example of early Colonial Revival in brick with a big Palladian window inserted into what originally was a church. The tiny frame office building at Number 49 served as Dover's first post office and, later, a law office. The brick Kent County Courthouse (c. 1875) was reconstructed in Colonial Revival in 1918, supposedly by Philadelphian Wilson Eyre. In 2003, the county left the Green for a new facility on U.S. 13 (Becker Morgan Group).

THE GREEN, PARKE-RIDGELY HOUSE (DV13) AT CENTER

DV14 OLD STATE HOUSE, photo during restoration, 1975

DV15 DELAWARE PUBLIC ARCHIVES (HALL OF RECORDS), before enlargement

agitated for restoration and brought in New York City architect Tilton to restore the exterior (no funds were available for the interior). Tilton made no effort at strict historical accuracy—he employed a gambrel roof, for example. The tower, if oversized, was aesthetically excellent. The legislature moved out in 1933, ending what was believed to be the longest continuous use of any American statehouse.

There were plans for restoring the two-story building to its original appearance, removing wings added at various times, but nothing was done. Eventually, it was determined to reconstruct an "authentic" replica. Architect George F. Bennett, however, denounced the project (1977) as "an architectural disaster," the restorers bent on "deliberately destroying a Delaware shrine." Although the facade and tower of 1912 were handsome and effective, the latter weighed heavily on the old walls; in order to strengthen the building, the restorers stripped away everything post-1790s, demolishing all additions and reducing the statehouse to a virtual shell. They were hampered by a paucity of pictures of the original edifice. In the end, roof dimensions and window details were determined from old bills that listed how many feet of shingling and cornices had been installed and how many window panes, and the cupola was copied from Wilmington's Old Town Hall (WL19). Inside, a spectacular stair (1791, John Howe) was recreated in part from the ghostmarks of balusters found on the wall. Today, the Old State House is open to the public and contains a small exhibition on its history and restoration. Exterior refurbishment was undertaken in 2005 (Bernardon Haber Holloway).

DV15 Delaware Public Archives (Hall of Records)

1938, Martin and Jeffers. 1998–2000, Moeckel Carbonell Associates. Legislative Ave. and Duke of York St.

This was the second building in the modern capitol complex, one that remedied a notorious problem, the poor treatment of the state's historic archives. The Delaware Tercentenary (1938) brought attention to the value of these records, housed in cramped quarters in the Old State House basement (DV14). Wilmington architect Ralph Walbree Jeffers and then-assistant archivist Leon deValinger visited the National Archives and the new Maryland Hall of Records (1934–1935, Laurence Hall Fowler) to see the latest trends. Great Depression–era PWA funds made the hipped-roof, Colonial Revival brick building possible, with its many innovations, including vaults that featured a special air-conditioning and fumigation system. Fearing aerial bombardment during World War II, many state agencies moved their records here. Quarters became very cramped before the 80,000-square-foot addition was undertaken. DeValinger lived long enough to attend its topping-off ceremony.

DV16 Legislative Hall (State Legislative Building)

1931–1932, E. William Martin, with Norman M. Isham. 1966–1970 extended, George F. Bennett. 1993–1994 eastern wings, Architects Studio. 411 Legislative Ave.

Delaware's state capitol is unique in the United States: it is the only one of Colonial Revival style or named a "Hall." The architect

DV16 LEGISLATIVE HALL (STATE LEGISLATIVE BUILDING), photo 1930s

E. William Martin had been working closely with Pierre S. du Pont on building Delaware schools. That it would be colonial was certain, given that H. Rodney Sharp and Mabel Lloyd Ridgely sat on the advisory committee and Isham, a Rhode Island antiquarian who was friends with H. F. du Pont of Winterthur (CH10), assisted. (Martin seems to have been brought in after Alfred Victor du Pont and others protested giving the Depression-era job to Isham, an out-of-stater.) The tiered tower was derived by Isham from the Old State House, Boston. Such details as the balcony over the front door, round-topped dormers, and pilaster-piers in the lobby recalled the Old Colony House, Newport, Rhode Island, which Isham had restored in 1932. Locher and Company of Glasgow, Virginia, provided handmade colonial bricks replicating those of the original state house nearby. The clay tiles of the hipped roof imitated cypress shingles. Fine woodwork in the House and Senate Chambers was executed by American Car and Foundry Company of Wilmington (murals by Bridgeville folk artist Jack Lewis in 1986 are a discordant addition). A pale green "colonial" paint scheme prevailed inside. The interior was refurbished in 1995–1997 (Moeckel Carbonell Associates). The park eastward, with handsome brick bridges over the St. Jones River, was constructed by the WPA (1936–1938).

DV17 Christ Church

1734–1760. 1859–1860 restoration. 1887 alterations. 1879–1889 bell tower and chancel. 1913–1914 west door cut and lych-gate added, *Frank R. Watson, George E. Edkins, and William Heyl Thompson. S. State and Water sts.*

The Anglican congregation, founded in 1707, moved to this site in 1734, occupying one of two public squares set aside for places of worship in the Dover town plan of 1717. "The walls are finished," a missionary reported in 1734, but the remainder of construction dragged on for years, and as late as 1750, the brick building resembled "a refuge for wild beasts." The door was originally in the middle of the south facade, which has glazed Flemish-bond brickwork with a chamfered watertable, in contrast to the plainer north side with its English bond. From the west end projected a vestry room, skillfully transformed into an entry porch in the early twentieth century. When the congregation dwindled to four communicants by 1834, the church was going to "ruin and waste," but Ann Ridgely and her husband Charles I. du Pont (see Breck's Mill, CH19) saw to its reopening shortly before the Civil War. Renovations were carried out with funds from the sale of the ancient glebe lands (agricultural properties that provided income for the local Anglican church). Cast-iron lotus leaf posts holding up the balcony date to this restoration. There have been many subsequent changes, including renovations that began in July 1913 under Thompson, a Philadelphia architect who had worked for Wilson Eyre in 1911–1917; years later he would design several Episcopal churches and associated buildings in Delaware (CH16, LN16).

The interior is painted in a cream color and is illuminated by dormer windows. A fine stained-glass window behind the altar has a

DV17 CHRIST CHURCH

strongly colored design of the 1870s. The surprisingly modernistic window high on the west wall (1929, James H. Hogan) was imported from White Friars Glass Works of James Powell and Sons, England; Senator Willard Saulsbury bequeathed four windows to Delaware churches, the others being Trinity, Wilmington (WL47); St. John's, Milton; and St. Paul's, Georgetown (ES4). Hogan visited Delaware in September 1928 to see the churches and plan the designs. The Dover window is opaque in order to hide the belfry just outside, which perches atop the west porch.

DV18 Hangar 1301, Dover Air Force Base

1944. Air Mobility Command Museum, DE 9, 3.5 miles southeast of Dover

The U.S. Army leased the Dover public airport within ten days of Pearl Harbor (December 7, 1941) and created Dover Army Air Field, today a 3,900-acre facility. Fighter pilots trained here. Building 1301—a combination of hangar, heating plant, and shop—housed top-secret facilities for testing air-launched rockets. The 155 × 160–foot hangar stands forty-two feet high, the steel truss roof system supported by concrete buttresses.

DV19 Dover Air Force Base Mortuary Facility

2002–2003, Becker Morgan Group. On the base; not open to the public

Dover Air Force Base is famous for the televised arrival of flag-draped coffins from foreign wars. After 9/11, the U.S. government accelerated plans for a new, 84,800-square-foot facility to receive the dead, allowing "efficient processing during mass casualty situations." At such times, 500 staff can perform one hundred autopsies a day. The first caskets came from the Iraq War. Inside the glass barrel-vaulted lobby, a curved "wall of honor" commemorates "each event that has sent Americans through the facility." With the opening of the new building, the arrival of coffins was no longer televised—to hide the true cost of war, critics charged.

DV19 DOVER AIR FORCE BASE MORTUARY FACILITY

Eastern Sussex County

For the purposes of this book, Sussex County is divided in two by U.S. 113, which runs in a north–south direction. Historically, Sussex was quite southern in flavor, as befits its location, lying almost entirely below the latitude of Washington, D.C. It was rather isolated, though the deepwater port at Lewes linked the eastern part of the county to the larger world. In 1790, the population of Sussex County was slightly larger than that of Kent or New Castle counties, but in the coming decades it fell far behind. The gap is starting to close today, however, with an epic explosion of development. From 1989 to 2003, almost 23,000 building permits were issued for homes and apartments alone, and the population grew more than 40 percent.

Historically, Sussex was overwhelmingly agricultural, and for many years Lewes was the only established town. Architectural historians Gabrielle Lanier and Bernard Herman (1997) stress that building traditions in Sussex County were generally very different from those farther north, originating as they did on Maryland's Eastern Shore. Early houses showed little variation in plan, being usually one-room, and were often built without excavated foundations, allowing them to be moved. As Lanier and Herman say, "Framing traditions associated with the Chesapeake region, such as common rafter roofs, board false plates, and hewn L-shaped corner posts, were also more characteristic of this area."

Lewes, on Delaware Bay near its confluence with the Atlantic, was founded in the early seventeenth century; the remainder of eastern Sussex County was settled much later as colonists slowly penetrated the dense forests and cypress swamps inland. Lower Coastal Plain deposits are sandy, and suitable clay for brickmaking is scarce. Brick houses were never common, and only a dozen or so eighteenth-century ones were found in Sussex in a survey of 1980. The historic architecture is overwhelmingly of wood (see Potter Mansion photograph on p. 9), as described in Bernard Herman's investigation of an area east of Dagsboro, *The Stolen House* (1992). The Cypress Swamp west of Selbyville was famous for the export of bald cypress and white oak. Sawmilling (along with grain milling) was a major industry, and newcomers to Sussex County may be forgiven for confusing the towns of Milford, Millsboro, Millville, and Milton. Stone is almost entirely absent, but "bog iron" ore

Railroads made possible the rise of early-twentieth-century tourism to the Delaware coast. Vacationers built shingled, screen-porched cottages at Rehoboth Beach. Photo c. 1940.

was dug and transported to Samuel G. Wright's Delaware Furnace, Millsboro (as well as to Pennsylvania and New Jersey). During its brief heyday (1821–1836), Delaware Furnace produced iron stoves, pipe, and railroad and fence rails, but also a variety of architectural items: steps, doors, window frames, and skylights. In 1831, architect John Haviland spurred this diversification by ordering 220 iron steps for his U.S. Naval Asylum in Norfolk, Virginia. Later came orders for Haviland's Eastern State Penitentiary and Thomas U. Walter's Moyamensing Prison—both in Philadelphia—as well as iron fittings for the Delaware Breakwater (ES25).

Population growth in Sussex County was stimulated by the coming of the railroad in the mid-nineteenth century, with several new towns established. A New Yorker laid out Lincoln on the railroad right-of-way in 1865, but he died suddenly and the community never grew to the metropolitan dimensions he expected. Today, houses are sparsely scattered about an enormous street grid. As in Kent County, the railroad fostered the development of crops that could be shipped to market in refrigerated cars. Chickens, strawberries, and sweet potatoes became predominant, and vernacular architecture evolved to suit new, specialized agricultural needs. The railroad also encouraged tourism to the scenic coast. Early tourism was religious, as Methodists attended camp meetings at Rehoboth Beach starting in the 1870s. Mosquitoes proved a deterrent to growth until the Civilian Conservation Corps (CCC) launched a massive drainage campaign; by late 1935, there were 240 men employed in six drainage projects in Sussex County, digging channels in lieu of using poison sprays. Over 44,000 acres were ultimately drained, encouraging a touristic boom. In the twenty-first century, new and dramatically better roads continue to bring huge summertime crowds, 160,000 visitors now converging on coastal Delaware in a single weekend—more people than inhabit the state's seven largest towns combined.

MILTON

First named in 1807, this town on the Broadkill River (pop. 1,657) grew quickly into a trading center with several shipyards and many grist and saw mills. The town prided itself on its Academy and on being the home of five governors (four of Delaware and one of Wyoming). Eighteen buildings in the business district burned in 1909, by which date the region around the community was largely deforested and growing vegetables for shipment to canneries. Many prominent nineteenth-century homes have disappeared from the compact and picturesque town, but some 200 buildings are on the National Register, including numerous small frame dwellings with scrollsawn porches. The Lydia B. Cannon Museum, Union Street, occupies a former Methodist church (c. 1855). The Governor Ponder House at 416 Federal Street (c. 1875) is Second Empire style. St. John the Baptist Episcopal (1875–1877, remodeled 1936) contains one of four English stained glass windows (1929) given to Delaware churches by bequest of Senator Willard Saulsbury, this one having been considered especially fine and replicated for Eton College museum, England.

ES1 Hazzard House

c. 1790. Early 19th century. 327 Union St.

Grandson of an English settler, the Revolutionary War soldier John Hazzard built this house and engaged in shipping and shipbuilding at the future site of Milton. His son, David, was a governor of Delaware from 1830 to 1833. The original section of the shingled dwelling was single-pile, hall-parlor in plan, with a heavy timber frame on English-bond brick foundations.

SOUTH OF ELLENDALE

ES2 Redden Lodge

1901, Wilson Eyre. 1996 renovated, Staikos Associates Architects. Ellendale/Redden State Forest, east of U.S. 113

Prominent Philadelphia architect Eyre designed a "shooting lodge" for Frank G. Thomson, son of a president of the Pennsylvania Railroad, and presumably this low, rustic building in the pine woods is that structure. The Maryland, Delaware and Virginia Railroad, incorporated in 1905, operated on the Pennsylvania Railroad line, and its executives established a hunting retreat here, "The Gun Club," coming down on a special train from Philadelphia with horses and dogs. Redden State Forest was founded in 1934 on 740 surrounding acres and subsequently expanded to 5,000. The hipped-roof, cypress-shingled lodge, with eleven bedrooms and a living room, had become run-down, but was repaired by the Civilian Conservation Corps (CCC) and made available for civic group outings for $2.50 a day as "by far the prize possession of the State Forestry Commission." The southern half of the building was destroyed by fire after a lightning strike and subsequently rebuilt (1971). Closer to the main road stands a shingled carriage house long used as a garage but redeveloped as an Environmental Learning Center (2000, Staikos Associates Architects). The CCC built the workshop and latrine, which now serve as two garages; on U.S. 113 nearby stands a rustic CCC roadside rest stop (1938–1939).

GEORGETOWN

The village was established in 1791 when Sussex County moved its seat here from Lewes, seeking a more central location, albeit one "16 miles from anywhere," as an early account had it, and landlocked. The town's grid plan was laid out around a central circle (The Circle, ES5) and bounded by a unique, circular outer border that was not broken until 1986. A series of prominent jurists lived in the 104 W. Market Street house now called "The Judges" (c. 1810), one of several frame dwellings that contain sections almost as old as Georgetown itself. These buildings were typically covered in shingles. The Joseph T. Adams House (1868) at 12 E. Pine Street shows how the traditional shingled aesthetic could later be combined with up-to-date gingerbread work. O. H. Bailey's bird's-eye view of Georgetown (1885) affords a glimpse of virtually every building in the thriving county seat. U.S. Government funds flowed to Georgetown during the Great Depression; a WPA Post Office went up on The Circle (1932), and Federal Arts Project murals by Edward L. Grant, Walter Pyle, and Andrew Doragh were installed in a local school. The Georgetown Armory (1939–1940, Martin and Jeffers) at 109 W. Pine Street is brick with limestone trim (over concrete and steel), with a slate roof, in Moderne style. A rare International Style postwar building in town is the International Order of Odd Fellows Hall on N. Bedford Street (1966). Georgetown has undergone rapid growth in recent years.

ES3 Masonic Lodge (Georgetown Academy)

1841–1842. 1920 alterations. 151 E. Market St.

With approval of the legislature, members of the Masonic Lodge and citizens jointly organized a public lottery to raise construction funds for the building. An advertisement in 1848 for the school, located on the first floor of the edifice, read, "The *Building* is one of the most commodious and comfortable in the State." The last students departed the Academy in 1885, and the Masons updated the structure with a mansard roof, removed in 1920 when a portico was added. The railroad was built alongside in 1867, and the town station stands not far away on Railroad Avenue; it was restored by French + Ryan in 2003.

ES4 St. Paul's Episcopal Church

1843–1844. 1880–1881 alterations. 122 E. Pine St.

A frame church (1804–1806) preceded this brick building on the site. The Gothic Revival interior and front that one sees today were

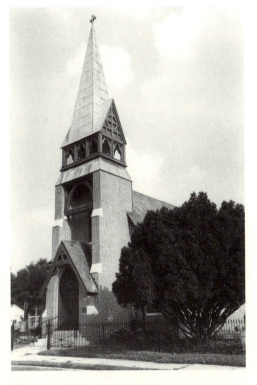

ES4 ST. PAUL'S EPISCOPAL CHURCH

added in the 1880s to the virtually unadorned structure of the 1840s under the supervision of a former rector, Reverend John Linn McKim. He was an uncle of Charles Follen McKim, partner in the famous New York City architectural firm of McKim, Mead and White, and so the project is frequently attributed to Charles McKim. Scholars of McKim, Mead and White make no mention of any Delaware commissions, but the heavy Stick Style of the St. Paul's alterations seems somewhat similar to the firm's contemporary work. Reverend McKim himself, however, had ably overseen the Gothic Revival transformation of Christ Church, Milford, when Charles Follen McKim was still a teenager, and his son, Reverend J. Leighton McKim, was likewise a talented church designer, as at St. Stephen's, Harrington (1875–1876). The tower is unusual: buttressed brick walls rise on either side of

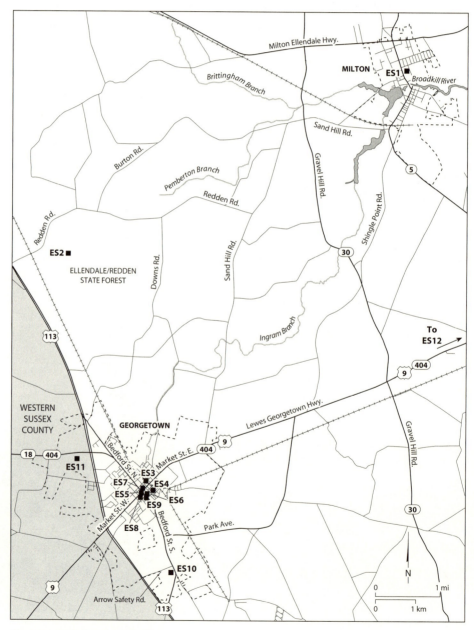

MILTON AND GEORGETOWN

the gabled entrance porch and support a complex, openwork wooden structure beneath the steeple. The interior is famous for its stained glass. The parish house (1940) was rebuilt in 1989–1990 after destruction by fire.

ES5 The Circle

1791, laid out. Center of Georgetown

At the heart of the town lies "The Circle," now a traffic roundabout and park inside a courthouse square. (The historic name for this park was "the circle of the Public Square.") Election results have long been delivered here in a Return Day ceremony, with a big cookout and a carnival atmosphere. Federal cavalry imposed order on election day 1862. The Circle was integrated into the state's paved highway system about 1921. As late as the addition of the Post Office (1932), with its colorful terracotta ornament, buildings around The Circle were modest in size. After World War II, however, several old structures were replaced with big Colonial Revival boxlike structures, including Farmers Bank (1971, R. Calvin Clendaniel Associates) and Sussex County Family Court (1986–1988, French + Ryan), the latter derived from the Governor's Palace in Colonial Williamsburg. Also echoing Williamsburg is the Sussex County Administration Building, for which the post office was nearly razed (1996, R. Calvin Clendaniel Associates). Only public outcry prevented the demolition of the Brick Hotel (ES8) in 1999 for another such modern building. The park within the Circle was refurbished in 2001–2002.

ES6 Sussex County Courthouse

1837–1839, William Strickland, with Joshua S. Layton and Caleb B. Sipple. 1914 portico and tower. 1969–1970 addition. The Circle

A lottery was authorized in 1835 for a new courthouse to occupy the site of the frame original (ES9). Famous Philadelphia architect William Strickland, then at work on the Delaware Breakwater (ES25), charged $60 for what he called "a *convenient plan.*" Fireproof offices lay below the big courtroom upstairs, with outside of the latter an "Iron Gallery . . . for the use of the Cryer of the Court . . . declaiming to a multitude beneath" (Gilchrist, 1954). With its Palladian window, Flemish-bond brickwork, and rubbed-and-gauged lintels (bricks

ES6 SUSSEX COUNTY COURTHOUSE, under restoration in 2004

shaped for a tight fit and rubbed to bring out their inner warm color), the two-story building clung to the old-fashioned Federal style as opposed to the newer Greek Revival. This was an economy measure; Strickland fretted in his letter of March 1837 to the commissioners: "If I have not been so happy in the front—your limits as to funds are the cause of the Brick Appearance, and I could have wished to have introduced a few columns and some other decorations, on the exterior but was afraid on account of the smallness of the sum to be appropriated." Two-story Ionic columns with a pediment over the central bay were added nearly eighty years later, along with a much larger tower. Crowds gathered in the courthouse yard for public whippings (until 1906) and hangings (until 1926). The wooden portico was reconstructed in 1969–1970. The state purchased the building in 1994, and its cupola was removed by crane nine years later for refurbishing.

ES7 Court of Chancery

2001–2003, R. Calvin Clendaniel Associates. The Circle

Since 1792, this court, a distinctively Delaware survival, has decided issues of equity. For 211 years, its judges periodically traveled from courtroom to courtroom, but with an expanding caseload it required a permanent home, for which planning started in 1995. The nearby Brick Hotel (ES8) was the favored site until preservationists protested. The architects for the red brick court building were a Lincoln, Delaware, firm, then in its fortieth year and one of the oldest in the state. The pedimented two-story front with Doric pilasters and an arcaded ground floor recalls both eighteenth-century market houses and the State Police headquarters north of Dover (1956, Pope and Kruse). A cherry-paneled courtroom has bulls-eye windows reminiscent of those at the Capitol in Colonial Williamsburg, Virginia.

ES7 COURT OF CHANCERY

ES8 BRICK HOTEL

ES9 OLD COURTHOUSE

ES8 Brick Hotel

1836, Joshua S. Layton and Caleb B. Sipple. 1955 altered. The Circle

Brick hotels were fashionable additions to early-nineteenth-century Delaware towns, as evidenced, for example, by the hotel in Odessa (LN9), but few were built in Sussex County, owing (it is usually said) to the scarcity of clay for brickmaking. Fortunately, a deposit was discovered just west of Georgetown. The two-and-a-half-story building was converted into a bank in 1955, at which time the picturesque nineteenth-century porch was replaced by an unpedimented portico of giant Doric piers, and unfortunate changes were made to the fanlit doors and window arrangement of the facade. The State of Delaware bought the old building in 1999 to demolish it for the Court of Chancery, but local residents lobbied successfully to save it.

ES9 Old Courthouse

1792–1793. 1837 moved here. 1974–1975 restored. 10 S. Bedford St.

Georgetown was founded to supplant Lewes as the county seat, and this two-story cypress-shingled building with gabled roof was among the first to be erected in "James Pettyjohn's old field," the tract upon which the new town grid was laid out. After being replaced in turn by the current courthouse, the structure was moved to a new location, where it served as a dwelling and, later, as a printing office. The state archives commission bought the abandoned and dilapidated building and heavily rebuilt it for the U.S. Bicentennial in 1976.

ES10 Nutter D. Marvel Carriage Museum

19th–20th centuries. 510 S. Bedford St.

A local businessman who eventually owned more than fifteen gas stations, Marvel began collecting old carriages as a hobby in 1926, acquiring and restoring eighty in all. In 1968, he established this outdoor museum, which has grown by the addition of small rural buildings brought in from near Laurel and elsewhere. One-room Ellis Grove School (1833) was moved here in 1979 and stands near Epworth Methodist Church (1890), moved in 1983, five years before Marvel's death. Carriages are stored in Barrel Barn, which used an innovative truss system of laminated rafters by a local builder (c. 1930, Rodney O'Neal). Georgetown Historical Society owns the museum and, as part of its mission, seeks to preserve threatened buildings throughout the town.

ES11 Jason Building, Delaware Technical and Community College (William C. Jason Comprehensive High School)

1949–1950, Victorine and Samuel Homsey. DE 404 and U.S. 113

Wilmingtonian H. Fletcher Brown (d. 1944) left money in his will for the establishment of a "Negro school" in southern Delaware. The resulting facility was the only one in the state outside of Wilmington offering four years of high school for African Americans. The design was modern: long and low, with no steps anywhere; enormous classroom windows, along with clerestories; suspended ceilings of perforated metal with recessed lighting; fluorescent bulbs in suspended racks; brick interior walls and polished Canadian birch plywood; and green Nucite chalkboards for use with powderless crayons. Exteriors were partly clad in California redwood. Initially, 300 students took general and vocational courses here, but as enrollments grew, the high school was enlarged. It closed in 1967 following desegregation and has been heavily remodeled as part of Delaware Technical and Community College.

EAST OF GEORGETOWN

ES12 Cool Spring Presbyterian Church

1854. Road 247, southwest of Lewes, Cool Spring

The cemetery here originated with a 4.5-acre grant by Pennsylvania Governor Thomas Penn to Reverend James Martin in 1737 and served a church already standing at that time. In its restrained, geometric simplicity, the current shingled frame sanctuary represents the unpretentious Greek Revival popular for religious structures downstate. A pedimented front gable stands above a small Doric porch. Three big windows along each side light the interior, which is distinguished by unusual, shallow-V-shaped pews and a gallery, a feature scarce today in the county. Early kerosene lamps were later converted to electricity.

ES12 COOL SPRING PRESBYTERIAN CHURCH

LEWES

Delaware's only seaport town, Lewes is named for a community in Sussex, England (hence "Sussex" County, Delaware). Lewes originated with an abortive Dutch effort, Swanendael (Valley of Swans) in 1631, the first European outpost on Delaware soil (ES13). Permanent occupation did not come until 1658, and then only slowly and with disheartening setbacks. "The houses are most of them built of wood," observed the evangelist George Whitefield when visiting in October 1739. Many dwellings, built of frame and shingle, have

DU PONT HIGHWAY

DU PONT HIGHWAY, UNDER CONSTRUCTION AT VIOLA IN 1923

T. Coleman du Pont will always be remembered for his highway (U.S. 13 and 113) that carries traffic ninety-seven miles north–south through Delaware. In 1908, looking for some contribution to make to the state, he considered a school, hospital, or fountain before deciding on a road to help farmers. "I will build a monument a hundred miles high and lay it on the ground," he is supposed to have said.

A builder of street railways in several cities, du Pont was a Good Roads advocate in the visionary National Highway Association, which pushed for 50,000 miles of paved Federal arteries. Du Pont saw in Delaware a chance to jumpstart the process, proposing to fund the ribbon of concrete himself, an extraordinary contribution to a state with notoriously bad roads (only 8 percent were then listed as "improved").

He hoped for a multilane thoroughfare with high-speed cars separated from trolleys, trucks, and horses, an ingenious suggestion not acted upon. The state legislature established a Boulevard Corporation in 1911, and by 1917, twenty miles of two-lane concrete road had been laid from Georgetown to the state line at Selbyville. Another ten miles was complete in the vicinity of Ellendale (a well-preserved segment today is Old State Road South through Ellendale Swamp, southwest of that town). The engineer was Frank M. Williams, formerly of the New York State highway department, working with the young future Delaware governor C. Douglass Buck.

The completion of the road (sixty-nine miles north to Wilmington) took place by 1923 under the new Delaware highway department, with Coleman paying up to $44,000 per mile. In total, he spent $3.9 million, double the initial estimate. Among the contractors providing concrete bridges and roadbeds were the Philadelphia firms of Field, Barker and Underwood and the Juniata Company, and some landscaping was done by Wheelwright and Stevenson of that city.

Du Pont Highway proved so popular for the shipment of produce by truck—by far its most important function in the early years—that it soon needed enlarging. In 1929–1933, the

been moved at one time or another. Lewes sank into some decay in the early nineteenth century, with loss of colonial fabric; unlike New Castle, it has no early church, courthouse, jail, or arsenal (though a much-altered Methodist meeting house of c. 1790 survives as a home on Mulberry Street). Nevertheless, Lewes boasts possibly the oldest building in Delaware, the Ryves Holt House (late seventeenth century; ES18). Mosquito control made the town forty-five miles from Wilmington to Dover were reconfigured as a divided highway, Delaware Dual Road—said to be the first highway in the world to adopt the "dual roadway" technique (well before the German autobahns opened in 1935–1936, and the Merritt Parkway in Connecticut, in 1938–1940). With a fifty-foot grass plot between them, the new lanes were for northbound traffic only, the old for southbound. By 1942, the dual road was handling more than a million crates each of poultry and cantaloupes, plus huge quantities of peaches, strawberries, and potatoes.

It was Coleman's idea that the original highway should bypass towns—five between Selbyville and Georgetown alone—a controversial idea at the time, but later standard practice everywhere. A surveyor of the initial route was Coleman's son, Francis V. du Pont, later head of the Delaware Highway Commission and a leading figure in the creation of the U.S. interstate highway system under President Dwight Eisenhower.

AERIAL VIEW OF DU PONT HIGHWAY AS EXPANDED TO A DUAL ROAD

more popular after 1935, and growth after World War II was steady as vacationers discovered the charming community, which faces the Lewes and Rehoboth Canal and has an appealing nautical flavor. A far greater boom came in the 1990s, with many dwellings expensively restored or rebuilt. A historic district covers much of the town, but explosive growth promises further change.

ES13 Fort Swanendael Site (possible) and DeVries Monument

1631. 1909. Pilottown Rd., west of Rodney Ave.

According to archaeologist Chesleigh A. Bonine, the roadway and a cemetery overlie the remains of the earliest European architecture in Delaware. The twenty-eight Dutch settlers who disembarked from the *Walvis* in 1631 under Captain David Pieterssen DeVries fashioned a palisade, inside of which is thought to have stood a house of yellow bricks brought from Holland. Indians soon massacred the settlers, and the fort vanished. Archaeology by Bonine in 1956 uncovered rows of nearly 200 postholes and postmolds (possibly from the palisade) inside the cemetery, which itself may date back to the burial of the Dutch victims. Pieces of yellow Dutch brick were also found. Plans of the 1970s to rebuild the fort nearby proved fruitless. Today, the nature of the site is controversial, some historians doubting that this was the earliest Lewes fort or even a fort at all; earthfast construction, we now know, persisted for generations, and this might be an eighteenth-century farmstead. A stone marker commemorates Captain DeVries.

ES14 Thomas Maull House

c. 1737. 542 Pilottown Rd.

Long beloved as the prototypical Sussex colonial cottage, this very early, 30 × 16–foot gambrel-roofed dwelling covered with cedar shakes exemplifies the growth of the community at Pilottown, home of many ship captains.

ES14 THOMAS MAULL HOUSE, photo 1936

Carpenter Samuel Paynter built the house, then sold it to the Maulls, who lived here for generations. The four-room plan is hall-parlor, making it larger and more elaborate than most of the now-vanished wooden dwellings of eighteenth-century Sussex County. The hall has a nicely paneled fireplace end. The Daughters of the American Revolution and architect George F. Bennett restored the house in 1962, in the process interviewing a woman who had lived there as a child in the 1880s, who recalled certain interior details.

ES15 Pagan Creek Dike

c. 1660. North bank of Canary Creek, just west of New Rd.

As in New Castle, Dutch settlers built a dike to carry a road across the marshes behind their riverfront habitations. This one, thirty feet wide and 700 feet long, crossed the "Great Marsh" and what is today called Canary Creek, presumably facilitating trade with the Indians. Archaeology took place on the overgrown dike in the 1950s.

ES16 Lewes Historical Society Complex

18th and 19th centuries. 3rd St. and Park Ave.

The outdoor museum mostly consists of frame properties moved here in the 1960s, to the yard of the Hiram Rodney Burton House (c. 1780). They include the Thompson Country Store (c. 1800, in use until 1962) and a temple-form Greek Revival doctor's office (c. 1850). Lewes's best Federal building is the Burton-Ingram House (1789, moved here 1962), a cypress-shingled building of side-passage plan that originally stood on 2nd Street; it was narrowly saved from destruction. The woodwork is excellent, as is the stair that rises free through three stories. A rear wing was brought from Milton in 1967, replacing one that burned c. 1922, and the whole was restored by architect George F. Bennett. The shingled Rabbit's Ferry House (1740s, kitchen section; moved here 1967) was scheduled for demolition on its original site at Robinsonville Road, southwest of Lewes. It is one of the few Delaware buildings on which dendrochronology has been carried out, the trees that form the kitchen wing having been felled after the

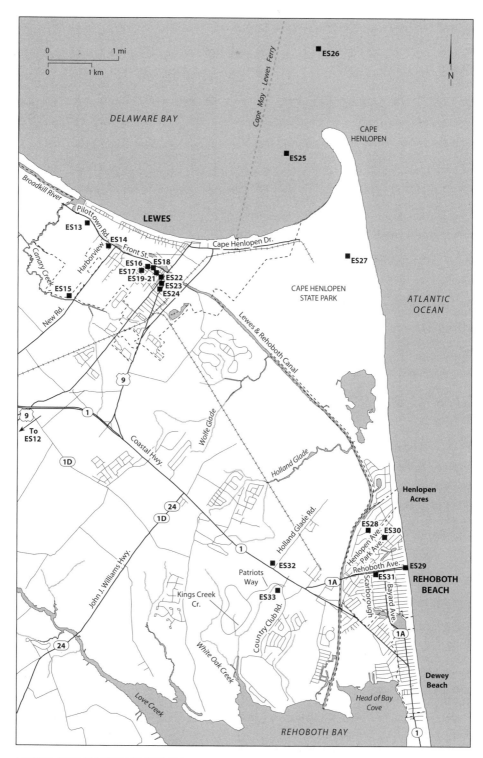

LEWES AND REHOBOTH BEACH

1741 growing season. Midway School No. 178 (c. 1890) was moved to the complex in 1998.

ES16.1 The Early Plank House (Swedish Log Cabin)

18th century. 1963–1964 moved and restored

Formerly called the oldest building in Lewes, nothing is known of the origins of this tiny house, except that its original location, at 314 Pilottown Road, formed part of the seventeenth-century patent of Swedish settler Helmanus Wiltbank, whose house was unfortunately demolished in the early 1930s. The plank floor suggests that it was used as a dwelling and, indeed, it might have been the original Wiltbank home, as some have speculated, and thus a rare survival of a seventeenth-century "Swedish" log house. Plank houses continued to be built for generations throughout the eastern United States, however, and are difficult to date; this one may be c. 1780. The original chinking was of clay, hair, and buckwheat shells. In the early twentieth century, the dwelling served as a smokehouse. Local carpenter Frederick Hudson restored it in 1964.

ES17 Shipcarpenter Square

1983 established. Park Ave., between 3rd and 4th sts.

A young banker from Washington, D.C., moved to Lewes and teamed up with a local restorer of old houses to create Lewestown Restorations, Inc., a real estate venture. They purchased eleven acres and, by 1988, had brought in twenty-six of a planned thirty-six historic houses, which they restored and sold. The houses were from Delaware, except for one from Virginia and one from Maryland. All were purchased for under $1,500; the move typically cost at least $10,000 and the restoration, $50,000. The developers used the historic Beers' *Atlas of Delaware* (1868) to identify potential houses for purchase. The oldest dwelling was said to be Mt. Pleasant, from Kent County (1730); there was a log house of 1795; and the youngest building dated to 1880. In order to make the houses attractive to buyers, each was massively rehabilitated and provided with a kitchen wing. Old rural dwellings are thus given a new lease on life in a pleasant suburb, but, some critics argue, the

ES18 RYVES HOLT HOUSE

houses have lost much of their interest by being shorn of their original context and heavily restored to suit modern lifestyles.

ES18 Ryves Holt House

Late 17th century west section, with additions. 2nd and Mulberry sts.

The date of "Delaware's Oldest House" continues to be debated. A study by the Center for Historic Architecture and Design (CHAD) at the University of Delaware (1998) argues that it is unlikely to predate 1685, when Phillip Russell got a license to operate a public house on the corner, and that it might be as late as 1710. This conflicts with the much-cited results of dendrochronology in the 1980s that showed a date of 1665, but the CHAD authors answer that the building's style surely belongs to a later decade and that the wood might have been curing. Whatever its date, the original section is one-and-a-half stories and 20 × 16 feet in area with a lean-to attached; a corner fireplace (removed by 1800) stood at left in the front room, with the door at right. H-bent construction recalls Dutch practice. Strikingly, all the joists are chamfered (with lambstongue stops) along with the studs and window and door jambs. Ryves Holt, captain and lawyer, occupied the house starting in 1723. Later additions resulted in unevenly grouped windows. It has been owned by the local Episcopal church since 1981 and lately has been leased to Lewes Historical Society. Delaware is notably lacking in seventeenth-century survivals, making this one exceedingly valuable (although Walnut Landing, near Seaford, is c. 1700). Curiously, it is of that most perishable of materials, wood. In all of Virginia, by comparison, only one wooden house of pre-1700 remains (Williamsburg's Nelson-Galt House, dated to 1695 by dendrochronology).

ES19 St. Peter's Episcopal Church

1853–1858, Sloan and Stewart. 1870 steeple. 1903–1904 sacristy and choir room. 2nd and Market sts.

The ninety-foot-high needle spire of this brick Gothic Revival church has long soared over Lewes as seen from the bay. Replacing a frame predecessor of 1808, the current church was initially meant to be frame, too; plans to this effect were purchased from important Philadelphia architects Samuel Sloan and John Stewart (partners, 1852–1857). A photograph shows the church before the buttressed tower was added and with the predecessor building still standing nearby. An altar of 1889 has been removed to the sacristy and replaced with the original eighteenth-century black walnut altar table. Colorful stained glass in the lancet windows ranges from nineteenth century with grisaille stenciling, to opalescent, to modernist examples of the 1950s by Wilbur Herbert Burnham of Boston. The graveyard is much older than the present church, with tombstones as early as 1707, the date of the first wooden church (relic stones from the foundation of which have been installed high on a side wall of the sacristy). One gravestone records a woman "born 1631," an extremely early date to find on any American stone. The old Sussex County courthouse (c. 1740, razed 1833) once stood at the edge of the same lot.

ES20 Robert Scott's Block

1885. 2nd and Market sts.

This commercial building is a tangible reminder of how the coming of the railroad in 1869 brought a boom and allowed the easy import of varied architectural materials and styles. The brick building shows sprightly decoration of black and white glazed bricks, white marble, and polychrome ornamental tile.

ES21 Cannonball House (David Rowland House)

Before 1797. 118 Front St.

Now a nautical museum, the plain, two-story cypress-shingled dwelling supposedly received damage to its brick foundation by a cannonball during the British bombardment of Lewes in 1813. In 1938, it housed offices, and later it became a restaurant. By 1961, however, it was vacant and had a laundromat attached, having become so decayed that brick nogging showed through the walls. The Lewes Historical Society was formed in the latter year to save the landmark and restore it (1964–1968, George F. Bennett). The wing was moved from a house in Millsboro. A nearby park, redesigned in 1914, features historic cannons memorializing the bombardment.

ES22 Commercial Building (Captain Charles W. Johnston House)

1899–1900. 3rd St. and Savannah Rd.

The frame Queen Anne–style house with ornate piazza was built for Johnston, a noted diver and salvager of wrecks, by his business partner, contractor William H. Virden. Inside is an elaborate, quartersawn red-oak stair. A mid-twentieth-century owner was Otis H. Smith, longtime mayor (1950–1968) and head of Fish Products Company, the town's largest and smelliest employer. Degenerated into a rundown rental property by the 1970s, it was restored and is currently occupied by a business, which has renamed it "Harvard House."

ES19 ST. PETER'S EPISCOPAL CHURCH, photo c. 1920

ES23 Zwaanendael Museum (Zwaanendael House)

1930–1932, E. William Martin. 102 King's Hwy.

With funds from the Delaware government, Wilmington architect Martin designed this step-gabled folly to commemorate the Tercentenary of Dutch settlement at Lewes and memorialize those massacred. Now a state museum, it occupies the site of the former Lewes Academy. Martin copied, at reduced scale, one-half of the double-gabled Town Hall at Hoorn, The Netherlands, from which David Pieterssen DeVries, organizer of the Swanendael colony, had come. Hoorn had given some historical mementos to Lewes as early as 1909. In Martin's papers at the University of Delaware are his Hoorn sketches "made under great difficulties in rain and hail" in October 1930. Small bricks were specially made to match the originals, one of which he sent back from Holland by parcel post. The trim is limestone, with red-and-white shutters in the official Hoorn colors. Window frames and doors were a deep Holland blue. The front is wildly picturesque, with richly embellished door surround, striped lintels over the windows, and scrolled crowsteps in the steeply pitched gable. A restoration (1998–2000, Bernardon Haber Holloway) rebuilt the heavy wood front doors and replaced the red tile roof. Inside, the museum has long since expanded to take over the library room upstairs. Among the displays are a chair belonging to a settler in Dagsboro in 1660, and the iron door of 1867 from the Cape Henlopen Lighthouse (1764–1767), a famous colonial landmark that toppled into the sea in April 1926.

ES24 Fisher-Martin House

1720–1760 period. c. 1790 extension. 1980 moved. 120 King's Hwy.

This gambrel-roofed wooden house, one of the oldest surviving in Sussex County, originally stood at Cool Spring, six miles southwest of its present location. It was targeted for preservation around 1960 by historian Harold D. Eberlein (who called it White Meadow Farm, and "an *architectural document of the first importance*") and state archivist Leon deValinger. Mabel Lloyd Ridgely, the Dover preservationist and a Fisher descendant, bought the decayed house and turned it over to the state. It was moved by truck to this location and now serves as an information center. Joshua Fisher, who prepared the first official charts of the Delaware Bay, inherited the Cool Spring property in 1713. After 1736, it was owned by the Martin family, who held it to 1959. The east part, until recently believed to date to 1728, is a two-bay, oak-framed structure with brick nogging. A molding of skinny dentils runs under the box eave, and the original siding was beaded. The house was expanded to the left by one bay, allowing the creation of a long stairhall, rather grand for such a tiny house. Historian Harold D. Eberlein was impressed by the dwelling's extremely simple "hall plan"—originally one room with a fireplace and winder stair—that was, he thought, a late medieval holdover. He called this type of plan "Resurrection Manor" for a Maryland house then thought to date to the 1650s and hence to be representative of practically the first phase of building in the colonies. But scholars today understand that the hall plan was a standard one for generations in the numerous, now-vanished, small wooden homes of the Tidewater.

ES25 Delaware Breakwater

1829–1869, William Strickland. In Delaware Bay, offshore from fishing pier, 2 miles northeast of Lewes

Maritime interests pleaded with the federal government for a breakwater protecting vessels that were riding out a storm in Lewes Harbor. The U.S. Navy surveyed the site in 1828 in preparation for what was said to be the third really sizeable breakwater in the world (after Cherbourg, France, and Plymouth, England) and the first ever built for nonmilitary purposes. Congress appropriated funds in May of that year, and Strickland was appointed engineer, working under the Army Quartermaster General in a tempestuous relationship. Strickland was already known in Delaware for his survey of the Chesapeake and Delaware Canal (C&D) (1822). Construction of the breakwater brought huge overruns in cost and time, even after the project was scaled back.

Strickland designed two sections, the breakwater itself (2,586 feet) separated by 1,350 feet of open water from an upriver icebreaker

ES23 ZWAANENDAEL MUSEUM (ZWAANENDAEL HOUSE), early view

ES24 FISHER-MARTIN HOUSE, photo 1980 prior to move

ES25 DELAWARE BREAKWATER, East End light, early view

(1,500 feet). During the 1829–1830 working seasons, stones up to two tons each were brought down from the Palisades of the Hudson River, New York. Tidal currents displaced them over the winter, so, in 1831, much larger stones were employed (up to six tons) and were positioned by four Strickland-designed derrick winches powered by hand. In 1833, 100,000 stones were delivered from quarries near Wilmington. Work was suspended in 1835 when it was discovered that Breakwater Harbor was silting up. Another campaign took place in 1836–1839, by which time the breakwater was serviceable, but stones continued to be added until 1869; 835,000 tons ultimately comprised the whole. Some blamed the gap of open water for causing harbor siltation, and it was filled in 1882–1898, as can be seen in the area of more neatly coursed stones. This failed to solve the problem, however. By that time, the total project costs over the decades had amounted to $2.6 million, and the breakwater had taken on a tragic association—the death of seventy sailors when their ships foundered here during the Blizzard of 1888.

Two lighthouses stood on the breakwater.

West End was designed by Strickland in 1833 in a fascinating, hefty design of stone. Finally built in 1849 in a different form, it served until 1903 and was removed in the 1950s; some ruins of the stone foundations are visible, which once had big arches through which storm surges could pass. East End (1885–1886) is a fifty-six-foot-tall cylindrical iron tower with a brick lining, bolted to a concrete foundation. Originally painted brown, it held a Fresnel lens and Daboll trumpet foghorn. It was automated in the 1950s and recently acquired by the State of Delaware as a landmark.

ES26 Harbor of Refuge

1897–1901. In Delaware Bay, north of Cape Henlopen (best seen from Cape May-Lewes Ferry)

This gargantuan engineering effort repeated the idea of Strickland's breakwater (ES25), but on a much larger scale (8,040 feet) and in deeper water. The earlier Breakwater Harbor had succumbed to siltation that accompanied the phenomenal nineteenth-century growth of the Cape Henlopen sand-spit (sixteen feet per year, so that it is now a mile longer than in 1765). The National Harbor of Refuge, well north from that spit, was authorized in 1896 and built from stones up to thirteen tons each. Steam power made the project go ten times faster than Strickland's earlier campaign. The huge steel caisson lighthouse (1926), a tapering white cylinder atop a round black base, still works but has been unmanned since 1973. A volunteer group has begun its restoration.

ES27 Fort Miles

1941–1945. Cape Henlopen State Park, east of Lewes

Anticipating war, the U.S. Army Corps of Engineers began surveying this site in 1940, establishing a 1,700-acre base by August 1941. Named for a former commanding officer of the Army, Fort Miles was one of the most heavily fortified locales in the United States. Bunker gun emplacements lay camouflaged beneath sand dunes. Eleven tall, cylindrical, concrete control towers directed the fire of eight-, twelve-, and sixteen-inch guns in the bunkers. The largest guns could lob a shell twenty miles with a concussion that broke windows in Rehoboth. They saw no action, and eventually Fort Miles housed German prisoners of war. The facility was gradually turned over to the state as a park between 1964 and 1996. Of the 250 original buildings, two thirds have been demolished. About a dozen standardized, concrete-block housing (or "cantonment") structures survive. The two-story park office was

ES28 HENLOPEN ACRES, photo 1936, with Lewes and Rehoboth Canal (1913–1916) at left

originally Building T-410; the nature center was a Guard House; the fishing pier, a wharf for mine-laying. Extant beneath seaside dunes is Battery Smith (1941–1942), principal armament of Fort Miles, which held two sixteen-inch guns on barbette carriages, located at either end of a transverse corridor. In between were rooms for shells, powder, and stores; air flues; latrines; and a muffler gallery. Just south is Battery Herring (1942–1943). Its concrete structure is exposed now that its sand covering has been removed; some later additions were demolished in 2003. A historical society was formed that year to restore the control towers and establish a museum.

ES28.1 THE HOMESTEAD (PETER MARSH HOUSE)

ES28 Henlopen Acres

1930, with additions. Wilbur S. Corkran. Entered by Dodd's Lane, north of Rehoboth Beach

This residential development beside the Lewes and Rehoboth Canal is considered one of Delaware's most desirable places to live. Colonel Corkran, raised and educated in Delaware, was an architect and engineer who had developed suburban housing in Short Hills, New Jersey. Around an existing house, The Homestead (ES28.1), he created Henlopen Acres, to be reached from eastern cities by automobile on "magnificent concrete roads [that] lead in all directions." A prospectus published by Newark's Press of Kells (NK13) touted it as offering "a pine woods setting on an ocean beach." Corkran, who called himself owner, supervising architect, and engineer, laid out streets (with such names as Tidewaters, Pine Reach, and Rolling Road) that "wind interestingly with the contour and shape of the property." Written restrictions were meant to safeguard the "exclusive residential park": lots were spacious (½ acre); all plans and specifications for houses and landscaping were to be approved; houses were set back irregularly and surrounded by native trees and shrubs—"each home site is a park within a park." Garages were attached to homes to avoid visual clutter, and behind each house was a bridle path along which the utility poles ran. Each dwelling had an incinerator, as no garbage cans were allowed. Billboards, livestock, and poultry were forbidden, too. Finally, "There are to be no residents in this development who are not of the Caucasian race—servants excepted." Corkran recommended Colonial Revival house designs, having stressed the historic nature of the area and named the development in part after the colonial lighthouse at Cape Henlopen. He dredged a yacht basin and drew unrealized plans for a Colonial Revival Beach Club, Yacht Club, and riding stables. The Great Depression hampered the development of Corkran's dream. Today, Henlopen Acres is Delaware's smallest incorporated town, with just 194 homes, twenty-two of which date from the 1930s.

ES28.1 The Homestead (Peter Marsh House)

1743. 1930 enlarged, Wilbur S. Corkran

Marsh and his descendants lived in this two-story shingled house until 1871, farming and making salt from sea water. The house was later given over to tenant farmers and had fourteen inhabitants at the time the Corkrans bought it in 1929. Louise Corkran described their Colonial Revival remodeling in *American Home* (August 1934), and the house and its quaint "wishing well" were depicted a year later in *National Geographic*. A paneled colonial partition-wall from Morristown, New Jersey, was inserted to create an entrance passage. Louise Corkran established the Rehoboth Art League in 1938, which occupied small buildings on the property before taking over The Homestead in 1979. Reverend Richard S. Bailey led the restoration of the house in 1979–1982, finding its black walnut framing (with brick nogging) still undecayed. Walnut was used inside the dwelling for paneled chimneybreasts. Forty-inch-long riven cypress shingles braved the weather for 230 years until a new set was applied in 1982. The Homestead's garden (1931), restored in 1998–1999 by A. C. Durham and Associates, has specimen trees. On The Homestead grounds, rustic studios are maintained for artists. The doors of one studio accumulated many autographs of vacationing painters and others, including architect Charles Z. Klauder.

REHOBOTH BEACH

Sometimes called the "The Nation's Summer Capital" for its many visitors from Washington, D.C., the town (see map on p. 269) had just 1,495 residents in 2000, but its population regularly soars to 25,000 on summer weekends. It was founded as a Methodist camp-meeting resort in 1872 and grew steadily after the railroad reached it six years later. A paved highway in 1925 supplanted the railroad and triggered a boom. Irénée du Pont improved Lake Gerar by dredging, and wealthy Wilmingtonians built around it. Rehoboth Heights ("Where Pine and Brine are Ever Wooing") was developed at the same time along Silver Lake. North of town, Mediterranean-style Henlopen Hotel flourished. A handful of early buildings survive today, including the Gables (1874) at 12 Lake Avenue on the eastern edge of Lake Gerar, once home to the Methodist bishop during camp meetings. The railroad station (1879), originally on Rehoboth Avenue near the beachfront, was moved by truck to the vicinity of the canal bridge and restored (1987–1988) as the Chamber of Commerce headquarters. All Saint's Episcopal Church at 18 Olive Avenue (1892–1893, Edward Luff Rice Jr.) was altered after a fire in the 1930s and again in the

ES29 BOARDWALK AND REHOBOTH AVENUE, photo 1940s

1950s. The rambling frame A. Felix du Pont house at 54 Oak Avenue serves as a church conference center. Rehoboth's tree-lined streets (some of which retain their original concrete surfaces) are good places to study cottage and bungalow design from many eras, but demolitions of old houses have lately increased, owing to escalating land values.

ES29 Boardwalk and Rehoboth Avenue

1873 established. Boardwalk frequently rebuilt. Oceanfront

The first, 1,000-foot-long boardwalk was installed a year after the initial Methodist settlement. Now a mile long and recalling those on the New Jersey Shore, it has been repeatedly reconstructed, including after a fierce storm in March 1962 that pulverized it and all the buildings directly on the oceanfront. A big sign advertises the shop selling Dolle's Salt Water Taffy, an institution here since 1927 and rebuilt after the storm. As at many East Coast resorts, the entire landscape is artificial; the beach is massively replenished every few years with sand dredged from offshore and smoothed out by tractors. Behind the boardwalk, Rehoboth Avenue retains its old-fashioned boulevard form, lined by shops and terminating in The Oval. Beautification of the avenue (2002–2006, Johnson, Mirmiran and Thompson) included a new gazebo that replaced the bandstand of the 1960s.

ES30 Mon Plaisir

1927, Mary Wilson Thompson with James H. W. Thompson. 35 Park Ave.

Indefatigable Mary Wilson (Mrs. Henry B.) Thompson of Wilmington was an activist in many causes: children's health, education, Red Cross, Association Opposed to Woman Suffrage, Anti-Prohibition, and historic preservation. She had a vague memory of visiting Rehoboth with her grandparents in 1872, when it was virtually uninhabited and an unspoiled paradise. When she built here in the 1920s, the village was rather seedy, but she soon saw to that, telling the 1932 edition of *Who's Who* that she had "improved Rehoboth Ave., planted and designed the gardens throughout the town." She bought a piney lot from Irénée du Pont well away from the beach with its undesirable surf-noise, wind, damp, and glare. She took great pride in designing her home herself. She visited old houses in Sussex County, taking photographs, and finally settled on one in Lewes as a model. A "young architect" drew up the specifications—no doubt her son, Jim, then an architecture student at Princeton. The two-story, shingled Mon Plaisir with its dormer windows (see p. 278) was meant to recall architecture of the 1790s and was fully paneled inside with pine. Screened French doors opened onto enormous porches.

ES31 ANNA HAZZARD MUSEUM

ES31 Anna Hazzard Museum

c. 1895. 1975–1976 moved and restored. Christian St.

The camp meetings that marked early Rehoboth were discontinued in 1881, but briefly revived in the mid-1890s. This little, shingled dwelling was built as a camp-meeting "tent," with the customary front-gabled arrangement plus porch, at Baltimore Avenue and 2nd Street. Its owners donated it to the town in 1975, and it was moved to this location, where it houses a historical society museum.

WOMEN AND DELAWARE ARCHITECTURE

Greenville socialite Mary Wilson Thompson was proud of having designed her own house at the beach, Mon Plaisir (ES30). This talented and forceful woman left her stamp on Delaware's architecture by overseeing construction of several homes of her own and helping preserve important buildings, including New Castle's Dutch House (NC7) and Wilmington's Bank of Delaware (WL89). She shaped the physical landscape, too, by promoting anti-mosquito campaigns. Working in her Rehoboth Beach garden, Thompson had to wrap newspaper around her ankles to ward off bites. This would not do, so she agitated for control efforts, first working with a local women's club, then with town officials, and finally (1933) with Governor Buck in establishing Civilian Conservation Corps (CCC) ditch-digging camps at Lewes and Slaughter Beach.

MON PLAISIR (ES30)

In Delaware as elsewhere, the architectural profession has long been dominated by men, but women have been active, too—including, most prominently, Victorine Homsey, who along with her husband and partner, Samuel, designed several buildings in this book (see Homsey Architects, WL87). As early as 1892, Philadelphia architect Minerva Parker Nichols created Wilmington's New Century Club (WL68). Mary Craig, an architect of Santa Barbara, California, designed a Mount Vernon replica called Dauneport on Old Kennett Road, Christiana Hundred (1932–1933), as a home for Amy du Pont. In progressive Arden, the school was built by a local female architect (1945–1947, Frances Harrison).

Recent years have seen many more women practicing in Delaware, including Marjorie Rothberg (NK7). But one does not have to be an architect to influence the built environment, as Mabel Lloyd Ridgely proved in early twentieth-century Dover, tirelessly advocating Colonial Revival and fending off modernism. Women's groups, including the Colonial Dames and the Junior League, have likewise lobbied for preservation.

Early in the twentieth century, du Pont women played a key role in laying out the elaborate gardens that made the Brandywine Valley one of the horticultural capitals of the country. In this, they were assisted by New York or Philadelphia professionals, including Marian Cruger Coffin, Ellen Biddle Shipman, and Annette Hoyt Flanders. They also funded historic preservation in Delaware and other states, with Jessie Ball du Pont (see Nemours, BR26) and Louise du Pont Crowninshield (see Eleutherian Mills, CH15.4) achieving national recognition.

WEST OF REHOBOTH BEACH

ES32 Dodd Homestead

c. 1830–1900. DE 1 and Holland Glade Rd.

When recorded in 1981, this nineteenth-century farm was found to be astonishingly intact, in spite of the proximity of modern development; the surveyors concluded, "Nowhere else in the Delaware coastal area is it possible to find such a complete and little altered complex." The Dodd family had owned it since the eighteenth century. The shingled house mixed Federal and Greek Revival details. Nearby, the researchers found an extraordinary array of outbuildings, some with early implements inside: poultry house, milkhouse, carriage house, root cellar, privy, woodshed, well and windmill, stable, corn cribs, dairy barn, and granary. Active farming had ceased here decades before, and many of these structures were dilapidated. Burgeoning new development seemed likely to claim the site.

ES33 The Village at Kings Creek

2002–2004, Dan F. Sater. Shuttle Rd. and Patriots Way

A local developer seeking to create a "beachy, Key West" feeling found Sater's firm (of Bo-

ES33 THE VILLAGE AT KINGS CREEK, under construction

nita Springs, Florida) on the Internet, where it markets home plans. This upscale community features closely spaced frame houses, and their complex massings, steep roofs, and traditional motifs, such as porches and cupolas, are used to lively effect. The development is one of many begun in the fast-growing west Rehoboth area after the completion of a sewer extension in 1995.

SOUTH ALONG THE INLAND BAYS AND OCEANFRONT

ES34 Indian Mission United Methodist Church

1921. DE 5 and Road 48, northwest of Fairmount

The Nanticokes are the only cohesive Native American tribe surviving on the Delmarva peninsula. Long a center of their culture, this Gothic Revival frame church replaced a simple chapel of the 1880s that had been built by a splinter group of Indians who left nearby Harmony Church when an African American minister was hired. That period saw a separatist movement rise within the Nanticokes, who had previously been assimilated into the larger black community. Another center of tribal life is the Nanticoke Indian Museum (DE 24 at Road 5). Built by the state as Harmon School in 1921, it closed in 1964 and was converted to a museum in the 1980s. The school was meant to educate both African Americans and Indians, but many of the separatists refused to attend and instead founded nearby Indian Mission School (rebuilt 1948).

ES35 McGee House

c. 1780, with additions. Road 298A, 0.5 miles northeast of intersection with Road 298, near Angola

Thanks to the Center for Historic Architecture and Design at the University of Delaware, much has recently been learned about early Sussex County buildings. One revelation is the persistence of the one-room "hall" plan house (even into the nineteenth century), often with relatively elaborate Federal interiors—a so-

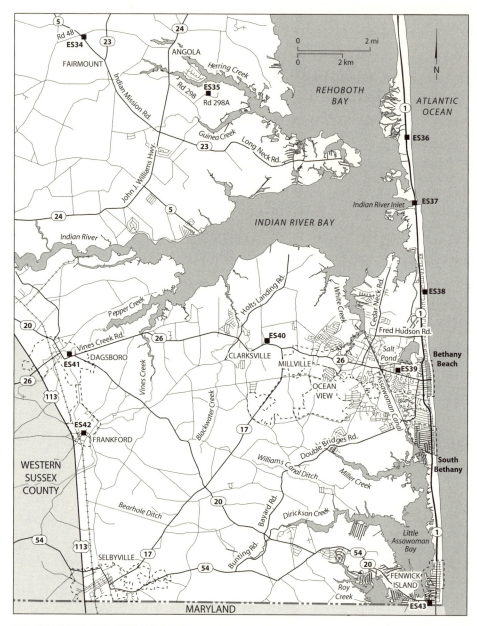

INLAND BAYS AND OCEANFRONT

called mansion. The McGee House, studied in 1986, originally consisted of a hall 16 × 18 feet in area. Federal paneling covered the fireplace wall and included glass-fronted bowfats (built-in cupboards). Later it was expanded into a hall-parlor plan and clad in cypress shingles. The house was built using H-bents, defined by architectural historians Gabrielle Lanier and Bernard Herman (1997) as "transverse, H-shaped structural units consisting of upper-story floor joists tenoned into principal posts." The house was moved here in 1960.

ES36 Indian River Life Saving Station

1874, with additions. 1997–1998 restored, Frens and Frens, with Bernardon Haber Holloway. DE 1, north of Indian River Inlet

Supposedly America's oldest coastal rescue station still on its original site, it was erected

ES37 INDIAN RIVER INLET BRIDGE, initial design

on the most inaccessible stretch of the Delaware shore just three years after the U.S. Life Saving Service was established. Original plans survive. Cladding was board-and-batten, with wide eaves above; there were frequent changes and additions over the years. In 1915, it became a Coast Guard Station. Construction of the road in 1934 linked it to the larger world, and summer tourists came by to admire the spit-and-polish conditions maintained by the crew, who were ready at any time to row into the surf to rescue shipwrecked sailors. The devastating storm of 1962 dumped four feet of sand inside. The place was subsequently abandoned and used for storage. A nonprofit group was founded in 1996 to save the building and return it to its appearance of 1905. The surroundings are part of Delaware Seashore State Park.

ES37 Indian River Inlet Bridge

2003–2010 est., Figg Engineering Group and others. DE 1 across the inlet

Historically, the tidal inlet through barrier dunes shifted frequently and sometimes closed altogether, as in the 1920s. During the subsequent decade it was reopened, bridged for the first time, then greatly widened by the federal government. In the early-twenty-first century, it was determined that the bridge of 1965 needed replacing, as swift currents had eroded the soil surrounding the support pilings. An initial design for the new bridge was unveiled in 2003, following considerable public input. It promised to be dramatic: a 1,000-foot span supported by a single, bowlike concrete arch from which stainless-steel cables descended in a single plane of radial stays. With this scheme, the engineering firm that had also built the DE 1 Bridge (PR13) intended to open a new era in the design of cable-stay bridges nationwide. Soaring project costs subsequently caused construction of the bridge to be delayed for redesign.

ES38 Kreindler Beach House

1993–1994, Michael R. Wigley for Davis, Bowen and Friedel. 27 Surfside Dr., north of Bethany Beach

Originally a religious colony, Bethany Beach was largely reconstructed after being flattened in the storm of 1962. One of Delaware's most novel recent houses stands just north of town. The owners had lived near the Connecticut estate of architect Philip Johnson and were attuned to modernism. The dramatic roof slope to the north shielded the occupants from cold winds, and windows and doors were recessed so mechanical shutters could slide across, protecting against hurricanes. A tall triangular gable is balanced by a projecting square block with echoing square window, and the whole is supported on piers. Davis, Bowen and Friedel began with a staff of four in 1983 and in ten years grew to one of the largest architecture and engineering firms on Delmarva, with offices in Milford and in Salisbury, Maryland.

ES39 Addy Cottage

c. 1901–1902. 807 Garfield Pkwy., Bethany Beach

The community of Bethany began in 1900 when the Disciples of Christ selected the locale for a seaside assembly and offered lots.

ES38 KREINDLER BEACH HOUSE

ES40 SPRING BANKE, photo 1978

Advertisements called the coast here "a bathing ground that cannot be surpassed. The sandy bottom is like a velvet carpet. No holes to terrify the timid bather. No treacherous undertow to swallow the unwary." Six Pittsburgh businessmen invested in the town, including English-born John M. Addy, who built this house near the beach, a balloon-framed, shingled bungalow with gambrel roof. It was moved and repaired after the Hurricane of 1927. The town took over the house in 2001, moving it to a new location and making plans for a museum. The Addy Sea (1902), a hotel since 1935 (Oceanview Parkway and North Atlantic), was also built by John Addy.

ES40 Spring Banke

Mid-18th century. c. 1835 addition. DE 26 and Irons Ln., between Clarksville and Millville

The small, two-part house is an extremely rare survival in the southeastern corner of the state. The 500-acre Spring Banke tract was granted to William Digges by Maryland in 1687. (This region, Baltimore Hundred, was claimed by Maryland as late as 1775.) The original one-story frame dwelling has a brick chimney partially exposed on the end wall, in Eastern Shore fashion. The place was occupied by tenants toward the end of the eighteenth century, but housed an owner for forty years in the mid-nineteenth century, widow Nancy Williams. She ran an adjacent store and held a half-interest in the sixty-five-foot schooner, *Mary Ann Catherine*. By then, the house was enlarged with a two-story cypress-shingled addition abutting the original, lower section. Both were framed with oak and gum timbers. Few changes were made prior to a restoration in the 1970s.

ES41 Prince George's Chapel

1755–1757, 1763. Vines Creek Rd. and Chapel Ln., Dagsboro

Named for the English prince soon to become King George III, this notable frame building was erected as a chapel-of-ease for Worcester Parish, Maryland, when the area was still part of that colony, in an oak grove at "Black Foot Town [Dagsboro] on the south side of Pepper's Creek" (Castrovillo, 1985). Two acres were purchased for 207 pounds of tobacco. James Johnson agreed to build the church for 39,200 pounds of the weed. Inside the barrel-vaulted nave (its ceiling is said to be a perfect semicircle) is a heart-of-pine interior, never painted. Galleries stood on three sides, and Daniel Hull was hired in December 1756 "to laying of the galleries floors . . . and wainscoating the gallaries all round." A T-shaped transept and chancel were added in 1763 to the east end. The church had deteriorated by 1850 and services were discontinued; during this decade, apparently, the transept was removed. But "Harvest Home" services opened the building once annually, and it was refurbished in 1893. The place was repaired and its walls shingled in 1928–1929. The Episcopal Church sold it to the state for a dollar in 1967. Subsequently, the missing transept was re-created, and the entire exterior and windows were renewed.

ES41 PRINCE GEORGE'S CHAPEL

ES43 FENWICK ISLAND LIGHT STATION, photo 1930s

moved the house back from the street after he bought it in 1918 and added the exterior decorative details. Chandler held seances on the third floor, and his wife always set a place at the table (with a single red rose) for their son who had died. In the 1960s, the house was converted into two apartments, fortunately preserving the character of the building, one of Delaware's more imaginative.

ES43 Fenwick Island Light Station

1858–1859 lighthouse. 1857–1858 and 1882 keepers' houses. Near corner of Lighthouse Rd. and DE 1, Fenwick Island

At the extreme southeastern corner of Delaware stands an old stone that has marked, since 1751, the start of the Transpeninsular Line, the state's southern boundary. Quarried and carved of oolitic limestone in England, it still shows the arms of Lord Baltimore (of Maryland) and William Penn (of Pennsylvania). The U.S. Lighthouse Board, established in 1852, reported to Congress three years later that a light was needed here to guide vessels from southern ports and Europe to the mouth of the Delaware River and to warn them of the "very dangerous" Fenwick Island Shoal. The resulting eighty-four-foot cylindrical brick lighthouse contained a third-order Fresnel lens manufactured in France. A ventilator ball stood atop the lantern assembly. The light burned whale oil for the first twenty years, then mineral oil, before conversion to electricity in 1899. It was automated in 1940 and, after twelve decades of continuous use, shut down in 1978. Popular with tourists, the lighthouse is the last to survive directly on the Atlantic coast of either Maryland or Delaware.

Historian Richard B. Carter notes that the church was originally shingled, so that today's weatherboards are not historically accurate.

ES42 Captain Chandler House

1880. 1918 altered. 13 Main St., Frankford

This sixteen-room gingerbread showpiece of the Queen Anne style was built by Captain Joshua Townsend. The two-story house has steeply pitched gables, the long porch terminates in steep-roofed gazebos with stained-glass windows in tiny gables, and the windows are variously shaped. The colorful Ebe T. Chandler, captain of a sea-going tugboat,

Western Sussex County

The state song "Our Delaware" (c. 1906) celebrates "Dear old Sussex . . . of the holly and the pine"—Coastal Plain flora abundant in the swampy woods of the western half of the county, culminating in the great Cypress Swamp between Gumboro and Selbyville. Huge bald cypresses hundreds of years old have escaped the axe at Trap Pond State Park near Laurel. In this land of abundant timber, wooden architecture was the norm, and much of it has disappeared with time. The Maryland influence in architecture was especially strong here: atypically for Delaware, the land drains *west* into the Nanticoke River basin, and early trade and settlement came up the many-pronged creeks from Caroline, Dorchester, and Somerset counties on the Eastern Shore. Only with the coming of the railroad in the 1850s was a full link established to Delaware itself. Towns sprang up along the line: Greenwood, Bridgeville, Delmar—the latter preserving a rare "highball" (a white ball that was raised and lowered to indicate track conditions) railroad signal device. Although industry transformed Seaford in the twentieth century with the coming of the DuPont nylon plant (WS17), most of the region remained a quiet rural enclave until development pressures began to grow in the 1990s.

WS1 Abbott's Mill Nature Center

Late 19th century. Abbott's Pond Rd., 0.7 miles west of DE 36, southwest of Milford

Mills in the Coastal Plain depended upon artificial ponds to provide a fall of water. A mill was first built on a dammed creek here in 1801–1802, and its foundations evidently support the current, two-story wooden facility, which Ainsworth Abbott operated starting in 1919. An unusual amount of milling equipment survives inside, from cloth chutes to carry grain from floor to floor to the diesel engine Abbott installed to run the facility when the pond was low. The state bought the property in 1963 and restored several structures, including the Gothic Revival miller's house (1905). Delaware Nature Society operates a solar-powered environmental education center (1986, Homsey Architects). One can canoe the millpond, visit a garden that models backyard wildlife habitat, or stroll along a boardwalk through a dark, mosquito-rich Sussex County swamp downstream from the dam.

WS2 Beracah Homes (Nanticoke Homes)

1970s–2000. West side of U.S. 13, 0.5 miles north of Greenwood

In 1971, poultry broker and politician John M. Mervine Sr. founded the Nanticoke Homes company inside an abandoned chicken house behind his Greenwood residence. Here he prefabricated modular homes for sale direct to the customer. Growth was swift, and by its

Early Sussex County chicken houses, photo 1930s

peak in 1989, the company occupied a large factory on this site and produced 1,183 homes. The only modular home manufacturer in Delaware, Nanticoke ultimately sold 20,000 houses throughout the Mid-Atlantic before going bankrupt in 2002. Two entrepreneurs immediately bought the plant and renamed it. Along with mobile homes, modular homes form a significant component of the housing stock in lower Delaware. The porticoed, Georgian Revival Administration Building at Beracah must be one of the biggest modular structures anywhere.

WS3 Poplar Level

c. 1758. Road 34 and Road 32, southwest of Greenwood

A descendant of seventeenth-century immigrants from England who settled near the Nanticoke River with its convenient shipping, John Richards built the frame house and farmed 1,271 acres. Features of the house are typical of southwestern Delaware and Eastern Shore Maryland, including the telescope arrangement of a big, three-bay unit with two increasingly smaller extensions in a line, and, also, the end brick chimneys flush with the wall and originally left exposed at the first story. The home remained in the family until 1952. A survey in 1980 found the early hall and parlor well-preserved, with outstanding Georgian scroll-cut designs on the stair ends. Other sections of the house suffered a late-nineteenth-century fire and were rebuilt in 1939. Except for the twin barns (c. 1850), the outbuildings mostly date to 1939–1955 and include machine shops and sheds, corncrib, pigpen, chicken house, and brooder house.

WS4 Locust Grove

1828. 1914 addition. North of corner of Road 34 and Road 32, southwest of Greenwood

John Richards, grandson of the builder of Poplar Level (ws3), erected Locust Grove in a conservative, Flemish-bond brick townhouse form, its plan derived from that earlier house. An original cypress-shingle frame section was replaced with a two-story Queen Anne structure in 1914. Inside the brick section, wooden Venetian blinds with richly carved valences above them are rare survivals, and there are fine Federal chimneypieces. Preservation ex-

WS4 LOCUST GROVE

WS5 Middle Space

1868. 1870s enlarged. Adjacent to Locust Grove

John Emory Richards grew up at Locust Grove (ws4) and fought for the Union (in the Sixth Delaware Regiment) in the Civil War, after which he built this house on 212 acres bought from his father's estate. He raised sheep, grew grain, and cultivated an orchard of 2,000 trees. The house of simplified Italianate style completes the important complex of Richards family homes. An associated structure nearby is the frame Epworth Church (1906), a deteriorating example of rural Sussex County's once-numerous Methodist places of worship.

pert T. Catherine Adams undertook an admirably detailed study of the house and outbuildings in 1978–1980.

BRIDGEVILLE

Long noted for its canneries, Bridgeville (pop. 1,436) still has a factory that makes scrapple. A gray, rock-faced cement brick was popular here and elsewhere in Sussex County in the early twentieth century, the railroad allowing easy distribution of such products. Several houses of that period are interesting for showing up-to-date architectural styles and materials, for example, Cannon House at 106 Main Street, in Arts and Crafts style with wide eaves. The Police Department in the former Baltimore Trust Company building (1903–1904; 302 Market St.) emulates the bold architectural style of Frank Furness and has metal cresting on the roof ridge; later, the diminutive building got a Beaux-Arts limestone facade in a stylish updating. The Gothic Revival St. Mary's Episcopal Church (1888–1889; 21 William St.) was built of inexpensive red brick with a trim of terra-cotta and yellow brick. A somewhat incongruous addition of 1969 partly surrounds the church and envelops its altar end. The Presbyterian Church of 1866 is now the town library (210 Market St.).

WS6 Sudler House

1750. c. 1795 enlarged. West side of N. Main St.

This two-story house, the oldest in town, contains a rare corner chimney in its original section. The Federal addition (making a rather stately six bays) has an end chimney with the lower few feet left exposed, in Eastern Shore manner. Cypress shingling is also typical of the area. Carving on the stair brackets is similar to that at Poplar Level (ws3). Dr. John R. Sudler, who promoted the cultivation of peaches and strawberries, bought the place in 1833; it remained in his family until 1971. Nearby, the colonial bridge crossed Bridge Branch, hence the name Bridgeville, adopted for the fledgling town in 1810.

WS6 SUDLER HOUSE

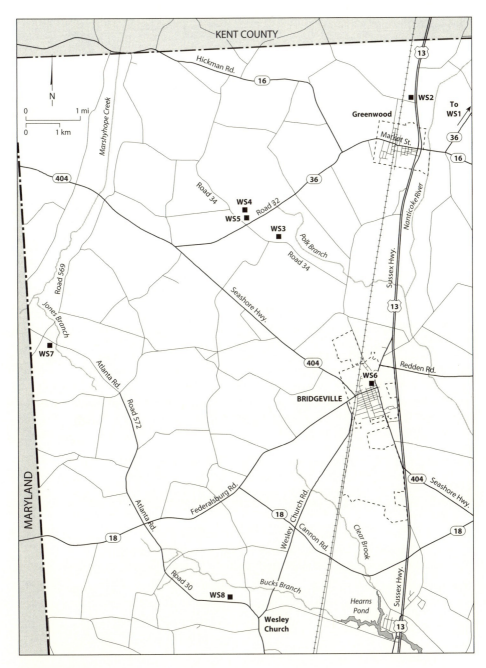

BRIDGEVILLE

WEST OF BRIDGEVILLE

WS7 Eratt House

Mid-18th century. Road 572, south of intersection with Road 569, near Maryland line

The rarity of eighteenth-century houses in Sussex County makes this semi-ruinous example especially significant. Little is known of the three-bay brick dwelling beyond the name of Eratt, its mid-nineteenth-century owner. The setting, near Marshyhope Creek, is remote. Some features are quirky, such as windows and doors unpredictably off-center and a long iron strap reinforcing the base of each gable. A frame extension has been removed. In time, the house was brutally converted into a mechanic's garage, a huge opening cut in the west wall and the entire first floor—even the floor joists—ripped out. The second floor remained eerily intact. Deteriorating rapidly, the Eratt House appears gravely threatened.

WS8 Maston House

1727. 1733 enlarged. Road 30, 0.4 miles west of Wesley Church, northwest of Seaford

One of the earliest brick houses in Sussex County, and long called Maston House after the man who bought it in 1851, it originally occupied a 450-acre tract called Cannon's Savannah, then in Maryland. Stylistically, it belongs to Maryland's Eastern Shore in its steep roof, brick corbeling at the eaves, chevron-shaped glazed-header diapering in the gables, and tilted-false-plate roof construction. Originally, it was single-cell, the simplest possible plan, but five years later it was expanded by one room. Inscribed bricks give the dates of both the original and second building campaigns. Interior chimneys stand at either end. They have a glazed pattern and show traces of pargetting in the band at top, features that suggest a lingering seventeenth-century aesthetic. In

WS8 MASTON HOUSE

the early twentieth century, the house became a garage, with a big door cut in (like the Eratt House, ws7). Photographer Frances Benjamin Johnston recorded the place, admired by historians as a colonial "Maryland house in Delaware." Architectural historian William Allen praises its brickwork as the best of any pre-Georgian house in the state.

SEAFORD

Largest incorporated town in Sussex County and the fifth-largest in Delaware, this community on the Nanticoke River once shipped fruit, oysters, and shad. Early photographs show the riverbanks lined with frame oyster houses (where shelling took place), boat yards, and canneries (for tomatoes, peas, and other vegetables), and streets crowded with wagons as farmers hauled in strawberries, watermelons, and other produce for shipment by refrigerated railroad cars. Several large homes and commercial buildings survive today to suggest Seaford's turn-of-the-twentieth-century agricultural prosperity. The town was abruptly modernized by the coming of the DuPont factory during the Great Depression (ws17), creating "Nylon City." About the same size as neighboring Laurel in 1930, Seaford now rocketed ahead of it. DuPont built some standardized worker housing and supported education. A Ralph Nader exposé published in 1971 of DuPont, *The Company State* (Center for the Study of Responsive Law, Washington, D.C.), uses Seaford as an example of capitalism's discontents, though more recently a geography student, Carmen Ann McWilliams, revisited the town and refuted most of Nader's findings (in a

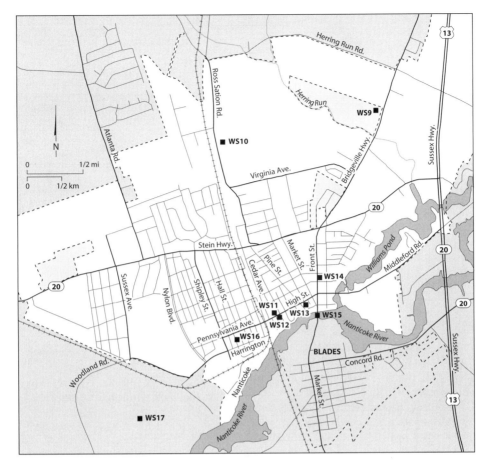

SEAFORD

M.A. thesis in 1998). In 2004, DuPont sold its plant to Koch Industries, ending an era. The Old Post Office (1935) at 105 New Street was bought and restored as a museum by Seaford Historical Society starting in 2001.

WS9 Lawrence

c. 1840. West side of Bridgeville Hwy., just north of Seaford

A rare example of a temple-front Greek Revival structure in southern Delaware, the elegant, white frame house was built for Charles Wright, tradesman and shipper of Seaford. Behind the four square columns that support the pediment, floor-length windows light the front parlor. A small north wing contained an office, whereas the south led to the kitchen and dining room in the service wing. When surveyed in 1977, the interior contained a remarkable array of period locks and other hardware. The whole complex was then in excellent condition, but by early in the twenty-first century, it was abandoned and facing possible demolition.

WS10 Governor Ross Mansion

1856–1860. 1101 N. Pine St. Extension

Among the state's best examples of the Italianate Villa mode, this was home to William Henry Harrison Ross, Delaware's governor in 1851–1855. He inherited the 1,400-acre farm from his father and at first (from c. 1845) lived in the eighteenth-century frame dwelling that forms a rear wing. The new two-story brick home featured wide, bracketed eaves; shaped chimneys; and an asymmetrically placed square tower. It is a free variation on a Richard Upjohn design published in Andrew

WS10 GOVERNOR ROSS MANSION

Jackson Downing's *The Architecture of Country Houses* (1850). Decorative plasterwork adorns the interior. A slaveowner and southern sympathizer, Ross smuggled arms to the Confederacy in 1861 before prudently fleeing to Europe. Returning after the war ended, he switched to fruit production. In the early 1880s, his son took over, and subsequent owners willed the estate in trust to the University of Delaware. Industrial and business parks now planned will largely surround the site, which is owned by Seaford Historical Society. That group is furnishing the numerous, high-ceiling rooms of the interior. The exterior has a rather stripped appearance, having lost the many balconies, canopies, and openwork finials that once enlivened it (these may eventually be replaced). Gone, too, is the veranda that once faced the road. Historian Harold D. Eberlein (1962) discussed the house only briefly before concluding, "the virtue of simplicity is wholly absent." Historians today, however, appreciate Ross Mansion as the consummate south-Delaware achievement of the antebellum villa movement.

An insurance policy in 1860 mentions several outbuildings, including carriage house, cart house, corn crib, two barns, stable, and stable-corn-crib combination. Seen at a distance across an expansive rear lawn, the outbuildings and big, wedge-shaped barn form an attractive group. The ancient-looking log corncrib (c. 1850), of white cedar, was moved from near Millsboro.

WS10.1 Honeymoon Cottage
c. 1860

By the road stands an entrance lodge now called Honeymoon Cottage, built for Ross's son, James Jefferson, at the time of his marriage. It was later moved away and narrowly escaped being destroyed in the early 1990s before being returned here and rebuilt (with a rear wing omitted). As with Ross Mansion (WS10), it copies the mid-nineteenth-century patternbooks of Andrew Jackson Downing, with board-and-batten siding, window hoods, ornamental vergeboards, and a projecting jetty above the door with three Gothic Revival windows. Across the road is James J. Ross's later Queen Anne–style house (1882), which has lost its original porches and trusswork in the gables.

WS10.2 Slave Quarter
c. 1855

This structure is described as Delaware's only documented slave building (but see KT38.1). The documentation consists of an insurance map and policy of 1860 that show "a Framed Quarter 16 × 24 1½ stories high with porch," worth $125, standing on this location. It housed ten men and four women ages twelve to sixty-four. Later, the building disappeared from the site, but twentieth-century researchers found it standing in a grove of trees across the fields, a log structure with frame additions. When studied in 1992, it was extremely dilapidated. The logs are oak and pine, dovetailed, and chinked with riven scrap and fragments of sawn scantlings. The roughly finished structure had an exterior chimney and a loft. On the plausible assumption that this building is the one mentioned in the 1860 policy—it is the same size and has a porch—it was returned to its original site and heavily restored.

WS10.2 SLAVE QUARTER

WS11 Ross-Allen House

c. 1880. c. 1925 altered. 114 High St.

Governor William Ross's son Willie built the big, frame Queen Anne house with dramatically steep and complex roofs, tall shaped chimneys, and decorative bracing in the gables. A narrow alley across the street conveniently took him to his yacht, moored on the Nanticoke. William F. Allen, produce broker and later a congressman, bought the house about 1916 and made changes along Colonial Revival lines, modifying the facade by adding a huge porch with archaeologically correct Ionic column capitals copied from the Erectheum in Athens, Greece, and a lower porch culminating in a porte-cochere. The result was a grandiose composition of the sort popular with the gentry in small towns nationwide. The interior was allowed to retain its original overmantels, tile hearths, staircases, doors (with wooden handles), and other details.

WS11 ROSS-ALLEN HOUSE

WS12 Reverend George A. Hall House

1860s. 1876 addition. 110 S. Conwell St.

Hall built the rather plain brick house while he served as rector of St. Luke's (ws14). (He also visited rural churches as a horse-and-buggy circuit preacher.) Shortly after enlarging the dwelling, he lost it in a sheriff's sale in 1879; subsequently, it was home to a prominent doctor. In recent years it has been a telephone company office, a private residence, and now a business in the rejuvenated Riverfront District.

WS13 BURTON BROTHERS HARDWARE STORE

WS13 Burton Brothers Hardware Store

1893. 407 High St.

Schoolchildren are brought to this two-story commercial building to see a business virtually unchanged for more than a century. It was owned by the Burton family until 1954, when the grandfather of the current owner took over after two decades working behind the counter. Calendars of the 1920s tacked to the wall give the store's telephone number as simply

WS15 SEAFORD BRIDGE (STATE BRIDGE NO. 151), view of counterweight and lift mechanism beneath bridge deck, photo 1991

"3." The counter, cash register, and wooden bins are original. Construction is frame, the exterior swathed in tin-colored galvanized sheet metal, pressed sheets imitating rusticated stone. The facade is a false front, as in a Western town, and is giddily embossed with friezes, swags, and elegant Renaissance-styled candelabra-and-dolphin panels, culminating in a big fleur-de-lis cornice.

WS14 St. Luke's Episcopal Church

1838–1843. 1904 tower. 1944 buttresses. Front and King sts.

In the early nineteenth century, the Episcopal Church was moribund in Delaware but eventually began to revive. The first bricks of St. Luke's were laid on May 1, 1838. Consecrating the Gothic Revival structure five years later, Alfred Lee, first Bishop of Delaware, praised its "very neat and appropriate style," Gothic Revival being a favorite mode for Anglican churches everywhere during this period (see NK9.16). The steeple was replaced by a tower in 1904, at which time the roof rafters were renewed, memorial windows added, and the building electrified. A Parish House came in 1931. When fissures appeared in the brickwork, the W. D. Haddock construction company of Wilmington undertook urgent renovations, adding twelve concrete buttresses, to some at the time "an eyesore."

WS15 Seaford Bridge (State Bridge No. 151)

1923–1925. 1992 partly rebuilt. Front St. over Nanticoke River

The towns of Seaford and Blades are divided by the Nanticoke, historically a busy navigational waterway. The current bridge, replacing an older steel and timber swing span, is a lift structure of a type called "trunnion bascule," the mobile "leaf" and its 305,000 pound concrete counterweight set in a pier below the bridge deck and rotating on a steel axle (the trunnion). The Chicago Bascule Bridge Company designed this fifty-five-foot span, built by Baltimore contractors. Chicago engineers also consulted on other Delaware bascule bridges of the 1920s—that first great era of highway construction—in Wilmington (S. Market St.), Newport, Milford, and Laurel.

WS16 Fairview (Dulaney House)

c. 1825 enlargement of earlier house. 119 South Hall St.

Before it was moved to this location in 1938, the frame house formed part of a 500-acre farm nearby on the Nanticoke, as described in the WPA *Delaware Guide*. Peter Rust of Virginia bought it in 1825 and added the larger two-story section with unusual twin fanlit doors and a Greek Revival portico around them (a house on Mt. Vernon Street in

WS16 FAIRVIEW (DULANEY HOUSE), prior to move

Smyrna has somewhat similar twin fanlights). "Planner" Williams was traditionally said to be the local architect of this and other homes. A chimneyed slave quarter appears in old photographs. William H. Dulaney acquired the place in the 1840s. A Southern sympathizer, he watched in outrage as Union troops from Baltimore disembarked from steamers and camped on his land, here to keep order in Seaford during the elections of 1862. When the complex was about to be razed for the DuPont plant, a local women's group, the Acorn Club, happily convinced the company to donate the house as their headquarters, and it was moved. It later served as the town library before being converted into a private home.

WS17 Invista Seaford Plant (DuPont Seaford Plant)

1938–1939, Walter R. Hope and others for DuPont Engineering Company. 400 Woodland Rd.

A pilot plant at the DuPont Experimental Station (BR25) produced the first run of an extraordinary new substance, "Fiber 66," in 1938. Various names were considered for the textile polymer, including "Delawear," before "nylon" was chosen. It was advertised to the public at the World's Fair of 1939 in New York City: "strong as steel, as fine as a spider's web." DuPont's siting of their nylon factory downstate in Seaford was regarded as a boon to Delaware. The Moderne plant came online with 850 workers in December 1939, which was about the time Japanese silk supplies were cut off by World War II. The product, of course, proved a sensation among consumers nationwide. Employment here peaked at 4,600 in the 1970s, but subsequently shrank to just 650 by 2004, the year DuPont sold the historic facility, part of which had previously been demolished. In its original form, the plant's buildings showed a complex rectilinear interplay between horizontals and verticals, at the time an architectural approach as innovative as the technology housed within.

WOODLAND AND BETHEL

WS18 Cannon Hall

c. 1820. Facing ferry landing, Woodland

A ferry carries travelers across the 500-foot-wide Nanticoke River at Woodland, a three-minute ride that represents a survival of a colonial institution into modern times, though the ferry is now diesel-powered and transports automobiles. The Cannon family operated it as early as the 1740s, and Jacob Cannon and his brother were merchants and traders who owned thousands of acres nearby. Jacob built Cannon Hall, a two-story frame house memorable for its big, original windows with curvy, folk-carved lintels. The date of the house is disputed; owners who restored the place in the 1960s tell me of a carpenter's diary of 1812 recording construction of the house, earlier than the usual c. 1820 date. Certain aspects of the dwelling, such as the tall brick foundations and center-passage plan, look back conservatively to eighteenth-century architecture and suggest Tidewater Maryland or Virginia. Architectural historian William Allen calls it "a wonderful transformation into wood of a

WS18 CANNON HALL

distinctly masonry form." A brick smokehouse stands nearby. Accounts of Cannon Hall recite its colorful lore: Jacob refused to move in after his fiancée jilted him, so the house stood empty for twenty years; a man he accused of stealing his "bee gum tree" shot him dead on the ferry landing in 1843.

WS19 Ship-Carpenters' Houses
Before 1868. Main St., Bethel

Shipbuilding once flourished on this tributary of the Nanticoke, a river that flows westward toward the Chesapeake Bay and markets in Baltimore. Bethel began as Lewisville in 1840 when a farmer laid out twelve lots adjacent to his wharf on Broad Creek; the current name came in 1880. Shipbuilders prospered here from the late nineteenth century through 1918. This side-by-side pair of weatherboarded houses facing south was built by two ship captains. One dwelling has Greek Revival corner pilasters, a treatment more common in Sussex County than elsewhere in Delaware. Simple pine paneling distinguishes the interiors. The modern bridge to Bethel (1967) replaced the original of 1887. An engaging ensemble of small frame houses, the entire town has been placed on the National Register.

WS19 SHIP-CARPENTERS' HOUSES

LAUREL

Old frame houses stand close to the twisting streets of Laurel (pop. 3,668), which radiate irregularly from the town center, elevated above Broad Creek. Land speculator Barkley Townsend, whose house still stands at 108 Oak Street, laid out Laurel Town at an Indian "wading place" in 1789. Streets were named for Lumber, Corn, Wheat, and Rye, staples of the local economy, all of which were shipped on the creek. The Delaware Railroad came through in 1859, allowing export of peaches, watermelons, berries, and corn to cities, along

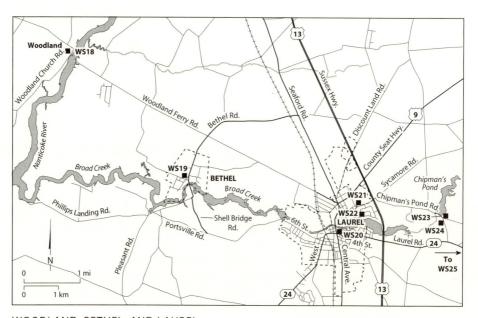

WOODLAND, BETHEL, AND LAUREL

with crates and baskets and five million feet of lumber annually (by 1860). Wealth ensued, and some large houses were built. The business district was entirely reconstructed after a disastrous fire in 1899 that consumed sixty-two of sixty-eight stores and twenty-eight houses. Up to 1,200 railroad cars filled with sweet potatoes left Laurel annually in the 1920s, and some sweet potato storage-and-curing houses survive. The 1920s also saw construction of a State armory (1926, Edward Canby May). Sussex County's third-biggest town, Laurel has the largest designated historic district in the state, with more than 800 buildings on the National Register. It is distinguished by its many late-nineteenth-century homes, of which local historian Ned Fowler singles out three as especially interesting: Dr. Joshua Ellegood House (1880s) and Daniel Fooks House, both Queen Anne style, and Hitchens House, which shows the influence of Andrew Jackson Downing's cottage designs.

WS20 Rosemont

c. 1763, with additions. 121 Delaware Ave.

This much-altered frame house just north of the town center was one of the first Georgian-style buildings erected in Sussex County; in the nineteenth century it received a Greek Revival portico. The dwelling was built for James Mitchell, whose son Nathaniel inherited it. Nathaniel was a prisoner of war in the American Revolution, a member of the Continental Congress, and finally governor (1805–1808). Homes of downstate governors survive in disproportionate numbers: of the eight men who served in 1797–1817 (all from Kent or Sussex counties), houses are still extant for seven. In addition to Rosemont, they are: Daniel Rodgers, Causey Mansion (KT38); Richard Bassett and James Sykes, homes on the Green, Dover; David Hall, 107 Kings Highway, Lewes; George Truitt, house on DE 33 outside Felton; and Daniel Rodney, 231 2nd Street, Lewes.

WS20 ROSEMONT, photo 1936

Massachusetts Institute of Technology chemical engineer Warren K. Lewis (b. 1882) grew up here.

WS22 Fowler House

c. 1770–early 19th centuries. 111 Lakeside Dr.

This many-sectioned frame dwelling in big house, little house, colonnade, and kitchen arrangement has been assembled from various old Laurel structures moved to this location by its owners, Ned and Norma Jean Fowler. The main block (c. 1770) was home to Robert Houston, builder of Christ Church (WS23), and has finely detailed features inside and out, including original beaded siding, modillion cornice, and elaborate parlor woodwork. The present kitchen was formerly the one-room Lowe House (c. 1800), discussed by Gabrielle Lanier and Bernard Herman (1997) as "the

WS21 Spring Garden

c. 1792 brick section. c. 1880 frame addition. 10905 Delaware Ave.

This house exhibits an L-shaped fusion of Georgian-style and Gothic Revival sections. The original brick Georgian part, with its substantial double-pile, center-passage plan, is a rare survival in the county. Paneling was once marbelized but stripped to natural wood by twentieth-century owners. An early-nineteenth-century barn is notable. Pioneering

WS22 FOWLER HOUSE

WS23 OLD CHRIST CHURCH

simplest form of hall dwelling [with] a single door, opening directly into the heated living space." It is one of the few fully paneled rooms in Sussex County.

WS23 Old Christ Church

1771–1772. 1952 foundation replaced. Chipman's Pond Rd. at Christ Church Rd., east of Laurel

Regular services ceased in 1850, so the church's subsequent survival in pristine condition seems almost miraculous. Robert Houston (not Holston, as sometimes given) sold land east of Chipman's Pond mill dam in September 1772 to Stepney Parish, Maryland, along with this church he had just built. The edifice served as chapel-of-ease for Stepney (chapels-of-ease made it more convenient for people in remote districts to attend services) and was, in fact, technically in Maryland until a boundary dispute was settled in favor of Delaware in 1775. Originally called Broad Creek Chapel, it was nicknamed "Old Lightwood" for its heart-pine construction, never painted inside or out (the exterior turned red from a coating of insect-and-rot repellent in c. 1951). The plan, a 40 × 60–foot, gable-roofed rectangle with two front doors leading to double aisles, was a traditional one on the Eastern Shore, and historian Harold D. Eberlein (1962) pointed out that the building was "virtually a replica in heart-pine planks of the brick Stepney parish church," Green Hill, eighteen miles away in Wicomico County, Maryland. The barnlike gables have a kick that overhangs a cove cornice along the eaves. Walls are of matched boards. The mellow interior with its shallow-vaulted wooden ceiling has become deservedly famous. The forty-three box pews show early graffiti—pew numbers, rents, and names of renters—and a Catherine Wheel inscribed on pew #13. The original east-end altar table, storage chest, and communion silver survive. In the middle of the north wall stand a raised pulpit with sounding board and a reading desk. John Chipman purchased the nearby mill from Robert Houston in 1812, and Chipman's Mill (1884) stood at the outflow of the pond. It was, until abandoned in the late 1940s, one of the few remaining Delaware gristmills powered solely by water. Intact with its water turbine grinding apparatus as late as 1977, it has subsequently disappeared.

WS24 Chipman Sweet Potato House

1913. Chipman's Pond Road, near Old Christ Church, 1.9 miles east of Laurel

Sweet potato production quadrupled in Sussex County after 1900, a boom that lasted until a root disease struck in the 1940s. Two-story,

WS24 CHIPMAN SWEET POTATO HOUSE

296 WESTERN SUSSEX COUNTY

CAMP MEETINGS

Lower Delmarva was a center of early Methodism—21 percent of its adults were Methodist by 1810—and western Sussex County still has many rural churches. A survey in 1976 found two score of them in a twenty-mile radius of Laurel, mostly Methodist. Camp meetings were widespread, too, this being a favorite recruiting device. Historically there were around forty on the peninsula, including at least fifteen in Sussex County, the first of which was Zoar Camp between Millsboro and Harbeson, about eighty-five years old when it closed in 1919.

At all the camps, tents of brushwood or, more elaborately, frame cottages (also called tents) encircled the preaching arena or tabernacle, where the itinerant preacher hoarsely harangued a sweat-drenched crowd. Illumination was provided by burning "lightwood knots" of heart pine. Food was standard: fried chicken, lima beans, sugar corn, and watermelon. The automobile greatly changed camp meetings, making their crowds more transient. Electric lights soon illuminated the camps, and according to some accounts, young people seemed more interested in flirting than in expressing religious fervor.

Established in 1890, Antioch Camp Meeting on Clayton Street, near Frankford (known as "Big Camp" or "Frankford Camp") served African Americans. The WPA *Delaware Guide* (p. 514) gives a lively account of the place before its destruction in a fire in 1943 and its subsequent rebuilding. Delmarva Camp, two miles north of Laurel (Cottage Circle Rd., off Camp Rd.), was founded in 1879 and was Delaware's largest, with some fifty frame tents in a circle around its tabernacle at the time of its abandonment in 1987. It is said that four camps survive in the state today, including Carey's (WS25) and Antioch.

---

houselike gabled buildings were used to store sweet potatoes over the winter, with chimneys to vent a stove that gave constant heat. Windows were few, but air circulation was provided by slatted floors and sliding panels. Today, these weatherboarded structures have all been converted for other uses—or, as here, abandoned.

SOUTHWEST OF MILLSBORO

WS25 Carey's Camp

1888, established. Carey's Camp Rd., 1 mile west of Millsboro Hwy.

Methodist camp meetings traditionally met for two weeks in August. Carey's, a rare survivor, occupies a white oak grove in flat, sandy countryside. It probably lasted so long because it was noted for its evangelical fervor, with spontaneous prayers, shouting, and old hymns without musical accompaniment. Fire-stands of pine "lightwood knots" were used as late as 1937, not electric bulbs (though these were introduced the next year). The forty-seven cabins, called tents, are mostly boarded-up when not in use. Individually owned and periodically repaired or rebuilt, they show subtle differences within a standard format, making them an intriguing study in architectural serialization. Tin-roofed and front-gabled, they are painted white and are, increasingly, sided with aluminum or vinyl. They crowd as close to each other as possible, with a window upstairs and the downstairs entirely open, so that one looks into each little parlor with its rug and furnishings as into a doll house. In front stands a porch. Formerly, weatherboards were omitted in a panel across the back for ventilation. The tents form an oval around the tabernacle (recently rebuilt), a big, cross-shaped

WS25 CAREY'S CAMP

structure supported by posts. Under electric lights and ceiling fans, the participants occupy seats recycled from an old theater or auditorium, with yellow sawdust thickly strewn underfoot. The preacher stands at a pulpit on a wooden stage, with "Jesus Saves" on a signboard overhead. Fascinating to visit during its brief summertime season, Carey's Camp is a nationally significant example of nineteenth-century architecture and religious culture. It truly brings the past alive.

GLOSSARY

Adamesque A mode of Neoclassical architectural design pioneered by eighteenth-century Scottish architects Robert Adam (1728–1792) and his brother James Adam (1732–1794), featuring attenuated proportions, bright color, and elegant, linear detailing; popular in America in the Federal Period.

AIA (American Institute of Architects) Leading professional organization of architects in the United States (established 1857). Among its hundreds of local chapters is AIA Delaware.

arcade A series of arches carried on columns or piers.

arch A curved construction that spans an opening. A masonry arch consists of a series of wedge-shaped parts called voussoirs.

architrave The lowest horizontal member of a classical entablature; also, the moldings around a door or window.

Art Deco A style inspired by the Exposition International des Arts Décoratifs et Industriels Moderne held in Paris in 1925; characterized by faceted forms and patterns, rich materials (including polished metal and exotic wood), and an overall sleekness of design.

Art Nouveau A style that originated in Belgium and France in the 1890s and flourished briefly across Europe and the United States, characterized by undulating lines and sensuous curvilinear forms inspired by the natural world and some nonwestern sources.

Arts and Crafts A late nineteenth and early twentieth century movement that emerged in England and spread to the United States. Inspired by William Morris (1834–1896) as a reaction to industrialization, it emphasized truth to materials and the importance of handicraft and beauty in everyday objects and environments.

ashlar Blocks of stone cut so that they fit tightly together in a wall.

balloon-frame construction A system of light frame construction, conceived in the United States in the 1830s and supplanting timber framing, in which single studs extend the full height of the frame (commonly two stories). Slender structural members (easily shipped by railroad) were sawn lumber, ranging from two-by-fours to two-by-tens, fastened with nails, not wooden pegs.

balustrade A row of balusters or posts; if supporting a stair rail, often called a banister.

bank barn A barn typically built into a bank or hillside, in which the barn is on two levels.

bargeboard An ornate fascia board that is attached to the sloping edges (verges) of a roof, covering the ends of the horizontal roof timbers (purlins).

Baroque A monumental and richly three-dimensional style of architecture, building upon the classical vocabularies of the Renaissance, that flourished in Europe during the seventeenth century.

barrel vault A semicircular ceiling forming a tunnel-like enclosure over a room or corridor.

baseboard A plank at the base of an interior wall at floor level.

batten A narrow strip of wood applied to cover a joint between two boards; used in board-and-batten siding.

Bauhaus Work in any of the visual arts by the faculty and students of the Bauhaus, the innovative design school founded by Walter Gropius (1883–1969) and an active force in German modernism from 1919 until 1933.

Also, work by individuals influenced by them.

bay Vertical division of a facade, generally embracing a single window or door. Facades are described as being three bay, four bay, and so forth.

bay window The horizontally grouped windows in a projecting bay, or the projecting bay itself, if it is not more than one story.

Beaux-Arts Historicist design on a monumental scale, generally classical, as taught at the Ecole des Beaux-Arts in Paris and disseminated internationally, c. 1850–c. 1930.

bent A transverse structural unit in a timber frame house, generally consisting of two posts and a tie beam.

blue rock Hard, bluish-gray stone used extensively as a building material in the Wilmington area, Delaware; also called "Brandywine granite," though it is actually gneiss.

board-and-batten A type of siding for wood-frame buildings, first popular in the early nineteenth century, that consists of vertical boards with narrow strips of wood (battens) covering the joints.

brace A wooden or metal member placed diagonally to stiffen the corner of a building frame; used in braced-frame construction.

bracket Supporting unit beneath a cornice or eave, often rendered decorative by carving.

broach spire A spire, usually octagonal, atop a square base with the transition between effected by partially pyramidal forms called broaches.

broiler house A farm building designed for the raising of chickens, which are sold as young birds ("broilers"), expressly for eating.

Brutalism An architectural style generally characterized by rough-looking, exposed concrete, and by a frank, often massive expression of structure and building systems. It was popular from the 1950s through the 1970s, especially for public buildings. Sometimes called New Brutalism.

bungalow A small, low, informal type of house with conspicuous porch and projecting eaves, popular in towns and suburbs in the early twentieth century.

buttress A pier of masonry abutting a wall that it strengthens or supports. Buttresses often absorb lateral thrusts from roofs or vaults, as in Gothic cathedrals.

Byzantine Term applied to the architecture and art of the Eastern Roman Empire centered on Byzantium (also known as Constantinople and Istanbul) from the sixth to the fifteenth centuries. It is characterized by domes, round arches, richly carved capitals, and mosaics.

campanile In Italian, a bell tower. While usually free-standing in medieval and Renaissance architecture in Italy, it was often incorporated as a prominent unit in the massing of picturesque nineteenth-century buildings.

cantilever A beam, girder, slab, or other structural member that thrusts out beyond the wall or column that supports it.

capital The topmost element of a classical column, above the shaft, adorned with moldings and carved enrichment.

Carpenter Gothic Gothic forms (1840s–1870s) rendered in wood, using lathes, jigsaws, and molding machines, often to fanciful effect. Sometimes called Gingerbread Style or Steamboat Gothic.

casement window A window that swings open from the side on hinges, like a door. An earlier window type than double-hung.

castellated Having elements of a medieval castle, such as crenellations and turrets.

cast iron Iron shaped by a molding process. It is strong in compression but brittle in tension. Distinguished from wrought iron, which has been forged to increase its tensile properties.

cast iron front A facade made of prefabricated, molded iron parts. Prevalent in American cities from the 1840s to the 1870s, especially for commercial buildings.

center passage A type of colonial house plan in which the ground floor consists of two rooms (the hall and the parlor) with a passage running through the building front-to-back between them. Historically, a later development than the simple hall-parlor plan.

chair rail Strip of molding running around a room at the height of a chair back; it is ornamental and at the same time protects the wall from damage.

chamfer On a wooden beam, an edge that is cut off to create an oblique surface that will not splinter.

chancel The end of a church (traditionally the east end) containing the altar and often set apart for the clergy and choir by a screen, rail, or steps.

chateau (plural, *chateaux*) In French, a large mansion or palace, sometimes with castle-like features. In the United States, a term applied to grand masonry houses that derive their forms from French Renaissance chateaux. Sometimes called Chateau Style or Chateauesque Revival.

Chateau Country A Delaware tourist-industry term for the scenic countryside near Wilmington that was historically owned by the du Pont family and that features large, handsome homes and country estates.

choir The part of the church chancel where the singers participate in the service.

City Beautiful A movement in architecture, landscape architecture, and planning (1890s–1920s) advocating the beautification of cities and employing a monumental Beaux-Arts classical style inspired in part by the World's Columbian Exposition in Chicago in 1893. City Beautiful schemes emphasized civic centers, parks, and boulevards.

clapboard A tapered board that is thinner along the top edge and thicker along the bottom, nailed horizontally with edges overlapping to provide weather-tight siding on a building of wood construction. Sometimes called weatherboard.

classicism, classical, classicizing Terms describing the application of architectural principles or elements derived from the ancient Greek and Roman world, especially temples, by any subsequent period of Western civilization, but particularly since the Renaissance.

clerestory A horizontal wall elevated high above the floor and fitted with a band of windows, as in a cathedral or factory.

coffer A recessed panel (usually square or octagonal) in a ceiling, as in the domes and vaults of classical architecture.

Collegiate Gothic The English Gothic or Tudor architecture of Oxford and Cambridge universities adapted for American colleges (1890s–1920s).

colonial Architecture surviving from the British, Dutch, French, or Spanish colonial periods in North America. In the northeastern states, usually applies to the British colonial period (c. 1607–1781). Eighteenth-century high-style (British) colonial architecture is usually classical in its approach and frequently called Georgian.

Colonial Revival The revival of forms, usually classical, from British colonial design. The Colonial Revival flourished after the U.S. centennial in 1876 and continues to the present, especially in domestic architecture and public buildings.

colonnade A running series of columns supporting an entablature or a simple beam.

colonnette A diminutive, often attenuated, column.

column A vertical supporting element typically consisting of a base, shaft, and capital. Also, any supporting element in a skeletal frame.

common bond A pattern of brickwork in which every fifth or sixth course consists of all headers, the other courses being all stretchers. Sometimes called American bond. Distinguished from running bond, in which no headers appear.

concrete A durable construction material made of cement, water, sand, and a coarse aggregate (gravel or crushed stone). The mix is poured into and shaped in molds called forms. Distinguished from cement, which is the binder without the aggregate.

coping The cap or top course of a wall, parapet, balustrade, or chimney, usually designed to shed water.

corbel A projecting series of brick or stone courses that step upwards and outwards to support a cornice.

Corinthian order In classical architecture, an elaborate ensemble of column and entablature elements, particularly characterized by carved acanthus leaves and small volutes in the capital of the column. See also the more general term *order*.

corner window In the International Style, a steel-framed window that occupies a corner, rather daringly replacing the expected masonry there; made possible by curtain-wall construction.

cornice The crowning member of a wall or entablature, usually right beneath the roofline, often richly ornamented.

country estate Large rural farmstead owned by wealthy industrialists, with a showpiece home. In Delaware's Chateau Country, the estates were often 500 acres or more and embraced diversified agricultural endeavors that were managed scientifically.

course A horizontal layer of bricks or stones extending the full length and thickness of a wall.

cove ceiling A ceiling in which the transition between wall and ceiling is effected by a sizeable curving panel or molding. Sometimes called a coved ceiling.

cove cornice A cornice that includes a curving panel, casting a deep shadow. Sometimes called a cavetto cornice.

Craftsman A style of furniture and interior design popularized by *The Craftsman* magazine (1901–1916), published by Gustav Stickley (1858–1942), a proponent of the Arts and Crafts movement, which emphasized handicraft and truth to materials.

crenellation A regular series of indentations (crenels) alternating with block-like rising projections on the parapet of a building, often associated with castles; also called battlements.

cresting An ornamental railing, usually of metal or tile, along the ridgeline of a roof.

crossing In a church with a cruciform plan, the area at the center of the building where the arms of the cross intersect; in technical terms, the space where the transept crosses the nave.

crowstep gable A gable that ascends in steps rather than in a continuous slope; typical of Dutch colonial architecture.

cupola A small structure, sometimes with windows and sometimes with a dome, on top of a roof.

curtain wall In post-1890 skeleton construction, a thin, nonstructural exterior wall. Distinguished from the traditional load-bearing wall.

dado The lower few feet of an interior wall between the chair rail and the baseboard, equivalent to a classical pedestal and sometimes decoratively paneled or wallpapered.

Decorated English Gothic see *English Gothic*.

DelDOT The Delaware Department of Transportation.

dentil In the moldings of a classical entablature, a small ornamental block forming one of a tooth-like series.

diaper pattern An overall repetitive pattern on a flat wall surface, especially diamond-shaped or checkerboard grid, Sometimes called diaper work.

dike A wall or embankment built to prevent flooding, or an earthen causeway over a marsh, as built by early Dutch settlers in Delaware.

dog-ear A squared projection at the top of a door architrave; also called a crossette.

Doric order In classical architecture, an ensemble of column and entablature elements, often characterized by an unfluted column shaft and the use of decorative elements called triglyphs and metopes in the frieze of the entablature. See also the more general term *order*.

dormer A window projected forward from the plane of a sloping roof, as is typical of some bedrooms (French *dormir*, to sleep).

double-hung window A window consisting of a pair of frames or sashes, one above the other, arranged to slide up and down.

double-pile A house that is two rooms deep in plan and any number of rooms in width; distinguished from single-pile.

drum The cylindrical or polygonal wall upon which a dome rests; also, one of the cylinders of stone that form the shaft of a column.

Dutch Colonial Refers to buildings dating from the Dutch occupation of the Hudson River Valley and adjacent areas, including Delaware (c. 1614–1664).

Early English Gothic see *English Gothic*.

earthfast construction A convenient but impermanent means of building in colonial America, in which the wooden posts of the house were set directly in holes in the ground.

eave The edge of a roof that runs horizontally and usually projecting beyond the wall below; distinguished from the rake or verge, which slopes.

Ecclesiological movement A movement begun in Oxford and Cambridge universities, England, in the 1830s to emphasize the rituals and ideology of the Anglican Church. In architecture, Ecclesiologists advocated a revival of Gothic architecture.

Egyptian Revival Term applied to works that emulate forms in the visual arts of ancient Egyptian civilization.

engaged column A half-round column attached to a wall; distinguished from a pilaster, which is a flattened column.

English bond A pattern of brickwork, particularly sturdy, in which the bricks are set in alternating courses of all-stretchers and all-headers. As Flemish bond became popular early in the eighteenth century, English bond was restricted to rear elevations and to the lower parts of walls, below the watertable.

English Gothic The Gothic architecture of England (1190–1520), characterized by stone construction, pointed arches, and vaulted ceilings. Divisions of English Gothic are: Early English (1190–1275), with columns composed of clusters of shafts; Decorated (1275–1350), with a more elaborate treatment of decorative elements and window tracery; and Perpendicular (1350–1520), with a greater emphasis on verticality, linearity of decoration, and fan vaulting.

English Perpendicular see *English Gothic*.

entablature The beam, often elaborately ornamented, that is supported by columns in a classical order. It is divided horizontally into three parts: architrave, frieze, and cornice. The decorative moldings of each part are distinctive of the order to which the entablature belongs, most commonly Doric, Ionic, or Corinthian. See also the related term *order*.

eyebrow window A dormer with a very low, curved top, barely rising above the level of the surrounding roof.

facade An exterior front of a building, especially the principal one that includes the main entrance.

fanlight A semicircular or elliptical window over a door, with radiating mullions in the form of a fan.

fascia A plain, molded, or ornamented board that covers the horizontal edges (eaves) or sloping edges (verges) of a roof.

Federal A version of Neoclassical architecture popular in the United States during the decades following the establishment of the Federal Government in 1789; many of its forms were derived from the English Adamesque.

fenestration Window treatment: arrangement and proportioning.

finial A vertical ornament placed upon the apex of a gable, turret, or other architectural element. Distinguished from a pinnacle, which is a larger feature.

Flemish bond A pattern of brickwork in which stretchers and headers alternate in every row. Because this creates a more animated texture than English bond, Flemish bond came to be favored for front facades.

fluting A series of parallel grooves or channels (flutes) that adorn the shaft of a classical column.

folk A general term for regional, often ethnic, architectural traditions that exist largely independent of high-style fashions and are passed down orally, not through any architectural literature. See also the related term *vernacular*.

four-square house A hip-roofed, two-story house with four principal rooms on each floor and a symmetrical facade, common in suburbs, 1890s–1920s.

French Renaissance A cultural and artistic movement in France from the late fifteenth century to the early seventeenth century. In architecture, it is associated with the chateaux on the Loire River with round towers with conical roofs, steep slate roofs, and grand interior spaces.

fret A latticelike repetitive ornament that runs across a band.

frieze The broad horizontal band that forms the central part of a classical entablature; also, any long decorated horizontal band near the top of a wall.

front-gabled Term applied to a building whose principal gable end faces the front of the lot. Distinguished from side-gabled.

gable The triangular wall area below the end of a gable roof (a roof in which the two planes slope equally toward each other to a common ridge, as in a child's simple drawing of a house).

galleting Chips of stone pressed into a mortar joint.

gambrel A roof that has a single ridgepole but a double convex pitch. The lower plane, which rises from the eaves, is rather steep, the upper plane less so.

Georgian A popular term for high-style architecture of the later colonial period in British North America (during the reigns of George I to George III). As applied to American architecture, Georgian has often been used to describe any boxy, relatively elaborate classical building of the colonial or even Federal era. Some architectural historians avoid the term as imprecise.

Georgian Revival The revival of Georgian period forms from the 1880s to the present.

glazed-header Flemish bond A fancy technique in colonial brickwork, with bricks laid alternately long-side-out and short-side-out in every row (Flemish bond) and the short-side bricks (headers) showing a green, glassy glaze that resulted from their particular position in the brick kiln during firing.

Gothic Revival A movement in Europe and North America devoted to reviving the forms and the spirit of Gothic architecture and art. Gothic was a style prevalent in Europe during the medieval period (from the twelfth century to approximately the sixteenth century) and characterized by pointed arches and ribbed vaults, as in the great cathedrals. Gothic Revival originated in the mid-eighteenth century.

Greco-Egyptian A term used for buildings that combine elements from Greek architecture and Egyptian architecture.

Greek cross A building plan that forms a cross with four equal arms.

Greek Revival A movement in Europe and North America devoted to reviving the forms and spirit of classical Greek architecture, sculpture, and decorative arts. It dominated architecture in the United States during the years 1825–1850, with the pedimented temple front becoming popular for public buildings and private residences, often rendered in wood.

groin vault A complex ceiling shape formed by the intersection of two pointed-arch vaults, as in a Gothic cathedral.

half-timber In English medieval architecture, a variety of timber-frame construction in which the framing members were exposed on the exterior of the wall, with the spaces between filled with brick or other materials and covered in stucco. Commonly used to describe modern buildings with merely decorative timbers that emulate such construction for picturesque effect.

hall-parlor plan A simple type of house plan in which the ground floor consists of only two rooms, a smaller one (the parlor) and a larger (the hall). Historically, an earlier type than the center-passage plan.

hammerbeam A short horizontal beam projecting inward from the foot of the principal rafter and supported below by a diagonal brace tied into a vertical wall post. Hammerbeams carry much of the load of the roof trussing above.

header A brick laid all the way through the thickness of a wall, so that the short end of the brick shows on the exterior. See the related term *glazed-header Flemish bond*.

high style A term referring to relatively expensive and elaborate architecture, often designed by an architect, that shows an awareness of larger, cosmopolitan stylistic trends and fashions. High style is typically contrasted with "vernacular" or "folk," these being the generally more modest productions of regional (often rural) building traditions that exist more-or-less in isolation from national or international currents. The ideas behind high style architecture are transmitted by books, whereas vernacular architecture is frequently oral.

High Victorian Gothic A version of the Gothic Revival (associated with theorist John Ruskin) that originated in England in the 1850s and later spread to North America; characterized by polychromatic exteriors of brick and stone inspired by the Gothic architecture of northern Italy.

hipped roof A roof that slopes inward on each of its four sides as it rises. The edge where any two planes meet is called a hip.

Historic American Buildings Survey (HABS) A branch of the National Park Service of the United States Department of the Interior, established in 1933 to produce detailed documentation of American architecture by means of photographs and measured drawings, deposited in the Prints and Photographs Division of the Library of Congress.

Historic American Engineering Record (HAER) A branch of the National Park Service of the United States Department of the Interior, established in 1969 to produce detailed documentation of sites and structures associated with industry, transportation, and other areas of technology.

historicism, historicist, historicizing Terms referring to the use of historical styles and details in architecture. Often opposed to twentieth-century modernism, which generally eschewed such borrowings.

hood A canopy, molding, or pediment over a door. Sometimes called a hood molding.

I-beam The customary form of a beam of iron or steel, named for its shape in cross-section.

in antis Columns in antis stand in front of a recessed portico or niche and are set between, and on the same plane as, two projecting sections of wall.

International Style A style that originated in Europe in the 1920s and flourished across the globe into the 1970s. It rejected historicizing ornament and traditional building aesthetics in favor of stripped, smooth surfaces; extensive use of steel, plate glass, and reinforced concrete; flat roofs and ribbon windows; and plans rigorously determined by the building's function. The term was originally applied by Henry-Russell Hitchcock and Philip Johnson in their 1932 exhibition at the Museum of Modern Art, New York, and an accompanying book, *The International Style*.

Ionic order In classical architecture, an ensemble of column and entablature elements, intermediate in elaborateness between the Doric and the Corinthian; characterized by the use of large scroll-like volutes in the capital of the column. See also the more general term *order*.

Italianate A popular architectural style, originating in England and Germany in the early nineteenth century and prevalent in the United States between the 1840s and 1880s; characterized by prominent window heads and bracketed cornices. A subtype is the *Italianate Villa*, with arcades, balconies, and a campanile-like tower.

jamb The vertical sides of a door or window opening, amounting to the full thickness of the wall.

jerkinhead A gable roof in which the upper portion of the gable end is clipped, or slanted inward along the ridgeline, forming a small triangle of roof surface; also called a clipped gable.

jigsaw work Elaborately machine-cut wooden decorative elements popular in the nineteenth century, especially on porches.

joist One of a series of small horizontal beams that support a floor or ceiling.

keystone The central wedge-shaped stone at the crown of an arch.

lancet A very narrow, tall, pointed-arch window typical of Gothic and Gothic Revival architecture.

lath Wooden strips or metal mesh nailed to walls to hold plaster.

Latrobe-Mills Survey The hand-drawn *Survey of New Castle* (1805) by architect Benjamin Henry Latrobe and his assistant Robert Mills, which shows the streets of the Delaware town as part of a scheme to excavate and grade them properly. It includes watercolor depictions of many local buildings. Two versions were produced (today at the Delaware Public Archives, Dover, and New Castle Historical Society).

leaded window A window in which lead strips are used to secure the small panes of glass; originally a medieval type.

lintel A horizontal structural member that supports a wall over a window or door opening.

lunette A semicircular or segmental window; also, a semicircular area, especially one that contains a decorative treatment.

mansard roof A hipped roof with double pitch. The upper slope may approach flatness, whereas the lower slope is much steeper. The name is a corruption of that of seventeeth-century French architect François Mansart, who designed roofs of this type. They were revived in Paris during the Second Empire in the nineteenth century and became popular in America around 1865.

masonry Construction using stone, brick, or some other hard and durable material laid up in units and usually bonded by mortar.

massing The grouping or arrangement of the primary volumetric components of a building.

medieval Term applied to the period in European civilization between Antiquity and the Renaissance (about the fourth to the fifteenth centuries).

Mediterranean style Design type popular for houses in the 1920s, featuring tile roofs, stucco, and arcades.

Moderne Design work (1920s to 1940s) blending historicism and modernism, often with stylized forms from historical and non-western cultures or the machine aesthetic. Sometimes called Modernistic. See also the related terms *Art Deco*, *PWA Moderne*, and *Streamline Moderne*.

modernism A twentieth-century movement in the visual arts and culture (among many other arenas) that deliberately broke from tradition and emphasized innovation and progress. In the visual arts, this meant rejecting classicism and historicism and seeking inspiration in the forms and ideas of the fast-changing present. One phase was the International Style.

modillion cornice A cornice ornamented with numerous small brackets, each of which has a scroll. A modillion is larger than a dentil, which lacks the scroll. Derived from the Corinthian cornices of classical temples, the modillion cornice is one of the most distinctive elements of high-style American colonial architecture.

molding A band or running surface that bears a distinctive decorative profile (squared, curved, rounded, and so forth).

mortise-and-tenon joint In timber framing, a connection between two wooden members, one with a projecting piece (tenon) that fits into a hole (mortise) in the other. Once joined, the pieces are held together by a peg that is hammered through.

mullion A post or similar vertical member (traditionally stone) dividing a window into two or more units, or lights, each of which may be further subdivided (by muntins) into panes.

nave The largest space within a church; the area between the entrance (or the narthex) and the crossing; also, the central space of a church between the aisles.

neoclassicism, neoclassical Terms referring to a broad movement in the visual arts (beginning in the mid-eighteenth century) which drew its inspiration from ancient Greece and Rome. In architecture it encompasses both a strict archaeological revivalism that copied classical models and motifs as well as more inventive reinterpretations.

Néo-Grec An architectural style developed in connection with the Ecole des Beaux-Arts in Paris in the mid-nineteenth century and characterized by the use of highly stylized Greek elements and incised decoration, often in conjunction with cast iron or brick construction.

New Urbanism A sometimes controversial new approach to suburban development, now gaining wider currency; emphasizes increased density, more sidewalks, a mix of shops and residences, houses of varying sizes and types, and diversity of ages and incomes among residents.

niche A semicircular recess in a wall, often meant to contain sculpture or an urn.

nogging Brickwork that fills the spaces between members of a timber-frame wall.

Norman A residential style popular in the 1920s, based on picturesque rural houses of the French provinces of Normandy and Brittany, often with turrets and stuccoed walls.

notching Deep cuts at the ends of the logs that form a log house, locking the members together. A common type is v-notching.

oculus A circular opening at the top of a dome; literally "eye."

order The most important constituents of classical architecture, first developed as a structural-aesthetic system by the ancient Greeks. An order consists of an upright column with its capital that supports a horizontal entablature. The Greeks developed three different types of order, the Doric, Ionic, and Corinthian, each distinguishable by its own decorative system and proportions. All were taken over and modified by the Romans, who added two orders of their own, the Tuscan, which is a simplified form of the Doric, and the Composite, which is made up of elements of both the Ionic and the Corinthian.

oriel window A projecting polygonal or curved window unit, supported on brackets from below. Distinguished from a bay window, which rises from the foundation and does not appear suspended.

outbuilding In vernacular architecture, a service building detached from the house, such as a kitchen, smokehouse, or privy.

Palladian, Palladianism Terms referring to work inspired by the Italian Renaissance architect Andrea Palladio (1508–1580), particularly by means of his treatise, I Quattro Libri dell'Architettura (*The Four Books of Architecture*), published in 1570 and later disseminated throughout Europe in numerous editions. For generations, the *Four Books* transmitted the details of the Roman orders to a wide audience of architects and builders. Much Anglo-American high style architecture of the eighteenth century is rooted in a Palladian aesthetic.

Palladian motif A distinctive window or door type popularized by Andrea Palladio: a three-part composition in which a taller round-headed opening is flanked by two lower flat-headed openings and separated from them by columns, pilasters, or mullions. Also called a Palladian window or Venetian window.

paneling Wooden panels applied to an interior wall for sumptuous effect, often with central raised panels and carved moldings.

parapet A low wall at the edge of a roof, balcony, or terrace, sometimes formed by the upward extension of the wall below.

pargeting Stucco or plasterwork surfacing to a wall, sometimes decorated with figures in low relief; also, sometimes undecorated and textured with sand or pebbles.

parlor Traditionally the most formal room in a house, where guests were received.

pattern book Architectural guidebook with text and illustrations to assist builders, primarily in matters of aesthetics; popular from the mid-eighteenth century on.

pediment In classical architecture, a low triangular gable, as on a temple front; also, any similar feature above a door or window.

pent eave A shingled, roof-like overhang that runs between the first and second stories of a masonry house.

Perpendicular Gothic see *English Gothic*.

piazza Eighteenth- and nineteenth-century term for a porch or veranda; also, a plaza or square.

pier A square column.

pilaster A flattened column attached to a wall.

pilotis Architectural supports (columns, pillars, stilts) which lift a building above ground level to create a tall space underneath. Typical of International Style buildings.

pit house Typical habitation of the Woodland Indians in Delaware, consisting of a shallow, sunken pit with a hearth, surrounded by a wigwam-like structure of saplings; known from recent archaeological investigation of pit house features in the earth.

plank house A log house in which the logs are squared on two sides and usually fixed into grooved corner posts.

pointing The finish treatment for a masonry joint. In colonial brickwork, a line was generally struck or jointed through the soft mortar with a tool called a jointer. Reapplication of mortar to a joint during a restoration is called repointing.

polychromy The use of combinations of materials of various colors or the application of surface color for lively architectural effect.

porte-cochere A porch projecting over a driveway and providing shelter to people leaving a vehicle and entering the building.

portico A porch at least one story high consisting of a low-pitched roof supported on classical columns; more generally, any classical porch supported by columns.

post A vertical element of construction, typically supporting a beam.

Postmodern, postmodernism A movement in architecture (1960s–1980s) that reacted against twentieth-century modernism, particularly the Bauhaus and International Style, by making use of historicist and populist elements that modernists had shunned.

powder mill Water-powered mill designed for the manufacture of black powder, the explosive used in gunpowder.

pressed metal Thin sheets of metal (usually galvanized or tin-plated iron; sometimes called pressed tin) stamped into patterned panels for covering ceilings or walls or forming cornices (1870s to 1920s).

purlin In roof construction, a structural member laid across the principal rafters and parallel to the wall and ridge beam and supporting the light common rafters or boards.

PWA Moderne A style popular for government and institutional buildings erected by the Public Works Administration (1933), which became a division of the Federal Works Agency in 1939 and was liquidated in the 1940s. Blends the Moderne (either Art Deco or Streamline) with stripped Beaux-Arts classicism.

Quaker plan Colonial house plan consisting of a large hall with two smaller parlors adjacent; no longer considered typically Quaker, however.

Queen Anne A popular architectural style of the 1860s through the 1910s in England and the United States that revived forms of seventeenth-century vernacular architecture as well as those popular during the reign of Queen Anne (1702–1714). It is characterized by asymmetry in plan, complex roof forms, projecting bays and oriels, and the quirky use of classical motifs such as broken pediments and pilasters.

quoin One of the bricks or stones laid in alternating directions, which bond and form the exterior corner of a building; sometimes simulated in wood or stucco and exaggerated in size.

race A ditch that conducts water from a point on a river to a mill downstream; at the end of the race, the water drops and turns a waterwheel.

Regency Term applied to the fashions and culture of the period between 1800 and 1830 and named for the Prince Regent (reigned as George IV, 1820–1830) in England.

Renaissance The period in European civilization identified with a rediscovery or rebirth (*rinascimento*) of classical Roman architecture and art. Renaissance architecture began in Italy in the mid-1400s and reached a peak in the mid-1500s. In England and France, it began in the late 1500s.

reredos A decorative screen or wall behind an altar.

ribbon window In the International Style, a continuous horizontal strip of steel-framed windows, as made possible by curtain-wall construction.

Richardsonian Romanesque A late-nineteenth-century style popularized by Henry Hobson Richardson (1838–1886), characterized by round arches, rustication, and Romanesque details; popular for public buildings such as courthouses and libraries.

ridgepole The horizontal beam at the apex of the roof, to which the upper ends of the rafters are attached.

rock-faced Term applied to stone that has been left very rough on the face of a building.

rolling mill Water-powered mill with huge iron wheels that grind the ingredients of black powder.

Roman Revival Architecture that emulates the heavy, formal styles of the Imperial Roman period, especially as promoted by the Ecole des Beaux-Arts.

Romanesque Revival A term that refers to the architecture that appeared in the United States from the 1840s that revived the forms of Romanesque architecture of the eleventh and twelfth centuries in Europe, or to the Richardsonian Romanesque architecture that appeared after the 1870s. It is characterized by round-arch construction and massive masonry walls.

rustication, rusticated Masonry in which the joints are emphasized by sunk channels or grooves at the edge of each block. Sometimes simulated in wood or stucco.

sash Any framework of a window, either movable or fixed, but generally used to describe a wooden framework that slides in a vertical plane, as in a double-hung window.

scagliola A colorful composite material imitating marble, used for interior decoration.

Second Empire Not strictly a style but a term for the period in French history coinciding with the rule of Napoleon III (1852–1870). Largely derived from Visconti and Lefuel's New Louvre in Paris, the Second Empire style is characterized by mansard roofs, pedimented dormers, classical columns, and French Renaissance decorative motifs. Popular in the United States from the 1850s through the 1880s.

serpentine Green metamorphic rock quarried at West Chester, Pennsylvania, and popular as a building material in Delaware in the 1870s.

setback A stepping-back of the upper stories of a skyscraper to allow more sunlight to reach the streets, as mandated by law.

sgraffito A form of decoration made by scratching through wet plaster on a wall to expose a different colored under-surface. From Italian, *sgraffire* (to scratch).

shaft The tall part of a column between the base and the capital.

shaped chimney A chimney the top of which has been rendered ornamental by giving it a complex visual form.

shed roof A roof having only one sloping plane; sometimes called a lean-to.

Shingle Style A mode of American domestic architecture (1870s–1890s) in which wood shingles cover the roof and flow across the exterior wall planes. An ample living hall or stair hall is often a dominant feature. The term was coined in the 1940s by architectural historian Vincent Scully.

shotgun plan Long, narrow, vernacular house of the American South with the front door in the short side.

single-pile A house that is one room deep in plan and any number of rooms in width; distinguished from double-pile.

skeleton construction A system of construction, first used widely in the late nineteenth century for skyscrapers, in which loads are carried by a rigid framework of iron, steel, or reinforced concrete and the exterior walls are not load-bearing (curtain walls).

skintled bricks Misshapen bricks, often irregularly laid, popular for decorative effects in the 1920s.

smokehouse Farm outbuilding designed for smoking meats to cure them.

snuff mill Water-powered mill that grinds tobacco leaves into snuff, which is powdered tobacco meant to be ingested by snorting.

soffit The exposed underside of an overhead component, such as an arch, beam, eave, cornice, or lintel.

springhouse Farm outbuilding erected over a spring and meant for the cool storage of milk and other perishables.

Stick Style A mode of American domestic architecture (1850s–1870s) in which exterior wall planes are subdivided into bays and stories outlined by narrow boards called stickwork, reminiscent of half-timbering, but lighter and more skeletal. The term was coined by Vincent Scully in the 1940s.

Streamline Moderne A later phase of the Moderne, popular in the 1930s and 1940s and characterized by smooth wall surfaces with rounded corners, horizontal banding, and details suggestive of modern Machine Age aerodynamic forms.

stretcher A brick laid so that its long side shows on the exterior of the wall, as distinguished from a header.

stringcourse In masonry, a projecting horizontal band that runs between the different stories of a building. Sometimes called a beltcourse.

stripped classicism Simplified classicism popular in the 1930s for federal buildings and other public structures, in which moldings are pared down and ornament is more or less abstracted.

stucco A hard exterior finish, often textured, composed of Portland cement, lime, and sand, mixed with water. Essentially, a harder version of the interior finish called plaster. Also, a material used for decorative work or moldings.

stud A relatively lightweight vertical member (typically a two-by-four) in a wall, as in *balloon-frame* and subsequent construction.

surround An encircling border or decorative frame around a door or window.

swag An ornamental motif representing a suspended fold of drapery hanging in a curve.

sweet-potato house Farm building designed for the curing and storing of sweet potatoes.

temple-front Referring to a building with a prominent classical portico and pediment on the front facade, as was popular in the Greek Revival.

terra-cotta A hard baked-clay material, especially popular from 1870 to 1930, used internally for fireproofing or externally as a finish surface, where it is often glazed and multicolored.

terrazzo A hard, often colorful material used for flooring in public buildings, consisting of marble chips mixed with cement and then polished.

tholos A circular temple; also a circular tomb.

timber-frame construction A type of construction in which heavy timber posts and beams (often six-by-sixes and larger) are fastened using mortise and tenon joints and wooden pegs. Sometimes called heavy timber construction, it was largely supplanted by the balloon frame after 1830, in which light pieces of wood were nailed together, not pegged.

tracery In Gothic and Gothic Revival architecture, the curved, interlocking stone bars that hold the leaded stained glass.

transept The lateral arm of a cross-shaped church, usually between the nave (the area for the congregation) and the chancel (the area for the altar, clergy, and choir).

transom A narrow horizontal window over a door.

triglyph-and-metope frieze In a classical Doric entablature, a band ornamented with imitation beam-ends (triglyphs, for the three channels inscribed on them) and square panels between these (metopes, sometimes bearing sculpture).

trompe l'oeil An art technique creating an optical illusion that the depicted objects exist, instead of being two-dimensional images. From French, "trick the eye."

truss A rigid framework made up of triangular arrangements of beams, posts, braces, struts, and ties and used for the spanning of large architectural spaces or the construction of bridges.

Tudor Revival Early twentieth-century style emulating the visual arts of the Tudor period in English history (1485–1603), including decorative half-timbering and steeply pitched gable roofs; popular for domestic architecture.

Tuscan order In classical architecture, an ensemble of column and entablature elements, similar to the Roman Doric order, but without triglyphs in the frieze and without mutules in the cornice of the entablature.

urban renewal Refers to efforts (1950s and 1960s) to combat the decline of American cities resulting from suburban expansion after World War II. Urban renewal involved the razing of dense, old commercial and residential districts and building new highways, public housing, and government centers. By the 1970s, urban renewal was widely considered a failure.

Usonian house Dwelling type developed by Frank Lloyd Wright in 1936; a small, relatively inexpensive house designed on a rational, modular plan and featuring a radiant heating system embedded in the concrete floor slab.

vault An arched ceiling or roof.

vergeboard A fascia board attached to the sloping edges (verges) of a roof, sometimes ornamented with carved or jigsaw work. Also called bargeboard.

vernacular A descriptive term for the vast range of common, everyday buildings that are produced not by architects but by ordinary people. The vernacular tradition includes the practices of regional and ethnic buildings whose forms often remained relatively constant through the years. Generally contrasted with high-style architecture.

Victorian A term for a period in British and Anglo-American history from the coronation of Queen Victoria in 1837 to her death in 1901; in architecture, it often connotes the Gothic Revival, High Victorian Gothic, and Queen Anne styles.

volute A spiral scroll, especially the one that is a distinctive feature of the Ionic capital.

voussoir A wedge-shaped masonry unit with tapering sides used in the construction of an arch.

wainscot A decorative or protective facing of wood paneling applied to the lower portion of an interior wall. Sometimes called wainscoting.

watertable In masonry, the horizontal line on a building at which the foundation courses of brick step inward and the main walls properly begin; often adorned with specially shaped bricks.

weatherboard Board siding on a house; often used synonymously with *clapboard*.

winder stair A step, more or less wedge-shaped, with its tread wider at one end than the other. Also, in colonial houses, a small, cramped stair without landings, set into a closet-like space and with each step wedge-shaped.

Works Progress Administration (WPA) A federal program (1935–1943) created to provide jobs during the Great Depression. Many of the jobs involved constructing public buildings and roads.

wrought iron Iron hammered to improve the tensile properties of the metal; typically used for railings. Distinguished from cast iron, a brittle material formed in molds.

BIBLIOGRAPHY

Many of the following sources (published through mid-2005) mention specific buildings, as indicated in brackets. Other resources (not listed here) include newspaper articles from files at Delaware Public Archives and Wilmington Public Library; National Register nominations; archival materials; personal communication; and Internet sources. Many communities throughout Delaware are covered by walking-tour booklets, and local historical societies can provide additional information.

Abbott, Charles D. *Howard Pyle: A Chronicle*. New York: Harper & Brothers, 1925.

Adams, Theresa Catherine. "The Richards House, Locust Grove, Greenwood, Delaware." Master's thesis, Columbia University, 1980.

Ames, David L. *Architectural Style in Delaware*. Newark: Center for Historic Architecture and Engineering, University of Delaware, 1992.

Ames, David L., and Robert Dean. *Projected Population Growth and the New Arithmetic of Development in Delaware 1990–2020*. Newark: Center for Historic Architecture and Design, University of Delaware, 1999.

Ames, David L., et al. *Evaluation of the Brandywine Historic District National Register Nomination*. Newark: Center for Historic Architecture and Design, University of Delaware, 1991.

Archdeacon, Herbert. "The Breakwaters." *Journal of the Lewes Historical Society* 3 (November 2000): 20–28.

"Architectural Engineering" [Christiana Towers]. *Architectural Record* 151, no. 4 (April 1972): 143–46.

Art Work of Delaware [historic buildings]. Chicago: Charles Madison Co., 1898.

Athan, Jean C., and John R. Ward. "Wilmington Architects: An Oral History" [cassette tape interviews]. Delaware Society of Architects, 1982. Historical Society of Delaware, Wilmington.

Ayres, Harry V. *Hotel du Pont Story*. Wilmington: Serendipity Press, 1981.

"B. & O. Bridge Is in Service." *Morning News* [Wilmington] (12 December 1910).

Bankert, Jean E. *A History of New Castle Presbyterian Church, 1651–1989*. 1989.

Beckman, Thomas. "The Etchings of Robert Shaw" [colonial Wilmington]. *Delaware History* 24, no. 2 (Fall–Winter 1990): 75–108.

Beers, D. G. *Atlas of the State of Delaware*. Philadelphia: Pomeroy and Beers, 1868.

Bell, Christina. "Harvard House." 1996. www.lewes.com.

Bennett, George Fletcher. *Early Architecture of Delaware*. 1932. Reprint, Wilmington: Middle Atlantic Press, 1985.

———. *The Perennial Apprentice*. Wilmington: TriMark, 1977.

Benson, Barbara E. "Delaware Goes to War." *Delaware History* 26, nos. 3–4 (Spring–Summer 1995, Fall–Winter 1995–96): 143–203.

———. "Vanished Estates of the du Pont Family." *The Hunt* (June–July 2000): 66–78.

Blake, Guilford. "Rockford Park, a New Section of an Old Town." *Indoors and Out* (October 1905): 42–52.

Blevins, Wiley O., Jr. *Dear Old High: The Story of Wilmington High School*. Wilmington: Cedar Tree Press, 2000.

Boeschenstein, Warren. *Historic American Towns along the Atlantic Coast* [New Castle]. Baltimore: Johns Hopkins University Press, 1999.

Bonine, C. A. "Archaeological Investigation" [Ft. Swanendael]. *Archelog* 8, no. 3 (December 1956): n.p.

Booth, James C. *Memoir of the Geological Survey of The State of Delaware*. Dover: S. Kimmey, 1841.

Borah, Leo A. "Diamond Delaware, Colonial Still." *National Geographic* 68, no. 3 (September 1935): 367–98.

Bowers, Martha H. *Architectural Investigations on State Route 7*. Dover: Delaware Department of Transportation, 1988.

———. *Architectural Investigations on State Route 7 North Corridor*. Dover: Delaware Department of Transportation, 1986.

Bridgeville, Delaware. Bridgeville: Chamber of Commerce, c. 1931.

Buck, C. Douglass, Jr. Editorial. *Center Line* 9, no. 1 (Summer 1967).

Buggeln, Gretchen T. "Architecture as Community Service: West Presbyterian Church in Wilmington." In David Morgan and Sally M. Promey, *The Visual Culture of American Religions*. Berkeley: University of California Press, 2001.

Bushman, Claudia L. "Oaklands in Newark, Delaware: Then and Now." *Delaware History* 24, no. 3 (1991): 141–63.

———. *So Laudable an Undertaking: The Wilmington Library, 1788–1988*. Wilmington: Delaware Heritage Press, 1988.

Bushman, Richard L. *The Refinement of America: Persons, Houses, Cities* [Corbit-Sharp House]. New York: Knopf, 1992.

Caley, George L. *Footprints of the Past*. Smyrna, Del.: author, 1978.

Cannon, Patt, and Carol Kipp. *Centreville: The History of a Delaware Village, 1680–2000*. Centreville: Centreville Civic Association, 2001.

Carter, Edward C., II, John C. Van Horne, and Charles E. Brownell, eds. *Latrobe's View of America, 1795–1820*. New Haven: Yale University Press, 1985.

Castellano, Gene. "The Artists of Brandywine Springs: Revelations of Design and Use." *Delaware History* 31, no. 1 (Spring–Summer 2005): 1–31.

Castrovillo, Eugene F. *The History of Prince George's Chapel Dagsboro*. Dagsboro, Del.: author, 1985.

Cathey, Jennifer A., et al. *Threatened Resources in Delaware 2001–2002*. Newark: Center for Historic Architecture and Design, University of Delaware, 2002.

Chance, Elbert. "The Motion Picture Comes to Wilmington, Part II." *Delaware History* 25, no. 1 (Spring–Summer 1992): 33–57.

Chandler, Alfred D., Jr., and Stephen Salsbury. *Pierre S. du Pont and the Making of the Modern Corporation*. 1971; reprint, Washington, D.C.: Beard Books, 2000.

Chase, Susan Mulchahey. *Forever Green: A Commemorative History of Tower Hill School*. Wilmington: Tower Hill, 1994.

———. [Historical articles on Brandywine Park and vicinity.] Friends of Wilmington Parks Newsletter (1998–2004). http://www.brandywinepark.org/published_works.html.

———. "The Process of Suburbanization and the Use of Restrictive Deed Covenants as Private Zoning, Wilmington, Delaware, 1900–1941." Master's thesis, University of Delaware, 1995.

———. *Within the Reach of All: An Illustrated History of Brandywine Park*. Wilmington: Friends of Wilmington Parks, 2005.

[Christ Church, Dover.] *Architectural Record* 59, no. 5 (May 1926): 445–49.

Claro, Daniel, and Rebecca J. Sheppard. *Addy Cottage*. Newark: Center for Historic Architecture and Design, University of Delaware, 2003.

Clemons, M. Thomas. *Wilmington: Wide Is the City*. Photos by Willard Stewart. Wilmington: Hambleton, 1947.

Coghlan, Glady Mason. "The Ridgely House." *Delaware Antiques Show* (1975): 69–75.

"Concepts for the Decades Ahead." Wilmington: AIA Delaware, 1963.

Construction in Delaware. Wilmington: Chamber of Commerce, n.d.

Cooper, Constance J. *Rockford Tower*. Wilmington: Cedar Tree Press, 1990.

———. *350 Years of New Castle*. Wilmington: Cedar Tree Books, 2001.

———. *To Market, To Market, in Wilmington: King Street and Beyond.* Wilmington: Cedar Tree Press, 1992.

Corkran, W. S. *Henlopen Acres.* Newark: Press of Kells, c. 1930.

Cottrell, Robert Curtice. "Town Planning in New Castle, Delaware, 1797–1838." Master's thesis, University of Delaware, 1991.

Craig, Peter Stebbins. *The 1693 Census of the Swedes on the Delaware.* Winter Park, Fla.: SAG Publications, 1993.

Cram, Ralph Adams. *American Church Building of Today.* New York: Architectural Book Publishing Company, 1929.

Cullen, Virginia. *History of Lewes, Delaware.* Rev. ed. Lewes: NSDAR, 1981.

Custer, Jay F. "Stability, Storage, and Culture Change in Prehistoric Delaware." Dover: Delaware State Historic Preservation Office, 1994.

Dalleo, Peter T., and J. Vincent Watchorn III. "Slugger or Slacker? Shoeless Joe Jackson and Baseball in Wilmington, 1918" [Harlan and Hollingsworth]. *Delaware History* 26, no. 2 (Fall–Winter 1994–95): 95–124.

Davis, Steven. "The Early History of Cloud's Row and Its Place in the Philadelphia Tradition." 1996. Old Court House archives, New Castle, Delaware.

Daynes, Gary. "Cars, Carports, and Suburban Values in Brookside, Delaware." *Material Culture* 29, no. 1 (Spring 1997): 1–12.

De Cunzo, Lu Ann. *A Historical Archaeology of Delaware.* Knoxville: University of Tennessee Press, 2004.

Delaware: A Guide to the First State (WPA guidebook). New York: Viking Press, 1938.

Delaware Historic Bridges Survey and Evaluation. Dover: Delaware Department of Transportation, 1991.

Delaware: Its Products, Resources, and Opportunities. Wilmington: National Publishing Co., c. 1925.

"Delaware's Governors" [inc. houses]. www.russpickett.com/history

Demars, Kenneth R., et al. "[Dayett] Mill on the Christina." *University of Delaware News* 47, no. 2 (March 1981): 16–23.

Dickey, John M. "Historic Structure Report: The Brandywine Manufacturers Sunday School." Media, Pa., 1980.

Dixon, Stuart Paul. "Organizational Structure and Marketing at Delaware Furnace, 1821–1836." Master's thesis, University of Delaware, 1990.

Dobbs, Kelli W., and Rebecca J. Siders. *Fort Delaware Architectural Research Project.* Newark: Center for Historic Architecture and Design, University of Delaware, 1999.

———. *The Joseph Cleaver House, Port Penn.* Newark: Center for Historic Architecture and Design, University of Delaware, 1999.

Domestic Architecture of H. T. Lindeberg [Owl's Nest]. 1940; reprint, New York: Acanthus Press, 1996.

Dooley, David W. "The Geographic Diffusion of Art Deco Architecture in Delaware." Master's thesis, University of Delaware, 1999.

Downing, Andrew Jackson. *The Architecture of Country Houses.* New York: D. Appleton & Company, 1853.

Downing, M. Catherine. "The Parson Thorne Mansion—Its Owners and Occupants." *Archeolog* 18, no. 1 (1966): 1–7.

Du Pont, Alfred V. "Gabriel Francois Massena, 1902–1945." 1946. Historical Society of Delaware, Wilmington.

Du Pont, Alfred V., to A. I. du Pont. June 17, 1933. Accession 1508, Hagley Museum and Library, Delaware.

"Du Pont Company in Peace and War." *The Mediator* 3, no. 21 (1920s): 79–87.

Eberlein, Harold Donaldson, and Cortlandt V. D. Hubbard. *Historic Houses and Buildings of Delaware.* Dover: Public Archives Commission, 1962.

Eckman, Jeannette. "Historical Research Old Court House New Castle Delaware." 1953. Old Court House archives, New Castle.

———. *New Castle on the Delaware.* New Castle: New Castle Historical Society, 1950.

Editorial. *Center Line* (AIA Delaware) 4, no. 3 (October 1962): 7.

Editorial [Independence Mall]. *Center Line* (AIA Delaware) 5, no. 3 (November 1963): 2.

Edwards, Eliza Harvey. "Arden: The Architecture and Planning of a Delaware Utopia." Master's thesis, University of Pennsylvania, 1993.

Essah, Patience. *A House Divided: Slavery and Emancipation in Delaware, 1638–1865.* Charlottesville: University Press of Virginia, 1996.

Evans, Douglas J. "The History of Cape Henlopen Lighthouse 1764–1926." Senior thesis, University of Delaware, 1958.

Ferris, Benjamin. "A Sketch of the Proceedings" [Wilmington Friends Meeting House]. *Delaware History* 13, no. 1 (April 1968): 67–80.

Fields, Dale. "Willingtown Square." *Delaware Antiques Show* (1976): 45–51.

Fleming, E. McClung. "History of the Winterthur Estate." *Winterthur Portfolio* 1 (1964): 9–51.

Fleming, Nancy. *Money, Manure and Maintenance* [Marian Cruger Coffin]. Weston, Mass.: Country Place Books, 1995.

Foster, William D. "New Castle, Delaware." *White Pine* 12, no. 1 (1926).

Fox, Susanne N. "The Vogl House." *Delaware Antiques Show* (1976): 53–61.

Frank, Bill. "Who's a True Blue Delawarean?" [New Castle preservation]. *Wilmington Morning News* (October 31, 1963): 32.

Frebert, George J. *Delaware Aviation History*. Dover: Litho Printing, 1998.

From Crossroads to County Seat: A Bicentennial Look at Georgetown Delaware. Georgetown: Rogers Graphics, c. 1991.

Garrison, J. Ritchie, et al., eds. *After Ratification: Material Life in Delaware, 1789–1820*. Newark: Museum Studies Program, University of Delaware, 1988.

Gestram, Iris. "The Historic Landscape at Gibraltar—A Proposal for Its Preservation." Master's thesis, University of Delaware, 1997.

Gibson, George H. "Fullers, Carders, and Manufacturers of Woolen Goods in Delaware." *Delaware History* 12, no. 1 (April 1966): 25–53.

Gilchrist, Agnes A. "Documentary Supplement" [Sussex County Courthouse]. *Journal of the Society of Architectural Historians* 13, no. 4 (October 1954): 1–16.

Githens, Alfred Morton. "The Complete Development of the Open Plan" [Wilmington Library]. *Library Journal* 58 (May 1, 1933): 381–85.

Govatos Collection. Architectural drawings from twentieth-century firms. Delaware Public Archives, Dover.

Gowdy, Jim, and Kim Ruth. *Guiding Lights of the Delaware River and Bay*. Egg Harbor, N.J.: Laureate Press, 1999.

Grosvenor, Jewitt A. "The Wooden Architecture of the Lower Delaware Valley." *White Pine* 6, no. 3 (June 1920).

A Guide Between Washington, Baltimore . . . New York: J. Disturnell, 1847.

Haden, Amy, et al. *Victorian Lewes and Its Architecture*. Lewes, Del.: Lewes Historical Society, 1986.

Hakutani, Yoshinobu. *Theodore Dreiser's Uncollected Magazine Articles, 1897–1902* [New Castle Jail]. Newark: University of Delaware Press, 2003.

Hale-Byrnes-Boyce House: The Story Behind a Delaware Jewel. Delaware Society for the Preservation of Antiquities, 1999.

Hammond, H. Edgar, and Ruth L. Springer. "The Hendricksons of Crum Creek and the 'Old Swedes House.'" *Pennsylvania Genealogical Magazine* 22, no. 2 (1961): 45–82.

Hancock, Harold B. *Bridgeville*. Bridgeville Historical Society, 1985.

———. *The History of Nineteenth Century Laurel*. Westerville, Ohio: Otterbein College, 1983.

Hancock, Harold B., and Russell McCabe. *Milton's First Century 1807–1907*. Westerville, Ohio: Otterbein College, 1982.

Harlan, Marion. *More Colonial Homesteads and Their Stories*. New York: G. P. Putnam's Sons, 1899.

Harper, Deborah Van Riper. "'The Gospel of New Castle': Historic Preservation in a Delaware Town." *Delaware History* 25 (1992–1993): 77–105.

Heacock, Walter J. "Eleutherian Mills." *Delaware Antiques Show* (1965): 51–57.

Hein, Kara K., and Rebecca J. Siders. *A Documentary History of the Arsenal, New Castle, Delaware*. Newark: Center for Historic Architecture and Design, University of Delaware, 1998.

———. *A Documentary History of the Sheriff's House and Jail, New Castle, Delaware*. Newark: Center for Historic Architecture and Design, University of Delaware, 1998.

Heite, Edward F. *Mills on Wilson's Run* [Winterthur Estate Stone Walls]. Dover: Delaware Department of Transportation, 1992.

———. "Old State House." *Delaware Antiques Show* (1977): 115–25.

Heite, Edward F., and Louise B. Heite. "Report . . . of Fort Casimir." *Bulletin of the Ar-*

chaeological Society of Delaware no. 25, n.s. (Summer 1989).

Hempstead, Joshua. Remarks on Delaware log houses, 1749. In *Delaware History* 7, no. 1 (March 1956): 96.

Henry, Allan J. *The Life of Alexis Irénée du Pont*. 2 vols. Philadelphia: William F. Fell, 1945.

"Hercules Incorporated Headquarters." *Architectural Record* 173, no. 7 (June 1985): 164–65.

Herman, Bernard L. *Architecture and Rural Life in Central Delaware, 1700–1900*. Knoxville: University of Tennessee Press, 1987.

———. "Eighteenth-Century Quaker Houses in the Delaware Valley and the Aesthetics of Practice." In Lapsansky, *Quaker Aesthetics*, 188–211.

———. *The Stolen House*. Charlottesville: University Press of Virginia, 1992.

Hewlett, Richard Greening. *Jessie Ball DuPont* [Nemours]. Gainesville: University Press of Florida, 1992.

Higgins, Anthony. *New Castle Delaware 1651–1939*. Boston: Houghton Mifflin, 1939.

Hinsley, Jacqueline A. "Three Decades of Growth and Change at the Hagley Museum." In Robert Weible and Francis R. Walsh, eds., *The Popular Perception of Industrial History* (Lantham, Md.: AASLH Library, 1989): 21–38.

Historic American Buildings Survey (HABS), Delaware. http://memory.loc.gov/ammem/collections/habs_haer/.

Historic Buildings of Newark, Delaware. Newark Planning Department, 1983.

Historic Wilmington: A Guide to Districts and Buildings on the National Register of Historic Places. Wilmington: Department of Planning, 2002.

History of St. Luke's [Seaford] 1843–1968. 1968.

Hoffecker, Carol E. *Brandywine Village*. Wilmington: Old Brandywine Village, 1974.

———. "Church Gothic: A Case Study of Revival Architecture in Wilmington, Delaware." *Winterthur Portfolio* 8 (1973): 215–31.

———. *Corporate Capital: Wilmington in the Twentieth Century*. Philadelphia: Temple University Press, 1983.

———. *Wilmington, Delaware: Portrait of an Industrial City, 1830–1910*. Charlottesville: University Press of Virginia, 1974.

Holmes, William F. "Canal Versus Railroad." *Delaware History* 10, no. 2 (October 1962): 152–80.

Hutchinson, Henry H. "Collected Notes on Christ Church, Broad Creek, and Her Neighbors." *Archeolog* 15, no. 2 (Summer 1963). Reprinted with additions, Summer 1971.

Industrial Wilmington. Wilmington: George A. Wolf, 1898.

Jordan, Terry G., and Matti Kaups. *The American Backwoods Frontier: An Ethnic and Ecological Interpretation* [log houses]. Baltimore: Johns Hopkins University Press, in association with the Center for American Places, 1992.

Kaynor, Fay Campbell. "Thomas Tileston Waterman: Student of American Colonial Architecture." *Winterthur Portfolio* 20, nos. 2–3 (Summer–Autumn 1985): 103–48.

Keebler, Patricia Heintzelman. "The Life and Work of Frank Miles Day." 2 vols. Master's thesis, University of Delaware, 1980.

Kenton, Dave. *Milford*. Charleston, S.C.: Arcadia, 2001.

Kershaw, Christina E. "Contradictions, Contextuality and the Campus" [Trabant Center]. Master's thesis, University of Delaware, 2001.

Lala, Aimee C. "Delaware's Small Town Theaters." Master's thesis, University of Delaware, 2002.

Lanier, Gabrielle M. *The Delaware Valley in the Early Republic: Architecture, Landscape, and Regional Identity*. Baltimore: Johns Hopkins University Press, in association with the Center for American Places, 2005.

Lanier, Gabrielle M., and Bernard L. Herman. *Everyday Architecture of the Mid-Atlantic: Looking at Buildings and Landscapes*. Baltimore: Johns Hopkins University Press, in association with the Center for American Places, 1997.

Lapsansky, Emma J., and Anne A. Verplanck. *Quaker Aesthetics: Reflections on a Quaker Ethic in American Design and Consumption*. Philadelphia: University of Pennsylvania Press, 2003.

Lesley, J. P., ed. *The Geology of Chester County*. Harrisburg, Pa.: Second Geological Survey, 1883.

Lewis, Michael J. *Frank Furness: Architecture and the Violent Mind*. New York: Norton, 2001.

Lidz, Margaret Renner. "Dueling Identities: The Influence of the Family on the Winterthur Museum." Master's thesis, University of Delaware, 1999.

Littleton, Harold J. "Lombardy Hall: Delaware's 'First' Treasure." *Northern Light* (September 1986): 10–12.

"Living with Antiques: The Delaware Home of Mr. and Mrs. Lammot Copeland" [Mount Cuba]. *Antiques* 62, no. 4 (October 1952): 292–95.

Long, Irene. "The Queen [Theater] of Market Street." *Delaware History* 24, no. 3 (Spring–Summer 1991): 187–211.

Longworth, Joyce K., and Marjorie G. McNinch. *The Church of Saint Joseph on the Brandywine 1841–1994*. Wilmington: Saint Joseph, 1995.

Looking Back: A Century of Life in Downstate. Dover: Delaware State News, 2000.

Macdonald, Betty Harrington. *Historic Landmarks of Delaware and the Eastern Shore*. Lancaster, Pa.: Intelligencer, 1963.

"Many Changes in 4 of 15 Surviving Sussex County Camps." *Journal Every Evening* [Wilmington], July 30, 1937.

Marine, David. "Examination of the Pagan Creek Dike." *Archeolog* 7, no. 3 (June 1955): 1–2.

———. "Further Work on the Pagan Creek Dike." *Archeolog* 10, no. 1 (April 1958): 1–8.

Marine, David, and C. A. Bonine. "Excavations at the Thomas Maull House." *Archeolog* 17, no. 2 (1965): 7–12.

Marshall, Karen S. "The American Country House in the Greater Brandywine Valley." Master's thesis, University of Delaware, 2002.

Marshall, Karen S., et al. *The Old Stone Tavern*. Newark: Center for Historic Architecture and Design, University of Delaware, 2002.

Martin, Roger A. *In Our Midst: Delaware Vignettes in Pictures and Prose*. N.p.: author, 2000.

May, Edward Canby. "Wilmington of the Colonial Period." *Wilmington Every Evening* (November 27, 1928): 6.

Maynard, W. Barksdale. *Architecture in the United States, 1800–1850* [Summit Bridge]. New Haven: Yale University Press, 2002.

———. "A Log House for an Architect: Benjamin Henry Latrobe at Iron Hill." *Delaware History* 31, no. 2 (Fall–Winter 2005–2006): 97–124.

———. "New Castle's Dutch Tile House of 1687: Fraud or Genuine?" *Delaware History* 29, no. 3 (Spring–Summer 2002): 141–68.

———. "The Road Not Taken" [1940s preservation, New Castle]. *Colonial Williamsburg* 23, no. 1 (Spring 2001): 36–41.

McAndrew, John. *Guide to Modern Architecture: Northeast States* [Homsey buildings]. New York: Museum of Modern Art, 1940.

McEwing, Barbara Y. *The Witness of Market Street*. n.p. 1975.

McNinch, Marjorie G. "The Changing Face of Rodney Square." *Delaware History* 21 (1984–85): 139–63.

———. *The Silver Screen* [Wilmington Theaters]. Wilmington: Cedar Tree Books, 1997.

———. *Wilmington in Vintage Postcards*. Charleston, S.C.: Arcadia, 2000.

McWilliams, Carmen Ann. "Seaford, Delaware: 1938–1998: DuPont's Cinderella Story?" Master's thesis, University of Delaware, 1998.

Meehan, James D. *Rehoboth Beach Memoirs*. Bethany Beach, Del.: Harold E. Dukes, 2000.

Meginnis, Susan. Henry Clay Village map, based on 1902 survey. Hagley Museum and Library, 1973.

Merriweather, James. "School's History Traced" [St. Joseph's, Clayton]. *News Journal* [Wilmington] (September 23, 2003).

Milford, Maureen. "MBNA Claims Pieces of Wilmington's Elegant Past." *New York Times* (November 19, 2003).

Miller, William J., Jr. *Crossing the Delaware: The Story of the Delaware Memorial Bridge*. Wilmington: Delapeake, 1983.

Monigle, Joseph P. "Reconstructing a Legend: Immanuel Church 1980–1983." *Delaware Antiques Show* (1983).

Moore, S. S., and T. W. Jones. *The Traveller's Directory*. Philadelphia: Mathey Carey, 1804.

Moqtaderi, Nedda E. "History of the Robinson House, with an Emphasis on the Robinson Family, 1745–1851." Wilmington: Naaman's Heritage Association, 2003.

Munroe, John A. *History of Delaware*. 2nd ed. Newark: University of Delaware Press, 1984.

"New [Wilmington] General Hospital Built

around Old." *Architectural Record* 90, no 2 (August 1941): 84–86.

Odessa Yesterday. Odessa, Del.: Corbit-Calloway Memorial Library, c. 1980.

1-2-1-4 [Wilmington building trades journal, 1920s–1930s].

"Our Wealth of Granite." [Wilmington] *Board of Trade Journal* (Fall 1900): 15.

Plank, Margaret O., and William S. Schenck. *Delaware Piedmont Geology*. Newark: Delaware Geological Survey, 1998.

Procter, Mary. *Gritty Cities* [Wilmington]. Philadelphia: Temple University Press, 1978.

Progress [WPA for Delaware] 1, no. 1 (November 1935).

Pulinka, Steven M. *Discover the Historic Houses of Odessa*. Winterthur, Del.: Winterthur Museum, 1999.

———. "Success and Failure in Cantwell's Bridge" [Wilson-Warner House]. *Delaware History* 21 (1984–85): 53–72.

[Pyle, Howard.] "A Peninsular Canaan." *Harper's New Monthly Magazine* 59, no. 350 (July 1879): 194–208.

Quimby, Maureen O'Brien. "Brandywine Valley Estates: Two Centuries of Garden Tradition." Greenville, Del.: Hagley Museum, 1991.

———. *Eleutherian Mills*. Greenville, Del.: Hagley Museum, 1973.

Quinn, Judith A., and Bernard L. Herman. *Sweet Potato Houses of Sussex County, Delaware*. Newark: Center for Historic Architecture and Engineering, University of Delaware, 1988.

Rae, John B. "Coleman du Pont and His Road." *Delaware History* 16 (Spring–Summer 1975): 171–83.

Rendle, Ellen. "Another Look at Frank Zebley's Churches of Delaware." *Delaware History* 31, no. 1 (Spring–Summer 2005): 53–64 and subsequent issues.

———. *P.S. [Du Pont High School] We Love You*. Wilmington: Cedar Tree Press, 1993.

Report of Washington Street Bridge Commission. Wilmington: Star Publishing, 1923.

The Restoration and Rehabilitation of Immanuel Episcopal Church. John Milner Associates, 1984.

Robinson, Robert H. *Visiting Sussex Even If You Live Here*. Georgetown, Del.: author, 1976.

Roland, Carolyn Z. "Rodney Street Chapel/Westminster Presbyterian Church: Its Architects and Architecture." Master's thesis, University of Delaware, 1985.

Rooney, Audrey. "The Old Library" [New Castle]. Master's thesis, University of Delaware, 1984.

Ross, Elizabeth G. R. "Fort Miles: A Military Legacy of Adaptation and Resilience." Master's thesis, University of Delaware, 2002.

Saltmarsh, John A. *Scott Nearing: The Making of a Homesteader* [Arden]. White River Junction, Vt.: Chelsea Green, 1998.

Sarrabezolles-Appert, G., and M.-O. Lefevre. *Carlo Sarrabezolles* [Nemours]. Paris: Somogy, 2002.

Scharf, J. Thomas. *History of Delaware*. 2 vols. Philadelphia: L. J. Richards, 1888.

Schiek, Martha, and Ray Hester. *Claymont*. Charleston, S.C.: Arcadia, 2000.

Seely, Bruce E. "Pennsylvania Railroad Improvements in Wilmington, 1901–1908." *Railway History Monograph* 5, no. 4 (October 1976): 1–32.

———. "Wilmington and Its Railroads: A Lasting Connection." *Delaware History* 19, no. 1 (Spring–Summer 1980): 1–19.

Selections from the Architectural Work of E. William Martin F.A.I.A. and Associates. Wilmington: author, 1960.

A Self-Guided Tour of Historic Middletown, Delaware. Middletown: Downtown Revitalization Office, c. 2000.

1705–1955, Celebrating the 250th Anniversary. Middletown: St. Anne's Church, 1955.

Shields, Jerry. "Achiever at the Archives: The deValinger Era in Dover, 1930–1972." *Delaware History* 26, no. 2 (Fall–Winter 1994–95): 63–94.

Siders, Rebecca J., et al. *Delaware Agricultural Landscapes Evaluation 1998–1999*. Newark: Center for Historic Architecture and Design, University of Delaware, 2000.

Silliman, Charles A. *The Episcopal Church in Delaware 1785–1954*. Wilmington: Diocese of Delaware, 1982.

———. *The Story of Christ Church Christiana Hundred and Its People*. Wilmington: author, 1960.

Silver, Robert T. "Monumental Outdoor Sculpture in Wilmington." Master's thesis, University of Delaware, 1984.

Sisson, William A. "From Farm to Factory" [Henry Clay Mill]. *Delaware History* 21 (1984–85): 31–52.

Smith, Barbara Clark. *After the Revolution: the Smithsonian History of Everyday Life in the Eighteenth Century* [Delaware log house]. New York: Random House, 1985.

Stapleton, Darwin H., and Thomas C. Guider. "The Transfer and Diffusion of British Technology: Benjamin Henry Latrobe and the Chesapeake and Delaware Canal." *Delaware History* 17, no. 2 (Fall–Winter 1976): 127–38.

The State House: A Preservation Report. Dover: Hall of Records, 1976.

Stewart, Willard. "Photographs for the WPA and HABS." www.lib.udel.edu/digital/wsp/index.htm.

Sweeney, John A. H. *Grandeur on the Appoquinimink: The House of William Corbit at Odessa, Delaware.* 2nd ed. Newark: University of Delaware Press, 1989.

Taggart, Robert J. "Everett C. Johnson (1879–1926): Political Visionary and Eternal Optimist." *Delaware History* 25, no. 4 (Fall–Winter 1993–94): 215–36.

Thomas, George E. *William L. Price: Arts and Crafts to Modern Design* [Arden]. New York: Princeton Architectural Press, 2000.

Thomas, George E., Michael J. Lewis, and Jeffrey A. Cohen. *Frank Furness: The Complete Works.* New York: Princeton Architectural Press, 1996.

Thomas, Selma, ed. *Delaware: An Inventory of Historic Engineering and Industrial Sites.* Washington, D.C.: U.S. Department of the Interior, 1975.

Thompson, Mary Wilson. "Memoir," pt. 4. *Delaware History* 23, no. 4 (Fall–Winter 1979): 238–66.

Thompson, Priscilla M. "Creation of the Wilmington Park System Before 1896." *Delaware History* 18, no. 2 (Fall–Winter 1978): 75–92.

Toro, Lucille P. "The Latrobe Survey of New Castle 1804–1805." Master's thesis, University of Delaware, 1971.

Travers, Jim. *New Castle.* Charleston, S.C.: Arcadia, 2005.

A Tricentennial View of Frederica, Delaware 1683–1983. Dover: Dover Public Library, 1984.

University of Delaware Library Postcard Collection. www.lib.udel.edu/digital/dpc/.

Vallandingham, J. L., et al. *History of Pencader Presbyterian Church.* Wilmington: John M. Rogers Press, 1899.

Van den Hurk, Jeroen, et al. *Threatened Buildings Documented in Delaware, 1998–1999.* Newark: Center for Historic Architecture and Design, University of Delaware, 2000.

———. *Threatened Resources Documented in Delaware, 1997–1998.* Newark: Center for Historic Architecture and Design, University of Delaware, 1998.

Vincent, Gilbert T. *Romantic Rockwood.* Wilmington: Friends of Rockwood, 1998.

Volkman, Arthur G. "Delaware Rocks." *Delaware Today* (December 1973): 55–62.

Wade, William J. *16 Miles from Anywhere: A History of Georgetown, Del.* Georgetown: Countain Press, 1975.

Wall, Joseph Frazier. *Alfred I. du Pont: The Man and His Family.* New York: Oxford University Press, 1990.

Ward, Christopher L. "Autobiography," pt. 2. *Delaware History* 15, no. 4 (October 1973): 220–255.

Ward, Mary Sam. "Inns and Taverns in Delaware (1800–1850)." Master's thesis, University of Delaware, 1968.

Warrington, C. W. *A Mighty Fort Called Miles.* n.p.: Idyllwood Publishers, 1972.

Welsh, Peter C. "The Brandywine Mills: A Chronicle of an Industry, 1762–1816," *Delaware History* 7, no. 1 (March 1956): 17–36.

Weslager, C. A. "The Excavation of a Colonial Log Cabin Near Wilmington." *Bulletin of the Archaeological Society of Delaware* 6, no. 1 (April 1954).

———. *The Log Cabin in America.* New Brunswick: Rutgers University Press, 1969.

———. "Log Structures in New Sweden during the Seventeenth Century." *Delaware History* 5, no. 2 (September 1952): 77–79.

———. *The Richardsons of Delaware* [John Richardson House, Latimeria, etc.]. Wilmington: Knebels Press, 1957.

Wheelwright, Robert. "Goodstay." 1960. Hagley Archives, Hagley Museum.

"The Whipping-Post and Pillory in [New Castle] Delaware." *Harper's Weekly* 12, no. 624 (December 12, 1868): 791.

Whitehead, Russell J. "Harrie T. Lindeberg's Contribution to American Domestic Architecture." *Architectural Record* 55, no. 4 (April 1924): 309–72.

Whiteside, G. Morris. "Architecture." In *Delaware: A Guide to the First State.*

Wildes, Kristen Laham. "The Preservation of Historic New Castle: A Study in Perceptions." Master's thesis, University of Delaware, 2003.

Willey, Shannon. *Seaford, Delaware.* Charleston, S.C.: Arcadia, 1999.

Williams, William H. *The Garden of American Methodism.* Wilmington: Peninsula Conference, 1984.

"Wilmington 'Red Brick Town' for Years, Capt. [Edward Luff] Rice Recalls." [Wilmington] *Sunday Star* (April 19, 1931): 3.

Wilson, Anita. "Arden Revels Unmasked: A History of Theatre in Arden." Master's thesis, University of Delaware, 1961.

Wilson, W. Emerson. "The Cooch House in Battle." *Delaware Antiques Show* (1977): 35–41.

The Winterthur Story. Winterthur, Del.: Winterthur Museum, 1965.

Wolcott, Daniel F. "The Restoration of the Courthouse in New Castle." *Delaware History* 7, no. 3 (March 1957): 193–206.

Wolcott, Eliza. "George Read (II) and His House [New Castle]." Master's thesis, University of Delaware, 1971.

"Wood Craft" [Kip du Pont Boathouse]. *Architectural Record* 178, no. 8 (July 1990): 58–59.

Woolard, Annette. "Heart of Wilmington: The Life and Times of 'Old' Town Hall." *Delaware History* 24, no. 1 (Spring–Summer 1990).

The Work of Wallace and Warner, Philadelphia [Westover Hills]. Philadelphia: Franklin Printing Co., 1930.

Wright, Robert B. *The Homestead.* Rehoboth, Del.: Rehoboth Art League, 1993.

Young, Toni. *The Grand [Opera House] Experience.* Watkins Glen, N.Y.: American Life Foundation, 1976.

Zebley, Frank R., photograph collection [almost 900 Delaware churches]. 1930–1947. Delaware Public Archives, Dover.

ILLUSTRATION CREDITS

DPC   Delaware Postcard Collection, University of Delaware Library, Newark, Del.
DSHPO   Delaware State Historic Preservation Office, Dover, Del.
HABS   Historic American Buildings Survey, Prints and Photographs Division, Library of Congress
HAER   Historic American Engineering Record, Library of Congress
HML   Hagley Museum and Library
HSD   Historical Society of Delaware
UDA   University of Delaware Archives

Photographs not otherwise credited were provided by the author.

Maps by Eliza McClennen, Cartographer.

INTRODUCTION
Page 6, HABS (top) and Robert Montgomery Bird (bottom); p. 9, HABS (top and bottom); p. 11, HSD; p. 12, UDA; p. 13, HSD; p. 15, HML; p. 16, HSD; p. 17, DPC; p. 20, HML; p. 22, DSHPO; pp. 25, 28, HML; p. 29, DSHPO

BRANDYWINE HUNDRED
Page 33, BR3 HSD; BR4 Archmere Academy; BR8, BR10 DSHPO; p. 42, DPC; BR17 DSHPO; BR18 HABS; BR22 DPC; BR25 HML; BR26, BR26.4 DPC

CHRISTIANA HUNDRED
CH5 DSHPO; CH10.2, p. 62, DPC; CH12 DSHPO; CH15, CH15.1, CH15.5, CH19, CH21, CH22, p. 77, CH33 HML

WILMINGTON
Page 83, HSD; pp. 84, 87, HML; WL3 HSD; WL5 DPC; WL10 HAER; pp. 93, 95, HSD; WL19 HABS; WL21 HSD; WL24 HABS; WL29 HML; WL30 DPC; WL32, WL37, WL41, WL45 HSD; WL46 DPC; p. 118, WL50 HSD; WL52 DSHPO; WL54 HSD; WL57, p. 123, DPC; WL58, WL61 HSD; WL62 HML; WL63 HAER; WL66 HSD; WL76 DPC; WL77, WL80 HSD; WL81 DSHPO; WL85 DPC; WL86 DSHPO; p. 140, DPC; WL89, WL91 HML; WL94 DSHPO

NEW CASTLE HUNDRED
NC3, p. 150, HSD; NC8, NC15 DSHPO; NC19 HABS; NC21 HSD; p. 162, DPC; NC23, NC24 HABS

MILL CREEK AND WHITE CLAY CREEK HUNDREDS
MC10, MC11, MC12 HABS

NEWARK AND WHITE CLAY CREEK VALLEY
NK1 DSHPO; NK6 HABS; NK9 UDA; NK9.1 HABS; NK9.7 UDA

PENCADER AND RED LION HUNDREDS
Page 193, HSD; PR3 DPC; PR8, p. 198, PR12 DSHPO; PR15 DPC; PR16 DSHPO; PR17 DPC; PR21 HABS

LOWER NEW CASTLE COUNTY
LN1 HAER; LN2 HABS; LN5 HSD; LN8, LN11, LN17 HABS; LN18 DSHPO; LN20 HAER; LN23 HABS; LN24 DSHPO

KENT COUNTY
KT1 HABS; KT12 DSHPO; KT14 DPC; KT15, KT16 HABS; KT17 DSHPO; KT18 HABS; KT21, KT22 DSHPO; KT23 HABS; KT25 DPC; KT26 HABS; KT27, KT28, KT29, KT31 DSHPO; KT33 HABS; KT36 DSHPO; KT38 HABS

DOVER
Page 247, DPC; DV1 Dover International Speedway, Inc., and Getty Images; DV6 DPC; DV7 HAER; DV8 HABS; DV11 DSHPO; DV12 DPC; DV13 HSD; p. 254, HABS; DV14 DSHPO; DV15, DV16, DV17 DPC; DV19 Becker Morgan Group

EASTERN SUSSEX COUNTY
Page 259, DPC; p. 266, Delaware Public Archives; p. 267, HML; ES14 HABS; ES18 DSHPO; ES19 HSD; ES23 DPC; ES24 DSHPO; ES25 DPC; ES28 HML; ES28.1 HABS; ES29 DPC; ES37 Figg Engineering Group; ES38 Davis, Bowen and Friedel, photo by Gary Marine; ES40 DSHPO; ES41 HABS; ES43 DPC

WESTERN SUSSEX COUNTY
Page 285, DPC; WS4 HABS, drawn by T. Catherine Adams; WS6, WS8, WS10 HABS; WS15 HAER; WS16, WS18, WS19, WS20 HABS; WS22 Ned Fowler; WS23, WS25 HABS

INDEX

Properties named for individuals or families with a given surname are indexed in the form *surname (first name)*, and page numbers in **boldface** refer to illustrations.

Abbott, Ainsworth, 284
Abbott's Mill Nature Center, 284
Academy Building, Middletown, 217
Academy Building, University of Delaware, 182–83
A. C. Durham and Associates, 276
Achmester, 15, 215, **215**
Acrelius, Israel, 89
Adams, John, 96
Adams, John M.: Smith Hall, University of Delaware, 186
Adams, Keith, 215
Adams, T. Catherine, 286
Adams (Joseph T.) House, 261
Addy, John M., 282
Addy Cottage, 281–82
African American history and architecture, 15–16
   Antioch Camp Meeting, 297
   and Barratt's Chapel, 239
   and Civilian Conservation Corps (CCC), 231
   Delaware State University, 248
   Hockessin Community Center (Hockessin School 107-C), 166, **166**
   Howard High School, 90–91
   Iron Hill Museum (Iron Hill School No. 112C), 193
   Jason Building, Delaware Technical and Community College (William C. Jason Comprehensive High School), 265
   Morning Star Institutional Church of God in Christ (Whatcoat Methodist Episcopal Church), 235–36
   Polktown, 203
   Providence Creek Academy (St. Joseph's Industrial School), 225, **225**
   See also slavery and slave trade
agricultural buildings, 14
   Chipman Sweet Potato House, 14, **296**, 296–97
   Delaware Agricultural Museum and Village, 14, 248–49
   Frink Center for Wildlife, Tri-State Bird Rescue Center, 176
   Winterthur Farms Dairy Buildings, 63
   See also barns; farms
A. I. du Pont Hospital for Children (A. I. du Pont Institute), 50–51
Aiken's Tavern (Glasgow Hotel), 196
Air Mobility Command Museum, 257
airports: New Castle County Airport (Greater Wilmington Airport), 149
Air Service hangar, 149, **149**
Aldersgate United Methodist Church, 26, 53
Alexander House, 159
Alexis I. du Pont Middle School (Public School, U.S. Districts 23 and 75), 72, **72**
Alison, Dr. Francis, 182–83
Allee, Abraham, 231
Allee House, 14, 231, **231**
Allee Mansion. *See* Tudor Manor Hotel, Dover
Allen, William F., 288, 291, 293
Allen J. Saville Inc.: Westover Hills, 72–73
Allison Platt and Associates, 118
Allmond, Henrietta, 89
Alrichs, Jacob: Wilmington Friends Meeting House, 113, **113**
American Automobile Association (AAA) headquarters, 92
American Car and Foundry Company, 21
American Decorative Glass Company, 116
American Institute of Architects (AIA), Delaware Chapter, 17, 26, 28, 99, 117–18, 122, 190
American Life Insurance Building, 109
Ames, David, 13, 231
Ammann, O. H.: Delaware Memorial Bridge, **148**, 148–49
Ammann and Whitney: Delaware Memorial Bridge, **148**, 148–49
Amstel House, 160, **160**, 233; garden, 160
Amtrak Bridge over Naamans Creek, 35
Amtrak viaduct arches (Pennsylvania Railroad), Wilmington, 46, 92, **92**
Amtrak Wilmington Shops (Pennsylvania Railroad), 92, 126–27, **127**
Anderson, Peter C.: Tower Hill School Library-Science Building, 144
Anderson and Barr: Fourteen Foot Bank Lighthouse, 238, **238**
Anderson Brown Higley Associates, 18–19
   Education and Technology Building, Delaware Technical and Community College, 111, **111**

Anderson Brown Higley Associates (*continued*)
   Grace United Methodist Church, addition, 115
   McLaughlin-Mullen Student Life Center, Archmere Academy, 36
   Memorial Hall, University of Delaware, restoration, 184–85
   St. Anne's School, Middletown, 219
Andrews, Doug, 109
Aniline Village, 36
Anna Hazzard Museum, 277, **277**
Ann Beha Architects
   Delaware Art Museum (Delaware Art Center), 142–43
   Portland Museum of Art, Maine, 142
   Taft Museum, Cincinnati, Ohio, 142
Anthony, John, 229
Antioch Camp Meeting, 297
apartments and condominiums
   Brandywine Park, 45
   1401 Condominiums, 137, **138**
   Olde Colonial Village, 51
   Westcourt Apartments (Foster Park Apartments), 135
Appoquinimink Friends Meeting House, 214, **214**
archaeology, 3–5, 7, 8, 153, 163, 268
Architects Collaborative, 144
Architects Studio, 19
   Legislative Hall (State Legislative Building), 255–56
   New Castle County Library Brandywine Hundred Branch, 52
Archmere, 24, 35–36, **36**
Archmere Academy, 36
Arden, 14, 17, 32, 37–40; map, 38
Arden Forge, 39, 40
Arden School, 40, 278
Arsenal, New Castle, 155–56, **156**
Art Deco style, 42, 76, 88, 97, 100, 102, 117, 118, 119, 133, 147, 252
Arthurs, Stanley, 124, 137
Artisan's Savings Bank. *See* Historical Society of Delaware (Artisan's Savings Bank)
Arts and Crafts movement, 14, 36, 37–40, 130, 190, 203, 286
Asbury, Francis, 239
Asbury United Methodist Church, Smyrna, 227, 228
Ashland and vicinity, 79–81; map, 80

Ashland Covered Bridge, 80
Ashland Nature Center, 79
Ashton, John, Jr., 208
Ashton, Robert, 208
Ashton (John) House, 208, **208**
Aspendale, 8, 224, **225**, 238
Associated Federal Architects: Wilmington Trust Center (United States Post Office, Court House, and Custom House), 105
AstraZeneca, 53
Astropower (former), 195, **195**
Atlas of the State of Delaware (Beers), 23, 270
Auburn Heights, 14, 80–81, **81**
Au Clair School (McCoy House), 199, **199**
Augustine Bridge, 126
Augustine Inn (Augustine Beach Hotel), 209–10
Augustine Mills, 45, 126
Aull Houses, 161
Automobile Row, west Wilmington, 42, 133, **133**
Avon Products Northeast Regional Headquarters, 42, 177, **177**
Ayers/Saint/Gross
   Lammot du Pont Laboratory, University of Delaware, 180–81
   Roselle Center for the Arts, University of Delaware, 181
   Wolf Hall restoration, University of Delaware, 183

Bachtle, Edward
   Fountain Plaza, northwest Wilmington, 136, **136**
   Hale-Byrnes House landscaping, 170
   Soldiers and Sailors Monument landscaping, 139
Bader, John A., 83, 216
Bailey, O. H., 261
Bailey, Richard S., 275
Baird, Stephen, 101
Baker, Louis Carter, Jr.: St. Francis Renewal Center (Samuel N. Trump House), 41
Baker and Dallett, 17
   Bassett Hall parsonage, Wilmington, 115
   Delaware Health and Social Services Herman M. Holloway Sr. Campus (Delaware State Hospital), 146–47, **147**
   Episcopal Church of Saints Andrew and Matthew (St. Andrew's), 113–14

Balano, Paula Himmelsbach, 134, 178
Baldwin, Joseph, 159
Ballinger and Perrot: Union Park Gardens, 134–35
Ballinger Company: John Bassett Moore Intermediate School, 226
Baltimore, Lord, 2, 283
Baltimore, Md.
   Enoch Pratt Library, 103
   Johns Hopkins University, 184–85
   Mount Vernon Place Methodist Episcopal Church, 114
   Peabody Institute, 108–9
   Sheppard and Enoch Pratt Hospital, 164
   World Trade Center, 109
Baltimore and Ohio (B&O) Railroad, 23
Baltimore and Ohio (B&O) Station, Newark, 173
Baltimore and Ohio (B&O) Station, Trolley Square, Wilmington, 16–17, 135
Baltimore Hundred, 282
Bancroft, Joseph, 143
Bancroft, Samuel, 139
Bancroft, William P., 123, 129–30, 140, 143
Bancroft Mills, 143, **143**
Bank of Delaware, 26, 278
banks
   Bank of Delaware, 26, 278
   Citizens Bank (Fruit Growers' National Bank and Trust Company), Smyrna, 228
   Delaware State Bar Association (Farmers Bank), Wilmington, 96
   Delaware Trust Bank, Dover, 246
   Farmers Bank, Georgetown, 263
   First National Bank, Harrington, 243
   Historical Society of Delaware (Artisan's Savings Bank), 97
   Levy's Loan Office (Central National Bank), 97
   Odessa Bank, 214
   office building (Bank of Delaware), 141–42, **142**
   Old Farmers Bank, New Castle, 161
   PNC Bank (National Bank), Smyrna, 228
   Wilmington, 85–86
   Wilmington Savings Fund Society, 102

Wilmington Trust Building (Brandywine Trust and Savings Bank), 118
Bannister Hall, **229,** 229–30
Banta, Claude, 43
Barber, Joel: Hotel du Pont, Wilmington, 106–7
Barczewski, Steven B., 196
barns
    Barrel Barn, Georgetown, 265
    Blue Ball Barn, 33
    Cherbourg Round Barn, 14, 234, **234**
    Cloud's Farm, 14, 80
    Corner Ketch Barn, **9**
    Simon Hadley Barn, 165
Barratt's Chapel, **239,** 239–40
Barrel Barn, Georgetown, 265
Bassett, Richard, 295
Bassett Hall parsonage, Wilmington, 115
Bates, Colonel Daniel Moore, 56, 144, 151–52
Bauduy, Pierre, 54, 98, 142, 146
Bayard, Thomas F., 140
Bayard (Thomas F.) House, 144
Bayard Sharp Hall (St. Thomas Church), 187
Baynard, Samuel H., 126
Baynard Boulevard Historic District, 126
Bear, 195
Beard, Duncan, 211
Beaver Valley, 5
Becker Morgan Group
    Dover Air Force Base Mortuary Facility, 257, **257**
    Dover Downs and Dover International Speedway, **247,** 247–48
    Kent County Courthouse (new), 254
Bedford, Gunning, Jr., 51–52
Bedford (Gunning) House, 161
Beers, D. G., 229, 270
Beitel, Jeffrey C.: Centreville Reserve, 57, **57**
Bell, John, 232
Bellanca, Giuseppe, 149
Bellevue Hall, 41, **41,** 43
Belmont Hall, 230, 233
Belville, Jacob, 156
Beman, Solon S.: Ursuline Academy Performing Arts Center (First Church of Christ Scientist), 130
Ben-Ami Friedman and Associates: Middletown plaza, 216
Beneficial Building, Wilmington, 110

Bennett, George F., 27
    Allee House restoration, 231
    and Brecknock, 235
    and Buck Tavern, 199
    Cannonball House restoration, 271
    Legislative Hall (State Legislative Building), 255–56
    Lewes Historical Society Complex restoration, 268
    Maull House restoration, 268
    and Old State House, 255
Beracah Homes (Nanticoke Homes), 284–85
Bernardon Haber Holloway
    Aldersgate United Methodist Church, 53
    Astropower (former), 195, **195**
    Buena Vista renovation, 164
    Dickinson Mansion renovation, 236
    George V. Massey Station (Pennsylvania Station), 251
    Indian River Life Saving Station restoration, 280–81
    New Castle Arsenal renovation, 156
    New Castle Court House renovation, 159
    office building (Bank of Delaware) renovation, 142
    Old State House restoration, 255
    Zwaanendael Museum (Zwaanendael House) restoration, 272
Betelle, James O., 17
    Howard High School, 90
    Iron Hill Museum (Iron Hill School No. 112C), 193
Bethany Beach, 281–82
Bethel, 293–94; map, 294
Beth Emeth Synagogue, 129, **129**
Beth Shalom Synagogue, 126
Bevan, Catherine, 159
Beyer, Joseph, 116
Biddle, George Read, 93
Bide-a-wee, 40
Biden, Joseph, 126–27
Bidermann, Evelina du Pont, 60
Bidermann, James A., 60
Biggs, Benjamin T., 217
Bird, John, 159
Bird, Robert Montgomery, 159
Bird (Thomas) House, **6,** 7, 88
Bird Transfer Company, 91
Birkenhead Mills, 66
Bissell, E. Perot: Winterthur, 17, 60–61
Björk, Reverend Eric, 89
Black, Samuel Henry, 196

Blake, Weston Holt, 17, 27
    Rodney Street Chapel remodeling, 138
    Wilmington Friends Meeting House, 113, **113**
Bleich, Morton E., 97; Dorset Apartment Building, northwest Wilmington, 137
Bloch and Hesse: Beth Emeth Synagogue, 129
Blocksom's Colored School, **15**
Bloor, Eva Reeve, 38
Blue Ball Barn, 33
Blue Ball Tavern, 33
blue rock, 10–11, 46–47
Boardwalk and Rehoboth Avenue, Rehoboth Beach, **276,** 277
Boden, Mrs. Harry C., 170
Boell, William, 92
Bombay Hook National Wildlife Refuge, 231
Bonine, Chesleigh A., 268
Bonner, William, 17
Booth, James, Jr., 159
Booth, James, Sr., 159
Booth, James C., 11, 46
Booth (James) House, 159
Boothhurst, 146
Borah, Leo, 200
Boston, Charles J., 116
Boston, Mass.
    Christian Science Administration Building, 109
    John Hancock Tower, 109
Bradbury, Calif.: Pearce (Wilbur) House, 43
Bradford, Thomas B., 251
Brambles, The, Arden, 38
Bramshott, 56
Brandywine Academy, 121–22
Brandywine Garden Club, 160
Brandywine Granite Quarry, 11, **11,** 46–47, 64, 126
Brandywine High School, 32
Brandywine Hundred, 32–54
    Arden, 37–40; map, 38
    Claymont, 33–36; and vicinity map, 34
    south and west, map, 49
    south of Arden, 41–45
    vicinity of Brandywine Creek and along Concord Pike, 45–54
Brandywine Manufacturers' Sunday School, 68, 69
Brandywine Park, 123, **123.** *See also* Brandywine Village and Park
Brandywine Park Condominiums, 45

Brandywine Pumping Station and Waterworks, 46, 118–19, **119**
Brandywine Springs Park, 168
Brandywine Village and Park, 22, 117–26, **118**; map, 121
Brandywine Zoo, 123
Brantwyn (Bois-Des-Fosses), 54
Breck, William, 71
Brecknock (Howell's Mill Seat), 235, **235**
Breck's Mill, 71, **71**
Breckstone Group, 102; The Mill at White Clay (Joseph Dean and Son), 178, **178**
Breuer, Marcel, 109
brick construction, 10, 82
Brick Hotel, Georgetown, 263, 264, **264**
Brick Hotel, Odessa, 214, 264
Brick Mill House. *See* Richardson (John) House (Brick Mill House)
bridges, 21–22
    Amtrak Bridge over Naamans Creek, 35
    Ashland Covered Bridge, 80
    Augustine Bridge, 126
    Cantwell's Bridge, 210
    CSX Railroad Bridge (Baltimore and Ohio Railroad Bridge), **125**, 125–26
    Delaware Memorial Bridge, 22, **148**, 148–49
    Indian River Inlet Bridge, 281, **281**
    I-95 Bridge, Wilmington, 125, **125**
    J. Tyler McConnell highway bridge, 47
    Marshallton Bridge, 77
    North Market Street Bridge, Wilmington, 21, 117, 119
    Old St. Georges Bridge, 200–201, **201**
    over Red Clay Creek, 55
    Paper Mill Road covered bridge, 173
    Pratt Truss Bridge, 79
    Reedy Point Bridge, 203
    Rising Sun Bridge, **71**, 71–72
    Rockland Bridge, 54
    Seaford Bridge (State Bridge No. 151), 292, **292**
    Senator William V. Roth Jr. Bridge (DE 1 Bridge, St. Georges Bridge), 199–200, 281
    Smith's Bridge, 22, 54
    Stanton Bridge, 170
    Summit Bridge, 197
    Summit Covered Bridge, **193**

Van Buren Street Bridge and Aqueduct, 124–25
Washington Memorial Bridge, 122, **122**, 124
Wire or Swinging Bridge, 126
Wooddale Covered Bridge, 22, **22**, 78, 80
Bridgeville, 24, 284, 286–87; map, 287; west of, 287–88
B. Ridgway and Son, 116
Brilmaier, E.: St. Hedwig's Roman Catholic Church, 131
Brinckle, John R., 144–45
Brinckle-Maxwell House, 171
Bringhurst Drugstore, Wilmington, 95
Bringhurst family, 44
Britt, John, 89
Brockhouse, John, 124
Brockie, Arthur Howell
    Founders Hall (main building), St. Andrew's School, Middletown, 219–20
    St. Andrew's School, Middletown, **219**, 219–20
Brongniart, Alexandre Théodore, 48
Brook Ramble, 221, 225
Brookside, 25, 190–91
Brookview Apartments, 36
Brown, H. Fletcher, 265
Brown, Walter Stewart, 108
Brown, William H.: Amtrak viaduct arches (Pennsylvania Railroad), Wilmington, 92, **92**
Brown and Whiteside, 17, 18, 42
    Alexis I. du Pont Middle School, 72, **72**
    Central Young Men's Christian Association (YMCA), **115**, 115–16
    Delaware Children's Theater (New Century Club) addition, 130
    Delaware Health and Social Services Herman M. Holloway Sr. Campus facilities, 147
    Delmarva Power and Light Company, 100
    First and Central Presbyterian Church, Wilmington, 108
    Historical Society of Delaware (Artisan's Savings Bank), 97
    Immanuel Episcopal Church, northwest Wilmington, 138
    Kuumba Academy Charter School, 99
    Read House renovation, 163

Tower Hill School, northwest Wilmington, 144
and Western Hills, 72
Wilmington Trust Center (United States Post Office, Court House, and Custom House), 105
Brown v. Board of Education, 91, 166
Bryan, William Jennings, 229
Brynberg, Peter: Old Town Hall, Wilmington, **98**, 98–99
Bryn Mawr College, Pa., 187
Buccini/Pollin Group
    Nemours Building, 107–8
    Residences at Rodney Square, 102
Buck, C. Douglass, 164, 203, 230, 266–67, 278
Buck, C. Douglass, Jr., 20, 26
Buck Simpers Architect + Associates
    Carvel State Office Building renovation, 102
    Central Young Men's Christian Association (YMCA) renovation, 116
    Community Service Building (Montchanin Building), Wilmington, 108
    Delaware Cadillac renovation, 133
    Enchanted Woods, Winterthur, 64
    Justin E. Diny Science Center, Archmere Academy renovation, 36
    May B. Leasure School, 195
    New Castle County Courthouse, 96, **97**
    Thurgood Marshall Elementary School, 195, **195**
    Town Hall, New Castle, renovation, 157
    William B. Keene School, 195
Buck Tavern, 29, 197, 199
Budovitch (Isaac) House, 52
Bue, John: Tower Hill School Library-Science Building, 144
Buena Vista, 164, **164**, 203
Buffalo, N.Y.: Larkin Building, 110
Buist, Robert, 163
Bulah, Sarah, 166
Bulfinch, Charles, 181
Burkavage Design Associates: Justin E. Diny Science Center, Archmere Academy, 36
Burkland, Raymond A., 190–91
Burnham, Wilbur Herbert, 116, 271

Burns, Charles M.: St. Peter's Episcopal Church, Smyrna, 227–28
Burr, Aaron, 96
Burr House, 34
Burton, William, 244
Burton Brothers Hardware Store, **291**, 291–92
Burton (Hiram Rodney) House, 268
Burton-Ingram House, 27–28, 268
Bushell, Robert, 167
Button, Stephen Decatur, 17
  Immanuel Episcopal Church on the Green, New Castle, 154–55
  Wilmington Almshouse, 146–47
Buzz Ware Village Center, 40
Byrnes, Daniel, 170

Cab Calloway School of the Arts (Wilmington High School), 26, 135, **135**
Caesar Rodney Equestrian Monument, 104
Camac, William M., 154
Camden, 234–36; map, 237
Camden Friends Meeting House, 235, **235**
camp meetings, 3, 276, 297–98
Canby, Henry Seidel, 116, 139
Canby, James, 116
Canby, Oliver, 117
Canby, Samuel, 123
Canby, William M., 123, 131, 140
Canby (Henry) House, 56
Cannon, Jacob, 293
Cannonball House (David Rowland House), 271
Cannon family, 293
Cannon Hall, Woodland, 293, **293**
Cannon House, Bridgeville, 286
Cantwell's Bridge, 210
Capaldi, Emilio
  Independence Mall, 51, **51**
  Olde Colonial Village, 51
Cape Henlopen Lighthouse, 26
Cape Henlopen State Park, 274–75
Carbonell, Joseph E., Jr.: Wilmington Public Library interior, 102–3
Carey's Camp, 297–98, **298**
carillon, Nemours, 50
Carlson, Walter: Beneficial Building, Wilmington, 110
Carman and Dobbins, 157
Carney Farm, 248
Carothers, Wallace, 47
Carpenter, J. L., 58

Carpenter, Robert, 106
Carpenter House (Riverview), 58
Carrcroft Meeting House, 32
Carrère and Hastings, 122
  Frick Mansion, New York City, 48
  Nemours, 21, **48**, 48–49
  Vernon Court, Newport, R.I., 48
Carroll, Armand: Edgemoor Theatre, 42
Carson, Charles L.
  Grand Opera House, Wilmington, 101, **101**
  Mount Vernon Place Methodist Episcopal Church, Baltimore, 114
  Queen Theater (Clayton House Hotel), Wilmington, 97
Carswell, Frank R.: Mechanical and Electrical Hall, University of Delaware, 182
Carter, Richard B., 283
Caruso, Enrico, 151
Carvel, Elbert N., 193
Carvel State Office Building, 102
C. A. Sims and Company, 125
casinos (Dover Downs), 248
Cathedral Church of St. John, Wilmington, 11, **120**, 120–21
Catherine the Great, empress of Russia, 49
Catholics. *See* Roman Catholics
Caudill Rowlett Scott: Education and Technology Building, Delaware Technical and Community College, 111
Causey, Peter F., 244
Causey Mansion, 15, 244–45, **245**, 295; kitchen and slave quarter, 245
Cavanaugh's Restaurant (Reynolds Candy Store), 100, **100**
Cecil Baker and Associates: ING Direct (Kent Building) renovation, 91
cemeteries
  Cool Spring Presbyterian Church, 265, **265**
  Odd Fellows Cemetery, Smyrna, 226
  Wilmington and Brandywine Cemetery, 116–17
Center for Historic Architecture and Design (CHAD), University of Delaware, 14, 86, 207, 213, 223, 270, 279
Center Friends Meeting House, 59, **59**
Central Hotel (Sterling Hotel), Delaware City, 204

Central Law Building, Dover, 243
Central National Bank. *See* Levy's Loan Office (Central National Bank)
Central Young Men's Christian Association (YMCA), **115**, 115–16
Centre Grove School, 59
Centreville, 22, 56–64; and vicinity map, 58
Centreville Lodge No. 37, Independent Order of Odd Fellow (IOOF), 56–57, **57**
Centreville Reserve, 57, **57**
Century Club, Dover, 254
Chalfant, Richard D., 117, 141
Chance, John, 232
Chandler, Abram, 169
Chandler, Alfred, 105
Chandler, Ebe T., 283
Chandler, Theophilus P., 20, 69
  Alexis I. du Pont Middle School, 72, **72**
  Christ Church Christiana Hundred alterations, 69–70
  New Castle County Courthouse, 104
  Opera House, New Castle, 151
  Pelleport, 70
  Trinity Episcopal Church, Wilmington, 116
  Winterthur, 60–61
Chandler (Captain) House, 283
Chandler-Dixon-Frederick House, 57
chapel, Delaware Health and Social Services campus, 147–48
Chapman Decorative Company, 163
Charcoal Pit restaurant, Concord Pike, 33
Charles Luckman Associates: Christiana Towers Apartments, University of Delaware, 188
Chase, Susan, 24, 32, 43, 83, 123
Chateau Meown, 56, 65
Cherbourg Round Barn, 14, 234, **234**
Chesapeake and Delaware (C&D) Canal, 21, 192, **193**, 196, 197–200, **198**, 203, 204, **204**, 207; along, map, 197
Chester County, Pa.: Mt. Pleasant, 160
Chevannes, 21, 60, 65
Chicago, Ill.: Transportation Building, 1893 World's Columbian Exposition, 32

INDEX 327

Chicago Bascule Bridge Company, 292
Chickadel, Joseph
   Independence Mall, 51, **51**
   Mike's Famous Roadside Rest, 148, **148**
chicken houses, 14, 248, **285**
Chipman, John, 296
Chipman Sweet Potato House, 14, **296**, 296–97
Christ Church, Dover, **256**, 256–57
Christ Church Christiana Hundred, 69–70
Christiana, 22, 24, 170–72
Christiana Hundred, 55–81
   Ashland and vicinity, 79–81; map, 80
   Centreville, 56–64; and vicinity map, 58
   Elsmere vicinity, 75–76; map, 75
   Greenville vicinity, 64–70; map, 67
   Newport, 76
   north along Red Clay Creek, 77–79
   northern, 55–56
   south of DE 141, 70–74
Christiana Towers Apartments, University of Delaware, 188
Chrysler Plant, Newark, 42
churches
   Aldersgate United Methodist Church, 26, 53
   All Saints Episcopal Church, Rehoboth Beach, 276–77
   Asbury Methodist Church, Harrington, 242
   Asbury Methodist Church, Wilmington, 86
   Asbury United Methodist Church, Smyrna, 227, 228
   Barratt's Chapel, **239**, 239–40
   Bayard Sharp Hall (St. Thomas Church), 187
   Cathedral Church of St. John, Wilmington, 11, **120**, 120–21
   chapel, Delaware Health and Social Services campus, 147–48
   Christ Church, Delaware City, 203
   Christ Church, Dover, **256**, 256–57
   Christ Church, Milford, 262
   Christ Church Christiana Hundred, 69–70
   Christiana Presbyterian Church, 171
   Church of the Ascension, Claymont, 35
   Church of the Holy City (Swedenborgian), 133
   Cool Spring Presbyterian Church, 265, **265**
   Cow Marsh Old School Baptist Church, 224
   Daugherty Hall (Old First Presbyterian Church), University of Delaware, 187
   diversity of, 3
   Ebenezer United Methodist Church, Delaware City, 203
   Episcopal Church of Saints Andrew and Matthew (St. Andrew's), 113–14
   Epworth Methodist Church, 264, 286
   First and Central Presbyterian Church, Wilmington, 108, 124
   First Presbyterian Church, Smyrna, 228, **228**
   Grace United Methodist Church, Wilmington, **16**, 101, 114–15, **115**, 187
   Hillcrest Bellefonte Methodist Church, 53
   Holy Trinity Greek Orthodox Church, west Wilmington, 131
   Immanuel Episcopal Church, northwest Wilmington, 138
   Immanuel Episcopal Church on the Green, New Castle, 8, 151, 154–55, **155**, 169, 183
   Indian Mission United Methodist Church, 5, 279
   Kingswood United Methodist Church, 191
   Morning Star Institutional Church of God in Christ, 235–36
   Mount Vernon Place Methodist Church, 187
   New Castle Presbyterian Church, **150**, 156
   Old Christ Church, Laurel, 156, 295, 296, **296**
   Old Drawyers Church, 183, 210–11, **211**, 239
   Old First Presbyterian Church, Wilmington, 26, 97, 124, **124**, 176
   Old Presbyterian Church, Dover, 5, 251–52
   Old St. Anne's Church, Middletown, **218**, 218–19
   Old Swedes Church (Holy Trinity), Wilmington, 5, 26, 88–90, **89**, 98, 121
   Old Union Methodist Church, Townsend, 221
   Pencader Presbyterian Church, 196, **196**
   Presbyterian Church, Bridgeville, 286
   Presbyterian Church, St. Georges, 200
   Prince George's Chapel, **282**, 282–83
   rural Kent County, 224
   St. Albans Episcopal Church, 53
   St. Anne's Church, Middletown, 217, 228
   St. Anthony of Padua Church, west Wilmington, 133–34, **134**
   St. Francis Renewal Center (Samuel N. Trump House), 41
   St. Hedwig's Roman Catholic Church, west Wilmington, 131
   St. James Episcopal Church, Newport, 76
   St. James Episcopal Church Millcreek Hundred, 169–70, **170**
   St. John the Baptist Episcopal Church, Milton, 257, 260
   St. John the Baptist Roman Catholic Church, Newark, 178
   St. Joseph on the Brandywine, 70
   St. Luke's Episcopal Church, Seaford, 292
   St. Mary's Church, Wilmington, 86
   St. Mary's Episcopal Church, Bridgeville, 286
   St. Paul's Catholic Church, west Wilmington, 131
   St. Paul's Episcopal Church, Georgetown, 257, **261**, 261–63
   St. Paul's Lutheran Church, Newark, 165
   St. Paul's Methodist Church, Odessa, 214
   St. Peter's Episcopal Church, Lewes, 271, **271**
   St. Peter's Episcopal Church, Smyrna, 227–28
   St. Philip Lutheran Church, Newark, 165
   St. Stephen's Church, Harrington, 262

St. Stephen's Lutheran Church, northwest Wilmington, 138
Star Hill A.M.E. Church, 236
Trinity Episcopal Church, Wilmington, 116, 257
Trinity Methodist Church, Frederica, 240
Ursuline Academy Performing Arts Center (First Church of Christ Scientist), 130, **131**
Welsh Tract Baptist Church, 191, **191**, 196
Westminster Presbyterian Church, northwest Wilmington, 133, 137–38
West Presbyterian Church, Wilmington, 113
White Clay Creek Presbyterian Church, 176, 183
Zion A.M.E. Church, Camden, 236
Zion Lutheran Church, west Wilmington, 130
Zoar Methodist Church, Odessa, 214
See also meeting houses; synagogues
Church of the Holy City (Swedenborgian), 133
Circle, The, Georgetown, 261, 263
Citizens Bank (Fruit Growers' National Bank and Trust Company), Smyrna, 228
City Beautiful movement, 104
city halls
  Dover City Hall, 247
  Frederica Town Hall and Firehouse, 240
  Old Town Hall, Wilmington, 26, 27, 96, **98,** 98–99
  Smyrna Opera House and Old Town Hall, 229, **229**
  Town Hall, New Castle, iv, 157
Ciukurescu, George, 70
Civilian Conservation Corps (CCC), 231, 259, 260, 278
Clapp, James Ford, Jr.
  Crowninshield Research Building, 61, 63
  Wilmington Public Library interior, 102–3
Clark, George W.: Wilmington Savings Fund Society, 102
Clark, Kenneth, 159, 163
Clark, Lulu, 39
Classical Revival architecture, 184
Clay, Henry, 68, 164
Claymont, 5, 32, 33–36; and vicinity map, 34
Claymont Stone School, 35

Clayton, John M., 164
Clayton, 225; map, 226
Clayton House Hotel. *See* Queen Theater (Clayton House Hotel), Wilmington
Cleaden, William, 68
Cleaver, Joseph, 209
Cleaver House (Linden Hall), 209
Clement, Samuel, 199
Clendaniel, R. Calvin. *See* R. Calvin Clendaniel Associates
Clinton, De Witt, 203
Cloak, Eben, 227
Cloud, Harlan, 158
Cloud's Farm, 14, 80
Cloud's Row, New Castle, 157–58, **158**
clubs
  Central Young Men's Christian Association (YMCA), **115,** 115–16
  Centreville Lodge No. 37, Independent Order of Odd Fellow (IOOF), 56–57, **57**
  Century Club, Dover, 254
  Delaware Children's Theater (New Century Club), 130, **130,** 278
  DuPont Country Club, 53, **53**
  Gild Hall (Arden Club House), 40, **40**
  Greenville Country Club (Owl's Nest), 21, **57,** 57–58
  International Order of Odd Fellows Hall, Georgetown, 261
  International Order of Odd Fellows Lodge, St. Georges, 200
  Masonic Lodge (Georgetown Academy), 261
  Monday Club, 16
  Wilmington Club, **108,** 108–9
Clyde Mansion, 35
Cobb, Henry
  John Hancock Tower, Boston, 109
  World Trade Center, Baltimore, 109
Cochran, John P., 217
Cochran Grange, 15, 24, **217,** 217–18
Coffin, Marian Cruger, 278
  Christ Church Christiana Hundred landscaping, 69
  Corbit-Sharp garden, 211
  Delaware College landscaping report, **180–81,** 182
  Gibraltar garden, 145
  Magnolia Circle, 185

  Mt. Cuba garden, 166–68
  St. Amour garden, 73
  Winterthur garden, 63–64
Coke, Thomas, 239
Colbert, Jean-Baptiste, 48–49
Colburn, Jane, 35
Cole, Thomas: Old Swedes Church (Holy Trinity), Wilmington, 88–90
colleges, universities, preparatory school campuses
  Archmere Academy, 36
  Delaware College of Art and Design (Delmarva Power and Light Company), 100
  Delaware State University, 248
  Education and Technology Building, Delaware Technical and Community College, 111, **111**
  Johns Hopkins University, Baltimore, Md., 184
  Princeton University, N.J., 179, 184
  University of Virginia, 180
  Ursuline Academy, 130
  Wilmington College, 13
  See also University of Delaware
Collins, Thomas, 230
Collins-Sharp House, 214, **214**
colonial architecture, 7–8, 10–11, 76, 111, 117, 160, 246, 253, 256–57, 268, 286, 287–88
Colonial Dames, 27, 160, 278
Colonial Revival architecture, 11–13, 27, 47, 53, 59, 70–71, 72–73, 92, 108, 128–29, 130, 132, 175, 180, 181, 183, 185, 213, 227, 229, 230, 242, 246–47, 253, 254, 263, 278
Columbus Square, northwest Wilmington, 136
Comegys Farm, 219
commercial building (Captain Charles W. Johnston House), Lewes, 271
Commodore Macdonough School, 200
Commonwealth Development Group, 178
Community Service Building (Montchanin Building), Wilmington, 108
Concord Pike, 32–33
Concrete-Steel Engineering Company, 124–25; Van Buren Street Bridge and Aqueduct, 124–25
condominiums. *See* apartments and condominiums
Conrad, Henry C., 75

INDEX 329

Converse, Bernard T.
  Bellevue Hall, 41, **41**, 43
  Residences at Rodney Square, 102
Cooch, Edward W., 194
Cooch, Thomas, 194
Cooch, William, Jr., 195
Cooch-Dayett Mill, 194–95
Cooch House, 194, **194**
Cooch's Bridge, Battle of, 191, 192, 196
Cook, Philip, 219
Cookman, William H.: George V. Massey Station (Pennsylvania Station), 251
Cook-Simms House, 98
Cool Spring, 272
Cool Spring Presbyterian Church, 265, **265**
Cool Spring Reservoir Pumping Station, 130–31, **131**
Cooperson, Jay N., 229
Cooperson Associates
  Ashland Nature Center, 79
  Smyrna Opera House and Old Town Hall, 229, **229**
Cope and Stewardson, 17, 133, 180, 219; University of Pennsylvania Law School, 183
Copeland, Lammot du Pont and Pamela Cunningham, 21, 166–68
Cope Linder Architects: Dover Downs Hotel, 247–48
Corbit, William, 172, 211, 222
Corbit family, 210
Corbit-Sharp House, 14, 172, 210, 211–12, **213**, 224, 227; smokehouse, 213, **213**
Corinne Court. *See* Villa Monterey (Corinne Court)
Corkran, Louise, 275
Corkran, Wilbur S.
  Henlopen Acres, **274**, 275
  The Homestead (Peter Marsh House) enlargement, 275–76
Cornelius, Charles O.
  office building (Bank of Delaware), 141–42
  and Winterthur, 61
Corner Ketch Barn, **9**
Cornwallis, Charles, 165, 194
Cossutta, Araldo
  Christian Science Administration Building, Boston, 109
  1105 North Market Street (Wilmington Tower), **109**, 109–10
Cotter, John S., 199
Couper, William, 163

Courland, Raphael: Beth Shalom Synagogue, 126
Court House, New Castle, 150, **158**, 158–59, 183
courthouses
  Court House, New Castle, 150, **158**, 158–59, 183
  Kent County Courthouse, 254
  New Castle County Courthouse, 96, **97**, 104
  Old Courthouse, Georgetown, 264, **264**
  Sussex County Courthouse, 263, **263**
  Sussex County Family Court, 263
  Wilmington Trust Center (United States Post Office, Court House, and Custom House), 105
Court of Chancery, Georgetown, 263–64, **264**
Cowgill, Daniel, 250
Cox, Robbi: Wilmington Trust Center (United States Post Office, Court House, and Custom House), 105
Cox, Warren J.: Winterthur Galleries, 63
Cox, William, 165
Coxe (Thomas) House, 98
Cox House, 79
Craft Shop. *See* Red House and Craft Shop, Arden
Craig, Mary, 278
Cram, Ralph Adams, 63, 120
Crapper, Levin, 244
Crawford, James, 221
Crawford family, 221
Crawford Greenewalt Laboratory, 47
Crenier, Henri, 49
Cresson, Hilborne T., 5
Cret, Paul, 105
Crisp and Edmunds: A. I. du Pont Hospital for Children (A. I. du Pont Institute), 50–51
Crouding, Peter, 154, 161
Crowninshield, Francis B., 69
Crowninshield, Louise du Pont, 27, 61, 68, 69, 153, 278
Crowninshield Research Building, 61, 63
CSX Railroad Bridge (Baltimore and Ohio Railroad Bridge), **125**, 125–26
Cummins, George W., 231
Cummins family, 227
Cummins (Alexander G.) House, 226, 251

Cummins Stockly House, 227
Curtis Cox Kennerly: Wilmington Trust Center (United States Post Office, Court House, and Custom House), 105
Curtis Paper Company, 173
Cypress Swamp, 258, 284

Dali, Salvador, 167
Dallas, Tex.: Municipal Center, 109
Dallett, Elijah James, 17, 99
  Delaware Health and Social Services Herman M. Holloway Sr. Campus (Delaware State Hospital), 146–47, **147**
  Episcopal Church of Saints Andrew and Matthew (St. Andrew's), 113–14
  office building (Harlan and Hollingsworth Company Office Building), 92
  St. Francis Renewal Center (Samuel N. Trump House), 41
  Wilmington and Brandywine Cemetery chapel, 116–17
dams: Hoopes Reservoir Dam (Old Mill Stream Dam), 78–79, **79**
D'Anastasio and Lisiewski: Valley Run, 36, **36**
Darley, Felix O. C., 35
Darley House, 14, 35, **35**
Daugherty Hall (Old First Presbyterian Church), University of Delaware, 187
Dauneport, Christiana Hundred, 278
Davies, Samuel, 199
Davies (Samuel) House. *See* Lum House (Lums Mill House, Samuel Davies House)
Davis, Benjamin H.: Washington Memorial Bridge, 122, 124
Davis, Bowen and Friedel
  Kreindler Beach House, 281, **281**
  Mispillion Riverwalk and Greenway, 244
Davis, Frank E.: Daugherty Hall (Old First Presbyterian Church), University of Delaware, 187
Dawes, Rumford, 66
Dawkins, Bill: Marim-Dawkins House (Ye Olde Log Cabin) reconstruction, 223, **223**
Day, Frank Miles, 99, 124
  Pyle (Frank) House, 132, **132**

Trinity Episcopal Church Parish House and Rectory, 116
Day and Klauder
   Congress Hall, Philadelphia, 182
   Harter Hall, University of Delaware, 183, **183**
   Memorial Hall, University of Delaware (proposal), **12**, 184
   Old College, University of Delaware, 181–82
   Trinity Episcopal Church Parish House and Rectory, 116
   University of Delaware work, 179–82, 185
   Wolf Hall, University of Delaware, 183, **184**
Dayett, John, 195
Day in Old New Castle, A, 27, 151
Dayton, Richard L.: Old Custom House (Old Federal Building) renovation, 99
DE 1 Bridge. *See* Senator William V. Roth Jr. Bridge (DE 1 Bridge, St. Georges Bridge)
Deakyne, Horace L., 158
Dean, Joseph, 178
DeArmond, Ashmead and Bickley
   Gibraltar, 21, 144–45, **145**
   Oberod, 21, 55–56
   Thomas (Stirling H.) House, 144
Deer Park Farm, 173
Deer Park Tavern (Deer Park Hotel), **188**, 188–89
de Foss, Mattias, 90
Delaplaine (James) House, 56
Delaware, 1–31
   African American history and architecture in, 15–16
   agriculture in, 14, 24
   architects in, 16–19
   building materials, 8, 10
   colonial architecture in, 7–8, **9**, 10–11
   Colonial Revival architecture in, 11–13
   Dutch in, 7, 21, 149–50, 152–53, 156, 207, 265, 268, 272
   Finns in, 5, 7
   geography of, 1
   historic preservation in, 26–30, 278
   influences on architecture, 1–3
   modernism in, 42
   nineteenth-century architecture, 13–16
   physiography, map, 4
   population growth, 25–26
   railroads, 1880s, map, 23
   roads, 1790s, map, 10
   state divisions, map, 2
   suburbs in, 24–26, 32
   Swedes in, 5, 7, 35, 86, 89, 93, 170–71
   transportation in, 21–24
   women and architecture in, 278
   Woodland Indians in, 3–5
Delaware Agricultural Museum and Village, 14, 248–49
Delaware Archaeological Museum (Old Presbyterian Church), 5, 251–52
Delaware Art Museum (Delaware Art Center), 42, 142–43, 167
Delaware Breakwater, 259, 272–74, **273**
Delaware Children's Theater (New Century Club), 130, **130**, 278
Delaware City, 14, 203–6; map, 205
Delaware City Hotel, 204
Delaware City Refinery (Tidewater Delaware Refinery), 201, **202**, 203
Delaware College of Art and Design (Delmarva Power and Light Company), 100
Delaware Department of Transport (DelDOT), 4–5, 22, 29–30, 44
Delaware Dual Road, 147, 267
Delaware Furnace, 259
Delaware Health and Social Services Herman M. Holloway Sr. Campus (Delaware State Hospital), 146–47, **147**
Delaware History Museum, 97
Delaware Hospital for the Chronically Ill (State Welfare Home), 230, **230**
Delaware Indian tribe, 5
Delaware Iron Works, 78
Delaware Land Development Company, 72–73
Delaware Memorial Bridge, 22, **148**, 148–49
Delaware Nature Society, 284
Delaware Paper Mill, 54
Delaware Park Racetrack, 3
Delaware Public Archives (Hall of Records), 151, 255, **255**
Delaware Railroad, 23, 294–95
Delaware Society for the Preservation of Antiquities, 27, 98, 153, 170
Delaware State Bar Association (Farmers Bank), Wilmington, 96
Delaware State Historic Preservation Office, 28
Delaware State Hospital. *See* Delaware Health and Social Services Herman M. Holloway Sr. Campus (Delaware State Hospital)
Delaware State Hospital, Farnhurst, 17
Delaware State University, 248
Delaware Technical and Community College, 111, 265
Delaware Tide Lock, Chesapeake and Delaware (C&D) Canal, 198, 204, **204**
Delaware Trust Bank, Dover, 246
Delaware Trust Building. *See* Residences at Rodney Square (Delaware Trust Building)
Delaware Turnpike, 26
Delaware Woolen Factory, 54
de la Warr, Lord, 1
Delmar, 284
Delmarva Camp, 297
Delmarva Power and Light Company. *See* Delaware College of Art and Design (Delmarva Power and Light Company)
Delwood, 32
Dennison, Ethan A.: Residences at Rodney Square, 102
Derrickson family, 215
Deshpande, Jag, 166
Design Collaborative, Inc.
   Juniper Financial Corporation (Gates Engineering Building) rehabilitation, 92, **92**
   Mike's Famous Roadside Rest, 148, **148**
   The Mill at White Clay (Joseph Dean and Son), 178, **178**
   west Wilmington work, 129
deValinger, Leon, 7, 28, 35, 231, 236, 237–38, 248–49, 255, 272
Devondale Hall, 146
DeVries, David Pieterssen, 268, 272
DeVries Monument. *See* Fort Swanendael site (possible) and DeVries Monument
Diamond State Engineering: Delaware Agricultural Museum and Village, 248–49
Dickens, Charles, 35
Dickinson, John, 236, 251
Dickinson, Samuel, 236

INDEX   331

Dickinson (John) Mansion, 14, 28, 234, 236, **236**
Digges, William, 282
dikes, 21, 149, 231, 268
Dilks, Albert W.: St. Amour site, 73
Dilworth House, 208
Dingee (Obadiah and Jacob) Houses, 98
Disciples of Christ, 281–82
Dixon, Jeremiah, 188
Dixon, Thomas
  Daugherty Hall (Old First Presbyterian Church), University of Delaware, 187
  Episcopal Church of Saints Andrew and Matthew (St. Andrew's), 113–14
  Grace United Methodist Church, Wilmington, **16**, 101, 114–15, **115**, 187
  Grand Opera House, Wilmington, 101, **101**
  Mount Vernon Place Methodist Episcopal Church, Baltimore, 114, 187
  Queen Theater (Clayton House Hotel), Wilmington, 97
Dixon, Thomas and James M.
  Fox Lodge at Lesley Manor (Allen Lesley House), 163–64, **164**
  Porter's Lodge, 44
  Sheppard and Enoch Pratt Hospital, 164
Dodd family, 279
Dodd Homestead, 279
Dogwood, 31n18
Dollar, Bonner, Blake and Manning
  Marbrook Elementary School, 78, **78**
  Tower Hill School preschool, 144
Dollar, Bonner and Funk: Tower Hill School Library-Science Building, 144
Dollar, Erling G., 17; Aldersgate United Methodist Church, 53
Dollar and Bonner, 19; Aldersgate United Methodist Church, 53
Doragh, Andrew, 261
Dorset Apartment Building, northwest Wilmington, 137
Douglass, Frederick, 229
Dover, 27, 224, 246–57, **247**; map, 249
  history, 246–47
  Post Office, **28**, 247

Dover Air Force Base, 246, 257; Mortuary Facility, 257, **257**
Dover Downs and Dover International Speedway, **247**, 247–48
Downing, Andrew Jackson, 44, 163, 251, 254, 289–90, 295
Downing, Catherine, 244
Downingtown, Pa.: Eagleview, 215
Downs, Frank B.: The Brambles renovation, 38
Downs, Joseph, 61
Draper House, Milford, 243
Draper Mansion, Wilmington, 14, 108
Dreiser, Theodore, 157
Drexel, St. Katharine, 225
Duck Creek Historical Society, 227, 229
Duck Creek Village, 225
Dulaney, William H., 293
Dunleith, 146
du Pont, A. Felix, 219; house, 277
du Pont, Mrs. A. Felix, 160
du Pont, Alexis I., 20, 69–70, 71; Middle School, 72, **72**
du Pont, Alfred I., 20, 33, 47–51, 65, 102, 105, 122, 230, 252; Hospital for Children, 50–51
du Pont, Alfred Victor (I), 60, 68, 69
du Pont, Alfred Victor (II), 17, 20, 50, 51, 73, 256
du Pont, Alicia, 48
du Pont, Amy, 278
du Pont, Bessie Gardner, 65
du Pont, "Boss Henry," 48, 60, 64, 68, 69
du Pont, Charles I., 71, 168, 256
du Pont, Eleuthère Irénée (E. I.), 65–66, 67, 68
  Eleutherian Mills, 68; gardens, 69
  Latimeria, 64
  Lower Louviers, 54
du Pont, Ellen, 74
du Pont, E. Paul, 65; House, 65
du Pont, Mrs. E. Paul, 160
du Pont, Ethel, 58, 70
du Pont, Eugene E., 133
du Pont, Eugene H., Jr., 57–58, 70
du Pont, Evelina. *See* Bidermann, Evelina du Pont
du Pont, Francis G., 72
du Pont, Francis V., 125, 267
du Pont, Colonel Henry Algernon, 60, 61, 63–64, **64**, 68
du Pont, Henry Belin, 136, 149, 175

du Pont, Henry Francis, 27, 29, 60–61, 63, 64, 68, 70, 179, 241, 256; Christ Church Christiana Hundred alterations, 69–70
du Pont, Irénée, 59, 73, 104, 144, 276, 277
du Pont, Irene Sophie, 59, 220
du Pont, Isabella. *See* Sharp, Isabella du Pont
du Pont, Jessie Ball, 48, 49, 51, 278
du Pont, Lammot (I), 70, 73
du Pont, Lammot (II), 179
du Pont, Louise. *See* Crowninshield, Louise du Pont
du Pont, Margaretta E., 74
du Pont, Mary Belin, 73
du Pont, Pete, 54
du Pont, Pierre S., 35, 50, 56, 65, 73, 99, 103, 105, 106, 133, 145, 181, 210, 252
  Elementary School, 128–29
  public school initiatives, 12, 15, 90–91, 128–29, 166, 178–79, 193, 200, 256
du Pont, Pierre S., III, 54, 72
Du Pont, Admiral Samuel F., 54, 69; statue, 140
du Pont, S. Hallock, 175
du Pont, Sophie, 68
du Pont, T. Coleman, 74, 78–79, 266–67
du Pont, Victor, 54, 67
du Pont, Victorine, 68, 69
du Pont, Victorine (II). *See* Homsey, Victorine du Pont
du Pont, William, 41, 70–71, 72, 139
du Pont, William, Jr., 41, 43
DuPont Building, Wilmington, 17–18, 82–83, **84**, **104**, 105–7, **106**
DuPont Company, 20, 46, 65–66, 84, 137, 288–89
  Engineering Department, 17, 97, 107–8, 144, 293
  Krebs Pigment and Chemical Company, 32, 76, **77**
  office building (Louviers Building), 175, 191
DuPont Country Club, 53, **53**
du Pont de Nemours, Pierre Samuel, 20, 48, 64
DuPont Experimental Station, 47, **47**, 71, 293
du Pont family estates, 19–21, 55, 62. *See also specific estates by name*
du Pont family genealogy, 18–19
Du Pont Highway, 24, 147, 210,

226, 242, 246, **266,** 266–67, 267
Du Pont Motors, 65
DuPont Seaford Plant. *See* Invista Seaford Plant (DuPont Seaford Plant)
DuPont Theatre, Wilmington, 106
Dutch House, New Castle, 7, 27, 68, 150, 153, **153,** 278
Dutch settlers, 7, 21, 149–50, 152–53, 156, 207, 265, 268, 272

Eagleview, Pa., 215
Eakins, Thomas, 37
Early Plank House (Swedish Log Cabin), The, Lewes, 27–28, 270
earthfast construction, 8
East Aurora, N.Y.: Roycroft, 37, 190
eastern Sussex County. *See* Sussex County, eastern
Eberlein, Harold D., 28, 176, 182, 210, 244, 253, 272, 290, 296
Eckhart, William, 106
Eddy, Mary Baker, 130
Eden Hill, 224
Eden Park, 146
Edgemoor, 32
Edge Moor Bridge Works, 140
Edge Moor Elementary School, 41, 42, **42**
Edge Moor Iron Works, 32, **33**
Edgemoor Terrace, **25**
Edgemoor Theatre, 42
Edison, Thomas, 73
Edison, William L., 73
Edkins, George E., 256–57
Edmonds, George P., 73
Education and Technology Building, Delaware Technical and Community College, 111, **111**
E. F. Hodgson Company: The Wren's Nest, Nemours, 49–50
Egyptian Revival style, 146
"Eight Square School," 232
Eleutherian Mills, 14, 21, 60, 65–66, 68; gardens, 69, **69**
1105 North Market Street (Wilmington Tower), **109,** 109–10
Ellegood (Dr. Joshua) House, 295
Ellendale, 260, 266–67
Ellerslie, 14
Elliott Hall, University of Delaware, 182
Ellis Grove School, 264
Elsmere viaduct, 76
Elsmere vicinity, 75–76; map, 75

Elton, 31n18, 160
Emalea Pusey Warner School, 84
Embury, Aymar, II
   DuPont Country Club, 53, **53**
   Old St. Georges Bridge, 200–201, **201**
England, John, 176
England, Joseph, 176
England (John) House and Mill, 8, **176,** 176–77
England (Thomas) House Restaurant (Woodlawn), 230–31, **231**
Episcopal Church of Saints Andrew and Matthew (St. Andrew's), 113–14
Episcopalians, 3
Eratt House, 287–88
Erickson, A. M., 68
Etzel (Gastho) House, 190
Eugene, Ernest K.: Holy Trinity Greek Orthodox Church, west Wilmington, 131
Evans, Oliver, 165, 168, 169
Evans, Robert: Hercules Inc. Headquarters, 110, **110**
Evans, Rosanna, 214
Evans, Walker, 66
Everett Theater (Middletown Theater), 216
Eyre, Wilson
   Kent County Courthouse, 254
   Mauchline, 132
   Redden Lodge, 260

factories. *See* industrial buildings; mills and mill complexes
Fagnani, Leon N., 136; St. Anthony of Padua rectory, west Wilmington, 133–34
Fairfax, 24, **52,** 52–53
Fairlamb, Jonas P., 68
Fairview, St. Georges, 201, **201**
Fairview (Dulaney House), Seaford, **292,** 292–93
Fall Line, 8, 11
Farmers Bank, Georgetown, 263
farms
   Carney, 248
   Cloud's, 14, 80
   Comegys, 219
   Deer Park, 173
   Selborne, 21, 56
   Winterthur Farms Dairy buildings, 63
   See also agricultural buildings; barns
Federal architecture, 110, 141–42, 159, 160–61, 169, 196, 197, 204, 209, 214, 229, 250, 268, 279–80

Federal Arts Project, 226, 261
Federal Job Corps Center, 118
Federal Writers' Project, 27
Feeder Canal, 192
Fels, Joseph, 37, 38–39, 40
Felton, 224
Fenimore family, 88
Fenwick Island Light Station, 283, **283**
Ferguson and Brown: Old Swedes Church (Holy Trinity), Wilmington restoration, 88–90
Ferris, Benjamin, 168
   Brandywine Academy cupola, 121–22
   Wilmington Friends Meeting House, 113, **113**
Ferris (Zachariah) House. *See* Jacobs House
Fiddeman, Henry B., 244
Field, Barker and Underwood, 266–67
Field, William M., 46
Figg Engineering Group
   Indian River Inlet Bridge, 281, **281**
   Senator William V. Roth Jr. Bridge (DE 1 Bridge, St. Georges Bridge), 199–200, 281
   Sunshine Skyway Bridge, St. Petersburg, Fla., 200
Filippakis, George, 131
Financial Center Development Act of 1981, 165
Finney, Dr. John, 160
Finnish settlers, 5, 7
First and Central Presbyterian Church, Wilmington, 108, 124
First Delaware Preservation Conference, 152
First National Bank, Harrington, 243
first office, Eleutherian Mills, 69
First Presbyterian Church, Smyrna, 228, **228**
Fisher, Joshua, 272
Fisher-Martin House, 28, 272, **273**
Fisler Memorial Chapel, Smyrna, 228
Fitzgerald, F. Scott, 14
Five Mile Run, 196
Flagler, Henry M., 48
Flanders, Annette Hoyt, 278
Fleming, Nancy, 185
Fletcher and Buck, 18, 155
Flint House, 59
Fooks (Daniel) House, 295

INDEX   333

Fort Casimir site, 7, 149, 152–53
Fort Christina, 35, 87
Fort Christina Monument, 88
Fort Christina Park, 5, 87–88, 93
Fort Delaware, 11, 203, 204, **205**, 206
Fort DuPont, 46, 203
Fort Miles, 274–75
Fort Mott, 46
Fort Swanendael site (possible) and DeVries Monument, 268
forts, fortifications. *See specific forts by name*
Fouilhoux, J. André: Hotel du Pont, Wilmington, 106–7
Foulke and Henry Dormitories, Princeton University, 121
Founders Hall (main building), St. Andrew's School, Middletown, 219–20
Fountain Plaza, northwest Wilmington, 136, **136**
401 Washington Street, Wilmington, 111
4614 Bedford, Forest Hills Park, 52
4615 Bedford, Forest Hills Park, 52
Fourteen Foot Bank Lighthouse, 238, **238**
1401 Condominiums, northwest Wilmington, 137, **138**
Fowler, Laurence Hall: Maryland Hall of Records, 255
Fowler, Ned, 295
Fowler, Norma Jean, 295
Fowler House, 295–96, **296**
Fox Lodge at Lesley Manor (Allen Lesley House), 163–64, **164**
Frank, Bill, 85, 109
Frankl, Ephraim J., 137
Frank Miles Day and Brother, 144
Frank Stephens Memorial Theater, 39
Frawley, Dan, 116
Frederica, 224, 240–42; map, 237
 Town Hall and Firehouse, 240
Frederick, William H., Jr., 69
Freemark, Kenneth M., Jr.: Old Custom House (Old Federal Building) renovation, 99
French + Ryan
 Georgetown Railroad Station restoration, 261
 Sussex County Family Court, 263
Frens and Frens
 Indian River Life Saving Station restoration, 280–81

New Castle Court House renovation, 159
Friendly Gables, Arden, 38–39
Friends of Old Dover, 246, 251
Friends of Old Drawyers, 26, 211
Frink Center for Wildlife, Tri-State Bird Rescue Center, 176
Fuller and McClintock: Hoopes Reservoir Dam (Old Mill Stream Dam), 78–79, **79**
Funk, Harley, 110
Furness, Evans and Company
 Kuumba Academy Charter School, 99
 Old Library, New Castle, 154, **154**
 Recitation Hall, University of Delaware, 182
 St. Francis Renewal Center (Samuel N. Trump House), 41
 Wilmington Station (Pennsylvania Railroad Passenger Station), **90**, 91
Furness, Frank, 16–17, 37, 41, 91, 154, 201, 286
 B&O Station, Newark, 173
 B&O Station, Wilmington, 135
 Pennsylvania Building, Wilmington, 91
 1315 Delaware Avenue, northwest Wilmington, 135
 University of Pennsylvania Library, Philadelphia, 154
 Water Street Station, Wilmington, 91
Furness and Evans: Fairview, 201, **201**

Gables, the, Rehoboth Beach, 276
Gabriel, A.-J., 48
Gaithersburg, Md.: Kentlands, 215
Gallagher, Hugh F., 189–90
Gambrill, Melville, 115
Gam's Store, St. Georges, 200
Garden City movement, 37
Garden Club of Wilmington, 55
gardens
 Amstel House, 160
 Brantwyn (Bois-Des-Fosses), 54
 Dutch House, 153
 Eleutherian Mills, 69, **69**
 Enchanted Woods, Winterthur, 64
 Gibraltar, 145, 185
 Goodstay, 74
 Mt. Cuba, 167
 Nemours, 20, 48–49; Sunken Garden, 50
 Owl's Nest, 58

Read (George) House, 163
 St. Amour site, 73, 167, 185
 Winterthur, 63–64, 185
 women's role in developing, 278
Garland, Sylvester, 159
Garrett, Ellwood, 111
Garrett, Thomas, 15, 159
Garrett (Thomas) House, 111
Gates Engineering Building. *See* Juniper Financial Corporation (Gates Engineering Building)
Gause, Henry, 56
Geddes, Robert L., 188
Geddes Brecher Qualls Cunningham: Rodney Complex (West Complex), **187**, 187–88
General Chemical Company, 33, 36
General Motors Plant, Newport, 76
George, Henry, 37
George Lynch Company, 175
Georgetown, 261–65; map, 262
 bird's-eye views, 261
 history, 261
Georgetown Academy. *See* Masonic Lodge (Georgetown Academy)
Georgetown Armory, 261
Georgetown Post Office, 261, 263
Georgetown Railroad Station, 261
George V. Massey Station (Pennsylvania Station), 251
George Yu Architects
 Westminster Presbyterian Church Community Hall, 137–38
 West Presbyterian Church, Wilmington, 113
Georgian Revival architecture, 54, 72, 142, 211–12, 213, 228, 234, 236, 240, 243, 244, 295
Giaroli, Egidio, 134, 136
Gibbons and Moore, 97
Gibbs, Abraham, 235–36
Gibbs, Absalom, 235–36
Gibraltar, 20, 21, 55–56, 144–45, **145**, 185
Gilchrist, Edmund B.: Goodstay, 74, **74**
Gild Hall (Arden Club House), 40, **40**
Gillette, Charles F.: Amstel House garden, 160
Gillmer, Thomas, 87
Gilpin, Richard A.: Christ Church Christiana Hundred alterations, 69–70
Giovannozzi, Frank, 83–84

Githens, Alfred Morton
    Enoch Pratt Library, Baltimore, 103
    Wilmington Public Library, 17, 102–3, **103**
Giusti, M. R., 107
Givan, Alexander: Old State House, 253, 255
Glasgow, 196–97; map, 194
Glasgow Regional Park, 197
Glassie, Henry, 80
Gleeson, Mulrooney and Burke: St. Anthony of Padua Church, west Wilmington, 133–34, **134**
Gleeson and Mulrooney
    St. Joseph on the Brandywine renovation, 70
    Salesianum, 126
Godley, Frederick
    Hotel du Pont, Wilmington, 106–7
    Nemours Building, 107–8
Goggin, Elizabeth, 235
Good, Stafford, 226
Goodman, James, 60, 68, 70
Goodstay, 74, **74**
Gore Hall, University of Delaware, 183–84
Gothic Revival architecture, 14, 39, 41, 43, 44, 70, 113, 114–15, 116, 120, 130, 133, 137–38, 156, 163–64, 171, 178, 179, 186, 187, 214, 217, 219–20, 221, 226, 228, 246, 261–63, 279, 284, 286, 290, 292, 295
Government Center, Wilmington, 101–2
Gowans, Alan, 29
Gowdy, Jim, 238
Grace United Methodist Church, Wilmington, **16**, 101, 114–15, **115**, 187
Graham, Chauncey G.: Rodney Street Chapel, 137–38
Grancell, William E.
    Founders Hall (main building), St. Andrew's School, Middletown, 219–20
    St. James Episcopal Church, Newport, 76
Grand Opera House, Wilmington, 101, **101**
Granite Mansion, Newark, 173
Granogue, 24, 59, 62
Grant, Edward L., 226, 261
Greater Wilmington Airport. *See* New Castle County Airport (Greater Wilmington Airport)

Greater Wilmington Development Council, 101
Great Geneva, 224
Greek Revival architecture, 13–14, 102–3, 164, 168, 173, 176, 203–4, 218, 231–32, 234, 244, 254, 265, 268, 289, 292–93
Green, the, Dover, 253, 254, **254**, 295
Green, the, New Castle, 150–51, 156
Green, the, University of Delaware, 179–80, 183
"green" architecture: Arden, 38
Greenbank Mill, 168, **168**
Greenberg, Allan
    Du Pont Hall, University of Delaware, 183–84
    Gore Hall, University of Delaware, 183–84
Greene, Nathanael, 192
Greenewalt, Mary Hallock, 147–48
Green Gate, Arden, 39
Greenlawn, **29**
Greenlawn Farm Manager's House, 221
Green Mansion, Newark, 178
Greenville Country Club (Owl's Nest), 21, **57**, 57–58
Greenville vicinity, 64–70; map, 67
Greenwood, 284
Gregg family, 64–65
Gregg (William) House (Ashland Mills), 79
Grieves, Armstrong-Child, and Baird: Grand Opera House, Wilmington restoration, 101, **101**
Grieves, James R., 101
Grubb, Charles E.
    North Market Street Bridge, 119
    Rising Sun Bridge, **71**, 71–72
Grubb (A. A.) House, 34
Guilbert and Betelle
    Commodore Macdonough School, 200
    Iron Hill Museum (Iron Hill School No. 112C), 193
Gustav Adolf, Swedish Crown Prince, 87

Hadley (Simon) Barn, 165
Hagley House, **20**, 31n18
Hagley Museum, 5, 46, **65**, 65–66, 168
Hagley Program, 29
Hagley Yard, **66**, 66–67

Hale, Samuel, 170
Hale-Byrnes House, 170, **170**
Hall, Albert E. S., 59
Hall, David, 295
Hall, George A., 291
Hall (Reverend George A.) House, 291
Hall of Records. *See* Delaware Public Archives (Hall of Records)
Hangar 1301, Dover Air Force Base, 257
Hankinson, H. B., 115
Hanson (Timothy) House, 247
H. A. Ramsay and Son, 238
Harbor of Refuge, 46, 274
Harding, Warren G., 229
Harking, Curtis: Ships Tavern Mews, Wilmington, restoration, 96, **96**
Harkins, William
    Hathorn-Betts House restoration, 240–41
    Old State House restoration, 253, 255
Harlan, Caleb, 169
Harlan, Marion, 230, 250, 253
Harlan and Hollingsworth, 82, 92; shipyard, **87**
Harlan Mill, 169
Harmon, Arthur Loomis: Shelton Hotel, New York City, 115
Harrington, 24, 242–43; map, 242
Harrington, Howard and Ash
    North Market Street Bridge, 119
    Rising Sun Bridge, **71**, 71–72
Harrington Post Office, 242
Harris, Philip Thomas
    Delaware Trust Bank, Dover, 246
    Residences at Rodney Square, 102
Harrison, Frances: Arden School, 40, 278
Harter Hall, University of Delaware, 183, **183**
Hartman-Cox Architects: Winterthur Galleries, 63
Harvey-Derickson-Bringhurst House. *See* Lea (Thomas) House
Haskell, Harry G., Jr., 99
Haslet, John, 220, 252
Hastings, Thomas, 50
Hathorn-Betts House (Hathorn-Lowber or Peter Lowber House), **240**, 240–41

Haviland, John
   Eastern State Penitentiary, Philadelphia, 259
   U.S. Naval Asylum, Norfolk, Va., 259
Hawkins, Jack. Sr., 146
Hay, Henry H., 160
Hayes, Manlove, Sr., 232
Hazzard, David, 260
Hazzard, John, 260
Hazzard House, 260
Heacock, Walter J., 29, 68
Heald, Joshua T., 135
Heap, D. P.: Fourteen Foot Bank Lighthouse, 238, **238**
Hedgelawn, 217
Heite, Edward, 28
Hellmuth, Obata and Kassabaum: Bob Carpenter Center, University of Delaware, 181
Hempstead, Joshua, 7, 170
Hendrickson House, 90
Henlopen Acres, 24, **274**, 275
Henlopen Hotel, 276
Henry, James, 203
Henry Clay Mill (Metal Keg Shop), 67–68, 71
Hercules Inc. Headquarters, 110, **110**
Herman, Bernard, 8, 159, 207, 208, 220, 258, 280, 295–96
Hetzel (Harry) House, 39
Hicks, Elias, 214
Hicks, Joseph, 187
Higgins, Anthony, 201
Higgins, John Clark, 201
Higley, Thomas E.: Education and Technology Building, Delaware Technical and Community College, 111, **111**
Hillier Architecture: New Castle County Library, Brandywine Hundred Branch, 52
Hills Mansion House, 171
Hillyard, Charles, 250
Hindu Temple of Delaware, 3, 166
Hirons, Frederic C.: Residences at Rodney Square, 102
Hirons, John, 74
Historical Society of Delaware, 99, 163
Historical Society of Delaware (Artisan's Savings Bank), 97
Historic American Buildings Survey (HABS), 27
Historic Houses of Odessa, 212
Historic Markers Commission, 27
Historic Red Clay Valley, 168
Hitchens House, 295
Hite, Geron S.: Hathorn-Betts House restoration, 240–41

Hizar, Thomas B., 132
Hockessin, 165–66
Hockessin Community Center (Hockessin School 107-C), 15, 166, **166**
Hockessin Friends Meeting House, 165–66
Hoffecker, Carol E., 29, 53, 125
Hoffman, F. Burrall, Jr.: Christ Church Christiana Hundred alterations, 69–70
Hogan, James H., 116, 257
Hoggson Brothers: Wilmington Savings Fund Society, 102
Holcomb, Frederick W., 54
Holden, McLaughlin and Associates: office building (Bank of Delaware), 141–42
Holloway, William E.: Aldersgate United Methodist Church, 53
Holmes-Hendrickson House, N.J., 153
Holt, Ryves, 270
Holt (Ryves) House, 7, 153, 266, **270**, 270–71
Holy Trinity Greek Orthodox Church, west Wilmington, 131
Homestead, The (Peter Marsh House), **275**, 275–76
Homestead cabin, Arden, 39
Homsey, Eldon, 63; Three Mill Road, 141, **141**
Homsey, Samuel: and Government Center, 102
Homsey, Victorine du Pont: Amstel House garden toolhouse, 160
Homsey, Victorine du Pont and Samuel, 20, 42, 155, 278
   Cathedral Church of St. John, Wilmington, **120**, 120–21
   chapel, Delaware Health and Social Services campus, renovation, 147–48
   Delaware Art Museum (Delaware Art Center), 142–43
   4615 Bedford, Forest Hills Park, 52
   Homsey Architects Office, northwest Wilmington, 141, **141**
   Jason Building, Delaware Technical and Community College (William C. Jason Comprehensive High School), 265
   Lower Louviers restoration, 54
   Mt. Cuba, 166–68

   Pavilion (Garden Tours Pavilion), 63
   St. Albans Episcopal Church, 53
   Trinity Episcopal Church chapel, 116
   Wilmington Drama League, 129
   Winterthur, South Wing, 63
Homsey Architects, 18, 278
   Ashland Nature Center Lodge, 79
   Bayard Sharp Hall (St. Thomas Church), University of Delaware, 187
   Brandywine Park Condominiums, 45
   Brandywine Zoo refurbishment, 123
   Delaware History Museum, 97
   Delaware Nature Society Educational Center, 284
   Delaware State University work, 248
   Elliott Hall renovation, 182
   Mt. Cuba adaptation, 166–68
   Old Custom House (Old Federal Building) renovation, 99
   Public Building of the City of Wilmington and County of New Castle (former) conversion, 105
   St. Joseph on the Brandywine, 70
   Ships Tavern Mews, Wilmington, restoration, 96, **96**
   Wilmington College, 13
Homsey Architects Office, northwest Wilmington, 141, **141**
Honeymoon Cottage, Governor Ross Mansion, 290
Hood, Raymond M.: Hotel du Pont, Wilmington, 106–7
Hoopes Reservoir, 74
Hoopes Reservoir Dam (Old Mill Stream Dam), 78–79, **79**
Hope, Clarence R.
   Cavanaugh's Restaurant (Reynolds Candy Store), 100, **100**
   St. Stephen's Lutheran Church, northwest Wilmington, 138
Hope, Walter R.: Invista Seaford Plant (DuPont Seaford Plant), 293
Hopkins, Alden, 236
hospitals
   A. I. du Pont Hospital for Children (A. I. du Pont Institute), 50–51
   Delaware Health and Social Services Herman M.

Holloway Sr. Campus (Delaware State Hospital), 146–47, **147**
Delaware Hospital for the Chronically Ill (State Welfare Home), 230, **230**
Delaware State Hospital, Farnhurst, 17
Veterans Administration Medical and Regional Office Center, 76, **76**
Wilmington Hospital (Delaware Hospital), 117
Hotel du Pont, Wilmington, **17**, 97, 106–7
Hotel Richardson, Dover, 246–47
hotels and inns
    Augustine Inn (Augustine Beach Hotel), 209–10
    Brick Hotel, Georgetown, 263, 264, **264**
    Brick Hotel, Odessa, 214, 264
    Central Hotel (Sterling Hotel), Delaware City, 204
    Clayton House (Queen Theater), Wilmington, 97
    Delaware City Hotel, 204
    Henlopen Hotel, 276
    Hotel du Pont, Wilmington, **17**, 97, 106–7
    Hotel Richardson, Dover, 246–47
    Inn at Montchanin Village, 65
    Jefferson Hotel, New Castle, 161
    Mary Bruce Inn (The Jungalow), 39
    Practical Farmer Inn, 33–34
    Robinson House (Naamans Tea House), 34–35
    St. Patrick's Inn, 188
    Shannon Hotel, 172, **172**
    Tudor Manor Hotel, Dover, 250
    Union Hotel, Frederica, 240
    See also taverns
Houdon, Jean-Antoine, 50
Houston, Robert, 295, 296
Howard, Ebenzer, 37
Howard, Needles, Tammen and Bergendoff
    Delaware Memorial Bridge, **148**, 148–49
    I-95 Bridge, Wilmington, 125
Howard, General Oliver O., 139
Howard High School, 90–91
Howe, John, 255
Howe, William, 192
Howell Lewis Shay and Associates, 187
Howell's Mill Seat. *See* Brecknock (Howell's Mill Seat)

Hubbard, Cortlandt, 28
Hubbard, Elbert, 37, 190
Hudson Mansion, 227
Huguenot House (Elias Naudain House), **221**, 221–22
Hull, Daniel, 282
Hull (Royal C.) House, 72
Hullihen, Walter, 184
Hummel, Charles, 63
Humphrey, Hubert, 149
Hunn House, 234
Huntington (Dr. Park W., Jr.) House, 52
Hutton, Addison: Wilmington Savings Fund Society, 102
Huxley, Elisha, 44
Hynes, John: Riverfront Parking Deck, 91

Ice Piers, New Castle, 163
IEI Group: Pennsylvania Building redevelopment, 91
Immanuel Episcopal Church on the Green, New Castle, 8, 151, 154–55, **155**, 169, 183
Immanuel Parish House, New Castle, 161
Independence Mall, 51, **51**
Indiana War Memorial, Indianapolis, Ind., 184
Indian Mission United Methodist Church, 5, 279
Indian River Inlet Bridge, 281, **281**
Indian River Life Saving Station, 280–81
industrial buildings
    Amtrak Wilmington Shops (Pennsylvania Railroad), 126–27, **127**
    Beracah Homes (Nanticoke Homes), 284–85
    Brandywine Pumping Station and Waterworks, 46, 118–19, **119**
    Cool Spring Reservoir Pumping Station, 130–31, **131**
    Delaware City Refinery (Tidewater Delaware Refinery), 201, **202**, 203
    Delaware Woolen Factory, 54
    DuPont Experimental Station, 47, **47**, 71, 293
    Edge Moor Iron Works, 32, **33**
    General Motors Plant, Newport, 76
    Invista Seaford Plant (DuPont Seaford Plant), 284, 288–89, 293
    Krebs Pigment and Chemical Company, 32, 76, **77**

    Madison Factory, 168
    Mrs. Steele's Broiler House, 14, 248
    New Castle Manufacturing Company, 151
    Porter Rapid Sand Filter Plant, 46, **46**
    State Office Building (Richardson and Robbins Cannery Complex), 250, **251**
    W. Compton Mills Pumping Station, 126
ING Direct Bank, 91
ING Direct (Kent Building), 91
I-95 Bridge, Wilmington, 125, **125**
I-95 Newark toll plaza (John F. Kennedy Memorial Highway, Delaware Turnpike), 192–93
Inn at Montchanin Village, 65
International Latex Company. *See* Playtex Products (International Latex Company)
International Order of Odd Fellows Hall, Georgetown, 261
International Order of Odd Fellows Lodge, St. Georges, 200
International Style, 42, 46, 47, 102, 108, 110, 126, 133, 135, 242, 261
Invista Seaford Plant (DuPont Seaford Plant), 284, 288–89, 293
Iris Brook (original), 31n18
Irisbrook (second), 70–71
Iron Hill, 192
Iron Hill Museum (Iron Hill School No. 112C), 15, 193
Isham, Norman M., 253; Legislative Hall (State Legislative Building), 255–56, **256**
Italianate architecture, 14, 36, 58, 91, 99, 101, 108–9, 115, 129, 133–34, 157, 210, 214, 216, 217, 227, 246, 286, 289–91
Ives, Albert Ely, 241
    Chateau Meown, 56, 65
    Chevannes, 21, 60, 65
    Gibraltar, 144–45, **145**
    Hull (Royal C.) House, 72
    Winterthur, 21, 60–61

J. A. Bader and Company, 106
Jackson, Andrew, 199
Jackson, C. Terry, II
    Schwartz Center for the Arts (Dover Opera House), 252, **252**
    Social Security Administration Office, Dover, 251

Jackson, Joseph "Shoeless Joe," 92
Jackson and Sharp, 82
Jacobs House, 98
jails: Sheriff's House and jail site, New Castle, 157, **157**
Jallade, Louis: Hartshorn Hall, 185
Jardel Co., 77
Jason Building, Delaware Technical and Community College (William C. Jason Comprehensive High School), 265
Jefferis, Jacob, 95
Jeffers, Ralph Walbree, 255
Jefferson, James, 290
Jefferson, Thomas, 54, 96, 180, 251
Jefferson Hotel, New Castle, 161
Jennings, Peter, 54
John Bassett Moore Intermediate School, 226
John Milner Associates: Immanuel Episcopal Church on the Green, New Castle, reconstruction, 154–55
Johns, Kensey, 159
Johns Hopkins University, Baltimore, Md., 184–85
Johns (Kensey) House, 159, **159**
Johnson, Edward L., 132
Johnson, Everett C., 184, 185; 318 South College (Press of Kells), 190
Johnson, James, 282
Johnson, Mirmiran and Thompson, 277
Johnson, Philip, 281
Johnston, Frances Benjamin, 288
Joselow, Evie, 49
Josephine Fountain (Josephine Tatnall Smith Memorial Fountains), 30, 124
Joseph Mandes Company, 219
J. Morton Poole Buildings, 91
J. Tyler McConnell highway bridge, 47
Judd, Henry: Old Town Hall, Wilmington restoration, **98**, 98–99
"Judges, The," Georgetown, 261
Juniata Company, 266–67
Junior League, 28, 119–20, 278
Juniper Financial Corporation (Gates Engineering Building), 92, **92**
Justin E. Diny Science Center, Archmere Academy, 36

Kahn, Louis I., 113
   Erdman Dormitory, Bryn Mawr, Pa., 187
   Richard Medical Research Building, Bryn Mawr, 187–88
Kalm, Peter, 222
Kalmar Nyckel shipyard, 87
Keast, Morton: Westcourt Apartments (Foster Park Apartments), 135
Keck, Charles, 105
Keebler, Patricia, 116, 132, 180
Keely, Patrick, 86
Keen, Charles Barton, 144
Kelly, Grace, 70
Kelly, James Edward, 104
Kelly and Johnson Architects: Tower Hill School renovation, 144
Kendall, William M., 104, 105
Kenmore, Va., 68
Kennedy, Jacqueline, 68
Kennedy, John F., 193
Kennett Square, Pa.: Chalfont House, 41
Kent County, 3, 224–45
   along DE 9, 231–34; map, 233
   brick construction in, 10
   Camden, 234–36, map, 237
   Clayton, map, 226
   Courthouse, 254
   Frederica, 240–42; map, 237
   Harrington, 242–43; map, 242
   Magnolia, 237–38; map, 237
   Milford, 243–45; map, 242
   Smyrna, 225–31; map, 226
   southeast of Dover, 236–40
   See also Dover
Kent Hall, University of Delaware, 185
Kentlands, Gaithersburg, Md., 215
Kentmere Parkway, northwest Wilmington, 140
Kenton, 224
Kimball, Fiske, 63
Kingston-upon-Hull, 236–37, **237**
Kip du Pont Boathouse, St. Andrew's School, Middletown, 220
Kirkwood Highway, 26, 190–91
kitchen and slave quarter, Causey Mansion, 245
Klair, Frederick, 169
Klauder, Charles Z., 276
   Memorial Hall, University of Delaware, 184–85
   Memorial Hall, University of Delaware (proposal), 179, 184
   Mitchell Hall, University of Delaware, 183
Klee, Jeff, 153
Kling Partnership, 47; Crawford Greenewalt Laboratory, 47

Klondike Kate's Restaurant, 178
Koch Industries, 289
Kohn Pederson Fox: Hercules Inc. Headquarters, 110, **110**
Kozloff, Joyce, 91
Krebs Pigment and Chemical Company, 32, 76, **77**
Kreindler Beach House, 281, **281**
Kruse, Albert, 105, 115, 129
   Camden Friends Meeting House annex, 235
   Collins-Sharp House restoration, 214
   Delaware Archaeological Museum (Old Presbyterian Church) restoration, 251–52
   DuPont Building remodeling, 106
   Dutch House restoration, 153
   and First Delaware Preservation Conference, 152
   Hale-Byrnes House restoration, 170
   and historic preservation, 27, 28, 98, 117
   Lea (Thomas) House restoration, 119–20
   New Castle and Frenchtown Railroad ticket office restoration, 162
   New Castle Court House restoration, 158–59
   New Castle Presbyterian Church restoration, 156
   office building (Bank of Delaware), 141–42
   Old St. Anne's Church restoration, 218
   Starr House restoration, 110
   Thorne (Parson) Mansion restoration, 244
Kuumba Academy Charter School, 99

Lackey Mansion, 34
Lafayette, Marquis de, 45, 68, 96, 97, 99, 168, 170, 192, 196
La Grange, 196–97, **197**
Laird, Philip and Lydia, 160, 163
Laird, Warren P., 104, 105
Lake Gerar, 276
Lammot, Daniel, 133
Landmark Engineering, Inc.
   Cooch-Dayett Mill restoration, 194–95
   Mill at White Clay, The (Joseph Dean and Son), 178, **178**
Langley, Batty, 166
Lanier, Gabrielle, 8, 208, 258, 280, 295–96

Lankey, John G.: Arsenal, New Castle, 155–56
Laskaris, Leo, 131
Latimeria, 61, 64
Latrobe, Benjamin Henry, 16, 71, 138–39, 151, 154, 155, 158, 159, 161, 192, 196, 198
Latrobe-Mills survey. See *Survey of New Castle* (Latrobe-Mills)
Laurel, 288, 294–97; map, 294
Laurel (Dudley W. Spencer House), **43,** 43–44
Lauritsen, Allen L., 83
Lawler, William, 17
Lawrence, 289
Layton, Joshua S.
   Brick Hotel, Georgetown, 264, **264**
   Sussex County Courthouse, 263, **263**
Lea, Thomas, 117, 119
Leach, George: The Brambles, 38
Lea-Derickson House. *See* Lea (Thomas) House
Lea (Thomas) House, 117, 119–20, **120**
Lea (William) House, 120
Lea Mills, 117, **118**
Leavitt, Greg, 168
Le Corbusier, 109
Ledoux, Claude-Nicolas, 48
Lee, Bishop Alfred, 113, 187, 203, 218
Leftovers House, 214
Legislative Hall (State Legislative Building), 12, 246, 253, 255–56, **256**
Leisen, Theodore A., 123
   Brandywine Pumping Station and Waterworks, 118–19, **119**
   Van Buren Street Bridge and Aqueduct, 124–25
L'Enfant, Pierre-Charles, 204
Lenni Lenape Indian tribe, 5
Leon N. Weiner and Associates, 190; Village of Eastlake (Eastlake Public Housing Project), 127
Lesley, Allen V., 163–64
Lesley (Allen) House. *See* Fox Lodge at Lesley Manor (Allen Lesley House)
Lesley Manor, 14
Levin/Brown and Associates: Beth Emeth Synagogue alterations, 129
Levy's Loan Office (Central National Bank), 97
Lewden family, 172
Lewden (John) House, 172, 213

Lewes, 7, 14, 21, 258, 265–76; map, 269
Lewes and Rehoboth Canal, 267
Lewes Historical Society, 27–28, 270, 271
Lewes Historical Society Complex, 268, 270
Lewestown Restorations, Inc., 270
Lewis, Jack, 256
Lewis, Warren K., 295
Lewis, Winslow, 181; Old College, University of Delaware, 181–82
Lexington, 14, 201
libraries
   Hagley Library, 66
   New Castle County Library, Brandywine Hundred Branch, 52
   Old Library, New Castle, 154, **154**
   Talleyville library, 33
   Wilmington Public Library, 17, 102–3, **103,** 124
Lidz, Margaret, 62, 63, 65
lighthouses, 21
   Cape Henlopen Lighthouse, 26
   Delaware Breakwater, **273,** 273–74
   Fenwick Island Light Station, 283, **283**
   Fourteen Foot Bank Lighthouse, 238, **238**
   Harbor of Refuge, 274
   Liston Range Rear Lighthouse, 207–8, **208**
limestone, 11
Limestone Road (DE 7), 165, 168–69
Lincoln, Abraham, 93, 259
Lind, Edmund G.
   Church of the Holy City (Swedenborgian), 133
   Peabody Institute, Baltimore, 108–9
   Wilmington Club, **108,** 108–9
Lindale, 14, 238
Lindeberg, Harrie T., 58; Greenville Country Club (Owl's Nest), 21, **57,** 57–58
Linden Hall, Newark, 173
Linden Hall, Port Penn. *See* Cleaver House (Linden Hall)
Lindens, The (Miller's House), 225, 229
Lindeström, Peter, 75, 87
Lindsey, Harry L.: Corbit-Sharp House restoration, 211
Liston House, 222

Liston Range Rear Lighthouse, 207–8, **208**
Little, Henry, 217
Llorens Stained Glass Studios, Atlanta, Ga., 69, 131
Locher, C. H., 166
Locust Grove, 285–86, **286**
Lodge, The, Arden, 39
Lofland, John, 1, 244
Log College, Pa., 176
log houses, 5, **6,** 7, 88, 169, 248–49
   The Early Plank House (Swedish Log Cabin), Lewes, 27–28, 270
   Marim-Dawkins House (Ye Olde Log Cabin), 223, **223**
   Merestone, 175, **175**
   Plank House, Smyrna, **228,** 229
   slave quarter, Governor Ross Mansion, 290–91, **291**
   "Swedish" Log House (Josh's Cabin), 248–29
Lombardy Hall, 51–52
Lone Pine. *See* Rest Harrow, Arden
Long Hook, 146
Longwood Gardens, Pa., 56, 62, 145
Lorimer, A. G.: Delaware Memorial Bridge, **148,** 148–49
Lorimer and Rose: Delaware Memorial Bridge, **148,** 148–49
Louviers Building. *See* office building (Louviers Building)
Louvier Stable, Odessa, 214
Lovatt, George I., 17; Providence Creek Academy (St. Joseph's Industrial School), 225, **225**
Lowber (Matthew) House, 237–38, **238**
Lowber (Peter) House. *See* Hathorn-Betts House (Hathorn-Lowber or Peter Lowber House)
Lowe, Harry, 138–39
Lowe House, 295–96
Lowell, Guy, 140
Lower Louviers, 54
lower New Castle County, 207–23
   Middletown, 216–20; map, 216
   Middletown vicinity, 215
   Odessa, 210–14; map, 212
   Port Penn, 208–10; map, 209
   Townsend vicinity, 221–23; map, 222
lower White Clay Creek Valley, 176–77; map, 177

Lueders, Albert D.: Wilmington Merchandise Mart, 46
Luke (James L., Jr.) House, 72
Lukeman, H. Augustus: Todd Memorial (Soldiers and Sailors of Delaware Monument), 122
Lum, John, 199
Lum House (Lums Mill House, Samuel Davies House), 29, 199
Lunger, Harry W., 55–56
Lunger, Jane du Pont, 55–56
Lunt, Dudley Cammett, 44
Lydia B. Cannon Museum, 260

Maass, John, 226
Mack, W. W., 76
Madison Factory, 168
Maene, Edward, 116, 121
Magnolia, 14, 237–38; map, 237
Magnolia Circle, University of Delaware, 185
Magonigle, H. Van Buren, 105
Maillol, Aristide, 74
Maloney, Tom, 99
Manahan, E. G.: Hoopes Reservoir Dam (Old Mill Stream Dam), 78–79, **79**
Mann, Frederick E.: Immanuel Episcopal Church, northwest Wilmington, 138
Mansell, T. Norman
   St. Paul's Lutheran Church, Newark, 165
   St. Philip Lutheran Church, Newark, 165
Mansfield, J. F., 214
Mansfield, Richard, 215
Manufacturers Contracting Company: DuPont Building, Wilmington, 105–7, **106**
Maples, The, 215
Marbrook Elementary School, 78, **78**
March, Leslie I., 241
Marcia Davis and Associates, 247–48
Marim, Richard, 223
Marim, Thomas, 223
Marim-Dawkins House (Ye Olde Log Cabin), 223, **223**
Marjorie Rothberg Architecture: Avon Products Northeast Regional Headquarters remodeling, 177
Market Street houses, Wilmington, 120
Marsh, Peter, 275–76
Marsh (Peter) House. *See* Homestead, The (Peter Marsh House)

Marshall, James, 119
Marshall, Tom, 81
Marshallton Bridge, 77
Martin, E. William, 42, 163
   Irisbrook, 70–71
   Legislative Hall (State Legislative Building), 255–56, **256**
   P. S. du Pont Elementary School (Pierre S. du Pont High School), Wilmington, 128–29
   Wilmington Trust Center (United States Post Office, Court House, and Custom House), 105
   Zwaanendael Museum (Zwaanendael House), 272, **273**
Martin, James, 265
Martin and Jeffers, 17–18
   Delaware Public Archives (Hall of Records), 255
   Georgetown Armory, 261
Martin family, 272
Marvel, Nutter D., 264–65
Marvel (Nutter D.) Carriage Museum, 264–65
Marx, Roberto Burle, 136
Mary Bruce Inn (The Jungalow), 39
Maryland Hall of Records, 255
Mason, Charles, 188
Mason-Dixon Line, 3
Masonic Lodge (Georgetown Academy), 261
Massena, Gabriel F., 50
Massena and du Pont, 17, 18
   A. I. du Pont Hospital for Children (A. I. du Pont Institute), 50–51
   Bellevue Hall, 41; gate lodges, 41
   Brantwyn (Bois-Des-Fosses), 54
   carillon, Nemours, 50
   Delaware Hospital for the Chronically Ill (State Welfare Home), 230, **230**
   Edison Tower, Menlo Park, N.J., 50
   1102 Hopeton Road, Westover Hills, 72
   office building (John Wanamaker Store), 45–46, **46**
   Old Town Hall (library), Wilmington, 99
   stained glass window, Nemours, 48
   Sunken Garden, Nemours, 50
   Veterans Administration Medical and Regional Office Center, 76, **76**

Wesley Church Educational Center (U.S. Post Office, Federal Building), 252–53, **253**
Westcourt Apartments (Foster Park Apartments), 135
Wilmington Hospital (Delaware Hospital), 117
Maston House, 10, 288, **288**
Mauchline, 132
Maull (Thomas) House, 268, **268**
Maxwell, Solomon, 171
May, Arthur: Hercules Inc. Headquarters, 110, **110**
May, Edward Canby, 17, 117, 194
   Delaware State Bar Association (Farmers Bank), 96
   Hotel du Pont, Wilmington, alteration, 106
   Josephine Fountain (Josephine Tatnall Smith Memorial Fountains), 124
   Nemours Main Gates, 48
   Old First Presbyterian Church restoration, 124
   State Armory, Laurel, 295
   Westminster Presbyterian Church Parish House, 137–38
May, Robert, 172, 211, 213
May B. Leasure School, 195
Mayer I. Blum and Sons, 137
MBNA, 86, 105, 175
McAndrew, John, 129
McArthur, J.: Old Farmers Bank, New Castle, 161
McBeath, Alexander, 181
McCaulley, H., 154
McClure and Harper: Archmere, 35–36, **36**
McComb, John W.: Westover Hills, 72–73
McComb House, 239
McCoy, Dr. John C., 199
McCoy, John W., Jr., 107
McCoy House. *See* Au Clair School (McCoy House)
McCune, John F., III: Old State House restoration, 253, 255
McDaniel, Harry, 234
McDermott, George: St. Norbert Hall, Archmere Academy, 36
McEwen, Lawrence D.: Volunteer Hose Company, Middletown, 217
McEwing, Barbara, 108
McGee House, 279–80
McIlvaine, John Gilbert: Mauchline, 132

McKennan, William, 169
McKennan-Klair House, 169
McKim, Charles Follen, 262
McKim, J. Leighton, 262
McKim, John Linn, 262
McKim, Mead and White, 48, 262; University of Delaware buildings, 180
McKinley, William, 201
McLane, Louis, 71
McLane-Spearman House, 227
McLaughlin-Mullen Student Life Center, Archmere Academy, 36
McWilliam, Richard: Court House, New Castle, **158**, 158–59
McWilliams, Carmen Ann, 288–89
McWilliams, William A., 54
meeting houses, 3
    Appoquinimink Friends Meeting House, 214, **214**
    Camden Friends Meeting House, 235, **235**
    Carrcroft Friends Meeting House, 32
    Center Friends Meeting House, 59, **59**
    Hockessin Friends Meeting House, 165–66
    Mill Creek Friends Meeting House, 166
    Wilmington Friends Meeting House, 8, 10, 111, 113, **113**
Mellor, Meigs and Howe
    Bramshott, 56
    Eleutherian Mills, 21, 68
    Selborne Farms, 21
Mellor, Walter: Bramshott, 56
Memorial Hall, University of Delaware, 184–**85**
memorials. *See* monuments and memorials
Mencken, H. L., 73
Mendenhall (Thomas) House, 86
Menlo Park, N.J.: Edison Tower, 50
Mente, Charles, 115
Merestone, 21, 175, **175**
Mermaid Tavern, 168–69
Merrick, John, 108–9
Mersereau, William H.: Old Swedes Church (Holy Trinity), Wilmington restoration, 88–90
Metcalf and Eddy: Porter Rapid Sand Filter Plant, 46, **46**
Methodists, 3, 239–40, 259, 276, 297–98

Meyer, Richard Conway
    Kip du Pont Boathouse, St. Andrew's School, Middletown, 220
    Volunteer Hose Company, Middletown, 217
MGZA
    Cool Spring Reservoir Pumping Station renovation, 131
    Rockford Tower restoration, 140
Middle Space, 286
Middletown, 14, 210, 216–20; map, 216
Middletown vicinity, 215
Mid-Town Parking Center, 114, **114**
Midway School No. 178, 270
Mifflin, Daniel, 235
Mifflin House, Dover, 249
Mike's Famous Roadside Rest, 148, **148**
Milford, 224, 243–45; map, 242
Milford Historical Society, 244
Mill at White Clay, The (Joseph Dean and Son), 178, **178**
Mill Creek Friends Meeting House, 166
Mill Creek Hundred, 165–72
    north, map, 167
    south, map, 171
    See also Christiana; Hockessin; Limestone Road (DE 7); Red Clay Creek: down; Stanton Vicinity
Milles, Carl, 87, 88
Milligan, George, 71
Mills, Robert, 16, 151, 154, 155
mills and mill complexes, 8, 82
    Abbott's Mill Nature Center, 284
    Augustine Mills, 45, 126
    Bancroft Mills, 143, **143**
    Birkenhead Mills, 66
    Brandywine Village district, 117
    Brecknock (Howell's Mill Seat), 235, **235**
    Breck's Mill, 71, **71**
    Cooch-Dayett Mill, 194–95
    Curtis Paper Company, 173
    Delaware Iron Works, 78
    DuPont gunpowder mills, 55, 65–66
    England (John) House and Mill, 8, **176**, 176–77
    Greenbank Mill, 168, **168**
    Hagley Yard, **66**, 66–67
    Harlan Mill, 169
    Henry Clay Mill, 67–68, 71
    Lea Mills, 117, **118**
    The Lindens (Miller's House), 225

    The Mill at White Clay (Joseph Dean and Son), 178, **178**
    Mill Creek Hundred, 165
    Noxontown Mill, 8, 220, **220**
    Rockland Mills, 54
    Rokeby Mill, 71
    Smith's Mill House, 54
    Sussex County, 258
    Walker's Mill, 71, **71**
    Yorklyn snuff mills, 55
Millsboro, 259; southwest of, 297–98
Milner, John, 155
Milton, 260; map, 262
Minuit, Peter, 5
Mispillion Riverwalk and Greenway, 244
Mitchell, James, 295
Mitchell, Nathaniel, 295
Mitchell, Richard: Smyrna Opera House and Old Town Hall, 229, **229**
Mitchell Associates, 247–48
Mizner, Addison, 60
modernism, 12, 32–33, 42, 46, 52, 53, 96, 106, 109–10, 129, 133, 177, 246. *See also* International Style; Streamline Moderne style
Moeckel, William, 42, 107, 133; Hendrickson House, 90
Moeckel/Carbonell + Partners
    State Office Building (Richardson and Robbins Cannery Complex), 250
    Wilmington Station (Pennsylvania Railroad Passenger Station) restoration, 91
Moeckel Carbonell Associates, 18, 44, 54
    Delaware Public Archives renovation, 255
    J. Morton Poole Buildings, 91
    Lammot du Pont Laboratory, University of Delaware, 180–81
    Legislative Hall refurbishment, 256
    Recitation Hall Annex (Agricultural Experiment Station) renovation, 182
    Recitation Hall renovation, 182
    Tower Hill School Arts Center, 144
Monaghan, Paul: Ursuline Academy, 130
Monday Club, 16
Mondrian, Piet, 110
Monmouth County, N.J.: Holmes-Hendrickson House, 153
Mon Plaisir, 277, 278, **278**

Montchanin Building. *See* Community Service Building (Montchanin Building), Wilmington
Montchanin Design Group: 906 Westover Road, 73
Monterey, 14
Montgomery, Charles F., 29, 61, 166
Montgomery, Tom, 48
Montgomery (Thomas) House, 173
Montpelier, Va., 41, 71
monuments and memorials
  Caesar Rodney Equestrian Monument, 104
  DeVries Monument, 268
  Fort Christina, 88
  Josephine Fountain (Josephine Tatnall Smith Memorial Fountains), 30, 124
  President McKinley Memorial, 124
  Samuel F. Du Pont Statue, 140
  Soldiers and Sailors Monument, northwest Wilmington, **138**, 138–39
  Thomas F. Bayard Statue, 140
  Todd Memorial (Soldiers and Sailors of Delaware Monument), 122
  William M. Canby Memorial, 140
  William Penn Statue, 157
Moonlight Theater, Arden, 40
Moore, W. Lee, 45–46
Mordington, 61, 241
Morning Star Institutional Church of God in Christ (Whatcoat Methodist Episcopal Church), 235–36
Morris, William, 40
Mortelido, 107
Mosca, Matthew, 154
Mott, Lucretia, 253
Mt. Airy No. 27 School, 56
Mt. Cuba, 21, 42, 79, 166–68
Mt. Pleasant, Kent County, 270
Mrs. Steele's Broiler House, 14, 248
Muir, John, 140
Mullett, Alfred B.: Soldiers and Sailors Monument, northwest Wilmington, **138**, 138–39
Mullins Store, Wilmington, 100
Mulrooney, Thomas F., 133–34
Munroe, John A., 29
museums
  Air Mobility Command Museum, 257

Anna Hazzard Museum, 277, **277**
Delaware Agricultural Museum and Village, 14, 248–49
Delaware Archaeological Museum (Old Presbyterian Church), 5, 251–52
Delaware Art Museum (Delaware Art Center), 42, 142–43, 167
Delaware History Museum, 97
Hagley Museum, 5, 46, **65**, 65–69, 168
Iron Hill Museum (Iron Hill School No. 112C), 15, 193
Lewes Historical Society Complex, 268, 270
Lydia B. Cannon Museum, 260
Marvel (Nutter D.) Carriage Museum, 264–65
Nanticoke Indian Museum, 279
Read (George) House, 163
Rockwood Museum (Shipley-Bringhurst Mansion), 14, **44**, 44
school buildings, 15
Smyrna Museum (The Barracks), 229
Winterthur House and Museum, 17, 19, 21, 29, 48, 55, 60–64
Zwaanendael Museum (Zwaanendael House), 272, **273**

Naamans Tea House. *See* Robinson House (Naamans Tea House)
Nader, Ralph, 288–89
Nanticoke Homes. *See* Beracah Homes (Nanticoke Homes)
Nanticoke Indian Museum, 279
Nanticoke tribe, 5, 279
National Aniline Chemical, 33
National Highway Association, 266–67
National Register of Historic Places, 38
National Trust for Historic Preservation, 27
Native Americans, 3–5, 192, 279
Naudain, Andrew, 222
Naudain, Elias, 221–22
Naudain (Elias) House. *See* Huguenot House (Elias Naudain House)
Nearing, Scott, 40
Nearing (Scott) Cottage, 39

Nelson, Jim, 19
  Claymont Stone School restoration, 35
  New Castle County Library, Brandywine Hundred Branch, 52
Nelson, Lee: Old Town Hall, Wilmington restoration, **98**, 98–99
Nemours, 20, 21, 33, 47–51, **48**, 62
Nemours Building, 107–8
Nemours Foundation, 51
Newark, 178–91
  Main Street, 178
  population, 173
  south of center, 190–91; map, 189
  west of University of Delaware, 188–90; map, 189
Newark Elementary School, 42
Newbold family, 203
New Castle, 22, 149–64, **150**; old, map, 152
  colonial architecture in, 8
  Court House, 150, **158**, 158–59, 183
  Dutch in, **6**, 7, 21, 149–50, 152–53, 156
  historical preservation in, 27
  pillory and whipping post in, 13, 157
New Castle and Frenchtown Railroad, 23, 158, 162; ticket office, 162, **162**
New Castle County, 3, 25–26
  brick construction in, 10
  Courthouse, 96, **97**, 104
  Library Brandywine Hundred Branch, 52
  log houses in, 7
  lower, 207–23 (*see also* Middletown; Middletown vicinity; Odessa; Port Penn; Townsend vicinity)
New Castle County Airport (Greater Wilmington Airport), 149
New Castle Hall, University of Delaware, 185
New Castle Historical Society, 151, 153
New Castle Hundred, 146–64; map, 147
  north, 146–49
  south, 164
New Castle Institute, 156
New Castle Manufacturing Company, 151
New Castle Presbyterian Church, **150**, 156

New Century Club. *See* Delaware Children's Theater (New Century Club)
Newell, Henry, 239
Newell-Sipple-Reed families, 239
New Haven, Conn.: Connecticut Hall, Yale University, 183
Newkirk, Matthew, 168
Newport, 22, 76–77, **77**
Newport, R.I.: Vernon Court, 48
Newport and Gap Turnpike toll road, 165, 169
New Sweden colony, 5
New York City, N.Y.
    Brooklyn Bridge, 32
    Empire State Building, 35
    Frick Mansion, 48
    Shelton Hotel, 115
Nichols, Minerva Parker, 278; Delaware Children's Theater (New Century Club), 130, **130**, 278
Nine Foot Road (Smith Mill Road), 175
906 Westover Road, 73
Nolen, John
    Overlook Colony, 36, 134
    Union Park Gardens, 134–35
Nones, Albert S., 138–39
Norbertine Order, 36
Norfolk, Va.: U.S. Naval Asylum, 259
Norman Day Associates, 254
North Cass Street houses, Middletown, 217
northeast Wilmington, 126–29; map, 128
North Market Street Bridge, Wilmington, 21, 117, 119
North Milford Historic District, 243
North State Street houses, Dover, 249–50
northwest Wilmington, 135–45; map, 139
Notman, John, 16
    Boothhurst addition, 146
    Cathedral Church of St. John, Wilmington, **120**, 120–21
    Dunleith, 146
    Immanuel Episcopal Church on the Green, New Castle, 154–55
Nottingham Green, Newark, 189–90
Noxon, Thomas, 220
Noxontown Mill, 8, 220, **220**
Number, Charles, 224
Nylon Suite, Hotel du Pont, Wilmington, **17**

Oaklands, Newark, 189–90
Oakley, Annie, 151
Oberly Brick Company, 83
Oberod, 21, 55–56
Octagonal Schoolhouse (District No. 12 Public School), 29, 232, **232**
Odd Fellows Cemetery, Smyrna, 226
Odessa, 210–14; map, 212
Odessa Bank, 214
office building (Bank of Delaware), 141–42, **142**
office building (Harlan and Hollingsworth Company Office Building), 92
office building (John Wanamaker Store), 45–46, **46**
office building (Louviers Building), 175, 191
office tower (Rollins International), 53
Ogletown, 7
Okie, R. Brognard
    Buena Vista library wing, 164
    1101 Hopeton Road, Westover Hills, 72–73
    Merestone, 21, 175
Old Academy, New Castle, 154
Old Brandywine Village, Inc., 117–18, 119–20
Old Christ Church, Laurel, 156, 295, 296, **296**
Old College, University of Delaware, 179, **181**, 181–82, 183
Old Courthouse, Georgetown, 264, **264**
Old Custom House (Old Federal Building), 98, 99, **100**
Old Delaware Bank Association, 142
Old Dover Day, 27, 246
Old Drawyers Church, 183, 210–11, **211**, 239
Olde Colonial Village, 51
Old Farmers Bank, New Castle, 161
Old First Presbyterian Church, Wilmington, 26, 97, 124, **124**, 176
Old Library, New Castle, 154, **154**
Old Post Office, Seaford, 289
Old Presbyterian Church, Dover, 5, 251–52
Old St. Anne's Church, Middletown, **218**, 218–19
Old St. Georges Bridge, 200–201, **201**
Old State House, 253, 255, **255**
Old Stone Tavern, 11, 232

Old Swedes Church (Holy Trinity), Wilmington, 5, 26, 88–90, **89**, 98, 121
Old Town Hall, Wilmington, 26, 27, 96, **98**, 98–99
Old Union Methodist Church, Townsend, 221
Oliver, Joseph, 243
Olmsted, Frederick Law, 123, 140
Olmsted, John C., 140
107 Kings Highway, Lewes, 295
116 Technologies, 91
123 Front Street, Frederica, 240
123 W. Main St., Middletown, 216
129 Front Street, Milford, 243
O'Neal, Rodney: Barrel Barn, Georgetown, 265
Onondaga Litholite Company, 104
Opera House, New Castle, 151
outbuildings, 14–15
    Causey Mansion, 245
    Cochran Grange, 218
    Corbit-Sharp smokehouse, 213, **213**
    Dickinson Mansion, 236
    Poplar Level, 285
    Ross (Governor) Mansion, 290
    Wheel of Fortune, 232
Overlook Colony, 24, 36, 134
Owl's Nest. *See* Greenville Country Club (Owl's Nest)

Pagan Creek Dike, 268
Palm, Per A., 88
Palmer, Hornbostel and Jones: Public Building of the City of Wilmington and County of New Castle (former), 105, **105**
Paper Mill Road covered bridge, 173
Parke, Thomas, 253
Parker, Donald H., 236
Parke-Ridgely House, 183, 253, **253**, **254**
parking garages
    Mid-Town Parking Center, 114, **114**
    Riverfront Parking Deck, 91
Parks, Charles C., 101, 102, 122, 136, 157
parks
    Brandywine Park, 123, **123**
    Brandywine Springs Park, 168
    Cape Henlopen State Park, 274–75
    Columbus Square, northwest Wilmington, 136
    Fort Christina Park, 5, 87–88, 93

parks (*continued*)
    Fountain Plaza, northwest Wilmington, 136, **136**
    Glasgow Regional Park, 197
    The Green, New Castle, 150–51
    Mispillion Riverwalk and Greenway, 244
    Rockford Park, northwest Wilmington, 140
    White Clay Creek State Park, 173
Parkside, Town of, 26, 215
Parrish, Maxfield, 59
Parsons, Klapp, Brinckerhoff and Douglas: Old St. Georges Bridge, 200–201, **201**
Pavlo, E. Lionel: Delaware Memorial Bridge, **148**, 148–49
Paynter, Samuel, 268
Peabody Institute, Baltimore, Md., 108–9
"Peach Mansions," 24
Peale, Charles Willson, 117
Pearce, John, 169
Pei, I. M., 42
    East Building for the National Gallery of Art, Washington, D.C., 109
    1105 North Market Street (Wilmington Tower), **109**, 109–10
    Municipal Center, Dallas, 109
    Society Hill Towers, Philadelphia, 42
Pelleport, 31n18, 70–71
Pels, Albert, 105
Pencader Hundred, 192–206. *See also* Chesapeake and Delaware (C&D) Canal; Delaware City; Glasgow; St. Georges and vicinity
Pencader Presbyterian Church, 196, **196**
Penn, John, 182
Penn, Thomas, 265
Penn, William, 2, 32, 150, 158, 191, 196, 246, 254, 283
Penn (William) Guest House, New Castle, 150
Pennsylvania Building, Wilmington, 91
Pennsylvania Railroad, 23
Pennsylvania Railroad Station, Clayton, 225
Penny House, 44, 45, **45**
Perkins House on Penny Hill, Wilmington, 160
Perot, Robeson Lea, 20
    Taylor Hall, University of Delaware, 182
    Winterthur, 60–61

Perry, Shaw and Hepburn and New Castle, 152, 156
    New Castle Court House restoration, 158–59
Philadelphia, Pa.
    Bingham (William) Mansion, 161
    Congress Hall, 182
    D'Ascenzo Studios, 129
    Delaware State Building, 1876 Centennial Exhibition, 16
    Divinity School, 121
    Eastern State Penitentiary, 259
    Guild House, 186
    Independence Hall, 185
    Main Building, 1876 Centennial Exhibition, 32
    Moyamensing Prison, 259
    Powel House, 212
    St. Paul's, Chestnut Hill, 120
    Society Hill Towers, 109
    Stamper House, 227
    Town Hall, 158
    260 Arch Street, 161
    University of Pennsylvania, 154, 180, 183, 187
    Valley Forge Memorial Chapel, 120–21
    Walnut Street Bridge, 46
    William Reith Studios, 115
Philadelphia Single Tax Society, 37
Philadelphia, Wilmington and Baltimore Railroad, 82
Philips family, 168
Pietrantonio, Father Thomas, 41
Pilchard, Sewell N., 239
pit houses, 3–5
Plank House, Smyrna, **228**, 229
plank houses, 7, 27–28, 34, **228**, 229, 270
Planning Design Research Corporation: office building (John Wanamaker Store) adaptation, 45–46
Platt, Charles A., 104
Platt Associates: office tower (Rollins International), 53
Playtex Products (International Latex Company), 246, 250
PNC Bank (National Bank), Smyrna, 228
Poe, Edgar Allan, 183, 188
Police Department, Bridgeville, 286
Polk, Robert, 203
Polk, William, 214
Polk-Henry House, 203–4
Pomada, Elizabeth, 244
Ponder (Governor) House, 260
Poole, William: Wilmington

Friends Meeting House, 113, **113**
Pope, George E.
    DuPont Building remodeling, 106
    Dutch House restoration, 153
Pope, John Russell, 104
Pope, Kruse and McCune
    New Castle Court House restoration, 158–59
    Old State House restoration, 253
Pope and Kruse, 18, 155; State Police headquarters, 264
Pope-Mustard Mansion, 227, **227**
Poplar Level, 285, 286
Port Penn, 208–10; map, 209
Porter, Alexander, 116
Porter Rapid Sand Filter Plant, 46, **46**
Porter's Lodge, 44
Portland Museum of Art, Maine, 142
postmodernism, 47, 58, 110, 111, 195, 220
postmolds, 3
post offices
    Dover Post Office, **28**, 247
    Georgetown Post Office, 261, 263
    Harrington Post Office, 242
    Old Post Office, Seaford, 289
    Smyrna Post Office, 229
    Wesley Church Educational Center (U.S. Post Office, Federal Building), 252–53, **253**
    Wilmington Trust Center (United States Post Office, Court House, and Custom House), **104**, 105
    Winterthur Railroad Station and Post Office, 63
Potter, William Appleton: Dover Post Office, **28**, 247
Potter, William Woodburn, 17, 72
    Church of the Holy City (Swedenborgian), 133
    Westminster Presbyterian Church, northwest Wilmington, 137–38
Potter (Benjamin) Mansion, **9**, 258
Practical Farmer Inn, 33–34
Pratt Truss Bridge, 79
prefabricated architecture, 32, 38, 50, 284–85
preparatory school campuses. *See* colleges, universities, preparatory school campuses

Presbyterian Church, St. Georges, 200
Presbyterians, 3
President McKinley Memorial, 124
Press of Kells, 184, 190, 275
Preston, W. Ellis, 18
    Asbury United Methodist Church education annex, 227
    Delaware Trust Building, 102
    Government Center plan, 101
    Hillcrest Bellefonte Methodist Church, 53
    New Castle County Airport control tower and terminal, 149
    office tower (Rollins International), 53
    Union Park Pontiac dealership, 133
Price, Isaac, 172
Price, James, 117
Price, William, 17, 37, 39
    Craft Shop, 40
    Friendly Gables, 38–39
    Gild Hall (Arden Club House), 40, **40**
    Green Gate, 39
    The Lodge, 39
    Rest Cottage, Arden, 40, **40**
    Rest Harrow, 40
Prices Corner Shopping Center, 26, 77
Priestman, Mabel Tuke, 38
Prince George's Chapel, **282**, 282–83
Princeton University, N.J., 179, 184
privies, 14
Proctor, Doug: St. Anne's School, Middletown, 219
Providence Creek Academy (St. Joseph's Industrial School), 225, **225**
P. S. du Pont Elementary School (Pierre S. du Pont High School), Wilmington, 83, 128–29
Public Building of the City of Wilmington and County of New Castle (former), **104**, 105, **105**
Pugin, A. W. N., 115
Pusey and Jones Company, 139
Pyle, Howard, 26, 34, 37, 74, 89, 106, 136–37, 139, 230
Pyle, Walter, 226, 261
Pyle (Frank) House, 132, **132**
Pyle (Howard) Studios, 14, 74, 136–37, **137**

Quaker Hill, Wilmington, 111
Quakers, 3, 8, 32, 59, 64–65, 111, 214, 224, 234, 250
quarries: Brandywine Granite Quarry, 11, **11**, 46–47, 64, 126
Queen Anne architecture, 14, 70, 73, 81, 97, 131, 132, 136–37, 182, 200, 217, 238, 243, 244, 247, 271, 283, 285–86, 290, 291, 295
Queen Anne houses, northwest Wilmington, 137, **137**
Queen Theater (Clayton House Hotel), Wilmington, 14, 97

Rabbit's Ferry House, 268, 270
racetracks
    Delaware Park Racetrack, 3
    Dover Downs and Dover International Speedway, **247**, 247–48
    McCoy harness-racing track, 3
Rahenkamp, Sachs and Associates: Valley Run, 36, **36**
railroads, 23–24, 259
    Baltimore and Ohio (B&O) Railroad, 23
    Delaware, 1880s, map, 23
    Delaware Railroad, 23, 294–95
    New Castle and Frenchtown Railroad, 23, 158, 162
    Philadelphia, Wilmington and Baltimore Railroad, 82
    Wilmington and Western Railroad, 23, 78, 79, 166, 168
railroad stations, 24
    Baltimore and Ohio (B&O) Station, Newark, 173
    Baltimore and Ohio (B&O) Station, Trolley Square, Wilmington, 16–17, 135
    Georgetown Railroad Station, 261
    George V. Massey Station (Pennsylvania Station), 251
    Pennsylvania Railroad Station, Clayton, 225
    Rehoboth Beach, 276
    Wilmington Station (Pennsylvania Railroad Passenger Station), 16, **90**, 91
    Winterthur Railroad Station and Post Office, 63
Rainier, Prince, of Monaco, 70
Raley, Robert L., 28, 35
    and "Delaware Plank House," 169
    and First Delaware Preservation Conference, 152

    Hendrickson House, 90
    Lea (Thomas) House restoration, 119–20
    and Old Brandywine Village, Inc., 117
    Parke-Ridgely House refurbishment, 253
    Wilson-Warner House and stable restoration, 213
Randel, John, Jr.
    Chesapeake and Delaware (C&D) Canal, 198
    Delaware Tide Lock, Chesapeake and Delaware (C&D) Canal, 204, **204**
    New Castle and Frenchtown Railroad survey, 162
Raskob, John Jacob, 35–36, 50, 70, 104, 106
Raskob, William, 70
Raskob Foundation for Catholic Activities, 70
Rawl, Allen, 87
Raymond Neck Historic District, 224
R. Calvin Clendaniel Associates, 19
    Court of Chancery, Georgetown, 263–64, **264**
    Dover Post Office, 247
    Farmers Bank, Georgetown, 263
    Sussex County Administration Building, 263
Read (George) House, 27, **150**, 154, 161, **161**, 163; garden, 163
Reading, Philip, 218
Recitation Hall, University of Delaware, 182
Recitation Hall Annex (Agricultural Experiment Station), University of Delaware, 182
Red Clay Creek, 55; down, 166–68
Redden Lodge, 24, 260
Redding, Louis L., 166
Red House and Craft Shop, Arden, 40
Red Lion Hundred, 192–206. *See also* Chesapeake and Delaware (C&D) Canal; Delaware City; Glasgow; St. Georges and vicinity
Red Lion Inn facade, 61, **61**
Reed, Jehu M., 239
Reed (Jehu M.) House, **13**, 238–39, **239**
Reedy Point Bridge, 203
Reese, John, 175
Rehoboth Art League, 275
Rehoboth Beach, 259, **259**, 276–78; map, 269

INDEX   345

Rehoboth Heights, 276
Rencourt, 31n18
Residences at Rodney Square (Delaware Trust Building), 102
residential developments
    Brandywine Hundred, 32
    Brookside, 190–91
    Centreville Reserve, 57, **57**
    Edgemoor Terrace, **25**
    Fairfax, 24, 52–53
    Henlopen Acres, 24, **274**, 275
    Oaklands and Nottingham Green, Newark, 189–90
    Residences at Rodney Square, 102
    Shipcarpenter Square, Lewes, 270
    Ships Tavern Mews, Wilmington, 96, **96**
    Town of Parkside, 26, 215
    Union Park Gardens, 24, 130, 134–35
    Valley Run, 26, 36
    Village at Kings Creek, 26, 279, **279**
    Village of Eastlake (Eastlake Public Housing Project), 127
    Villa Monterey (Corinne Court), 24, 43, **43**
    Westover Hills, 43, 72–73, **73**
    Willard Street vicinity houses, 143–44, **144**
    Wilmington-area, 83
    See also apartments and condominiums; worker housing
Rest Cottage, Arden, 40, **40**
Rest Harrow, Arden, 40
Reyam, David, 160
Reybold, Philip, 201
Reynolds Candy Store. *See* Cavanaugh's Restaurant (Reynolds Candy Store)
R. Graham and Sons: Hudson Mansion, 227
Rhodes Pharmacy, Newark, 178
Rice, Edward Luff, Jr., 16
    All Saints Episcopal Church, Rehoboth Beach, 276–77
    Schoonover (Frank E.) Studios, **138**, 139, 141
    Shortlidge School, 126
    Westminster Presbyterian Church nave and transepts, 137–38
    Willard Hall School, 125
Rich, Charles A.: DuPont Theatre, Wilmington, 106
Richards, John (I), 285

Richards, John (II), 285–86
Richards, John Emory, 286
Richardson, Harry A., 249–50
Richardson, H. H., 113
Richardson, John, 75
Richardson and Robbins Cannery Complex. *See* State Office Building (Richardson and Robbins Cannery Complex)
Richardson (Harry A.) Hall, 249–50
Richardson (John) House (Brick Mill House), 75
Ridgely, Ann, 256
Ridgely, Charles G., 253
Ridgely, Henry, 249
Ridgely, Mabel Lloyd, 28, 253, 255, 256, 272, 278
Rising, Johan, 35
Rising Sun Bridge, **71**, 71–72
Ritchie, Effie Stillman, 140
Riverfront Development Corporation, 86
Riverfront Parking Deck, 91
Riverview. *See* Carpenter House (Riverview)
Rizzo, Joseph C.: New Castle County Library Brandywine Hundred Branch, 52
roads, 10, 22–23, 24, 32–33, 56, 165, 168–69, 175, 192–93, 210, 226, 266–67; Delaware, 1790s, map, 10
Robbins, Roland Wells, 67
Robbins Hardware Store, Frederica, 240
Robert May and Company, 211
Robert Scott's Block, Lewes, 271
Robertson (Henry B.) House, 42
Robinson, Hanson, 41
Robinson, Reah de B., 108, 115, 144; Delmarva Power and Light Company, 100
Robinson, Rodney
    Gibraltar garden restoration, 145
    Magnolia Circle redesign, 185
    Rodney Square redesign, 104
Robinson, Stanhope and Manning
    Edge Moor Elementary School, 41, 42, **42**
    Silverside Carr Executive Center (Silverside Elementary School), 41
    Wilmington Trust Center (United States Post Office, Court House, and Custom House), 105
Robinson, Thomas, 34
Robinson House (Naamans Tea House), 34–35

Rockford Park, northwest Wilmington, 140
Rockford Tower, northwest Wilmington, 52, 140, **140**
Rockland Bridge, 54
Rockland Mills, 54
rock shelters, 5
Rockwood Museum (Shipley-Bringhurst Mansion), 14, 44, **44**
Rodgers, Daniel, 295
Rodney, Caesar, 220; Equestrian Monument, 104
Rodney, Caesar A., Jr., 130
Rodney, Daniel, 295
Rodney Complex (West Complex), University of Delaware, **187**, 187–88
Rodney House, New Castle, 159
Rodney Square, Wilmington, 103–4, **104**, 121
Rodney Street Chapel, northwest Wilmington, 137–38
Rogers, Daniel, 244–45
Rogers, Laussat R., 146, 155, 222
    Amstel House restoration, 160, **160**
    Arsenal, New Castle, 155–56
    Immanuel Parish House wing, 161
    New Castle Court House restoration, 158–59
    Warner Hall, University of Delaware, 185
Rohrbach, Edward, 40
Rokeby House, 71
Rokeby Mill, 71
Rollins, John W., 53, 247
Roman Catholics, 3
Roman Revival architecture, 119
Roosevelt, Franklin, Jr., 58
Roosevelt, Franklin D., 58, 65, 70, 88, 135
Rose Cottage, 251, **251**
Rosemont, Laurel, 295, **295**
Rosemont House, New Castle, 150
Rosenblum, Martin, 163
Rose Valley, Pa., 37, 39
Ross, James J., 290
Ross, William Henry Harrison, 289
Ross, Willie, 291
Ross-Allen House, 291, **291**
Ross (Governor) Mansion, 14, 15, 289–91, **290**
Rothberg, Marjorie, 177, 278
Roudebush, Rhoda B., 244
Rouse and Wilmington Renaissance Corporation: Ships Tavern Mews, Wilmington, restoration, 96, **96**
Rowland (David) House. *See*

346   **INDEX**

Cannonball House (David Rowland House)
Royer Brothers, 101
Rubin, Richard I., 77
Russell, Phillip, 270
Russum, F. W.: DuPont Building, Wilmington, 105–7
Rust, Peter, 292
Ruth, Kim, 238

Saarinen, Eliel: Crow Island School, Winnetka, Ill., 41
Sachse, Edward, 82, 86
St. Amour site, 31n18, 73, 167, 185
St. Andrew's School, Middletown, 11, 219, **219**
St. Anne's Church, Middletown, 217, 228
St. Anne's School, Middletown, 219–20
St. Anthony of Padua Church, west Wilmington, 133–34, **134**
St. Francis Renewal Center (Samuel N. Trump House), 41
Saint-Gaudens, Augustus, 122
St. Georges and vicinity, 200–203; map, 202
St. Georges Bridge. *See* Senator William V. Roth Jr. Bridge (DE 1 Bridge, St. Georges Bridge)
St. Giles, 31n18
St. James Episcopal Church Millcreek Hundred, 169–70, **170**
St. Joseph on the Brandywine, 70
St. Luke's Episcopal Church, Seaford, 292
St. Norbert Hall, Archmere Academy, 36
St. Paul's Catholic Church, west Wilmington, 131
St. Paul's Episcopal Church, Georgetown, 257, **261**, 261–63
St. Petersburg, Fla.: Sunshine Skyway Bridge, 200
St. Peter's Episcopal Church, Lewes, 271, **271**
St. Peter's Episcopal Church, Smyrna, 227–28
Salesianum, 126
Salisbury, Eve, 242
Salsbury, Stephen, 105
Sandtown, 224
Sarrabezolles, Carlo, 50
Sater, Dan F.: Village at Kings Creek, 279, **279**

Saulsbury, Willard, 116, 257, 260
Savage, George D.: Kingswood United Methodist Church, 191
Saxelbye, Powell, Roberts and Ponder: A. I. du Pont Hospital for Children (A. I. du Pont Institute), 50–51
Scharf, Thomas, 248
Scheiner, James M., 64
Schenck, William S., 232
Schine Theater (Plaza Theater), Milford, 243
school buildings, 18
  Academy Building, Middletown, 217
  Alexis I. du Pont Middle School (Public School, U.S. Districts 23 and 75), 72, **72**
  Arden School, 40, 278
  Au Clair School (McCoy House), 199, **199**
  Blocksom's Colored School, 15
  Brandywine Academy, 121–22
  Brandywine High School, 32
  Brandywine Manufacturers' Sunday School, 68, 69
  Cab Calloway School of the Arts (Wilmington High School), 26, 135, **135**
  Centre Grove School, 59
  Claymont Stone School, 35
  in Colonial Revival style, 12
  Commodore Macdonough School, 200
  Edge Moor Elementary School, 41, 42, **42**
  "Eight Square School," 232
  Ellis Grove School, 264
  Emalea Pusey Warner School, 84
  Frederica Public School, 240
  Georgetown Academy, 261
  Hockessin Community Center (Hockessin School 107-C), 15, 166, **166**
  Howard High School, 90–91
  Iron Hill Museum (Iron Hill School No. 112C), 15, 193
  Jason Building, Delaware Technical and Community College (William C. Jason Comprehensive High School), 265
  John Bassett Moore Intermediate School, 226
  Kuumba Academy Charter School, 99
  Marbrook Elementary School, 78, **78**
  May B. Leasure School, 195
  Midway School No. 178, 270

Mt. Airy No. 27 School, 56
Newark Elementary School, 42
Octagonal Schoolhouse (District No. 12 Public School), 29, 232, **232**
Old Academy, New Castle, 154
Providence Creek Academy (St. Joseph's Industrial School), 225, **225**
P. S. du Pont Elementary School (Pierre S. du Pont High School), Wilmington, 83, 128–29
Pyle (Howard) Studios, 14, 74, 136–37, **137**
St. Andrew's School, Middletown, 11, 219, **219**
St. Anne's School, Middletown, 219–20
Salesianum, 126
Shortlidge School, 126
Silverside Carr Executive Center (Silverside Elementary School), 41
Thurgood Marshall Elementary School, 195, **195**
Tower Hill School, northwest Wilmington, 144
Willard Hall School, 125
W. T. Chipman Middle School, 242
See also colleges, universities, preparatory school campuses
Schoonover, Frank, 76, 137, 138, 139, 141
Schoonover (Frank E.) Studios, **138**, 139, 141
Schwartz, George M., 252
Schwartz, Milton: 1401 Condominiums, northwest Wilmington, 137, **138**
Schwartz Center for the Arts (Dover Opera House), 252, **252**
Scott, George Gilbert, 114
Seaford, 14, 270–71, 284, 288–93; map, 289
Seaford Bridge (State Bridge No. 151), 292, **292**
Seaford Historical Society, 289, 290
Sears, Thomas Warren: Mt. Cuba, 166–68
Seattle Art Museum, 186
Second Empire architecture, 227, 260
Second Homestead, Arden, 39, **39**
Security Trust and Safe Deposit Company. *See* Kuumba Academy Charter School

Seeler, Edgar V.: Old Town Hall, Wilmington restoration, **98**, 98–99
Selborne Farms, 21, 56
Senator William V. Roth Jr. Bridge (DE 1 Bridge, St. Georges Bridge), 199–200, 281
Seybold, Joanne: Nylon Suite, Hotel du Pont, Wilmington, **17**, 107
Shannon, William, 172
Shannon Hotel, 172, **172**
Sharp, H. Rodney, 12, 256
   and Chevannes, 65
   and Gibraltar, 144–45
   and Odessa, 210, 212, 214; Corbin-Sharp garden, 211
   travels, 20
   and University of Delaware, 178–79, 180, 181, 183, 184, 185
Sharp, Isabella du Pont, 56
Shaw, Robert, 26, 44, 45, 89
Shay, Howell L.: Recitation Hall, University of Delaware, 182
Shepley, Bulfinch, Richardson and Abbott
   Crowninshield Research Building, 61, 63
   Wilmington Public Library interior, 102–3
Sheriff's House and jail site, New Castle, 157, **157**
Sherwood Forest, 37
Shingle Style, 132
Ship-Carpenters' houses, Bethel, 294, **294**
Shipcarpenter Square, Lewes, 270
Shipley, Joseph, 44
Shipley-Bringhurst Mansion. *See* Rockwood Museum (Shipley-Bringhurst Mansion)
Shipley (Thomas) House, 61
Shipley Run, Wilmington, 111
Shipman, Ellen Biddle, 57–58, 278
Ships Tavern Mews, Wilmington, **95**, 96, **96**
shipyards
   Harlan and Hollingsworth, **87**
   Kalmar Nyckel, 87
shooting lodges, 24, 260
shopping centers. *See* stores and shopping centers
Shortlidge School, 126
shutters, 8
Sign of the Ship Tavern, 96
Sigstedt, Karl, 220
Sigstedt, Thorsten, 69
Silver, Frank, 61

Silver Lake, 276
Silverside Carr Executive Center (Silverside Elementary School), 41
Silverside Elementary School. *See* Silverside Carr Executive Center (Silverside Elementary School)
Simon, Louis A., 242
Sims, Joseph E.: Walker's Mill, 71, **71**
Sinclair, Upton, 38, 39, 40
Sipple, Caleb B.
   Brick Hotel, Georgetown, 264, **264**
   Sussex County Courthouse, 263, **263**
Sipple, Sally A., 254
Sipple (Sally A.) House, 233–34
slave quarter, Governor Ross Mansion, 290–91, **291**
slavery and slave trade, 3, 15, 207, 245, 290–91. *See also* Underground Railroad
Sleeper, Henry D., 60
Sloan, Samuel, 16, 271
   Church of the Ascension, Claymont, 35
   Lexington, 14, 201
   Odessa Bank, 214
   St. Paul's Methodist Church, Odessa, 214
   Sheriff's House and jail site, New Castle, 157, **157**
   West Presbyterian Church, Wilmington, 113
Sloan and Stewart: St. Peter's Episcopal Church, Lewes, 271, **271**
Smart, John, 89
Smith, Al, 35
Smith, Barbara Clark, 169
Smith, Duncan, 107
Smith, J. Ernest, 124
Smith, John Rubens, 54
Smith, Otis H., 271
Smith, W. Gary: Enchanted Woods, Winterthur, 64
Smith Hall, University of Delaware, 12, 186
Smith's Bridge, 22, 54
Smith's Mill House, 54
smokehouses, 14, 213, **213**
Smyrna, 7, 224, 225–31; map, 226
Smyrna Museum (The Barracks), 229
Smyrna Opera House and Old Town Hall, 229, **229**
Smyrna Post Office, 229
Smyth, James M., 48, 72, 83
Smyth Construction Company, 73

Snapp Site, St. Georges Creek, 3–4
Social Security Administration Office, Dover, 251
Society for the Propagation of the Gospel, 169
Society of Colonial Wars, 124
Society of Friends. *See* Quakers
Society of Natural History of Delaware, 131
Society of the Colonial Dames, 124
Soldiers and Sailors Monument, northwest Wilmington, **138**, 138–39
Sommer, Frank H., 29
South Milford Historic District, 243
Spahr, Albert H.: Granogue, 59
Spanel, Abram N., 250
Spanish House, 31n18
Speakman, Cummins, 230
Spencer (Dudley W.) House. *See* Laurel (Dudley W. Spencer House)
Spikeman, Thomas, 161
Spring Banke, 282, **282**
Springer, Lewis R.: Recitation Hall Annex (Agricultural Experiment Station), 182
Springer (Thomas) log house, 7, 169
Spring Garden, 295
Squirrel Run, 175
Staikos, Mary, 54, 176
Staikos Associates Architects, 176; Redden Lodge renovation, 260
Stalcop (John) Log House. *See* Bird (Thomas) House
Stanhope and Manning, 19
Stankiewicz, Richard, 102
Stanton Bridge, 170
Stanton vicinity, 169–70
Starr, Jacob, 110
Starr House, Wilmington, 110
Starr-Lore House, Odessa, 210
State Armory, Laurel, 295
State Legislative Building. *See* Legislative Hall (State Legislative Building)
State Office Building (Richardson and Robbins Cannery Complex), 250, **251**
State Police headquarters, 264
statues. *See* monuments and memorials
Stees, Hubert Sheldon, 17
   DuPont Building, Wilmington, 105–7
   Nemours Building, 107–8

office building (Louviers Building), 175
Steinlein, Fred, 39
Stephens, Don, 40
Stephens, Frank, 37, 40
    Frank Stephens Memorial Theater, 39
    Mary Bruce Inn (The Jungalow), 39
    Second Homestead, 39, **39**
Sterling Hotel. *See* Central Hotel (Sterling Hotel), Delaware City
Stevenson, Robert, 162
Stewart, Dr. David, 208
Stewart, John, 271
Stewart, Willard S., 27
Stewart and Donohue, 50
Stewart House, 208–9
Stickley, Gustav, 38; 300 Clinton Street, Delaware City, 203
Stick Style architecture, 242, 262
Stillman, Michael, 140
Still Pond, 31n18
Stiner, A. E., 56
stone construction, 8, 10–11, 82, 83–84, 232
Stone Mountain, Ga., 122
stores and shopping centers
    Automobile Row, 42, 133, **133**
    Boardwalk and Rehoboth Avenue, Rehoboth Beach, **276**, 277
    Burton Brothers Hardware Store, **291**, 291–92
    commercial building (Captain Charles W. Johnston House), Lewes, 271
    Fairfax, **52**, 52–53
    Gam's Store, St. Georges, 200
    Independence Mall, 51, **51**
    Market Street, Wilmington, 95
    Mike's Famous Roadside Rest, 148, **148**
    Prices Corner Shopping Center, 26, 77
    Robbins Hardware Store, Frederica, 240
    Robert Scott's Block, Lewes, 271
    Thompson Country Store, 268
    Wanamaker's, 26, 45–46, **46**
    Wilmington Merchandise Mart, 46
Strand, the, New Castle, 149, **150**, 160–61
Strand Millas, 8, 64–65, **65**
Stratford, Richard: Riverfront Parking Deck, 91
Stratford Hall, Va., 49
Streamline Moderne style, 42, 68, 107, 250, 261, 293

Strickland, William, 16, 198
    Delaware Breakwater, 272–74, **273**
    Immanuel Episcopal Church on the Green, New Castle, 154–55
    Sussex County Courthouse, 263, **263**
Struever Brothers Eccles: Ships Tavern Mews, Wilmington, restoration, 96, **96**
Studio Group, 137
Stuyvesant, Peter, 152
Sudler, John R., 286
Sudler House, 286, **286**
Summerton, 217
Summit Bridge, 197
Summit Covered Bridge, **193**
Sunken Garden, Nemours, 50, **50**
Survey of New Castle (Latrobe-Mills), 151, 155, 158, 159, 161, 163
Sussex County, 3, 258–98
    Administration Building, 263
    brick construction in, 10
    Courthouse, 263, **263**
    Family Court, 263
    See also Sussex County, eastern; Sussex County, western
Sussex County, eastern, 258–83
    east of Georgetown, 265
    Georgetown, 261–65; map, 262
    history, 258–60
    Lewes, 265–76; map, 269
    Milton, 260; map, 262
    Rehoboth Beach, 276–78; map, 269
    south along the inland bays and oceanfront, 279–83; map, 280
    south of Ellendale, 260
    west of Rehoboth Beach, 279
Sussex County, western, 284–98
    Bethel, 293–94; map, 294
    Bridgeville, 286–87; map, 287
    Laurel, 294–97; map, 294
    Seaford, 288–93; map, 289
    southwest of Millsboro, 297–98
    west of Bridgeville, 287–88
    Woodland, 293–94; map, 294
Sussex Hall, University of Delaware, 185
Sutton House, 200
Swamp Hall, 31n18
Swan, Abraham, 159, 212
Swanendael, 7, 265
Swanwyck, 146
"Swedish" Log House (Josh's Cabin), 7, 248–49
Swedish settlement, 170–71

Swedish settlers, 5, 7, 35, 86, 89, 93
Sweeney, John, 210, 211
Sykes, James, 295
synagogues
    Beth Emeth Synagogue, 129, **129**
    Beth Shalom Synagogue, 126

Tafel, Edgar: Budovitch (Isaac) House, 52
Taft Museum, Cincinnati, Ohio, 142
Talbot County, Md.: St. John's Chapel, 187
Talleyville library, 33
Tallman, Frank G., 132
Taney, Roger B., 159
Tatnall, Edward, 120
Tatnall, Joseph, 98, 117
Tatnall-Febiger House, 120
Tatnall Houses, 120
Tattoni, Joseph G.: New Castle County Library, Brandywine Hundred Branch, 52
taverns, 22
    Blue Ball Tavern, 33
    Buck Tavern, 29, 197, 199
    Deer Park Tavern (Deer Park Hotel), **188**, 188–89
    Mermaid Tavern, 168–69
    Old Stone Tavern, 11, 232
    Sign of the Ship Tavern, 96
    Tweed's Tavern, 165
    Witherspoon Building, Middletown, 216–17
Ted Harvey Wildlife Area, 236
Temple of Love, Nemours, 50, 230
Tennent, Charles, 176
Tennent, Gilbert, 156
Terry, Charles, 250
Terwilliger, Violet, 107
Tevebaugh Associates
    American Automobile Association (AAA) headquarters, 92
    Bob Carpenter Center, University of Delaware, 181
    Federal Job Corps Center, 118
    ING Direct (Kent Building) renovation, 91
    Riverfront Parking Deck, 91
Thacher, Edwin, 125
Tharp House, 242
theaters
    Delaware Children's Theater (New Century Club), 130, **130**, 278
    DuPont Theatre, 106
    Edgemoor Theatre, 42
    Everett Theater (Middletown Theater), 216
    Frank Stephens Memorial Theater, 39

theaters (*continued*)
  Grand Opera House, Wilmington, 101, **101**
  Moonlight Theater, Arden, 40
  Opera House, New Castle, 151
  Queen Theater (Clayton House Hotel), Wilmington, 14, 97
  Schine Theater (Plaza Theater), Milford, 243
  Schwartz Center for the Arts (Dover Opera House), 252, **252**
  Smyrna Opera House and Old Town Hall, 229, **229**
  Ursuline Academy Performing Arts Center (First Church of Christ Scientist), 130, **131**
  Wilmington Drama League, 129
1315 Delaware Avenue, northwest Wilmington, 135
Thomas E. Hall and Associates: 1105 North Market Street (Wilmington Tower), 109–10
Thomas (Charles) House. *See* Immanuel Parish House, New Castle
Thomas (Stirling H.) House, 144, **144**
Thompson, A. W.: CSX Railroad Bridge (Baltimore and Ohio Railroad Bridge), **125**, 125–26
Thompson, Henry B., 116, 124, 132, 179–80
Thompson, James H. W., 20–21
  Dutch House restoration, 153
  Mon Plaisir, 277, **278**
Thompson, John Dockery, Jr.: Public Building of the City of Wilmington and County of New Castle (former), 105, **105**
Thompson, Launt, 140
Thompson, Mary Wilson, 278
  and Delaware Society for the Preservation of Antiquities, 27, 153
  Mon Plaisir, 277, 278, **278**
  and Old Delaware Bank Association, 142
Thompson, Priscilla M., 140
Thompson, William Heyl
  Christ Church, Dover, 256–57
  Christ Church Christiana Hundred Education Building and Children's Chapel, 69–70
  Founders Hall (main building), St. Andrew's School, Middletown, 219–20

St. Anne's Church chapel and parish house, 217
St. James Episcopal Church, Newport, 76
Thompson Country Store, 268
Thompson Homes, Inc.: Centreville Reserve, 57
Thompson's Loss and Gain, 8
Thomson, Frank G., 260
Thorne, Edwin: 401 Washington Street, Wilmington, 111
Thorne, Sydenham, 243
Thorne (Parson) Mansion, **243**, 243–44
Three Mill Road, 141, **141**
300 Clinton Street, Delaware City, 203
310 West Street, Wilmington, 111
318 South College (Press of Kells), 190
Thurgood Marshall Elementary School, 195, **195**
Tidewater Oil Company, 201, 203
Tiffany Studios, 116
Tijou, Jean, 49
Tile House, New Castle, **6**, 7, 90, 149–50, 151
Tilghman Moyer Company: Citizens Bank (Fruit Growers' National Bank and Trust Company), 228
Tilton, Edward L.
  Enoch Pratt Library, Baltimore, 103
  Old State House restoration, 253, 255
  Wilmington Public Library, 102–3, **103**
Tindall, Roscoe Cook
  Etzel (Gastho) House, 190
  Grubb (A. A.) House, 34
Toaes, Daniel, 235
Todd, William H., 122
Todd (Henry) House, 254
Todd Memorial (Soldiers and Sailors of Delaware Monument), 122
Torbert, Vance W.: Washington Memorial Bridge, 122, 124
Totten, Charles, 185
tourism, 259, 276
Tower Hill School, northwest Wilmington, 144
Towers, The, Milford, 244, **244**
Town, Ithiel, 80
Town Hall, New Castle, **iv**, 157
townhouses
  Cloud's Row, New Castle, 157–58, **158**
  "The Flats," west Wilmington, 129–30

Market Street houses, Wilmington, 120
New Castle, 7
North Cass Street houses, Middletown, 217
North State Street houses, Dover, 249–50
Queen Anne houses, northwest Wilmington, 137, **137**
Willingtown Square, Wilmington, 97–98
Town of Parkside, 26, 215
Townsend, Barkley, 294
Townsend, George A., 15, 250
Townsend, Joshua, 283
Townsend vicinity, 221–23; map, 222
Trabant University Center, University of Delaware, **186**, 186–87
Trap Pond State Park, 284
Tribolo, Niccolo, 124
Trinity Episcopal Church, Wilmington, 116, 257
Trinity Vicinity, Wilmington, 111
Tri-Valley Trail, 175
Truitt, George, 295
Truman, Harry, 135
Trump (Samuel N.) House. *See* St. Francis Renewal Center (Samuel N. Trump House)
Trustees of New Castle Common, 150, 155, 156, 157, 158
Tubman, Harriet, 236
Tucker, Father Francis, 133–34
Tuckerman, Arthur Lyman, 253
Tudor Manor Hotel, Dover, 73, 250
Tudor Revival architecture, 72, 132, 141, 190, 240
Tull, Alfred H., 53
Turner Construction Company, 219
Tweed's Tavern, 165
231 2nd Street, Lewes, 295

Underground Railroad, 3, 15, 111, 214, 234, 235–36, 250
Union Hotel, Frederica, 240
Union Park Gardens, 24, 130, 134–35
universities. *See* colleges, universities, preparatory school campuses
University of Delaware, 17, 132, 173, 178–88, 246; map, 179
  Academy Building, 182–83
  Alumni Hall, 182
  architectural programs, 29
  Bayard Sharp Hall (St. Thomas Church), 187
  Center for Historic Architec-

ture and Design (CHAD), 14, 86, 207, 213, 223, 270, 279
Christiana Towers Apartments, 188
Colonial Revival architecure, 12
Daugherty Hall (Old First Presbyterian Church), 186, 187
Du Pont Hall, 183–84
Elliott Hall, 182
Gore Hall, 183–84
Graham Hall, 42
Harter Hall, 183, **183**
Hartshorn Hall, 185
Kent Hall, 185
Magnolia Circle, 185
Mechanical and Electrical Hall, 182
Memorial Hall, 184–85
Memorial Hall (proposal), **12**, 184
Mitchell Hall, 183
New Castle Hall, 185
Old College, 179, **181**, 181–82, 183
plan, 178–81, **180–81**
Recitation Hall, 182
Recitation Hall Annex (Agricultural Experiment Station), 182
Robinson Hall, 185
Rodney Complex (West Complex), **187**, 187–88
Roselle Center for the Arts, 181
Smith Hall, 12, 186
Sussex Hall, 185
Taylor Hall, 182
Trabant University Center, **186**, 186–87
Warner Hall, 185
west of, 188–90; map, 189
Wolf Hall, 183, **184**
University of Pennsylvania
Annenberg Center, 180
Law School, 183
Library, 154
Pender Labs, 187
University of Virginia, 180, 251
Upjohn, Richard, 69, 187, 289–90
Upper Louviers, 31n18, 54
upper White Clay Creek Valley, 175–76; map, 174
Ursuline Academy Performing Arts Center (First Church of Christ Scientist), 130, **131**
utopian communities: Arden, 37–40

Valley Run, 26, 36, **36**
Van Buren Street Bridge and Aqueduct, 124–25
Vanderbilt, William K., 92
Vandever, Harry: The Brambles, 38
Van Kirk, Augustin, 164
Van Kirk, Michael: Starr House, 110
Van Leuvenigh House, 161
Van Valkenburgh, Michael, 143
Vaules-Grier House, 243
Venturi, Robert, 195, 220; Flint House, 59
Venturi, Scott Brown and Associates
Guild House, Philadelphia, 186
Seattle Art Museum, 186
Trabant University Center, University of Delaware, **186**, 186–87
Venturi and Rauch: Flint House, 59
Vergnaud, N., 60
Vertol Aircraft, 90
Veterans Administration Medical and Regional Office Center, 76, **76**
viaducts
Amtrak viaduct arches (Pennsylvania Railroad), Wilmington, 46, 92, **92**
Elsmere viaduct, 76
Victorian architecture, 14, **28**, 247
Victorian Dover Historic District, 14
Village at Kings Creek, 26, 279, **279**
Village of Eastlake (Eastlake Public Housing Project), 127
Villa Monterey (Corinne Court), 24, 43, **43**
Vilone, Alfred J., 52–53
Vincent G. Kling and Associates: Amy du Pont Music Building, University of Delaware, 180
Vincent G. Kling and Partners: Wilmington City-County Building, 102
Virden, William H., 271
Vision for the Rivers report, 86
Vista, Arden, 40
Vogl, John and Wilhelmine, 241–42
Vogl House, **241**, 241–42
Volunteer Hose Company, Middletown, 217
Voorhees, Walker, Foley and Smith: office building (Louviers Building), 175
Voorhees, Walker, Smith, Smith and Haines: Hagley Library, 66
Vulcanized Fiber Company, 201

Wagoner, Harold: Zion Lutheran Church, west Wilmington, 130
Wains, William, 160
Walker, Frank B., 184
Walker and Gilette: Wilmington Trust Center (United States Post Office, Court House, and Custom House), 105
Walker's Mill, 71, **71**
Wallace, McHarg, Roberts and Todd, 102
Wallace, Roberts and Todd: Glasgow Regional Park, 197
Wallace and Warner, 17; 1109 Hopeton Road, Westover Hills, 72
Walnut Landing, Seaford, 270–71
Walter, Thomas U., 16, 168
Devondale Hall, 146
Moyamensing Prison, 259
Walter Dorwin Teague Associates, 68
Wanamaker's Department Store, 26, 45–46, **46**
Ward, Christopher, 56, 144
Warner, Emalea Pusey, 185
Warner, Mary Tatnall, 213
Warner, William, 64
Warner Hall, University of Delaware, 185
Washington, George, 22, 24, 34, 45, 61, 96, 120, 122, 160, 168, 170, 172, 192, 199
Washington, D.C.: East Building, National Gallery of Art, 109
Washington Memorial Bridge, 122, **122**, 124
Waterman, Thomas T.: The Cottage, Winterthur, 63
Waterman, Thomas Tileston, 61
Water Street Station, Wilmington, 91
Watson, Frank R., 256–57
Watson, John Fanning, 151
Wawaset Park, west Wilmington, 130
Way, John: Old Town Hall, Wilmington, **98**, 98–99
Wayne, Anthony, 120
W. Compton Mills Pumping Station, 126
W. D. Haddock Company, 292
Weaver, John, 211
Weavers Plant, Arden, 40
Webb, George R., 106
Weeks, Harry E., 184

Weldin House, 29, 44
Wellford, Robert, 161
W. Ellis Preston, 18
Welsh Tract Baptist Church, 191, **191**, 196
Wenner and Fink: Wilmington Conference Academy, Dover, 246
Wernwag, Lewis, 54, 119
Wertmüller, Adolph-Ulrich, 35
Weslager, C. A., 7, 88, 158, 249
Wesley Church Educational Center (U.S. Post Office, Federal Building), 252–53, **253**
Wesley College, 246
Westcourt Apartments (Foster Park Apartments), 135
western Sussex County. *See* Sussex County, western
Westminster Presbyterian Church, northwest Wilmington, 133, 137–38
Westover Hills, 43, 72–73, **73**
West Presbyterian Church, Wilmington, 113
west Wilmington, 129–35; map, 132
Wetmore, James A.
  Smyrna Post Office, 229
  Wesley Church Educational Center (U.S. Post Office, Federal Building), 252–53, **253**
Weymouth Architects, 19
Wheel of Fortune, 15, 231–32, **232**
Wheelwright, Robert, 74, 136, 153
Wheelwright and Stevenson
  Du Pont Highway landscaping, 266–67
  Fort Christina Park, 87–88
  Goodstay garden, 74
  St. Andrew's School, Middletown, 219
White, William D., 252
White Clay Creek Hundred, 165–72
  north, map, 167
  south, map, 171
  See also Christiana; Hockessin; Limestone Road (DE 7); Red Clay Creek: down; Stanton Vicinity
White Clay Creek Presbyterian Church, 176, 183
White Clay Creek State Park, 173
White Clay Creek Valley
  lower, 176–77; map, 177
  upper, 175–76; map, 174
Whitefield, George, 176, 265
White Friars Glass Works, 257

Whiteside, G. Morris, 17, 26, 98, 234
  Brandywine Pumping Station Office Building, 119
  Central Young Men's Christian Association (YMCA), **115**, 115–16
  Mullins Store, Wilmington, 100
  Rodney Street Chapel remodeling, 138
  Village of Eastlake (Eastlake Public Housing Project), 127
Whiteside, G. Morris, II, 108
  chapel, Delaware Health and Social Services campus, 147–48
  Delaware Art Museum (Delaware Art Center), 142–43
  DuPont Building dining room, 107
  Hale-Byrnes House restoration, 170
  Tower Hill School gym, 144
Whiteside, Moeckel and Carbonell
  Aldersgate United Methodist Church, 53
  Avon Products Northeast Regional Headquarters, 177, **177**
  Brandywine High School, 32
  Cab Calloway School of the Arts (Wilmington High School), 135, **135**
  Congress Hall, Philadelphia, 182
  Historical Society of Delaware (Artisan's Savings Bank) restoration, 97
  Mid-Town Parking Center, 114, **114**
  Old Town Hall, Wilmington restoration, **98**, 98–99
  Smith Hall, University of Delaware, 186
  Talleyville library, 33
  318 South College (Press of Kells), 190
  Wilmington City-County Building, 102
  Wilmington Public Library interior, 102–3
  Wolf Hall extension, University of Delaware, 183
Whiteside and Carbonell: and Government Center, 102
Whitman, Requardt and Associates: Cool Spring Reservoir Pumping Station renovation, 131
Whittingham, Richard A.

Old College, University of Delaware, 181–82
Rhodes Pharmacy, Newark, 178
Wigley, Michael R.: Kreindler Beach House, 281, **281**
Wiley (John) House, 159
Wilkie, Wendell, 104
Willard Hall School, 125
Willard Street vicinity houses, 143–44, **144**
Willet, Henry Lee, 121
William B. Canby Memorial, 140
William B. Keene School, 195
William Penn Statue, 157
Williams, Frank M., 266–67
Williams, George Monier: Rockwood Museum (Shipley-Bringhurst Mansion), 44, **44**
Williams, Nancy, 282
Williams, "Planner," 293
Williamsburg, Va.
  Governor's Palace, 263
  Nelson-Galt House, 271
William Shinn and Company, 100
Willing, Sims and Talbutt: Selborne, 56
Willing, Thomas, 82
Willingtown Square, Wilmington, 97–98
Wills, W. Compton: Hoopes Reservoir Dam (Old Mill Stream Dam), 78–79, **79**
Wilmington, 14, 22, 82–145, **84**
  bird's-eye views, 82, **83**, 86, **93**
  Brandywine Village and Park, 117–26; map, 121
  Christina Riverfront and East Side, 86–92, **87**; map, 88
  City-County Building, 102
  historic districts, 85, 111, 135
  history of, 82–86
  Market Street, **95**
  Market Street corridor, 93–110; map, 94
  neighborhoods, map, 85
  northeast, 126–29; map, 128
  northwest, 135–45; map, 139
  population, 82, 86
  suburbs of, 24
  Swede settlement, 5, 86, 89, 93
  urban renewal in, 84–86, 96, 101–2, 111
  west, 129–35; map, 132
  west center city, 111–17; map, 112
Wilmington Almshouse, 146–47
Wilmington and Brandywine Cemetery, 116–17
Wilmington and Western Railroad, 23, 78, 79, 166, 168

Wilmington Board of Park Commissioners, 123
Wilmington Club, **108,** 108–9
Wilmington College, 13
"Wilmington Complex" gneiss, 11
Wilmington Conference Academy, Dover, 246
Wilmington Drama League, 129
Wilmington Friends Meeting House, 8, 10, 111, 113, **113**
Wilmington High School. *See* Cab Calloway School of the Arts (Wilmington High School)
Wilmington Hospital (Delaware Hospital), 117
Wilmington Merchandise Mart, 46
Wilmington Public Library (Wilmington Institute Library), 17, 102–3, **103,** 124
Wilmington Savings Fund Society, 102
Wilmington Station (Pennsylvania Railroad Passenger Station), 16, **90,** 91
Wilmington Tower. *See* 1105 North Market Street (Wilmington Tower)
Wilmington Trust Bank, Newark, 178
Wilmington Trust Building (Brandywine Trust and Savings Bank), 118
Wilmington Trust Center (United States Post Office, Court House, and Custom House), **104,** 105
Wilson, David, Jr., 213
Wilson, David, Sr., 214
Wilson, Jack, 51
Wilson, General James H., 122
Wilson, L. Waring: Wilmington Trust Building (Brandywine Trust and Savings Bank), 118
Wilson family, 210
Wilson (David) House. *See* Wilson-Warner House and stable
Wilson-Warner House and stable, 11, 14, 172, 211, 213
Wiltbank, Helmanus, 270
Windrim, James H.
  Old State House, 253, 255
  Wilmington Conference Academy, Dover, 246

Winnetka, Ill.: Crow Island School, 41
Winterthur, 19, 60–64, 241
  The Cottage, 63
  Crowninshield Research Building, 61, 63
  Enchanted Woods, 64
  estate stone walls, 48, 64
  Farms Dairy buildings, 63
  Galleries, 63
  garden, 63–64, 185
  House and Museum, 17, 21, 29, 55, 60–61, **62**
  Montmorenci staircase, **62**
  and Odessa properties, 210, 212
  Pavilion (Garden Tours Pavilion), 63
  Red Lion Inn facade, 61, **61**
  tulip poplar tree, 254
Winterthur Program in Early American Culture, 29
Winterthur Railroad Station and Post Office, 63
Wire or Swinging Bridge, 126
Wise, Herbert C., 17, 27, 180, 185
Witherspoon Building, Middletown, 216–17
Wolf Hall, University of Delaware, 183, **184**
women and Delaware architecture, 278. *See also specific women by name*
Women's College, Newark, 130
Wood, Alan, 78
Woodburn, 15, 250, **250**
wood construction, 8, 10, 258, 265–66
Wooddale Covered Bridge, 22, **22,** 78, 80
Woodin, Richard, 215
Woodland, 293–94; map, 294
Woodland Indians, 3–5
Woodlawn. *See* England (Thomas) House Restaurant (Woodlawn)
Woodlawn Trustees, Inc., 83, 129–30, 143–44
Woods, Walter Scott: 4614 Bedford, Forest Hills Park, 52
Woolworth (F. W.) Store, 97
worker housing
  Aniline Village, 36
  Brookview Apartments, 36
  Claymont, 33–34
  Inn at Montchanin Village, 65
  Overlook Colony, 24, 36, 134
  Seaford, 288

Wawaset Park, west Wilmington, 130
Worthland, 36
Works Progress Administration (WPA), 24, 72, 155–56
Worthland, 36
Worth Steel, 33, 36
Wren's Nest, The, Nemours, 49–50
Wright, Benjamin
  Chesapeake and Delaware (C&D) Canal, 198
  Delaware Tide Lock, Chesapeake and Delaware (C&D) Canal, 204, **204**
Wright, Charles, 289
Wright, Frank Lloyd, 52
  Larkin Building, Buffalo, 110
  Laurel (Dudley W. Spencer House), **43,** 43–44
Wright, Samuel G., 259
W. T. Chipman Middle School, 242
Wyeth, Andrew, 89
Wyeth, N. C., 102, 137, 141, 220
Wyoming, 224, 234

Yale University (Connecticut Hall), New Haven, Conn., 183
Yamasaki, Minoru, 53
Yellin, Samuel, 56, 59
Yorklyn, 55
York Seat, 232
Young, Ammi B.: Old Custom House (Old Federal Building), 99, **100**
Young, Henry Wynd, 70
Young, William, 54
Young and Banwell, 18; office building (John Wanamaker Store) addition, 45–46

Zantzinger, Borie and Medary
  Cathedral Church of St. John, Wilmington, **120,** 120–21
  Foulke and Henry Dormitories, Princeton University, 121
  Philadelphia Divinity School, 121
  Rodney Square, Wilmington, 103–4, **104,** 121
Ziegler, Charles A., 99
Zimmerman, Herman H., 105
Zoar Camp, 297
Zwaanendael Museum (Zwaanendael House), 272, **273**

BUILDINGS OF THE UNITED STATES is a series of books on American architecture compiled and written on a state-by-state basis. The primary objective of the series is to identify and celebrate the rich cultural, economic, and geographical diversity of the United States as it is reflected in the architecture of each state. The series has been commissioned by the Society of Architectural Historians, an organization dedicated to the study, interpretation, and preservation of the built environment throughout the world.

PUBLISHED BY THE UNIVERSITY OF VIRGINIA PRESS

Buildings of Delaware, W. Barksdale Maynard (2008)

PUBLISHED BY THE SOCIETY OF ARCHITECTURAL HISTORIANS AND THE CENTER FOR AMERICAN PLACES

Buildings of Pittsburgh, Franklin Toker (2007)

PUBLISHED BY OXFORD UNIVERSITY PRESS

Buildings of Alaska, Alison K. Hoagland (1993)

Buildings of Colorado, Thomas J. Noel (1997)

Buildings of the District of Columbia, Pamela Scott and Antoinette J. Lee (1993)

Buildings of Iowa, David Gebhard and Gerald Mansheim (1993)

Buildings of Louisiana, Karen Kingsley (2003)

Buildings of Michigan, Kathryn Bishop Eckert (1993)

Buildings of Nevada, Julie Nicoletta, with photographs by Bret Morgan (2000)

Buildings of Rhode Island, William H. Jordy; Richard Onorato and William McKenzie Woodward, contributing editors (2004)

Buildings of Virginia: Tidewater and Piedmont, Richard Guy Wilson and contributors (2002)

Buildings of West Virginia, S. Allen Chambers Jr. (2004)